FROMMER'S
INDIA ON
$25 A DAY

by Jan Aaron

1988–1989 Edition

Published by Prentice Hall Press
A Division of Simon & Schuster, Inc.
Gulf + Western Building
One Gulf + Western Plaza
New York, N.Y. 10023

ISBN 0-13-456872-9

Manufactured in the United States of America

*Although every effort was made to ensure the accuracy
of price information appearing in this book,
it should be kept in mind that prices
can and do fluctuate in the course of time*

CONTENTS

MAPS

Acknowledgments

*I gratefully acknowledge the patient planning assistance of
Leela Nadan and Sudha Kothary, and the much-needed
research backup provided by these two and the staff of the
India Tourist Office in New York City. Other thank-yous
for guidance and assistance go to India's Department of
Tourism, the India Tourist Offices, and the state
Departments of Tourism in India, and those helpful
individuals who work in and manage them; to airlines, bus,
and railway personnel for giving me updated information
and getting me to everywhere; to guides who never
tired . . . and to the many other individuals at hotels,
restaurants, museums, monuments, and shops, who allowed
me to look around and who supplied more answers to
questions. Research assistance by Edwin K. Hudson is
acknowledged. Finally, thanks also to Lettergraph, Inc., of
New York City for supplying the historical chronology and
the Hindi phrases.*

INFLATION ALERT: I don't have to tell you that inflation has hit India as it has everywhere else. In researching this book I have made every effort to obtain up-to-the-minute prices, but even the most conscientious researcher cannot keep up with the current pace of inflation. As we go to press, I believe I have obtained the most reliable data possible. Nonetheless, in the lifetime of this edition—particularly its second year (1989)—the wise traveler will add 15% to 20% to the prices quoted throughout these pages.

A DISCLAIMER: Although every effort was made to ensure the accuracy of the prices and travel information appearing in this book, it should be kept in mind that prices do fluctuate in the course of time, and that information does change under the impact of the varied and volatile factors that affect the travel industry.

No hotel, restaurant, shop, or tour operator paid to be in this book, nor did any other commercial enterprise. The recommendations in this book are purely personal. You may find minor discrepancies throughout these chapters—color schemes change if hoteliers decide on a new look; an exotic curry can no longer be on the menu if the chef has quit and no one else knows how to make the dish. Prices may vary slightly too. There were rumors of minor increases while I researched this edition, but they could not be pinned down. Even with slight increases, the dollar stretches far in India.

RESTRICTIONS: Some parts of India are politically sensitive and/ or designated as protected areas and certain restrictions apply to traveling to them. These include Punjab, Darjeeling, parts of Assam, Chandigarh, Kaziranga Sanctuary and parts of the Andaman Islands. In the introduction and the chapters dealing with specific locations, instructions are given on how and where permits are given. Currently (April 1988), tourist travel is not advised to Chandigarh and Punjab is completely off-limits for tourists.

INDIA ON $25 A DAY

1. India Past and Present
2. Food
3. Essential Information
4. The $35-A-Day Travel Club—How to Save Money on All Your Travels

MY FRIENDS SEEMED divided in their reactions when I first informed them that I was going to India. A substantial minority managed to look vaguely mystical, placed their hands together in a prayerful salute, and rolled their eyes reverentially as if they were already in the presence of holiness.

And then there were the others who sneered—"Ugh, you'll hate it; full of snakes and beggars, and so *poor,* and besides that, it's *filthy.*"

Now that I'm back in New York, with India fully researched and documented, my suitcase full of knickknacks and my head a montage of overlapping images, it's easy to understand the differing reviews. India undeniably has beggars (so does New York, for that matter)—they are there, but so are many other things.

As for snakes, I never saw one, except for the sluggish specimens displayed in the baskets of professional snake-charmers or the occasional exotic breed to be found in a zoo. The average Indian's familiarity with snakes is about equal to an American suburbanite's encounters with foxes.

Holiness, though, is more pervasive: India is full of reverence. There are scores of religions (with Hinduism overwhelmingly preponderating), and apart from sporadically bitter factionalism, they have made much the same accommodations toward each other as those in other countries. But somehow, in India, religion is more than that: it has endured as a reverence for life itself—a tolerance for and protection of every living thing. There are people who won't swat a fly, millions more who won't touch meat, much less allow a cow to be harmed. If a man wants to abandon the day-to-day cares of this mundane life and return to nature by becoming an itinerant ascetic in search of higher truths, there are few who would not pay respect to the humble sadhu's robes he dons. If a woman decides to dedicate her life to similar pursuits, the path is hers to follow.

For above all else—despite independence as a modern nation, since

1947, and a century and half before that of colonial rule; despite foreign aid, five-year plans, increasing industrialization, a nuclear blast and space experimentation—India is still very close to nature.

In the countryside—and about 75% of the nearly half a billion population lives in rural areas—families share their work, food, and sometimes the roofs above their heads with their animals. And sometimes, when they move to the city, little is changed. True, there is no longer the plowing to be done, and there are cars to dodge, modern buildings and broad avenues to contend with; but amazingly, the beloved animals are still there—meandering without fear in this society that pleasantly accommodates all animal life.

Caught in a metropolitan traffic jam, cows and goats wander, oblivious to taxis, cars, buses, bikes, rickshaws, and horse-drawn tongas. Occasionally, elephants, monkeys, donkeys, camels, and performing bears and parakeets are there too.

There is no such thing as a dull Indian street. A typical panorama seems an endless extravaganza of faces and physical types in saris, flowing dhotis (skirt-type male garments), impeccably tailored business suits, jeans, shorts, even loincloths. The range of activities, even on the smallest street, can include: cycle rickshaws (bearing ads for family planning) waiting for customers, balloon sellers, squatting peanut vendors roasting their wares, fortune-tellers, a man being shaved, another carving chair legs, fruit stalls, boys squirting each other at the water pump, a string of burros laden with newly baked bricks, women spreading their colored wash to dry on the sidewalk, a group of customers gathered at the tailor's hookah (water pipe), a bullock cart slantwise across the road blocking a half dozen trucks, bike riders, buses, the "pan wallahs" wrapping spices into betel leaves for the favorite after-meal snack. All of the above were hastily noted as my taxi wove slowly through a village street. Invariably, Indian streets offer more than a passerby can possibly absorb all at one time.

One's memories of India become a shifting kaleidoscope of fragmentary images—from the happy faces of the children at the Tibetan self-help (refugee) center in Darjeeling to the morose expressions of the water buffalo hauling timber at the Pondicherry ashram; from the flight over the snowcapped Himalayas and descent into the Shangri-la of the Kashmir valley to the tropical lagoons of Cochin, lined with coconut palms, to the Chinese fishing nets gracefully rising and dipping into the tranquil waters.

For India is not one but many countries, a fusion of many races, traditions, and influences. To sit in a garden in Darjeeling sipping tea and nibbling cheese toast is to return to the leisurely days of the British Raj; to view the outlines of Mughal palaces against the skyline at dusk or to attend the centuries-old rites of cleansing and worship on the banks of the Ganges at Varanasi is to plunge back into an even older era.

And there's the India of today: the gigantic steel and electrical plants at Jamshedpur and Bhakra Nangal, the skyscrapers lining Bombay's waterfront, the discotheques of New Delhi, the sleek modern architecture of Chandigarh.

And there is the India of tomorrow—seen in glimpses today in the modern health services, electricity, improved water supplies, schools and transportation systems that are constantly being expanded to improve villagers' lives. There's also the steadily rising literacy rate, up from 16% at independence in 1947 to 36% in 1981, date of the last census, to open increasing opportunities to more people.

The '80s too have also seen the launch of India's space program and the future holds more experimentation along these lines. Indeed, scientific and technical manpower in India is said to be 2.3 million.

Yet despite all these impressive gains, India still has much to do and is still a developing nation.

For those fortunate enough to go to India today, there awaits a ringside seat at a simultaneous extravaganza of the past, present, and future.

First, about the past. . . .

1. India Past and Present

EARLY ORIGINS: Who the early peoples of India were is not known for certain. Possibly the original Dravidians became partially submerged by waves of Aryans who, as far back as 2000 B.C., poured into the country from the northwest.

The Aryans were pastoral. Their lives depended on the elements and so they worshipped the sun, moon, and rivers. Their mystics and philosophers composed songs in praise of nature, two of which, lyrical poems, the *Ramayana* and *Mahabharata,* influence the people to this day. These epics were not just the work of one poet but were the creations of generations who embellished the basic legends over thousands of years. The Aryans also laid the cornerstone of Hinduism, the principal religion of present-day India.

The early peoples of India blended with the Aryans and organized themselves into states. Led by the Aryans, they were not content with just farming: they contributed two basic mathematical concepts to the world, the decimal system and the zero, and the stories with which they amused their youngsters are those that entertain children now—*Aesop's Fables.*

As civilization spread, religious unrest grew and found expression in the *Upanishads* (Forest Books), written between approximately 1000 and 500 B.C. by philosophers who retired to the hills to contemplate. As doubt increased, many religious leaders arose, each claiming to have the answer. One of these was to change the lives of millions. He was Gautama, the future Buddha, who led a revolt against the established order in the 6th century B.C. Buddha urged people to lead ethical lives, thereby eliminating sorrow. He spoke in plain language and without regard for caste or creed. About the same time, Mahavira, the Jain prophet, laid the foundation for the creed of nonviolence—still an influence on current Indian thinking.

The West made contact with India, and Alexander the Great invaded the country in 326 B.C. This Greek invasion enriched Indian art and mythology and the West in turn extended its knowledge of science and mathematics.

A few years after Alexander's departure the first great Indian empire, the Mauryas, was formed in 323 B.C., lasting more than 150 years and producing among its monarchs Ashoka, during whose exceptional reign the arts and architecture flourished.

Originally a warrior, Ashoka foreswore war and violence after embracing Buddhism and decided to conquer the world with love. Monolithic pillars inscribed with his gentle rules of conduct were erected throughout his huge empire. Ashoka's stupas (memorial shrines to Buddha, which can still be seen at Sanchi and Sarnath), now more than 2,000 years old, were crowned with stylized lions—that emblem is now the symbol of the Indian Republic. Ashoka sent Buddhist missionaries to preach his word in central Asia, Kashmir, Burma, and Ceylon (now Sri Lanka).

At the dawn of Christianity, merchants, priests, and artists departed from India and founded settlements in Java and Sumatra, Cambodia, Thailand, and Malaya, spreading India's art, philosophy, and religion throughout Southeast Asia.

The second great dynasty, the Guptas, in power from A.D. 320 to 495, ushered in the Golden Age of Indian history, a time of impressive achievements, including the fine frescoes and sculptures still to be seen at Ellora and Ajanta.

Islam came to India in the 8th century with Arab traders and invaders, followed by the Turks and Afghans, and finally the Mughals, who made India their homeland in the 16th century, ruling for about 250 years. They were the builders of the memorable Taj Mahal, the Red Fort, the now deserted city of Fatehpur Sikri, and more. During this period, miniature painting flourished, as did court music and a dance form known as Kathak.

The British came as traders in the 18th century and by the beginning of the 19th century were ruling most of the country, except for small French, Portuguese, and Dutch enclaves.

The British influence still persists in India in the system of law and government, in education, and also in the widespread use of the English language.

In 1947, after years of sporadic struggle for independence under Mahatma Gandhi, India emerged as a sovereign nation. That same year, two primarily Muslim portions of the country—East Bengal and Northwest India—were partitioned and became East and West Pakistan. Kashmir, claimed by both, remains part of India. East Pakistan is now Bangladesh, following the war in 1971.

India became a republic in 1950 under the late Prime Minister Jawaharlal Nehru, who, with the All-India Congress, governed until his death in 1964. The prime minister from 1964 to 1966 was Lal Bahadur Shastri.

From 1966 to 1977 Mrs. Indira Gandhi (no relation to Mahatma Gandhi, but Nehru's daughter) was prime minister. She was voted out of office in favor of the Janata party and Morarji Desai became prime minister, followed briefly by Charan Singh.

Mrs. Gandhi and the Congress party returned in 1979. She was prime minister until her assassination on October 31, 1984, purportedly by two of her Sikh security guards. The prime minister today is her son, Rajiv Gandhi.

India is governed by a president who is advised by a Council of Ministers. The country's constitution stipulates freedom for all, and discrimination is strictly forbidden by law. This means that the once-rigid caste system is slowly dissolving into a more flexible society.

To telescope the major events in India's long history, here is a chronology:

326 B.C.—*Alexander the Great invades India*

323 B.C.—*Death of Alexander at Babylon*

322 B.C.—*Accessions of Chandragupta Maurya*

273–232 B.C.—*Emperor Ashoka*

185 B.C.—*The last Maurya king killed*

320 A.D.—*Chandragupta I; beginning of Gupta era*

330 A.D.—*Samudragupta*

380 A.D.—*Chandragupta II*

405–411 A.D.—*Travels of Fa-hien in the Gupta empire*

415 A.D.—*Kumaragupta I*

455 A.D.—*Skandagupta*

476 A.D.—*Aryabhata the astronomer born*

480–490 A.D.—*Breakup of the Gupta empire*

505 A.D.—*Varahamihira the astronomer born*

606 A.D.—*Harsha-Vardhana; beginning of Harsha era*

622 A.D.—*Flight of Mohammed to Medina*

629–645 A.D.—*Travels of Hiuen Tsang*

647 A.D.—*Death of Harsha*

740 A.D.—*Defeat of Pallavs by Chalukyas*

973 A.D.—*Taila founded second Chalukya Dynasty of Kalyani*

1175–1290—*Rise of Muslim power in India and establishment of the Sultanate of Delhi*

1290–1340—*The Khilji and Tughlak dynasties*

1340–1526—*The decline and fall of the Sultanate of Delhi; end of Tughlak dynasty; end of Lodhi dynasty*

1336–1646—*The Hindu Empire of Vijayanagar*

1526–1556—*The Mogul Empire: Babur, Humayun, and the Sur Dynasty*

1600–1708—*The Early European Voyagers—The East India Company*

1498 (May 20)—*The Portuguese explorer Vasco da Gama landed at Calicut*

1510—*Portuguese conquest of Goa*

1555–1605—*Emperor Akbar*

1605–1627—*Jehangir*

1628–1666—*Shah Jahan*

1659–1707—*Aurangzeb*

1627–1680—*Shivaji*

1632–1653—*The Taj Mahal built as tomb for Queen Mumtaz Mahal by Shah Jahan*

1600–1858—*The East India Company*

1857—*The Sepoy Mutiny*

1858—*The end of the rule of the East India Company and the taking over of all its powers and obligations in India by the British Crown*

1877—*The Queen was proclaimed Empress of India*

1905—*First partition of Bengal aroused nationalist opposition*

1919 (April 13)—*Jallianwala Bagh Massacre*

1920—*First noncooperation movement launched by Mahatma Gandhi*

1931—*The First Round Table Conference*

1935—*The Government of India Act*

1942—*Quit India Movement*

1947—*Independence of India; partition of the country into India and Pakistan*

1948 (January 30)—*Assassination of Mahatma Gandhi*

1950 (January 26)—*Inauguration of the Republic of India and Rajendra Prasad became the first president of India*

1947–1964—*All-India Congress ruled the country under Prime ministership of Jawaharlal Nehru*

1964–1966—*Prime ministership of Lal Bahadur Shastri*

1966–1977—*Congress party in power under prime ministership of Indira Gandhi*

1977–1979—*Janata party in power under prime ministership of Morarji Desai*

1979—*Janata party in power under prime ministership of Charan Singh*

1979–1984—*Congress party government under the prime ministership of Indira Gandhi*

1984 (October 31)—*Assassination of Indira Gandhi*

1984–Present—*Congress party government under prime ministership of Rajiv Gandhi*

POPULATION: With 748 million people (according to 1984 statistics), India is the second most populous country in the world. The most heavily populated state is Uttar Pradesh, with 110 million; next is Bihar, with 69.3 million; and then West Bengal, with 54.4 million.

GEOGRAPHY: Of all the places that come to mind, none more quickly evokes a tropical image than India. Yet India's most significant geographic feature is the massive Himalaya Mountains to the north, as well as some of the country's most beautiful resorts in Kulu and Kashmir. The great Himalayan peaks rise to average heights of 17,000 feet, with 40 higher than 24,000 feet. The mountains that form the border between Burma and Bangladesh are slightly lower, but snow falls and the wind blows. So much for wall-to-wall tropics!

As to vital stastistics: India is almost half the size of the U.S., or about the same size as Europe, less the U.S.S.R. The seventh-largest country in the world, India is commonly referred to as a subcontinent because of its size and also because it is geographically a unit separated from Asia by mountains and seas. India stretches 1,930 miles from the northern Himalayas to the southern lagoons of Kerala, and 1,760 miles from the Arabian seacoast in the west to the Bay of Bengal in the east, with half of the country lying on either side of the Tropic of Cancer.

South of the Himalayas, India's heavily populated, flat, fertile Indo-Gangetic plain (150 to 200 miles broad) is formed of the rich alluvium of the Rivers Indus, Ganges, and Bhramaputra. In this region is the capital, Delhi with its layers of civilizations; to the northwest, the prosperous Punjab and the monument that virtually symbolizes India to many Westerners, the Taj Mahal, and the lesser-known Khajuraho; and to the east, fascinating Calcutta.

Then, south of the plains is the triangular peninsula, with its heartland the Deccan plateau. In this area the sights are richly varied from the glamorous city of Bombay to the ancient Buddhist shrine at Sanchi and the soaring temples of the south. Finally, at India's southwesternmost state, Kerala, are some of the country's most splendid tropics.

WHAT'S WHAT AND WHO'S WHO IN THE RELIGIOUS PANTHEON: Always remember to remove your shoes at temples, mosques, and other holy shrines. You also remove your belt (if it's leather) at some Hindu temples. Cover your head when visiting any Sikh temple. Dress decorously at holy places.

Hinduism

About 82% of India's total population is Hindu. Although Hinduism teaches belief in one Supreme Being, the religion's vast mythology includes numerous gods, goddesses, and avatars (incarnations). To understand, even superficially, you should know that when the Aryans arrived in India, the Dravidians had already established some religious beliefs and gods. The Aryans were smart enough to realize that if they were to make any headway, they had to adopt some of these gods—and so the synthesis began and continued through the ages. When gods were not assimilated or combined, they were welcomed as relatives of major gods' families or made into incarnations. Indian gods, unlike their fickle Greek "brothers," tend to be monogamous, and some of the most impressive powers were assigned to their female consorts, centuries before women's lib. There are, without exaggeration, millions of gods dealing with all forms of life and nature. Listed here are only the major deities to be encountered on tours to temples.

Brahma (The Creator): Once the mightiest of the Hindu gods because he set the world in motion. He lost importance with the emergence of Shiva and Vishnu. Brahma has four heads, each one looking over one quarter of the universe. From his quartet of heads sprang the *Vedas* (the four ancient Hindu scriptures). He carries these along with a scepter and other symbols. He wears white robes, rides a goose, and is considered the god of wisdom.

Saraswati: Brahama's consort. She rides a white swan and is the goddess of learning.

Shiva (The Destroyer): One of the two greatest gods of Hinduism, he represents power in its many aspects—war, famine, and death, for example, are under his control. He frequently wears a tiger skin, and carries an axe, a trident, and a bowl made of a skull, itself sometimes adorned with snakes. He is worshipped as a lingam (a phallic symbol) and is also seen, in South Indian bronzes, as Nataraj, the God of Dance.

Parvati (Also Mahadevi): Shiva's wife, she is often seen with him in statues and paintings looking like the model of the loving consort. In her incarnations she is **Durga,** ten-armed goddess of battle; or **Kali,** who wears snakes and desires blood; or **Uma,** the Beautiful, who sometimes acts as a moderator between Brahma and the other gods. Her transport is the tiger.

Nandi (The Bull): Shiva's sacred mount and his musician. Shiva wears Nandi's insignia, a crescent moon, on his brow.

Ganesh: The chubby, elephant-headed son of Shiva and Parvati, a very popular god and worshipped before new ventures to ensure success. He rides on a mouse.

Vishnu (The Preserver): The other great god, Vishnu usually holds four symbols: a discus, conch, mace, and lotus. He appears in incarnation whenever mankind needs kind assistance. It is believed that he has had nine avatars, and the tenth is yet to come. Two of his most popular incarnations are **Krishna** and **Rama,** the latter representing the ideal husband, wise ruler, and of greatest importance, a valiant crusader against evil. He inspired the *Ramayana* by killing the demon Ravana, a deed which is celebrated each year with the Dussehra festivities of the fall. Sita is Rama's wife, an incarnation of Lakshmi, and the symbol of the perfect wife.

Krishna, the other important incarnation of Vishnu, plays the flute, is usually blue in color, and is the god of love. He is prominent in the *Bhagavad Gita.* Tales of his childhood pranks, his adolescent adoration by the gopis (milkmaids), and his heroic deeds have inspired a great many works of art.

Yet another incarnation of Vishnu is Buddha—a choice example of how

Hinduism assimilates beliefs of other religions. In Hinduism, Buddha represents compassion toward animals.

Lakshmi: The wife of Vishnu, often shown seated on a lotus. She represents wealth and prosperity. Her attendants are white elephants. She is also worshipped as Sita.

Garuda: Vishnu's mount, Garuda is a huge bird with the head and wings of an eagle and the body and limbs of a man. He carries his god on his gleaming golden back.

Islam

About 11% of India's population are Muslims. The holy *Koran* is their sacred book and their greatest prophet is Mohammed.

Christianity

About 2.6% of the population is Christian. St. Thomas ("Doubting") was said to have been martyred at Madras in A.D. 78. St. Francis Xavier was an early missionary in Goa in the 16th century; the Franciscans preceded him.

Sikhism

About 1.9% are Sikhs. Founded in the 15th century as a branch of Hinduism and as a bridge between that religion and Islam, it gathered its greatest strength in the 17th century. The Sikhs' religion does not permit them to cut their hair, which is usually neatly tucked up into a turban at all times.

Jainism

Less than 0.5% of the population practice Jainism. Nonviolence in deed and thought plus complete tolerance for other religions are basic concepts.

Buddhism

About 0.7% are Buddhists. Born in Nepal, probably around 567 B.C., Buddha preached his first sermon at Sarnath in India. Basic to his doctrine was that worldly desire was at the root of all that is bad. The ultimate goal is Nirvana, attained by following a fourfold path to awaken and free the heart and mind.

Zoroastrianism

About 0.3% of the population are Zoroastrians. In the 7th century the Parsis fled Persia because of religious persecution and since earliest days have remained in and about Bombay. Their holy book is the *Zend Avesta;* they follow the Path of Asha—good thoughts, words, and deeds. Fire worship is part of the religion.

Sadhus

It is estimated that about six million orange-robed sadhus (holy men) live in India. They lead solitary lives as hermits or beggars near shrines and will take anyone into their fold. The sincere ones are searching for very deep truths indeed.

CASTE SYSTEM: This serious subject is so complex that I offer only an elementary explanation here. The intricacies of the caste system, going back two millennia or more, involve literally thousands of communities divided by taboos about foods, occupations, intermarriage, and all manner of social inter-action. Originally, there were four main castes: priests (Brahmans), warriors and administrators (Kshatriyas), businessmen, farmers, traders, and shop-keepers (Vaishyas), and craftsmen and hired help (Shudras)—each allegedly born from a part of Brahma. The four major castes were further divided into countless subcastes. Under all were the Untouchables (Gandhi's "Children of God") who did the most disagreeable tasks.

In the early villages this was a good arrangement—ensuring a steady labor supply in various occupations to satisfy all needs. It did not encourage change or upward mobility by moving away. Punishment for leaving home was to become an outcast.

Obviously, this kind of system, inhibiting progress, splitting rather than uniting, would not work in building a democracy. Through the untiring ef-forts of Mahatma Gandhi and legislation, discrimination is forbidden by law. This is especially encouraging to the lower castes. But just because a law is passed doesn't mean the immediate dissolution of worn-out practices and deeply ingrained beliefs. (We can all cite examples of this in Western socie-ties.) Traces of the caste system still remain, but they are changing—in cities, all kinds of people are working together in new businesses and industries; in villages, people are moving away from home motivated by new opportunities and are being absorbed into the mainstream; there are intercaste marriages, and even the army plays a part by encouraging men to mingle and moving them about.

Bigger changes have occurred in India in the past half century than in all past millennia. To Westerners accustomed to rapid and extreme change, these may not seem like much, but to Indians they are huge and irreversible. Each future generation of Indians will live less and less like the one before: rigidity is being replaced by a more accepting way of life.

2. Food

GOURMET GLOSSARY: If *curry* is the limit of your knowledge about Indian food, then you have a lot to learn about one of the most exotic and varied cuisines in the world. Curry dishes spiced just enough to be interesting can consist of meat, fish, eggs, or vegetables. They are served with rice or one of India's tasty breads and will taste very different from the curry you've had in the Western world. The spices that go into them will be freshly ground and no two cooks will make exactly the same mixture of seasonings.

There's terrific variety, too, in the way the same dishes are spelled on res-taurant menus. But even the most far-out spellings you'll encounter will match up to the dishes described below and elsewhere in this book.

Mulligatawny, a soup with a curry base, is world famous.

Chapatis, parathas, and *puris* are Indian breads made of whole-wheat flour, shaped into flat cakes and grilled, roasted, or sautéed. Another popular bread is *naan,* made from white flour and long in shape. *Pappadums* are crispy cracker-like concoctions, seasoned with peppers and anise seed and very tasty with any food. *Dosas,* thin pancakes made with a rice base and pop-ular in the south, are often stuffed with vegetables, turnover style. *Idlis* are steamed rice and lentil cakes, and are served with chutney and ground spices —a popular breakfast dish in South India.

Vindaloo is a marinated meat dish popular in Goa.

Biryani, a dish for a special occasion, is made of chicken or lamb with fragrant whole spices and rice, and is garnished with raisins, cashews, al-monds, and a sprinkling of rose water.

Tandoori defines a method of cooking, something like our barbecue except in a clay oven. Chicken tandoori is very popular, and sometimes lamb and fish are cooked this way.

Seekh kebabs are skewered pieces of meat broiled over an open fire. Kebabs are minced pieces of meat, patty shaped, and are filled with chopped onion, green pepper, and fresh ginger.

Patrani machli is fish stuffed with chutney and baked in banana leaves—popular in Bombay.

Dhal or *dal, chutney,* and *raita* are side dishes. Dhal will look like soup or gravy to you. It is made of lentils or dried peas and other ingredients, and is served with the main course as a bland partner to other more highly seasoned foods. Chutneys are made with fruit or vegetables in a sweet-and-sour sauce. Mint and mango chutneys are especially good. Green coriander (Chinese parsley) makes another delicate chutney.

Pickles are also popular and can be made out of fruits or vegetables.

Raita is a yogurt preparation with vegetables or fruit. *Dhai* is yogurt and is used to tone down more spicy foods; it is also used in salads and as a marinade for vegetables.

Cooked vegetables include *brinjals* (eggplant), *bhindi* (okra), and *mattar* (peas). Vegetarian dishes are especially good in India, prepared with unusual sauces, combined with cheese and delicately spiced. Rice is also excellent in India and is served many ways, with vegetables, nuts, fruits, and spices.

Firni is pudding made with rice; *barfi,* a sweet similar to fudge; *jalebi* are pretzel-looking sweets in syrup; *sandesh,* a dessert made with milk; and *rasgullas,* a light dessert made with yogurt.

Carrots are disguised at dessert time and come to the table as *halwa.* India's ice cream is rich and creamy and often filled with chunks of fresh fruit. Any dessert may appear looking very dressy with a coat of thin edible silver or gold, which is not only pretty but practical, as it is supposed to aid digestion.

To top off any feast, there are a variety of fruits, some familiar (bananas, apples, incredibly tasty mangoes) and some exotic, such as *chikoos* (a cross between the fig and the russet apple) or the custard apple, which looks like an artichoke but is not.

Indian-grown tea is excellent; coffee, also locally grown, is very good. Be sure to specify if you want your coffee black—the Indian way is to mix it with steaming milk before serving it. Local beer is very good and a fine partner to Indian foods. There is a large selection of fruit drinks, of which apple is excellent (but relatively expensive), so too fresh lime and soda. Water should be boiled to stay on the safe side. You can ask politely and get this in most restaurants.

After a big meal, try *paan,* an Indian digestive sold by vendors near restaurants. This is made of betel nuts, and sweet and aromatic spices, and wrapped in crisp betel leaf. Ask for it not too hot. Paan leaves the mouth refreshed, as if you had just brushed your teeth.

3. Essential Information

What follows next is a quick survey of useful knowledge to prepare you for India.

DOCUMENTS NEEDED: A **passport** is required, and all tourists from the U.S. must have a **visa.** (U.S. residents used to be able to stay in India for 30 days without a visa, but this is no longer the case.) A visa costs $15 in person and an extra $2 (per passport) if you want it mailed. Your fee must be accompanied by a visa form available through the Indian Embassy in Washington, D.C., or the Consul-General's offices in New York, San Francisco, and Chicago.

All tourist visas are triple-entry visas and valid up to three months, which simplifies visiting neighboring countries like Nepal and getting back in India again. They can be extended for a maximum of six months.

There are also transit visas issued for stays of 15 days. To get a transit visa you must fill out an application form and produce a ticket showing your on-going destination.

Tourist visas are issued within 24 to 48 hours if you apply in person, but take up to two weeks by mail.

If you arrive in India without a visa, *you won't get in.* After 72 hours in the airport, or until a flight leaves for your home, you'll be sent out of the country. There are no visitors' permits.

For travel in restricted or protected areas foreigners require **special permits.** For Sikkim, Darjeeling, Jaldapara (West Bengal), permission for a one-week visit can be given by Indian missions abroad by making an endorsement in your passport, as well as by the Foreigners' Registration Office in New Delhi, Bombay, Calcutta, and Madras. Foreign tourists can visit Darjeeling and nearby places without permits for a period of 15 days if they arrive and depart Bagdogra by air. The permit situation often changes so quickly that even state authorities in India are unaware that the Central authorities have changed the rules. Many a time, conflicting information about travel strictures can add up to a frustrating experience. To avoid them, be sure to contact the local tourist office in your area. At press time, the Government of India was printing a brochure that would outline all the restrictions in force. It is highly advised that you consult with the tourist officers and the personnel at the states in northeastern India, Port Blair (Andamans), wildlife sanctuaries in the restricted areas, pick up forms from the Indian missions and route the application through their offices to the Ministry of Home Affairs, Department of External Affairs (Foreigners IV Section), North Block, New Delhi—110001. Allow a minimum of eight weeks for processing.

Other Useful Documents

International Student Identity Card: You qualify if you're a full-time junior or senior high, college, university, or vocational school student at least 12 years of age, enrolled in a program of study leading to a diploma or a degree at an accredited secondary or postsecondary educational institution during the current academic year. The card costs $10 and can be obtained from the Council on International Educational Exchange, 205 E. 42nd St., New York, NY 10017 (tel. 212/661-1450).

Student I.D. cards are no longer the magic wands they once were when it comes to getting special deals on train and air fares, and in India most of the old deals have been discontinued and replaced with new across-the-board concessional fares. However, your student I.D. card still has a number of uses. For instance, it entitles you to travel assistance by the Student Travel Office in New Delhi, which can save you a bundle when you're looking for a bargain fare home. The card also entitles you to automatic accident/sickness insurance anywhere outside the U.S. If you're already in India and it occurs to you how useful a card can be, you can still get it—at the Student Travel Information Center, Imperial Hotel, Janpath, New Delhi 110001. This is also the place to get your card renewed. Proof may be required for cards issued in New Delhi: You may have to show a letter from your educational institution or similar identification vouching for your student status. Verification may also be required from the U.S. Embassy in New Delhi, which is usually quite helpful.

International Youth Hostel Membership Card: You don't have to have one to use the youth hostels in India, nor do you have to be young to be a hosteler. But in some hostels preference is given card-holders, and most hostels grant members discounts on already-cheap dorm accommodations (about 60¢ for members; 80¢ for nonmembers). For details on Youth Hostel membership, write: National Headquarters, American Youth Hostels, National Office, P.O. Box 37613, Washington, DC 20013.

INOCULATIONS: If you're coming from an infected area, you'll need a smallpox vaccination and proof of yellow fever inoculations. A cholera shot is not necessary but some tourists take it anyway. Make sure any inoculation you have is entered on your World Health Organization card. Cholera shots are given in two doses if you've never had them before (make sure you allow enough time), and must be renewed every six months so keep them up-to-date if you plan an extended stay in India. A smallpox vaccination lasts three years. The lowest-budget travelers might consider a more extensive series of inoculations, including tetanus, typhoid, typhus, and bubonic plague. Some people take a gamma globulin inoculation right before leaving. Requirements change from time to time, so you'll want to check on the latest as you prepare for your India trip. For up-to-the-minute requirements, call the U.S. Public Health Service's Quarantine Department, located in the following cities: Boston, Washington, Atlanta, Miami, Los Angeles, San Francisco, Seattle, Anchorage, Chicago, and New York. Check your local directory for the number.

CURRENCY: The Indian rupee is worth, at press time, 7.6¢ U.S., but the value fluctuates from day to day. As for the dollar amounts appearing in parentheses following prices quoted in rupees throughout this book—they were calculated on the basis of $1 U.S. = Rs. 13. Barring any significant alteration in the rate of exchange, these dollar equivalents will give you a fairly good idea of what you'll be spending. If you wish, check with a banker before you leave home to determine the latest official rate of exchange. Or pick up a copy of the *New York Times* or the *Wall Street Journal,* which lists daily values of world currencies in its "Foreign Exchange" column.

There are 100 paise to each rupee. In some country towns, people still talk about annas—currency about as useful as a trading bead. (For the record, one-half rupee is worth eight annas.) You are not permitted to take rupees in or out of India. You can bring any amount of foreign currency or traveler's checks into India. If you have more than $1,000 with you, you'll have to declare your money on an official form when you arrive. Whatever you do, don't discard the form: you have to show it again when you leave the country, along with receipts for changing traveler's checks and dollars. And when you declare, be accurate—or be prepared for trouble when you leave. You'll need written permission from the Reserve Bank of India to transport undeclared currency over the border. Changing your money in India only at authorized places is advised. On the black market, your seemingly fantastic deal may turn out to be counterfeit, or your dealer may well disappear with your hard-earned dollars without giving you a rupee. When there's a favorable rate of exchange, the few paise gained is hardly worth the risk.

Traveler's checks are the best and safest way to carry your money. Major credit cards are widely accepted in India. At all but the smallest, low-budget hotels you're required to pay your bills in foreign currency, which includes credit-card transactions.

Authorized money-exchanging facilities are available at the front desks of major hotels—for guests only—and for the general public in some hotels at branch banks. Its faster to change your money at hotel banks and you get the official rate of exchange. International airports also have banks to change currency.

Be warned: when you change money, stock up on a plentiful supply of small change. It's an annoying fact (or fiction) that there isn't a curio or soft-drink seller or rickshaw wallah in India with small change. You also need plenty of small change for tips. Further, check all notes for holes and tears. Indians won't accept damaged currency. You have to take it back to the bank to redeem it or keep it as a souvenir. It's especially unfortunate to have some vendor reject your damaged currency when you've found a special treasure in an out-of-the-way bazaar and you're miles from the nearest money changer. At times like these, you might barter by offering the merchant something of your own in exchange for the coveted merchandise.

$25 A DAY—WHAT IT MEANS: The title of this book refers to a self-imposed allowance of $25 a day for basic living costs in India—that is, for a room and three meals. Before breaking this down, let me say that you can get by for less in India, but it would be living a spartan life. For those who wish to try it, the $15 and $10 standards are included as my lowest budget recommendations as well throughout this book. On the other hand, $25 a day stretches far in India in a comparison with the West.

What brings the average cost up into the $25 level in India are luxury and food taxes that affect all travelers. These taxes vary from place to place, but have been factored into the overall cost of living during your stay. Also figured into the $25-a-day cost are service charges and gratuities in connection with accommodations and meals.

Now, what you get for your money: Hotel rooms in India are usually almost two-thirds of your budget. This means $14 to $15 a day for a room, and $1 to $2 for breakfast, $2.50 to $3 for lunch, and $4 to $5 for dinner. This will cover a comfortable stay even in the most popular, and therefore most expensive, cities; in off-the-beaten-path places, this budget will permit a surprisingly high standard for the money.

Many travelers choose to modify the above budget. For instance, there are those who prefer to stay at more modestly priced hotels and eat in higher priced restaurants, or vice versa. More frequently, travelers do a bit of both. This is, of course, a matter of personal preference. Nearly all travelers put something aside for a few splurges in accommodations and meals during their India tour.

The costs of transportation to and within India, of sightseeing, and of entertainment are generally not included in the $25 figure. But in some cases—especially where two people traveling together have $50—they will find that this amount stretches to include a splurge or two, coach tours, and a number of other tourist essentials. In addition, every effort has been made to locate bargains in tours and transportation to help budget tourists keep expenditures in line.

This book is not a guide to mere subsistence living, but deals instead with clean and comfortable accommodations that can be used safely by people of all ages and both sexes.

Bon Voyage! And don't forget to pack your sense of humor with your other travel essentials.

ACCOMMODATIONS: Throughout India there are Western-style hotels with every amenity, classified by the government according to the star system, from five-star deluxe (top) to one-star. They include some fabulous palaces turned into hotels, houseboats, and hunting lodges, as well as sleek, modern international-style structures.

There are also many well-run starred **Indian-style hotels,** especially in the south. They are usually clean, functional, but comfortable places, with few frills, whitewashed walls, and stone floors. But newer Indian-style hotels are adding more of the interior decoration associated with Western-style places, racking up high star ratings and hiking room rates as well. Plain or fancy, the main difference between these hotels and their Western counterparts is the food—Indian-style hotels are strictly vegetarian.

Everywhere, **budget hotels** offer lower rates for non-air-conditioned rooms. Virtually all rooms have swirling ceiling fans to stir the breezes and many have windows or balconies opening onto gardens. So to conserve funds, you might try to get by without air conditioning. In cooler seasons, you won't need air conditioning; then hoteliers will charge you for a heater.

Be sure to pay attention to check-out times to avoid being charged for a full day by missing your deadline. And if you're traveling in the off-season, ask about discounts which may be in effect, but are not well publicized. No matter your budget, if you've made a reservation, be sure and indicate an arrival time so your room will be waiting if you get in at some offbeat hour. If you're going to be delayed, get through to the hotel about it or you may find your star accommodations those you sleep under outdoors.

Additionally, there are no-star, low-priced hotels that are great finds; and the lowest-priced hotels, usually clustered around bus and railway stations, often offer nothing more than cells with cots.

Guesthouses are other possibilities in major cities. They range greatly, from a notch or several above or below the three-, two-, and one-star hotels. The major difference between a guesthouse and a small hotel is limited meal service. Guesthouses don't have restaurants, but will send food to your room. Then there are families that take in paying guests. You'll find some mentioned on the following pages in the accommodation sections. For others, the Government of India or state tourist offices have lists.

Out of the mainstream, where sights are plentiful but tourists are not, **government-run lodges, bungalows, and forest rest houses** offer comfortable places to stay. PWD Inspection Bungalows, also usually off the beaten path, are intended for government officials, but if no inspector is expected, tourists can move in for a modest fee.

Inns run by charitable organizations, temples, or towns, known as *dharamshalas,* will put you up for a few rupees. These truly humble places, meant primarily to house traveling pilgrims, have strict rules for all guests: they are purely vegetarian and do not permit alcohol or tobacco. In dharamshalas there are no cots or restaurants, and few or no toilets.

Sooner or later you'll learn to deal with Indian-style toilets, which are as hygienic as Western styles, but take some getting used to. Indian toilets are sunk in the floor with little footpedals to either side. You squat—not sit—on them and supply your own toilet paper. Indians use water to cleanse themselves, which explains the bowls and faucets near the toilets. The left hand is for cleansing. The right hand is for eating.

The best way to experience India is to vary your accommodations. No one would want to pass up the opportunity to spend a night or two in a fabulous marble palace turned into a luxury hotel, or to relax for a few days on a well-appointed houseboat in the Vale of Kashmir. It's also enjoyable to stay in some of the splurgey hotels, where other Westerners gather.

But be sure to stay in some of the Indian-style hotels and mix with Indian travelers. This can lead to wonderful new experiences—perhaps an invitation to visit new Indian friends when they are at home or the unexpected treat of going to a wedding (which is why they may be away from home).

At the lowest end of the accommodations, the humble life might be hard to take day after day. If, however, you have little money and want to stretch it as far as possible, there's nothing unsafe about living on the cheap in India. Many travelers do it all the time. Taking a backpack and heading into the hills is yet another splendid way to enjoy India and spend little money. In some remote villages foreigners and trekking are big tourist attractions.

RESTAURANTS: There are restaurants all over India where you can get good food for budget prices. Some of these restaurants specialize in Western fare and some in Chinese dishes. In some top hotels you'll find French, Italian, and Spanish restaurants. But the reason to go to India is to sample some of the regional fare. These days managements in a number of five-star hotels have gone back in history to find authentic dishes to serve in their Indian-style restaurants. It's worth a splurge or two ($14 to $40 for two) to sample some of these rarely prepared recipes. Often they're Mughali in style, and lamb or chicken based in a never-ending variety of subtle sauces.

Table Manners

In most restaurants, you will be served by snappy waiters (bearers) at tables with plates and gleaming flatware. In traditional restaurants you will get the same efficient service, but instead of plates there will be a banana leaf or a thali (brass, stainless-steel, or bell-metal platter) to hold all your foods. Porcelain plates, which contain bone ash, are not acceptable to orthodox Hindus. Banana leaves are further washed with water at the table—a step you may wish to forgo if you are concerned over the water—before foods are placed on it.

On thalis, little metal bowls called *katoris* hold portions of each of your foods—vegetable mixtures, or meat, fish, or chicken curry, dal (lentils), raita (yogurt with chopped vegetables), achar (pickles), and papads (cracker bread) will be placed around the outer rim, while the center is crowned with a snowy mound of rice or wheat puris or both. Traditionally, there were rules about the placement of dishes, but these have been relaxed over the years. Water, however, is placed to the left, not the right, and is the traditional drink with an Indian meal. Order it bottled or boiled, if in doubt. Beer and wine are not served with these Indian meals, but in sophisticated restaurants they can be ordered.

After washing your hands at the tap, the food is eaten with the fingers of your right hand only, which is quite an art in itself. The best technique is to take a little of the dry food such as rice or bread and use it to scoop up the less solid foods like curry or dal. You might also pour some dal on your rice to make a pickupable combination. In the north of India, only the tips of the fingers are used; in the south, more of the hand is employed, including the palm. In the western section, wheat is eaten before the rice is served, although it's hardly necessary for you to worry about regional techniques. Your main concern will be to eat as neatly as possible without getting your meal all over yourself.

Alcoholic Beverages

There is total prohibition of alcohol only in Gujarat (at this writing). In other states the laws range from certain dry days to no prohibition at all, to other rules restricting drinking—and all these laws change from time to time. None of these need faze you if you have an **All-India Liquor Permit** (issued free at India Tourist Offices) to produce when you purchase drinks or bottles. You show your permit whenever you purchase a drink or bottle and your name is recorded in a large Dickensian ledger, along with your permit number and other details. Waiting around for this paperwork, W. C. Fields might have switched to soda. However, there is no problem in buying alcohol from stores in the major cities of India.

NIGHTLIFE AND ENTERTAINMENT: This is not India's strong point. There are **discothèques** in some top hotels in the major cities, and most of these hotels also have **supper clubs** with dance bands and singers. Some hotels have Indian folk and classical **dance performances** in the evenings. While less-than-authentic versions, they're pleasant diversions at dinner.

Some sleazy cabarets with half-nude dancers are found in a few cities, but these are diminishing. At these performances, dancers wiggle around in something more covered-up than we do at the beach, but get a big round of applause nonetheless. The statues on some of the celebrated temples are far more revealing.

Where more **movies** are made than anywhere else in the world, there are always movies to see. More than 700 feature films a year are produced annually in India, mainly of the boy-meets-girl, morality-and/or-mythological-themed type, although splat-and-gore action films are produced as well. Almost all movies have elaborate musical scores and singers. As a matter of fact, people go to the films to hear the dubbed-in voices of their favorite singers as much as they do to see the stars. When these favorite singers go on tour, they attract crowds larger than those who flock in the U.S. to see Madonna or Bruce Springsteen. No overt lovemaking is permitted on screen. Indeed, so extraordinary was India's recent first on-screen kiss—itself hardly more than a peck—that is merited coverage by *Life* magazine. Most often, however, the would-be passionate scene shifts to something symbolic of tenderness, while dancers dance and singers sing. English-language films also play in major cities, often after they have been censored to nonsense.

The best films are always on a reserved-seat basis, so you have to call or drop by the box office early in the day to book. There's almost always a local English-language newspaper which carries details of schedules. There are no subtitles, but even in Hindi, Tamil, or Bengali the plots are easy to follow.

The **son-et-lumière** (sound-and-light) performances at such attractions as Delhi's Red Fort, Madurai's palace, Ahmedabad's Sabarmati Ashram, and Srinagar's Shalimar Gardens commence around sunset, offering poetical and colorful presentations of various aspects of Indian history. Top price is around a dollar. Performances are in English as well as local languages.

There are dance and music **recitals** where you can see authentic *bharata natyam,* for example, one of the graceful classical dances of India, or hear the sitar, sarod, or other instruments and singers. Check the newspapers' events listings for places and times of performances. These opportunities should not be overlooked.

The Media

Television stations are government run, and programs are sometimes in English. Color television is a fairly recent innovation. Most locally produced programs are on in the evenings; on weekends there are some daytime shows. The top hotels' guest rooms have television sets that are equipped for closed-circuit transmission of a range of videotapes, viewable without extra charge. Offerings range from such screwball comedies as Woody Allen's *Bananas* to spy melodramas. Indeed, through modern technology East has finally met West. Now in this land for centuries renowned for yoga, you can, if you wish, start your day with a new guru—Jane Fonda on videotape.

The 85 **radio** stations in India are government run. News is broadcast in English frequently throughout the day.

Most **newspapers** are privately owned, and of the 17,168 newspapers published in a plethora of languages and dialects, 3,288 are in English. Two major wire services, Press Trust of India and United News of India, relay national news in English. The *International Herald Tribune* and *Wall Street Journal*'s Asian edition are sold in India.

There are news, business news, economic, feature, and movie **magazines** in English throughout the country. In addition, you can buy the Asian editions of *Time* and *Newsweek,* though the prices are high—Rs. 15 ($1.15) a copy plus a newsstand markup.

Speaking of reading, excellent **bookstores** are found all over India with many fascinating titles, some familiar and some new to Westerners.

TO YOUR HEALTH: Water is said to be potable in many large Indian cities, but I recommend drinking it boiled, bottled, or filtered—or stick to hot tea instead. Many hoteliers and restaurateurs offer boiled or specially treated water; but if not, don't be shy—ask for it. You'll probably worry about the water if you don't, and worry in itself can cause upsets. Also, remember that ice is made of water. Take it easy on exploring new foods until you are adjusted to India. A spicy curry after a long and tiring international flight is too hard to digest if you're not used to it, and any sudden change in diet can cause your stomach to play tricks in revenge. Use good sense when buying fresh foods, as you would anywhere. When in doubt, don't. Peeling your own fruit is advised; buying from street stalls is not. India is exciting, different, stimulating. There will be a tendency to overdo, which also can invite temporary upsets. Finally, if you do get a "bug," there are good doctors, drugstores, and hospitals in all towns and cities. In some places, the doctors have studied abroad. Your hotel reception desk can recommend a good doctor or point out the nearest pharmacy.

WHAT TO PACK: Here are some guidelines on what you need to get by in India. First, you should know that it's not a dressy country, and casual clothes will do for just about every occasion except a big event (and if something big comes up, you can buy something locally). Nor is India always hot: if you're going to be in northern India, mid-November to mid-February, you'll need woolens, and the farther north you go during those months, the heavier the woolens. After mid-February, summer clothes will do everywhere, except Kashmir, Ladakh, and other mountain regions, where you'll need a sweater and you should dress in layers so you can strip down during the warmth of the day. Summertime, you'll need summer clothes everywhere, though in the mountains you may need a light wrap at night.

Jeans or something comparable are acceptable almost everywhere (except, again, at a big occasion), and they're positively essential in outlying areas. Shorts are not worn in city streets, although some Westerners who don't take Indian sensitivities into consideration, do. Generally, women's shoulders are covered in India. You need shoes easy to get in and out of at temples and other shrines. Plus, you'll need beachwear for beach resorts and trekking gear for trekking. Take sunblock, sunglasses, and insect repellent, the latter for jungly places. An umbrella and raincoat are necessary for visiting during the monsoon.

Imported cosmetics are expensive, as is imported film, so take a plentiful supply of both. (The domestically made products are not as good.) Also, if you take any medication, bring it along, as well as a prescription for a refill. An extra pair of glasses or a prescription for a new pair is a good idea in case you lose or break yours.

In the "other items" area, take a fits-it-all sink stopper. Some budget hotels don't always have them (and it's impossible to make one). Take a small padlock, some of the lowest-budget hotels expect guests to bring their own. Take a flashlight—power failures occur. And remember your Swiss army knife for peeling fruits and dozens of other uses.

The best advice of all is to travel light: there are *dhobis* (clothes washers) all over India who can wash and press clothes in hours—and while at times I've found the job less than perfect, I've never had anything totally ruined. This is not the case with dry cleaners, which are not always top-notch.

Don't worry about running out of clothes. You can always buy something good to wear everywhere in India at surprisingly affordable prices.

CUSTOMS: There is virtually no restriction on the importation of personal effects—a modest amount of jewelry, one watch, two still cameras and five rolls of film (you may want to bring more), one 8-mm movie camera and ten reels or cartridges of film, and many other items are permitted without special declaration. You're also allowed one quart of liquor. If, however, you've got a lot of high-priced photographic equipment, transistor radios, tape recorders, and the like, you'll have to fill out a re-export form. You can bring in up to Rs. 500 ($38.50) in articles as gifts for Indian friends; tourists of Indian origin are permitted Rs. 1,250 ($96) in gifts.

All items brought into India are to be re-exported when you leave. You can also take out souvenirs of Indian silk, wool, art wares, and other items without limit. As long as you're not a resident of India, you can take out gold jewelry up to Rs. 2,000 ($155); a Rs. 10,000 ($770) limit is applied to items set with precious stones. Items of peacock feathers can be taken out in a reasonable amount. Banned entirely from export are articles made of animal or snake skin. There are restrictions on the exportation of antiquities (more than 100 years old). To check on whether your purchases are considered antiquities, you may wish to consult the director of antiquities, Archaeological Survey of India, Janpath, New Delhi 110001, or the local superintending archeologist at three offices around the country: Eastern Circle, Archaeological Survey of India, Narayani Building, Brabourne Road, Calcutta 700013; Southern Circle, Archaeological Survey of India, Fort St. George, Madras 600001; Frontier Circle, Archaeological Survey of India, Minto Bridge, Srinagar 190001.

SHOPPING: In a vast country with people of highly diverse backgrounds and talents, crafts are varied and plentiful. Indeed, artisans work the same way as they did centuries ago, with secrets fathers handed down to their sons. It still takes the same incredible patience and skill (one whole day to weave an inch of elaborately patterned silk) as it did many years ago. Some silk like that might cost as much as Rs. 800 ($61.50) per yard; but it is also possible to buy six yards of a simpler fabric for Rs. 180 ($13.85) and a cotton sari for half that or less.

Here is what to look for, in general, as you go to some of the popular places in this book:

Delhi: Crafts from everywhere in India. Local specialties are ivories, carved so fine that you need a magnifying glass to see each perfect figure; pottery in blue and black, painted in bright designs; gold-embroidered handbags; copper made into lamps and other useful items.

Agra: Inspired by the Taj Mahal, local craftsmen make use of inlays of petal-thin strips of cornelian, lapis lazuli, and mother-of-pearl to create stunning boxes, coasters, plates, and even table tops.

Jaipur: Headquarters for jewelry. Gems are set into enameled brooches, necklaces, and bracelets similar to those worn in the 18th century. Stones are carved into flowers and fanciful beasts. Another specialty is colorful enamelwork on brass, made into carafes, ashtrays, and other items. Pretty embroidered slippers, with turned-up toes, are another good buy, as are tie-dyed silks.

Madras: Fabrics, especially the famous cotton. Silks from the nearby temple city of Kanchipuram are very beautiful. Alligator cigar and cigarette cases and wallets are other specialties. Bronzes, old and new, and elaborate woodcarvings can also be found locally.

Cochin: Ivory statues and coir mats, made of coconut fiber, are inexpensive, durable buys.

Bhopal: Chanderi, a sheer fabric often shot with gold and silver, and zari, a combination of silver and gold threads on black velvet, are local items.

Bhubaneswar: A silver filigree made into lovely bracelets, pins, necklaces, and small ornamental items. Paintings in primary colors from nearby Puri can make interesting accents in any home.

Hyderabad: Bangles, more than anywhere else; bidriware, an unusual mixture of stones and wires, inlaid in black or white alloy, comes in all shapes and sizes and types of useful items—from pins to pitchers. Amusing toys are cheap; pearls, expensive.

Mysore City: Fragrant sandalwood used for carvings and as the base of exotically scented soaps and oils.

Calcutta: Unusual toys in pottery and wood.

Ahmedabad: Stunning embroidery studded with mirrors, suitable for dramatic wall hangings, pillow covers, or a dressy vest or skirt.

Kashmir: Thick hand-loomed rugs rich with flowers; papier-mâché objects coated with gold leaf and decorated with vines, flowers, and unusual figures; fine paisley shawls, caftans, and silver and turquoise jewelry.

Bombay: Boutiques for ready-made or tailor-made dresses. Men's clothes also can be made up quickly. Ceramic tiles are a modern specialty. Many antique stores are filled with items left behind by the British Raj and others.

Amritsar: Embroidery work, shawls, and metalware; sheer kurtas (billowing embroidered shirts) from nearby Lucknow.

Varanasi: Silks richly woven with silver and gold; also cutwork and embroidery on cotton, in saris or to make up into dresses.

Darjeeling: Rugs, shawls, jewelry, furs.

Note: Specifics on shopping appear in the area chapters, and include not only what to buy, but where to buy it.

The Art of Bargaining

Bargaining goes on almost everywhere except in such government-run stores as Central Cottage Industries Emporium, and it's a way of life in bazaars like Chandni Chowk. In posh shops, merchants who claim they don't probably will bargain if you tactfully suggest that their prices are out of line.

Patience is rewarded when it comes to driving a good bargain. For example, you find the perfect woodcarving for your collection at home. When the merchant asks Rs. 500 [$38.50] for the item, look at him passively and say, "For this? It's not that I don't like it. But who would pay more than Rs. 150 [$11.50] for this?" Pick up the carving and look at it carefully and remark on its "flaws." "It's damaged, and the workmanship is not really good." Then quickly offer Rs. 200 ($15.40) for the carving, put it down, and start to walk off. Don't worry. As soon as you've set foot in the direction of the door, you'll get another offer and finally settle on Rs. 250 ($19.25) to Rs. 300 ($23).

If you think in terms of dollar equivalents, you'll be doomed when bargaining. Start equating rupees with dollars—Re. 1 to $1—and see how your perspective changes about how much you are willing to pay even for the piece of your dreams.

Always shop without your guide or driver, and shun shops they suggest since the merchants probably give commissions to those who steer buyers their way—commissions that are tacked onto bills in the form of higher prices.

Remember, too, that there are restrictions on exporting antiquities (items more than 100 years old). If you buy a fabulous antique or think you have, be sure that you get the proper permits through the merchant or consult the director of antiquities, Archaeological Survey of India, Janpath, New Delhi 110001, or the equivalent authority in Madras, Bombay, or Calcutta, about getting it out of the country.

FESTIVALS: India shines at festival times. The following include only major celebrations. Be sure to check with local tourist offices to see if others are going on while you're around. As for dates, with the exception of Republic Day, they vary slightly from year to year. Again, check local tourist offices for details.

January

Republic Day—always on the 26th and, in New Delhi, lasting for four days. This is the most spectacular of the festivals. It starts with a big parade down the majestic Rajpath. There are decorated elephants, camels, girls with flowers in their hair, floats from every region, and a shower of rose petals from above. The nation's leaders are in the grandstands. The parade is followed by folk-dance exhibitions and a military display, on Victory Square, facing the main government buildings and Presidential Palace.

Pongal—In Madurai, Thanjavur, and Tiruchirapalli. There are special foods, and in some places you can see an extraordinary bullfight where money is tied to the horns of the animals and young boys pull it off.

March

Holi—very spirited. Mainly celebrated in the north. It's the time when everyone throws colored water and powder on each other and everything in sight. It symbolizes tarnishing the old and beginning the new—wear your oldest clothes.

June

Cart Festival—when the gods go on their summer holiday, thousands go to Puri to see them off down "Main Street."

August

Onam—Kerala's harvest festival; includes a great "snake" boat race through the lagoons.

October-November

Dussehra—in the fall (October or November), commemorates the killing of the demon King Ravana by Rama and symbolizes the destruction of evil by good. It differs from place to place. For example, in Delhi the evil king literally gets blown up: giant effigies are stuffed with firecrackers and set off. In Calcutta it's called **Durga Puja,** and pandals (displays) of traditional scenes bring out the best in the bustling city. In Kulu, gods are paraded on special palanquins with musical accompaniment.

Diwali—very pretty. Every house, village, and public building is lit with tiny flickering oil lamps (although the public buildings sometimes use electricity). The goddess of prosperity, Lakshmi, reputedly comes to call on lighted homes and scorns those that are not. Gifts are exchanged; mountains of sweets, mostly silver-wrapped, appear in the bazaars.

Pushkar—a fair in Rajasthan, in November, where there is camel racing and spirited folk dancing.

December

Vaikunta / Ekadasi—procession of beautifully adorned gods from Srirangam's Temple in Tiruchirapalli.

Christmas—gift-giving goes on almost everywhere, even among non-Christians. In Goa and Kerala, where there are large numbers of Christians, the celebration is carried out traditionally.

WILDLIFE: About one-fifth of India's land is covered with a wide variety of wildlife. Rare species such as the Asian lion, one-horned rhinoceros, black buck, Kashmiri stag, and white tiger (seen today mainly in zoos) are protected animals. India's 20 national parks, 191 wildlife sanctuaries, and 9 bird sanctuaries all over the country make it possible to see rare animals and beautiful birds in various striking settings somewhere during your journey. Be sure to check with the tourist office on the best seasons to visit before you take off. Some preserves are inaccessible during the monsoon, and others have limited populations at some seasons. You'll read about a few of India's major sanctuaries in the following chapters. These, and some others equally worthwhile, are:

Bandipur (Karnataka): elephants, bison, panthers, tigers, and spotted deer.

Corbett National Park (Uttar Pradesh): tigers, sambhar, and chital.

Kaziranga National Park (Northeast Frontier): one-horned rhinoceros and bison.

Palamau National Park (Bihar): tigers and panthers.

Periyar Wildlife Sanctuary (Kerala): elephants and wild boars.

Gir Lion Sanctuary (Gujarat): Asian lions.

Jaldpara Wildlife Sanctuary (West Bengal): rhinoceros, kakar, and peafowl.

Sariska Wildlife Sanctuary (Rajasthan): tigers, nilgai, and deer.

Dandeli Wildlife Sanctuary (Karnataka): tigers, elephants, sloth bear, gaur, chowsingha, and wild dogs.

Nagarhole (Karnataka): tigers, elephants, sambar, and wild boar.

Bharatpur Bird Sanctuary (Rajasthan): rare birds come from as far away as Siberia in winter.

Chilka Bird Sanctuary (Orissa): waterbirds.

Ranganathittu Bird Sanctuary (Karnataka): stork, ibis, white heron, Indian darter, and others.

Three **lion safari parks** have also been developed, at Hyderabad, at Borivili near Bombay, and at Nandankanan in Orissa.

MARIJUANA SMOKING: It comes as no surprise to anyone from here to Kathmandu that ganja is readily available in India, where it not only grows but is sold. What you may not know is that, contrary to popular mythology, the attitude in India is not "anything goes toward smokers," no matter what you've heard. It's not legal to smoke the weed in India unless you're a sadhu or an addict. Discretion is advised: don't smoke in public, and keep it out of sight wherever you're staying. Searches are conducted from time to time in suspect areas. For instance, Pharaganj in Delhi, Stuart Lane in Calcutta, and some borders leading to Nepal and Sri Lanka are some of the well-publicized places where there have been searches. "Hippy" looks are often associated with soft- and hard-drug problems in the eyes of some Indian authorities. You might want to dress extra-conservatively on days you're apt to cross paths with officialdom.

TIPPING: Some hotels and restaurants add a service charge to your bill. You might tip over and above this service charge in hotels where you have a bearer (personal servant) to see to your every need. Two rupees a night would be adequate. In a restaurant where there's a service charge and the service has been exceptionally good, you might leave some small change as well.

At hotels and restaurants without service charges, tip 10% to 12½% for services rendered, unless the bill is moderate, and then probably 5% would do. Hotel porters get Rs. 2 (15¢) per bag; coat room attendants, Rs. 2 when you retrieve your coat. Doormen do not get tipped.

About Rs. 26 ($2) per day should be given to a driver if he has done an excellent job. This can apply to individual travelers and does not increase when the party is made up of a carload. You might increase the driver's tip to Rs. 30 ($2.30) for an especially challenging mountainous trip. Cab drivers don't get tipped, unless they've performed some special service for you, such as locating a hard-to-find address or watching your packages while you go off to admire the view. Little boys who appear from nowhere to carry packages deserve a few paise for their help. Sometimes a guide won't accept a tip, but a small gift such as a box of sweets is well received.

Porters at railway stations get Rs. 2 (15¢) per bag. At major airports, you buy a porterage ticket, usually Rs. 2 per bag. Porters don't get tipped on top of this, but they'll hang around looking like they do. At airports where there's no porterage fee, stick to the Rs. 2 rule.

Don't tip the help at hotels who crawl out of the woodwork and hover when you leave unless they've actually done something for you.

Finally, a tip for you: Don't overdo when tipping in India. Service in India is far less expensive than it is at home. One or two rupees go a long way and is considered a generous tip.

GUIDES: English-speaking guides are available through the India Tourist Offices throughout the country. For local sightseeing for a group of four or fewer the fee is Rs. 48 ($3.70) for a half day, Rs. 72 ($5.50), varying modestly in some places, for a full day. Transportation charges for the guide going out of town are not included in the above fees, nor are entrance charges to museums, monuments, etc. If the guide has to spend the night, the cost of board and lodging is paid by the tourist or group. Government-approved guides are also stationed at some of the country's leading monuments, and non-approved guides also hang around. If in doubt, ask the guide to produce his certificate issued by the Department of Tourism. Foreign-language guides, available in some larger cities, cost Rs. 25 ($1.90) extra.

BEGGING: Make a contribution at a temple, mosque, or charity if you wish, but the government asks that you not give to beggars who hang around the hotels, restaurants, and shops, and creep up when your car is caught in traffic. You may find it hard to resist some of these pathetic types, but please do. According to my Indian friends, these are professionals who are often more well off than you.

TIME: There is a 10½-hour time difference between New York and India. In other words it's 5½ hours ahead of Greenwich Mean Time.

VOLTAGE: 220 volts A.C., 50 cycles. You'll need to take a transformer and special plugs for American gadgets; they are not easily available in India. Some of the high-priced hotels have dual current for Western travelers.

LANGUAGE: While there are 15 major regional languages, and over 250 minor regional ones, English is widely spoken. It's one of the things the Raj left behind.

HELP!: For free aid in planning your trip, for assistance while traveling in India, or simply for pamphlets and brochures, consult any of the **Government of India Tourist Offices,** at the following places: In the U.S. and Canada at 30 Rockefeller Plaza, 15 North Mezzanine, New York, NY 10112 (tel. 212/586-4901); 3550 Wilshire Blvd., Suite 204, Los Angeles, CA 90010 (tel. 213/380-8855); 230 N. Michigan Ave., Chicago, IL 60601 (tel. 312/236-6899); West Suite 1003, Royal Trust Tower, 60 Bloor St., Toronto, ON, Canada M4W 3B8 (tel. 416/962-3787). In India at 88 Janpath, New Delhi 110001 (tel. 32005); Willingdon Island, Cochin 682009 (tel. 6045); Communidade Building, Church Square, Panaji, Goa 303001 (tel. 3412); Tourist Bhawan, Bir Chand Patel Marg, Patna 800001 (tel. 26721); Middle Point, Port Blair, 744101 (tel. 3006); G.S. Road, Police Bazar, Shillong 793001 (tel. 25632); 123 M. Karve Rd., Bombay 400020 (tel. 293144); 154 Anna Salai Road, Madras 600002 (tel. 88686); 4 Shakespeare Sarani, Calcutta 700071 (tel. 441402); State Hotel, Jaipur 302001 (tel. 72200); 191 The Mall, Agra 282001 (tel. 72377); 15 B The Mall, Varanasi 221002 (tel. 43189); Krishna Vilas, Station Road, Aurangabad 430001; (tel. 4817); Near the Western Temples, Khajuraho 471690 (tel. 47); K.F.C. Building, 48 Church St., Bangalore 560001 (tel. 579517); B.K. Kakati Road, Ulubari, Guwahati 751007 (tel. 31381); B-21 Kalpana Area, Bhubaneshwar, Orissa 751014 (tel. 54203); 25 Sandozi Bldg. (2nd Floor), 26 Himayat Nagar, Hyderabad 500029 (tel. 66877).

A WORD FROM OUR READERS: All of us share a common aim—to travel as widely and as well as possible, at the best value for our money. In achieving that aim, your comments and suggestions can be of aid to other visitors. Therefore if you come across an appealing hotel, restaurant, nightclub, shopping bargain, sightseeing attraction, please don't keep it to yourself. And the letters need not only apply to new establishments, but to hotels and restaurants already recommended in this guide. The fact that a listing appears in this edition doesn't give it squatter's rights in future publications. If its services have deteriorated, its chef grown stale, its room prices risen unfairly, whatever, these failings need to be known. Even if you enjoyed every place and found every description accurate, a letter letting me know that too can cheer many a gray day. Send your comments to Jan Aaron, c/o Frommer Books, Prentice Hall Press, Gulf + Western Building, One Gulf + Western Plaza, New York, NY 10023.

4. The $35-A-Day Travel Club—How to Save Money on All Your Travels

In this book we'll be looking at how to get your money's worth in India but there is a "device" for saving money and determining value on *all* your trips. It's the popular, international $35-A-Day Travel Club, now in its 26th successful year of operation. The Club was formed at the urging of numerous readers of the $-A-Day and Dollarwise Guides, who felt that such an organization could provide continuing travel information and a sense of community to value-minded travelers in all parts of the world. And so it does!

In keeping with the budget concept, the annual membership fee is low and is immediately exceeded by the value of your benefits. Upon receipt of $18 (U.S. residents), or $20 U.S. by check drawn on a U.S. bank or via international postal money order in U.S. funds (Canadian, Mexican and other foreign residents) to cover one year's membership, we will send all new members the following items:

(1) Any *two* of the following books

Please designate in your letter which two you wish to receive:

Frommer's $-A-Day Guides
> Europe on $30 a Day
> Australia on $30 a Day
> Eastern Europe on $25 a Day
> England on $40 a Day
> Greece (including Istanbul and Turkey's Aegean Coast) on $30 a Day
> Hawaii on $50 a Day
> India on $25 a Day
> Ireland on $30 a Day
> Israel on $30 & $35 a Day
> Mexico (plus Belize and Guatemala) on $20 a Day
> New York on $50 a Day
> New Zealand on $40 a Day
> Scandinavia on $50 a Day
> Scotland and Wales on $40 a Day
> South America on $30 a Day
> Spain and Morocco (plus the Canary Is.) on $40 a Day
> Turkey on $25 a Day
> Washington, D.C., and Historic Virginia on $40 a Day

Frommer's Dollarwise Guides
> Dollarwise Guide to Austria and Hungary
> Dollarwise Guide to Belgium, Holland, & Luxembourg
> Dollarwise Guide to Bermuda and The Bahamas
> Dollarwise Guide to Canada
> Dollarwise Guide to the Caribbean
> Dollarwise Guide to Egypt
> Dollarwise Guide to England and Scotland
> Dollarwise Guide to France
> Dollarwise Guide to Germany

Dollarwise Guide to Italy
Dollarwise Guide to Japan and Hong Kong
Dollarwise Guide to Portugal, Madeira, and the Azores
Dollarwise Guide to the South Pacific
Dollarwise Guide to Switzerland and Liechtenstein
Dollarwise Guide to Alaska
Dollarwise Guide to California and Las Vegas
Dollarwise Guide to Florida
Dollarwise Guide to the Mid-Atlantic States
Dollarwise Guide to New England
Dollarwise Guide to New York State
Dollarwise Guide to the Northwest
Dollarwise Guide to Skiing USA—East
Dollarwise Guide to Skiing USA—West
Dollarwise Guide to the Southeast and New Orleans
Dollarwise Guide to the Southwest
Dollarwise Guide to Texas
(Dollarwise Guides discuss accommodations and facilities in all price ranges, with emphasis on the medium-priced.)

Frommer's Touring Guides
Egypt
Florence
London
Paris
Venice
(These new, color illustrated guides include walking tours, cultural and historic sites, and other vital travel information.)

Serious Shopper's Guides
Italy
London
Los Angeles
Paris
(Practical and comprehensive, each of these handsomely illustrated guides lists hundreds of stores, selling everything from antiques to wine, conveniently organized alphabetically by category.)

Arthur Frommer's New World of Travel
(From America's #1 travel expert, a sourcebook with the hottest news and latest trends that's guaranteed to change the way you travel—and save you hundreds of dollars. Jam-packed with alternative new modes of travel that will lead you to vacations that cater to the mind, the spirit, and a sense of thrift.)

A Shopper's Guide to the Caribbean
(Two experienced Caribbean hands guide you through this shopper's paradise, offering witty insights and helpful tips on the wares and emporia of more than 25 islands.)

Beat the High Cost of Travel
(This practical guide details how to save money on absolutely all travel items —accommodations, transportation, dining, sightseeing, shopping, taxes, and more. Includes special budget information for seniors, students, singles, and families.)

Bed & Breakfast—North America
(This guide contains a directory of over 150 organizations that offer bed & breakfast referrals and reservations throughout North America. The scenic attractions, and major schools and universities near the homes of each are also listed.)

Dollarwise Guide to Cruises
(This complete guide covers all the basics of cruising—ports of call, costs, fly-cruise package bargains, cabin selection booking, embarkation and debarkation and describes in detail over 60 ships cruising the waters of Alaska, the Caribbean, Mexico, Hawaii, Panama, Canada, and the United States.)

Dollarwise Guide to Skiing Europe
(Describes top ski resorts in Austria, France, Italy, and Switzerland. Illustrated with maps of each resort area plus full-color trail maps.)

Guide to Honeymoon Destinations
(A special guide for that most romantic trip of your life, with full details on planning and choosing the destination that will be just right in the U.S. [California, New England, Hawaii, Florida, New York, South Carolina, etc.], Canada, Mexico, and the Caribbean.)

Marilyn Wood's Wonderful Weekends
(This very selective guide covers the best mini-vacation destinations within a 175-mile radius of New York City. It describes special country inns and other accommodations, restaurants, picnic spots, sights, and activities—all the information needed for a two- or three-day stay.)

Motorist's Phrase Book
(A practical phrase book in French, German, and Spanish designed specifically for the English-speaking motorist touring abroad.)

Swap and Go—Home Exchanging Made Easy
(Two veteran home exchangers explain in detail all the money-saving benefits of a home exchange, and then describe precisely how to do it. Also includes information on home rentals and many tips on low-cost travel.)

The Candy Apple: New York for Kids
(A spirited guide to the wonders of the Big Apple by a savvy New York grandmother with a kid's-eye view to fun. Indispensable for visitors and residents alike.)

Travel Diary and Record Book
(A 96-page diary for personal travel notes plus a section for such vital data as passport and traveler's check numbers, itinerary, postcard list, special people and places to visit, and a reference section with temperature and conversion charts, and world maps with distance zones.)

Where to Stay USA
(By the Council on International Educational Exchange, this extraordinary guide is the first to list accommodations in all 50 states that cost anywhere from $3 to $30 per night.)

(2) A one-year subscription to *The Wonderful World of Budget Travel*

This quarterly eight-page tabloid newspaper keeps you up to date on fast-breaking developments in low-cost travel in all parts of the world bringing you the latest money-saving information—the kind of information you'd have to pay $25 a year to obtain elsewhere. This consumer-conscious publication also features columns of special interest to readers: **Hospitality Exchange** (members all over the world who are willing to provide hospitality to other members as they pass through their home cities); **Share-a-Trip** (offers and requests from members for travel companions who can share costs and help avoid the burdensome single supplement); and **Readers Ask . . . Readers Reply** (travel questions from members to which other members reply with authentic firsthand information).

(3) A copy of *Arthur Frommer's Guide to New York*

This is a pocket-size guide to hotels, restaurants, nightspots, and sightseeing attractions in all price ranges throughout the New York area.

(4) Your personal membership card

Membership entitles you to purchase through the Club all Arthur Frommer publications for a third to a half off their regular retail prices during the term of your membership.

So why not join this hardy band of international budgeteers and participate in its exchange of travel information and hospitality? Simply send your name and address, together with your annual membership fee of $18 (U.S. residents) or $20 U.S. (Canadian, Mexican, and other foreign residents), by check drawn on a U.S. bank or via international postal money order in U.S. funds to: $35-A-Day Travel Club, Inc., Frommer Books, Prentice Hall Press, Gulf + Western Building, One Gulf + Western Plaza, New York, NY 10023. And please remember to specify which *two* of the books in section (1) above you wish to receive in your initial package of members' benefits. Or, if you prefer, use the last page of this book, simply checking off the two books you select and enclosing $18 or $20 in U.S. currency.

Once you are a member, there is no obligation to buy additional books. No books will be mailed to you without your specific order.

Chapter I

GETTING THERE AND GETTING AROUND

1. Getting There
2. Getting Around India

INDIA IS A FAR THROW from the Western world when it comes to culture—and a far throw in terms of distance too. That and the cost of fuel these days are the main factors in determining how much your plane ticket to this exotic land will cost. And before I even tell you about the options, let's say that all fares in this chapter, while accurate at press time, *are subject to change.*

1. Getting There

Now in considering some options on Air-India, the national carrier, which has daily flights from New York to India, via London, to either Bombay or New Delhi, let's look first at:

THE MOST FREQUENTLY USED BUDGET FARE: It's the **120-Day Round-Trip Excursion Fare,** which gives you 14 to 120 days to savor the temples, marble palaces, Mughal archways, and other exotic sights. It costs $1,415 from New York to Bombay/Delhi, and $1,477 to Calcutta/Madras.

With this fare, you not only get your flight to one of the cities above to begin your visit to India, but one stopover in each direction between the U.S. and India in a city served by Air-India. Since the carrier always stops in London, you might want to spend a few days there before or after your India journey for one of your stopovers, and select another stop from the cities served by the carrier.

You also get an additional stop at Bombay or Delhi. So if you go first to Bombay, then Delhi is thrown in at no extra charge, and vice versa. Try to take off during midweek; otherwise, on Friday or Saturday when eastbound, and Saturday or Sunday when westbound, there's a $15 surcharge. The 120-Day Round-Trip Excursion ticket can be purchased at any time prior to departure, and if you change your mind about routing, adjustments can be made at any time

There's also a **60-Day Round-Trip Excursion Fare** which gives you from 21 to 60 days to savor the sights, carries no weekend surcharge, and permits one stop in each direction, but not more than one in the Middle East. This ticket can be purchased anytime before departure, and rerouting is allowed. From New York it costs $1,604 to Bombay/Delhi, and $1,732 to Calcutta/Madras.

Additional Cities at No Extra Fare

While the additional-cities offers have changed over the years, it's still worth pointing up again that both the 120-day and the 60-day Round-Trip Excursion fares give you one stopover in each direction. This means that your air fare for India may not be as costly as it appears since it can also transport you to two other points of interest.

Higher-priced air fares permit you to travel to a number of different places en route to or from India, based on the mileage to India. For big-spenders, Air-India offers two other fares from New York: Executive Class (costing $1,168 to Bombay/Delhi, $1,219 to Calcutta/Madras) and First Class ($2,473 to Bombay/Delhi, $2,557 to Calcutta/Madras).

Flights in the U.S. that bring you to New York for your Air-India departures, and your return home, are special add-on fares at lower-than-usual prices.

One-way fares are also offered—$979 is the lowest—but are generally not useful to tourists.

West Coast Departures

From the West Coast, both San Francisco and Los Angeles can be gateway cities. Your 14- to 120-Day Round-Trip Excursion fares from Los Angeles or San Francisco to Delhi or Bombay would be $1,171 ($1,325 between December 1 and December 26). If your visit will be less than two weeks, you can book Pan Am's fare of $2,648—valid year round. You can enjoy the little extras if you book the business class fare of $3,776 round trip also valid year 'round.

If your destination is Madras or Calcutta, Pan Am can book you on an Indian Airways connecting flight.

PACKAGE TOURS: If you're short of time, you might seriously consider a package tour to avoid on-the-spot planning and that sort of thing. Currently there are more than 30 tours to India, catering to diverse tastes and interests, and often including neighboring Nepal, Sri Lanka, or China. The lowest price is something like 16 days for $695, which takes in highlights of India and Nepal; the highest is about 45 days for $5,795, which includes highlights in India, Nepal, and Sri Lanka. To get an "India Tour Digest" describing these and many other tours at various prices, contact Air-India, 400 Park Ave., New York, NY 10022 (tel. 212/407-1377).

CHOOSING AN AIRLINE: Despite deregulation, all airlines flying to India charge about the same fares and fly almost the same equipment. That said, I'll point out that my favorite airline is Air-India and for good reason: it offers a most pleasurable preview of the country you're about to visit. Even before boarding the 747, the mood is set—bordering the exteriors of the windows on the gigantic plane are distinctive Indian designs. Once aboard, the plane is further enhanced by colorful Indian motifs. More likely than not, your hostess will be wearing a shimmering sari, and your steward will change to a raw-silk, high-necked serving jacket en route. Both will pamper and please, gliding up and down the aisles, offering curries and international cuisine, tending to your every need with true Indian hospitality. Air-India's business class flights offer all the extras for much less than other airlines.

OVERLAND TO INDIA: There are overland tours by coach that go through Europe, the Near and Middle East, and across India to Kathmandu. There are tours by train and variations on these themes. To get there from here isn't possible without going partway there—to London. Two good London-based resources for traveling overland to India are **Hann Overland,** 288-270 Vauxhall Bridge Rd., 2nd Floor, Victoria, London SW1V 1EJ (tel. 01/834-7337), and **Encounter Overland Ltd.,** 267 Old Brompton Rd., London SW5 (tel. 01/370-6845), both offering tours for those 18 to 40; and **Sundowners,** 267 Old Brompton Rd., London SW5 (tel. 01/370-1482), with tours for any adult age, but the average participant is 20 to 45.

Prices for overland tours start around $695 for a 24-day trip covering 2,000 miles to around $2,000 for a 15-week, 10,365-mile trip that meanders through a number of countries before getting to India, and exits in Nepal. Considering the current political situation in a number of countries en route, American travelers should check with the State Department's Citizens Emergency Center (CEC), 2201 C St., NW, Room 4811, Washington, D.C. 20520 (tel. 202/647-4000) for up-to-the-minute situation reports.

2. Getting Around India

BY AIR: Indian Airlines, one of the country's carriers, is the largest regional carrier in South Asia, operating to 73 stations, including nine cities in seven neighboring countries. Its fleet consists of 10 wide-bodied Airbus aircraft and 25 Boeing 737s, besides 19 turboprops for short sectors.

Vayudoot, the other carrier, was originally launched to link inaccessible areas in the northeast and now flies to a number of areas in India, both off the beaten path and in the mainstream. Aircraft used by Vayudoot are smaller than Indian Airlines, but fares and all rules regarding passengers are the same. The rupee/dollar rates, set by the airlines, are not pegged to any current rate of exchange but to a formula developed to serve the airlines. This explains why the Rs. 13 to $1 used throughout this book does not apply to the air fares you'll find in the "Getting There" sections throughout this book.

For foreign travelers, the **Discover India fare** can be a good deal. It permits you to fly anywhere in India for $375 within 21 days. You can buy this ticket before you leave home and make reservations for the flights when you book your flight to India.

Booking your reservations for flights within India is a good idea, especially if you don't have all the time in the world. Planes in some sectors in India are heavily booked with business travelers who must travel long distances in the shortest time to keep their appointments, and who therefore go by plane rather than train. And in the last few years the domestic airlines have installed computerized reservations. Thus booking errors are fewer than in pretechnology days when flights listed as booked were often half full and those listed as available were overbooked, and other variations on the seat theme.

Other concessional fares of interest are the 30% **South India Excursion Rebate.** This fare gives a discount on the U.S. dollar tariff when the gateway points are Madras, Tiruchirapali, or Trivandraum for passengers originating in Sri Lanka or Maldives. In addition, there's a 25% **Youth Discount** on U.S. dollar fare for ages 12 to 30, applicable on domestic and India-Nepal routes only. Student discounts of 25% are also given to those aged 12 to 30.

Always remember to confirm your domestic flights 48 hours in advance or you may be cancelled. Keep in mind that arrival time at the airport is one hour before flight time, not the skid-to-the-finish-line margin at home. It takes a while in India to check in at ticket counters, and security checks are very thorough, which accounts for the early arrival time.

It is SOP to go through the electronic devices, then a personal hands-on checkup, in addition to an open-baggage inspection. You will be asked to identify your luggage on the field before it is placed on the aircraft. Any luggage not identified is left behind.

If you have a Swiss army knife or other items that are remotely sharp, don't attempt to carry them aboard. They will be taken from you during the security check and given to the pilot to carry for you. You get them back once you've reached your destination.

When going through electronic security, don't leave exposed film in the pockets of your carry-on bag. The X-ray can ruin the film. There are special containers you can buy to carry film safely through checkpoints.

Note also that unlike in the West, where the bulk of each plane is nonsmoking, in large Indian aircraft there are only eight rows for nonsmokers. If you're like me, you'll show up early just to get a nonsmoking seat.

BY BUS: Indian buses are always crowded, but convenient for getting to someplace, and the fares are dirt cheap. In many cases the only discernible difference between "Ordinary," "Deluxe," and "Luxury" buses—aside from the ticket prices—is that the higher priced buses hold fewer people, have leatherette seats, and at the very top, have push-back seats. An innovation in recent years is video buses—taking a cue from the airlines, films are shown (but the Indian movies are played at a blast-you-out-of-your-mind sound level).

One highly recommended bus journey is the mountainous trip between Srinagar and Ladakh, described fully in Chapter VI.

In some cases the bus is preferable because it's faster or more direct if your only alternative is a narrow-gauge train. This is not true in Darjeeling, where the "Toy Train" or Ooty, and the mountain railway, are delightful rides at a creeping pace.

The general rule about buses in India is this: the longer the trip, the more comfortable you will be on trains or planes.

BY CAR: There are no self-drive cars in India, but you can hire a car and driver for splurge-high rates for budget travelers, yet lower than the comparable deal at home. For instance, a 16-hour round trip between Delhi and Agra (440 km, 265 miles) will cost about Rs. 1,200 ($92.25) in a small car without air conditioning.

BY TAXI: The charges for yellow-topped black taxis vary from place to place, but average around Rs. 2 (15¢) to Rs. 30 ($2.30) per kilometer, plus another couple of rupees for waiting charges while you go off to discover some intriguing sight. Meters are rarely up-to-date, so you must consult the fare chart when you pay.

Watch out for taxis that are not yellow and black. These are tourist taxis, unmetered, and a bit costlier than taxis. For instance, in Delhi, five hours of local sightseeing by tourist taxi would run about Rs. 70 ($5.40).

Scooters, or auto-rickshaws, are about half the price of black-and-yellow taxis, and fun for scooting here and there.

On some routes, such as Jammu to Kashmir, Bangalore to Mysore, and

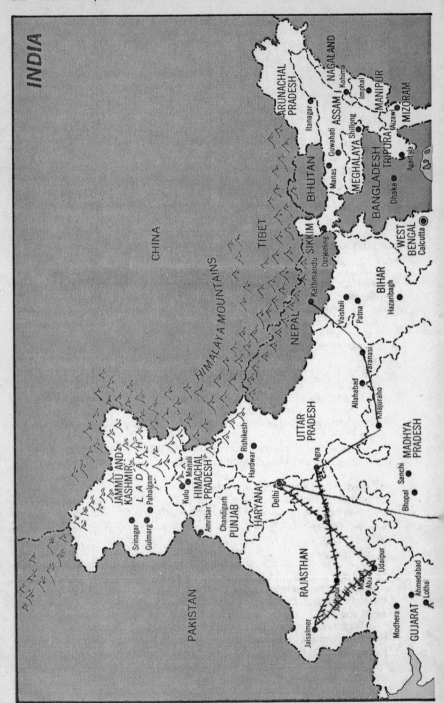

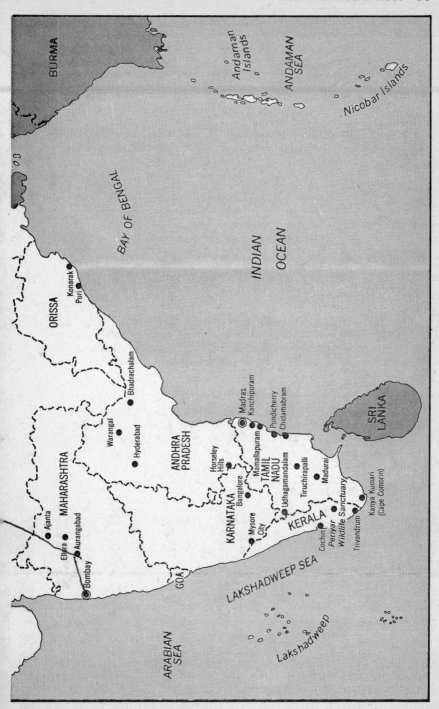

Abu Road Station to Mount Abu, you can get share taxis, where you buy a seat to your destination. These are more comfortable than the bus, and of course, more expensive. For instance, a trip between Jammu and Srinagar costs about Rs. 155 ($12).

Finally, travel from major international airports to destinations in cities by taxi can be prepaid at the airports. This keeps the cab from overcharging you. Be sure to save your receipt—you must turn it over to the driver when you get where you're going. If not, you will (as happened to me) have a little shadow that goes in and out with you, until you find the receipt or fork over another fare. The receipt is the proof the driver needs to be paid by the company for his work.

BY TRAIN: Indian Railways, the fourth-largest railway system in the world, moves about 9 million people over a route covering 60,000 km every day and offers two classes of accommodation: first and second. But there are other variations: Air-Conditioned, AC Two-Tiered Sleeper, AC Chair, and Express Second Class as well as Ordinary Second Class.

Not all classes are offered on all trains: Air-Conditioned is found mainly on the top express trains. There are also some special express trains like the *Rajdhani Express,* which have only Air Conditioned Class and Air-Conditioned Second. They cut down the time considerably between Bombay and Delhi, and Delhi and Calcutta, lopping off five hours on the Delhi–Calcutta run and seven from the Delhi–Bombay run, making them each 18 hours.

For a bit of exotica on the rails, there's another special train. It's the "Palace on Wheels," which uses historic old coaches of the former Maharajas on two- to seven-day package tours from Delhi through Rajasthan. For information, contact Central Reservations, Rajasthan Tourism, Chandralok Building, 36 Janpath, New Delhi (tel. 321820).

Indrail Pass

A good deal for foreign tourists can be the Indrail Pass for anywhere from 7 to 90 days. The ticket can be purchased only in India and only with foreign currencies, and can be an excellent value for the traveler making an extended trip. The table lists the prices for 1987.

Period of Validity	Fares (in U.S. Dollars)					
	A.C. Class		First Class/2-tier AC/AC Chair Car		Second Class	
	Adult	Child	Adult	Child	Adult	Child
7 days	$180	$ 95	$ 95	$ 50	$ 45	$ 25
15 days	230	115	115	60	55	30
21 days	280	140	140	70	65	35
30 days	350	175	175	90	75	40
60 days	520	260	260	130	115	60
90 days	690	345	345	175	150	75

These tickets are sold at the Railway Central Reservation Offices at Bombay, Calcutta, Madras, and New Delhi; at Reservation Offices at Secunderabad/Hyderabad, Rameswaram, Bangalore, Vasco-Da-Gama, Jaipur, Trivandrum Central, Chandigarh, Agra Cantt. Aurangabad, Ahmadabad, Vadodara, Varanasi, Amritsar, and Gorakhpur; and also by certain recognized tourist agencies in metropolitan cities.

Having the Indrail Pass entitles the ticket holder to travel on all trains, including the Rajdhanis, at all times anyplace in India.

Indrail passes should be handled with care: they are neither refundable nor replaceable if lost, stolen, or mutilated. Nor are the passes transferrable, and the tourist must be prepared to show his or her passport whenever asked. Refunds are rendered at the office of issue before commencement of the first rail journey, provided that no advance reservation has been made. Otherwise, the Indrail Pass is subject to the same deductions as the regular refund rules, mentioned below.

To help you map out your tour, Indian Railways "Trains at a Glance," costing Rs. 4 (30¢), lists key trains, timings, and fares. To help you make reservations or purchase your Indrail Pass there are Tourist Guides at the Bombay, Calcutta, and New Delhi railway stations. If you have trouble finding your train, ask for the station superintendent and you'll get assistance.

Rules of the Rails

Generally, when traveling by train, reservations should be made as far in advance as possible to make sure you get what you want. You're expected to get to your train ten minutes before departure or your reserved seat will be assigned to someone else—but the earlier the better. There's lots going on (to say the least!) at the stations.

There is a cancellation charge. Best bet is to make sure of your plans before you purchase your tickets. You can lose up to 50% if you cancel on the day of your journey on the *Rajdhani Express,* and up to 36% if you cancel six hours before on some other trains. And whatever you do, don't miss your train. You'll be plum out of luck—there's no refund.

You'll be expected to pay a reservation fee, from Rs. 10 (75¢) for Air-Conditioned Class chair seats to Rs. 1 (7½¢) for Second Class seats. There are also fees for bedding: Rs. 5 (38¢) per night in the top-price accommodation, Rs. 5 (38¢) on some Second Class accommodations. Bedding is reserved when making your reservations for tickets.

There are dining cars on some important trains where you can get Western and Indian foods. There are restaurants at important stations serving Indian vegetarian and nonvegetarian foods.

Chapter II

NEW DELHI: WHERE THE TOUR BEGINS

1. Hotels
2. Restaurants
3. Seeing the City
4. Nightlife
5. Shopping
6. Useful Information

FROM A TRAVELER'S point of view, New Delhi is both the best and the worst place to start one's itinerary in India: the best because making the transition from a Western environment to an Indian one is easier in a city that is relatively clean and uncluttered (New Delhi is similar in style to Washington, D.C.); the worst because in some respects New Delhi is at once the least exotic and least "Indian" town in India.

Because it's on most international air routes, however, it's where most visitors to India start spending a few pleasant days easing themselves into the leisurely Indian life. Some tourist "musts" are within one day's trip from the capital, so it makes a suitable base for visiting such spots as Agra (Taj Mahal), Khajuraho (erotic sculptures), and Chandigarh (a Punjab city modernistically designed).

GETTING TO DELHI: Delhi is a major stop for **airlines** serving Asia and can be reached with ease from either the East or West Coast of the U.S., Western European cities, the U.K., the Middle East, Australia, and East Africa. You can reach Delhi by air from Nepal, Sri Lanka, Pakistan, Bangladesh, and Afghanistan. Within India, flights between Bombay and Delhi take under two hours and cost Rs. 1,007 ($77); Calcutta to Delhi takes about two hours and costs Rs. 1,142 ($88); and Madras to Delhi takes 2½ hours and costs Rs. 1,428 ($109), to name only a few of the many domestic flights.

Best **trains** are the speedy *Rajdhani Expresses,* which cover the distance in about 18 hours five times a week between New Delhi and Calcutta or New Delhi and Bombay. The 1,441-km (865-mile) trip between New Delhi and Howrah costs Rs. 1,090 ($83.85) in air-conditioned class, Rs. 330 ($25.40) for an air-conditioned chair, and Rs. 615 ($47.30) in two-tier air-conditioned. Between New Delhi and Bombay Central, the distance is 1,002 km (600 miles) and the cost is Rs. 1,065 ($81.90) in air-conditioned class, Rs. 325 ($25) in air-conditioned chair, and Rs. 605 ($46.50) in two-tier air-conditioned.

Among the less expensive and slower trains, the *Howrah-Delhi-Kalka Mail* takes 22 hours and costs Rs. 400 ($30.75) in first class and Rs. 97 ($7.45) in second; from Bombay Central, the *Frontier Mail* takes 24 hours and costs Rs. 312 ($24) in first class, Rs. 76 ($5.85) in second. From Madras, the *Tamil Nadu Express* covers the 1,171 km (715 miles) in 30 hours and costs about Rs. 358 ($27.50) in first class and Rs. 78 ($6) in second.

For inquiries, call the station in Old Delhi (tel. 255560), New Delhi (tel. 3313585), or Nizamuddin (tel. 683942).

ORIENTATION: Delhi is actually two cities with a combined population of eight million: **New Delhi,** with its broad boulevards, parks, fountains, impressive government buildings, and embassies, plus most of the modern hotels and restaurants; and **Old Delhi,** with its historic landmarks, crowded streets, bazaars, and peripatetic cows. Needless to say, Old Delhi is much more interesting.

A sketchy knowledge of three areas will orient you sufficiently to find your way around. The place where you'll probably spend most time, apart from your hotel room, is the busiest area of New Delhi, **Connaught Place,** a completely circular traffic "wheel" lined with shops, restaurants, movie theaters, etc., and encircling a grassy center. Around Connaught Place is an outer "wheel" called **Connaught Circus,** so that on the map, or from the air, the whole area looks like an enormous wheel of concentric circles with a green ring of grass in the center and radial roads as spokes running outward from the center in all directions. Among the things clustered around one of these radial roads, **Janpath,** at the outer part of the wheel, are the tourist office, most airline offices, and the regional handcraft shops operated by India's different state governments.

Most of the scenically interesting parts of New Delhi are farther south (farther away from Connaught Place) from this point. If you head southward along **Parliament Street** or Janpath, you'll eventually reach the big open space known as the **Rajpath,** which culminates in the **India Gate** and, southeast of that, the zoo and **Humayun's Tomb.**

The other major center of Delhi is the region around the **Delhi Gate,** which actually separates the old and new portions of the city. Just to the west of Delhi Gate itself is **Asaf Ali Road,** on which are located several budget-priced hotels. From the Delhi Gate you can head into Old Delhi via either **Chitilikabar Street** or the wide road named **Netaji Subhash Marg.** Either way you'll eventually reach the famous **Red Fort** and the equally renowned **Jama Masjid,** an immense mosque.

The streets around the mosque, in particular **Chandni Chowk,** are among the most interesting of any to be found throughout India. Scores of narrow alleyways run off in all directions and an exploration of any of them is fascinating. Don't worry about getting lost; if you keep going long enough on any street you'll always hit a bigger (wider) one along which you can find a taxi or a pedicab—or something.

Most first-time visitors to Delhi make the mistake of being overly cautious. They allocate one day to visiting Chandni Chowk for "shopping," completely forgetting that the Golden Rule for this country is: There's no such thing as a dull Indian street—the less-traveled (by tourists) the street, the more interesting it is.

1. Hotels

A good budget room is hard to find in Delhi. But, believe it or not, there are still some $10-a-day places. Most budget hotels are in the Connaught area or around Paharganj, near the New Delhi Railway Station.

Still, most budget rooms in Delhi are overpriced for what you get in terms of atmosphere and charm. More important, many mid to low-priced rooms are not well maintained.

Throughout India, as mentioned in the introduction, most budget hotels offer lower rates for non-air-conditioned rooms. In Delhi, from October to March you won't need air conditioning. You might get by without it at other times as well. Almost every budget room has a big overhead fan. So you can try the swirling breezes before spending extra rupees for air conditioning.

If you travel off-season, be sure to inquire about discounts. You may well get a price break if you remember to ask about it. In addition, if occupancy is down considerably, as is often the case in the off-season, bargaining a little is not unheard of even in the best of places. However, some hotels in the upper range never offer discounts for a number of reasons, not the least of which is full occupancy. When a convention moves into Delhi, all but the cheapest hotels are generally fully occupied. At convention times, just be happy you have a room—any room, at any price.

If Delhi is your arrival city, you might want to reserve a room in advance to make sure you have a place to stay when you get in. This is especially advised for peak months when many mid- and splurge-priced hotels are full of tour groups. Once you get to Delhi and size up the accommodation situation, you can move if you find a room better suited to you and your budget.

Should you have difficulty getting accommodation, India Tourist Office and DTDC representatives at the airports, DTDC representatives at the railway stations in Old and New Delhi and at the Interstate Bus Station will be happy to help you find a place to stay. In town, the **India Tourist Office,** 88 Janpath, will try to help as well with hotels and all kinds of information to make your stay most pleasant.

Finally, tasty, filling meals can be had inexpensively, in a number of Delhi's restaurants you'll read about later on. So even if you have to go over budget on your room, the low cost of food will help you even out your expenditures.

BUDGET CHOICES: I'll begin with the best budget choices in the central area and then spread out. For readers willing to spend a bit more, the moderate and splurge choices are at the end of this section.

Centrally Located—In and Around Connaught Place

The **YMCA Hostel,** Jai Singh Road, New Delhi 110001 (tel. 311915 or 311847), a ten-minute stroll from Connaught Place, is a good buy—more like a resort than a Y, with gardens, tennis courts, and a shopping arcade. It caters mainly to budget-minded adults and families. There are 55 economy doubles and 35 economy singles. In these you share a bathroom, the phone is down the hall, and there are fans but no air conditioning, for Rs. 90 ($6.90) single and Rs. 150 double ($11.50). With private attached bathrooms, telephones, and air conditioning, rates are Rs. 160 ($12.30) single and Rs. 270 ($20.75) dou-

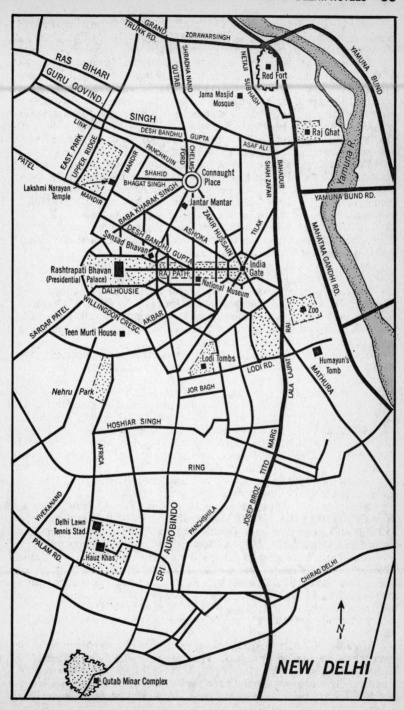

NEW DELHI

ble. A double on a single-occupancy basis is Rs. 220 ($16.90). All rates include breakfast. A transient membership fee costs Rs. 5 (38¢) for 30 days. There's a 5% service charge. To reserve, write to the manager.

Just a stone's throw from Connaught Circus is the friendly and pleasant **YWCA International Guest House,** Sansad Marg (formerly Parliament Street), New Delhi 110001 (tel. 311561, 311562, or 311563). The rooms could use a coat of paint, but are bargains when you consider that they include air conditioning, little verandas, telephones, and private bathrooms, as well as breakfast, all for Rs. 140 ($10.75) single, Rs. 230 ($17.70) double, Rs. 180 ($13.85) for a single in a double room. The 24-room complex caters to men, women, and families. Service charge is 10%.

Neat, wallpapered rooms, some with such luxury touches as room refrigerators, can be found at the **Hotel Asian International,** Janpath Lane, New Delhi 110001 (tel. 321636), one of the nicest budget places in this city. Air-conditioned singles run Rs. 220 ($16.90) and doubles cost Rs. 280 ($21.50). Non-air-conditioned singles are Rs. 160 ($12.30), and doubles are Rs. 220 ($16.90). All have attached bathrooms. The Bhagat family, owners of the hotel, personally see that guests are happy and comfortable. The hotel's Bamboo Hut restaurant is for hotel guests only.

At the clean and neat **Janpath Guest House,** 82 Janpath, New Delhi 110001 (tel. 321935, 321936, or 321937), air-conditioned rooms cost Rs. 150 ($11.50) for singles and Rs. 185 ($14.25) for doubles; non-air-conditioned singles are Rs. 115 ($8.85); and doubles, Rs. 150 ($11.50). Of the 25 rooms, 23 have private bathrooms; two rooms have a common bathroom. There's hot and cold running water in winter only; otherwise hot water in buckets, upon request. Air conditioning is offered in summer only.

You can still get by for $10 a day at some centrally located guesthouses, long the favorites of young travelers. While they won't appeal to the overly fastidious for the most part, they'll do for the not-too-fussy. At 3 Janpath Lane, New Delhi 110001, is **Mrs. Colaco's** (tel. 312558), which has declined over the years and is now recommended only in a pinch. Here a bed in a dorm costs Rs. 25 ($1.90) per night, and a double is Rs. 70 ($5.40) to Rs. 80 ($6.15).

Nearby and better, and popular with backpackers, is **Sunny Guest House,** in the lane behind the India Tourist Office, 152 Scindia House, New Delhi 110001 (tel. 3312909). Singles with a common bath run Rs. 30 ($2.30) and doubles with a common bath are Rs. 45 ($3.45). In the six rooms with attached bathrooms it's Rs. 55 ($4.25) for a single and Rs. 65 ($5) for a double. Dorm beds are Rs. 12 (90¢) per head.

Not quite as nice but just as popular is **Ringo Flat,** 17 Scindia House, New Delhi 110001 (tel. 3310605), where singles run Rs. 40 ($3.05) to Rs. 50 ($3.85), with a common bath. Doubles are Rs. 75 ($5.75) with a common bathroom and Rs. 85 ($6.55) for doubles with attached bathrooms.

Run-down, but higher in price is the **Asian Guest House,** 14 Scindia House, Kasturba Gandhi Marg, New Delhi 110001 (tel. 331393), where rooms face the outside. Doubles with air conditioning and attached bathrooms are Rs. 160 ($12.30) and singles are Rs. 130 ($10). Air-cooled doubles with attached bathrooms are Rs. 140 ($10.75); singles, Rs. 110 ($8.45). With a common toilet and ceiling fans, singles run Rs. 70 ($5.40); doubles, Rs. 100 ($7.70).

Up a flight of narrow, dingy stairs is a favorite of backpackers from all over the world, the low-priced, clean but austere, **Gandhi Guest House,** 80 Tolstoy Lane, New Delhi 110001 (tel. 351113), located in a 100-year-old building. There are only seven doubles, at Rs. 80 ($6.15), and two singles, at Rs. 50 ($3.85), all with shared bathrooms. Hot water is on tap in winter only (but bring a towel and some soap). There are sheets for the bed, and in winter, quilts are free to guests. According to the manager, G. M. Parmar, most other guesthouses have a Rs.-5 (38¢) quilt fee.

Now for some budget hotels in the Connaught area. A most convenient budget hotel in Delhi, the very simple **Palace Heights,** D Block, Connaught Circus, New Delhi 110001 (tel. 351369 or 351419), has 20 sparsely furnished but clean rooms and an elevator. Breakfast can be sent in for a modest charge, but generally no food is served. Since there are numerous inexpensive restaurants nearby you can eat out and merely pay for an inexpensive room. Rates for a single without private bathroom are Rs. 35 ($2.70) to Rs. 95 ($7.30); the higher priced is a big room. Doubles go for Rs. 80 ($6.15) to Rs. 120 ($9.25), the higher price with a private bathroom. There is no service charge. A heater (needed in winter) will cost Rs. 25 ($1.90) a day; air cooling in summer is free, as is hot water, which is supplied in buckets.

The pleasant, well-run, ten-room **Metro,** N-49, Connaught Circus, Janpath, New Delhi 110001 (tel. 3315481), has some roses blooming on the terrace, but little else in the way of ambience. Cleanliness and value are the main attractions. The four doubles with air conditioning are Rs. 250 ($19.25); when let as singles they cost Rs. 200 ($15.40). Five non-air-conditioned rooms run Rs. 105 ($8) single and Rs. 165 ($12.70) double. There is one air-conditioned suite, at Rs. 250 ($19.25) to Rs. 300 ($23), single or double. All rooms have attached bathrooms, with hot and cold water. There is no restaurant, but snacks can be sent in or you can eat out in one of the many budget restaurants nearby.

Hotel Fifty-Five, H-55, Connaught Circus, New Delhi 110001 (tel. 321244 or 321278), is a good buy. The 15 clean rooms are vest-pocket sized and air-conditioned, with attached baths that have hot and cold running water, and are budget-right: Rs. 210 ($16.15) single, Rs. 270 ($20.75) double. There is no restaurant, but you can get light snacks on site or eat out at one of the inexpensive restaurants nearby.

The **Bright Hotel,** M Block, Connaught Circus, New Delhi 110001 (tel. 350444 or 351545), has 18 rooms, 7 of them single. Amusing touches are the old bathtubs used as planters in the courtyard. Overall, the hotel needs care and will not appeal to the fastidious. With private bathroom, singles run Rs. 80 ($6.15) and doubles go for Rs. 110 ($8.45). Without attached bathrooms, charges are Rs. 10 (75¢) less. Air conditioning will run Rs. 60 ($4.60) extra per day, and an air cooler, Rs. 10 (75¢), both only necessary in summer. There's a 10% service charge.

Right above the Bright, with similar rates and also a do-in-a-pinch place, **Blue** (tel. 312100 or 352222) has singles at Rs. 50 ($3.85) to Rs. 70 ($5.40), and doubles for Rs. 90 ($6.90) to Rs. 110 ($8.45), the higher rates for attached bathrooms. A number of the centrally located guesthouses are better choices than the above two hotels.

Nirula's, L Block, Connaught Circus, New Delhi 110001 (tel. 352419), is ringed with popular snack shops—Rs. 10 (75¢) for Indian snacks or ice cream dip-chocolate topping. There's also a pastry shop and a Chinese restaurant. Indeed, Nirula's is well known for snack shops around town. The hotel rooms are large and have attached bathrooms, air conditioning, phones, and some have balconies, but alas, they've seen better days. Doubles run Rs. 410 ($31.50); singles, Rs. 300 ($23). A small suite is Rs. 475 ($36.50); a deluxe suite, Rs. 600 ($46.25). This could be your choice if central location means more than decor or tidiness.

The **York Hotel,** K Block, Connaught Circus, New Delhi 110001 (tel. 353769), is a cut above some others in this area. An upstairs location removes it from the bustling street, and rooms are nicely, if not spectacularly, furnished. They're all air-conditioned and all have attached bathrooms, music, and telephones. Rates are Rs. 275 ($21.25) single and Rs. 375 ($28.85) double.

Hotel Alka, 16/90 Connaught Circus, New Delhi 110001 (tel. 344328), is centrally air-conditioned, and has carpeting and modern furnishings, music in all rooms, well-appointed bathrooms, and an overall cozy feeling. There are 23 rooms: 4 singles, 14 doubles, and 5 suites (meaning the rooms face outside and have television sets). Singles run Rs. 300 ($23); doubles Rs. 400 ($30.75); suites Rs. 75 ($36.53).

The Host Inn, F-33, Connaught Place, New Delhi 110001 (tel. 3310704), above the Host Restaurant, has gone downhill when it comes to maintenance. Rates are Rs. 250 ($19.25) single, Rs. 300 ($23) double, and Rs. 350 ($26) deluxe. They have attached tiled bathrooms, air conditioning, telephones, and piped-in music.

Hotel Marina, G-59, Connaught Circus, New Delhi 110001 (tel. 344658), has French antique tapestries in marble halls, a sweeping marble staircase, and reasonably clean, well-appointed air-conditioned rooms with bathrooms attached. Rates are Rs. 390 ($30) for singles and Rs. 460 ($35.40) for doubles—getting a bit high for our budget.

Slightly lower in price, but moving up our budget scale, is the delightful Jukaso Inn Downtown, L-1, Connaught Circus, New Delhi 110001 (tel. 351223), with lots of charming atmosphere. The building dates from the 1940s, but was totally renovated in 1984 when it was converted into a cozy 25-room hotel. There are flowering plants at the entrance, and green plants as well in the lounge and reception, further accented with handsome antiques. All is centrally air-conditioned. The rates are Rs. 300 ($23) to Rs. 405 ($31.15) single, and Rs. 375 ($28.85) to Rs. 450 ($34.60) double for rooms. Lowest-price rooms have no television or refrigerator, but all have attached bathrooms. In the dining room, Indian and Western foods are cooked to order.

Central Court Hotel, N Block, Connaught Circus (opposite Scindia House), New Delhi 110001 (tel. 3515013), needs a paint job, but it has a nice terrace. Singles cost Rs. 195 ($15) to Rs. 230 ($17.70), and doubles run Rs. 290 ($22.30) to Rs. 325 ($25); the lowest prices are rooms without an attached bathroom. The rooms and restaurant are air-conditioned.

The garden's a main attraction at the Centre Point Tourist Home, 13 Kasturba Gandhi Marg, New Delhi 110001 (tel. 324478 or 324805), where a new 70-room wing, under construction when I was there, should be completed by the time you arrive. The rooms off the main building have been recently renovated and have new tiled bathrooms. Doubles cost Rs. 325 ($25), and singles run Rs. 250 ($19.25), all air-conditioned. A rooftop restaurant was planned for the new wing. From here it's about a three-minute stroll to Connaught Place and the tourist office.

Two kilometers (1½ miles) from the New Delhi Railway Station and one kilometer (about half a mile) from Connaught Place, ITDC's Ashok Yatri Nivas, 19 Ashok Rd., New Delhi 110001 (tel. 344511), offers 558 rooms in an 18-story building. This modern hotel was built around 1982 just for budget travelers. While the prices are still in line—Rs. 95 ($7.30) single, Rs. 130 ($10) double—the premises have deteriorated over the years (lack of maintenance has been cited in several readers' letters). Services still include air-conditioned restaurants, 24-hour money changing, a post office, and a shopping arcade. The staff is helpful and friendly, so it's too bad about the conditions at the hotel. With care, it could again be a special place for us.

Near the New Delhi Railway Station

The **Hotel Tourist**, Ram Nagar, New Delhi 110055 (tel. 524397 or 524255), is probably the nicest of the hotels near the New Delhi Railway Station. It's set off from the street by a driveway and a strip of garden, and there are plants to decorate the first floor hall. Doubles on the one air-conditioned floor are Rs. 190 ($14.60) to Rs. 210 ($16.15), and singles run Rs. 165 ($12.70), making them right in line with our budget. Even lower priced are the non-air-conditioned rooms, which range from Rs. 50 ($3.85) to Rs. 100 ($7.70) single and Rs. 130 ($10) to Rs. 140 ($10.75) double. All rooms have attached bathrooms. There is an all-vegetarian restaurant on the premises.

Nearby, with no connection with the Hotel Tourist, is the newer and slightly more expensive **Hotel Tourist Deluxe** (tel. 770985). It has wall-to-wall carpeting, color TV, and air-conditioned rooms at Rs. 200 ($15.40) single and Rs. 250 ($19.25) double, with attached baths. The hotel does not have a restaurant, but food can be ordered through room service or you can eat out.

In the Paharganj Area

About a mile west of the New Delhi Railway Station and a 25-minute walk from Connaught Place is the Paharganj area, a main shopping center, with row-upon-row of fruit and food stalls, and a number of moderate to low priced accommodations. The following are some of the better selections:

Worn around the edges, with faded wallpaper and in need of a paint job, but rated at the top of the scale for friendliness and enthusiasm, the **Hotel Natraj**, 1750 Chirta Gupta Rd., Paharganj, New Delhi 110055 (tel. 522699), is managed by the hospitable Jagjit Singh. The rooms are fairly clean, if worn, and compact. Singles run Rs. 80 ($6.15) to Rs. 145 ($11.15); doubles, Rs. 110 ($8.45) to Rs. 165 ($12.70). Bathrooms are attached and air-conditioned.

The 50-room **Vivek Hotel**, 1550 Main Bazaar, Paharganj, New Delhi 110055 (tel. 621948), has a fancy lobby off a dismal-looking entryway. Rooms are small and basic, but better maintained than many others in the area, and all but five have bathrooms attached. You get running hot water only in the deluxe rooms; otherwise it comes in buckets upon request. Rates are Rs. 50 ($3.85) single, Rs. 80 ($6.15) double, Rs. 120 ($9.25) for a deluxe double with hot shower.

The **Hotel Avtar**, 3425 Desh Bandu Gupta Rd., Paharganj, New Delhi 110055 (tel. 527295), has modest, air-cooled rooms at Rs. 70 ($5.40), single, Rs. 90 ($6.90) double.

If you shop around the Paharganj area, you can find lower-priced rooms for around Rs. 45 ($3.45) to Rs. 50 ($3.85). They have minimal comforts and cleanliness. Still, some of the most casual travelers don't seem to mind putting up with primitive conditions.

Hotels in Old Delhi

Note that while the next three hotels have New Delhi postal zones, they are nonetheless Old Delhi hotels.

Almost halfway around the world from New York's "Great White Way" is another Broadway, this one the very nice, neat, and clean budget **Hotel Broadway**, Asaf Ali Road, New Delhi 110002 (tel. 273821), similar to some small European hotels. Literally astride two worlds—the back faces Old Delhi and the front New Delhi—the hotel stands on the site of part of the old city wall. There's a comfortable lounge for guests, and all rooms are tidy and adequately furnished with attached bathrooms and air conditioning. Singles are Rs. 250 ($19.25) and doubles are Rs. 225 ($17.30).

The **Hotel President,** 4/23-B Asaf Ali Rd., New Delhi 110002 (tel. 277836), also straddles Old and New Delhi with reasonably clean and comfortable, if not imaginatively done-up, rooms in line with our budget. It's air-conditioned throughout. Singles run Rs. 225 ($17.30) and doubles are Rs. 325 ($25). All rooms have telephones and attached bathrooms.

The **Flora,** Dayanand Marg, Daryaganj, Delhi 110002 (tel. 273634), up a flight of stairs off the busy street, is a modest place with a friendly management and clean, simply furnished rooms. The rooms are air-conditioned, and there is hot and cold running water in the attached bathrooms, some with Western-style toilets. The rates are Rs. 135 ($10.40) single, Rs. 240 ($18.45) double.

Paying-Guest Accommodations

A number of Delhi's families welcome tourists as guests in their homes. Time permitted visiting only those described below; for a more complete list, consult the **Government of India Tourist Office,** 88 Janpath (tel. 320005).

According to readers Janet Reiser and Aasha Gopal, both of New York City, a top choice in guest accommodation is **Singhal's,** K-13 Green Park Main, New Delhi 110016 (tel. 668761). Mrs. Singhal is a gracious hostess, and this home is located on a quiet residential street. Doubles run Rs. 150 ($11.50), less if the room is small. Rooms have desert coolers. There is also a kitchen with a two-burner gas stove and a refrigerator for guests' use (separate from the household kitchen), plus a nice living room on the second floor. Readers noted that it was clean as well as comfortable, and close to the South Extension Shopping Centre and 20 minutes away from Connaught Place.

Out this way two other neighboring families have turned their homes into guesthouses. **Ashton Motel,** C1/6 Safdarjung Enclave, Mehrauli Road, New Delhi 110016 (tel. 668326), has singles with attached bathrooms for Rs. 100 ($7.70) non-air-conditioned, and Rs. 150 ($11.50) for doubles. Air-conditioned singles run Rs. 150 ($11.50) and doubles with air conditioning cost Rs. 200 ($15.40). The owner, Mr. Lal, will take you to town when he goes and save you cab fare. Otherwise, scooters from here cost about Rs. 8 (60¢) to Rs. 10 (75¢), or you can take bus 502 to the center. In the lounge are some lovely antiques—a Victorian setee, figures of Ganesha (the elephant-headed god of good luck), and embroideries for good luck frame the doors. The rooms could use more care. For extended stays, the rates are adjusted down.

Next door at **Lord's,** C-1/5 Safdarjung Enclave, Mehrauli Road, New Delhi 110016 (tel. 665442), the family is a follower of Swami Paramahansa and offers guests free instruction in yoga and meditation. Outsiders are welcome on Sunday if they call in advance. Rates are Rs. 80 ($6.15) single and Rs. 110 ($8.45) double, in the economy block, with Indian-style toilets. Non-air-conditioned rooms run Rs. 120 ($9.25) to Rs. 150 ($11.50) single, Rs. 160 ($12.30) to Rs. 200 ($15.40) double; air-conditioned accommodations cost Rs. 180 ($13.85) to Rs. 250 ($19.25) single and Rs. 230 ($17.70) to Rs. 300 ($23) double. A full English breakfast is Rs. 15 ($1.15). There's a 10% service charge. A little sprucing up would do no harm.

Both Ashton and Lord's are near Green Park Church, should you have trouble finding them.

New Delhi Low-Budget Hotels

Vishwa Yuvak Kendra (International Youth Center), Circular Road, Chanakyapuri (opposite the police station), New Delhi 110021 (tel.

3013631), has 36 rooms for travelers of any age for Rs. 85 ($6.50) to Rs. 90 ($6.90) double occupancy with private attached bathroom (the higher price for a room with a telephone), Rs. 65 ($5) double occupancy without a private bathroom. In the 16-bed women's and men's dorms, it's Rs. 15 ($1.15) per person. Modestly priced breakfasts, lunches, and dinners are served in the cafeteria. There's a 10% service charge and an admission charge of Rs. 15 ($1.15) per person for rooms and Rs. 5 (38¢) per person for the dorm, valid for one month. To reserve, write the manager. From here, bus 620 goes to the Connaught area for around Rs. 1 (7¢) deluxe or 50 paise regular.

Nearby is the **Youth Hostel,** 5 Nyaya Marg, Chanakyapuri, New Delhi 110021 (tel. 3016285), with dorms for Rs. 15 ($1.15) to Rs. 18 ($1.40) per head for foreigners, the lower price for members of the International Youth Hostel Association. This place needs sprucing up, but would do in a pinch, if you can get in—the hostel gives members preference and is often full. Breakfast, which is required, costs Rs. 4.50 (35¢), including eggs and toast.

You won't need your pup tent at the **New Delhi Tourist Camp,** at J. Nehru Marg, opposite Jai Prakash Hospital, New Delhi 110021 (tel. 272898 or 272899), which has clean rooms surrounded by gardens for Rs. 24 ($1.85) single, Rs. 36 double ($2.75). Deluxe rooms run Rs. 32 ($2.45) to Rs. 48 ($3.70). There is a restaurant serving budget priced meals in Indian, Chinese, and continental styles. Hot showers and money-changing facilities too. You're a stone's throw from Connaught Place and the New Delhi Railway Station. "Don't be put off by anyone advising we're full up, because accommodation is generally available at the camp," says camp employee Vivek Bhushan.

Another **Tourist Camp** is located at Oudsia Gardens, opposite the Interstate Bus Terminus (tel. 2523121), with similar rooms and rates.

At the Airport

International flights often leave between midnight and 5 a.m. from Delhi's Indira Gandhi International Airport, so it's less of a struggle to be on time if you stay nearby. It's also a good place to stay if you're spending an overnight between one domestic flight from Palam and another with a crack-of-dawn departure.

Airport Retiring Rooms, at Rs. 200 ($15.40) double and Rs. 100 ($7.70) single, offer simple, basic accommodation which could use sprucing up. For reservations, contact the airport manager, Delhi Airport (tel. 391351)—on a first-come, first-served basis and with confirmed tickets only.

ABOVE-BUDGET HOTELS: I'll begin with the top hotels in New Delhi, and then cover moderate and splurge choices around town.

The Top-Priced Splurge Hotels

IDTC's **Ashok Hotel,** 50B Chanakyapuri, New Delhi 110021 (tel. 600121), with 589 rooms, has a huge comfortable lounge and several interesting restaurants including the popular Frontier, built partly of stones from nearby ruins. The hotel is often home to visiting diplomats, as well as large international conferences. Singles are Rs. 900 ($69) and doubles run Rs. 1,000 ($77); suites go up to Rs. 5,500 ($423).

Standing alongside the Ashok and also run by ITDC is the pentagon-shaped **Samrat,** Chanakyapuri, New Delhi 110021 (tel. 603030), with beautiful terraces outdoors and Agra-inspired marble inlay in the reception area. It was the first hotel in Delhi (and, as far as I know, in India) to have hair dryers in each bathroom. The room rates are Rs. 800 ($61.50) single, Rs. 900 ($69) double. Between the two hotels—Ashok and Samrat—there are nine restaurants. A connecting passageway and a walk through the gardens gives guests easy access to both hotels. Both hotels have swimming pools.

WelcomGroup's **Maurya Palace Sheraton,** Sardar Patel Marg, New Delhi 110021 (tel. 3010101), has 510 rooms making excellent use of India's textiles and handcrafts in their decor, and a spacious lounge with a vaulted ceiling inspired by ancient temple architecture. Rooms cost Rs. 1050 ($80.75) for singles, Rs. 1150 ($88.50) for doubles; suites are much higher. Swimming pool and tennis courts.

At the **Oberoi,** Dr. Zakir Hussain Marg, New Delhi 110003 (tel. 699571), mirror-bright black granite floors contrast with huge arrangements of fresh red roses in the reception area. The club-like lounge recalls the Raj with its handsome leather furniture and the swimming pool has been newly redesigned so the water is level with the ground instead of the usual step or two down. The hotel would have made a Mughal emperor proud. The rates begin at Rs. 1,100 ($84.50) single and Rs. 1,200 ($92.25) double, and go up. The coffeeshop is refreshing with its palm decor.

In the lounge at the **Taj Mahal Hotel,** 1 Singh Rd., New Delhi 110011 (tel. 3016162), the striking ceiling has concave canopies and the wall panels are brightly painted and plastered to look like lavish zari embroidery, the celebrated local craft. There are views of the Parliament buildings from some of the western-exposure rooms. Gorgeous gardens make the hotel seem far from the center, which in fact is only minutes away. Rates are Rs. 950 ($73) single and Rs. 1,100 ($84.50) double; suites range up to Rs. 3,500 ($269).

Under the same management, and with similar rates, is the **Taj Palace Hotel,** 2 Sardar Patel Marg, Diplomatic Enclave, New Delhi 110021 (tel. 3010404), where gleaming marble halls and a motif of regal-looking peacocks give it a palatial look indeed. Both hotels have swimming pools and a number of well-decorated restaurants.

The 580-room **Hyatt Regency Delhi,** Bhikaiji Cama Place, Ring Road, New Delhi 110066 (tel. 609911), has a handsome cream-and-brown lobby, with a refreshing waterfall and cushy brown leather and chairs. Rates are Rs. 950 ($73) single, Rs. 1,050 ($80.75) double, and up. Facilities include a swimming pool and other diversions.

The **Siddarth,** 3 Rajendra Pl., New Delhi 110008 (tel. 571250), in a busy business center, is a rather intimate place with only 96 rooms. There's a copper mural in the lobby and flowered spreads on the beds. Rates are Rs. 695 ($53.50) single, Rs. 795 ($61.15) double. It's a Rs.-8 (60¢) scooter-rickshaw ride from here to Connaught Place and Rs. 20 ($1.55) by taxi. Outsiders can use the swimming pool on a membership basis.

In a garden setting, **Claridges,** 12 Aurangzeb Rd., New Delhi 110011 (tel. 3010211), dates from the days of the British, and is still a favorite of British visitors. It's as modern as tomorrow as far as amenities go. The hotel prides itself on personalized service. For an eccentric repeat visitor who dislikes sunlight, the management takes extreme precautions: they not only draw the drapes in his room, but sew them shut so the guest will not be disturbed by a sliver of sun. There's a clean marble lobby with a sweeping staircase and some interesting restaurants (see my restaurant recommendations). Room rates are Rs. 695 ($53.50) single, Rs. 795 ($61.15) double.

Getting set to open was the **Meridien Hotel,** Windsor Place, New Delhi 110001 (tel. 383960), a franchise of the exclusive French group of hotels with the same name. Rates were projected at Rs. 1,200 ($92.25) single, Rs. 1,300 ($100) double. Also fairly new is the sleekly modern **Hotel Sofitel Surya,**

Friends Colony, New Delhi 110065 (tel. 635070). Rates are Rs. 675 ($52) single and Rs. 775 ($59.50) double.

Splurge Hotels Near Connaught Place

The **Janpath,** an ITDC hotel, on Janpath, New Delhi 110001 (tel. 350070), is right of the entrance to Connaught Place and worthy of consideration. An old hotel that's been modernized with air conditioning, it has rooms that are more spacious than many newer hotels, and they are well furnished with beds, desks, tables, and silk-framed prints on the walls. The big bathrooms have marble floors. Rates are Rs. 400 ($30.75) single and Rs. 500 ($38.50) double. Like other hotels in this price range, there's a 24-hour coffeeshop, restaurants (see my recommendations of buffets and Mughlai choices), a bar, and a shopping arcade.

Hans Plaza, 15 Barakhamba Rd., New Delhi 110001 (tel. 3316861), is located on the top four floors of a modern white balcony-trimmed 20-story office building, the tallest in the Connaught Place area. The splendid view is a big attraction. The neatly furnished rooms have twin beds, settees, and dressing tables, and are all pretty much alike except for their color scheme which changes with the floor: 16 is green, 17 is pink, 18 is blue, and 19 is blue and white. Other amenities are attached modern bathrooms and central air conditioning. Rates are Rs. 460 ($35.50) single and Rs. 595 ($45.75) double. There's a coffee shop, restaurant and bar on the premises.

An oasis in the heart of town, the **Imperial Hotel,** Janpath, New Delhi 110001 (tel. 311511), the city's first hotel way back when travelers arrived with steamer trunks, is set in a palm-studded garden. The bustling arcade still looks like a throwback to the old days. The bedrooms are well maintained, big, and have attached tiled bathrooms. Rooms cost Rs. 700 ($53.85) single; Rs. 800 ($61.50) double; suites go up to Rs. 2,000 ($154). There's a restaurant and outdoor tea service in fair weather, but one big drawback: the hotel is usually booked months in advance by tour groups.

Away from Connaught Place—Moderate to Splurge

On Ring Road are several modest, moderately priced (but overpriced for what you get) guesthouses, near some main commercial centers and therefore convenient for business travelers, but out of the mainstream for most tourists. From here to Connaught Place, you can expect to pay about Rs. 35 ($2.70) by taxi, about half that by scooter rickshaw—one way. Many buses ply the same route.

Sun Village, A-14 Ring Rd., Lajpat Nagar, New Delhi 110024 (tel. 6436052), charges Rs. 250 ($19.25) single and Rs. 300 ($23) double, with deluxe rooms for Rs. 375 ($28.85) to Rs. 425 ($32.70); under the same ownership, with similar prices, is the **Shyama International Inn,** C/532 Safdarjung Enclave Development Area, New Delhi 1100021 (tel. 665222), near Palam airport. Again on Ring Road is the **International Inn,** 9-A Ring Rd., Lajpat Nagar IV, New Delhi 110024 (tel. 6430980), charging Rs. 110 ($8.45) to Rs. 200 ($15.40) for singles and Rs. 155 ($11.90) to Rs. 250 ($19.25) for doubles, the higher prices for air conditioning. A bit better maintenance is found at the similarly priced **Bawa Inn,** 34 Ring Rd., Lajpat Nagar, New Delhi 110024 (tel. 6418545). The nearby **Kumar Holiday Home,** 33 Ring Rd., Lajpat Nagar IV, New Delhi 110024 (tel. 6411874), needed more tender loving care. These places do not have restaurants. There is room service for food.

Set amid pretty gardens, ITDC's **Lodhi Hotel,** Lala Lajpat Rai Marg, New Delhi 110003 (tel. 619422), is named for the nearby Lodhi Tombs. Centrally air-conditioned, if it were painted and perked up it would be a nice place indeed. The rates—Rs. 300 ($23) single, Rs. 400 double ($30.75)—are on the expensive side for budgeteers. The hotel has a swimming pool and a shopping arcade. On the premises is the well-known South Indian Woodlands Restaurant (see my restaurant recommendations).

Not far from the Lodhi is the pleasant **Tourist Holiday Home,** 7 Link Rd., Jangura, New Delhi 110014 (tel. 618797). The 15 simple rooms with air conditioning and private bathrooms have price tags right in line with this book: Rs. 125 ($9.60) single and Rs. 200 ($15.40) double. Service charge is 10%.

Where Old and New Delhi meet is the ITDC's **Hotel Ranjit,** Maharaja Ranjit Singh Road, New Delhi 110002 (tel. 331256). The location is superb, just a short metered-motorized rickshaw drive from the Red Fort and Chandni Chowk, the old bazaar with lanes bursting with silver, ivory, and brocades. To the Connaught area, a rickshaw would cost around Rs. 4 (about 30¢) and the stand is almost at the hotel's doorstep, or you can walk in about ten minutes. The Ranjit's exterior with blocks of color might have been inspired by a Mondrian painting. From the individual covered balconies off the rooms you can see the immense Jama Masjid, India's largest mosque. The 188 rooms, and indeed the entire hotel, were undergoing massive renovations when I looked in. It was to be reincarnated as a strictly vegetarian hotel with splurge rates for lone travelers, but in line for two on our budget: Rs. 215 ($16.50) to Rs. 280 ($21.50) for singles, Rs. 270 ($20.75) to Rs. 380 ($29.25) for doubles, the higher rate for air conditioning. There's a swimming pool and shopping arcade for your amusement. It should be all spruced up by the time you arrive should you want to give it a try.

Bordering on Old Delhi is the **Oberoi Maidens,** 7 Sham Nath Marg (formerly Alipur Road), Delhi 110054 (tel. 2525464), a moderate splurge worthy of your consideration. This gracious old 60-room hotel still has many old-fashioned touches of luxury in renovated surroundings. There are spacious, well-appointed rooms with some nice old dark wooden chests, chairs, and tables, and many have dressing rooms and extra windows into hallways for added light and ventilation. Rooms have small refrigerators and color televisions. Rates run Rs. 495 ($38) single, Rs. 595 double ($45.75); suites go up to Rs. 1,250 ($96). There's a swimming pool and tennis courts in the flower-filled garden.

More moderate rates at the pleasant but much simpler **Sartaj,** A-3 Green Park, New Delhi 110016 (tel. 663277 or 667759), which has a tiled mural in the lounge and archways looking from the lounge into the wood-paneled dining room. Near the All-India Medical Institute and on the road to the famous Qutb Minar tower, the hotel is about a Rs.-15 ($1.15) taxi ride to Connaught Place. The rates are Rs. 275 ($21.15) for singles and Rs. 330 ($25.40) for doubles with attached bathrooms. There's 24-hour room service from the Daawat, a modern decorated restaurant with Indian and Mughali food.

The 73-room **Hotel Ambassador,** at Sujan Singh Park, New Delhi 110003 (tel. 690391), is on the edge of cool and inviting Sujan Singh Park and the Delhi zoo. It's an old hotel which has been updated with air conditioning, but the rooms are clean, spacious, with some nice furniture from bygone days. They have attached bathrooms and piped-in music. Rates are Rs. 395 ($30.40) single; Rs. 495 ($38) double. There's a 10% service charge. Dasaprakash, the famous South Indian restaurant, has a branch in this hotel, which is well worth trying and is described in the restaurant section under thalis.

On the pricey side is the **Hotel Vikram,** Ring Road, Lajpat Nagar, New Delhi 110024 (tel. 6436451), where crewel printed fabrics have been used extensively throughout. All rooms are air-conditioned with attached bathrooms, and cost Rs. 500 ($38.50) to Rs. 600 ($46.25) for deluxe doubles, Rs. 420 ($32.30) for twins, and Rs. 300 ($23) for singles. A swimming pool, terrace, and gardens are pleasant features. The Sakura Room (meaning "cherry blossom") serves Oriental specialties in the Rs. 25 ($1.90) range. A taxi to Connaught Place will cost around Rs. 25 ($1.90), and a scooter rickshaw, Rs. 12 (90¢). There's a 10% service charge.

About the same price is the **Hotel Rajdoot,** Mathura Road, New Delhi, 110014 (tel. 69983 to 69992), where there's a garden, a swimming pool, and air conditioning. Rates are Rs. 400 ($30.75) for singles, Rs. 500 ($38.50) for doubles. The hotel's cabaret and discothèque are covered in the nightlife section.

The former U.S. AID headquarters was some time ago turned into the ITDC's **Qutab Hotel,** off Sri Aurobindo Marg, New Delhi 110016 (tel. 660060). Inside many of the old AID furnishings remain, including some leather settees, cozy wing chairs, and abstract paintings in the lounge. The Paul Revere Bar is still there too, looking like an Early American colonial tavern, as well as the similarly themed Williamsburg restaurant. There's a swimming pool, tennis courts, and bowling alley (India's only one, as far as I know), and air conditioning throughout. Rooms run Rs. 500 ($38.50) for single occupancy, Rs. 600 ($46) for double; apartments are much higher. Rooms on the south side have views of the Qutb Minar. The hotel is six to eight miles from Connaught Place and a taxi from here would run about Rs. 30 ($2.30).

Near the Airport

Out near the airport, the **Hotel Diplomat,** 9 Sardar Patel Rd. (Diplomatic Enclave), New Delhi 110021 (tel. 3010204), has the atmosphere of a private club. The rooms are clean, quiet, and air-conditioned, with private attached bathrooms. Doubles for Rs. 545 ($42), and singles for Rs. 360 ($27.75), or Rs. 400 ($30.75) for single occupancy of a double, are splurges for this book. There is frequent bus service to Connaught Place, or a scooter rickshaw would cost about Rs. 10 (75¢) to take you to the same place.

The nearest hotel to the airport is the splurge-priced, white-and-red stone-accented **Centaur,** on Gurgaon Road, New Delhi 110037 (tel. 391411), with singles at Rs. 640 ($49.25) and doubles at Rs. 730 ($56). Modern, functional rooms are above an atrium lounge, swimming pool, and health club. Bus service to the airport is every 30 minutes, and seven times a day to and from Connaught Place.

2. Restaurants

The authentic dishes of India's capital, such as tandooris (delicately spiced and baked in a special clay oven), kebabs (food on a skewer), and biryani (meat or chicken on a rice base garnished with nuts, pomegranate seeds, and other tasty tidbits) had their origins in Mughal days and once graced the table of Emperor Shah Jahan. This is the origin also of such northern curries as *korma,* made with meat that has been tenderized in yogurt, and *rogan josh,* an elaborate curry which is indebted to saffron for its color and taste. *Pulau,* also typical of the North, is a less elaborate version of biryani; sweet pulau, very tasty, combines rice, spices, vegetables, fruit, and nuts. North India's bread is the chapati, which may remind some of the tortilla. Of course, you can get dishes from the other regions of India too, and from the Far East and West, because Delhi, like other cosmopolitan cities of the world, has a large population of foreigners and visitors, whose tastes are catered to by many restaurants. A 7% tax is added to the prices in Delhi's restaurants.

BOUNTIFUL BUFFETS: A good transition from West to East and an excellent way to sample some Delhi specialties are these eat-as-much-as-you-like buffets featuring foods from both sides of the globe. Served at many Delhi hotels at lunchtime, and occasionally at dinner, the meals start with soup, usually a choice of cream or clear, served at the table. Waiters assist in the selection of outstanding arrays of Indian and Western foods at the main table: sliced cold meats and pâtés studded with amber aspic jewels; "veg" and non-"veg" curries; hills of pearly rice; piles of chapatis; strips of raw vegetables; shredded, chopped, and tossed salads. A roast perhaps, or a little chicken? Try the chutney, pickle, and raita (curds). Return again, if one abundantly full plate was not enough. Or toss your calorie counter out and head for the desserts—sweets topped with mounds of whipped cream, cheese, fruits. Sample one or sample them all, then settle back over coffee or tea.

As the competition increases, so the Delhi buffets have become increasingly elaborate feasts presented with a great deal of showmanship. Menus are changed daily to keep regulars from growing bored and going elsewhere. Still, with so many choices there's a lot of buffet-hopping. Experienced buffet-goers arrive early to get the best selections, although it's not necessary as foods are replenished throughout the meal. Reservations are advised, especially during the peak season and always on the weekends. In summer when crowds taper off some of these buffets might be cancelled.

Prices for buffets have risen over the years, and indeed some are now in the splurge range. Taxes of 7% and gratuities add to their costs. They still qualify as bargains: since you can eat as much as you want of many different foods, you can make this your main meal of the day; your other meals can be lighter and less expensive. Here are costs per person of the leading buffets in Delhi:

Ashok Yatri Niwas, managed by ITDC, 19 Ashok Rd. (tel. 344511), in the cozy brick-walled, plaid-cushioned Caravan, charging Rs. 20 ($1.55) at lunch (noon to 2:30 p.m.), is a good value for budget travelers. Almost in the same price league, the **Regency Restaurant,** in the Talkatora Swimming Pool Complex (tel. 385679), charging Rs. 28 ($2.15) from noon to 3 p.m., is convenient when sightseeing around the Presidential Palace or Sri Lakshmi Narayan Temple.

Both lunch (1 to 3 p.m.) and dinner (8 p.m. to midnight) are tasty buffet arrays at Rs. 60 ($4.60) in the dimly lit Orbit Room of the **Janpath,** Janpath (tel. 3500700). A tradition with many Delhites is the Rs.-60 ($4.60) buffet of Hyderabadi and Lucknawi dishes, some of the richest of the North Indian cuisines, served in the appropriately Mughali-domed **Durbar,** in the Ashok Hotel, 50-B Chanakyapuri (tel. 600121), where lunch is served from 12:30 to 2:45 p.m. and dinner is 8 to 11:30 p.m. Across the street at the **Baradari,** in the Samrat Hotel, Chanakyapuri (tel. 603030), the buffet is Rs. 50 ($3.85), served from 12:30 to 2:45 p.m.

At **Hotel Kanishka,** 19 Ashok Rd. (tel. 343400) in the Dilkusha (meaning "heart pleasing"), the Rs.-85 ($6.50) buffet is on 1 to 3 p.m. At the Vaishali, in the **Hotel Siddarth,** 3 Rajendra Pl. (tel. 571250), the buffet costs Rs. 60 ($4.60) from noon to 3 p.m. On Sunday at the Siddarth there's a vegetarian buffet in the Chandan for Rs. 25 ($1.90) from noon to 3 p.m. Sure to be a splurge (it was in the planning stages when I looked in) is the lunch buffet in the beautiful **La Rochelle** in the Oberoi, Dr. Zakir Hussain Marg (tel. 699571).

For a delicious change of pace, there's an Italian accent to the splurge buffet at the **Casa Medici** in the Taj Mahal Hotel, 1 Man Singh Rd. (tel. 3016162), from 1 to 3 p.m., featuring soup, pasta selections, ten salads, three meat platters, fish, and dessert. At Rs. 100 ($7.70), it's not extravagant in terms of value. Less expensive—and a delight—is the Rs.-55 ($4.25) Indian buffet lunch at **Aangan,** in the Hyatt Regency Delhi, Bhikaiji Cama Place, Ring Road (tel. 609911), on Sunday only from 12:30 to 2:45 p.m.

Copper caldrons brim with delicately seasoned Indian, Chinese, and continental dishes served from a copper-accented counter at the buffets in the **Shatranj** in the Hotel Maurya Sheraton, Sardar Patel Marg (tel. 3010101), for Rs. 65 ($5) at lunch (12:30 to 3 p.m.) and dinner (7:30 to 11:30 p.m.). In the same hotel, a Sunday buffet of Polynesian and Chinese foods costs Rs. 45 ($3.45) in the rooftop Bali Hi.

In the rustic-looking **Handi,** in the Taj Palace, Sardar Patel Marg (tel. 3010404), there are 12 different dishes—six vegetarian and six nonvegetarian —prepared and served from clay pots called *handis,* the popular Gujarati cooking style for which the restaurant is named. Lunch, served from 12:20 to 3 p.m., costs Rs. 65 ($5).

At the **Imperial Hotel,** Janpath (tel. 311511), buffets are served in the coffeeshop from 12:30 to 3 p.m. for Rs. 75 ($5.75). The buffets at the **Centaur Hotel,** Delhi Airport, Gurgaon Road, (tel. 391411), are on Sunday only at poolside in the warm months, for Rs. 65 ($5).

Back in town, there's a French-accented buffet at the **Hotel Meridien,** Windsor Place (tel. 383960), for Rs. 60 ($4.60), from 12:30 to 3 p.m. every day but Sunday. The **Jade Garden,** in Claridges, 12 Aurangzeb Rd. (tel. 3010211), has a Chinese buffet for around Rs. 50 ($3.85) from 12:30 to 3 p.m. Another Chinese buffet can be found in South Delhi at **Chopsticks,** in the Village, Asian Games Complex (tel. 6447154), for Rs. 70 ($5.40), served from 12:30 to 3 p.m. Monday to Saturday. In the planning stages was a vegetarian buffet for the newly renovated **Kamal** in the Ranjit Hotel, Maharajah Ranjit Singh Marg (tel. 331256).

Finally, the **El Arab,** 13 Regal Building, Connaught Place (tel. 311444), Delhi's only restaurant serving Middle Eastern and Mediterranean cuisine, has a buffet with delectable roast lamb stuffed with delicately seasoned rice and grilled fish outstanding among the spread of 16 delicious dishes: Rs. 35 ($2.70) at lunch (1 to 3:30 p.m.) and dinner (7 to 11 p.m.).

THALIS FOR $3 OR UNDER: Here are some of the tastiest thali meals in Delhi. Prices do not include the 7% tax or tip. (For an explanation of thalis and traditions, see the "Gourmet Glossary" in Section 2 of the Introduction, "Food.")

At the **Woodlands,** in the Lodhi Hotel, Lala Lajpat Marg (tel. 619422), overlooking a lovely garden, a light and airy place with mirrored murals and terracotta wall designs, the thali is strictly vegetarian like those served in the restaurant's South Indian namesake. The thali meal, at Rs. 30 ($2.30), starts with an appetite-arousing soup and is followed by an array of several distinctive South Indian vegetable dishes such eggplant and okra simmered in unusual sauces and green beans sautéed with fresh coconut. There will also be dal (a lentil sauce), spicy pickles, dahi (curds) to cool down spicy dishes, mango and tamarind chutneys, chapatis, and steaming rice. Waiters circulate frequently offering seconds or thirds. A rich Indian-style dessert, perhaps perfumed with rosewater, doesn't have to end your meal—it can set you up for paan, a digestive made from a betel leaf, enclosing betel nuts, sweet lime paste, mild spices, and sometimes tobacco (omitted upon request), topped with shredded coconut . . . a typical Indian finale to a special meal. Paan isn't on the menu, but can be ordered. It's extra, as are soft drinks, tea, or coffee.

The additions should set you back another Rs. 10 (about 75¢). If you're not in the mood for such a hearty meal, try the excellent the masala dosa (paper-thin rice-and-lentil pancake) stuffed with curried potatoes and cashew nuts. Idli (steamed rice and lentil-flour cake) is served with sambar (soup-like and spicy) and chutney. Woodlands is open every day from 8 a.m. to 11:30 p.m.: the thali is served at lunch only; at dinner there are many delicious à la carte vegetarian selections, including butter masala, a pancake with peas, potato and onion, and cashews. Lunch is served from noon to 3 p.m.; dinner, from 8 to 11 p.m. Come early for lunch or dinner, and reserve in advance or wait in a long line.

An equally famous South Indian transplant, **Dasaprakash,** in the Ambassador Hotel, Sujan Singh Park (tel. 690391), open from noon to 11 p.m. daily, has a temple flagpost as the decorative focal point in the center of the room and gods and goddesses are displayed in niches here and there. A strictly vegetarian thali meal of South Indian curries and perhaps rice with rasam (a fiery broth) and the usual curds, pickle, chutney, and sweet, then polished off with South Indian coffee, costs Rs. 30 ($2.30) at lunch and dinner. For the not-so-hungry, a wide range of snacks are served for Rs. 7 (55¢) to Rs. 8 (60¢); outstanding among these is a ravi dosa, a rice-and-lentil pancake with onion stuffing, at Rs. 8 (60¢). The restaurant's black grape juice, at Rs. 10 (75¢) for a small glass, is supposedly unavailable anywhere else in Delhi. A wide range of ice-cream flavors, from rare fruits such as fig to more ordinary flavors such as vanilla, cost Rs. 10 (75¢) to Rs. 15 ($1.15) and are shipped in from Madras, according to the maître d'.

Then there are North Indian thali meals, enjoyed at tiny **Vega,** in the Alka Hotel, 16/90 Connaught Circus (tel. 344328), where according to a religious belief banning consumption of odorous foods, no onion or garlic is used. The thali dishes, richly prepared in ghee (clarified butter), might include curried cauliflower, rajma (red kidney beans), pappadams ka rayta (yogurt with deep-fried chickpea balls), matter paneer (peas and cheese in a savory gravy); rice and vegetable pilaf, puris (whole-wheat puffed bread), mint chutney, and more, for Rs. 28.50 ($2.20) or Rs. 39.50 ($3) depending on the lavishness of the assortment. Be sure to save room for kulfi, a type of ice cream, scented with cardamom and studded with dried fruits and nuts, for Rs. 10 (75¢), served in a traditional clay cup.

Less expensive is the oldtime favorite of many Delhi residents, the plain-looking **Shudh** (meaning "pure"), in the Regal Building at Connaught Place, a purely vegetarian restaurant where a sign says "Why Kill for Food?" The thali costs about half those in the fancier places and includes three different vegetable dishes, pappadams (wafer-thin bread), pickles, rice, curds, and chapatis. Hours are 11:30 a.m. to 10 p.m. every day.

For a nonvegetarian thali, with chicken or lamb curry for Rs. 35 ($2.70), try the self-service **Coconut Grove,** in the Ashok Yatri Niwas, 19 Ashok Rd. (tel. 344511), open 24 hours a day.

At **Kamal,** in the Hotel Ranjit, M. R. Singh Road (tel. 331256), the thali costs Rs. 35 ($2.70) and features both Rajasthani and Gujarati vegetarian specialties, served from 12:30 to 3 p.m. and 8 to 11 p.m.

Above our $3-and-under budget is the elaborate thali at **Rasoi,** in the Centaur Hotel, Delhi Airport (tel. 391411), decorated to resemble a simple villager's kitchen in every way but one—prices. Each thali has seven dishes, including a sweet, at Rs. 70 ($5.40) for a nonvegetarian thali and Rs. 60 ($4.60) for a vegetarian.

RESTAURANTS AROUND THE CONNAUGHT AREA: A gold-domed ceiling and muraled walls decorate the neat, well-tended, and moderately priced **Minar,** L-11, Connaught Circus (tel. 311778), concentrating mainly on Indian specialties. Good choices among these are any of the chicken dishes, at Rs. 19 ($1.45) for a curry to Rs. 64 ($4.90) for a full buttered chicken; the vegetarian foods, at Rs. 12.50 (96¢) to Rs. 18 ($1.40); and kababs, at Rs. 16 ($1.25) to Rs. 20 ($1.55). Rice dishes run Rs. 8 (60¢) for plain rice to Rs. 21 ($1.60) for a fancy pulao. Dessert and coffee or tea would add another Rs. 15 ($1.15) to Rs. 20 ($1.55). Hours are 11:15 a.m. to 11:30 p.m.; closed Tuesday.

At 11-D Block, Connaught Place, the **Embassy** (tel. 350480) is a fancy-looking place with rust-and-brown decor on the upper level, and mirror-spangled pink walls, beaded curtains, and orange table tops on the ground level, all reflected in a mirrored ceiling. Among the many specialties are chicken tandoori, the Indian dish akin to barbecue; murg masalam (spiced chicken); and Embassy mixed vegetables. Prices range from Rs. 9.50 (73¢) for vegetarian dishes to Rs. 49 ($3.75) for a full tandoori chicken. There's also a delicious tomato fish at Rs. 26 ($2). The Embassy special pudding, a caloric combination of cake and brandied cream, is both a caloric and financial splurge at Rs. 15.50 ($1.20), but worth the expenditure if you crave something rich.

In many of India's major cities you'll find a **Gaylord's** restaurant, and Delhi's, at 14 Regal Building (tel. 352677), one of the oldest, has, sad to say, seen better days. Still you can get a passable three- to four-course meal here in Indian, Chinese, or Western cuisines pleasantly served for about Rs. 50 ($3.85). Now if only they'd spruce up the place. It's open from 10:30 a.m. to 11 p.m. daily.

The triple-decker treat at 13 Regal Building, Connaught Place, starts on top with **El Arab** (tel. 311444). Already mentioned for its lavish buffets, the restaurant also has a Middle Eastern à la carte menu served by waiters in kurtas (tunics). Most of the foods are delicately seasoned to provide a nice change if you've been eating spicy fare. A satisfying salad platter gives you a chance to sample a number of such specialties as hummus (sesame paste, chickpeas, lemon, garlic, and oil), baba ghanoush (combining hummus and charred eggplant), tabouleh (wheat, chopped vegetables seasoned with fresh mint, parsley, and lemon), and pita bread, at Rs. 30 ($2.30). Other popular choices a bit higher in price include samak iskanderani (whole herbed fish, grilled over charcoal), shish kebab do jaj (chicken cubes on a skewer with eggplant, onions, and tomatoes), and shish kebab (using lamb cubes instead of chicken on skewers). There's a choice between pita bread or rice with main courses. A popular dessert is fritters doused with orange syrup and rosewater. Moroccan mint tea makes a refreshing finale. Open from 1 to 3:30 p.m. and 7 to 11 p.m.

Sharing the entrance with El Arab, and under the same management, **Degchi** is named for a type of saucepan found in most Indian kitchens. It serves Indian specialties, in about the same price range as El Arab. Still another restaurant under the same management in this building is **The Cellar,** where you can get a filling meal of continental-style foods for Rs. 45 ($3.45) à la carte. All three restaurants share the same telephone number: 311444. The Cellar and Degchi have the same hours: 8:30 a.m. to 11 p.m.

Popular for a quick snack or a full meal is yet another Regal Building restaurant, the **Standard,** 44 Regal Building (tel. 352588), with two main sections. The plain, crowded, noisy windowless rear is, for some reason that eludes me, immensely popular for an espresso at Rs. 5.50 (42¢) or a cold coffee at Rs. 10 (75¢) to Rs. 11 (85¢), the higher price with ice cream; and sandwiches for Rs. 2.75 (21¢) to Rs. 18 ($1.40). The pleasant air-conditioned front section is set off by glass doors and has huge windows. The reasonably priced

Indian and continental specialties add to its attractiveness, with many main dishes costing Rs. 25 ($1.90) to Rs. 30 ($2.30); the Indian foods are better than the others. Hours are 9:30 a.m. to 11 p.m. every day.

You won't find any blini or borscht on the menu of **Volga,** 11-B Connaught Place (tel. 351744), but there is a hint of Russian in the dishes on the menu and the stylized balalaikas appearing in the murals. Chicken Petrograd (à la Kiev) is breast of chicken with butter inside, as it should be, at Rs. 38 ($2.90); a non-Russian, but delicious poulet à la Volga (with chicken and mushrooms, peas, and carrots in cream sauce) is a house specialty, at Rs. 38 ($2.90). The chef also prepares vegetables à la kiev, for Rs. 24 ($1.85), and there are also Indian, Chinese, and Italian dishes on the menu, starting at Rs. 9 (70¢) and going up to Rs. 26 ($2). The hours are 10 a.m. to midnight seven days a week.

There are only a few Japanese specialties at **Ginza,** K Block, Connaught Circus (tel. 46714), named for the famous Tokyo street. The pleasing decor combines bamboo-paneled walls with brocade chairs. Most main dishes run Rs. 21 ($1.60) to Rs. 35 ($2.70). These include sukiyaki (vegetables, pork, or chicken in a special sauce) for Rs. 28 ($2.15) to Rs. 30 ($2.30), and Chinese foods such as sweet-and-sour chicken at Rs. 28 ($2.15), shark's fin soup at Rs. 14 ($1.05), and pork with mushrooms and bamboo shoots at Rs. 24 ($1.85). There are many vegetarian choices too, including some unusual wonton for Rs. 17 ($1.30) to Rs. 25 ($1.90). It's open from noon to 3 p.m. and 6:30 to 11 p.m. every day.

Yorks, also in K Block, Connaught Circus (tel. 353481), is under the same management as Ginza, but serves everything from milkshakes to midnight snacks. The tandoori kebabs, for Rs. 28 ($2.15) to Rs. 48 ($3.70) are specialties here. The fish tikka tandoori, at Rs. 27 ($2.10), is a tasty change from the usual chicken tandoori. On the continental side, a chicken sizzler on a piping hot platter, at Rs. 36 ($2.75), is another good choice. Open from 9 a.m. to midnight daily.

Kwality, Sansad Marg, near Connaught Circus (tel. 311752), has a full menu, but is especially nice for tea and Indian snacks. The attractive setting combines tiled walls contrasting with wood panels. Vegetable samosas (turnovers) and cheese pakoras (fritters) run Rs. 4 (30¢) to Rs. 12 (92¢). Sandwiches cost Rs. 8 (60¢) to Rs. 12 (92¢). Tea and a range of rich ice creams go for Rs. 8 (60¢) to Rs. 12 (92¢). Open from 9 a.m. to midnight; closed Sunday. You'll find Kwality restaurants throughout India. At one time, they were a nationwide chain, but they are no longer all under the same ownership. But they still have these common attributes: those checked for this edition in such cities as Bombay and Calcutta were generally well maintained and offered good value and quality foods.

A step away from the center at the entrance to Connaught Place is the pricey, silk-paneled, lantern-lit **Mandarin Restaurant,** in the Hotel Janpath, Janpath (tel. 350070), with deep red chairs and tablecloths, accented by amber drapes. The restaurant serves mainly Cantonese-style foods in the Rs.-45 ($3.45) to Rs.-65 ($5) range. A satisfying meal for two might run about Rs. 100 ($7.70) and include hearty sweet-corn soup, sliced pork or lamb or chicken with bamboo shoots, chicken with almonds, a single portion of egg, ham, or vegetarian fried rice, generous enough to share, and a non-Oriental ice-cream dessert. A vegetarian meal for two would cost about Rs. 70 ($5.40). Open from 1 to 2:30 p.m. and 7 to 11 p.m. every day.

Also in the Janpath Hotel, at the **Gulnar Restaurant** (tel. 350070) you're seated under a dark-mirrored ceiling and near a splashing waterfall, while enjoying some delicious Indian dishes named for famous Mughals and renowned cities. Figure on paying Rs. 125 ($9.60) for a nonvegetarian meal and Rs. 60 ($4.60) for a vegetarian meal for two. For this, you'll get such dishes as murg Mumtaz (chicken with dried fruits) at Rs. 45 ($3.45), biryani Jodhpuri (rice, chicken, and spices) at Rs. 38 ($2.90), and less expensive vegetarian dishes for Rs. 13 ($1) to Rs. 17 ($1.30). Rich Indian desserts cost Rs. 24 ($1.85), and coffee and tea, Rs. 6 (46¢) to Rs. 8 (60¢). Hours are 1 to 2:30 p.m. and 8 to 11:30 p.m. You'll hear ghazals (Indian love songs), accompanied by sitar and tabla, at night. Also on site is the **Orbit Room,** where a meal with continental foods should run two people about Rs. 135 ($10.40). Hours: 1 to 2:30 p.m. and 8 to 11:30 p.m.

Very popular in the Connaught area is **The Host,** F-8, Connaught Place (tel. 3316381), in the hotel of the same name. A vaulted ceiling, mirrors, stone walls, and amber velvet chairs make this a cozy, attractive place to dine up-stairs on Chinese foods, but especially to sample such well-prepared Indian dishes as murg Mumtaz (chicken tandoori made with cream) at Rs. 34 ($2.60); mutton rogan josh at Rs. 30 ($2.30) is one of the highest-priced dishes on the menu. Or go continental with fish Portuguese (made with tomatoes) or Western with fried chicken, both also around Rs. 34 ($2.60). There are sweets and ice creams to round off your feast; Rs. 12 (92¢) to Rs. 21 ($1.60). Open from 10 a.m. to 11:30 p.m. seven days a week.

Finally, in the outer circle of Connaught, opposite Nirula's, are a whole row of **dhabas** ("truck stop restaurants"): Punjabi, Kake de Hotel, Bhape de Hotel, Royal, National, Sindhi, and Glory, to name a few, where you can get a plate of meat, rice, and vegetables to eat in or in a handi (clay pot) to take out for a dollar or so. The foods are not hygienically prepared and many sensible Delhites steer clear of them. A lot of visitors go to these places thinking they are cheap. Yet for more or less the same amount you can go to any number of places and get better food, more safely prepared. For instance, you could go almost next door to **Bankura,** the clean little restaurant attached to Cottage Industries Emporium, and have a price-fixed lunch of mutton cutlets, salad, and bread for Rs. 16 ($1.25) or vegetable chow mein for Rs. 10 (75¢). Or buy a thali, as mentioned, or go to one of the fast-food places below.

FAST FOODS, DELHI STYLE: Self-service fast-food restaurants reminiscent of those in the West are springing up all over Connaught Place, and below are some I found most promising:

The **Regency Midtown,** B-29, Connaught Circus (tel. 321171), is an at-tractive self-service fast-food place, with green-and-white walls and soft amber globe lights. There are little counters for stand-up eaters, and places to sit as well. Rs. 10 (75¢) to Rs. 14 ($1.05) is the cost of a curry meal with rice, plus an additional Re. 1 (7½¢) for roti (bread). Rs. 32 ($2.45), for a full chick-en tandoori, is the highest price on the menu. Light-meal items such as masala dosas are Rs. 4 (30¢); cheese pakoras run Rs. 6 (45¢). Or you can stop in for a quick espresso at Rs. 3 (23¢) and syrup-soaked gulab jamun at Rs. 4 (30¢). It's open from 8 a.m. to 11 p.m.

The **Treat,** in the Palika Market Complex, across from British Airways on Connaught Circus, has no decor, but houses three fast-food places under one roof: Ting Ming, for Chinese lunch or dinner at Rs. 10 (75¢) to Rs. 15 ($1.15); the Fast Food Counter, for veggie burgers and other sandwiches at Rs. 12 (90¢) to Rs. 14 ($1.05), and omelets at Rs. 10 (75¢); and Kulfi Parlor, where Indian ice cream costs Rs. 6 (45¢) and up. Open for lunch and dinner: noon to 3 p.m. and 7 to 11 p.m.

Wimpy's, 5 Janpath, Connaught Place (tel. 3313101), is modeled after a U.K. chain of the same name and looks somewhat like U.S. McDonald's, with order-takers calling out selections from behind a counter and realistic pictures of foods near the billboard-type menus. However, this Wimpy's is in a grand old building with regal marble stairs and huge mirrors, and the burgers are veggie or mutton. For Rs. 18 ($1.40) you can get a chicken-in-a-bun meal which includes fries and a Coke or Indian version of the latter. (More Wimpy's are to be opened in other cities, starting in Bombay.) It's open Monday through Saturday from 9 a.m. to 11 p.m., on Sunday from 11 a.m. to 11 p.m. A new idea to Delhites and very popular.

Next store is **Kings Food World,** with a decor in orange, black, and yellow, and waiters in coordinating shades of orange uniforms. Featured here are inexpensive Italian dishes, such as pizzas at Rs. 14 ($1.05) to Rs. 18 ($1.40); also sandwiches at Rs. 14 ($1.05) to Rs. 22 ($1.70) and soft drinks at Rs. 4 (30¢) to Rs. 11 (85¢). Hours are similar to Wimpy's.

Finally, there's an old standby in the light-meal line, the **Snack Bar,** in Nirula's Hotel, L Block, Connaught Circus (tel. 352491), with hours from 10:30 a.m. to 8 p.m. You can get pizzas and frankfurters for Rs. 10 (75¢) to 14 ($1.05), and there are cold drinks and espresso and a dozen or more ice creams.

MUGHLAI DELICACIES IN OLD DELHI: The best-known restaurant for tandoori chicken, the unpretentious **Moti Mahal** (meaning Pearl Palace), Daryaganj (tel. 273011), had been closed for two years and just reopened when I saw it, looking much the same as it ever did. The old bedraggled menu, however, had been newly printed, with all the familiar favorites. Newer restaurants have glassed-in kitchens so you can peer in and see chefs preparing tandoori foods in clay ovens mounted in the tile counters. At Moti Mahal the process is done the old-fashioned way—the clay ovens are buried in the earth and perspiring cooks squat next to them, turning and basting their chickens or kebabs sputtering on iron spikes above the red-hot coals. You are invited behind the scenes to see all this, but frankly it can be a bit of a turnoff. Two notable breads also come out of these ovens, kulcha (round and flat) and nan (teardrop shaped). The chicken runs Rs. 18 ($1.40) for a half and Rs. 35 ($2.70) for a whole. The breads cost Rs. 3 (23¢) for nan and Rs. 30 ($2.30) for keema (stuffed with meat) nan. Good with the tandoori dishes are plain rice, at Rs. 9 (70¢), with one portion large enough to serve two people. Kulfi falooda, at Rs. 12 (90¢), is Indian ice cream with dry fruits and sweet vermicelli. After dinner, ask for anise seeds to refresh your palate. You'll want to eat outdoors under the colorful tent (heated in winter), not in the aggressively plain indoor section. Reservations are advised for the evenings when there is Indian music, and always on Saturday and Sunday when families go out. Hours are noon to midnight; closed Tuesday.

Almost next door is **Peshawari,** 3707 Subhash Marg, Daryaganj (tel. 262168), a tiny restaurant with tiled walls and a clean kitchen, serving delicious buttered chicken at Rs. 48 ($3.70) for a whole, Rs. 25 ($1.90) for a half. Curries run Rs. 12 (90¢) to Rs. 13 ($1) and breads cost Rs. 3 (23¢) to Rs. 6 (45¢), Rs. 5 (40¢) for rice. Hours: noon to 4 p.m. and 6 to 11:30 p.m.; closed Tuesday.

The **Tandoor,** in the President Hotel, Asaf Ali Road (tel. 277836), has modern Indian murals and traditional Mughal decor to make it attractive, and a number of unusual dishes that make it worth a visit. Most of the main-dish selections are in the Rs. -30 ($2.30) to Rs. -35 ($2.70) range, with a few higher. Interesting items are khurmee (garlic toast) and kebabs mahi (boned, skewered fish); tandoori salad (pineapple, cheese, and tomatoes in a rich sauce) cost Rs. 25 ($1.90). One of the elaborate pulaos (rice dishes) combines fried rice with vegetables, subtly flavored with rosewater. An appetite stimulant, jeera pani (literally, spiced water) is an acquired taste. But the soups, good from the first spoonful, range from Rs. 10 (75¢) to Rs. 12 (90¢). Beer, a perfect partner to almost any Indian meal, runs Rs. 28 ($2.15) for about a quart. If you have room after your main course, try the kulfi (Indian ice cream). The glassed-in kitchen enables you to watch the chefs deftly preparing exotic foods. It's open from 12:30 to 3:30 p.m. and 7 p.m. to midnight daily.

Highly regarded by Delhites are the Mughlai dishes at **Flora,** opposite the Jama Masjid (tel. 264593). You can eat in the cozy dining hall which glows from tiny lights illuminating Mughal-style archways inset with scenic murals, or Indian style in the Dastarkhwan, seated on floor cushions around a low table. The house special, chicken Flora, at Rs. 16 ($1.25), is made with a rich butter-cream tomato sauce; chicken and fish tandoori dishes are also available, costing around Rs. 36 ($2.75) for a full chicken to serve two. Nan (bread baked in a tandoor) is Rs. 2.25 (17¢); other Indian breads run Rs. 6.50 (50¢) and there are pulaos (rice) with vegetables and lamb to eat as side dishes. Shahi tukra is a fudge-like dessert, or halwa (a sweet made from fruits or vegetables) are Rs. 6.50 (50¢) each. Hours are 9 a.m. to 12:30 a.m. daily. There's a little gift shop in front of the restaurant.

EATING HERE AND THERE: Two innovative restaurants are **Dhaba** (meaning "truck stop") and **Corbett's,** inspired by Jim Corbett National Park, in Claridges Hotel, 12 Aurangzeb Rd. (tel. 3010211). Dhaba, though indoors, is decorated with a realistic replica of a brightly painted truck pulled into a rustic village café. Corbett's is in the garden, now landscaped as a jungle with a brook, machans (lookouts), recorded bird and animal calls, and waiters in forest ranger outfits. Well-prepared Indian foods are served at both places. Dhaba offers mainly tandooris, while Corbett's accents kebabs and grills. A meal for two at either will run about Rs. 125 ($9.60). Both are immensely popular. Indeed, reservations are essential, and for the weekends it's necessary to book five days in advance. Hours are noon to 3 p.m. and 7:30 to 11:30 p.m.

Four popular restaurants in two fashionable neighborhoods are under the same management as the centrally located York Hotel and restaurant and Ginza, and also have similar menus with prices in the same range. Three of the restaurants are in Defence Colony, and attract embassy people. They are **Shiraz** (tel. 690083), with Mughlai and Indian cuisines; **Akasaka** (tel. 628640), offering predominantly Chinese dishes, despite the Japanese name; and **Chungwa** (tel. 625976), which is mainly Chinese. The fourth, **Fujiya** (tel. 3760590), is in the Malcha Marg Shopping Center, and has Japanese dishes sprinkled among the Chinese. Figure on the lowest entrees averaging Rs. 18 ($1.40) to Rs. 20 ($1.55) and the highest at Rs. 26 ($2) to Rs. 28 ($2.15). Hours for all four may vary slightly, but are basically noon to 3 p.m. and 7 p.m. to midnight daily.

One of the most attractive Oriental restaurants in town is the wood-paneled **Golden Dragon,** C/2 Vasant Vihar, Main Market (tel. 670426), where you're surrounded by tapestries and tinkling bells and a fiery dragon surveys all from above your head. The cuisine is Mandarin, Szechuan, Cantonese, and Japanese. From Japan comes the interesting mizutaki (prawns and pork in a hot pot), at Rs. 65 ($5). The Golden Dragon is popular with diplomats who live in the area as both a take-out and an eat-in place. Open daily from noon to 3 p.m. and 7 p.m. to midnight.

At the **Mehrab,** in the Lodhi Hotel, Lala Lajpat Rai Marg (tel. 619422), there are white stucco walls, a fountain, and graceful archways to set the scene for notable Mughlai foods. Specialties include biryanis (rice with chicken or meat, fruits, nuts, and spices), and tender chicken masala (rich curry). The Kashmiri kofta curry (minced mutton balls stuffed with sultanas, nuts, and eggs in curry sauce) and the shahi paneer (vegetables in cheese sauce) are also recommended. Most of the main dishes cost Rs. 45 ($3.45), though a few go as high as Rs. 60 ($4.60), but nearly all are large enough to serve two. Figure on Rs. 100 ($7.70) for a three-course meal for two. Hours are 12:30 to 3 p.m. and 8 p.m. to midnight.

Most of the top hotels have 24-hour coffeeshops for light meals and snacks. Three that are exceptionally nice and extremely popular with everyone are the **Machan** (meaning "jungle lookout"), in the Taj Mahal Hotel, 1 Man Singh Rd. (tel. 3016162), where a "Peaceable Kingdom" of animals and Rousseau-like foliage decorate the walls and the rich pastries will drive you wild. The **Promenade,** in the Hyatt Regency, Ring Road (tel. 609911), beside a 90-foot cascade and surrounded by plants, is especially pleasant for an as-you-like-it breakfast: Indian style, with such tasty items as masala dosa (paper-thin rice-and-lentil pancake, stuffed with potatoes and cashews), sambar (spicy and soup-like), fresh fruits, and coffee or tea; or English style, with eggs and all the trimmings; or continental, with croissants and coffee or tea. **Isfahan,** in the Taj Palace, Sardar Patel Marg, Diplomatic Enclave (tel. 3010404), is decorated with a prized antique collection of Persian copper samovars and coffee pots, and wood dividers break up a large room into intimate settings. Foods are Persian accented as well as Central Asian and Afghani. Filling soups such as gosht goli shorba (made with lamb dumplings) are Rs. 16 ($1.25), or meat and spinach gulyas (at the same price) are, with bread or a roll, meals in themselves. The Isfahan meal-size platters give you a taste of various dishes, at Rs. 40 ($3.05) for vegetarian to Rs. 45 ($3.45) for nonvegetarian. Rich pastries and Indian desserts cost Rs. 15 ($1.15) to Rs. 20 ($1.55).

Also pleasant is **Samovar,** in the Ashok Hotel, 50B Chanakyapuri (tel. 600121), where you'll find some of the richest cappuccino in town for about Rs. 10 (75¢).

SPLURGING AROUND TOWN: Delhi's splurge restaurants are located in the top hotels. Only part of their enjoyment is dining in glamorous, evocative settings. The real reason to splurge is to try some highly varied, well-prepared regional fare.

Foods of India's northern frontier region, hot from the tandoori or sizzling on skewers, are especially well made at **Bukhara,** in the Maurya Palace Sheraton Hotel, Sardar Patel Marg (tel. 3010101). The same hotel's Mayur Restaurant specializes in richly prepared foods of the old Newabs. Frontier foods at the aptly named stone-walled **Frontier,** in the Ashok Hotel, 50B Chanakyapuri (tel. 600121), include a remarkably tasty dish, murg darranpur, a chicken stuffed with minced chicken, cheese, and spices.

For the saffron-spiked, charcoal-cooked dishes of Lucknow, go to **Haveli,** in the Taj Mahal Hotel, 1 Singh Rd. (tel. 386162), especially recommended at dinner when Indian dancers perform. **Aagan,** in the Hyatt Regency, Bhikaiji Cama Place, Ring Road (tel. 609911), excels in Peshawari foods such as fruit-filled nan (tandoori bread) seasoned with onion and fennel, and tangri kebab Peshawari (chicken legs stuffed with minced chicken, and laced with yogurt and spices). In the same restaurant, Hyderabadi foods on the menu include the elaborate gosht biryani (lamb and nut-studded spiced rice). Lucknowi and Hyderabadi cuisines are also featured at **Dilkusha,** in the Hotel Kanishka, 19 Ashok Rd. (tel. 343400).

A three- to four-course lunch or dinner for two at these restaurants should cost around Rs. 200 ($15.40) to Rs. 250 ($19.25) without drinks. Beer, the ideal drink with spicy Indian foods, will add about $4 when one large bottle is shared by two diners. Most of the restaurants are open for lunch from around 12:30 or 1 p.m. to 2:30 or 3 p.m., and again for dinner from around 7:30 or 8 p.m. to 11:30 p.m. or midnight. You can check exact timings when you make your reservations, which are advised—the top Indian restaurants are popular for family gatherings as well as for tourists. Live Indian music is played nearly everywhere.

All the top hotels also have other specialty restaurants for non-Indian cuisines. Chinese restaurants include **House of Ming,** in the Taj Mahal Hotel, 1 Singh Rd. (tel. 3016162), and the **Teahouse of the August Moon,** in the Taj Palace Hotel, 2 Sardar Patel Marg (tel. 3010404), with a bridge, pond, and bamboo grove, the first and only restaurant in Delhi to serve dim sum (dumplings and other small dishes) and undoubtedly the first in the world to offer this typical Chinese lunch in a setting inspired by a play based in Okinawa. **China Town,** in the Ashok Hotel, 50B Chanakyapuri (tel. 600121), serves both Szechuan and Cantonese dishes, in a room with foods displayed on colorful carts.

Casa Medici, in the Taj Mahal Hotel, 1 Singh Rd. (tel. 3016162), mentioned under buffets, also has an extensive à la carte menu for Italian foods. In this same hotel, is **Captain's Cabin** for fish and seafood. For French and continental dishes, try the elegant new **La Rochelle,** in the Oberoi, Zakir Hussain Marg, (tel. 699571); the **Burgundy Restaurant,** in the Ashok Hotel, 50B Chanakyapuri (tel. 600121); or the **Takshila,** in the Maurya Palace Sheraton, Sardar Patel Marg (tel. 3010101), which has Spanish dishes. **Taverna Cyprus,** in the Ashok Hotel, 50B Chanakyapuri (tel. 600121), features Cypriot foods which, like other Middle Eastern cuisines, rely on grilled lamb, tomato sauces, eggplant in various guises, yogurt dressings, and honey-drenched desserts. **Valentino's,** in the Hyatt Regency, Bhikaiji Cama Place, Ring Road (tel. 609911), and the **Brasserie,** in the Hotel Meridien, Windsor Place (tel. 383960), are other choices.

Possibly the most unusual setting for continental dinner is the **Orient Express,** in the Taj Palace Hotel, 2 Sardar Patel Marg (tel. 3010404), a replica of the dining car of the famous Belle Époque train. The menu is inspired by the cuisines of cities through which the recently renovated real train still passes—Paris, Lausanne, Milan, and Verona among them. Figure on Rs. 250 (about $20) per "traveler" for a meal on the legendary train, add Rs. 450 ($34.60) for a bottle of French wine, and call four days in advance if you hope to hop aboard. These prices would be typical of any of the splurge-priced restaurants above—with the exception of Chinese foods, which could be a slightly less expensive.

Hours are basically the same as the hotels' Indian restaurants. Live (sometimes much too loud) Western music is often played. Reservations are advised, especially on weekends and in peak season.

SNACKING: There are countless snack stalls in Delhi, but for the veritable snack-of-snacks, head to Bengali Market (about a 50¢ scooter-rickshaw ride from Connaught Place) and settle into one of the cozy booths at **Bhim Sain's Sweet House.** Walking in, you pass a great array of sweet and savory foods neatly displayed under glass. They taste as good as they look. On the sweet side, a plate of halwa (made of fruit, nuts, or vegetables) is about Rs. 20 ($1.55) per heaping plate. You get two or three gulab jamuns (choose the darkest ones) dripping with rosewater and syrup for about the same price, or you might like some jalebi, pretzel-looking sweets. From the savories, chaat (lentils, grains seasoned with tamarind) is around Rs. 2 (15¢) to Rs. 5 (40¢) per plate, and puffy puris and samosas (turnovers filled with vegetables or meat) cost about the same. One taste of anything at this shop and you'll know why Bhim Sain's is always recommended by loyal fans. On Diwali, the fall festival, when giving sweets is a tradition, customers stand in long lines in order to buy their gifts. It's open daily from 7:30 a.m. to 10:30 p.m.

Another famous and equally good sweet shop, **Nathus,** is directly across from Bhim Sain's.

If you've got about 30 rupees and you're in the mood for a light meal, do as many Delhites do: spend about 45¢ on a three-kilometer (two-mile) motorized-scooter ride to a snack shop few tourists know, **Roshan-Di-Kulfi,** in Ajamul Khan Market, Karol Bagh, among the best known of the many sweet shops here. Once there, use all but your return fare on a snack spree of fresh, piping hot puris (puffy fried breads), best eaten on the spot; chaat (a salty-grain snack), to eat at once or save for later in the day; or kulfi (Indian ice cream), in a little clay pot. This little snack feast should cost about Rs. 20 ($1.55), if you order a number of things.

Feeling like a "nosh" in the center of town? Go to Shah Jahan Road, not far from the Taj Mahal and Claridges Hotels, and stop at the **chaat walla** (snack seller's) cart near the Union Service Commission. You'll have no trouble finding it because everyone knows it and can point it out. Besides, there are always some fans buying spiced grains and other goodies, made so well by this vendor that many people make it a special point to stop for a nibble whenever they're passing by. For Rs. 10 (75¢) you can get a lot of tasty things to eat.

At **Maharajah,** in the Indian Oil Building, opposite the India Tourist Office on Janpath, a popular place about as big as a thumbprint, you can get crispy masala dosa (rice-and-lentil pancake) with vegetarian stuffing for Rs. 5 (40¢) to Rs. 6 (45¢), and a cold drink runs Rs. 5 (40¢). Open 9 a.m. to 7 p.m. daily, except closed on Sundays. In the same building, **Havro Sweets** has a similar array of inexpensive foods. The plainer-than-plain **Trap Snack Bar** sells the aforementioned, as well as light Chinese foods and sandwiches for Rs. 7 (53¢) to Rs. 8 (60¢). The most popular stall outside the Indian Oil Building features Bombay's favorite snack, bhel-puri (puffed rice, spiced grains, and chutney), served in little individual throw-away bowls made of banana leaves. For a few paise you can have a spicy treat.

After a bargaining session at Chandni Chowk, or anytime you're in Old Delhi, stop for refreshment at Delhi's only tea parlor, **Aap Ki Pasand** (meaning "as you like it"), opposite the Golcha Cinema, 15 Netaji Subhash Marg (tel. 260373), run by Sanjay Kapur, Delhi's only tea taster. Choose your cup from 20 different kinds of tea. Is it from Assam, Darjeeling, the Nilgiri Hills? You'd have to check the label to make sure, but Kapur, with years of experience in tea tasting, can sip and tell. Your own tastebuds will tell you you're onto something deliciously different with badam Kashmiri kahwa (almond- and spice-flavored) or sample the fragrant Darjeeling clonal leaves and buds that go into an "Iced Tea Holiday." A cup of tea costs about Rs. 3 (23¢), and for a bit more you can buy a neatly done-up drawstring packet of tea for sipping or gifting later on. Many herbal teas, such as chamomile and rosemary, are available as well.

3. Seeing the City

A stop by the American tourist should be at the handsome **American Embassy,** designed by architect Edward Durrell Stone and opened in 1959. It's a graceful building, cool, spacious, dignified, and yet welcoming. It is fronted by a mosaic grillwork of white stone and enhanced by a fountain-filled reflecting pool. The embassy sits way up in the south of town in what is known as **Chanakyapuri** (the Diplomatic Enclave), not far from the Ashok Hotel.

The **National Gallery of Modern Art,** Jaipur House, just off Rajpath, near the India Gate (tel. 382835), deals with Indian art from the middle of the last century on, and is an object lesson in the sensitivity of artists to foreign influence. Since 1930 the major star has been the half-Indian, half-Hungarian painter Amrita Shergil (1913–1941). The museum owns almost 100 examples of his work, including a self-portrait. Another gallery is devoted entirely to the drape-covered paintings and etchings of Rabindranath Tagore, India's Nobel Prize-winning poet, who started "doodling" after his reputation as a poet was well established and who eventually, in the opinion of some art critics, deserved another prize for his art. Since 1952 Indian contemporary art has almost paralleled that of New York or any other of the international centers. The gallery is open from 10 a.m. to 5 p.m. every day but Monday and some national holidays. Admission is 50 paise (3½¢). If there's a special exhibition, hours are extended to 8 p.m. and there's an additional charge.

Commissioning art and encouraging artists always held a high priority for India's rulers through the centuries, and so it is not surprising that the **National Museum,** about two miles farther out of town from the Janpath Hotel, on Janpath (tel. 385441), should possess a rich collection of works. Archeology rooms, with intricately carved stone groups and 3,000-year-old stone beads that could have been strung together but yesterday, are on the ground floor, while the upper rooms are devoted to Indian textiles, silver tables and trays, robes and costumes, and cotton temple hangings embellished with the story of Krishna—all full of toy-like elephants, voluptuous dancing girls, and paunchy little men on horseback with curved swords. Indian and Persian miniatures (the Persian influence is manifest in more detailed backgrounds) bear study for the delicately presented everyday scenes they unfold. Reproductions of frescoes from the Ajanta Caves (near Aurangabad) are more interesting in light of the fact that they are the earliest-known Indian paintings, dating back maybe 2,300 years. One section of the second floor is devoted to charts—different facial structures illustrating man's family tree and the different physical types to be found in India's heterogeneous population; the symbolic meaning of illustrations on early coins; and the development of different letters in Indian script. Reproductions of some of the more interesting pieces can be obtained cheaply at an office on the ground floor. The museum is open daily (except Monday) from 10 a.m. to 5 p.m. There are free film shows at 2:30 p.m. daily, and free guided tours every day. Admission is 50 paise (3½¢) Tuesday to Saturday, free on Sunday.

The Maharajah of Jaipur, a noted astronomer and mathematician of his time, built a series of observatories during his reign, 250 years ago, and you can still see the remains of some of them today. Just off Parliament Street (walk over from the Air-India office and turn left) is one of these, the **Jantar Mantar,** a series of red-stone structures built for astronomical purposes in 1719 and still impressive today. The centerpiece is an enormous stone sundial, fully 40 feet high, and around it are various structures with carved dials to ascertain longitudes and latitudes of various time zones around the world. Two circular buildings at the far end of this little park measure respectively the sun's and moon's rays, to determine via astrology the auspicious times for action. There's a narrow slit in one wall through which the sun shines only twice a year, on March 23 and September 21.

HUMAYUN'S TOMB: It isn't any startling new idea for people to erect dramatic monuments to their dead, as witness the Egyptian pyramids, but the enormous sandstone and marble mausoleum of Emperor Humayun began a new style in monuments of this kind. It was built by the emperor's widow, Haji Begum, in the 6th century and may have been the inspiration for the later Taj Mahal at Agra. Many similar architectural wonders were constructed by other Mughal rulers of this era.

The tomb holds not only the body of Humayun, but also that of his widow and later members of the dynasty, as is the custom with family mausoleums of today. Set in attractive gardens, it's an impressive sight, topped with a symmetrical dome and lined on the bottom with what appear to be guest rooms but which of course are different vaults for other members of the royal line, many of whom met violent deaths.

Entry fee is 50 paise (3½¢), free on Friday. Open from sunrise to sunset.

QUTAB MINAR AND VICINITY: It seems an obvious idea, but very few builders have constructed towers that are noticeably wider at the bottom than at the top.

The fluted tower of Qutab Minar, built of hard, red sandstone nearly 800 years ago, once seen is never forgotten. Imposingly fat at the bottom, it tapers to a narrow platform at the top, 230 feet above. Its interior spiral stairway is as sound today as when it was first built. It has survived earthquake, wind, and rain—and the recent experiments of a Delhi professor who tried to disprove the law of gravity by projecting stones from an intricate bamboo and string contrivance halfway up.

First begun in 1199 by Qutab-ud-Din, Delhi's first Muslim sultan, it was subsequently added to and for years has been a favorite picnic spot.

The beautiful tower (entry fee 50 paise, 3½¢) stands in the attractive gardens of India's first mosque, whose intricately carved pillars belong to an earlier structure and were plastered over when the mosque was first built. The covering has since been worn away, revealing the attractive carvings. In the ruins of the mosque stands a 24-foot shaft of iron, worn shiny about a fifth of the way up by the arms of countless people who believe the legend that it brings good luck to join their hands behind their back behind the pole.

The column, which has remained free of rust—much to scientists' amazement—ever since it was built in the 5th century, is a monument to "the divine Vishnu," according to a legend in Sanskrit translated in extravagantly flowery terms nearby (". . . he, by the breezes of whose prowess the southern ocean is even still perfume . . .").

Two hundred yards from the ruins, past the keekar trees, whose branches are used as toothbrushes, is the never-completed **Alai Minar,** a much wider tower that was meant to loom over its fluted neighbor, but after two years of building, was abandoned when its designer died.

The tower and the grassy lawns at its base are open from sunrise until sunset daily. It is a tranquil place, populated by tiny squirrels and wild green parrots which flutter among the ruins. Qutab Minar can be reached by city bus, motor-scooter taxi for Rs. 20 ($1.55), or a regular taxi from downtown Delhi, costing about Rs. 40 ($3.05).

IN OLD DELHI: For just over 300 years much of India's history has ebbed and flowed around its magnificent **Red Fort,** an immense, heavily guarded palace built of red sandstone by the Mughal emperors and the symbol of the oligarchy that ruled into this century. Magnificent as it is, with its inner gardens, marble buildings, and tricky architectural perspectives, it was once even more so. Until the 18th century its pride and joy was the world-famous Peacock Throne, situated in a room whose ceiling was solid gold and whose walls were studded with valuable gems. "If paradise be on the face of the earth, it is here, it is here, it is here" reads a couplet still engraved on the portico. Then came the reign of a merry monarch, the legend goes, who failed to safeguard this trust. The Persians invaded and looted almost everything of value.

There have been continuing attempts to restore the ornate decorations on the marble pillars, but it is slow and costly work. At one time water flowed through the palace, but today the marble channels are dry and the Pearl Mosque no longer gleams as it did when copper covered its dome. Aurangzeb, son of Shah Jahan, built this mosque in 1659 for Rs. 160,000.

The entrance to the fort (open from sunrise to sunset daily; entrance fee is 50 paise, 3½¢, free on Friday) is lined with small stores that don't have any particular bargains to offer but are fun to look at anyway, especially the old print stall. Centuries ago it was at this point that all visitors had to dismount and proceed on foot with heads bowed.

Probably the least painful history lesson you'll ever have is that presented by **Son et Lumière** (sound and light) at Delhi's Red Fort at sunset each night—except during heavy rains (July to September) or some chilly evenings in January. In fact, "lesson" would give the wrong impression, because although you'll learn quite a lot of Indian history, the sound-and-light experience through which it comes to you is pleasantly aesthetic. Unlike some examples of its kind, this particular Son et Lumière is extraordinarily interesting and presented with a great deal of imagination. On the face of it you wouldn't think that the simple ingredients—static buildings, lights, and noises—could be combined into anything very attention-getting, but the people responsible for this show have many surprises up their sleeves. Gently they'll lull you into a sort of reverie as you watch the light patterns play on the palaces of the inner courtyard and listen to the commentary, and then—suddenly—your attention will be cunningly diverted by the sound of horsemen rapidly approaching from behind. A measure of how well the trick works is that most people instantly turn around—only to see that the lights have shifted to another area. Attend Son et Lumière early in your Indian trip and then again just before you leave the country. You'll be amazed at how much you've learned in between visits.

Top price for the Son et Lumière is Rs. 8 (60¢), and this may well increase by the time you visit. English performances are usually at 7:30, 8, 8:30, or 9 p.m., depending on the sunset. There is a Hindi performance too. You almost always need a wrap from October to February. Reservations can be made through the Hotel Ashok, (tel. 600121, ext. 2155). Tickets are also available at the Naubat Khana in the Red Fort. Current booking, at the gate, is 15 minutes before show time.

THE "NOW" NEW DELHI: Go through the India Gate and you'll be on Rajpath, the scene, each January 26, of the spectacular Republic Day parade, and the site of the main governmental buildings. India's **Parliament** is the circular structure where members of the two houses (Peoples and States) come from every region—Bombay to Assam, Kashmir to Kerala. Also on the Rajpath, and very impressive, is **Rashtrapati Bhavan**, the Presidential Palace, with 340 rooms and 330 surrounding acres of Mughal-style gardens (open to the public twice a year, usually in February and March). This was the imperial abode of the viceroy when India was the brightest jewel in England's crown of colonies.

About 1½ km from Parliament is the **Nehru Memorial Museum and Library** (tel. 3015333), in Teen Murti House, Teen Murti Marg, where the late Prime Minister Jawaharlal Nehru lived for 16 years. The interior has been preserved just as he left it. It is open daily except Monday from 10 a.m. to 5 p.m. At night you can see a compelling **Son et Lumière** (sound and light) show here every evening after sunset, except during the rainy season, roughly mid-July to mid-September. It tells the story of the movement that brought to an end the days of the British Empire in India, and the life of the late prime minister during the country's first two decades of independence. An effective, often poetic show, it's well worth seeing. Performances are in Hindi (at 6:30 p.m.) and English (at 7:45 p.m.) and each lasts one hour. For details, telephone 375333, or inquire at the Delhi Tourist Office, 88 Janpath, or at the reception or travel desk in your hotel. Admission is Rs. 5 (40¢) and Rs. 2 (15¢).

Up the road from Teen Murti House, the white bungalow at 1 Safardjang Rd. (tel. 3012843) was the residence of the late Prime Minister **Indira Gandhi.** Now it, too, is a museum and through her personal effects and a photographic mural are told the story of her life and times. In the well-tended garden, Mrs. Gandhi can be heard via tapes addressing the public on various subjects, her voice blending with the rustling trees. A highly polished black granite slab with rough-hewn edges, guarded by soldiers, marks the place she was standing when assassinated on October 31, 1984. The bright flowers always near the stone are brought by the many visitors to the memorial. The museum is open from 10 a.m. to 5 p.m.; closed Monday.

Churches aren't always the most interesting or joyful places to browse for an hour or two, but there's something indefinably intriguing about Asian religions and that "something" manifests itself in the buildings connected with them. Delhi has at least two interesting examples. The **Jama Masjid Mosque,** begun in 1644 and completed in 1658, is an impressive elevated sandstone edifice almost opposite the Red Fort. Its two 130-foot-high, striped-with-white-marble minarets dwarf the hundreds of jam-packed stalls nearby. But, interesting as the huge 120- by 201-foot mosque is, it is overshadowed by the variety of life in the adjoining streets. The mosque is open from 7 a.m. until noon and 2 to 5 p.m. each day. Entry fee for the minarets is 50 paise (3½¢) per person, free on Friday (but Friday is not recommended, as it's a prayer day for Muslims).

On the other side of town, the **Sri Lakshmi Narayan Hindu Temple** houses a colorful collection of carved and decorated marble, plus turrets and towers of red and yellow sandstone. It was built in 1938 but appears to be a classic collection of all the facets of the Hindu faith. It is always thronged with white-robed pilgrims, some of whom will invariably be squatting before the full color statue of Lord Krishna in the main hall. The marble walls are etched everywhere with drawings and admonitory texts such as: "Just as the bird loses its freedom when enchained, so are those doomed to bondage who are enslaved to desire." Behind the temple is a small, pleasantly informal garden, and at the front is a small room where visitors can leave their shoes while walking around the temple itself.

The place where Mahatma Gandhi was cremated in 1948 (he was shot by a Hindu fanatic at a meeting on January 30 of that year) is maintained as a tranquil open-air shrine open to all every day from 5:30 a.m. to 7 p.m. It is just off Ring Road, the popular old name for Mahatma Gandhi Road, not far from the Red Fort, and can be reached by taxi from the latter for about Rs. 10 (75¢) to Rs. 12 (90¢), about half that by scooter rickshaw.

After a walk through a grassy park, you come to the **Gandhi Shrine** proper, a stone-enclosed garden in the center of which is a black marble slab inscribed with the Gandhi's last words, "O God," in Hindi.

A museum with books, photographs, and personal mementos of Gandhi is opposite the park and is open from 9:30 a.m. until 5:30 p.m. daily, except Monday. Films on Gandhi's life are shown on Sunday from 4 to 5:30 p.m. The museum itself attracts about 1,000 visitors a day. Admission to the museum and the films is free.

The **Delhi Zoo** (open from 9:30 a.m. to 4:30; closed Friday; admission is 50 paise, 3½¢) is like a spacious park in which many of the animals roam under keekar trees and beside pools. It's a lovely place to wander around, so big that it could easily provide a full day's outing. Be sure to buy some peanuts from one of the sellers; you'll find plenty of birds to give them to. (Don't feed the animals.) And don't miss the rare white tiger or the harmonica-playing elephant.

The zoo is located in the shadow of the Purana Qila, a 15th-century fort, at the far end of Rajpath. Buses go to the zoo (check the tourist office for numbers); a scooter rickshaw should cost Rs. 5 (40¢).

4. Nightlife

Entertainment centers around the top hotels where there are bars, supper clubs, and discos, as follows:

BARS, DANCING, MUSIC: Drinks are expensive everywhere. At top hotels expect to pay something like Rs. 45 ($3.45) for beer and Rs. 270 ($20.75) for 60 milliliters (about the equivalent of a U.S. double) for the imported whisky, about Rs. 55 ($4.25) for local gin, vodka, or rum; Rs. 100 ($7.70) for a glass of wine. Fruit juice costs about Rs. 20 ($1.55). Snacks in bars cost around Rs. 34 ($2.60) for shish kebab and Rs. 25 ($1.90) for cashews, to give two typical examples. Most of the top hotels have dance bands and, as they say in India, "crooners," in their top continental restaurants. The Garden at the Hotel Ashok has a crooner, guitarist, and piano; the Connaught Bar at the Oberoi has live jazz, and the Madira Bar at the Maurya Sheraton has music inspired by Omar Khayyam.

DISCOTHÈQUES: In top hotels they operate like private clubs for hotel residents, who are permitted one guest. For those not staying at the hotel, there's a temporary membership fee of around Rs. 50 ($3.85). (Regular memberships run about $200.) East meets West when it comes to the music, but the local dancers are always a step or two behind the times.

Some choice spots are **Number 1** in the Taj Mahal Hotel, hung with blow-ups of Indian movie stars and a sound system initially supervised by a New York disc jockey. For some strange reason, the lighting effects at Number 1 show butterflies on the ceiling (movie stardom is as fragile as a butterfly's wing?); **Ghungroo**, in the Maurya Sheraton, inspired by Juliana's in London, has a glass-brick dance floor. Other discothèques include **Wheels** in the Ambassador Hotel and **Pussycat** at the Rajdoot, which are less expensive. Generally, things get under way around 10 p.m. and wind up around 3 a.m.

MOVIES: Most of the movie programs are listed daily in the newspapers. Showings are usually at 3, 6, 9, and 11 p.m. (but you'd better double-check).

Top price for a reserved seat is about Rs. 8 (60¢). You can call in advance at the box office to book your seat. Though buying a ticket when you get there is cheaper, you probably won't get in because of the crowds. Some movie theaters show English-language films, usually censored of sexy parts.

CABARETS: Once the rage, these are dying out, but can still be found at the **Eldorado** in the Hotel Rajdoot, with shows at 8 p.m. and midnight, an entry fee of Rs. 35 ($2.70), and beer priced at Rs. 28 ($2.15); and the similarly priced **Lido Restaurant,** M Block, Connaught Circus (tel. 353010), with shows at 5:30, 7:45, and 10 p.m. Should half-nude dancing girls with considerable lack of talent appeal, then these shows and the expenses involved are for you. Frankly none of the performers is anywhere near as revealing or one iota as graceful as the statues on some of the celebrated Indian temples.

Better by far is the Indian dancing and music offered at Indian restaurants in the better hotels. For instance, there are always shows in the evenings at the restaurants **Haveli** at the Taj Mahal Hotel and the **Handi** at the Taj Palace. While these performances are not as authentic as classical concerts in recital halls, they are diverting for an evening.

As in major cities the world over, special events and entertainment possibilities change rapidly. To keep up-to-date, watch the daily papers or buy a copy of *Delhi Diary* for Rs. 2 (15¢) or *Genesis, The City Guide,* for Rs. 5 (40¢) at any newsstand.

5. Shopping

Remember that bargaining goes on just about everywhere, except in government emporia. For how to bargain and other overall shopping tips, see the Introduction.

SHOPPING HOURS: In the government Cottage Industries on Janpath, and state government emporia on Baba Karak Singh Marg off Connaught Place, hours are 10 a.m. to 6 p.m., with a lunch break from 1:30 to 2:30 p.m. Other stores are open from 9:30 a.m. to 7:30 p.m., with a lunch break sometime between 1 and 3 p.m.

Shops popular with tourists in the Connaught Place area, Sunder Nagar, and Chandni Chowk, are closed on Sunday; shops elsewhere are closed either Monday or Tuesday, so check if you are shopping off the beaten path. Hotel shops are open Monday through Saturday, and some stay open on Sunday as well.

BEST SHOPPING STRATEGY: Always head first to the government-run stores—to survey the merchandise, if not to buy. It gives you a clue to the standard of goods and prices before you venture into the privately owned shops and bazaars.

If you've only got one shopping stop to make, go to the three-story **Central Cottage Industries Emporium,** Janpath (tel. 311506), the government-run department store of arts and crafts from all over India. From the Delhi area are embroidered slippers with turned-up toes, and zari (gold embroidery aglow on dark velvet bags), costing Rs. 20 ($1.55) to Rs. 2,000 ($155) or more, depending on the amount of work and metal; copper shaped, shined, and made into lampshades with tiny floral cutouts to cast a soft glow; pottery from nearby kilns, in blue or black, with bright designs, made into pitchers, vases, plates, and pencil jars, with prices ranging from Rs. 250 ($19.25) for a large shade down to Rs. 25 ($1.90) for a pottery pencil jar. Among the other items found in this store are silk dresses, wool and cotton robes, and flowing embroidery-trimmed cotton caftans. If you'd rather sew your own, there are hand-block-printed silk and cotton printed fabrics that go up to the thousands for hand-woven silks. Easy to pack are men's ties and women's silk clutch bags. Papier-mâché boxes from Kashmir, painted with magical gardens and mythical beasts, are here as well. In the precious-jewelry section, glittering diamond ear studs start at Rs. 2,500 ($192); semi-precious stones are less. The antique department has shawls, decorative wall hangings, and wood and brass sculpture prominent among many other items. At this government-run emporium, you are assured that the antique you buy today was not made yesterday to look old today.

REGIONAL SHOPPING: Stroll off Connaught Place to the three-block stretch of state- and territorial-run shops on **Baba Kharak Singh Marg** for some unusual wares from all over India, including rarely visited remote places.

One of the best selections can be found at **Gujari** (Gujarat), no. A6 (tel. 343287), where you'll find attractive ankle-length salwar (tunics) embroidered and accented in tiny mirrors, matching kamiz (trousers that snap at the ankles and tie at the waist), and coordinating scarves, the cost depending on whether the fabric is cotton or silk. Decorative mirrored wall hangings and tie-dyed scarves, both moderately priced, make nice gifts; a bit more are nubby or smooth-textured hand-loomed woolen shawls.

At **Trimourti** (Maharastra), no. A8 (tel. 343747), cotton saris, to wear as is or to whip up into a skirt or dress, cost less than you think, as do printed cotton salwar-kamiz. **Zoon** (Kashmir), no. A7 (tel. 344723), features rugs, patterned papier-mâché boxes and bowls, wool and silk caftans and robes, and elegant carpets at wide-ranging prices, depending on the intricacy or pattern, number of knots, and whether the carpet is silk or wool. Other **Kashmir Emporia** are at 5 Prithviraj Rd. (tel. 611096) and 25-B Connaught Place (tel. 320581).

For arts and crafts from little-traveled regions, visit **Ambapali** (Bihar), no. A5 (tel. 343081), which has striking paintings of gods and goddesses done by villagers, priced according to size and intricacy of design.

Or go to **Utkalika** (Orissa), no. B4 (tel. 343326), for delightful primary-colored paintings showing Krishna cavorting with the gopis (milkmaids), dancers, and fanciful animals, as well as bright appliquéed hand-held fans and garden umbrellas. From distant **Nagaland,** at no. C2 (tel. 343161), hand-looms with traditional spear patterns are made into shawls, shoulder bags, and skirts. From **Assam** at no. B1 (tel. 344784), come gleaming heavy-textured silks by the meter at various prices, or made into quilted bedspreads; and from **Himachal Pradesh,** at no. C3 (tel. 343087), are embroidery-edged woolen caps and woolen shawls, dyed jute slippers for about $1, and bargain-priced papier-mâché dolls.

Black Partridge (Haryana), no. C8 (tel. 343021), displays goods from one of Delhi's neighbor states, including necklaces of polished semiprecious stones and boxes inlaid with stone fragments (priced according to box size box and the number of inlaid stones used in the designs).

Phulkari (Punjab), no. C6 (tel. 343747), is not only the name of the shop, but also of the renowned intricate Punjabi silk-embroidered cotton fabric, a traditional gift to North Indian brides. Useful for pillow covers, upholstery and spreads, it is priced up or down depending on the ornateness and size of the piece. About the same price structure covers another textile specialty, khes, which is cleverly embroidered for use on both sides. It's also ideal for draperies or covering pillows, but could be used for an interesting jacket or vest. At **Gangotri** (Uttar Pradesh), no. B5 (tel. 343559), also in the northern region, look for kurtas, the long flared shirts popular since Mughal days, priced at Rs. 25 ($1.90) or more, depending on the fabric and intricacy of embroidery trimming; they now make attractive beach cover-ups, cool summer shirts, or nighties.

Lepakshi (Andhra Pradesh), no. B6 (tel. 343892), has bidriware, stones and wires embedded in black or white alloy made into dozens of items including buttons, boxes, and bangles, priced from Rs. 10 (75¢) to Rs. 1,000 ($75) or more, depending on the size of the piece and the intricacy of the work; decorative scrolls, woodcarvings, perfumes, and gleaming glass bangles start under $1 and go up, but not sky high.

Mrignayani (Madhya Pradesh), no. B8 (tel. 343320), is the place to find hand-loomed fabrics so sheer that the 17th-century diarist, Bernier, said they'd wear out in a day. For a modest amount of money you can get enough of this gossamer material to make a pretty and cool summer dress—which will wash easily and wear about as well as any other, despite the diarist's dire prediction.

At the **Poompuhar** (Tamil Nadu), no. C1 (tel. 343161), there are lustrous Kanchipuram silks for a sari; famous Madras plaids to make a dress, skirt, or a couple of tailored shirts; and gaudy but nice, ornate and gilded Tanjore paintings of deities. **Kairali** (Kerala), no. B7 (tel. 243326), has ivory carvings (supposedly African tusks to conserve India's) of various subjects, some so intricate they look like fine lace, and placemats and doormats of palm-leaf fiber and rugs made of coir (coconut husk fiber), both durable and cheap. At **Kaveri** (Karnataka), no. C4 (tel. 343202), you'll find ivory-inlaid ebony walking sticks, bangles, boxes; rosewood and sandalwood carvings of deities and elephants; and jasmine and sandalwood soaps.

On Baba Kharak Singh Marg are also shops with merchandise from **West Bengal** (at no. A2; tel. 344745), **Tripura** (B3; tel. 344610), and **Manipur** (C7; tel. 310917), not to mention Delhi's own emporium at no. A3/4 (tel. 343287) with a varied selection of the cut-out copper shades, pottery, and zari (embroidered) bags, slippers, and belts. In addition, **Gram Shilpa** is a shop for khadi cloth and village industries.

MARTS, MARKETS, STALLS, STORES, SHOPS:

For other shopping opportunities, head to the countless stores and stalls in and about Connaught Place. To cite a few, **Bansal Brothers** (also called, "Jean Junction"), E-5, Connaught Place, is the place to pick up bargains in ready-made salvar-kamiz in a wide range of sophisticated colors and prints. It's **The Shop,** 10 Regal Building, run by sisters Kamal Singh and Nimma Mehra, when you want traditional fashions adapted to contemporary Western taste. Look for drindl skirts, pretty, full cotton dresses trimmed with tie-dyed fabrics, and jumpers with embroidery accenting the tops, as well as the store's cotton handbags.

A sightseeing tour in itself, and virtually a supermarket of gems and gold, is **Tribhovandas,** 2 Scindia House, Janpath. Even if you can't afford to buy in this store, you might like to stop in and look at some of the incredible pieces which cost up to many thousands of rupees. Some smaller items, such as pavé diamond earrings or studs, will cost around $200, and there are slender gold bangles starting at that price as well. Should you splurge here, you're guaranteed quality (the gold is 18K and up) and authenticity at a price somewhat less than you'd probably pay at home. Another reliable jeweler, not far from Connaught, **Narain,** in Showroom 2 (ground floor), New Delhi House, 27 Barakhamba Rd., which carries both set and unset stones, ivories, and carpets, will give clients a certificate vouching for the authenticity and quality of their purchases.

For affordable chunky jewelry studded with semi-precious stones, go to any of the Tibetan-run stores on Janpath. For T-shirt printing, it's **Giggles,** E-24, Connaught Place (tel. 310139).

Shimmering silks, mainly from Benares, Bhawalpur, and Bangalore, are found at **Benares House Ltd.,** N Block, Connaught Place. The dazzling selection includes silk and gold brocades (the price per meter depends on the amount of gold in the material). Less expensive are the scarves and shirts.

At the **Ivory Palace,** 19-F, Connaught Place, you can find ivory and other gift items at prices from low to very high. In Old Delhi's Ivory Palace, Northern Gate, Jama Masjid, craftsmen at the entrance show how they make some of the items sold inside. Among these are zari (gold- and silver-embroidered) clutch bags, with some garnets added to the design. Ivory bangles and miniatures painted on ivory are also sold here. You need a certificate to get sizable ivory pieces out of the country, and the shop's manager, Ananad Solomon, says that it's gladly provided. Such bulky ivory pieces would not include the uncomfortable-looking elaborately carved-ivory drawing suite which took two craftsmen 25 years to complete—it's on permanent display.

At Sunder Nagar Market

Easily one of the most enjoyable places to shop is Sunder Nagar Market, a group of well-appointed stores not far from the bustling center, but in comparison an island of serenity. This is where serious collectors from all over the world hunt for rare miniatures and bronzes, antique jewelry, woodcarvings, and unusual household objects. Prices for the extremely valuable items may seem high until you compare them with prices for similar objects in the West —providing you could find them at home. In some of these shops, subtly suggesting that the price might be out of line could get you a slight markdown. There are some inexpensive wares also. If you have more time than money to spend, then you can browse to your heart's content.

The following listing will give you a some idea of what's in store for you:

Bharany's, 14 Sunder Nagar Market (tel. 618528), is run by Chhote Bharany, the world-famous collector-merchant-author who has exhibited his heirlooms in museums and sold them abroad at such well-known department stores as Bloomingdale's in New York. A writer of books and plays, he inherited some of his valuable artifacts and purchased others from maharajas in distress. Among his most costly wares is a Tibetan necklace-set of emeralds and 24-karat gold pieces studded with precious stones. Down the price scale are pretty garnet necklaces, enamel earrings, and strands of seed pearls. Bharany also collects antique textiles, some as costly as his gems.

Ellora, 9 Sunder Nagar Market, is headquarters for stunning antique silver jewelry, including belts and bangles. Silver and gold items are sold by the gram, and will be weighed for you. Since there are only 25 grams to an ounce, several ounces of silver belt can easily run up a bill. Here also are unset stones and miniature paintings. Pre-18th-century miniatures are very rare, and those painted in 19th century are fast becoming hard to find, but you might find one here (at an understandably high price). Ellora has branches at no. 17 in the Red Fort and in the Great Eastern Hotel in Calcutta.

Indian Arts Corner, 30 Sunder Nagar Market, carries old silver belts that harem charmers once swiveled around their hips, and ankle bangles, now bracelets (sold by the gram), and semiprecious and precious stones, set and unset.

Kumar Art Gallery, 11 Sunder Nagar Market, specializes in rare antique rugs and equally rare Tantric art (symbolic, occult, diagramatic stuff), both of which cost thousands of rupees depending on the age, size, and intricacy of the piece. Branches of this store can be found in the Ashok and Maurya Sheraton Hotels in Delhi and on Madison Avenue in New York City.

T. Kishanchand, 22 Sunder Nagar Market (tel. 618466), the famous Bombay jewelers, and **Nav Rattan Arts,** at no. 26, both have gems, jewelry, and handcrafts. Nav Rattan also has brass, copper, and tapestries.

Lall's, 8 Sunder Nagar Market, has antique and new jewelry and interesting jewelry boxes to keep it in, as well as metal chests for safekeeping other precious possessions. **Nirula's Copper Bazaar,** 8 Sunder Nagar Market, has collector's items in copper, as its name implies, brass, and wood sculpture, and paintings.

La Boutique, 20 Sunder Nagar Market, has antique silverware, paintings, and ivory carvings.

Mascot's Book Shop, 6 Sunder Nagar Market, carries a large selection of art books.

Mohanjordaro, 25 Sunder Nagar Market, has woodcarvings and old bronzes, as well as handcrafted items. Like other places, the price depends on the condition and age of the item.

BARGAINS IN BANGLES: Every Tuesday at **Hanuman Mandir** (Temple), dozens of vendors display a dazzling array of bangles from near and far. You'll get an education in the diversity of the simple circle—there are bangles in every color; bangles embedded with chips of other colors, with metal, mirrors, and fake gems; candy-striped bangles, faceted bangles, flowered bangles— and that hardly covers the assortments at this bazaar. Two of the best selections can be found at the **Jagni Churi Walla** and **Babu Churi Walla** stalls. Ask anyone to point them out. With a little bargaining, for Rs. 13 ($1) to Rs. 30 ($2.30) you can dress up your wrists and take some bangles home for gifts.

If you're not in Delhi on a Tuesday, both sellers have shops in Old Delhi: Jagni's is at 3023 Mohd Ram Bazaar, and Babu's is 5243 Bazaar Ballimaran (tel. 238019).

Hanuman Mandir Bazaar is also a little mela (fair) where you can get your palm read by a strolling fortune teller or get your palm red by having an artist paint it with henna designs. These days Indian women have their palms painted for good looks or good luck. In earlier times henna painting was a ritual for new brides only, and it's still a bridal tradition. It takes some time for the henna designs to wear off, so one sure way to pick out a new bride in a crowd is to look for the young woman with designs painted on her hands and feet.

THE BIG BAZAAR: If you don't mind being hassled and hustled, bustling **Chandni Chowk,** famous for bargaining since the 18th century, can be a lot of fun. My favorite is Dariba Kalan, the fascinating lane of silversmiths, where you'll find rings for your fingers, toes, ears, and nose; bangles for your arms and ankles; and necklaces and combs. In other winding lanes are perfume oils, sparkling garlands, baskets, brocades, and copper pots—all for prices you can almost name yourself—but you have to bargain. While you look for bargains, be sure to keep an eye on your handbag and wallet.

6. Useful Information

AIRLINES: You'll find **Indian Airlines** at Kanchenjunga, 18 Barakhamba Rd. (tel. 343400), and at the airport (tel. 3310071); there are also offices in the PTI Building, at Palam Airport, in the Ashok and Siddarth Hotels, and in the Banarjee Building on Asaf Ali Road. The main **Vayudoot** office is in the

Malhotra Building, Janpath (tel. 3315768), with other offices at Palam Airport and Safdarjang Airport.

ARRIVAL: Coming in without reservations? Always check with the **India Tourist Office** counters at Indira Gandhi International or Palam Airport. In town, the tourist office is located at 88 Janpath (tel. 320005). In addition, the **Delhi Tourism Development Corporation (DTDC)** maintains a 24-hour counter at Indira Gandhi International Airport (tel. 391213), and counters at the New Delhi (tel. 321078), Old Delhi (tel. 2511083), and Nizamuddin (tel. 611712) Railway Stations, and the Inter-State Bus Terminus (tel. 2512181).

BIKE RENTALS: Shops are near Minto Bridge, not far from Connaught Place, and on Mohan Singh Place near the Rivoli Cinema. Rentals cost Rs. 4 or 5 (under 40¢) per hour to Rs. 10 (75¢) to Rs. 15 ($1.15) a day, plus a small refundable deposit. Shops in Pharaganj also rent bikes for similar rates.

CARS: There are no self-drive rental cars in Delhi or anywhere in India. A small, non-air-conditioned car with a driver will cost Rs. 305 ($23.50) for eight hours, Rs. 250 ($19.25) for four hours. Before you make a deal, consult the **India Tourist Office,** 88 Janpath (tel. 320005 or 320008), for a list of approved operators or the **India Tourism Development Corporation (ITDC)** car-rental desks in these hotels: Ashok, Ashok Yatri Niwas, Janpath, Kanishka, Lodhi, Qutab, and Samrat.

CURRENCY EXCHANGE: Most major hotels have money-changing permits for guests—the Ashok Hotel branch of the Central Bank open 24 hours a day. Banks outside of hotels are open from 10 a.m. to 2 p.m. Monday through Friday and 10 a.m. to noon on Saturday. They can be very busy so you may have to wait a long time to exchange your money. There is a 24-hour bank at Palam Airport and a bank at Indira Gandhi International that operates during flight times. Whenever you change your money, be sure to save your receipts; you'll have to show them when you leave and want to convert your leftover rupees into dollars. For overall rates and rules about rupees, see "Essential Information" in the Introduction.

DRUGSTORES: Here they're called chemists shops, and in Super Bazaar, Connaught Circus, are open 24 hours a day (closed Sunday).

MAGAZINES: *Illustrated Weekly of India* is a news-feature magazine with some interesting articles. On the other hand, if you've been traveling a lot, you might be interested in the periodicals at the **American Library,** 24 Kasturba Gandhi Marg (tel. 3314251), open from 9:30 a.m. to 6 p.m. daily except Sunday. The Asian editions of *Time, Newsweek,* the *International Herald Tribune,* and other Western periodicals can be found in the bookstalls at many larger hotels and as well as many bookshops.

MAIL: Can be received at **Post Restante, G.P.O.** (care of the postmaster), Baba Karak Singh Marg, New Delhi 110001 (and be sure to specify New Delhi), from 8 a.m. to 7 p.m.; at the **Tourist Office,** 88 Janpath, New Delhi 110001; and at **American Express,** Hamilton House, A Block, Connaught Place, New Delhi 110001.

NEWSPAPERS: Every city and large town has at least one, and often two or three English-language papers. The nationally circulated ones are the *Hindu-*

stan Times (Delhi), the *Times of India* (Delhi and Bombay), the *Statesman* (Delhi and Calcutta), *Indian Express* (Delhi, Madras, and Bombay), and *The Hindu* (Madras).

POSTAGE: Airmail letters to the U.S. and Europe cost Rs. 6.50 (50¢) for 20 grams; an aerogram is Rs. 5 (40¢). Rates are slightly less to the Asia-Pacific region, and they don't apply to Bangladesh, Bhutan, Nepal, Pakistan, or Sri Lanka. Airmail postcards are Rs. 4 (30¢). It takes about five days for mail to travel by air from India to the U.S. It's wise to count your change carefully when buying stamps from hotel clerks; at post offices you'll be given the correct change and probably a detailed handwritten receipt, even for the smallest purchases. Like the banks, the uncrowded post offices are the hotel branches located at the Ashok, Ashok Yatri Niwas, Kanishka, and Lodhi—very handy if you purchase something super-sized in the bazaar and would rather ship than schlep it home.

PROHIBITION: Alcoholic beverages are available without a permit at bottle shops. They are also served in bars and restaurants of major hotels. Restaurants outside of hotels do not presently serve liquor; they serve beer, however, which compliments spicy foods. Dry days are the first and seventh of every month, and three national holidays when bottle shops are closed.

RADIO: News in English is broadcast periodically throughout the day, from 8 a.m. to 9 p.m. Special bulletins are broadcast in English when something extra newsworthy occurs.

REPUBLIC DAY: Tickets in the seating enclosures for the big event, January 26, cost Rs. 10 (75¢) to Rs. 200 ($15.40). Tickets for the Beating of the Retreat, which closes the festivities, are Rs. 5 (40¢) to Rs. 10 (75¢). Children under 12 are admitted to both at no charge. Consult the India Tourist Office, 88 Janpath, for details and reservations.

SHOESHINE: Indians usually spend one to two rupees. If you're a tourist, shoeshine boys will pretend it isn't enough.

STUDENT INFORMATION CENTER: Located in the Students Travel Center Hotel, Imperial, Janpath (tel. 344965), the place to go for renewing or issuing International Student Identity Cards.

SWIMMING: Budget hotels don't have swimming pools, but budget travelers can still be in the swim by paying a fee at some hotels. For example, Rs. 50 ($3.85) at the Imperial or Rs. 20 ($1.55) at the Centaur. To find out about other hotels, check with them directly. Changing rooms and towels are available at the hotels.

TAXIS AND OTHER TRANSPORT: Both four-seater taxis and three-wheel, two-seater, semi-enclosed scooter rickshaws are metered. It's always a good idea to make sure the driver drops the flag on the meter before you take off. Officially, the taxi meter should start at Rs. 3 (23¢). Scooter rickshaw fares begin at Rs. 2.30 (18¢). But not all the meters have been recalibrated, and if they have not, they will start at Rs. 2.60 (20¢) on taxis and Rs. 2 (15¢) on scooters. Additional charges are tacked on both taxis and scooter rickshaws for heavy luggage and waiting. Between the hours of 11 p.m. and 5 a.m. there's a 25% surcharge. When in doubt about your fare, ask to see the driver's rate card for verification. If you think you have been overcharged or have any other complaints about taxi or scooter-rickshaw drivers, call tel. 230782 or 3014896. Neither taxi or motorized-rickshaw drivers are tipped. But so many tourists have been tipping them that some drivers seem to expect it from foreigners. Be firm.

Six-seater scooter rickshaws, found around Connaught Place and near popular neighborhood shopping centers, take off when they get a load of passengers going the same way. Supposedly, they charge by the sector; for example, a trip from Connaught Place to the Red Fort should cost about Rs. 2 (15¢). But to be on the safe side, set the fare before you get in. For cycle rickshaws and tongas (horse-drawn carts), found in Old Delhi, you bargain and set your fare before you get in.

Always make sure your driver understands where you're going before you get in. And if you take one of the share vehicles, know where it's heading before you take off. You can usually find someone to interpret if the driver doesn't understand English. And if he doesn't, a little pantomime goes a long way toward international understanding everywhere in India.

TELEVISION: There are only two channels in Delhi, with programs from 6 a.m. to 11:30 p.m. There's special programming for children on Sunday morning and Indian movies on Sunday evening; other times, you'll find news and feature programming and live telecasts of important events. Hotels in the medium to upper price ranges have installed television in guest rooms or created television rooms. Closed-circuit television is also being used in middle-bracket to splurge hotels to show Indian films in which songs and dances stand in for hugs and kisses. Western films and reruns of TV programs such as "The Cosby Show" are also channeled into hotel rooms. Television is still somewhat a novelty, and fascination with it is intense, especially during cricket season when sets are on everywhere all day long.

TELEPHONES: Pay phones take one 50-paise (3½¢) coin. Found in shops and shopping centers, they are in short supply. If there's no pay phone around, usually the receptionist at any good hotel will let you use the phone for a small fee. You can direct-dial to most cities in India, and to many European and some Southeast Asian countries, Japan, and the U.S. Direct dialing is one thing—getting through is quite another. Circuits are often busy.

TEMPERATURES: In the summer the temperature in Delhi ranges between 70° and 100° Fahrenheit; in winter, 45° to 90°.

TIPS: In Delhi, a service charge is added to some bills at hotels and restaurants, and any tip above that is at your own discretion. Private car drivers who've done an excellent job get a maximum tip of Rs. 10 (75¢) to Rs. 15 ($1.15) a day. Don't ask your guide's advice about tipping your driver as you may end up paying a sum large enough to be split between the two of them. Some guides prefer small gifts to rupee tips. For overall tipping advice, see Section 3, "Essential Information," in the Introduction.

TOURS: Budget-priced tours are conducted daily by IDTC, DTDC, and Travelite to all major points of Delhi: of New Delhi from 9 a.m. to 1 p.m. and of Old Delhi from 2 to 5 p.m. IDTC's tours cost Rs. 20 ($1.55) for New Delhi and Rs. 24 ($1.85) for Old Delhi.

Reservations and information are available at Ashok Travel and Tours Counters in the Hotels Ashok (tel. 600121, ext. 2155 or 2156), Janpath (tel.

350070, ext. 814), Lodhi (tel. 619422), Ranjit (tel. 3511256), Kanishka (tel. 343400), Samrat (tel. 603030, ext. 2848 or 2849), and Ashok Yatri Niwas (tel. 344611), plus at Palam Airport (tel. 392825). All tours operate from Ashok Travel and Tours, L Block Office, Connaught Circus, New Delhi 110001 (tel. 350331).

The DTDC's Delhi tours cost Rs. 14 ($1.05) for each tour. If both tours are taken on the same day, the total cost is Rs. 25 ($1.90). The DTDC also has an evening tour which includes the floodlit monuments, Birla Mandir and the Son et Lumière, and dinner. It costs Rs. 50 ($3.85) per head and departs at 6 p.m.

The DTDC's Museum Tour operates on Sunday only for Rs. 30 ($2.30) and will give you a glimpse of the Air force, Rail and Transport, and National Museums, the Indira Gandhi Memorial, Nehru Planetarium, Museum of Natural History, and Dolls Museum. For information on DTDC tours and reservations, call tel. 3313637. Departure point is DTDC, N Block, Bombay Life Building, Connaught Place.

Travelite's tours cost Rs. 35 ($2.70) each or Rs. 55 ($4.25) if both tours are taken on the same day. The coach picks you up at your hotel. To make reservations, see your hotel reception or call Travelite (tel. 353830) or Karachi Cab Company (tel. 322994).

Five hours of sightseeing in a non-air-conditioned car with a driver costs about Rs. 220 ($16.90).

TOURS BEYOND DELHI: ITDC, DTDC, and Travelite offer same-day coach tours to Agra from 6:30 a.m. to 9:30 p.m. Covered on all three tours are the Taj Mahal and Agra Fort. The DTDC's tour also includes the ghost city of Fatehpur Sikri. ITDC charges Rs. 225 ($17.30); DTDC, Rs. 185 ($14.25); and Travelite, Rs. 235 ($18). Reservations and pickup points are generally the same as for the Delhi tours above, except for IDTC's: for the Agra tour, the pickup points are the Hotels Janpath, Ashok, and Lodhi. Travelite also offers an overnight Agra trip for Rs. 685 ($52.75), including hotels and meals. By car to Agra and Fatehpur Sikri and return to Delhi the same evening via the Bharatpur bird sanctuary costs Rs. 1,330 ($102.25) plus waiting charges.

A day tour to the pink city of Jaipur run by ITDC tour, 6:30 a.m. to 10 p.m., will cost Rs. 225 ($17.30). The tour includes lunch in Jaipur, soft drinks, and entrance fees.

TOURIST GUIDES: Guides are available through the India Tourist Office at 88 Janpath (tel. 321078). The fees for one to four people for a half-day tour is Rs. 48 ($3.70) and for a full day, Rs. 72 ($5.55). There's a Rs.-15 ($1.15) lunch allowance if the guide is booked for the entire day.

TRAINS: A good train ride from New Delhi is the *Taj Express* to Agra, leaving Delhi daily at 7 a.m., arriving in Agra at 10:15 a.m., and returning the same day, leaving Agra at 6:50 p.m. and arriving in New Delhi at 10:15 p.m., costing Rs. 205 ($15.75) air-conditioned, Rs. 101 ($7.75) in first-class, Rs. 62 ($4.75) in a chair, Rs. 26 ($2) in second class. The train is met in Agra by tour buses to take you sightseeing. To make reservations for air-conditioned and first class, contact the Northern Railway Reservations office, State Entry Road, Connaught Place (tel. 345221 or 344877); open from 8 a.m. to 8 p.m. Monday through Saturday, 8 a.m. to 1 p.m. on Sunday and holidays; for second class, go to the New Delhi Railway Station, near Connaught Place.

The *Pink City Express* for Jaipur leaves Delhi daily at 5:50 a.m. and arrives in Jaipur at 11:05 a.m.; leaving Jaipur at 5 p.m. and arriving in Delhi at

10:15 p.m. The cost is Rs. 124 ($9.55) for first class, Rs. 29 ($2.25) in second class.

TRANSFER FROM AIRPORT: The **E.A.T.S. (Ex-Servicemen's Airlink Transport)** will take you from and to Palam domestic airport for Rs. 10 (75¢) and to and from Indira Gandhi International Airport for Rs. 15 ($1.15). There's no extra charge for luggage. The city/airport transfers begin at 4:40 a.m. and run frequently until 11:30 p.m. They leave the airport for the city when flights arrive. There is also a prepaid taxi service from Indira Gandhi to Delhi hotels. Tickets are purchased at the Pre-Paid Taxi Booth in Indira Gandhi Airport; the prepaid plan was to about to go into effect at Palam as well and may well be operating by now. The charges vary with your destination. Hold onto the receipt, as the driver will need it when you reach your destination.

WHEN TO VISIT: Delhi's top season is from mid-October through March. April, May, and June are very hot. The rainy season is roughly June through September. November to January is pleasant, with clear skies and cool to chilly temperatures. February is lovely and spring-like.

Chapter III

EXCURSIONS FROM THE CAPITAL

1. Agra and the Taj Mahal
2. The Erotic Statues of Khajuraho
3. Bhopal and Sanchi

TO ALL INTENTS and purposes, the sleepy little town of Agra began its career in the 16th-century era of the Mughal emperors. Today its population numbers about 770,000, but it still gives every appearance of an overgrown village sprawled on both sides of the muddy Jumna River. Its single-track, century-old iron bridge is thronged at all times with the heterogeneous traffic that amply illustrates the town's character: tumble-down camel carts, decrepit bicycles, overloaded trucks, ox-drawn wagons, automobiles, and scores of pedestrians in every conceivable garb.

Most of the tourists who visit Agra today see little of this—perhaps an occasional glimpse of street life through the windows of the deluxe coaches that take them from the station to the hotel to the Taj Mahal and back again. For the famous marble tomb is what they all come to see and rarely do they stay longer than one night. A pity.

1. Agra and the Taj Mahal

THE TAJ MAHAL: That famous marble tomb was built between 1631 and 1653 (with features added until 1657). It took 20,000 laborers, masons, stone cutters, and jewelers to complete the task. Marble was brought from one part of India, sandstone from another, semiprecious stones from all over Asia, Russia, Egypt, Baghdad, and other places. The final product is a masterpiece of symmetry: a landmark so famous that every visitor's first reaction is to exclaim how much smaller it is than they had believed.

The size is an illusion, as you discover when walking toward it. It actually seems to float in the air (an impression that is much heightened at sunrise) and somehow it is so delicately balanced that it fosters countless optical illusions. The main illusion is experienced if you face the Taj from the entrance gate, walking forward a few steps and then back: the whole building appears to move toward you. Atop this gate, incidentally, are 22 small domes, ostensibly recording the number of years the mausoleum took to build.

And it was constructed as a monument to love. Mumtaz Mahal was 20 when she was married to Shah Jahan, fourth in the illustrious line of Mughal rulers that began with Babar. The lovely Mumtaz was Shah Jahan's second wife, but his favorite, and she bore him 14 children before dying in childbirth in 1631. Hearing of her death while away at battle, he vowed to build her the most extravagant monument the world had ever seen. That monument became the Taj Mahal, universally acknowledged for centuries to be one of the world's most perfect pieces of architecture.

A fountain-filled reflecting pool leads up from the entrance gate, and the mausoleum itself is flanked by four gentle minarets (which lean slightly outward, so that they'd fall without damage to the main structure in case of an "accident"). A red sandstone mosque to the left is matched by an identical building to the right, purely for the sake of architectural harmony. Around the 90-foot-high entrance portico are quotations from the Koran in Arabic script. Inside the Taj itself, an intricately carved marble screen shields the tombs of Mumtaz and her husband. These tombs are fakes placed directly over the real tombs, which are in the chamber underneath. The marble walls are exquisitely decorated with pietra dura inlay, the method of setting semiprecious and precious stones into marble tile. Some of the decorative flowers are composed of as many as 64 separate inlays, so skillfully placed in a one-inch square that even your fingers cannot detect the joints. The ceiling of this inner dome is 80 feet high, and the guard delights in demonstrating the 15-second echo.

Behind the mausoleum, an open terrace looks across the river to a crumbling red stone wall that is generally believed to have been the site for a replica of the Taj in black marble for Shah Jahan. Upon its completion, the two were to be linked by a black and white marble bridge. Before this could be built, Shah Jahan was deposed and arrested by his son, Aurangzeb. When he died in 1666 he was buried beside his beloved wife.

During the 1971 war between India and Pakistan, the Taj Mahal was closed to the public for the only time in its more than 300-year history. The renowned monument also was covered over with straw matting, wildflowers, vines, and grass. This camouflage kept Pakistani bombers from using the reflection cast by the Taj under moonlight to lead them to important Agra targets.

For years, tourists made special trips to see the unforgettable sight of the Taj on full-moon nights. Many of these visitors would spend the entire night gazing at the Taj until the sunrise made the dome seem to be tinted pink. Now, however, it is not the possible to see this sight—the Taj is closed on full-moon nights, as it is on all others.

As Agra develops economically there's been widespread concern over the effects on the Taj of industrial pollution. Now as a safeguard, nearby foundries are being shut down and relocated away from the Taj, where they can do it no harm. To continue to check air quality as well, pollution-monitoring devices have been concealed in the garden and under the Taj dome.

The Taj Mahal is open daily from dawn to 7:30 p.m.; admission is Rs. 2 (15¢), free on Friday. The museum in the Taj compound is open from 10 a.m. to 5 p.m., and the entry fee is included in the Taj ticket. It's easy to find the Taj Mahal from almost anywhere in Agra: many signposts around town bear its silhouette and an arrow.

OTHER MAJOR SIGHTS IN AGRA: Although the Taj is the major attraction in Agra, it is by no means the only one. In fact, there are two other incredible spots and a myriad of less significant ones.

Itimad-ud-Daula

Building just seemed to come naturally to those old Mughals. Fourteen years before Shah Jahan started on the Taj Mahal, during the reign of his predecessor Jahangir, between 1622 and 1628 the magnificent tomb of Itimad-ud-Daula was built. This was the work of Jahangir's wife, Nur Jahan, who constructed it in memory of her parents. It is chiefly notable for being the first example of pietra dura inlay, precious stones intricately recessed in marble tile. The whole place is covered in it. Like the Taj, it has the real tombs downstairs and the replicas above. This was common practice so that visitors would not walk across the real graves. The woman's tomb, incidentally, is usually identifiable by the replica of a slate on its surface—the implication being: "Here is my heart, as clear as a slate, write on it what you will." Two of the tombs look exactly like wood, but they are actually made of yellow marble. The bodies are buried seven feet below, in accordance with Muslim custom.

The engraved walls bear some inspection. A recurring theme is a wine flask with snakes for handles, supposedly a sly reference by Nur Jahan to her husband's poisonous drinking habits. Atop the marble arches in some places is delicate carving copied from Nur Jahan's real-life embroidery. The mosaic marble floor of the tomb is designed like a Persian carpet.

Itimad-ud-Daula is just beyond the Jumna bridge on the east side of the river.

Agra's Red Fort

Agra's famous fort predates the Red Fort in Delhi by more than three-quarters of a century, having been built from 1565 to 1573. Although designed by Akbar, the third Mughal emperor, it was added to and improved by three of his successors and has changed little since the 17th century—still an impressive combination of military fortress and delightful palace.

It is massive in size and strategically located—the outer wall is almost two miles long and 70 feet high, adjoining the broad Jumna River. A moat and another wall are supplemented by a semitropical jungle area so wide that the fort's guardians would gather on the palace roof high above to watch staged fights between tigers and elephants. Monkeys play among the trees there today. Adjoining the palace at this point within the walls is another richly decorated palace, the octagonal **Musamman Burj,** of richly inlaid marble, where Shah Jahan spent his final years (after being imprisoned by his son, Aurangzeb) gazing up the river at his beloved Taj Mahal.

The most romantic and least military part of the fort is undoubtedly the area around the **Anguri Bagh,** or grape garden, where the women of the harem lived and played. Here the walkways were covered with rich Persian carpets, silken drapes hung over the doorways, and green parrots fluttered around the rosewater swimming pool, which had seats for the harem women between the two-score fountain jets. Nearby is the **Palace of Mirrors,** thousands of tiny, concave reflecting glasses inset into its walls, in which were the hot- and cold-water baths and a stairway leading down to the moat, for those athletic women who wished to swim in the open.

Under the grape garden, subterranean chambers offered a welcome cool respite from the summer heat. Here, too, dungeons were located, a couple of marble grills allowing unfortunate prisoners to see their friends still at play in the garden.

The women had their own little mosque too, but a bigger one, the **Moti Masjid** (Pearl Mosque), is the largest of its kind in the world and took Shah Jahan seven years to build.

Another inner courtyard of the fort, **Machchi Bhawan,** is a neat garden today, but once it was filled with water and stocked with colored fish which the various emperors delighted in catching as they sat languidly on a throne above.

The Red Fort is open daily from sunrise (around 6 a.m.) to sunset (usually about 6 p.m.). Admission is Rs. 2 (15¢), free on Friday.

Other Landmarks Worthy of Inspection

Chini-ka-Rauza (China Tomb), burial place of Afzal Khan (a Persian poet, he was Shah Jahan's prime minister) and his wife, **Rambagh,** said to be India's first Mughal garden (both are north of Itimad-ud-Daula); and finally near the railway station, the **Jami Masjid,** built in 1648 by Shah Jahan in honor of his daughter, Jahanara—the same who looked after him in his dying days. It doesn't hold a candle to the Delhi mosque near the Red Fort, but as long as you're here. . . .

AGRA HOTELS: Remember, in calculating your budget, that there's a 7% room tax and 5.5% sales tax.

For budget travelers in Agra, **Lauries,** Mahatma Gandhi Road, Agra 282007 (tel. 72536), an oldtime favorite, still has low rates: Rs. 65 ($5) for a single and Rs. 110 ($8.45) for a double, non-air-conditioned; with an added Rs.-10 (75¢) charge for air conditioning. To be sure, the hotel could use some painting and polishing, yet it's a warm and friendly place. The 20 decently furnished rooms have window seats, rugs, and swirling overhead fans, and the attached bathrooms have big old-fashioned tubs. All rooms open off a marble-floored pillared veranda, which stretches out on either side of the lobby. You can have snacks or a meal by the pool or in the garden under the gulmohar and kachnaar trees shading the 24 acres of lawns and land on which the hotel is set. Close to the railroad station and ten minutes from the airport, Lauries offers free taxi service from both, if asked in advance. In the dining room, you can have a full breakfast for Rs. 15 ($1.15), and lunch and dinner for around Rs. 30 ($2.30) to Rs. 35 ($2.70). Ask about the 20% discount from April to September. Nonresidents can use the pool for a Rs.-15 ($1.15) fee.

A good choice at a higher price is **Mayur Tourist Complex,** Fatehabad Road, Agra 282001 (tel. 67301), composed of 23 rooms and two suites in cottages partly concealed by bougainvillea vines and set in a rambling garden. Each of the rooms is done up in a different Indian style—there are rooms with big double beds overhung with printed fabric canopies, twin-bedded rooms with brightly lacquered furniture, and rooms decorated with beaded designs above their doors. The rates for air-conditioned rooms are Rs. 250 ($19.25) double and Rs. 200 ($15.50) single. Non-air-conditioned rooms run Rs. 190 ($14.60) double and Rs. 115 ($8.85) single. In a separate block are some clean, neat rooms without atmospheric decor but with bargain rates: Rs. 145 ($11.15) double and Rs. 115 ($8.85) single. All rooms have private bathrooms. The dining room has a building all its own and there's a swimming pool. Colored lighting illuminating fountains and bright flowering potted plants make everything as vivid as a *mayur* (peacock), for which the hotel was named.

At the **Mumtaz Hotel,** 181/2 Fatehabad Rd., Agra 282001 (tel. 64711), 60% of the rooms have a view of the Taj—keep this in mind when booking accommodations at this simply but adequately furnished place under the same management as the splendid Mughal Sheraton. The rates are a bit of a splurge: Rs. 225 ($17.30) single and Rs. 350 ($27) double. Guests at the Mumtaz can use the Mughal Sheraton's pool without charge, providing they're not part of a group. They also get a 15% discount on food and drinks at the Mughal Sheraton.

Easier on the budget is the **Jaiwal Hotel,** 3 Taj Rd. (next to the Kwality Restaurant), Agra 282001 (tel. 64141). It's not luxurious, but it is clean and comfortable. Of the 17 rooms, all opening onto balconies or the central courtyard, those in front are a bit nicer than the others. All are air-conditioned and have attached private baths. Rates are Rs. 125 ($9.60) single and Rs. 175 ($13.45) double. There's a 10% service charge. In the restaurant, a satisfying thali lunch costs Rs. 15 ($1.15).

In the city where replicas of the Taj are everywhere, the **Hotel Amar,** Tourist Complex Area, Fatehabad Road, Agra 282001 (tel. 65696), goes a different route with a huge mural of mountains dominating the reception and lounge. All 68 rooms are doubles with attached bathrooms, telephones, and piped-in music. Cleanliness and maintenance leave much to be desired in the rooms and restaurant, a fact that reader Linda Kamoji of Bloomington, Ind., noted in her letter to me. Therefore, this would be a last resort. Rates are Rs. 170 ($13) double; Rs. 115 ($8.85) single, non-air-conditioned; air coolers cost an additional Rs. 15 ($1.15). Air-conditioned rooms are Rs. 170 ($13) single, Rs. 220 ($17) double. A few deluxe rooms—meaning they're a little more spacious, with refrigerators—cost Rs. 300 ($23). The non-air-conditioned rooms are on the plain side; the air-conditioned rooms have printed spreads and wallpaper on the walls. In the wood-paneled dining room with parquet floors, a full breakfast is Rs. 25 ($1.90), lunch runs Rs. 45 ($3.45), and dinner, Rs. 50 ($3.85), with a choice of Western, Indian, and Mughali cuisines.

Near the splashy Taj View, the pleasant, budget-priced **Hotel Ratandeep,** Fatehabad Road, Agra 282001 (tel. 63098), has 24 rooms with attached baths and carpeted floors, and partly air-conditioned. Prices range from Rs. 130 ($10) single, Rs. 180 ($13.85) double, for air-cooled rooms; and Rs. 200 ($15.40) single and Rs. 250 ($19.25) double, with air conditioning. The hotel's restaurant serves the usual Indian, Chinese, and continental foods.

The not-really-grand, but okay, **Grand Hotel,** on Station Road, Agra 282001 (tel. 76311), is a two-story pink building on pleasant grounds which bears a striking resemblance to a motel. The rooms have attached baths, some with Indian-style toilets. There's a pleasantly lit small dining room and a glittering mirrored bar room. Without air conditioning, rates for singles are Rs. 70 ($5.40); doubles, Rs. 120 ($9.25). The inflated rates for air-conditioned rooms are Rs. 140 ($10.75) single, Rs. 175 ($13.45) double. Four rooms are classified as "deluxe," which means that they have refrigerators, a few extra rugs, curtains, and air conditioning. These rooms cost Rs. 200 ($15.40). Breakfast costs Rs. 30 ($2.30); lunch or dinner, Rs. 45 ($3.45).

Under the same ownership as the Grand is the **Hotel Ranjit,** Station Road, New Agra Cantonment, Agra 282001 (tel. 62416), which could use some tender loving care. Still, the price isn't too high: Rs. 95 ($7.30) for doubles and Rs. 70 ($5.40) for singles. The rooms are not air-conditioned, but there are air coolers for an additional Rs. 20 ($1.55). All rooms have balconies and attached bathrooms with hot and cold running water.

Located near Agra's main market, a mile and a half from the Taj Mahal and under a mile from the bus station, is the **India Hotel,** in the Priya Lall & Sons, Photographers, Building, Agra 282001 (tel. 72326). A nice feature is the roof garden. The carpeted rooms have attached bathrooms with hot and cold running water showers. Rates are Rs. 75 ($5.75) double, Rs. 45 ($3.45) single. Five rooms are air-cooled and cost Rs. 15 ($1.15) extra. Room service provides inexpensive snacks, Rs. 5 (40¢) to Rs. 10 (75¢). Dinner can be sent on special request.

The **Khanna Hotel**, 19 Ajmer Rd., Agra 282001 (tel. 66634), is a small, two-story 14-room hotel arranged around a garden courtyard. It's pleasant, bright, and fairly clean, with no frills. About half a mile from the bustling town near St. Anthony's School, it's about 1½ miles from the Taj. All the plain, simply furnished rooms have overhead fans and attached bathrooms with Western-style plumbing, some with cold running water only and hot water in buckets for an extra Rs. 15 ($1.15), and some with hot water geysers. Doubles run Rs. 60 ($4.60) to Rs. 75 ($5.75); singles go for Rs. 40 ($3.05). The seven newer rooms are your best choice.

A private home during the Raj period, the green-accented pink **Agra Hotel**, General Cariappa Road, Agra 282001 (tel. 72330), established in 1926, is said to be the oldest hotel in Agra. The rooms, which could be tidier, have more than adequate furnishings: beds, tables, chairs, cupboards, dressing tables, and overhead fans. There's hot and cold running water in the bathrooms, some with Indian-style toilets. Of the 18 rooms, four doubles are air-conditioned and cost Rs. 125 ($9.60). Other rooms cost Rs. 40 ($3.05) for singles; doubles range from Rs. 60 ($4.60) to Rs. 90 ($6.90), depending mainly on size. Air coolers for summer comfort and heaters in the winter cost an additional Rs. 15 ($1.15) per day. In the high-ceilinged dining room, you can get Western, Chinese, and Mughali, as well as other Indian-style cuisines. There are lawns and a view of the Taj from them.

Rugged, basic, and overpriced are the accommodations at the **Hotel Sarang**, Baluganj, Gwalior Road, Agra 282001 (tel. 63894), where doubles are Rs. 100 ($7.70) and Rs. 80 ($6.15), and singles go for Rs. 40 ($3.05) and Rs. 60 ($4.60). Rooms have attached bathrooms. In the ten-bedded, two-bathroom dorm, it's Rs. 20 ($1.55) per head. The hotel adjoins a restaurant, open from 7 a.m. to 10 p.m., where Indian and Western foods range from Rs. 8 (60¢) to 12 (90¢) per dish.

Low Budget Choices

Very pleasant management and low rates make the **Jaggi Hotel**, 183 Taj Rd., Agra 282001 (tel. 72370), popular with young travelers. The 15 modest rooms could be tidier, but all have swirling fans to cool the high-ceilinged rooms with stone floors and private cold-water-only bathrooms with showers, some with Western fixtures and two with geysers. You must ask to have the hot water turned on, however; otherwise hot water comes in buckets upon request. Singles cost Rs. 25 ($1.90) and doubles go for Rs. 45 ($3.45) to Rs. 75 ($5.75). In the back of the hotel are four truly cheap rooms with charpoys (cots) and shared bathrooms for the very unfussy, at Rs. 15 ($1.15) single, Rs. 25 ($1.90) double. Campers can park vans here for Rs. 10 (75¢). The dining room serves mainly Indian dishes, at reasonable prices. In fair weather you can have dinner by candlelight in the popular Jaggi's Open-Air Restaurant, adjoining the hotel, where a full Indian meal costs Rs. 15 ($1.15), and Pran Jaggi, the owner's son, will help you decide what to order.

In Baluganj is the **Tourist Rest House**, Kachahari Road (tel. 64961), which attracts young backpackers. If friendliness of management were furniture and cleanliness, this basic, untidy place would be a lavishly decorated palace. Yet there's more good hygiene here than meets the eye: according to the manager, the drinking water is boiled and filtered. Of the 30 rooms, those upstairs are the nicest. They cost Rs. 45 ($3.45) double, including an air cooler and running hot and cold water in the bathroom. Other rooms are priced anywhere from Rs. 10 (75¢) to Rs. 30 ($2.30), depending on whether they're single or double. An air cooler for a cheap room will cost an additional Rs. 10 (75¢) a day. All rooms have attached bathrooms, 18 of which have Western toilets. In the cheaper rooms, hot water is supplied in buckets. There's a pleasant roof garden. Both Indian and Western foods are available, with lunch (either style) costing around Rs. 12 (90¢). The management will confirm train and bus reservations without charge, and supplies all kinds of helpful advice on touring the area.

"Splendid" is the word to describe the full view of the Taj Mahal from the hilltop at the **Hotel Taj Khema** ("Tents"), at the eastern gate of the Taj Mahal, Agra 282001 (tel. 65383), which started as a tent ground, but now has six simple double rooms with connecting Indian-style stone bathrooms. Plans are to add eight more rooms and bathrooms. Doubles go for Rs. 60 ($4.60). The snackbar's pleasant for a sandwich—Rs. 6 (46¢) to Rs. 13 ($1)—and tea or coffee at Rs. 1 to 3 (under 25¢).

To wind up this low-budget section, there's the **State Government Tourist Bungalow**, opposite the Raj-ki-Mandi Railway Station (tel. 72123), with doubles for two people as low as $3 and as high as $17. Ordinary rooms are Rs. 50 ($3.85) single and Rs. 75 ($5.75) double; deluxe rates are Rs. 75 ($5.75) single, Rs. 125 ($9.60) double. Air-conditioned rooms cost Rs. 175 ($13.45) single and Rs. 225 ($17.30) double. Inexpensive meals are available.

Still looking for a cheap room? Follow Taj Road toward the Yamuna to Kinara Road behind the Taj and you'll find some low-priced hotels, but I found nothing appealing about them except their prices.

Guesthouses

The top guesthouse in Agra is the **New Bakshi House**, 5 Laxman Nagar, Agra 282001 (tel. 282001), first mentioned to me in a letter from reader Jack Wood of Kentwood, Mich., as the nicest thing that happened to him during his entire India trip. Indeed, this is an attractive, spotlessly clean place run by a hospitable couple, retired army Col. S. S. Bakshi and his wife, Rani, who genuinely enjoy making visitors feel at home. Rates, inclusive of continental breakfast, are Rs. 150 ($11.55) for single occupancy of a double room, and Rs. 200 ($15.40) to Rs. 225 ($17.30) for doubles with attached bathrooms. A single without an attached bathroom is Rs. 100 ($7.70). Meals other than breakfast will be prepared upon request for an additional fee. Service charge is 10%. The house is less than a mile from the Taj Mahal and not far from the airport, bus stand, and railway station. The Bakshis are glad to help with ongoing travel itineraries and local sightseeing. Indeed, they'll send you off with a car and driver for a full day, including a trip to Fathepur Sikri, for Rs. 300 ($23). A guest book bulges with compliments from many Westerners.

Recommended as well is another guesthouse, **Major Bakshi's**, 33/83 Ajmer Rd., Agra 282001 (tel. 76828), formerly run by the colonel mentioned above, whose late father started this guesthouse (it is now run by other members of the family). This is another hospitable place where visitors are treated as part of the family. Rates are Rs. 130 ($10) for a clean, neat double with a connecting bathroom and dressing room. There's a four-bedded room for Rs. 200 ($15.40). Some of the 12 rooms have little knickknack cabinets, and there's even a typewriter around in case the Taj brings out the poet in you. The Bakshis let guests use their big collection of books on India. Meals can be provided for an extra charge, upon request. You can get help here with your travel and sightseeing arrangements.

Splurge Hotels

The **Taj View**, Fatehabad Road, Taj Ganj, Agra 282001 (tel. 64171), a member of the Taj Group, is white with filigreed concrete screens across its balconies. The 95 attractively done-up rooms are modern with Indian-accented decor. Rooms on the north side have views of the Taj, and from the top floor you get a splendid Taj view. Rooms elsewhere overlook the swimming pool with its floating bar, and gardens and Agra countryside. Doubles cost Rs. 600 ($46.25) and singles go for Rs. 500 ($38.50). On the walls of the restaurant are more grillwork and works of Mughal art. Western dishes on the menu range from around Rs. 14 ($1.05) to Rs. 42 ($3.25); Indian foods run Rs. 10 (75¢) to Rs. 52 ($4). On the grounds there's a sauna and health club, and a full range of shops. Nonresidents can use the pool for about Rs. 50 ($3.85).

Hotel Clark's Shiraz, 54 Taj Rd., Agra 282001 (tel. 68654), is set in a garden with well-manicured lawns and a mango-shaped swimming pool. The rooms are comfortably furnished in modern international style, and the management is friendly and eager to please. Doubles are Rs. 550 ($47.25) to Rs. 600 ($46.25), singles run Rs. 500 ($38.50) to Rs. 550 ($47.25), and suites are many times higher. There are good views of the Taj from some rooms and from the rooftop Mughal Room restaurant, which features continental entrees averaging Rs. 70 ($5.40), Indian meat main dishes starting at Rs. 35 ($2.70), and vegetarian dishes at Rs. 15 ($1.15) to Rs. 35 ($2.70). At the hotel gate are snake charmers. As you go in or out, the music starts up and goes down, and so do the cobras.

Recently opened, the ITDC's **Hotel Agra Ashok**, 6B The Mall, Agra 2822001 (tel. 76223), is a white 58-room two-story hotel set on spacious lawns. Rooms also are spacious, with all the five-star deluxe amenities as well as some of its own, like hair dryers in the bathrooms and small dressing areas. Rates are Rs. 650 ($50) single and Rs. 750 ($57.75) double. The lobby is accented with grillwork and inlaid marble to pay homage to the Taj. The Shalimar Restaurant serves both Indian and Western foods. There's a swimming pool and health club, and a shopping arcade. An ITDC travel and tour counter is on site.

If you're in the mood for a good old splurge in Agra, go to the **Mughal Sheraton**, Taj Ganj, Agra 282001 (tel. 64701), because if you crave comfort and cheerful service in innovative surroundings, this hotel will fill the bill. It's easy to understand why in 1980 it was awarded the first Aga Khan Prize for Architectural Excellence. What makes the hotel so special is the way architect Ramesh Khosla blended the red-brick two-story hotel with the finely crafted Mughal masterpieces of the area. From the inside there are views out to lush landscaped gardens accented with cascades. From the white marble lobby, glass-enclosed marble bridges lead to spacious guest rooms in two styles—international, with comfortable, tasteful contemporary furniture; and Indian, with smooth marble floors, marble platform beds partly shaded by embroidered canopies, and simple stone bathrooms with showers only. In all rooms are double-bed-size window seats for relaxing and viewing the other guests enjoying the swimming pool or walking in the lotus-pool-accented gardens. Soundproofing in the rooms makes all the outside world a pantomime. Paths winding through the tranquil 21-acre gardens lead walkers beside flower beds, shrubs, and trees, where unobtrusive birdwatcher signs tell the species you might see. There's also a herb garden and orchard, which supply the hotel's kitchen. Facilities for croquet, tennis, archery, and mini-golf are also in the garden. Ordinary rooms cost Rs. 725 ($55.75) single and Rs. 775 ($59.50) double; deluxe rooms run Rs. 900 ($69.25) single and Rs. 1,000 ($77) double, with suites going as high as Rs. 4,500 ($346).

Even if you can't afford to stay here, you can drop in for tea or a drink in the main lounge where musicians play at various times every day, or in the tiny tea lounge from which the Taj looks like an exquisite miniature. There are three other restaurants, discussed later, and a shopping arcade. The best buys are not in the arcade but at the bangle seller's, right off the main lobby.

WHERE TO EAT IN AGRA: At **Kwality**, Taj Road (tel. 72525), a longtime favorite with visitors, a three-course soup-to-dessert lunch or dinner for two runs about Rs. 100 ($7.70). Most popular on the extensive menu are Cantonese Chinese dishes such as chicken with almonds, and sweet-and-sour fish, vegetables, or pork, in the Rs. 24 ($1.85) to Rs. 30 ($2.30) range, as are Italian dishes with pasta. The usual Indian dishes, such as curries and tandooris, are similarly priced, with breads such as nan at Rs. 9 (70¢). Among the rich desserts, chocolate eclairs and pineapple pastries, at Rs. 24 ($1.85), are especially recommended. Open every day from 9 a.m. to midnight.

The lantern-lit **Chung Wah**, on Taj Road (tel. 72370), the only exclusively Chinese restaurant in town, is owned by Jaggi's Hotel and shares its phone number. The chef, Lee Shi Kung, prepares some good Mandarin specialties such as a special fish dish. He recommends hot-and-sour soup as an appetizer and piquant ginger rice or ginger noodles as a side dish. Cantonese dishes on the menu include chicken sweet-corn soup, wonton, and pork with mushrooms, bamboo shoots, or vegetables. Most entrees cost about Rs. 20 ($1.55), with rice dishes about half that amount. There's fragrant jasmine tea to sip as you sup. Hours are 10 a.m. to 3 p.m. and 6 to 11 p.m. every day.

Prakash, on Taj Road (tel. 74593), has leatherette booths and chairs, Formica tables, and stone floors in two dining rooms—the front being most pleasant. Featured are such Indian specialties from the north as tandoori chicken, Rs. 32 ($2.45) for a whole chicken and Rs. 18 ($1.40) for a half; butter chicken (similar to tandoori, but richer) is about the same price. From the south are masala dosa (rice-and-lentil pancakes stuffed with potatoes) at Rs. 5 (40¢) and other snacks. There are a few Western dishes on the menu. Prakash is open every day from 10 a.m. to 11 p.m.

Taj Restaurant (tel. 76644) is right outside the western gate of the Taj Mahal itself. It consists of an air-conditioned section and bar, and a quick self-service cafeteria. The restaurant is pretty, the walls decorated with glass-covered peacock feathers with contrasting wood paneling and green-cushioned chairs. The menu features tandooris (clay-oven-baked foods): at Rs. 25 ($1.90) for half a chicken, Rs. 48 ($3.70) for a whole, they are among the highest-priced dishes on the menu. Vegetarian dishes range from Rs. 10 (75¢) to Rs. 15 ($1.15); thalis, served only in the cafeteria section, are Rs. 12 (90¢) for vegetarian and Rs. 15 ($1.15) for nonvegetarian. Hours are 8 a.m. to 10 p.m. every day.

A Buffet

In the marble and red-brick restaurant **Taj Bano** at the posh Mughal Sheraton, Taj Ganj (tel. 64701), the sumptuous breakfast buffet at Rs. 50 ($3.85) offers fresh fruits and fruit juices, eggs, omelets, cereals, breads and pastries, and coffee and tea. It's served from 6 to 10 a.m. Like buffets from here to Timbuktoo, you can return to the table to refill your plate as often as you wish. An interesting aspect of the Mughal Sheraton's decor is the way diners in Taj Bano or the hotel's other two restaurants—Nauratna (Indian foods) and Bagh-e-Bahar (Indian, Chinese, and European foods) can see each other in these different settings. The other restaurants are open for lunch from 12:30 to 3 p.m. and for dinner from 7:30 p.m. to midnight. In the evenings, ghazals are sung in Nauratna and there's dance music in the Bagh-e-Bahar.

Other Mughal Sheraton restaurants are the Mahjong Room (Chinese) and Roe's Retreat in the Garden, with barbecue and cold cuts and salads.

AGRA SHOPPING: From the days of the Mughals, Agra's artisans have excelled in marble inlay work. Today craftsmen—some claiming to be direct descendants of the early artists—still lay petal-thin strips of mother-of-pearl and semiprecious stones in translucent marble that tourists take home. Other popular crafts sold in Agra are brassware, carpets, ivory and wood carvings, textiles, and ready-made clothing. Merchants in Agra are generally less inclined to bargain than in off-the-beaten-path places where sales are harder to make, but some will give in to attractive offers. Here are just a few shopping opportunities in Agra.

At **Krafts Palace**, 506 The Mall (open from 9 a.m. to 7 p.m. every day), artisans at the entrance show how the exacting inlay work is done. On sale are inlaid plates, boxes, trays, and paperweights, easy to take home as souvenirs, costing from Rs. 30 ($2.30) to many times higher, depending on the intricacy of the inlay design. The store also has a full range of other gift items such as costume jewelry with dangling phony stones for Rs. 50 ($3.85) to Rs. 600 ($46), plus ivory, brass, sandalwood, and silks. A good buy are scarves, which cost Rs. 20 ($1.55) to Rs. 145 ($11.15) for large squares or oblongs in lustrous silk prints. Precious stones are purchased by the carat, with unset star rubies at Rs. 80 ($6.15) per carat.

At **Subash Emporium**, 18/1 Gwalior Rd. (open from 10 a.m. to 8 p.m. daily), especially fine inlaid marble table tops, costing Rs. 75,000 ($5,770), resemble elaborate tapestries. Much easier to carry home, and cheaper as well, are the inlaid boxes, letter openers, and fruit plates.

Jewel House, opposite Circuit House on Taj Ganj (tel. 75633; open from 9:30 a.m. to 7:30 p.m. every day), as its name implies, has jewelry both fine and costume, and gems set and unset. But the most attractive buys are salvar (shirts) and kamiz (full pants tied at the waist and snapped at the ankles) in bright cottons, at Rs. 125 ($9.60) for the set.

More sparklers at the famous **Kohinoor Jewellers**, 41 Mahatma Gandhi Rd. (tel. 76858; open from 10 a.m. to 7 p.m. daily), precious stone merchants for five generations. Among the unusual stones are rare emeralds costing up to Rs. 10,000 ($770) per carat. Much less rare, and therefore cheaper, are the smoky topaz for under $1 a carat. You might pick up some blue sapphire stud earrings for around Rs. 155 ($11.90) and up. Ivory bangles run Rs. 130 ($10) and up. On display is an elephant inlaid with 5,000 jewels—made for the 1970 World's Fair in Japan, it is now among the Kohinoor's priceless treasures.

Interesting among the many shops on shop-studded Munro Road is **Oswal Emporium**, 30 Munro Rd., Agra Cantonment (tel. 75168; open from 10 a.m. to 7 p.m. daily), with some of the highest-priced and most handsome inlay in town: elaborate inlaid table tops cost from Rs. 3,000 ($231) to Rs. 20,000 ($1,540), depending on size. Marble boxes can be had for as little as Rs. 50 ($3.85); trays and plates, Rs. 200 ($15.40) to Rs. 8,000 ($615).

Continuing down this road you'll find a full range of such items as brassware, wood, and ivory seen around the shops in Agra.

Rather have a carpet? **Bansal Carpets**, Naulakha Market (open from 10 a.m. to 7 p.m. every day), has four- by six-foot Persian-like carpets from Kashmir in silk for $1,000 to $3,000. Smaller woolen rugs, measuring two by three feet, are $50 to $75. Something in between these two runs around $200 to 300. Prices depend on quality and workmanship.

AN EXCURSION TO FATEHPUR SIKRI: For 14 years the glorious city of Fatehpur Sikri was the talk of the civilized world. Visitors from Shakespeare's

England returned with wondrous stories of this fairytale city of marble and sandstone. It grew out of nothing in the first place and almost as suddenly it was abandoned. By the end of the 16th century it had been forgotten, a ghost town in the desert, and it has remained that way ever since.

Only the tiny village of Sikri, home of some stonecutters, existed at the site when the Mughal emperor Akbar first came this way in 1568 to seek out the blessings of a mystic named Salim Chishti. Akbar was childless and badly wanted a son. Anyway, whatever the holy man put into those blessings seemed to work, and when Akbar's wife became pregnant, the emperor was so overjoyed he decided to build a fabulous city overlooking the village.

Construction began in 1569; an artificial lake was dug out (it has since been drained), a magnificent mosque, **Jami Masjid,** was built, and by 1575 Fatehpur Sikri was completed. Even today it's quite a place, and it's not hard to imagine what the court life must have been like in the days of its grandeur. There are marked tiles in the big courtyard where Akbar is said to have sat on a low stool and played parcheesi—dozens of dancing girls in bright-colored dresses were the living pawns. In a three-room house known as **Ankh Michauli,** Akbar supposedly played blindman's bluff with members of his harem, although it is more likely that this was the treasure house and the narrow passage surrounding the rooms a walkway for the guards.

The recessed stone tank in the courtyard, now dependent on the rains, used to be regularly filled up with water—and with coins, which were distributed to the poor.

Most of the buildings are outstanding: **Maryam's House,** for example, with its gilded frescoes, brightly painted ceilings, and portrait of a lady riding a parrot. And the house of the Turkish sultan, said by some to be the most richly decorated building in the world: every inch is ornamented with elaborate carvings, like having 3-D pictures chiseled onto your wall instead of hung on it. (The carvings containing birds and animals were later mutilated by Akbar's great-grandson, Aurangzeb, 1655–1706, a puritanical monarch who also happened to be a Muslim, a faith that prohibits the representation of living creatures.)

The most noticeable buildings at Fatehpur Sikri are the tapering **Panch Mahal,** so called because of its open five-storied structure, each floor with half the pillars of the preceding one; and the red sandstone **Diwan-i-khas,** or Hall of Special Audience, with its carved "elephant-tusk" props and enormous octagonal center pillar fed by four walkways from the upper balcony. The wise and tolerant Akbar used to sit on his throne on the top of the pillar and his representative Hindu, Muslim, Buddhist, and Christian advisers would toss ideas at him from each of the four walkways. Later he became interested in astrology and consulted an astrologer daily about what to do.

There are many other buildings worthy of attention, most of them an amalgam of the Hindu and Muslim styles. The impressive mosque, with its vast courtyard, at night lit by flaming torches (and a perfect place for the staging of a colorful historical pageant today), is flanked by rooms of what once was an Arabic university. The white marble mausoleum contains the tomb of the respected Salim Chishti, the holy man who first brought Akbar to this remote place. Delicate, lace-like carved marble screens and a chamber of mother-of-pearl and sandalwood house the holy man's remains.

Colored threads flutter from the marble screen, tied by pilgrims (usually childless women) from all over India who hope a visit to the mausoleum will bring them luck.

At the south end of the mosque, overlooking the village of Fatehpur, is the enormous **Buland Darwaza,** a lofty gate 134 feet high, built in 1602 to commemorate Akbar's victories in the south. Inscribed on one side, in Persian, are these words: "He that standeth up to pray and his heart is not in his duty, does not draw nigh to God but remains far from Him. Your best possession is what you give in alms; your best trade is selling this world for the next. Said Jesus—on whom be peace—the world is a bridge, pass over it but build no houses on it. He who hopes for an hour may hope for eternity. The world is but for an hour; spend it in devotion. The rest is unseen."

A deep well sits below the wall which adjoins the gate, and into this a local daredevil dives 80 feet down from the wall. He expects Rs. 50 ($3.85) for the jump, but will settle for Rs. 20 ($1.55) or less.

In 1584, before Akbar was able to move with his Hindu wife, Jodh Bai, into the big palace built specially for them (to the southwest of Maryam's house), the whole court shifted from Fatehpur Sikri to Lahore, possibly because political troubles had broken out, but more probably because the water supply at Sikri was running out. It was 15 years before Akbar disentangled himself from these troubles, and when he returned it was not to Sikri, but instead to Agra, where he remained until his death in 1605.

These days, it's souvenir sellers you'll disentangle yourself from. Be firm! The entry fee for Fatehpur Sikri is 50 paise (3½¢), and it's open from sunrise to sunset.

A Room and a Meal

For those who would like the adventure of spending the night in the ghost town, there's an **Archaeological Survey Inspection Bungalow** right in Fatehpur Sikri with six simple, clean, cheap rooms and a pretty garden: Rs. 9 (70¢) double and Rs. 6 (45¢) single. A cook prepares meals. Dinner or lunch costs Rs. 10 (75¢) vegetarian and twice that price for a meat meal. Frequent (and crowded) bus service to Agra costs Rs. 4 (30¢) and takes an hour. To book your rooms, you must write at least four days in advance to the Superintending Archaeologist, Department of Archaeology, Archaeological Survey of India, Agra Circle, 22 The Mall, Agra Cantonment, Agra 282001, India (tel. 74017).

SIKANDRA: This tomb is six miles north of Agra and is well worth seeing. Several years before Akbar died in 1605, he began work on his own mausoleum, as was the custom, and his son, Jahangir, took until 1613 to finish it. It stands today at Sikandra, an ornate tomb in 150 acres of lovely gardens, its four minarets situated in such a manner that only three can be seen from the minarets of the Taj Mahal, and vice versa. The gatehouse to Akbar's tomb is more impressive than the tomb itself, the latter having been ransacked by vandals late in the 17th century.

TOURS OF THE TAJ AND BEYOND: The **Uttar Pradesh State Road Transport Corporation** buses met the *Taj Express* daily at 10:20 a.m. and go to Fatehpur Sikri, Agra Fort, and the Taj, returning to the station at 6 p.m. The fares are Rs. 26 ($2) in an ordinary coach, Rs. 38 ($2.90) in a deluxe coach, and Rs. 54 ($4.15) in an air-conditioned coach. Fares are about Rs. 4.50 (35¢) less on Friday.

Making the same sightseeing stops is the **Uttar Pradesh Tourism** daily tour, which also meets the train at 10:20 a.m. and terminates at the station at 5 p.m. This bus stops at 9:15 a.m. to pick up passengers at the Government of India Tourist Office, 191 The Mall (tel. 72377), and the U. P. Government Tourist Bungalow, opposite the railway station. The fares are Rs. 35 ($2.70) for adults and Rs. 30 ($2.30) for children, deluxe coach. It's Rs. 4.5 (35¢) less on Friday.

Both tours include guide services and entry fees. Tickets are sold on the train and in the station.

USEFUL INFORMATION: The **Tourist information counters** at the airport or Agra Cantonment Railway Station, or the **India Tourist Office,** 191 The Mall (tel. 72377), can help with hotel reservations and information. . . . Approved guides, also available through the tourist offices, for parties of one to four persons cost Rs. 48 ($3.70) for a half day, Rs. 72 ($5.55) for a full day, with an added Rs. 20 ($1.55) for lunch allowance if booked for a whole day, plus Rs. 30 ($2.30) as an allowance for traveling outside Agra town. . . . The **Book Depot,** on Taj Road next to the Jaiwal Hotel, has Asian editions of Western news magazines, bestsellers, and loads of postcards. . . . The **photographic supply shop** in the India Hotel, Priya Lall & Sons, Photographers' Building, sells and develops film. . . . **Taxis** are unmetered and charges vary with time and mileage. Check rates before you get in. There are no fixed rates for scooters, rickshaws, and tongas. Bargain hard to get the best. . . . The **swimming pools** at the Hotels Clark's Shiraz, Mughal Sheraton, and Lauries are open to nonguests for a fee. . . . Gentle black-faced monkeys at Sikandra wait patiently along the path for peanuts. Better buy them in town as the peanut vendor at the monument is often sold out.

GETTING TO AGRA AND FATEHPUR SIKRI: The daily *Taj Express* is a pleasant **train** excursion from Delhi. Fares (as mentioned in the Delhi chapter) are Rs. 205 ($15.75) in air-conditioned class, Rs. 62 ($4.75) for an air-conditioned chair, Rs. 101 ($7.75) in first class, and Rs. 25 ($1.90) in second class. Sightseeing buses meet the trains.

From Delhi with a **car and driver** to Agra, Sikri, and returning to Delhi via the Bharatpur Bird Sanctuary costs Rs. 1,560 ($1.20); but it's cheaper to take the train from Delhi to Bharatpur (see Chapter IV).

A popular **plane** routing connects Delhi, Agra, Khajuraho, and Benares. The flying time between Delhi and Agra is about 35 minutes and the trip costs Rs. 191 ($15); between Agra and Jaipur the flying time and costs are about the same as the Delhi–Agra run.

Bus sightseeing trips from Delhi (described in Chapter II) compress the famous sights in a one-day blur and are recommended only for those truly pressed for time.

2. The Erotic Statues of Khajuraho

In one of the quietest villages in India sit some of the world's most celebrated statues. Khajuraho (pop. 4,000) is literally miles from anywhere. Inaccessible by train, barely reachable by road, and so isolated that the nearest movie house is 30 miles away, it is nonetheless an important day's outing by plane from Delhi (about 400 miles away), or more frequently, a stopover between Agra and Varanasi (Benares).

Tourists who come to Khajuraho dip briefly into a way of life that has remained virtually unchanged for 1,000 years, apart from the imposition of a handful of modern amenities—a jet strip in the midst of fields for the daily Boeing 737 flight, a photo supply shop with a very limited supply of film, souvenir and gem shops, and a few hotels that import from hundreds of miles away everything needed to make guests comfortable.

WHEN TO VISIT KHAJURAHO: October to end of March is best. Rains during July and August are heavy and constant, causing the closing until October of the Bandhavgarh National Park, a popular day trip during dry months.

Very special times to visit are during Shiva Ratri (February or March), when people stream in from all around the area for a big bazaar and other merriment, and for the week-long dance festival, sometime between March 1 and March 20 when well-known dancers perform with the temples as their backdrop. Summer sizzles around 100° F.

WHERE TO STAY IN KHAJURAHO: There are seven main choices. Among the best for budget travelers is the **Payal Hotel** (tel. 76), run by the Madhya Pradesh Tourist Development Corporation (MPTDC), with 25 nicely done-up rooms, each with a little veranda and private bathroom. Doubles and singles, non-air-conditioned, are Rs. 120 ($9.25) and Rs. 90 ($6.90) respectively. Air-conditioned doubles are Rs. 220 ($16.90) and singles are Rs. 160 ($12.30). There's an air-conditioned dining room with coir (coconut fiber fabric) paneled walls and ebony finished chairs.

Also run by MPTDC is the **Hotel Rahil** (tel. 62), with 19 clean, cool, and breezy, simply furnished rooms and comfortable rates: Rs. 50 ($3.85) single and Rs. 60 ($6.15) double; Rs. 15 ($1.15) extra for an air cooler. Dorm beds are Rs. 10 (75¢) in the four ten-bedded dorms. There are also four five-bedded rooms. All rooms have private stone bathrooms. Meals, on an à la carte basis, can run about Rs. 25 ($1.90) for a satisfying lunch or dinner. The extensive gardens are delightful.

Another clean, simple, low-budget place also run by MPTDC is the **Class I Tourist Bungalow** (tel. 64), charging Rs. 40 ($3.05) double and Rs. 80 ($6.15) for a quad. All rooms are clean with fans and private bathrooms, with cold-water showers only and hot water in buckets upon request. Some have Indian-style toilets. The reservation authority for the above three is Senior Regional Manager, MP State Tourism Development Corporation, Regional Office, Khajuraho 471606 India. If you just drop in, reception will give you a room—if it's available.

A cross between a splurge and a budget accommodation is the **Hotel Khajuraho Ashok** (tel. 24), run by the India Tourism Development Corporation (ITDC), with pleasant, functional rooms all with attached modern bathrooms. Rates for the 40 air-conditioned splurge-class rooms are Rs. 395 ($28.85) single and Rs. 475 ($36.50) double. The eight non-air-conditioned rooms with overhead fans run Rs. 190 ($14.60) single and Rs. 250 ($19.25) double. The tariff does not include meals. You'll need an additional Rs. 130 ($10) to Rs. 150 ($11.50) for breakfast, lunch, and dinner. A garden and swimming pool are other attractions. The view from the second floor is terrific—the temples rising from the plains and stretching up to the heavens.

The **Hotel Chandela** (tel. 54), about one kilometer from the temples, with sweeping marble halls and central air conditioning, is expensive: Rs. 600 ($46.25) single and Rs. 785 ($60.50) double. If you want to eat your three meals here, add Rs. 185 ($14.25) to your bill for each person. There's miniature golf, tennis, and a swimming pool. When the staff worships at the small temple in the hotel's garden, guests are welcome to watch the rituals, but they must be up by 5 a.m.

An imposing red statue of beloved Ganesh (elephant-headed god of good luck) dominates the reception area at the elaborately decorated 50-room, five-star, centrally air-conditioned **Jass Oberoi Hotel** (tel. 66), the top choice among splurgers from the States. There is an impressive, palatial circular marble staircase and an extensive collection of miniature paintings and bronze statues (some valuable antiques among them). Yet the overall ambience created by the friendly management evokes the feeling of a private country estate rather than an impersonal hotel. Of the rooms on two floors, those upstairs or away from the reception downstairs are preferred for quiet. Rates are Rs. 500 ($38.50) single and Rs. 725 ($55.75) double. There's a swimming pool, tennis courts, and shopping arcade. If you don't stay in the hotel, you might enjoy dropping in for tea and a snack to see some of the works of art.

The nicest of the Indian-style hotels, but not for the fastidious, is the **Temple Hotel** (tel. 49), with 11 double rooms all with attached bathrooms, where hot water is supplied in buckets upon request. None of the rooms is air-conditioned. Rates are Rs. 60 ($4.60) double and Rs. 40 ($3.05) single. An air cooler costs an additional Rs. 25 ($1.90). Indian vegetarian and nonvegetarian foods are available. The hotel is in the same building as Indian Airlines.

FOR A SNACK WITH A VIEW: Raja Restaurant, across from the western group of temples, is owned by a Swiss couple and prominently displays a sign-board menu in French and English—a pleasant place to stop for tea or a snack. You can also have a meal here for around Rs. 35 ($2.70) with chicken. The little boutique on the premises has T-shirts in three or four colors printed on the front with "Khajuraho" in English and Hindi—a status symbol for you to wear at home.

KHAJURAHO'S TEMPLES: For the four centuries from A.D. 900 to 1300, the region around Khajuraho—the name probably comes from "Khajurvahak," meaning date palms—was ruled by the Chandella kings. They left a legacy of 85 temples, built mainly between A.D. 950 and 1100, of which only 22 remain.

Despite their international reputation as a sort of repository of sexual sculptures, these temples offer more than erotic tableaux. But the extraordinary explicitness of the statues makes them the outstanding feature, even though they comprise only 10% of the carvings to be seen.

The Khajuraho Temples were built before the Muslims put women in purdah (seclusion). The Chandellas were richly bejeweled, scantily clad followers of a Tantric form of Hinduism that saturated sexual pleasures with divine qualities. The kingdom ended in 1200 when Turkish powers won the holy war they had waged for 100 years.

Couples were shown in a variety of postures that have been reproduced too often for them to be worth describing, and there are occasional scenes of soldiers, cut off from their women by war, taking animal lovers. In light of today's sexual permissiveness in the West, it is hard to imagine anyone being shocked.

The main temples, called the **Western Group,** are clustered in a pleasant park—50 paise (3½¢) admission. Like the others, it's built in a series of "hills" building up to a towering peak, symbolizing the Himalayas, where the gods were supposed to reside.

It's best not to approach any of them too academically, but just to appreciate them for what they are—a jubilant paean to life, built by thousands of craftsmen working every daylight hour during the century or so that it took to build the temples.

The first temple, **Lakshmana,** is typical of the rest. The incredible plasticity of the carvings is one of the first things you'll notice: bodies twisted in all directions displaying supple limbs, as though permanently frozen in a graceful dance. Young maidens are a favorite subject (women were worshipped as the main force of creation), and their hair styles and facial expressions, on even the smallest figures, are exquisitely portrayed.

The artists took the entire range of human activity as their subject, but dwelled most lovingly on females at their daily chores—washing their hair, writing letters, looking in mirrors, applying henna to the hair, playing with balls, singing, strumming instruments. There are delicate scenes of couples kissing and mothers with babies.

Around the Lakshmana Temple, about six feet off the ground, runs a long continuous frieze in which erotic scenes are more or less interlaced with military processions of horsemen, camels, elephants, and musicians. Wild boar and crocodiles underfoot denote the procession is through jungle and not on the road.

Originally, the Western Group of temples was set in an artificial lake and people went from one temple to another by boat. Another batch of temples, the Eastern Group, half of these of the Jain faith, are within walking distance.

The three **Jain temples** occupy their isolated compound in a rather modern tableau: sheets hanging to dry on an outdoor line alongside the temple, an old man squatting quietly in the yard chanting to himself, children skipping about, and the inevitable well on the temple grounds, and workmen standing ready with a bucket for the just-as-inevitable tourist camera.

Not as interesting as the Western Group, the Eastern temples display the 23 Jain teachers and Mahavira, who came last, and is most revered as the religion's founder. To identify a Jain prophet is easy: they're always shown nude with a diamond shape on their chests. At the adjacent **outdoor museum** are more Jain sculptures and free pamphlets on Jainism. In the Eastern Group there are also three Hindu temples. Of these, **Vamana,** dedicated to Vishnu's dwarf incarnation, also carries the erotic motifs of the Western Group.

The Southern Group of temples, about two kilometers (1¼ miles) from the tourist office, are the least interesting, and are visited mainly for **Chaturbujha** temple, which has a huge well-carved image of Lord Vishnu. The sculpture has a special glow at sunset.

All temples are open sunrise to sunset. At the Western Group there's a 50-paise (3½¢) entry fee. The entry fee also permits you to visit the small archeological museum (tel. 23), with galleries of stone-cut art (open from 10 a.m. to 5 p.m.; closed Friday).

USEFUL INFORMATION: The **Government of India Tourist Office,** near the Western Temples, Khajuraho 471690 (tel. 47), open from 9 a.m. to 5:30 p.m., is where you can pick up pamphlets, get help with plans, and hire an approved guide. The guide fee, as elsewhere in India, is Rs. 48 ($3.70) for four hours and Rs. 72 ($5.55) for eight hours for one to four persons. There is a Rs.-20 ($1.55) lunch allowance. Guides also congregate at Raja's Restaurant or the Western Group's gates, but only those with special I.D.'s are supposed to enter the temple grounds. . . . There's a **bottle shop** near Raja's Restaurant (open from 10 a.m. to 9 p.m.; closed on national holidays). . . . Among the newest buildings in town is the Post and Telegraph Office. . . . Interesting crafts are for sale at the **Madya Pradesh Emporium.**

GETTING TO KHAJURAHO: The easiest way is, alas, the most expensive— by air on the daily service that links Khajuraho to Delhi, Agra, and Varnasi. Delhi to Khajuraho costs $36; from Agra or Varanasi, $25.

The most convenient railhead from Delhi is Jhansi, from which you catch one of the three daily buses for the 175-km (105-mile) trip. From Varnasi, the railhead is Satna, on the Dombay Allahabad line, from which you take a 50-km (30-mile) bus trip to Khajuraho.

From Agra, there's a UP government bus going first to Gwalior and then on to Khajuraho. Buses also link Khajuarho with Bhopal (372 km, 223 miles) and several other cities of no great interest to the tourist.

3. Bhopal and Sanchi

Half-hidden among the mountains of Madhya Pradesh is the beautiful town of Bhopal, with its two picturesque lakes providing a beautiful background for each and every sunset. Bhopal (pop. 672,000) was ruled mostly by Begums, enlightened women of the 19th and 20th centuries, one of whom, Shah Jahan Begum, could have been right at home with today's women's liberation movement so vast was her work for equal rights, albeit within the confines of her Muslim beliefs.

In true Mughal fashion, lakes and gardens are among Bhopal's attractions. The city also has beautiful mosques, one of which, Taj-ul Masjid, is billed as India's largest (although the claim is also made for the Jama Masjid in Delhi).

Ironically, the world learned of Bhopal through the worst industrial accident in history on December 3–4, 1984, when clouds of toxic gases from the Union Carbide plant spread throughout this central Indian city, killing and harming hundreds. A huge white statue of a woman and child has been erected to commemorate the dreadful event, but all is safe now.

As always, the main reason for visiting Bhopal is as a gateway to Sanchi, 42 miles away, which is famous throughout the world as a 2,000-year-old center of Buddhist art.

BHOPAL: Bhopal's history goes back to the 11th century, when the Raja Bhoj built the two impressive lakes around which the city is still clustered. The most outstanding is the **Great Lake,** 4½ miles long and nearly two miles wide, which is separated by a bridge from the two-mile-long **Lower Lake.**

Apart from the three mosques, about which there is nothing special to note, except possibly their size, Bhopal's major architectural attraction is a 12th-century **Shiva Temple** at **Bhojpur,** 24 miles from town. It was never completed, but even in its semi-finished state it is an impressive pile of purple sandstone, its dome lying nearby on the grounds as if waiting for someone to get on with the job.

While moseying around town, be sure to note some of the schools, the Lady Landsdowne Hospital, and the waterworks, built by the Begums.

In your shopping around town, be sure to visit the **Women's Cooperative Zari Center,** at Peer Gate, where richly embroidered bags with gold and silver threads, plus chiffon saris, are the major attractions. Another stop on the shopping route might well be the **Madhya Pradesh State Emporium,** on Sultania Road, which specializes in the local fabric called chanderi, a combination of silk and cotton so sheer that Emperor Aurangzeb insisted that his daughter wear seven layers of this transparent cloth—when he allowed her to wear it at all.

Where to Stay in Bhopal

Rated tops is the 23-room **Jehan Numa Palace,** Shamla Hills, Bhopal 462013 (tel. 76080), with air conditioning and other three-star amenities. Rates are Rs. 320 ($24.60) single, Rs. 400 ($30.75) double in the main wing; Rs. 250 ($19.25) and Rs. 360 ($27.70) respectively in the annex. A restaurant and bar are in the hotel.

In town, Hamidia Road might be named "hotel road," for almost all the hotels are on it. In case you want to write for a reservation, they all have the same postal code: 462001. Here are a some moderate places: **Manjeet,** 3 Hamidia Rd. (tel. 74664), good for readers with its bed lamps; **Ranjit** (tel. 75211); and the **Blue Star** (tel. 75526), the latter a little more expensive than the others. Manjeet and Ranjit have tariffs ranging from around Rs. 55 ($4.25) for a single and Rs. 75 ($5.75) for a double. The Blue Star's rooms start at the same prices, but go up to Rs. 140 ($10.75) single and Rs. 160 ($12.30) double for air-conditioned rooms. Most of the rooms have attached bathrooms with Indian-style toilets.

The **Rajdoot Hotel,** 7 Hamidia Rd. (tel. 72691), has little to recommend it except the low price for some of its rooms: Rs. 40 ($3.05) to Rs. 70 ($5.40) single, Rs. 50 ($3.85) to Rs. 95 ($7.30) double. With air conditioning, the rooms run Rs. 110 ($8.45) to Rs. 165 ($12.70) single and Rs. 140 ($10.75) to Rs. 195 ($15) double.

Nicer, and pricier, the **Hotel Ramsons,** Hamidia Road. (tel. 72299), has an attractive lobby and such amenities as air conditioning, room radios, phones, and balconies. Rates range from Rs. 110 ($8.45) to Rs. 295 ($22.70) single, and Rs. 160 ($12.30) to Rs. 390 ($30) double. Some accommodations are in cottages, and the in-house restaurant's specialty is Mughali food.

Also similarly priced on Hamdia are the 50-room **Hotel Taj** (tel. 73161), charging Rs. 110 ($8.45) to Rs. 275 ($21.15) single, and Rs. 160 ($12.30) to Rs. 450 ($34.60) double, the higher prices for the 28 air-conditioned rooms; and the **Hotel Surya Sheraton** (tel. 76925), with a dubious relationship to the well-known Sheraton chain, charging Rs. 110 ($8.45) to Rs. 200 ($15.40) single, and Rs. 150 ($11.50) to Rs. 250 ($19.25) double, the lower rates for non-air-conditioned rooms. The **Hotel Siddhartha,** also on Hamidia Road (tel. 75680), has only 16 simple rooms renting for Rs. 105 ($8.05) to Rs. 240 ($18.45) for doubles and Rs. 110 ($8.45) to Rs. 195 ($15) for singles. The lower-priced rooms are air-cooled; the more expensive are air-conditioned and a bit larger.

A commercial hotel, the **President International,** Berasia Road, Bhopal 462029 (tel. 77291), is fairly clean and attractive, with comfortable rates: Rs. 70 ($5.40) single and Rs. 110 ($8.45) double without air conditioning; with air conditioning, the rooms cost Rs. 175 ($13.45) single, and Rs. 200 ($15.40) double. Some non-air-conditioned rooms have Indian-style toilets.

Pricey on Berasia Road is the **Hotel Mayur** (tel. 76418), where singles run Rs. 110 ($8.45) to Rs. 400 ($30.75) and doubles go for Rs. 150 ($11.50) to Rs. 450 ($34.60), the higher rate for air conditioning.

Hotel Shiraz, opposite Board Office on Shivaji Nagar (tel. 64513), has rooms and four cottages accommodating eight persons, and could use a paint job. Rates are Rs. 125 ($9.60) for the cottages, rooms cost Rs. 225 ($17.30), single or double. Non-air-conditioned rooms run Rs. 75 ($5.75).

Station Road is the other place to find budget hotels. Among these are the bright **Rainbow** (tel. 76395), **Meghdoot** (tel. 76961), **Samrat** (tel. 77023)—all with singles for Rs. 35 ($2.70) to Rs. 55 ($4.25) and doubles for Rs. 60 ($4.60) to Rs. 70 ($5.40)—and the higher-priced **Sangam** (tel. 77161), with some air-conditioned rooms at Rs. 130 ($10) single and Rs. 150 ($11.50) double.

The super-budget choice is the **Youth Hostel** (tel. 63671), offering the not-at-all-fastidious no frills at Rs. 8 (60¢) and Rs. 10 (75¢) per head.

Where to Eat

There are two **Kwality Restaurants** in town, on Hamidia Road and in the New Market. Both are cool and comfortable, offering inexpensive snacks and reasonably priced main dishes. The **India Coffee House,** for coffee and snacks, is popular at both its locations: Hamidia Road and T. T. Nagar.

Information and Tours

For information and pamphlets on Bhopal and Sanchi, check with the **Government of Madhya Pradesh Tourist Information Office,** 5 Hamidia Rd. (tel. 3400), or the **MPTDC,** 13-G, T. B. Complex, T. T. Nagar (tel. 64388).

The MPTDC runs tours to Sanchi in a 24-passenger coach three times a week, on Saturday, Monday, and Wednesday, from 9 a.m. to around 7:30 p.m., for Rs. 30 ($2.30) per person. The price does not include lunch—you buy it or bring your own. Another tour, in the same 24-passenger coach, offered on Sunday, Tuesday, and Thursday, from 9 a.m. to 4 p.m. takes in Bhopal and the surrounding area for Rs. 24 ($1.85), again not including lunch. For information and reservations, call the MPTDC (tel. 64388).

SANCHI: Everything about Sanchi is awesome. For 2,000 years it has been the site of what is now renowned as one of the major archeological prizes in the world. Buddha never set foot here, but in the 3rd century B.C. Emperor Ashoka did, after he had adopted Buddhism. He chose this site for the construction of his monuments because his wife, Devi, who came from nearby Vidisha, had established a monastery here and because there was already an important religious center nearby.

The eight stupas, vast stone mounds, he erected at Sanchi were memorial shrines to house relics of Buddha and his disciples; three of them remain. As Buddhism went into a decline in India, these stupas lay neglected on their hilltop, camouflaged by sand and vines and undiscovered even by the Mughal emperor Aurangzeb, who mercilessly desecrated most Buddhist shrines that he came across.

Sanchi's stupas were rediscovered in 1811 by a British military officer, but were not cleared away by archeologists until Sir Alexander Cunningham dug here in 1851. Sloppy archeologists damaged some of the monuments later in that century and they were not properly restored until about the time of the First World War.

At the Site

The structures at the archeological site consist of stupas, pillars, shrines, and convents, and a 50-paise (3½¢) charge admits you to all of them and the archeological museum. The periods covered are from the 3rd century B.C. to the 10th century A.D.

High spot, of course, is the **Great Stupa,** its shape representing the heavens embracing the earth. At the top is a square surrounded by a balustrade, symbolizing the heaven of the gods, with the umbrellas pointing upward like a spire as if they were reaching for the heavens. A platform around the stupa was used by the pious, who would walk in the direction of the sun. The stupa is guarded by a stone fence with four gateways corresponding possibly to the seasons of the year, and the inscriptions on the balustrades represent the names of the people who contributed to its building.

The Great Stupa, 106 feet in diameter and 42 feet high, was built originally of brick by Ashoka and embellished into its present shape in the 1st or 2nd century A.D. The toranas, pale stone gateways, were originally inspired by crude bamboo village fences. They are made of two pillars surmounted by three horizontal bars and were constructed from stone quarried at nearby Udaygiri.

Only a profound student of Buddhism could possibly identify all the carvings and legends on the gateways, but it might be helpful to know that (1) *Birth* is signified by a lotus, either alone or in a bouquet; (2) *Enlightenment* is shown by the Bo-tree; (3) *The Great Sermon* is symbolized by the Wheel of Law; and (4) *Death* is represented by stupas. Buddha, according to the religious custom of the time, was never depicted except in disguise. Other common symbols of Buddha are footprints, umbrellas, deer (for the first sermon given, at Deer Park near Sarnath), ducks and geese (perhaps standing for Buddha's flock), and the peacock, symbol of Ashoka's empire.

One of the more interesting toranas is the **South Gateway,** the carvings atop which depict the birth of Buddha: Maya, the mother, stands on an open lotus while elephants shower water on her and the dwarfs bestow garlands.

The **East Gateway** shows Buddha renouncing wealth and leaving his father's house to begin his search for truth. On the left pillar you can see a miracle—Buddha walking on water, one of the miraculous deeds he performed to dispel doubts among the incredulous.

On the **North Gateway,** Buddha not only walks on water, he does so while flames issue from his feet and angels bang drums to draw everybody's attention.

Near the South Gateway are the remains of **Ashoka's Pillar,** once 42 feet high and weighing 40 tons. It is believed to have been brought from Chunar near Benares by waterways. The four lions that once adorned the pillar are now in the small museum and are, of course, the emblem of the Indian republic. Ashoka originally erected 30 pillars throughout India, 10 of which remain. Some pillars mark sites made holy by Buddha; others mark the route for pilgrims on their way to holy places. All bear inscriptions asking the people not to swerve from the path of truth. Also of note near the South Gateway is the 7th-century **Chaitya Hall,** with its classic columns.

Where to Stay and Eat in Sanchi

You will need about a day to look around Sanchi, so it would be best to stay overnight at the **Travellers Lodge,** Sanchi 464661 (tel. 23). Its veranda overlooks the ancient shrines. In fact, both the Great Stupa and railway station are within walking distance of the lodge, which is itself attractively designed with ancient motifs. There is a long covered passage leading from the lounge to the rooms, all of which have attached baths and ceiling fans. A banyan tree and mango grove in the adjoining garden make the place even more attractive. Single rooms cost Rs. 90 ($6.90); doubles, Rs. 120 ($9.25); Rs. 70 ($5.40) to Rs. 100 ($7.70) per day more for air conditioning. You can eat here, even if you don't stay here. All three meals will cost about Rs. 65 ($5) per day. Reservations are advised at the lodge. Write to the Manager, Travellers Lodge, Sanchi 464661, Madhya Pradesh, India.

More than 50 years ago a woman from Sanchi visited the U.S.A. and fell in love with gingerbread houses, their peaks, porticos, and porches, so her husband built a place like that at home. This bit of stranded Americana is now the **P.W.D. Resthouse.** This, too, has only a couple of rooms, costing about Rs. 15 ($1.15) per day. For Resthouse reservations, write to Sub-Divisional Officer, Raisen; but it's doubtful that you'll get in. The Resthouse, like the **Circuit House,** charging Rs. 60 ($4.60), is mainly for government officials.

Another possibility is the **Railway Retiring Rooms**—two in all—at Rs. 20 ($1.55) to Rs. 30 ($2.30). Clean.

You can take your meals at the MPTDC's Bungalow or bring something with you for a picnic or two. Bringing some oranges or other fruit is a good idea, as there is nowhere nearby to get it.

If you want to mingle with monks in residence and pilgrims visiting the shrines, you apply at the **Buddhist Guest House** (tel. 39), where there are 20 rooms for Rs. 50 ($3.85) double; dorms cost Rs. 5 (40¢) per head. It is necessary to write in advance to Bhikku-in-Charge, Mahabodhi Society, Sanchi, 464661, Madhya Pradesh, to reserve a room. Each room contains a large ceiling fan. If you eat here—under $1 per meal—you must inform the cook in advance so that he can stock up on food. Otherwise, you can eat at the Traveller's Bungalow, but, to reiterate, the manager here must be forewarned as well. Also, it is a nice gesture to leave a small donation for the society.

GETTING TO BHOPAL AND SANCHI: **Bhopal** is on the Bombay Central–Delhi railway line. From Delhi it's a 705-km (440-mile), 17-hour ride, costing Rs. 236 ($18.15) in first class, Rs. 58 ($4.45) in second class. From Bombay, it's about 837 km (523 miles), and costs Rs. 275 ($21.15) in first class and Rs. 69 ($5.30) in second. **Sanchi** is on the Jhansi Itarsi section of the Central Railway. First-class passengers in mail and express have to ask the guard or stationmaster to stop at Sanchi, 68 km (42 miles) north of Bhopal; the fare is Rs. 42 ($3.25) in first class. Second-class passengers should check on train service when buying tickets. Buses go regularly between Bhopal and Sanchi; fare is about Rs. 10 (75¢).

Flights connect to Bhopal from Bombay, at Rs. 619 ($48); from Delhi, at Rs. 550 ($42); and Gwalior, at Rs. 314 ($24) to name the most popular routings.

Chapter IV

RAJASTHAN: DESERTS, HILLS, AND PALACES

1. Jaipur
2. Jodhpur
3. Jaisalmer
4. Udaipur
5. Mount Abu

RAJASTHAN OFTEN GETS in the news in India because of its comparative poverty, aggravated by the occasional droughts that come as an unwelcome reminder of how much of the state is desert.

But in some ways it's also one of the most attractive states, with numerous distinctive assets: the marble mines of **Makrana** (from whence came the stone for Agra's Taj Mahal); the forests of **Sawai Madhopur,** filled with wild animals; that otherwise rarely seen beast of burden, the aloof camel; and the artificial lakes that have made lovely cities bloom.

Not to mention the people: women in swirling bright skirts, literally covered from head to toe in bangles, balancing brass jugs on their heads; men with rose-red and pink turbans like full-blown roses in a desert. (It takes ten yards of silk to wind that headgear—amateurs need not even try.) Alas, these colorful outfits are rarely seen in Jaipur anymore.

Still, they are trying to preserve some of the traditional atmosphere of this city by painting all of the buildings in the old part of town their original pink shade and printing all signs in the local language.

1. Jaipur

Jaipur (pop. 1,500,000), the most renowned of Rajasthan's cities, is often referred to as rose-pink because of the delicate flamingo color with which so many of the most arresting buildings were painted.

Mirza Ismail Road separates the new city from the old, but to the visitor's surprise, once through the ancient **Sanganer Gate,** he finds the centuries-old

Johri Bazar as wide a street as in any modern city in the world. Truly it is an example of foresighted planning: by Sawai Jai Singh (1699–1743), who founded the city in 1727 and determined that it should be the best-planned metropolis of its time.

The streets, 110 feet wide (to accommodate oldtime elephant processions), were laid out to intersect at right angles in the now-familiar grid system; eight gateways were built in the surrounding city wall, 20 feet high and eight feet thick.

Jai Singh, who was only 13 when he became ruler, was dubbed "Sawai" (prodigy) by the Mughal emperor Aurangzeb ruling in Delhi at the time, and the title is still borne today by the princely house of Jaipur. Jai Singh, not content with city planning, went on to become one of the world's major astronomers, building observatories not only in Jaipur but also in Delhi and other cities.

WHERE TO STAY IN JAIPUR: Jaipur is bursting at the seams with former palaces turned into hotels—grand palaces, small palaces, parts of palaces. While none of these is quite up to the ethereal fairytale beauty of Udaipur's, they, too, have past grandeur, and even the very modest among them has great charm. Indeed, the most famous of these former palaces is one of India's most beautiful hotels and another, more recently converted, is also quite splendid. The following are palaces splurge and moderate, and then more conventional places to stay:

Staying in a Palace

The **Rambagh Palace,** Bhawani Singh Road, Jaipur 302005 (tel. 75141 to 75146), in the southwest corner of town and formerly the home of the late maharaja, has 105 rooms and suites done up with works of art, freshly potted plants, lovely local decorative themes, and every conceivable comfort you can possible imagine. The hotel's public rooms—the lounges and dining rooms, and the attractive Polo Bar—are definitely in the palatial style: fresh flowers everywhere complement the elegant furnishings and mirrored and marble halls. The extensive 25-acre park-like grounds, where peacocks strut and spread their fan-like tails, house a glass-enclosed swimming pool which adjoins a nine-hole golf course. Rates are Rs. 600 ($46.15) single occupancy, Rs. 700 ($53.85) double occupancy; garden suites cost Rs. 1,300 ($100) to Rs. 1,500 ($115.50), and bed/sitting rooms run Rs. 800 ($61.50); other suites go up to Rs. 3,000 ($230). At these prices, it's no surprise that the rooms are heated in winter and air-conditioned in summer.

Nonresidents can sample some of the opulence at the Rambagh by having a meal in the Suvarana Mahal (Golden Hall) Restaurant which, appropriately enough, is done up in golden brocade. The food is definitely prepared for the most timid Western palate, with very little seasoning in either Eastern- or Western-style dishes. Snacks are served on the garden terrace if you want to drop in for tea and a quick look at the palace's public rooms. There's a shopping arcade, travel counter, and post office on the premises—and usually lots of tour groups too.

Another pretty palace, the **Jai Mahal Palace Hotel,** Jacob Road, Civil Lines, Jaipur 302006 (tel. 73215), newer to the hotel scene, is located near the main shopping center. This former palace has 100 rooms with every conceivable amenity, plus a quality of intimacy and charm. Beautiful lawns with live peacocks and a rooftop terrace for sitting with drinks are nice attractions.

Rates run Rs. 500 ($38.50) to Rs. 600 ($46). There's a swimming pool, shopping arcade, jogging track, and horseback riding for your amusement.

For those who want top accommodations without the high prices, there's the **Hotel Arya Niwas,** behind the Amber Cinema on Sansar Chandra Road, Jaipur 302001 (tel. 73456), part of which was an old palace. Now with additions and renovations, it's a spotlessly clean, friendly hotel run by the hospitable M. K. Bansal and family, who will treat you royally. The rates are Rs. 60 ($4.60) single, Rs. 75 ($5.75) double; deluxe doubles run Rs. 110 ($8.45) to Rs. 130 ($10), the latter with a Western toilet. Single occupancy of a deluxe room is Rs. 20 ($1.55) less. There's no service charge and tipping is not encouraged. One of the delights of staying here is the delicious vegetarian food (eggs are served), supervised carefully when it's prepared for good hygiene (more about this in "Where to Eat").

Still hunting for a palace to call home for the night? Try the **Hotel Narain Niwas,** Kanota Bagh, Narain Singh Road, Jaipur 302004 (tel. 65448), which advertises itself as "an Ancient Palace in a Shady Grove." Ancient might be stretching it as the palace was started by Narain Singhji, chieftain of Kanota, in the 19th century as a garden house. But palatial it is and in a grove it stands, with many regal trappings—huge rooms, high ceilings, big fireplaces, attached bathrooms, Rasjasthani portraits of the Singhji's going back through the years, guns, rugs, and crystal chandeliers. All 22 rooms are air-cooled (which, as you probably know, is not air conditioning, but quite effective). In the winter months (the peak time for visiting Jaipur) it gets chilly here—the last thing you need is any kind of cooling. A sweater is nice though. Rooms go for Rs. 135 ($10.40) to Rs. 225 ($17.30); or Rs. 165 ($12.70) to Rs. 300 ($23.10) for deluxe rooms. With nonvegetarian meals and a full breakfast, add Rs. 125 ($9.60) per person; with a continental breakfast and vegetarian meals, Rs. 92 ($7.05).

Another intimate palace is the **Hotel Bissau Palace,** outside Chandpole Gate, Jaipur 302006 (tel. 303006), once the home to the Rawal (like Duke) of Bissau, with lots of charm and beautiful public rooms: a book-lined library, a small armory with valuable antique weapons, a family portrait gallery stretching back centuries, and a handsome dining room. You'll be happy in this little palace if you don't expect the bedrooms to live up to the public rooms—they need care—and will overlook slight sluggishness in the service. The rates, however, are right for the budget traveler: Rs. 110 ($8.45) for bed-and-breakfast single, Rs. 180 ($13.85) for bed-and-breakfast double. Lunch and dinner will each run Rs. 30 ($2.30) per head. All rooms are air-cooled, and there's a swimming pool, garden, and grand view of the Amber Palace and fort looming above the hotel.

Almost next door is the **Khetri House Hotel Jaipur,** outside Chandpole Gate, Jaipur 302006 (tel. 69183), a down-at-the-heels former palace: only 13 rooms, some with pieces of handsome 1930s furniture that could use care and repair. Yet you could be happy here in the large rooms with a bathroom and perhaps your own sitting room. It would be remote for singles as few people stay here these days: without meals, singles run Rs. 90 ($6.90), and doubles go for Rs. 180 ($13.85). With meals, add Rs. 80 ($6.15) to the single rate and Rs. 160 ($12.30) to the double. The service charge is 10% and the garden is one of the best features.

Hotels

Centrally located in town, the box-like, modern **Hotel Gandharva,** Station Road, Jaipur 302006 (tel. 72365), has 24 simple, clean rooms with wallpapered walls, carpets, and attached bathrooms. Prices are Rs. 160 ($12.30) single and Rs. 200 ($15.40) double, air-conditioned; Rs. 110 ($8.45) and Rs. 140 ($10.75) without air conditioning. There's a restaurant, open from 7 a.m. to 11 p.m.

Another downtown place near the Central Bus Stand, the **Chandragupt,** on Station Road, Jaipur 302006 (tel. 75001), has a marble lobby but rather dark rooms. They have everything you need to be comfortable, however, without any frills. There's a vegetarian restaurant and Chinese and Indian food as well. Of the 40 rooms, 15 have air conditioning, at Rs. 125 ($9.60) single and Rs. 175 ($13.45) double; Rs. 90 ($6.90) single and Rs. 110 ($8.45) double without. Suites have the rates, but not the personality or comforts, of some of the palace hotels.

A nice feature of the otherwise rather plain **Hotel Mangal,** Sansar Chandra Road, Jaipur 302001 (tel. 75126), is the roof terrace where barbecues are held at night. The 65 rooms run from Rs. 75 ($5.75) for an ordinary single to Rs. 200 ($15.40) for a super-deluxe single with air conditioning; doubles range from Rs. 100 ($7.70) to Rs. 250 ($19.25). There's a pure vegetarian restaurant in addition to the rooftop barbecue.

Off in the western part of town, the **Khasa Kothi,** Mirza Ismail Road, Jaipur 302001 (tel. 75151), is government-operated and shares a huge lawn-filled compound with the Government of India Tourist Office and a local radio station. The once-attractive chambers need sprucing up; it's adequate however, and there are such nice features as verandas to sit out on, from which you can admire the well-trimmed shrubs, trained and cut into various shapes, nice examples of the art of topiary. Rates are Rs. 150 ($11.55) for a single, Rs. 225 ($17.30) for a double, and from there they go up to Rs. 400 ($30.75) for a suite, and all prices in between, depending on size and occupancy, whether single or double. All rooms and the restaurant are air-conditioned.

In the center, at the **LMB Hotel,** Johari Bazar, Jaipur 302003 (tel. 48844), guests are instructed to keep their windows closed so the monkeys can't scamper in and make off with something. This is a nice hotel with 33 attractive, if not imaginative, rooms, 11 of them with Eastern-style toilets in their attached bathrooms. Rates are Rs. 190 ($14.60) single, Rs. 230 ($17.70) double, and there is a 10% service charge. The adjoining inexpensive restaurant serves delicious vegetarian foods.

Back in the higher price bracket, the ITDC's comfortable, although not highly imaginative **Hotel Jaipur Ashok,** Jai Singh Circle, Bani Park, Jaipur 302006 (tel. 75171), has singles for Rs. 320 ($24.60) and doubles for Rs. 435 ($33.45), with all the amenities you'd expect at such a high price. There's also a swimming pool.

Out near the airport is the high-priced **Clark's Amer,** Jawaharlal Nehru Marg (P.O. Box 222), Jaipur 302001 (tel. 822616), where singles cost Rs. 500 ($38.45) and doubles go for Rs. 550 ($42.30). It's a favorite of Russian tour groups, and there's a swimming pool.

The **Meeru Palace,** 14/1–2 Ram Singh Rd., Jaipur 300004 (tel. 61212), is not a palace at all but a pleasant, 48-room hotel with marble-accented interiors. Rooms cost Rs. 350 ($26.90) single and Rs. 425 ($32.70) double. Three restaurants, shopping arcade, bar.

Looking much like a palace in red sandstone and marble is Welcomgroup's posh **Mansingh,** Sansar Chandra Road, Jaipur 302001 (tel. 78771), with marble interiors and spacious rooms renting for Rs. 550 ($42.30) single and Rs. 660 ($50.75). Very attractive restaurants and good food are features.

Tourist Bungalows

Now more for the budget-minded, the bungalows run by the RTDC. The **Gangaur Tourist Bungalow,** on Mirza Ismail Road (tel. 60231), charges Rs. 165 ($12.70) and Rs. 200 ($15.40) for air-conditioned single and double rooms, Rs. 80 ($6.15) and Rs. 100 ($7.70) for deluxe singles and doubles. At the **Teej Bungalow** in Bani Park (tel. 74206), charges are Rs. 40 ($3.05) to Rs. 80 ($6.15) for a single, Rs. 80 ($6.15) to Rs. 100 ($7.70) for a double; with air conditioning, rooms cost Rs. 150 ($11.55) to Rs. 200 ($15.40), single or double. Both are near the railway and bus stations.

Super Budget

The RTDC also runs the lower-priced **Swagatam Tourist Bungalow,** near the railway and bus station (tel. 67560), with deluxe doubles at Rs. 55 ($4.25) and deluxe singles at Rs. 40 ($3.05); ordinary doubles run Rs. 40 ($3.05), and ordinary singles, Rs. 25 ($1.90). The dorm is Rs. 10 (75¢) per person.

The **Youth Hostel,** S.M.S. Stadium Road (tel. 67576), in front of the Rambagh Palace, charges Rs. 10 (75¢) single and Rs. 15 ($1.15) double for members, Rs. 20 ($1.55) and Rs. 35 ($2.70) for nonmembers, Rs. 8 (60¢) each in the dorm.

At the pink-painted **Bombay Hotel,** outside Chandpole Gate, opposite St. Andrews Church (tel. 68112), the reception is up a narrow flight of stairs, with decorated and mirrored ceilings (is this truly a hotel?). Rooms with attached bathrooms, with Western-style toilets and hot water on request in buckets (but cold water on tap), cost Rs. 40 ($3.05) to Rs. 80 ($6.15); Rs. 10 (75¢) less with a common bathroom.

Hotel Rose, B–6 Shopping Centre, Bani Park (tel. 77422), has three rooms at Rs. 60 ($4.60) to Rs. 75 ($5.75)—highly overpriced and nothing to recommend it. There is also a ten-bed dorm at Rs. 10 (75¢) per head—cheap but in the cellar.

In addition to the aforementioned, there are many other cheapies, but not necessarily goodies, outside Chandpole Gate, a mile away from town. The same goes for the area near both the railway and bus stations.

Finally, for a former palace at a low-budget rate, there's the **Kaiser-I-Hind,** near the railway station (tel. 74195), charging Rs. 65 ($5) to Rs. 80 ($6.15) single, Rs. 80 ($6.15) to Rs. 130 ($10) double, all rooms with attached bathrooms. Everything about this place is run-down—even the peacocks stroll rather than strut on the lawns. But the rooms are big, ceilings are high, and you probably won't find a palace room at a lower price. There's a restaurant with the usual ho-hum Indian, Chinese, and continental dishes.

EATING OUT: Most Westerners still eat in their hotels here, which is truly a pity because they miss some excellent, well-prepared foods available at the restaurants in town.

Niro's, on M. I. Road (tel. 74493), with its excellent food has been a favorite for many years of residents who enjoy their meals in the two cozy air-conditioned rooms. It is the only restaurant in Rajasthan that has been on the government-approved list since 1962. The food is Indian, continental, and Chinese, but I suggest the Indian specialties, for which this restaurant is so justly famous. Tandoori (clay-oven-baked) chicken and chicken kebabs (skewered) are popular, but more unusual and worth trying is the chicken or lamb cooked first in the tandoor and then simmered in special sauce. (Ask the steward for it.) If you start this meal with soup and Indian nan (bread baked in the tandoor) and end with Niro's special dessert—a caloric concoction of egg whites whipped to a froth, accompanied by fruits and nuts—it will cost around Rs. 48 ($3.70) to Rs. 56 ($4.30). If you're confused and don't know what to order, don't worry, just ask the gracious owner, V. P. Pardal, to help you. If he's not around, one of the English-speaking supervisory staff will be glad to advise. Hours: 9 a.m. to 11 p.m. daily.

The **LMB,** Johari Bazar (tel. 61261), has wonderful vegetarian foods, which are quite reasonable. A spacious place that can accommodate 500 people, the restaurant has brocade chairs and playing-card murals. But there is no gamble in trying any of the foods. Eat the local vegetable curry (kaddi) with rice, tandoori roti (special bread) and dahi badi, a famous sweet, for a satisfying lunch which will set you back about Rs. 23 ($1.75). Many palate-pleasing snacks too, and rich milkshakes, ice creams, and an impressive selection of homemade Indian sweets. Indeed, LMB started as a sweet shop some years ago and now is also a hotel as well as a restaurant. One interesting fact: no onions are served here because of the religious belief that anything plucked from the ground with such a strong odor should not be ingested. Open from 8 a.m. to 10:30 p.m. daily.

The outdoor sweet stall at LMB features LMB kulfa (Indian ice cream), which smells as good as it tastes—made with saffron and dry fruits. The other famous sweet here is rasmalai (cheese cooked in milk), garnished with nuts and flavored with saffron, at Rs. 8 (60¢) per plate.

At **Arya Niwas,** behind the Amber Cinema (tel. 73456), a lunch or dinner of special vegetable curry will cost Rs. 15 ($1.15) and include an assortment of well-prepared dishes. The chutney is especially good as the owner's mother supplies it homemade. She also supervises the clean kitchen and the preparation of food. You can get a good Western breakfast here for about Rs. 20 ($1.55), which would include fresh juice, eggs, and tea and toast. The chutney made such a hit with reader Cheryl Davies of Newcastle-upon-Tyne, England, that she managed to get a jar to take home—Rs. 20 ($1.55).

On Mirza Ismail Road, **Kwality** (tel. 72275), with 64 seats, has the usual Indian, Chinese, and continental dishes. Tandooris are priced at Rs. 20 ($1.55) to Rs. 35 ($2.70); continental or Chinese dishes, Rs. 22 ($1.70) to Rs. 33 ($2.55). Open from 11:30 a.m. to 10:30 p.m.

In the gracious Rajasthani mirror-studded **Shivir,** in the Mansingh (tel. 78771), open from noon to 3 p.m. and 7 p.m. to midnight, there's a Rs. 55 ($4.25) buffet at lunch, and a host of well-prepared, well-served Mughali dishes at all times. Noon and night, live ghazals add to the atmospheric ambience. A good place for a splurge.

Across the street from the Hotel Mangal is the new **Eats Restaurant** (tel. 69098), two-storied and tiled, which boasts of being the first fast-food place in Rajasthan. All-vegetarian, the restaurant also has a cake shop, and the cakes are all made on site, as are the ice creams. Main dishes are in the Rs.-10 (75¢) to Rs.-20 ($1.55) range. Ghazals at night. According to their advertising, the vegetables and fruits are the greenest and the freshest that Mother Nature could give us. What more could we ask in a meal?

The Rambagh's **Polo Bar** is one of the most popular meeting places in town.

THE PALACE AND OBSERVATORY:
In the center of the old town is the **City Palace,** built by Maharaja Sawait Jai Singh in 1728, with additional sections added by later rulers. The palace, half of which is still a private residence, is a treasure trove of royal acquisitions and is occasionally used as a setting for special events.

One of the latest additions to the palace is the **Mubarak Mahal,** built by Sawai Madho Singh II in 1900 and today housing the **Textiles and Costumes Museum**—worth some attention. The building itself looks as if it had been made of marble "lace," while some of the costumes inside are probably the best example you'll see of the way Rajput women dressed.

Another interesting collection is located in the **Pothikhana.** Originally this was the coronation hall of the palace—it's a huge room with an enormous venetian glass chandelier, extensive ceiling decorations painted 75 years ago, and large carpets made in the early 1600s from Pakistan (when it was part of India), Afghanistan, and Persia around the walls.

Filled with interesting and beautiful artifacts, this museum is both a repository of the culture and a family album of the long line of maharajas who ruled this area for so many years.

Among the lovely Rajput miniatures is one of the Shah Jahan and Mumtaz Mahal—the "lovers" of Taj Mahal fame. Another shows a battle with ying ships and a third illustrates an Indian elopement (but instead of the perennial ladder, the suitor has brought his elephant upon which to whisk his love away). For the visitor with lots of time, there are about 2,000 of these fine miniatures, illustrating rulers, holymen, and the way of life of the people (usually the noble-type people).

Other cases display fascinating and rare manuscripts written in very fine and very beautiful Persian, Arabic, and Sanskrit script. Sawai Jai Singh's works on mathematics and astronomy are here too. Scattered among these are extremely delicate paperwork cutouts, including one done in 1743 by the second ruler of Jaipur, Ishwari Singh, when he was a young boy.

The doors throughout the palace are worth noting: some are huge brass ones, others are of delicately carved ivory (real ivory, by the way—like wood —always has a grain). Passing through the gate flanked by two large marble elephants, you come to the **Sharbata,** a deep-pink colored court with white patterns. Here the marble-pillared **Diwani-i-Khas** (Hall of Private Audience) is located. Connected to its patio is the **Diwan-i-Am** (Hall of Public Audience); festivals are still celebrated in its large courtyard in the months of March, April, and September. Flanking this yard is the screened latticework gallery from which the royal ladies would view the proceedings below. As you enter the **Ladies' Apartments,** you will see a large photograph, taken in 1926, of the late maharaja atop his elephant, en route to his first marriage. The foreign community of that time can be seen in the left corner watching the procession. This is a tinted enlargement of the original photo.

Dominating the palace is the majestic **Chandra Mahal,** the towering yet delicate seven-story white building that was started in 1728 by Sawai Jai Singh—who built the ground-floor **Chandra Mandir** (Moon Palace)—and was added to by later rulers. Gold leaf was used in the ceiling decorations and again there are portraits of the Kachhawa monarchs, dating back to 958 when the court resided at Amber. On the wall, a large mural resembling the sun is made of alternating guns and arrows, with a warrior's shield at the center. One room is furnished the same way as when it was lived in: a rug, canopy, backrest pillow, gadi (floor cushion), spittoon, and hookah.

Tucked into a lovely leaf-filled niche along the passageway to the Chandra Mahal are a number of 14th-century sandstone statues representing a group of musicians, each playing a different instrument. Found 70 miles from Jaipur, they're interesting because they are much less stylized and look-alike than the statues usually seen in temples.

The **Silehkhana** (Armory) is famous for the finest collection of armor and arms in India; it contains 2,000 weapons dating from 1580 onward. Maharaja Man Singh's sword weighs at least ten pounds.

Easily one of Sawai Jai Singh's greatest feats was the construction of the adjoining **Jantar Mantar,** the still futuristic-looking observatory, which has justly been described as "the most surrealistic and logical landscape in stone." A passionate and knowledgeable student of astronomy, Jai Singh often spent hours among these massive yet precise structures, which are even more impressive when one remembers that they were built in the very early 1700s.

The sun dial gives the actual local time in Jaipur, accurate to the minute, although this differs, of course, from Indian Standard Time by varying amounts throughout the year.

The largest structure—90 feet high—gives time in units of two seconds. The high steps were used both to take the reading and to forecast the weather.

The structure that looks a bit like a tilted twin-faced clock is really the equinox dials. Only one of the two circular surfaces is ever touched by the sun's rays at one time: in winter one side is lit, in summer the other; March 21 and September 21 the sun passes from one side to the other.

Horoscopes have played—and still do play—a large part in Indian life, so it is not at all surprising to find here a separate structure for each of the 12 signs of the Zodiac. Someone skilled in taking the readings can ascertain from these structures the position of the dominant planet in relation to the earth and the sun, and if supplied with such information as the exact local time and the time of birth of the "subject," can chart a full-fledged horoscope. The scales are devised also to allow calculation of each person's most auspicious time of day.

Jai Singh built five observatories throughout India but this one is the largest, and certainly—even without any knowledge of how to read or utilize the information these grand structures provide—the intrinsic beauty of construction is impressive.

The palace and observatory are both open daily, the palace from 9:30 a.m. to 5 p.m.; the observatory opens at 9 a.m. and closes at 4:30 p.m. The museum is closed on some holidays. The entry fee for the palace is Rs. 6 (45¢); Rs. 1 (7½¢) for students and on special holidays. The entry fee for the observatory is Rs. 1 (7½¢).

The best-known landmark in Jaipur reproduced in innumerable pictures, is the **Hawa Mahal** (Palace of the Winds), also in the palace compound but best seen from the front, on the main street called Siredeori Bazar. With its semi-octagonal overhanging windows it's a distinctive example of architectural delicacy, but is today really only a suggestion of what was once a palace of great beauty (and coolness, hence the name).

AMBER PALACE: Northwest of the old town, the roads lead to the fabulous Palace of Amber, seven miles away. Maharaja Man Singh, a contemporary of the Mughal emperor Akbar and one of his most successful generals, began to construct the Palace of Amber back in the early 17th century; subsequent rulers added bits and pieces. As it was never threatened, much less conquered, it remains today in much of its original pristine state and is proudly regarded, rightly or wrongly, as being one of the most glorious palaces of India.

Traditionally, tourists navigate the hill to the palace via elephant, sitting on a kind of padded box atop the gaily painted animal. The local joke is to convince unsuspecting tourists that they must allow the elephant to wrap his trunk around each customer and swing him up and over, into position—the only way to mount. In actual fact, the mounting is performed rather more prosaically by climbing the stone steps to the ancient platform at the level of the patient creature's back.

The ride is not particularly comfortable . . . but where else can you ride an elephant to a palace? Why is the elephant ride so expensive? Because even lady elephants, like these, eat 200 pounds of fodder a day.

At the top of the hill is the palace, its marble pillars topped with elephants' heads, each animal holding a lotus in its trunk. The **Ganesh Pol** (gate), covered with 300-year-old paintings, leads into an inner courtyard whose garden is patterned like a Persian rug. To the east of this inner court stands the **Jai Mandir,** literally a glass palace whose walls and ceilings are covered with mirrors and spangles. The concave ceiling in one room is shaped so that it would fit snugly over an elephant's back. The guides in the palace are wont to light candles, demonstrating thousands of overhead reflections, like shimmering stars in the sky.

The maharani's apartments are adjoining, all rooms and balconies connected by a ramp, up which the royal mistress was carried in a rickshaw (one of the original rickshaws, its wheels padded to eliminate unnecessary noise, can be seen behind a glass door in the courtyard below). From the upper vantage point of the maharani's quarters one can peer discreetly through filigree marble "windows" into the public courtyard below, or gaze out at the brightly colored gardens laid out in pretty **Maota Lake.** Through the gorge at the foot of the hill—a narrow, well-defined pass—a winding road eventually leads to Delhi.

At the back of the palace, the servants' quarters are naturally much sparser. From here an underground tunnel once led to another fort on the hill to the rear, but this tunnel has now been filled in.

Back in the inner courtyard at the entrance to the palace, visitors can admire the primitive air-conditioning system of three centuries ago: water pouring down a ribbed marble channel, cooled by winds blowing through the perforated marble screen at each side.

Just outside, off the public courtyard where the elephants wait to begin their downward journey, is the small **Kali Temple** in which a five-minute ceremony takes place five times each day.

WALKING AND SHOPPING: Walking about Jaipur's bustling streets is a rewarding experience and, not surprisingly, it's popular with photographers. The flower sellers with their bright piles of marigolds in the bazaars, the delicately carved tiny sandstone "windows" (to keep the women unseen) in some of the old houses of the nobles, the occasional camel, and the ubiquitous oxcarts—all catch the eye.

The town is rich in handcrafts—more than 50,000 locals are said to be so employed—and the best place to find them under one roof, price-fixed, is the **Rajasthan Government Handicrafts Emporium** (open from 10 a.m. to 1 p.m. and 3 to 8 p.m.; closed Sunday and holidays), opposite the **Ajmeri** gate on Mirza Ismail Road and also in the Amber Fort. Look for tie-dyed and block-painted textiles, enameled household objects, filigree, bold folk paintings on cloth, but above all, jewelry. Jaipur sparkles here with gems faceted or carved into fanciful creatures or bright blossoms and oft-times mounted into enameled settings painted so delicately that you can see each tiny bird, flower, leaf, and scroll quite plainly—even on the smallest of pieces.

Many of the town's leading jewelers and curio dealers are located on **Mirza Ismail Road,** among them the reliable **Rakyan's,** who have been known to send out for a piece of jewelry tucked in some secret cache to make a sale.

They'll be glad to let you look at their beautiful jewelry, think it over at your hotel, and send someone over with your piece when and if you're ready to buy. Or try **Jewel's Emporium** (tel. 75767).

Other jewelers line the road to the Amber Palace and some have good selections of silver. Many of the jewelers also have hotel branches.

For tie-dyes, jewelry, lacquerwear, it's **Johri Bazar.** The big brass pots always appeal to me as simple, useful objects and not expensive. Buying such a bargain is one thing; schlepping it home, another.

TOURS: There are daily city tours offered by the **Rajasthan Tourism Development Corporation** (RTDC), at the railway station (tel. 69714), for Rs. 15 ($1.15) from 8 a.m. to 1 p.m. and from 1:30 to 6:30 p.m. Another RTDC tour from 9 a.m. to 6:30 p.m., for Rs. 35 ($2.70) covers the city sights and other temples, museums, gardens, and Nahargarh Fort. Be sure to take Rs. 65 ($5) for the elephant ride. The **India Tourism Development Corporation (ITDC)** conducts city tours for the same price, same timing. Check with the Hotel Jaipur Ashok (tel. 75171) or the ITDC (tel. 65451) for information and reservations.

INFORMATION: The **Government of India Tourist Office,** Hotel Khasa Kothi (tel. 72220), also with a counter at the airport (but at flight times only), and the **Rajasthan Government Information Bureau,** at the railway station (tel. 69714), are at your disposal for information, pamphlets, and guides.

GETTING TO JAIPUR: From Delhi, planes take off twice a day for Jaipur, 35 air-minutes away, for Rs. 296 ($23). There are daily flights from Jodhpur, at Rs. 296 ($23); from Udaipur, at Rs. 306 ($24); and from Bombay flights three times a day (except one, which goes six days only), at Rs. 862 ($66).

By train, the *Pink City Express* from Delhi takes five hours and costs Rs. 140 ($10.75) in first class and Rs. 32 ($2.45) in second class. Should you want to stop in Agra first, take the Agra–Jaipur Express.

Bus service from Delhi, Agra, Jodhpur, and other cities is frequent and the roads are pretty good. Buses also connect from Bharatpur.

TOURING BY SPLURGE TRAIN: A once-in-a-lifetime train trip aboard the **Palace on Wheels,** a train made of former maharajas' railway coaches now restored to elegance, starts in Jaipur for a seven-day trip through the region. After Jaipur, the unforgettable journey goes to Chittorgarh, Udaipur, Jodhpur, Jaisalmer, Bharatpur, and Agra. It's strictly for those with lots of time and big bankrolls—Rs. 18,850 ($1450). The cost includes meals, entrance and guide fees, elephant and camel rides, but not those thirst-quenching Rs.-30 ($2.30) bottles of beer. Drinks, laundry, and tips are extra. The trip can be booked through the Rajasthan Tourism Development Corporation, 36 Chandralok Building, New Delhi 110001 (tel. 321820).

AN EXCURSION TO THE BIRDS OF BHARATPUR: Bharatpur, in the 18th century an important fortified city, now is chiefly renowned as the location of the nearby **Keoladeo Ghana Bird Sanctuary,** a sight no birdwatcher will want to miss.

Once a royal hunting preserve, Keoladeo, comprising 52 square miles, is one-third marshland where babul trees, however thorny, are the favorite nesting places for many different exotic birds. Indeed, the sanctuary is a nesting ground for around 150 birds; and said to be one of the best places in the world to see nesting herons. Among the 350 of their nesting species, belonging to 56 families, seen here are painted stork, egret, pelican, ibis, cranes, and purple moorhen. Birds from Siberia, the Arctic, central Asia, Afghanistan, and elsewhere can be sighted here.

No matter when you visit you'll find some birds here, but there are some seasons noted for certain species: April to June for arboreal birds, August to October for nesting resident water birds, and November to February for migratory birds. Winter is key season for birds of prey.

Taking a cycle rickshaw (Rs. 5, 40¢, for two) or bike (Rs. 5, 40¢ for half a day), is the best way to go on a birdwatching tour. Not half as much fun is the minibus, at Rs. 10 (75¢), which goes if there is a minimum of six; or the park's Jeep, at Rs. 2.50 (20¢) per kilometer. At certain seasons, you can see marshland birds by boat. However or whenever you go, be sure to take along the park's helpful pamphlet, available for Rs. 5 (40¢), with information, checklists, and bird sketches. Keeping careful watch, you're almost certain to see more than birds—spotted deer, wild boar, sambar, and black buck also live in this park.

The sanctuary is open from sunrise to sunset throughout the year. Sunsets can be as colorful as the finest Rajasthan tie-dyes. Entry fee is Rs. 10 (75¢), and there are camera fees of Rs. 2 (15¢) per still camera and Rs. 50 ($3.85) for movie or video cameras.

At the sanctuary, there's a **Forest Rest House,** charging Rs. 65 ($5) and Rs. 90 ($6.90), the higher rate for air-conditioned rooms.

The **Forest Lodge,** at the park entrance (tel. 2260), is less a lodge than a little hotel, and prices are accordingly higher: Rs. 175 ($13.50) single, Rs. 250 ($19.25) double. For meals, add Rs. 130 ($10) per person. Air conditioning costs Rs. 90 ($6.90) to Rs. 100 ($7.70) more. From April to September the rates are reduced by Rs. 50 ($3.85) to Rs. 90 ($6.90), depending on the room. For more information, contact the Rajasthan Tourist Office, in Jaipur or elsewhere.

In town, there's a pink-painted palace with inlaid floors and designs on the walls; the 18th-century fort commemorates both victories over the British and the Mughals.

Getting There

Bharatpur is 184 km (110 miles) from Delhi by road, via Mathura (frequent buses). It can be an interesting tour in combination with Agra (55 km, 33 miles, away), Fatehpur Sikri, and Jaipur: Rs. 1,560 ($120) by car, but bus service is available. There's also direct rail service from Delhi, at Rs. 157 ($12.10) in first class, Rs. 22 ($1.70) in second class; and from Bombay, at Rs. 400 ($30.75) in first class, Rs. 97 ($7.45) in second.

2. Jodhpur

To many Westerners, Jodhpur is the name of a tight-fitting riding trouser, flared at the hips. It's actually been a main city of the Great Indian Desert since medieval days. The focal point here, the **Mehrangarh Fort,** is so fantastic that you think if you blink it will vanish. From the local men's attire came the name of the breeches.

More than in Udaipur or Jaipur, and despite this Rajasthani city's abundant flowers, trees, vast artificial lakes, and lawns, in Jodhpur you sense that only a step away is a desert landscape, almost as barren as the moon. This makes the medieval fort seem more magical—a larger-than-life version of an idealized illustration in a child's book.

And talk about pink—horseshoe-shaped Jodhpur blushes like a bride as it nestles into the ridge of rosy sandstone hills whose quarries gave birth to the stones for the major structures. Less majestic buildings in white or yellow are dazzling against a flawless blue sky.

Jodhpur (pop. 500,000), once the state of Marwar, meaning land of death, was actually founded in 1211. The city was built by Rao Jodha in 1459. His descendants, some among the residents today, ruled these parts for half a millennium, until Indian independence in 1947.

The city's walls are almost six miles in circumference. Through its seven huge gates—five are named for the towns to which the roads go that pass through the gate—passed some of Rajasthan's most valiant warriors. As with all Rajputs, they claimed that their history of heroic deeds went back as far as the epic poems, the *Ramayana* and *Mahabharata*, and they upheld their heritage with honor.

Jodhpur is visited with Mandore, a few miles away, the earlier capital of Marwar.

WHERE TO STAY: Rajasthan means land of kings, and so here again in Jodhpur we find another palace—one of the most imposing in all of India—**Umaid Bhawan,** Jodhpur 342006 (tel. 22316), 22516, or 22366), turned into a hotel. If you've been traveling around Rajasthan, you may be getting blasé about palace hotels. Well, wait till you see this one. How do you begin to describe it? For openers, it's a sensational pink sandstone structure, reminiscent of New Delhi's Parliament House and Secretariat Building. One of the architects, H. U. Lancaster, had in fact worked with Sir Edwin Luytens, renowned planner of New Delhi. The immense structure, built at the twilight days of India's maharajas, lacks the lightness of the palaces at Udaipur.

Behind the building of Jodhpur palace is this interesting story: The foundation was laid in November 1929 by the late Maharaja Sri Umaid Singhi, who commissioned the building to give jobs to thousands of his subjects during several years that severe drought resulted in famine. Employing 3,000 workers over 13 years, the palace was completed in 1942. It took a few more years to put all the finishing touches on it so the royal family could live in it.

Everything needed to enjoy and embellish life is under one roof. A huge dome, 105 feet high, crowns the central marble hall, itself circled with ornate balconies spiraling higher and higher. Thirty feet underground is an immense swimming pool, surrounded by archways painted with fantasy fish and undersea plants. Private chambers adjoin for changing. In other rooms, gold ceilings and parquet floors seem awaiting elegant couples arriving for official receptions. An intimate movie theater is in another wing. At present, 62 bedrooms are open for guests. Some have private sitting rooms. They all open onto cool shady loggias. One of the suites is a knock-out with its white-painted, intricately carved, wooden furniture, patterned rugs, and cushioned, carved white chairs—like an early Hollywood set for an exotic movie queen. There are spacious private bathrooms with the latest fixtures throughout. The grounds, landscaped as formal gardens, with broad avenues, contain tennis, squash, and badminton courts, and there's a billiard room. The Welcomgroup now manages the palace. Rates are high, but not as high as you might imagine for such a splendid chunk of history: Rs. 550 ($42.30) single, Rs. 650 ($50) double. The restaurant serves buffet meals: Rs. 45 ($3.45) at breakfast, Rs. 85 ($6.55) at lunch and dinner.

Much lighter in mood, lower in price, and lots of fun is **Ajit Bhawan,** near the Circuit House, Jodhpur 342006 (tel. 20409), run by Maharaj Swaroop Singh, of the former maharaja's family. A small palace in an earlier day, it still has many regal trappings in the main building where there are ten well-appointed guest rooms. Better by far are the 30 stone cottages dotting the spacious gardens—each cottage done in a different motif and accented with antiques. For this delightful place, rates are realistic for our budget: Rs. 250 ($19.25) single, Rs. 350 ($26.90) double, without meals; Rs. 375 ($28.85) single, Rs. 600 ($46.15) double, with meals. There's a 10% service charge. Featured is Marari food, the richest of the Indian cooking styles. Singh himself takes guests on tours to give them an inside look at village life. Tours cost Rs. 800 ($61.50) for four people per day in a Jeep.

Recently opened, the **Sardar Guest House,** Residency Road, Jodhpur 342006 (tel. 20009), is opposite the Collector's Residence in the quiet Ratanada area, and easy on the pocketbook. It is a former royal guesthouse, still furnished with a 1930s flavor. There are five doubles, each with a large dressing room and attached bathroom. Rates are Rs. 125 ($9.60) single and Rs. 225 ($17.30) double, inclusive of continental breakfast. Meals cooked to order are available upon request for an additional charge. A small swimming pool and garden are attractions.

Also on Residency Road is a hotel for those who crave modernity, the **Hotel Ratanada International,** Residency Road (P.O. Box 63), Jodhpur 342001 (tel. 2591). Nothing antique here—everything is sleek and streamlined, and fairly splurgey in price: Rs. 340 ($26.15) single, Rs. 440 ($33.85) double, all air-conditioned. A swimming pool, restaurants, and bar are features. For all meals taken here add Rs. 160 ($12.30) per person.

Photographers Porterfield and Chickering of New York City called to my attention the **Hotel Karni Bhawan,** Defence Laboratory Road, Ratanada, Jodhpur 342006 (tel. 20157). A Rajput home, it's now an intimate 12-room hotel with neat, clean rooms. At night dinner is sometimes served up on the roof along with a view of the floodlit fort. Breakfast is in the court; lunch and dinner are in dhanis, which means "huts away from the village," these in the garden. There is also a courtyard for meals. Rates are Rs. 175 ($13.45) single, Rs. 250 ($19.25) double. Meals run Rs. 20 ($1.55) for breakfast and Rs. 60 ($4.60) each for lunch and dinner, with the exception of the roof dinner which is Rs. 100 ($7.70).

The Government of Rajasthan's **Ghoomar Tourist Bungalow,** High Court Road, Jodhpur (tel. 21900), has 60 rooms, all doubles with attached bathrooms. Built in 1972, it's an unpretentious place with some very grand adornments, such as marble floors and a sweeping staircase, but it could use a little tender loving care. Cheap meals are served in the dining room, Indian-style foods only. Birds often take shortcuts through the bungalow, though some stay on as guests, building their nests in the window grills. Offices of the Tourist Bureau and Indian Airlines are on the premises. Rates for non-air-conditioned rooms are Rs. 80 ($6.15) single and Rs. 100 ($7.70) double; with air conditioning, Rs. 100 ($7.70) to Rs. 125 ($9.60).

Super-Budget Choices

Neat and basic, the **Railway Retiring Rooms** (tel. 22741)—four rooms with four beds each and two rooms with two beds each—run Rs. 20 ($1.55) per bed. Bathrooms are attached, but there is a small fee for towels. As elsewhere, these rooms are usually reserved for rail travelers.

It will come as no surprise that cheap hotels are clustered around the railway station where they are convenient to travelers. They aren't as cheap as they were—but what is? These days the average charge is Rs. 50 ($3.85) to Rs. 60 ($4.60). Of these, the barely passable **Ardash Niwas** (tel. 23936) is best, but that's saying very little. Rates here start at Rs. 35 ($2.70) single and Rs. 60 ($4) double, and then go up to Rs. 150 ($11.55) for a suite. Some others are the Agarwal Lodge, Alpana Hotel, and Shanti Bhawan Lodge—strictly for penny watchers who will stay almost anywhere.

EATING OUT: The **Kalinga Restaurant** (tel. 246066), in the Ardash Niwas Hotel, is pretty good for nonvegetarian foods. In the old city, **Pankaj,** near Jalori Gate (tel. 24974), has good vegetarian foods.

In the old city, also near Sojati Gate, is the **Agra Sweet Home**—worth a special trip to try the local specialty, makhania lassi (a creamy, saffron-scented yogurt drink). You may have to elbow your way in; it's such a favorite, they sell more than 1,000 glasses a day. You'll understand why when you taste it. During your stay you might also like to try another local specialty, mauakachori, cake filled with sweet syrup.

Buffets are served at the **Umaid Bhawan** (tel. 22316): Rs. 45 ($3.45) at breakfast, Rs. 85 ($6.55) at lunch or dinner.

LOOKING AROUND: Most people start in **Mandore,** which is a very wise thing to do. Now a pretty park, five miles north of the city, it was the early capital of Marwar. The park contains the shrine of **300 Million Gods,** a series of gigantic painted figures, some covered by the pious over the years in layer upon layer of silver leaf and looking strangely like enormously oversize foil-wrapped sweets. Nearby, the **Hall of Heroes** was carved from a single rock wall. These brightly painted figures represent local heroes and more deities. (Sadly some were damaged by flooding monsoon waters a few years back, but are still well worth seeing.)

The park's other main attraction are the cenotaphs of former rulers, handsomely constructed in a combination of Saivite and Buddhist styles with Jain details on the columns. These structures—pink sandstone again—stand on places where cremations took place. Above the cenotaphs, and a perfect vantage point to view it all, is a two-mile reservoir overlooking some fairly new Mughal-style gardens. It's a pleasant place to sit and rest, when it's hot.

Before leaving Mandore, stop in at the small museum.

Jodhpur's massive **Victory Gate** was erected by Ajit Singh to mark a military defeat of the Mughals in the 18th century. Above it, medieval Mehrangarh Fort looms almost 500 feet, is more than 500 years old, and dominates the entire landscape. Now your entry fee permits you to pierce its grim, once nearly impenetrable wall, concealing extraordinary palaces, spanning five centuries of Rajput glory. A steep zigzag ascent goes to the summit where there are handprints of 15 maharajas' widows who committed suttee (death by immolation when husbands died in battle) rather than suffer at the enemy's hands.

Inside, behind the lotus-patterned, lacework, sandstone façade are many palaces to be inspected. The muraled-mirrored rooms start from the 15th century and were added to even in the 20th. There are sumptuous brocades and marble-topped furnishings from the 18th century. From an early day also is the **Deepak Mahal** (Children's Palace), where gold-encrusted cradles wait still to rock royal infants. Nearby, the **Moti Mahal** (Throne Room) is golden and mirrored.

In the 300-year-old **Rose Palace,** the windowpanes are tinted pink in keeping with the theme. From other halls you can glance through perforated marble screens, as did the ladies in the chambers years ago, at a view of the countryside and town below—a view that probably summed up their universe.

The 200-year-old **Thakat Vilas Palace** has splendid floor-to-ceiling murals showing—in minute details—marchers, feasting, wars, games, weddings, religious rites, beautiful women, proud warriors, and even palace pets.

Room after room houses fantastic collections of folk instruments, miniature paintings, jewel-studded robes, howdahs, and many other relics of the old regal life. On the outside the display continues with a collection of old canons.

The fort is open from 9 a.m. to 5 p.m. The entry fee is Rs. 10 (75¢). Still cameras are Rs. 10 (75¢), Rs. 15 ($1.75) with flash, and movie cameras are Rs. 25 ($1.90). Musicians drum and pipe you in. They get a tip.

On the way down is **Jaswant Thada,** the 19th-century white marble cenotaph to Maraja Jaswant Singh, which houses portraits of Jodhpur's rulers. Bits of colored thread, tied to the decorative marble, have been left by local women who consider the place a shrine.

Five miles out of town are the 12th-century **Balsamand Lake** with a 20th-century palace, open from 8 a.m. to 6 p.m. for an entry fee of Rs. 2 (15¢), a pretty garden spot for picnics. About two miles from town is **Manamandir, a** small, old walled city, with a temple noted for 100 pillars.

TOURS: Daily tours departing from the Ghoomar Tourist Bungalow, 9 a.m. to 1:30 p.m., and 2 to 6:30 p.m. (but less frequent out of season, so check) take in the fort, Jaswant Memorial, Umaid Bhawan, and Mandore for Rs. 20 ($1.55).

GETTING AROUND: There are unmetered taxis and metered auto rickshaws. Perhaps their meters are good-luck charms like the baby shoes in the West. They are definitely not used as meters. Bargain!

SHOPPING AND WALKING: The enormous **Sardar Market** is spread around the Old Clock Tower in the old city. It's interesting to wander in the lanes off the market. One lane, not far from the Agra Sweet Home, is the red-light district.

There are numerous antique sellers in Jodhpur, but they seemed unwilling to bargain and prices were generally high. However, some of the merchandise—old bronzes and nutcrackers—was quite interesting, and perhaps even valuable.

GETTING TO JODHPUR: There are two daily **flights** from Delhi, at Rs. 489 ($56); two daily flights from Jaipur, at Rs. 296 ($34); one from Udaipur, at Rs. 228 ($28); and two a day from Bombay, at Rs. 750 ($87).

By **train,** the **Jodhpur Mail** from Delhi takes 17 hours and costs Rs. 220 ($16.90) in first class, Rs. 55 ($4.25) in second; the train goes on to Jaisalmer, and so should you when the time comes to move on. If you want to stop in Agra and Jaipur en route from Delhi, take the Agra–Barmer Express. From Jaipur to Jodhpur by train is a seven- to eight-hour ride, costing Rs. 128 ($9.85) in first class, Rs. 33 ($2.55) in second.

If public transport isn't adventurous enough for you, there are always **camels.** Travel agent Suman Singh of Peacock Travels Limited, 2 Rai Ka (tel. 27176), will be glad to fill one up and send you on your way. He'll also arrange private cars and guides for the conventional.

From Jodhpur, the former maharaja's wood-paneled train takes groups of 20 to Jaisalmer. But, you say, you are not a group of 20. If they're not all sold out, they'll let you hop aboard.

3. Jaisalmer

In every adventurous traveler's imagination is a city like Jaisalmer—a rarely visited golden city rising from the wilderness waiting to be discovered. Relatively difficult to reach, but well worth the effort, Jaisalmer (pop. 238,000), founded in 1156 by Rawal Jaisal, lies at the western end of Rajasthan, in the heart of the **Great Indian Desert.**

When camel caravans carried precious cargos to central Asia, Jaisalmer was in its glory days as a trading center and stop en route to Delhi. Traces of this former opulence are seen in lace-like buildings of luminous sandstone. New construction today must also be ochre toned to blend with the old. Against this theatrical background are handsome Rajasthanis in bright turbans and vivid skirts and blouses.

As Bombay rose in importance as a seaport, Jaisalmer began to lose its luster. After the 1947 partition, the trade routes to Pakistan were closed and Jaisalmer went further into decline. During the 1965 and 1971 wars with Pakistan, Jaisalmer, with its strategic border position, was reborn as an important military base. Today the army is Jaisalmer's main industry.

While a good paved road makes it a six-hour run from Jodhpur to Jaisalmer, there are no flights, which deters many travelers, and also there are no big hotels to hold tour groups. In Jaisalmer they wish there were jet flights so tourism would further shore up the economy. But for now at least it's possible to be among the few visitors wandering in the magic streets of this golden and glowing city rising in the desert wilderness.

WHERE TO STAY: Other cities in Rajasthan have palaces, but Jaisalmer has **Jaisal Castle** (tel. 62), right in the fort, a unique place to stay. It's modest for a castle—more a private-home atmosphere—with ten pleasant rooms, all with bathrooms attached. From the roof there's a wonderful view of the desert, especially beautiful at sunrise and sunset. Room rates are Rs. 115 ($8.85) single and Rs. 140 ($10.75) double, without meals. With meals, single rates go up to Rs. 240 ($18.45), and doubles, Rs. 390 ($30).

The government's **Moomal Tourist Bungalow** (tel. 92) is outside the city walls, and has 32 rooms in a nice-looking building and 20 huts, but all of them could use better upkeep. Still, it's a more than adequate place to stay. Air-conditioned accommodations run Rs. 155 ($11.90) to Rs. 200 ($15.40); non-air-conditioned singles run Rs. 90 ($6.90) to Rs. 125 ($9.60) and doubles go for Rs. 120 ($9.25) to Rs. 160 ($12.30). Huts are quite basic, but so are the prices: Rs. 40 ($3.05) single, Rs. 50 ($3.85) double.

Not far from Moomal, a beautiful old haveli in typical golden sandstone was once a royal guesthouse. It's now the **Hotel Jawahar Niwas Palace,** with 15 spacious rooms and antique furnishings, high ceilings, and big bathrooms in the main building. An annex has smaller, more modern rooms. Rates are Rs. 200 ($15.40) single, Rs. 350 ($26.90) double. The hotel will arrange a camel-cart tour of town for you.

One of the ritziest places in town, the **Narayan Niwas Palace,** near Malka Prol, Jaisalmer 345001 (tel. 108), was an old caravanserai, and still has the camel mangers and other trappings. Built into the old structure is a modern hotel with wall-to-wall carpeting and attached bathrooms. Rates are Rs. 230 ($17.70) single, Rs. 210 ($16.15) double, without meals; Rs. 355 ($27.30) single and Rs. 530 ($40.75) double, with meals. More rooms were under construction, as was a roof garden, and they should be ready by now. Rajasthani music in the evenings here.

Next to the Narayan is the **Hotel Sri Narayan Vilas,** Jaisalmer 345001 (tel. 283), another converted caravanserai. Built in 18th-century Rajasthani style, the rooms have all the 20th-century conveniences, carpeting, and modern bathrooms, for Rs. 175 ($13.45) single, Rs. 200 ($15.40) double, without meals; Rs. 280 ($21.55) single and Rs. 410 ($31.55) double, with meals. Trio is the hotel's tented restaurant, where you can get Rajasthani dishes as well as continental foods. Average entree price is Rs. 20 ($1.55) and the highest is around Rs. 40 ($3.05), and Rajasthani musicians are featured at night.

For low-budgeteers, the **Golden Rest House** (tel. 226) has clean, basic rooms with bathrooms attached, a friendly atmosphere, and low rates: Rs. 20 ($1.55) single, Rs. 80 ($6.15) double. Similarly modest rooms and rates are found at the **Tourist Hotel** and the **Hotel Swastika** (the swastika is a Vedic good luck sign).

Rs. 10 (75¢) to Rs. 30 ($2.30) are the prices at the **Hotel Fort View, Rama Guest House, Hotel Pleasure, Sun Ray Hotel,** and **Sunil Bhatia Rest House.** These are little more than mud-walled huts with cots. Many of these lowest-price places are clustered around the railway station.

The best place near the railway station is the 15-room **Hotel Neeraj** (tel. 142), with plain but adequate rooms and private bathrooms for Rs. 120 ($9.25) to Rs. 150 ($11.55).

Finally, a new luxury hotel, the Thar, was under construction outside the city walls, and it should be open by the time you arrive.

WHERE TO EAT: There are no restaurants to speak of except in the Moomal Tourist Bungalow and the top-priced hotels.

For the vegetarian, there are the ultra-simple **Purohits** and **Shama Lodges** in Gandhi Chowk. By the time you get there, a branch of **Trio Restaurant** now in the Hotel Sri Narayan Vilas is expected to open in the central market. As with all Indian cities, there are many tea and soft-drink stalls.

SEEING THE SIGHTS: From a distance, the fort built in 1156 by Rawal Jaisal looks like a rich fantasy of golden crenelated walls outlined against a sapphire-blue sky. Nor does it disappoint on closer inspection. What makes this fort fascinating is that about a quarter of Jaisalmer's residents live inside its walls. Within the first gate of the fort is the Rawal's seven-story palace, with beautifully carved balconies and crowns of pagoda-shaped cupolas. The fort is situated on a hill 262 feet high, and offers a magnificent view of the town and desert.

In the fort, and open only from morning till noon, are a group of **Jain temples** dating from the 12th to the 15th centuries, richly sculpted with friezes showing the sensuous and the divine. There are hundreds of Jain images to see, some with jewel-studded eyes. Jain priests, with scarves across their mouths lest they inadvertently swallow an insect, minister to the deities and tend the temples.

The **Jain Bhandar** (library), established in 1835, is within the temple group and contains 3,000 manuscripts written on palm leaves and paper and composed between the 11th and 13th centuries. They discourse on religious as well as secular subjects. There are also Shiva and Ganesh temples in the fort.

Off the main market, and remarkably preserved, are five handsome, lavishly carved golden sandstone mansions built by the wealthy, mainly in the 19th century, and known as havelis. Most extravagant of all is **Patwon ki Haveli,** a flamboyant fantasy of intricate designs. The building is closed up except for one narrow staircase, which leads to an old chamber decorated with murals.

Salim Singh ki Haveli was built by a former prime minister when Jaisalmer was in its heyday. His mansion is identified by the blue cupola. The extravaganza of sculpture on Singh's mansion virtually covers the entire house. Its most outstanding figures are the beautiful peacocks with fan-shaped tails melding into the designs on the richly carved support brackets.

Nathmalji ki Haveli, while also handsomely carved, is somewhat of a curiosity. The former prime minister who built this lace-like house hired two brothers to delicately sculpt the right and left sides, and while similar, they are slightly different from each other.

Slightly south of the city is **Gadi Sagar Tank,** once a reservoir for the city, and site of some small temples. The striking stone gateway across the road leading to the tank was supposedly built by Telia, a favorite courtesan of one of the rawals. When the royal family found out who was responsible for the gate, they threatened to destroy it. But the clever courtesan topped it with a statue of Krishna and had the gate consecrated as a temple. Not even royalty would tear down a sanctified gate, although they never again used the tank.

North of Jaisalmer is **Bada Bagh,** a garden oasis and old dam, where a great deal of the town's produce is grown. There are graceful cenotaphs over-looking the garden. This place is positively magical in the late afternoon as the last rays of the sun turn Jaisalmer into a golden ochre town.

There are no coach tours of Jaisalmer but they are not necessary. Meandering through the town is the best way to experience it. Below the walled fort is the **main market,** where there are always vibrantly dressed women bargaining for their wares. Another shopping area is near the Amar Sagar Gate, to the west. The bus stand is near this gate, as is the Tourist Bungalow. Out this way also is **Mool Sagar,** a pretty garden and tank, which you'll need a taxi or tonga (horse-drawn cart) to reach. In this direction, 25 miles (40 km) from town are Sam sand dunes. The railway station is at the end of town near the fort. You can get a Jeep and a driver for Rs. 30 ($2.30) for sightseeing.

There are a number of shops selling antiques and made-to-look-like antiques near the fort, and some guides and rickshaw wallahs around there. You'll find it interesting to look in the shops, although the prices are rather high. From the fort you can take a taxi out south to Gadi Sagar and eventually north to Bada Bagh for the sunset. The taxis are unmetered. Be sure to bargain and set the price before you get in.

GETTING AROUND: The Tourist Office's Jeep can be rented for sightseeing for Rs. 2 (15¢) per kilometer and a minimum of Rs. 25 ($1.90) for half a day. Some travel agents will also rent Jeeps. **Bikes** are available for rental in the central market; bargain for the best price.

Jaisal Tours, Jaisal Castle (tel. 62), will fix you up with a camel tour around town. Figure on Rs. 25 ($1.90) for half a day.

A CAMEL SAFARI: Recommended by readers Susan Timmons of Chugwater, Wyoming, and her sister, Patricia Timmons Keach of Algona, Iowa, the Camel Safari into the Thar Desert can be booked through Mahendra Singh Ujjwal, in the New Tourist Hotel, near Fort Gate, Besa Para (tel. 282). It's not necessary to stay at the hotel to book the trip. Jeep trips are also available.

Mahendra promised them a desert trip that would be a true glimpse at area life, and he lived up to that promise, in both three- and seven-day safaris.

The cost, if you wish to participate, is Rs. 450 ($34.60) to Rs. 850 ($65.40) for the three-day two-night safari, the higher rate if Mahendra himself comes along; the seven-day trip was Rs. 1,100 ($85) per day. Included are a camel driver, cook-bearer, guide, and three meals a day (beverages purchased as needed). Memorable moments included an impromptu concert by local musicians and ghost-city visit, and the fact that there was no discomfort or physical stiffness after their camel trip atop well-upholstered camel saddles.

GETTING TO JAISALMER: There are day and night trains from Jodhpur, a ten-hour run, costing Rs. 125 ($9.60) in first class, Rs. 31 ($2.40) in second. The bus from Jodhpur, 179 miles (287 km) away, takes seven hours and costs Rs. 37 ($2.85). There are also buses from Ajmer, Bikaner, and Pokhran.

If you go by road, you may want to stop in **Pokhran** to see the fortress. Pokhran is also the site of Indian's nuclear test explosion on March 18, 1974. Road travelers should be sure to take plenty of bottled water; this is an exceptionally dry area. You'll need it and there are no places en route to get safe drinking water. You can find tea, however, and tepid soft drinks (no refrigeration in most wayside stands).

There is said to be a three-times-a-week Vayudoot flight from Delhi, Jaipur, Jodhpur, and Bikaner to Jaisalmer, but the schedule at this writing does not list it. Vayudoot has changes at short notice, so you may wish to check it out. However, the road trip through the desert from Jodhpur is an unforgettable journey through villages and desertland, relieved by patches of green, not to be seen from the plane.

4. Udaipur

The picturesque town of Udaipur (pop. 230,000) is a fertile oasis in the scratchy deserts of Rajasthan. Three large artificial lakes built centuries ago for irrigation still form the heart of the city, which is enclosed on all sides by mountains.

Udaipur is a colorful place, with beautiful murals on the whitewashed walls of many of its homes—it's a local custom to paint a horse and an elephant on each side of the gateway when a marriage takes place. The women here prefer the royal colors of orange and red for their saris.

The city, originally capital of the State of Mewar, was founded in the 16th century by Udai Singh, its first maharana—a "prince among princes" title bestowed only upon this Rajput royal family for valorous deeds and its longer-than-other-Rajputs' resistance to the Muslim rulers in Delhi. They gave in to the Muslims in 1614, but the city remained, until Indian independence, under the rule of this same royal family, who built many gorgeous palaces over the years.

WHERE TO STAY IN UDAIPUR: The opportunity to sleep in one fabulous palace, let alone two of them, doesn't come often for most people, so if you can possibly manage to stretch your budget you should try to spend at least one night in either of Udaipur's two marble palaces turned into hotels.

The most famous of the two, the **Lake Palace Hotel**, Pichola Lake, Udaipur 313001 (tel. 23421), is perhaps the quintessential palace hotel of the world. Originally the summer residence of the maharana and supposedly converted into a hotel at the suggestion of Jacqueline Onassis (when she was Kennedy), its marble halls have since played host to kings and commoners—so many in fact that the interiors, having gotten run-down, have recently been done up anew to look properly palatial again. Architecturally a place of classic beauty, this palace of curved archways, domes, and cupolas appears to be floating in the lake. Throughout the interior there's a blending of furnishings with carved marble and mirror-studded murals. Some of the suites are truly splendid, with stained-glass windows, marvelous views across the lake, rooftop-terraces, and cupolas that overlook courtyards and lotus-filled pools. For its opulence, the rates are not unreasonable: Rs. 600 ($46.25) single occupancy, Rs. 700 ($53.75) double. They get higher for bed/setting rooms and small suites: Rs. 950 ($73) to Rs. 1,250 ($96.25), single or double occupancy. The splendid multiroom suites cost Rs. 2,000 ($154) to Rs. 2,500 ($192.25).

Regular launch service connects the hotel with the mainland, and launches also take hotel guests around the lake on sunset tours. The three-mile-square lake, built in the 14th century, is 30 feet deep.

The palace, once known as Jag Niwas, has a companion piece, Jag Mandir, on a nearby island. A charming but apocryphal tale says that Emperor Shah Jahan hid out on this island after feuding with his father, and got the inspiration for the Taj Mahal while here.

In the main building, puppet shows and dance displays are often held for guests' entertainment.

Across the way on the mainland, at the south end of the imposing group of white buildings making up the City Palace, is now the exclusive and intimate **Shivniwas Palace,** Udaipur 313001 (tel. 28239, 28240, 28241, or 28251), a former guesthouse of the maharana for entertaining such dignitaries as the Queen of England and the King of Nepal. It's now a health resort hotel, with only 24 sumptuous multiroom suites—Rs. 1,500 ($115.50) to Rs. 3,000 ($231)—furnished with the maharana's treasured antiques, blended with new custom-made furnishings, and eight beautifully appointed rooms— at Rs. 500 ($38.50)—done up in red and blue with hand-cut glass inlaid work and crystal chandeliers. (All prices will have risen by the time you arrive, perhaps by as much as 25%.) There are crested towels and terrycloth robes in the marble bathrooms. All the elegant suites have secluded terraces for sun or moonbathing in the buff, and other terraces for partying. Some of the suites have rooms enough to make a summer bungalow—a study dressing room, bathroom, pantry, baggage room, in addition to a bedroom and bathroom and terraces.

All rooms have commanding views of the gardens, lake, or city. They're entered from a private courtyard, hidden from the road, with an oval mosiac-tiled swimming pool in the center. There's a lounge with cut-crystal furniture and hand-cut glass inlaid flowers and animals on the walls and ceilings. A cozy bar is adjacent to the restaurant. Food is prepared with many herbs to accent healthful living. If you're a James Bond film fan, the Shivniwas may look familiar to you: some of the sexiest scenes of *Octopussy* were shot at this hotel. The Lake Palace across the way played a role in the Bond movie as well.

If the palaces are a little too rich for your diet, then stay on the mainland at the **Laxmi Vilas Hotel,** Udaipur 313001 (tel. 24411, 24412, or 24413), once a guesthouse for VIPs visiting the maharana (so why not you?). There are 34 spacious rooms in the main palace (26 with air conditioning) and 23 neat rooms in a new wing. The view, which is very good, makes up for a certain lack of opulence in the furnishings—though there are still many beautiful rugs and other trappings of earlier, more regal days. Rates are Rs. 210 ($16.15) to Rs. 425 ($32.70) single, and Rs. 270 ($20.75) to Rs. 520 ($40) double, the higher rates for air conditioning. Suites run Rs. 450 ($34.60) to Rs. 950 ($73), depending on occupancy, air conditioning, and degree of lavishness. Breakfast runs Rs. 40 ($3.05); lunch and dinner, Rs. 60 ($4.60) each.

Almost adjoining the Laxmi Vilas, and also on a hilltop with a spectacular view, is the 20-room **Anand Bhawan,** Fateh Sagar Road, Udaipur 313001 (tel. 23256 or 23257), with wide balconies overlooking the lake. It's a bit plainer than its neighbor, but was, at one time, a royal guesthouse. Now it's a buy in line with this book—but you must reserve very far in advance. The spacious rooms have carpets, comfortable couches and chairs, dressing rooms, and high ceilings. There is a pleasant garden with huge tamarind and mango trees. Rates are Rs. 150 ($11.55) single and Rs. 200 ($15.40) double, and they include air conditioning. Rs. 40 ($3.05) more will get you a deluxe room. Excellent curries are served in the restaurant.

Also overlooking Fateh Sagar Lake, the modern **Hotel Hilltop,** 5 Ambavgarh, Udaipur 313001 (tel. 23708), has 24 double rooms with baths attached and comfortable rates, especially when not air-conditioned: Rs. 100 ($7.70) to Rs. 200 ($15.40) single and Rs. 150 ($11.55) to Rs. 275 ($21.15) double; air-conditioned rates are Rs. 275 ($21.15) for singles and Rs. 325 ($25) for doubles, but only seven rooms are air-conditioned.

Hotel Lakend, Alkapuri, Fateh Sagar, Udaipur 313001 (tel. 23841), offers rooms with and without meals, and a view of the lake. This is a modern, casually run hotel where warmth of personality makes up for a lack of professionalism. Rates are Rs. 205 ($15.75) single and Rs. 310 ($23.85) double, with meals; Rs. 140 ($10.75) single and Rs. 200 ($15.40) double, without meals. All rooms are air-cooled, not air-conditioned, and have attached bathrooms. There is a 10% service charge.

The very pleasant **Chandralok Hotel,** 123 Saheli Marg, Udaipur 313001 (tel. 28109), has only 14 well-kept rooms, with attached bathrooms; all are doubles, but are let as singles. Six are air-conditioned. Rates are Rs. 150 ($11.55) to Rs. 200 ($15.40) for single occupancy, Rs. 200 ($15.40) to Rs. 250 ($19.25) for double (the higher rates are for air conditioning). For all meals, add Rs. 110 ($8.45) per person.

The **Shreenath** (or Shrinath) **Tourist Hotel,** near Court Chouraya, Udaipur 313001 (tel. 24422), has ten simply furnished, wallpapered rooms with flagstone floors and attached bathrooms (two with Western-style toilets). Air coolers should be installed by now. Rates are Rs. 105 ($8.05) single, Rs. 175 ($13.45) double, Rs. 225 ($17.30) for a deluxe double.

Simple but adequate, the **Hotel Damanis,** opposite the telegraph office, Udaipur 313001 (tel. 5675), has 26 rooms in the heart of the city for Rs. 65 ($5) to Rs. 100 ($7.70) double, Rs. 45 ($3.45) to Rs. 75 ($5.75) single. Only three doubles are air-conditioned and they cost Rs. 140 ($10.75) double and Rs. 110 ($8.45) single, so upper prices get into the moderate range.

The government's 34-room **Kajri Tourist Bungalow,** Shastri Circle, Udaipur 313001 (tel. 23509), in the center of town, charges Rs. 40 ($3.05) for an ordinary single to Rs. 150 ($11.55) for an air-conditioned single and a couple of other single rates in between. For doubles, the range is Rs. 50 ($3.85) to Rs. 200 ($15.40). The dorm is Rs. 12 (90¢) per head.

Back to higher budgeting, the **Hotel Rajdarshan** on the banks of Swroop Sagar, Udaipur 313001 (tel. 24088), has 34 centrally air-conditioned rooms with modern furniture, marble and tile bathrooms, and small balconies offering panoramic lake and city views. Rates are Rs. 325 ($25) single and Rs. 400 ($30.75) double.

Hotel Chandra Prakash, Lake Palace Road, Udaipur 313001 (tel. 28109), almost next door to the posh Shivniwas, is a casual, family-run hotel where visitors are made to feel at home. A pleasant garden, a neat room, and an attached bathroom with hot and cold running water for Rs. 40 ($3.05) make it an attractive low-budget find; the Rs.-200 ($15.40) rooms are okay, but somewhat overpriced. There is a restaurant open 24-hours a day.

On a plot of land jutting into Lake Pichola is the nicely sited, appropriately named **Lake Pichola Hotel,** outside Chandpole, Udaipur 313001 (tel. 24497). Although brand-new, it has the domed and balconied look of traditional Udaipur architecture and interiors with the same traditional flavor. There are balconies on all 18 rooms (two are suites) overlooking the lake for sitting out and admiring the view. Prices run Rs. 250 ($19.25) single, Rs. 350 ($26.90) double, with attached bathrooms. Breakfast costs Rs. 25 ($1.90), and lunch and dinner run Rs. 50 ($3.85) each. The hotel offers boat rides to take guests around the lake.

Finally, a splurge away from the city, the **Hotel Shikarbadi,** Goverdhanvilas, Udaipur 313001 (tel. 25321 to 25325), a former royal hunting lodge, offers an offbeat place to stay. The tariff is offered without or with meals—a consideration since the hotel is three miles from town in a dense jungle. It is still the private residence of Maharaj Kumar Arvind Singh, a son of the Maharana of Mewar. Singles cost Rs. 325 ($25) to Rs. 500 ($38.40); doubles, Rs. 500 ($38.40) to Rs. 800 ($61.50). The higher prices include meals. The grounds house a small stud farm for those who like to ride. There is an elephant in residence for venturing into the bush, an animal park, and a swimming pool for a refreshing dip. A 50% discount, offered from April 1 to September 30, can also be refreshing to your pocketbook.

Super Budget

Alka Hotel, opposite Shastri Circle, Udaipur 313001 (tel. 23611), is managed by the very pleasant Pratap Bhandari, whose brother runs the previously mentioned Lakend. While this place is not fancy, you could be happy here in rooms that are simple, fairly neat and clean, and have a balcony. Rates are low as far as Udaipur hotels go: Rs. 25 ($1.90) to Rs. 60 ($4.60) single, Rs. 50 ($3.85) to Rs. 80 ($3.05) double. There are 55 rooms, of which 20 have Western toilets. A real find!

The **Hotel Keerti,** Airport Road (tel. 36389), has only nine rooms, all doubles, all with bath attached, for Rs. 15 ($1.15) singles occupancy, to Rs. 75 ($5.75) for two people, air-conditioned. There is a 10% discount in May and June, and a service charge of 10%. The hotel also runs **Pratap Country Inn,** four miles out of the city. If you go to the Keerti, they'll see that you get out to the other place. The rates are the same as at the Keerti, but there is a swimming pool and horses and camels to ride. The atmosphere is casual. Bus service to downtown Udaipur from Pratap is frequent so you can go to and fro without depending on taxis.

Back in town, the rooms at the **Rangniwas Hotel,** Lake Palace (tel. 23891), are ringed around a big garden popular for weddings. They are modest rooms in a pleasant setting, and worth the Rs.-15 ($1.15) low price, but not the Rs.-200 ($15.40) highest price. They have bathrooms with Indian toilets, cold-water showers, and basic furnishings.

Low-budgeteers should also remember the Rs.-12 (90¢) dorm accommodations at the government's **Kajri Tourist Bungalow,** Shastri Circle (tel. 23509). Rooms here start at Rs. 40 ($3.05).

EATING OUT IN UDAIPUR: It isn't done much here as most tourists prefer to eat where they stay. There are some restaurants in Chetak Circle—**Kwality, Berry's, Chetak**—with the by-now memorized Indian, Chinese, and so-called continental menu. They're open from around 9 or 10 a.m. to 11 p.m. The **Coffee House,** also in Chetak Circle, has good coffee and Indian snacks, and is open from 7:30 a.m. to 10 p.m. The **Mayur,** 155 Jagdish Chowk (opposite Jagdish Temple), has a wide range of South Indian foods.

TOURS: From the Tourist Bungalow, you can catch the government's coach tour daily at 8:30 a.m. (to 1:30 p.m.) and cover the city's highlights for Rs. 15 ($1.15). A tour in the afternoon (from 2 to 7 p.m.) for Rs. 35 ($2.70) takes in the outskirts: Elinkgji, a temple village; Haldighati, a former battle site; and Nathdwara, an 18th-century temple (which non-Hindus can't enter).

Unless you're a compulsive sightseer or have loads of time on your hands, you can pass up the afternoon tour without missing a lot and have a far more interesting time exploring the city on your own. You can stroll, take a scooter rickshaw, or rent a bike (rates vary, but bargaining keeps them moderate) from one of the shops near the tourist information bureau in the Tourist Bungalow and you can make your own tour at your own pace.

GETTING AROUND: If a bike is not your thing, then there are auto-rickshaws with meters, which apparently are for decoration since drivers don't bother to use them. Haggle (don't just bargain) and set the rate before you get in. The local people complain that ever since they shot *Octopussy* here and the film people threw money around, the drivers expect visitors to do more of the same.

SIGHTS AROUND TOWN: The **City Palace** is now public property and can be visited. Its upper balconies are the highest point in town and offer a splendid view of Pichola Lake at one side and the city at the other—it's easy to visualize the royal guests sitting up here watching the elephants at play in the spacious courtyard below. Although the 20 elephant stables remain untouched, they are unoccupied today. The government of Rajasthan, which now administers the palace, has higher priorities for its funds than maintaining elephants.

The palace is an intricate warren of inner patios, courtyards, and balconies, connected by narrow passageways and flights of stairs. The Peacock Courtyard features beautiful glass peacocks, composed of thousands of tiny colored glass slivers inset into the walls. Above is the maharana's private apartment, occupied until but 30 or so years ago; below that is a tiny room containing a "golden sun" which could be illuminated on days the real sun was obscured by the monsoon.

There are rooms with mirrored walls and ivory doors, colored-glass windows and carved and inlaid marble balconies. The pièce de résistance must be the tiny room in which every inch of space, even the ceiling, is covered with brightly colored painted miniatures of festivals, flowers, jungle scenes, and dancing girls. Adjoining are portraits of all the maharanas.

Attached is a small and somewhat indifferent museum containing textiles, armor, inscribed stone blocks, and row upon row of turbaned plaster heads.

City Palace is open from 9:30 a.m. to 4 p.m. daily. Entry fee of Rs. 3 (23¢) for ladies' apartments, plus Rs. 3 (23¢) for still cameras and Rs. 10 (75¢) for movie cameras.

Until the death of the last maharana, the City Palace was the major one in use. On a distant hill can be seen the "monsoon palace"; the "summer palace," Jag Niwas, is the one now turned into the Lake Palace Hotel. The other island palace, **Jag Mandir,** was the one in use in the 17th century, and it has a lovely black marble pagoda and eight life-size stone elephants guarding its entrance.

Fateh Sagar is the more northern of the two lakes, and along its eastern bank (town side) twists a serpentine road. On the landward side of this road, ascending the hillside, is attractive **Nehru Park,** topped off by **Pratap Smarak,** a hilltop rock garden dominated by the black bronze statue of the 16th-century Rajput patriot, Maharana Pratap.

Also caressed by this lake are the lovely gardens known as **Sahelion-ki-Bari** whose pathways and courtyards feature fountains (turned on by attendants only when someone pays a rupee) in ingenious combinations. A square tank in the inner courtyard contains a white marble cupola in the center—whose roof turns into a waterfall—and black marble pavilions at each corner, on the roofs of which birds revolve in a circle of spray. In another part of the garden, four marble elephants spray water through their trunks as birds emit jets from their teeth.

The gardens themselves, which are lovely, date back to the 18th century. They were used to amuse young ladies who had been sent as a peace gift from Delhi's ruler. The fountains were not added until later, in the last century. A sign at the entrance commands, "Let thy voice be low." Open from 8 a.m. to 6 p.m. The entry fee of Rs. 2.50 (20¢) also includes the fountains.

The maharanas were apparently great ones for entertainment. The **Gangor Ghat,** a stone gateway opening on to lakeside steps just north of the City Palace, is where dancing girls used to perform, watched from an elevated barge on the lake by all the nobility and their guests.

Just behind this gate is the **Jagdish Temple,** a richly carved structure dating back three centuries. Today it possesses such a valuable collection of treasures that an armed guard stands perpetually on duty.

Toward the south end of town, on the way to the railroad station, are the public gardens containing a small but interesting zoo, and a train for children.

The "center" of Udaipur could be regarded as **Chetak Circle,** up in the northeast section of town. Here are the **Jumma Mosque,** the offices of Indian Airlines, the **Chetak Cinema** (Indian movies), and the aforementioned **Kwality** and **Berry's Restaurant,** the former air-cooled. The narrow streets to the older part of town and bazaar lead off from here; up one of them, only about 100 yards from the Circle, are two shops, the **Curious House** and **Eastern Antiquity,** with some overpriced and dubiously dated miniatures and carvings. Udaipur is renowned for its carved and painted wooden toys, and numerous shops up these little streets stock them in great quantity. Search, also, in the **City Bazaar** for bargains on silver, a local specialty.

Just north of Chetak Circle is the nationally celebrated **Folk Art and Puppet Museum** (known as **Bhartiya Lok Kala Mandal**), which, since its founding in 1952, has been collecting, recording, filming, practicing, and performing folk art and dancing of the region. It's open from 9:30 a.m. to 6 p.m. Admission is Rs. 2 (15¢) and puppet shows are a regular feature.

WHEN TO VISIT: Most people visit Udaipur—and Rajasthan—from September to March. But the dry and arid area is beautiful when fringed with green during the monsoon, July to September. Rainfall is light in this desert region. It's very hot from the end of March until the rains come.

INFORMATION: For information or brochures, or to hire approved guides, stop at the **Tourist Information Bureau** in the Kajri Tourist Bungalow (tel. 23605). For information on festivals, fairs, and other special events throughout the Rajasthan area, check with the **West Zone Cultural Centre,** Bagore-Ki-Haveli, Gangaur Ghat, near the City Palace (tel. 23858).

SHOPPING: Udaipur is noted for silver jewelry, tie-dyes, and folk toys. The **Rajasthan Government Emporium** is price-fixed. Shops near the Clock Tower have good assortments of local wares. At one of these, **Ashok Art,** 96 Patwa St., near Jagdish Temple, artisans are at work on ivory miniature paintings. Some of these run as high as Rs. 15,000 ($1,155), but you can get something small for Rs. 300 ($23) as well (less if you bargain).

GETTING TO UDAIPUR: Daily flights connect Udaipur with Delhi at Rs. 236 ($18), Jaipur at Rs. 306 ($24), Jodhpur at Rs. 226 ($17), Bombay at Rs. 615 ($47), and Aurangabad at Rs. 556 ($43).

The **train** from Delhi takes 22 hours and costs Rs. 250 ($19.25) in first class and Rs. 65 ($5) in second class. The respective prices for trains from Bombay are Rs. 264 ($20.30) and Rs. 34 ($2.60); from Jodhpur, Rs. 128 ($9.85) and Rs. 18 ($1.40); from Aurangabad, Rs. 124 ($9.55) and Rs. 15 ($1.15).

5. Mount Abu

The colorful city of Mount Abu (pop. 14,000), in southern Rajasthan, is both a charming hill resort and an important place of pilgrimage for the Jains who come to visit the beautiful Dilwara Temples. Celebrated as a Jain religious site since the 11th century, Mount Abu was earlier important to Shiva worshippers. Today the many centuries-old archeological treasures found here remain relatively unknown to Westerners, who rarely visit here.

On a plateau 4,000 feet above sea level, the 25-square-mile resort has a terrific climate. When the plains sizzle, the local temperature rarely goes above 85°; in winter temperatures reach highs of 75° and lows of about 55°. Even the rainy season, June to September, is relatively light. So it's not surprising that in summer whole families make their way to Mount Abu by train, bus, or car for a breath of cool air. The crush is on again during the ten-day fall Diwali holiday.

WHERE TO STAY: Many hoteliers' peak-season rates apply during Diwali (in October / November; see "Festivals" in the Introduction) and May through June, although Mount Abu is officially in season from March to June and September to December. So it's possible to find bargains even when the resort is in season, but not at its peak in terms of numbers of guests to fill the hotels. Sales taxes add about 5% to your food and board. The following are only a few of the hotels found in Mount Abu. You will undoubtedly make your own discoveries, so let me hear about them if you do.

If you've been staying in palace hotels in Rajasthan, you can also have a royal resting place here at the stately **Palace Hotel,** Bikaner House, Dilwara Road, Mount Abu 307501 (tel. 21 or 33), about a kilometer (half a mile) from town. This imposing granite-and-sandstone mansion, with acres of gardens and a lake, was from 1893 until 1961 the summer palace of the Maharaja of Bikaner. Inside are many old furnishings, tiger heads and faded photos of the tiger hunts at which they met their fates, and photos of the family and visiting friends. The place is loaded with atmosphere, but could use a lot of tender loving care (renovation was mentioned during my visit). If you stay here before it becomes modernized, you will undoubtedly have a regal-size room, with a bathroom large enough to hold a polo team, at Rs. 200 ($15.40) for a single and Rs. 285 ($21.90) for a single in a suite, Rs. 275 ($21.15) for a double and Rs. 400 ($30.75) for two people in a suite, all with continental breakfast included. Having all your meals here will cost about an additional Rs. 155 ($11.90) per head, including the aforementioned continental breakfast. Overhead in the dining hall you can see carved perforated granite wall screens which permitted the harem ladies to see below without being seen. Aside from the price, a drawback is that you are away from the center of town. Hiring a cab for a day around town costs Rs. 250 ($19.25) for eight hours, less after bargaining.

Not a palace but still owned by the former Maharaja of Jodhpur is **Connaught House,** Rajendra Marg (tel. 20941 in Jodhpur), formerly the summer residence of Sir Donald Field, chief minister of the state of Marwar-Jodhpur. On the pricey side, the six-room bungalow set in a pretty terraced garden is walking distance from town. The entire house, which can accommodate 12 people, can be rented for Rs. 1,200 ($92.25) per day; or rooms are available at Rs. 250 ($19.25) for doubles and Rs. 200 ($15.40) for singles. Meals, including a full English breakfast, will cost another Rs. 125 ($9.60) or so per person. The rooms are simply but adequately furnished with white iron bedsteads, and big adjoining bathrooms. The lounge has chintz upholstered wicker settees and chairs.

Downtown prices are lower, and one of the nicest places is the family-run **Hotel Swaraswati,** opposite the taxi stand, Mount Abu 307601 (tel. 7), where owner Trilok Jani oversees every detail. No fancy furnishings here, but the rooms—especially those in the annex—are clean and moderately priced. All are doubles: Rs. 120 ($9.25) to Rs. 200 ($15.40) in season, Rs. 40 ($3.05) to Rs. 60 ($4.60) off-season. The lower-priced rooms are off the courtyard, not in the annex. There are Indian-style attached bathrooms, and hot water on tap from 7 to 9 a.m. The dining hall is open from 11 a.m. to 1:30 p.m. and 6:30 to 8:30 p.m. A vegetarian thali for lunch or dinner costs Rs. 10 (75¢)—you eat breakfast out.

Nearby, the blue-painted 50-room **Hotel Maharaja International** (tel. 61), is reasonably clean, but run-down and overpriced at Rs. 150 ($11.55) to Rs. 300 ($23.05) for various rooms from doubles to suites, or Rs. 60 ($4.60) to Rs. 70 ($5.40) per person in the blocks with five to seven beds in them. There's a 20% discount off-season.

Across the way, set back from the road by a small courtyard bordered by potted plants, are two hotels painted yellow and green and under the same management. They are **Hotel Navjivan** (tel. 53) and the **Hotel Samrat International** (tel. 73). They also share a glitzy reception area which has a mirrored ceiling, crystal chandeliers, a sunken conversation pit, surrounded by a marble rail, wood and metal molded doors, and pictures of Shiva, Ganesha, and Krishna on the walls.

The Samrat International, the fancier of the two hotels, has suites as high as Rs. 400 ($30.75) to Rs. 460 ($35.40), singles for Rs. 250 ($19.25) in season and Rs. 160 ($12.30) off-season, and doubles for Rs. 300 ($23.05) in season and Rs. 200 ($15.40) off-season; deluxe rooms run Rs. 450 ($34.60) and Rs. 400 ($30.75) respectively. Western-style tile bathrooms predominate. Punjabi vegetarian food is available at the Samrat. Taking all your meals here would come to about Rs. 100 ($7.70) extra a day, per person.

At the Navjivan, rooms are Rs. 150 ($11.55) double and Rs. 120 ($9.25) single off-season, Rs. 350 ($26.90) in season; in triple- and four-bedded rooms, add Rs. 100 ($7.70) for each additional person in season and Rs. 50 ($3.85) off-season. Taking all your meals here would add around Rs. 75 ($5.75) to Rs. 100 ($7.70) per person per day. At lunch a vegetarian meal in Gujarat style with four vegetable curries and wheat breads and rice is Rs. 12 (90¢); curds and a sweet are extra.

Near the bus stand, the **Hotel Madhuban,** Mount Abu 307501 (tel. 121), was undergoing massive renovation and adding ten rooms when I visited. So far everything appeared to be shaping up so nicely that you might want to check it out for yourself. No tariff had been set, but it was thought that doubles would run Rs. 300 ($23.05) in season and Rs. 150 ($11.55) off-season.

A short walk up the road, the **Hotel Sheratone** (hoteliers in Mount Abu like to approximate famous Western chain names), Mount Abu 307501 (tel. 273), was adding 16 rooms to its existing 27 when I dropped in. When completed, 20 rooms will have balconies—good for admiring the view. All rooms have connecting baths, some with Indian-style toilets. Some of the rooms are plain with absolutely no frills; others have tweed-finish Formica headboards and wardrobes. Rates are Rs. 80 ($6.15) to Rs. 150 ($11.55). There is a 20% to 30% discount off-season. The atmosphere seemed cheerful and unprofessional.

The red-and-yellow building opposite the polo grounds is the **Hotel Abu International,** P.O. Box 29, Mount Abu 307501 (tel. 177), and was about to undergo renovations. There are 43 rooms in all, all with bathrooms attached, mainly Western-style plumbing. The prerenovation rooms were simple and clean with granite floors. The new rates were not set, but they would be worth checking into—let's hope renovation doesn't drive them through the roof. The hotel serves both Punjabi- and Gujarati-style foods.

About half a kilometer from downtown, the delightful **Mount Hotel,** Dilwara Road, Mount Abu 307501 (tel. 55), is clean and cozy, and run by the Bharucha family in what was once a British officer's bungalow. There are six rooms in all, three double- and three triple-bedded. Single rates are Rs. 80 ($6.15) to Rs. 150 ($11.55); double, Rs. 100 ($7.70) to Rs. 200 ($15.40); triple-bedded, Rs. 175 ($13.45) to Rs. 350 ($26.90). There is a 30% discount off-season. Taking your meals here will add about Rs. 50 ($3.85) to Rs. 75 ($5.75) a day. There are no restaurants nearby so you may want to have some, if not all, of your meals here. The cuisines are Indian, continental, Gujarati, and Parsi, and all foods are made to order.

On your way into town, you pass the turnoff to the Rajasthan government-run—or more accurately, government-run-down—**Shikhar Tourist Bungalow.** A beautiful view is about all that recommends it; the rooms are in bad condition (although a fraction better in the annex) and the rates are high for what you get: doubles range from Rs. 90 ($6.90) to Rs. 180 ($13.85) in season, and Rs. 40 ($3.05) to Rs. 140 ($10.75) off-season. In the dorm, it costs Rs. 12 (90¢) per person with a bedroll and Rs. 7 (55¢) without. You'd be better off with a bedroll judging from the condition of the bedding. There are cottages on the grounds, renting from Rs. 150 ($11.55) to Rs. 300 ($23.05). The annex has the super-deluxe rooms at the highest rates above. They're a cut above the others, but nothing to rave about. Indian-style attached bathrooms are found throughout.

Opposite the Tourist Bungalow is the **Hotel Aravali,** near the Veterinary Hospital, Mount Abu (tel. 216), with 18 rooms, pleasantly furnished and surprisingly well maintained. No English is spoken or understood. However, the rate sheet is in English and the rooms, all doubles, range from Rs. 150 ($11.55) to Rs. 250 ($19.25) for bed-and-breakfast in season, and Rs. 40 ($3.05) to Rs. 100 ($7.70) off-season. The rooms are grouped in little buildings around the pretty terraced garden with plants lining the walks and stairs.

Up the road, near the Toll Tax Office, the gray-stone green- and cream-trimmed building is the **Hotel Veena** (tel. 280), with eight reasonably clean, snug rooms opening onto a spacious veranda and garden aglow with tiny lights at night. The bathrooms have hot and cold water on tap from 7 to 11 a.m. A dining hall was to be added, and could be functioning by the time you read this. If not, you can have snacks on order and meals sent in, or eat out. The busy road in front quiets down after 10 p.m. Rates are Rs. 150 ($11.55) to

Rs. 300 ($23.05) in season, Rs. 75 ($5.75) to Rs. 100 ($7.70) off-season. Under the same management downtown is another **Hotel Veena** (tel. 133) also with eight rooms, a mite simpler, not as tidy, and with no running hot water. Rates are Rs. 100 ($7.70) to Rs. 250 ($19.25) in season, Rs. 60 ($4.60) to Rs. 80 ($6.15) off-season.

Crowning a hilltop three kilometers from the bazaar off the main road on the way to Gaumukh Temple, the neat and clean **Gujarat Bhavan** (tel. 182) is run by the government of Gujarat for visiting officials. If there's a vacancy, then you can move in for Rs. 60 ($4.60) in season, Rs. 30 ($2.90) off-season. All the rooms have balconies and attached private bathrooms, though the seven with Western plumbing are in a bit better condition than the others. But, overall, the place is well maintained. You can take your chances and drop in or write in advance for reservations to Engineer, B & C Dept., Palanpur, Banaskatha, Gujarat (tel. 2323).

Finally, downtown there's the splurgey, three-star **Hiltone Hotel,** P.O. Box 18, Mount Abu 307501 (tel. 137 or 237), with 38 rooms and six village-hut–style cottages, set on the two acres of landscaped grounds. The rooms are cheerful with twin beds; some have mirrored dressing tables, while others have plainer furnishings. A single costs Rs. 260 ($20); a double, Rs. 330 ($25.40). One of the best cottages is round with a big round bed, peaked beamed roof, straw matting on the floor, and drum-shaped tables and rustic chairs, rented for Rs. 360 ($27.70) single and Rs. 430 ($33.05) double. Mount Abu is a popular for honeymoons and the cottages often house newlyweds. All the rooms have modern tile bathrooms with hot and cold running water. You must inquire about off-season discounts. The Handi Restaurant serves breakfast, lunch, and dinner, and there are vegetarian and nonvegetarian entrees (see "Where to Eat").

WHERE TO EAT: The Hotel Hiltone's **Handi** is decorated with clay pots ("handis") and serves many dishes in metal handis. This is a splurge place to head for if you're tired of all-vegetarian food. You might start with a vegetable soup at Rs. 10 (75¢), followed by Adrak chicken made with ginger-cream sauce, coriander, and tomatoes, at Rs. 30 ($2.30), and ice cream at Rs. 6 (45¢) to Rs. 10 (75¢). Or try one of the nonvegetarian or Chinese specialties at Rs. 15 ($1.15) to Rs. 20 ($1.55). The chef has a tendency to oversalt dishes. Hours are 7 to 10 a.m. for breakfast, noon to 3 p.m. for lunch, and 7 to 11 p.m. for dinner. The Kalali Bar is open from 10 a.m. to 11 p.m.

The plain, no-frills **Angan Dining Hall** in the Hotel Navjivan serves an excellent, abundant Gujarati thali with wheat bread and rice and four vegetable curries for Rs. 12 (90¢). If you want curds or a sweet, it will cost a bit more. Hours are 1 to 2:30 p.m. and 7 to 9 p.m. Very popular with Indian tour groups.

Other places for good thalis include the **Hotel Maharaja International,** charging Rs. 15 ($1.15). The hotel serves South Indian snacks as well. There's a Rs.-10 (75¢) thali at the **Swaraswati Hotel,** served from 11 a.m. to 1:30 p.m. and 6:30 to 8:30 p.m.

For various à la carte Indian and Rajasthani foods in the Rs.-20 ($1.55) range for entrees, try the **Dilwara,** a two-minute stroll from the Samrat.

THE SIGHTS OF MOUNT ABU: Follow the main road from the bus stand for a pleasant walk of about three minutes through the bazaar and you will be at **Nakki Lake,** one of the main centers of activity. The many photographers' stalls near the lake display velvet robes in royal blue and deep red trimmed with gold braid—costumes to rent for a picture to take home. Nakki Lake's landmark is **Toad Rock,** so named because it looks like a toad about to leap into the water. Locals are fond of pointing out other rocks with resemblances to Nandi and camels, but they are open to many interpretations.

For Rs. 20 ($1.55) to Rs. 30 ($2.30) per hour you can rent a **boat** with or without a boatman to row you and explore the lake. **Ponies** with handlers to lead you around the lake can be hired for Rs. 15 ($1.15) to Rs. 20 ($1.55). It's a nice walk as well, with a stop to see **Raghunath Temple.** Or you can head away from the Lake up Raj Bhavan Road to the **Art Museum and Gallery** (hours are 10 a.m. to 5 p.m.; closed Friday; free), opposite the post office. In the small collection are some textiles and stone pieces from the 9th to 12th centuries.

Early morning is the best time go three kilometers (two miles) from town to join the pious for the steep climb up 226 stone-cut steps to the old **Adhar Devi Temple** dedicated to Durga. The goddess's shrine is carved into a natural cleft in a huge rock. To enter, you bend down and slide·in.

The two **Dilwara Temples,** five kilometers (three miles) from town, visited from noon to 6 p.m., are the outstanding sight of Mount Abu. Before entering them, you must remove all leather, shoes, belts, handbags, and camera cases, and pay Rs. 5 (40¢) for your camera—although you cannot take pictures of the images.

These temples are very beautiful and some of the most deftly carved in all of India. The older of the two temples was built in 1031 by Vimal, a minister under an early Gujarati ruler, Bhim Deva. One of the earliest Jain temples in India, it is made of pure white marble, austere outside and extravagantly sculptured inside with deities and dancing figures and fantastic lace-like designs. In a hall outside the temple, images of Vimal and his family ride marble elephants in a procession to the handsomely carved domed portico. Inside the temple, within his little shrine, the smooth bronze statue of Adinath sits cross-legged, adorned with jewels and gazing out at passing pilgrims. The elaborately carved dome is supported by richly carved pillars. More carved pillars—48 freestanding in all—lead to the temple courtyard enclosed by a wall with 52 little cells, each a house for seated image of a Jain saint.

The second temple was built about 200 years later by the brothers Tejapal and Vastupal, ministers to Raja Viradhawaler, a ruler of Gujarat. While this temple follows the same general plan as the first, it is even more richly ornamented, resembling a marble tapestry. Here, however, marble carving reaches its apogee in the partly opened lotus flower drooping like a pendant from the dome. The mason-laborers were surely a dedicated group of craftsmen. They were also encouraged to do carvings of the utmost delicacy with gifts gold and silver coins equal to the weight of the marble shavings.

There are three other temples in this complex, but they don't rival the aforementioned two.

Another five kilometers (three miles) from town is the **Achalgarh Fort** housing the **Achaleswhar Temple.** Instead of a lingam in this temple, there's a deep pit which is supposed to go to the netherworld. My guide told me that Shiva jumped in and made the pit, leaving behind his right toe, which is now worshipped here. Shiva's sacred bull, Nandi, is handsome here in bronze; the wounds on his back were made long ago by Muslims searching for riches they thought were inside. A path lined with souvenir stalls leads up to a notable group of Jain temples (there's a Rs.-5, 40¢, camera charge; no leather, no pictures of idols) not as minutely decorated as the Dilwara temples, but eloquent on their own and on a higher plateau with fine views of the valley. Down in the parking area is an empty tank and some stone statues of buffalos and a king taking aim at them with a bow and arrow. The grouping illustrates this old legend about the tank. It was once filled with ghee, which greedy demons disguised as buffalos drank at night until the king put an end to their pleasure by piercing them with his arrows.

Another nine kilometers (5½ miles) is the end of the plateau and **Guru Shikhar,** 5,653 feet, the highest point in Rajasthan. On top is **Ari Rishi Temple,** nearly always full of tourists admiring the view.

Off the main road, beyond the Government of Gujarat Bungalow, a flight of 700 stone stairs gently descends through the lush valley to **Gaumukh Temple,** where a small stream flows through the mouth of a marble cow and gives this temple its name. According to ancient legend the tank here, Agni Kund, marks the spot where the sage Vashista ignited the fire that created the four Rajput clans. On this site is a stone figure of Vashista, with Rama and Krishna on either side. Around the ashram are a number of interesting stone carvings excavated nearby. Before you climb up, monks will ask you to sign their guestbook and give you a write-up to read.

There are many lovely viewpoints in Mount Abu. At least once during any visit every tourist joins the huge crowd on the rocks and steps at **Sunset Point** to see the surroundings at the end of day. **Honeymoon Point** is also popular in the flush of sunset. Other viewpoints are the Crags and Robert's Spur.

TOURS: The **Rajasthan Tourism Development Corporation (RTDC)** conducts daily tours to Dilwara Temples, Alchalgarh, Guru Shikhar, Nakki Lake, Sunset Point, and Adhar Devi, for Rs. 14 ($1.05). They take off two times a day, from 8 a.m. to 1 p.m. and 2 to 7 p.m. Get details at the Tourist Bureau (tel. 51), open from 8 to 11 a.m. and 4 to 8 p.m. in season, 10 a.m. to 5 p.m. out of season; and while you're at it, check to make sure the guide speaks English.

Among the travel agents in town that put together tours by Jeep at Rs. 15 ($1.15) per person is **Gujarat Travels** (tel. 218). All tours are heavily booked in season, so make your reservation in advance. You probably won't get on otherwise.

SHOPPING: The **Rajasthan Emporium,** on Raj Bhavan Road, features such typical crafts as carved agate boxes, soft marble figures of lions and other animals, and bangles.

The main reason to go to the **Chacha Museum,** one of the best-known stores in town, is to check out the one-of-a-kind and unusual items kept in a special room. They may not be antiques, but they'll be treasures you aren't apt to find all over the place. Hours are 9:30 a.m. to 10 p.m. every day, including Sunday. Price fixed.

One of the best selections of silver in town is found at **Roopali,** near Nakki Lake, open from 9 a.m. to 9 p.m. every day. Silver is sold by weight (recently Rs. 6, 45¢ per gram). A number of shops in town will make to order salwar and kamiz in a few hours and sell them ready-made at Rs. 80 ($6.15) and up.

GETTING TO MOUNT ABU: Most people travel by **bus** to Mount Abu from any of a number of cities in Rajasthan and Gujarat. Good roads in Gujarat make Ahmedabad a popular starting point for a seven-hour bus trip, at Rs. 60 ($4.60) in a deluxe bus, run by travel agents. Alternatively, there are four state roadways buses from Ahmedabad, at Rs. 23 ($1.75). From Udaipur, the seven-hour trip by deluxe coach costs Rs. 55 ($4.25); by state-run buses, the trip takes 7 to 11 hours, depending on the route, and costs Rs. 26 ($2).

By **train,** you arrive at Abu Road, the railhead, 27 km (16½ miles) below

Mount Abu, where you can pick up a bus from 6 a.m. to 9 p.m., at Rs. 5 (40¢), for the one-hour trip to Mount Abu. You can also buy a seat in a taxi or Jeep for Rs. 10 (75¢) per person.

When you arrive in Mount Abu you'll be on the main street in town. Here are the bus stand, and opposite it, the tourist bureau (tel. 51), bazaar, travel agents, and many hotels.

Chapter V

HEADING NORTH

1. Hardwar and Rishikesh
2. Chandigarh
3. Amritsar and the Golden Temple
4. Kulu and Manali

THOUSANDS OF HINDUS every year make their pilgrimage to the little town of Hardwar (pop. 114,000), whose major claim to fame is that it's about as near as most people can get to where the holy River Ganges emerges from the mountains and meets the plains.

It's an article of faith among many people who can afford it to carry to Hardwar the ashes of a dead relative and to carry away some sacred water from the river—the same river that is treated with equal devotion in the holy city of Varanasi, which nestles alongside its bank so many hundreds of miles to the south.

1. Hardwar and Rishikesh

From Delhi, 263 km (160 miles) away, the visitor can make his own pilgrimage to Hardwar by either train or road, the road passing through countryside thick with sugarcane fields and clay pits, the latter studded with primitive brick-making plants to mold the raw material.

There are two trains a day from Delhi—Rs. 111 ($8.55) first class, Rs. 27 ($2.05) second class—but the trip takes almost seven hours; the bus is faster by a couple of hours. By car it's a leisurely drive of about four hours; the **Polaris Motel** at **Roorkee,** about 30 km (20 miles) from Hardwar, is a suitable stop for lunch. There's also an outdoor snackbar about two hours out of Delhi (your driver will know it).

A car and driver for a two-day trip to Hardwar/Rishikesh runs about Rs. 1,200 ($92.25), with seating capacity for four. A four-passenger car costs about Rs. 1,470 ($113), air-conditioned—pricey but a possible splurge.

Supposedly Vayudoot flies in, but this was not so recently. Call 699272 in Delhi to check.

HARDWAR: Because pilgrims come to Hardwar in such numbers in the warmer months, it's best to try and reserve a room.

Where to Stay

Be sure to check on out-of-season rates wherever you stay. They are given below, where known. Remember that in both Hardwar and Rishikesh all nonvegetarian foods (including eggs) and alcoholic drinks are prohibited at all times.

There is a Tourist Bungalow, **Belwala** (tel. 379), on the far side of the Ganga Canal—isolated by the wide canal from all the noise and crowds, yet near enough so you won't miss the action. There are 22 simple rooms, for which the rates are Rs. 75 ($5.75) for a double and Rs. 125 ($9.60) for deluxe double. Meals will cost you about Rs. 10 (75¢) to Rs. 12 (90¢) more.

Among the long row of Indian hotels on the opposite (main) bank of the canal, the **Arya Niwas,** near Modi Bhawan (tel. 272), is recommended for foreigners. It's extensively used by pilgrims, who cook in the simple kitchen (strictly vegetarian, of course). Arya Niwas is on the riverbank right across from the Tourist Bungalow and has simple but extremely clean two-bed and four-bunk rooms for Rs. 15 ($1.15) per person, a bathroom shared by two.

Another good place for tourists to stay is at the **Inspection Bungalow** (tel. 107), at the junction of the two canals at the bottom end of town. This house, comfortable and well situated, is maintained by the Irrigation Department for its visiting inspectors, but the two rooms are usually available when no inspecting is going on—at around Rs. 15 ($1.15) per person. You'd have to bring your sleeping bag, sheet, and towel as no linens are provided here.

A new choice is the **Hotel Arti,** Enterprises, Railway Road (tel. 456), with 33 rooms, all doubles and all air-cooled. The no-frills rooms are clean. In season, double occupancy is Rs. 125 ($9.60) and single occupancy costs Rs. 100 ($7.70); off-season, Rs. 25 ($1.90) is taken off each of these rates. Half the bathrooms are Western style, and hot water is available without extra charge in buckets. There is no restaurant, but you can get snacks.

Another newcomer, **Gurder,** Railway Road (tel. 101), has 30 rooms. The seven rooms with air-conditioning cost Rs. 180 ($13.85) single and Rs. 250 ($19.25) double; non-air-conditioned rooms run Rs. 80 ($6.15) single, Rs. 120 ($9.25) double, and Rs. 150 ($11.55) triple. Off-season there are discounts ranging from Rs. 20 ($1.55) to Rs. 40 ($3.05). Hot water is available free in buckets. No restaurant, but there's room service for food service.

Recently renovated, the **Kailash Hotel,** Shiv Murti, near the railway station (tel. 789), is clean and comfortable. There are 70 air-cooled rooms, all with baths attached, half with Western-style toilets. The furnishings are modern and in the 24 deluxe rooms are such amenities as telephones, carpeting, TVs, and running hot water. Rates are Rs. 120 ($9.25) single, Rs. 150 ($11.55) to Rs. 170 ($13.05), the higher rate for a deluxe room. The restaurant is open from 6 a.m. to 10 p.m. Off-season reductions range from Rs. 40 ($3.05) on the singles up to Rs. 50 ($3.85) on the deluxe rooms.

On Jassa Ram Road are three hotels, the Panama, Ashok, and Mansarovar. The best of the lot is the **Hotel Panama,** Hardwar 249001 (tel. 1506), has simply furnished rooms with Indian-style toilets and is certainly all right for a short stay. Rates are Rs. 35 ($2.70) to Rs. 40 ($3.05) single, Rs. 55 ($4.25) double; hot water costs Rs. 1.50 (11¢) per bucket. Off-season rates are Rs. 10 (75¢) to Rs. 15 ($1.15) less.

The other two are not highly recommended. The **Hotel Ashok,** Jassa Ram Road, Hardwar 249001 (tel. 788), has 30 rooms with attached baths, six with Western toilets, all with hot running water supplied from geysers. Rates are Rs. 25 ($1.90) single, Rs. 40 ($3.05) to Rs. 55 ($4.25) double, and Rs. 60 ($4.60) to Rs. 90 ($6.90) double with air cooling. There are reductions of Rs. 20 ($1.55) to Rs. 40 ($3.05) off-season, depending on the room size. The restaurant serves a variety of regional vegetarian foods, and is open from 6 a.m. to 10 p.m. The **Hotel Mansarovar,** Jassa Ram Road, Hardwar 249001 (tel. 1487), has 12 rooms with showers and Indian toilets in attached bathrooms.

Towels and soap are provided on request, as is hot water in buckets. Doubles cost Rs. 48 ($3.70) in season, Rs. 30 ($2.30) to Rs. 35 ($2.70) off-season.

The tourist office near the railway station can refer you to **dharmashalas** (simple housing for pilgrims) that take in foreigners. The floor is your bed, you share the bathrooms, and the charge is your small contribution.

Eating Out

Chotiwala Restaurant, Railway Station Road across from the tourist office, has tasty vegetarian curries for Rs. 5 (40¢) to Rs. 8 (60¢), and rice dishes for Rs. 1 (7½¢) to Rs. 7 (55¢). It's open from 8 a.m. to 10 p.m.

Two blocks up the road is the **Brijwasi Mathura Wak Sweet Center,** with all kinds of Indian sweets in clean glass cases. One of these is chandralaka, at Rs. 2 (15¢) per piece, a crisp pastry with syrup and nut filling.

When to Visit

Best time to be in Hardwar is for the Hindu New Year, sometime between March 20 and April 10, or in mid-April for Bishwawat Sankranti, a huge fair. But the fall, too, is very pleasant from September to November, and because this is a holy city there can be festivals at any time.

Around the Town

There are two main centers of attraction in Hardwar. First is the **Har Ki Pairi,** or main bathing ghat, and second, the winding streets of the fascinating bazaar that lead off it.

The time to get to Har Ki Pairi, the steps on which the priests perform their blessings, called "Arti of Ganja," is about 6 p.m. Then the whole area, including the area beside the clock tower across the water, as well as the Centenary Bridge that leads to it is thronged with pilgrims.

Many of the faithful float lotus leaves as candlelit boats on the river. Each tiny boat filled with flower petals finally becomes a mere twinkle downstream.

Conch horns sound, bells ring, holy chants fill the air. Saffron-robed sadhus and beggars compete for the goodwill of Hindus intent on immersing themselves in the holy waters—which flow so fast that chains anchored to the steps are used for support by bathers.

All around are stalls from which visitors can buy every possible kind of container to carry home the holy water. It is said to be so pure that it will remain fresh for years. There are brass and copper bowls as well as cheap vessels converted from old ghee or beer cans sold for a few paise.

RISHIKESH: About 16 miles away (regular connecting buses) is Rishikesh (pop. 29,000), whose very name brings to mind religious sages. It's a small and not particularly fascinating town, although there are some pretty views where the River Ganges first emerges from the Himalayan foothills. The **Divine Life Society** is probably the best-known organization in a town positively filled with ashrams and other religious organizations. Started by Swami Sivananda in 1936, it maintains a lovely blue-domed temple on the hillside, always filled with adherents from many countries chanting prayers, consonant with the society's theme that all religions are one and have more to share than to fight about. Just in front of the temple, at river's edge, is the society's office with plenty of literature available, and if you wait patiently, a boat (free) will ferry you across the swift-flowing Ganges to some well-worth-visiting temples and ashrams on the opposite bank. A one-mile walk on the far side will bring you to the ashram of the Maharishi Mahesh Yogi, one-time guru to the Beatles and other well-known Westerners.

Plans are under way for Rishikesh to have an evening "Arti of Ganga" ceremony as in Hardwar—with torches and little lotus-leaf candlelit floats. To find out if this ritual is a reality, ask at your hotel reception or the tourist bureau at the bus station.

Where to Stay

The best hotel in town is the centrally located **Inderlok Hotel,** Railway Road, Rishikesh 249201 (tel. 555), with a plant-decked patio and roof garden with mountain views. The 50 double rooms are clean and functionally furnished with moderate rates of Rs. 100 ($7.70) to Rs. 150 ($11.55) single, Rs. 150 ($11.55) to Rs. 205 ($15.75) double, the higher rates for air conditioning. They all have attached bathrooms. The Indrani restaurant serves Indian foods and some Western dishes.

Hotel Menka, opposite the Roadways Bus Stand, Rishikesh 249201 (tel. 285), has, of all things, an oversize photo of Marilyn Monroe behind the reception desk. The tidy rooms cost Rs. 35 ($2.70) double and Rs. 25 ($1.90) single, and you'll need your own towel as none is supplied. About half the toilets are Indian style. There's no restaurant, but they'll bring breakfast to your room.

Hotel Ashoka, also near the Roadways Bus Stand, Rishikesh 249201 (tel. 715), is clean and the rooms have overhead fans and connecting private bathrooms with Indian-style toilets. Rates are Rs. 40 ($3.05) double and Rs. 25 ($1.90) if occupied by one person.

A new hotel near the Roadways Bus Stand parking lot is **Rajhan's,** Rishikesh 249201 (tel. 126), with 17 double rooms, all with attached bathrooms, Indian-style toilets, and cold showers. A bucket of hot water costs Rs. 2 (15¢). Price is Rs. 35 ($2.70) per person.

The almost brand-new **Hotel Girwar,** 154 Ashutosh Nagar, Rishikesh 249201 (tel. 1076), has 21 double rooms, six of them air-cooled. All rooms have attached Indian-style bathrooms with running hot water. The no-frills rooms cost Rs. 40 ($3.05) to Rs. 80 ($6.15), Rs. 20 ($1.55) less off-season. The pleasant, helpful proprietor is a plus here.

Finally, popular with trekkers is the **Tourist Bungalow Complex,** Rishilok, Rishikesh 249201 (tel. 373), of cottages, some having rooms with private bathrooms and some share-a-bathroom accommodations. Rates are Rs. 40 ($3.05) double and Rs. 35 ($2.70) single. Chinese and Indian foods are served, and full board will cost Rs. 35 ($2.70) to Rs. 45 ($3.45), depending on the type of food you select.

Two miles from the center of town on a steep hill overlooking the river is the **Hotel Luxman Jhula,** Rishikesh 249201 (tel. 442). The rooms aren't fancy, but the view is fine. Rates range from Rs. 55 ($4.25) air-cooled to Rs. 155 ($11.90) air-conditioned, all with attached bathrooms, most of which have Western toilets; hot water is in buckets. The more expensive rooms are carpeted and have telephones.

Useful Information

In Hardwar, the address of the **regional tourist bureau** is Lalta Roa Bridge, Station Road (tel. 19), and an information counter (tel. 817) is in the railway station. At Rishikesh, the **tourist bureau** is on Railway Road (tel. 208) and in the Yatayat bus station (tel. 209) . . . To sightsee an entire day in either Hardwar or Rishikesh by scooter rickshaw should cost Rs. 50 ($3.85), after bargaining to set the rate . . . For a conducted tour, contact the **Uttar Pradesh State Road Transportation Corporation** in Hardwar (tel. 37). You might try some of the local travel agents as well. Bamboo baskets are the local craft.

2. Chandigarh

"The ivory tower school of architecture" is the way iconoclasts describe Chandigarh (pop. 421,000), capital of Punjab and Haryana states. Supporters say it's the prototype of all Indian cities to come. Looking around is the best way to understand these widely disparate views. Chances are, if you're an architect, you'll like the city better than other travelers do.

Chandigarh, coordinated by Le Corbusier, was designed by a team of international architects, including the master's cousin, Pierre Jeanneret, England's E. Maxwell Fry and Jane Drew, and a number of Indians. It was planned, like Brasilia, solely as a capital.

Gaudily painted cycle rickshaws are about the only visible links to the past here, outside of the saris, churidars, and other traditional clothing, museum exhibits, an occasional camel looking as abstract and committee-constructed in shape as some of the buildings, and numerous wandering highly revered cows, which span all centuries. In Chandigarh there are no winding lanes, cozy bazaars, and rakish houses, but a rigidly laid-out, 50-sector city that looks cubistic and cold. The designers made extensive use of readily available concrete in its natural state, and as a result Chandigarh looks like a cement prairie, relieved only by some pastel-painted buildings.

The modern structures look more harmonious together than they might if grafted onto an older city—which almost was the case. After the Partition of 1947, when Lahore, then the capital of the Punjab, went to Pakistan, both Simla and Jullundur were used as new seats of government. When it was decided to start from scratch, the site for Chandigarh, at the base of the Shivalik Hills, was selected for its good soil and water supply, accessibility, and beauty. Construction was carried out mainly between 1951 and 1965.

Chandigarh was named a double capital when Haryana state was created out of the eastern portion of the Punjab in 1966. The state was further divided in that same year—the hilly areas are now part of Himachal Pradesh. Simla, the hill station summer seat of government during British days, is now year-round capital of Himachal Pradesh.

Note: As of this writing, travel to this area is restricted to foreign travelers with special permits. Permits are obtained by writing, at least six weeks in advance, to Ministry of Home Affairs Govt. of India (F-IV Section), New Delhi 110001.

WHAT TO SEE: The focal point of Chandigarh is the **Government Complex** at the city's northern end. The Secretariat, an elongated structure, cost Rs. 14,049,000 to build. Tours are given every half hour; ask at Main Reception. Usually 15 go together, but if that number doesn't show, you can go with those on hand, or by yourself for that matter. The nicest part about this building is the roof garden. It provides a refreshing vantage point for surveying the other buildings and the bustling officials below.

Nearby, the multipillared **High Court,** with its strange stucco sun screen, stands in a reflecting pool. This is the most frequently photographed of the government buildings. Primary-color panels break up gray expanses. There is no organized tour—you are permitted to look around on your own. This building cost Rs. 6,465,000.

Atop the huge chamber room in the **Assembly,** there's a dome that can be removed to let in light. Here you also can see a mural by Le Corbusier. It was given to Chandigarh by the French government and symbolizes evolution. The cost of this building—nearly 12 million rupees. There are tours on the half hour from 10:30 a.m. to 12:30 p.m. and again from 2:30 to 4:30 p.m., or you can go on your own. Ask at the public reception desk.

Under construction in this same sector is a huge **Open Hand,** to symbolize the unity of man. A Museum of Knowledge is to be built.

The **Cultural Zone,** in the west part of town, harbors a museum and an art gallery, well worth seeing. Exhibits, which include modern works, go back 5,000 years or more to the Indus Valley Civilization. Hours: 10 a.m. to 4:30 p.m.; closed Monday. Admission: 20 paise (1½¢).

Connected with the Cultural Sector is a park in which the colleges are situated. More colleges—Engineering, Architecture, Medicine, and Research —to the north.

In other sectors, each approximately half a mile wide and three miles long, are housing, medical, shopping, and educational facilities for the residents. The city, home to 421,000, was planned for 500,000 maximum. There are 14 ranks of housing for government employees, from multiroom mansions for chief ministers to two rooms for the lowest-paid employees. Each sector supplies each family's basic needs, as did the old-style villages of India. Newly arrived villagers, seeking work, live outside of town.

Beyond the Government Enclave—Fantasies and Flowers

Three of the best sights in and about Chandigarh are striking gardens, two in the city and one about ten miles from town.

Almost in the shadows of Le Corbusier's geometric buildings in Sector 1 is the extraordinary 12-acre (and still growing) **Garden of Nek Chand,** the highly talented, self-taught artist who has created an epic out of found objects. One of the most remarkable aspects of Chand's park is that he got hold of so many castoffs. In India, almost nothing is thrown away: what can't be used again may be sold for some other use.

Entering Chand's fantastic park, you first encounter several hundred courtesans made from bicycle frames. But this is no X-rated show: in fact, meandering on the curving paths may take you back to the imagined wonderlands of your childhood.

In this remarkable community are hundreds of glistening birds made from over a million broken-glass bangles, thousands of dancers molded from motorcycle mudguards, and intricate mosaics created from 10,000 electrical outlets. There are block-long fences constructed from burnt-out fluorescent tubing, and warriors fashioned from cloth scraps astride scrap cloth steeds.

To go from one delightful section to another, you have to bend through archways suitable for Lilliputians. Chand's reason for constructing the three-foot-high passageways was to make sure that visitors bowed to the many gods and goddesses making their kingdom in his garden.

About two hours is needed to savor the garden, pausing in shady nooks where terracotta tykes forever play soccer in pottery-shard shorts, cork musicians strum sitars, and airy castles are splashed with waterfalls. Be sure you see the lovely Japanese-style garden imagined by this Indian artist who's never been to the Orient or seen pictures of this kind of architecture.

Chand, in his late 50s, constructed his garden over the last 30 or so years. At first he worked secretly at night because he was afraid that if his creation was discovered it might be destroyed by officials as not in keeping with the carefully planned new city. In 1972, as his accomplishments became known and acknowledged by respected artists and intellectuals, a city official also recognized his genius and got the local government to back him. Now Chand gets a salary of about $150 a month and a staff of 100 assistants. He plans eventually to cover 40 acres with castles, creatures, waterfalls, and other figments of his fertile imagination.

Chand is also becoming known outside India: he has exhibited his work at the Museum of Modern Art in Paris and was given a high French award. A book on his garden has also been published in France, and Australians have made a documentary about him. Recently Chand was honored with India's highest artistic award.

But he prefers to stay home and add to his garden and have everyone come to admire his work. In his huge guest ledger are comments from visitors the world over. You may ask for the book if you'd like to add your reactions.

In his youth Chand was a road laborer. Later, as a supervisor at a warehouse and storage yard that stood on his present site, he began scavenging the surrounding area for interesting discards from which his wonderful garden grew.

To see Nek Chand's Sculpture Garden (open every day from 10 a.m. to sunset) costs 25 paise (about 2¢). Early morning or late afternoon are recommended times. There are plenty of benches so you can relax while admiring the remarkable creations. Snacks and soft drinks are available in the garden.

Since Chand works alongside his staff as many as 12 hours a day, he's often around and glad to answer visitors' questions about new sections or show them his workrooms. If he's busy, one of his assistants gladly supplies the facts about the fantasies.

In Sector 16 is the handsomely landscaped **Zakir Rose Garden.** With 30 acres it's supposed to be the largest garden in Asia. Featured in the immense tract are 2,400 varieties of roses.

The peak time to see many of the roses in full bloom is February during the Rose Festival, when activities include naming a Prince and Princess of Roses. Zakir Rose Garden is open year round. From April 1 to September 30 the hours are 5 a.m. to 9 p.m., and from October 1 to March 31, 6 a.m. to 8 p.m. From 5 to 9 p.m. throughout the year the ornamental fountain is turned on.

Travel ten miles from Chandigarh and you'll find yourself back in the 17th century at **Mughal Pinjore Gardens.** They're cool and green and as carefully planned as Chandigarh, but delightfully frivolous compared with the severely designed city. The Pinjore Gardens, once the private preserve of the Maharaja of Patiala, are now a popular picnic spot.

The gardens are open from 8 a.m. to 10 p.m. daily. Special lighting effects on Saturday and Sunday evenings draw crowds. Best time for a visit is during the week when fewer people go. Buses for the garden leave the Bus Terminus, Sector 17, about every half hour and cost about Rs. 3.50 (25¢) one way. In a four-seater taxi, it's about Rs. 75 ($5.75) round trip, including a one-hour stay.

WHERE TO STAY: A clean room at almost any price is hard to find in Chandigarh.

You can try the **Union Territory State Guest House,** Sector 6, Chandigarh 160007 (tel. 27231, 27232, or 27233), primarily for government officials, also takes other travelers in its 27 rooms, if vacancies permit. It's not overly tidy, but better than some hotels in town. Rates are Rs. 70 ($5.40) single and Rs. 110 ($8.45) double. Rooms are air-conditioned, and have ceiling fans and attached private bathrooms. The seven acres of landscaped gardens surrounding the guesthouse is its outstanding feature. Meals cost Rs. 12 (90¢) for breakfast, Rs. 22 ($1.70) for a nonvegetarian Indian lunch or dinner, and Rs. 20 ($1.55) for vegetarian meals. Continental food, not advised, is slightly higher. On each meal, there's a 20% tax. For reservations, write: Director of Hospitality and Tourism, Chandigarh Administration (U.T. State Guest House) Union Territory, Sector 6, Chandigarh 160007.

Very so-so are the 14 rooms at the **Hotel Alankar,** Sector 22-A, (tel. 21303), where doubles cost Rs. 60 ($4.60) to Rs. 70 ($5.40) and singles are Rs. 45 ($3.45), all with bathrooms attached and hot and cold running water. The more expensive doubles have room telephones and air conditioning. Next door, the **Hotel Amar,** Sector 22-A, (tel. 26608), has similar rates and amenities: Rs. 45 ($3.45) for singles, Rs. 60 ($4.60) to Rs. 70 ($5.40) for doubles. The higher priced rooms are air-conditioned.

Also in Sector 22-A, the **Hotel Pankaj** (tel. 41906) is a cut above the aforementioned two with a red-carpeted stairway and small wood-paneled lobby. All 14 rooms are doubles and have bathrooms attached. Doubles cost Rs. 195 ($15) air-conditioned and Rs. 155 ($11.90) air-cooled. Single occupancy runs Rs. 180 ($13.85) air-conditioned, Rs. 145 ($11.15) air-cooled. The Noor restaurant, attached to the hotel, serves everything from snacks to full meals, and for about Rs. 20 ($1.55) you can have Chinese almond chicken, the house specialty. Noor is open from 7 a.m. to 11:30 p.m. every day.

Hotel Piccadily, Himalaya Marg, Sector 22-B (tel. 32223 to 32227), is supposed to be a four-star hotel. The public rooms are nice, but the bedrooms and halls upstairs need better maintenance. Rates are Rs. 240 ($18.45) single and Rs. 320 ($24.60) double. The premises are air-conditioned and all the rooms have bathrooms attached.

In Sector 22-C is the **Hotel Aroma** (tel. 26415), which is overpriced for what it offers in the way of comfort and cleanliness. This is not your choice if you're fussy to any degree. Rates are Rs. 90 ($6.90) to Rs. 125 ($9.60) single, Rs. 100 ($7.70) to Rs. 135 ($10.40) double; the higher-priced rooms are air-conditioned and have private bathrooms, some with Western fixtures.

The centrally air-conditioned **President Hotel,** Madya Marg, Sector 26 (tel. 40840), has a gleaming marble lobby and doubles for Rs. 395 ($30.40) and singles for Rs. 295 ($22.70). There are print bedspreads, bird prints, and cushy carpeting in all the bedrooms, which also have attached modern bathrooms. There are two restaurants—Indian and Chinese—and a health club on the premises. From here it will cost about Rs. 5 (40¢) by motorized scooter rickshaw to Sector 17, the part of town for the most action.

Chandigarh Mountview, Sector 10, Chandigarh 160010 (tel. 41773), once part of the well-known Oberoi chain, is now government run. Set in a lovely old-fashioned garden, the modern, well-appointed rooms cost Rs. 250 ($19.25) single and Rs. 320 ($24.60). There's a buffet on Saturday, and the hotel is a popular local gathering place all the time.

Not seen by me, but worth checking into, the **Hotel Sunbeam,** Udyog Path, Sector 22-B (tel. 32057), charges Rs. 240 ($18.45) single and Rs. 340 ($28.15) double. All rooms are centrally air-conditioned and have most other modern amenities.

WHERE TO EAT: Sector 17 (location of all the following places) is the place to head for a snack or a meal. For inexpensive snacks, there are three **Indian Coffee Houses,** open from 9 a.m. to 10:30 p.m. in summer and 9 a.m. to 10 p.m. in winter. South Indian coffee (with hot milk) is a specialty. **Piccad's** stand-up bar, serving samosas (turnovers), pakoras (fritters), sandwiches, and ice cream, is open from 9 a.m. to 11 p.m. Try **Milk Food,** open from 9:30 a.m. to midnight, for ice cream in butterscotch delight and a dozen more flavors, for Rs. 4 (30¢) and up per dip.

Kwality (tel. 31383) serves affordable full meals as well as snacks, from 8 a.m. to 11 p.m. Also for meals and snacks, there are two nicely decorated, dimly lit restaurants with extensive Indian, continental, and Chinese menus: **Mehfil** (tel. 29439), open from 9 a.m. to 11 p.m. daily; and **Gazhal** (tel. 42548), open from 8 a.m. to midnight. The former has blue banquettes and mirrored murals; the latter a fancy doorway, wooden grillwork, and mirrors. At both, most dishes—the usual Indian, Chinese, and continental—run Rs. 14 ($1.05), but grills go as high as Rs. 20 ($1.55).

Other restaurants to check out as splurges would be the **Mezbaan,** in the Hotel Picadilly (tel. 44996), open from 12:30 to 3 p.m. and 7 to 11 p.m.; and the **Shaolin,** in the Hotel President (tel. 33233), open from noon to 3 p.m. and 8 p.m. to midnight.

TOURS: Tuesday to Friday local sightseeing tours go to the Zakir Rose Garden, the University Campus, the Museum and Art Gallery, Secretariat, High Court, Assembly Hall, Nek Chand's Sculpture Garden, and Sukhna Lake. The tour takes three hours, costs Rs. 8 (60¢), and lasts from 10:30 a.m. to 1:30 p.m. or 3 to 6 p.m. in summer and 10 a.m. to 1 p.m. or 2:30 to 5 p.m. in winter. On Sunday the local tour is from 2:30 to 5 p.m.

Saturday's tour, at Rs. 30 ($2.30), lasting from 8 a.m. to 6 p.m., goes to Bhakra-Nanagal dam, at 740 feet high said to be the highest dam in the world. It was supervised by the well-known American dam builder Harvey Slocum. The massive dam provides valuable electrical energy and irrigation, which has speeded the development of this part of India.

On Sunday there are tours to Chhat Bir Zoo and the Pinjore Gardens, from 9 a.m. to 12:30 p.m., each Rs. 6 (45¢). To make reservations, check with the Tourist Reception Office in the Bus Terminus, Sector 17 (tel. 21076), or your hotel reception.

GETTING AROUND: Scooter rickshaws are metered and the minimum fare is Rs. 1.50 (about 10¢) for the first 1.5 km and 10 paise for every part thereof. Waiting while the meter is on adds another 10 paise for every eight minutes. If you take a scooter rickshaw to the airport, there's a charge of 25% more than the one-way fare. Rates may be higher by publication time, and they're also negotiable.

Cycle rickshaw rates vary, but start at Rs. 1.50 (10¢); better set the fare before getting in.

Tourist cars charge Rs. 1.60 (12¢) per kilometer for straight runs and Rs. 2 (15¢) per kilometer if you head for the hills. Buses are crowded, as in all Indian cities, connect various sectors, and cost 30 paise (2½¢) to 80 paise (6¢).

USEFUL INFORMATION: English-language films play at the four theaters in Sector 17 about once a week. Admission is Rs. 4.60 (35¢) and Rs. 2.50 (about 20¢), and you book seats in advance . . . In Sector 17 are banks and a number of state emporia, among them those selling wares from the Punjab, Haryana, Uttar Pradesh, and Kashmir . . . Also in Sector 17, the Tourist Reception Office, Administration, First Floor, Bus Stand (tel. 21076), can provide help.

WHEN TO VISIT: October to March is the best time for Punjab and neighboring Haryana. April, however, is the time of the Baisakhi festival, when bhangra dancers perform with wild abandon—their movements include standing on their fellow dancers' shoulders to form a human tower.

GETTING TO CHANDIGARH: Ordinary buses from Delhi, 250 km (152 miles) away, run every 10 to 15 minutes, take five hours, and cost about Rs. 25

($1.90); air-conditioned buses are less frequent and more costly, at Rs. 65 ($5). Buses also come from many other northern cities, most frequently from Amritsar, 240 km (145 miles) away, take five hours, and cost about Rs. 20 ($1.55) for an ordinary bus and Rs. 30 ($2.30) for a deluxe; and from Pathankot for similar fares.

Trains from Delhi cost Rs. 104 ($8) in first class, Rs. 26 ($2) in second. The train station is ten kilometers from the city, but trains are met by taxis, rickshaws, and scooters.

Chandigarh is connected by Indian Airlines flights with Delhi, Jammu, Srinagar, and Kulu. The fare from Delhi is Rs. 272 ($21); from Kulu, also Rs. 272 ($21). Vayudoot also flies in here, with prices the same as Indian Airlines.

3. Amritsar and the Golden Temple

Amritsar (pop. 589,000), the busiest city in Punjab, is famous for its Golden Temple (formerly known as Hari Mandir), which is of great religious importance to the Sikhs, who form the bulk of the population here. The city (its name means Tank of Nectar) was founded in 1579, and the old city is still surrounded by a wall in which there are about 20 city gates.

Aside from the old sights, looking around Amritsar provides a prime glimpse at what may be India's most prosperous region. Modern farming methods are reaping success for the Punjabis and bringing some of the luxury goods that go with it to mingle with the old traditions. All around Amritsar (and elsewhere in Punjab) turbaned Sikhs drive their motor scooters and automobiles like fury, and numerous television antennas (Punjab is third after Delhi and Bombay when it comes to television sets) share the skyline with the resplendent gold-domed temple. Beyond these material possessions is undoubtedly a more important result of the new prosperity: all the villages in Punjab have electricity.

Modern history in Punjab since 1983 has seen hostility toward the central government increase as Sikhs pressed for greater autonomy.

Note: As of this writing, travel to this area is restricted to foreign travelers with special permits. See introductory chapter for permit information.

THE TEMPLE: The Golden Temple, besides being the centerpiece of Sikh devotion—it is every Sikh's desire to visit it at least once—is one of the most interesting temples in the world. This is not said lightly. Contained in an immense wall-enclosed patio, the temple sits in the center of a vast pool, several feet deep, a causeway connecting it to the marble-tiled courtyard.

At one end of the compound is the ornate Akal Takht (Immortal Throne) for the temple priests. Normally, the compound is a scene of fascinating activity. All around the pool, squatting cross-legged on the carved and decorated marble tiles, sit hundreds of men, women, and children—thinking, sleeping, talking, eating, and reading. Occasionally an elderly woman will step gingerly into the water and immerse herself. Men in bright-blue robes, sheathed swords at their waist and steel-tipped pikes in their hands, stride proudly past. Flower-sellers dispense garlands of golden marigolds. Old ladies sit behind a stall filled with shiny brass saucers offering free drinks of water.

The panorama continues for 24 hours each day the temple is open. And when it is closed, many of the homeless visitors stay in a free hostel that adjoins the temple precincts, and as many as 10,000 hungry will file through to sit on stone floors and be served a kind of gruel by volunteers passing back and forth with buckets and ladles. Even between mealtimes the kitchens are a beehive of activity, with volunteers preparing the chapatis. An old man sits beside a boiling tank of syrup making sugar candies, while piles of firewood are busily being stacked to keep the ovens going. All this charity is a constant feature of Sikh temples: there is even a section to which private citizens are invited to bring their home-cooked food and give it away to the poor.

Before entering the temple precincts, visitors must empty their pockets of cigarettes (Sikhs are not supposed to smoke or drink); they must cover their heads and go barefooted or don special socks that have never been used before. And right at the entrance, feet must be dipped in a tank of water, a ceremonial cleansing.

Then, crossing the covered portico where whole families lie resting on straw mats under the spreading branches of the 400-year-old jamun tree, visitors make their way around the edge of the tank (pool), noting underfoot the occasional marble tile engraved with a donor's name. They pass the Akal Takht, which has been the administrative center of Sikhdom since it was built three centuries ago. Then they traverse the walkway into the center of the pool and the Golden Temple itself, so called because the dome and upper part are covered with fine filigree and enamel work in gold.

There is no admission charge to the temple, but it is customary to make a small donation in return for several hours of entertainment and enlightenment.

The temple was built in the 16th century by Guru Arjan, the fifth of ten gurus, or masters, who shaped and directed the Sikh religion over a period of two centuries. Many times the temple changed hands, the Sikhs driven out and the premises desecrated by different rulers. In 1740 the local Mughal commandant was using it as a dance hall when two valiant Sikhs disguised themselves to enter the precincts and assassinate him. On another famous occasion, in 1758, a Sikh named Baba Dip Singh led an avenging body through to the temple where, legend says, he finally let go of his already-severed head "and went to the eternal abode of martyrs." A mausoleum named after him stands within the temple precincts. Nine years later the Sikhs reconquered Punjab and have remained in possession of the temple ever since.

THE FLAME OF LIBERTY: Amritsar's other major monument is the **Jallianwala Bagh** (Flame of Liberty), which is not far from the Ghee Mandi Gate in the crowded city center. The monument, an impressive red sandstone pillar, commemorates the miserable day in 1919 when British General Dyre ordered his soldiers to fire on a gathering of about 1,500 people who were meeting at this spot to demonstrate for Indian independence. Independence finally came, but not until 29 years later when the British left.

WHERE TO STAY: The most pleasant place is just outside town—**Mrs. Bhandari's Guest House,** 10 Cantonment, Amritsar 143001 (tel. 43737). The rate is for $10-a-dayers if you stay without meals: Rs. 45 ($3.45) single, Rs. 80 ($6.15) double. This might present a problem, however, as there are few other places to eat. With meals, add another Rs. 50 ($3.85) to Rs. 60 ($4.60) per person. For these rates, you get a nice clean room in a well-maintained place that was Mrs. Bhandari's private home until the early 1950s. She grows her own fruits and vegetables, and has her own cows and poultry too. Mrs. B. will also arrange transfers to and from the airport and sightseeing for additional fees.

Here is a partial listing of hotels in town:

Airlines, Cooper Road, Amritsar 143001 (tel. 44545), is not excessively tidy, but it does have carpeting, air conditioning, and private bathrooms. Without air conditioning, singles are Rs. 75 ($5.75); doubles, Rs. 100 ($7.70).

With air conditioning it's Rs. 125 ($9.60) and Rs. 150 ($11.55), single and double respectively.

Hotel Amritsar International, City Centre, Amritsar 143001 (tel. 31991, 31992, or 52814), run by the Punjab Development Corporation, is an angular modern building with reasonably clean rooms and fairly high prices. All the rooms are air-conditioned, with modern functional furniture, scenic wall murals, and attached bathrooms. There's a 24-hour coffeeshop. Rates are Rs. 100 ($7.70) to Rs. 120 ($9.25) single and Rs. 125 ($9.60) to Rs. 250 ($19.25) double. On the expensive side also is the **Hotel Mohan International,** Albert Road, Amritsar 143001 (tel. 34146, 52864, or 52865), where singles are Rs. 195 ($15) and doubles are Rs. 275 ($21.15). It's centrally air-conditioned and has a 24-hour coffeeshop.

Other choices are the 20-room **Hotel Blue Moon,** The Mall (tel. 33759), where rates are Rs. 125 ($9.60) single and Rs. 175 ($13.45) double with air conditioning, Rs. 80 ($6.15) single and Rs. 85 ($6.55) double without; or the 44-room **Grand Hotel,** Queens Road, Amritsar 143001 (tel. 33821), conveniently located near the railway station, which charges Rs. 60 ($4.60) to Rs. 125 ($9.60) single and Rs. 90 ($6.90) to Rs. 150 ($11.55) double, the higher rate for air conditioning. Both hotels have such amenities as attached bathrooms, telephones in the rooms, and service charges of 10%. They both also have restaurants.

Super Budget

The **Youth Hostel,** Mall Mandi, Grand Trunk Road (tel. 48165), charges Rs. 7.50 (60¢) per person. **P.W.D. Bungalow,** Court Road, will take you in if there's is no official in town, for Rs. 20 ($1.55) to Rs. 30 ($2.30).

INFORMATION: The Government of Punjab Tourist Bureau is in the Palace Hotel, opposite the railway station (tel. 42164).

GETTING TO AMRITSAR: The frequent bus service from Chandigarh takes five hours and costs around Rs. 32 ($2.45) deluxe. There are daily trains from Delhi, nine hours away, for Rs. 168 ($12.90) in first class, Rs. 42 ($3.25) in second. The train goes on to Jammu Tawi, the jumping-off point for Srinagar. Daily flights from Delhi take under an hour and cost Rs. 455 ($35); from Srinagar, Rs. 388 ($30).

4. Kulu and Manali

Two of the most enchanting mountain towns in the world—Kulu (4,000 feet) and Manali (6,000 feet)—in the "valley of the gods" offer everything mortals need for heavenly holidays. Perched above the thundering Beas (pronounced Beahs) River in the lower Himalayas, these mountain hamlets are only half as far from Delhi as celebrated Kashmir, but they seem many times more remote—and are much less expensive.

For centuries, missionaries, traders, and adventurers have traveled through here, but not one developer has exploited the potential of this remarkably beautiful real estate. Basically, the fertile valley, about 1 mile wide and about 50 miles long, is a major fruit-producing region.

Everywhere en route in the fall are little apple-juice bars for the traveler's refreshment. Spring turns the valley into a flower basket filled with bouquets of blossoming fruit trees against a background of giant red rhododendrons brightening the upper slopes. In summer, tiny buttercups spread an elusive mist from gold to red and spears of purple iris sway in the fields. The winter colors Kulu nutty brown with a cloak of green from the cedars and pines.

In any season and at any time the sturdy valley people are the main delight. The aspect of their life you'll find most interesting is their division of labor: women tend the house and fields while men stay indoors and weave wool into warm shawls, blankets, and textiles for their homespun clothing. Not surprisingly, hand-woven shawls are among the items, as are the distinctive embroidered caps and heavy silver jewelry, often sold by the towns' Tibetan merchants.

In the late 1960s the valley was high on the list of hangouts for Western wanderers shuttling between Goa and Nepal. The permanent Western hippie residents community in the surrounding villages shuttled here back then and never shuttled on. Enjoying another kind of highlife are trekkers, especially in the spring and fall, and the Japanese who come to ski in winter.

Yet the only time during the year there's anything approaching a crowd is during the week-long Dussehra festival in October or November. This annual fall festival, hailing Rama's victory over the evil King Ravana, marked all over India, is so spectacularly celebrated in Kulu that it attracts visitors from all over the country, and since the 1960s many Westerners have been turning up for the event as well. The main festival attraction is a procession in Kulu of more than 100 gods from all the valley temples. Thus the name "valley of the gods." There is also dancing and music and an extra-tempting array of wares on sale in the market.

Still, modern times are knocking on the valley's door. Video-equipped buses and jet planes are bringing more travelers in. But for a few more years anyway you can enjoy the simple pleasures of the past.

BUDGETING YOUR VALLEY VISIT: The Himachal Pradesh government levies a luxury tax on rooms: 3% on rates from Rs. 25 ($1.90) to Rs. 50 ($3.85); 5% on rates from Rs. 50 ($3.85) to Rs. 75 ($5.75); and 8% above Rs. 75. You'll want to remember this when budgeting. You might get a break during the mid-November to mid-April off-season when some managers reduce their rates. Be sure to ask about these special rates during these times. Reductions may not be offered if you don't.

Basically, the season is April 15 to July 30 and again from September 1 to October 30, although some accommodations may be discounted during September as well. The fall festival of Dussehra, usually in October, is especially colorful in Kulu and attracts many visitors. Be sure to make reservations if you hope to share in the excitement yourself!

WHERE TO STAY IN KULU: In Kulu choices are very limited. Among the best, the Himachal Pradesh Tourist Development Corporation's (HPTDC) **Travellers Lodge,** Kulu 175101 (tel. 79), perched on a hill at the entrance to town, has six doubles, with attached bathrooms, and hot and cold running water, and window-enclosed sitting rooms. The rooms contain more than adequate furniture: beds, dressing tables, wardrobes, lamps, plus lounge chairs and tables in the sitting rooms. There are rooms on the first floor, but those upstairs are quieter and brighter. Rates for singles are Rs. 230 ($17.70) without meals and doubles cost Rs. 285 ($21.90) without meals. Some deluxe rooms are about Rs. 100 ($7.70) more. Add Rs. 130 ($10) per person to take all your meals here. If you prefer buying provisions to picnic in the hills at lunch, you can take only two meals a day for around Rs. 80 ($6.15) per day per person.

Nearby, the **Hotel Empire** (tel. 97) is seedy but passable. All the rooms are modest, but those upstairs are better than those on the ground floor. There are six doubles at Rs. 60 ($4.60), two three-bedded rooms at Rs. 100 ($7.70), four five-bedded rooms at Rs. 150 ($11.55), and one single at Rs. 24 ($1.85).

A good bet is the HPTDC's **Hotel Servari** (tel. 81), located near town on a big grassy lawn and offering better-than-average accommodations and great big rooms: eight doubles and four dorms with six beds each. Two Western-style bathrooms are attached to two of the doubles, Indian-style toilets with the others, and common toilets and showers for dorm-users. The dorm fee is Rs. 20 ($1.55) per person. A heater, which you will need in the winter and early spring, runs Rs. 10 (75¢). Double rooms cost Rs. 125 ($9.60) to Rs. 175 ($13.45) per day, linens included—not cheap, but a fairly good buy since cheap meals are close at hand in the restaurant near the tourist office.

Off a road to the Mall is **Sa-Ba** (tel. 118), which has nothing but low price to recommend it and is typical of a number of other small guesthouses in Kulu: Rs. 90 ($6.90) single and Rs. 110 ($8.45) double. All the attached bathrooms have Indian-style plumbing, and hot water in buckets—not for you if you're at all fussy.

The fairly new **Hotel Rothan** (tel. 303) has 12 rooms, coir-carpeted floors, and hot showers in attached Western-style bathrooms. Rates are Rs. 60 ($4.60) to Rs. 200 ($15.40) for ordinary to deluxe rooms. There are also some rooms for Rs. 110 ($8.45) and Rs. 150 ($11.55). In the more expensive rooms there is a TV, which doesn't really amount to much so save your rupees. A restaurant on the premises is open from 9 to 11 a.m., 1 to 3 p.m., and 7 to 10 p.m., serving Indian and Chinese foods with entrees under $1.

Hotel Bijleswar View (no phone yet) is a new arrival, with eight clean, simply but attractively done-up large doubles with antique furniture, fireplaces, and cement floors for Rs. 75 ($5.75) plus Rs. 3 (25¢) tax. There are Indian toilets in two of the attached bathrooms and the others have Western. The café next door is open from 7 a.m. to 10 p.m., and serves thali meals for Rs. 10 (75¢) to Rs. 15 ($1.15).

WHAT TO DO IN KULU: There are no taxis here, so you walk, Jeep, or bus it, unless of course you've come by car. And now here are some suggestions on how to spend your time:

1. Stop in at the tourist office (tel. 7), right of the maidan (grassy center), anytime between 10 a.m. and 5 p.m. Buy an area map for Rs. 2 (15¢). If you fish and it's March to mid-April, arrange for your license, rent a rod and line. For a day, all this should cost around Rs. 5 (40¢) to Rs. 7.50 (60¢) a day. Go to **Aut** (pronounced "out"), 20 miles away, where trout are plentiful.

2. Wander around the maidan, which looks strangely like an American frontier town movie set, with villagers playing a variety of roles. Even before 10 a.m., the scribe is under his tree typing letters for residents. The barber holds a mirror for a satisfied customer—it costs 50 paise (3½¢) for a shave with lotions and a facial massage. No one's at the dentist's, so he dozes in his chair. Tibetans carefully string up blankets to sell to passersby; children, giggling, run through and knock them down. A patent-medicine seller spellbinds a huge group of healthy-looking people; a holy man ambles over the green; apple, nut, and bangle sellers hawk their wares; lollers loll. By mid-morning almost the entire perimeter is a pageant of activity. In the fall the maidan is the focal point of the great Dussehra festival.

3. Shop in the stores off the maidan, or stop at the **Himachal Pradesh Handicraft Emporium** for locally made woolen items.

4. Trek 28 miles (or take the luxury coach) to **Manikaran,** purportedly the hottest springs in the world. Orchards and river scenery on the way.

5. Play table tennis at the tiny **Kulu Club.**
6. Leave for Manali.

ON THE WAY TO MANALI: Of the two roads running the 26 miles (42 km) to Manali, the old circuitous bumpy backroad, which can take four hours, is full of fascinating sights and is therefore recommended over the direct route taking about two hours. Buses leave every two hours on the direct route and twice a day via the old road. If it's raining, you'll want to wait for dry weather or take the direct route (the old road turns to instant slither when wet).

You'll also want to check bus timings so you can either stop at Naggar (about the halfway point) to see the famous **Naggar Castle,** and continue later by bus, or plan far enough ahead to reserve one of the seven rooms in the Hotel Castle Naggar, on the Naggar Castle grounds: Rs. 150 ($11.55) to Rs. 200 ($15.40) per room. For reservations, contact the Tourism Development Officer, Kulu (tel. 7). The castle itself, built by Raja Sidh Singh more than 400 years ago, remarkably withstood the earthquake of 1905 when other buildings around here collapsed like cardboard cartons.

On the grounds, **Jagti-Pat Temple** has a stone slab which is off-limits because it's supposed to hold all the deities. To test this, a foreigner once stepped on this forbidden territory and was swallowed up by a huge crack that mysteriously opened. Since then no one's ever slipped up by stepping on the slab.

For temple-trotters, there's a **Shiva temple,** perhaps 900 years old, on the approach to Naggar Castle, a Vishnu temple almost at the entrance, and Devi and Krishna temples above it.

Also a steep climb from behind the castle is the charming old stone cottage in which the Russian adventurer/artist Nicholas Roerich lived more than 50 years ago. It's now a small **museum** full of his paintings of the valley, some abstract and others realistic. All around the house, the foundations of the house, and in the garden are marvelous stone carvings, and of course, the view is quite a special sight.

Only 10 miles (16 km) from Kulu is a camping site at **Raison,** if you're trekking through, where there are also rooms in huts for Rs. 50 ($3.85) per day.

At **Katrain,** two miles farther along, there's the well-located Hotel Apple Blossom. The spectacular view and cleanliness makes up for the rather spartan furnishings. Some of the bathrooms have Western toilets; some also have geysers to supply hot water and in others you pay Rs. 1.50 (10¢) for a bucket of the hot stuff. Rates are Rs. 50 ($3.85) single and Rs. 75 ($5.75) double; there are nine rooms in all. There is also a charming three-bedroom cottage, renting for Rs. 275 ($21.15) per day.

For reservations at the Hotel Apple Blossom or in the camping ground huts, contact the Tourism Development Officer, Kulu (tel. 7).

Also near Katrain is the romantic **Span Resorts** (tel. Katrain 40), a series of well-appointed stone cottages overlooking the Beas River. In the main building are a big well-stocked bar, video room, and lounge. Even with meals included, rates are a splurge for us—Rs. 1,100 ($84.50) double and Rs. 950 ($73) single—and isolated if you're on your own. It's also the place to stop for a special meal between Kulu and Manali: breakfast costs Rs. 45 ($3.45); lunch and dinner, Rs. 65 ($50). Should you care to stay here, reservations are made through Span Motels Ltd., GF-7, Surya Kiran, 19 Kasturba Gandhi Marg, New Delhi, India 110001 (tel. 3311434).

WHERE TO STAY IN MANALI: The HPDTC's **Travellers Lodge,** Manali 175131 (tel. 31), has ten double rooms with high ceilings and attached bathrooms with hot and cold running water; some rooms also have sitting rooms. It has the gracious look of olden days. The furniture, like its counterpart lodge in Kulu, is functional and modern, and everything you need for a mountain holiday. Without meals, rates are Rs. 230 ($17.70) single, Rs. 285 ($21.90) doubles. If you take all your meals here it will add about Rs. 130 ($10) more per person; two meals, Rs. 70 ($5.40) additional. Off-season, from July 15 to September 30 and again from December 15 to March 31, rates are about Rs. 130 ($10) less per person.

At the **Hotel Rohtang Manalsu** (tel. 32), for Rs. 100 ($7.70) to Rs. 200 ($15.40) you can get rooms with twin beds in the new section, and for Rs. 125 ($9.60) you can get a four-bedded room in the old section. All rooms have attached bathrooms (no showers) and the necessities you need, but are a mite overpriced in view of what you get for the such a basic place. There's a Rs.-20 ($1.55)-a-day charge for heaters, which you need except in summer. A restaurant is on the premises.

Away from the center, there's a newcomer, the **Hotel Greenfields** (tel. 39), with 18 rooms in an attractive stone building. The neat, clean rooms have modern furniture, carpeted floors, and mountain views. The rate is Rs. 200 ($15.40) per room, plus Rs. 25 ($1.90) additional for heaters. The hotel's restaurant serves Indian and Chinese dishes.

About two kilometers (1¼ miles) from the center, and bearing a resemblance to an old-style U.S. motel, the **Tourist Cottages** (tel. 34) are extremely pleasant. The interior decoration is very simple, but with the Himalayas outside your window, who's looking inside? If you did, however, you'd see a double-bedded room, kitchen, and dining room—cozy, cheerful, and clean. There are 12 cottages, at Rs. 300 ($23.05) per day.

Would you believe Lincoln Log Cabins in Manali? Well, they're here, but Abe Lincoln never had it so good. Each of the 12 cabins, called **Log Huts** (tel. 39), has two neatly furnished bedrooms with carved bedsteads and velvet settees, a kitchen, pantry, and two bathrooms. Cabins 1, 2, and 3, lower down in the hills and therefore less tiring to reach, are priced highest: Rs. 1,100 ($84.50). Cabins 4 to 12 run Rs. 900 ($69.25). Throughout the year, there's a caretaker for each hut.

Hamta and Birch View are two romantic cottages, with deep sloping roofs, that are popular with honeymooners. Brightly printed drapes and outdoor verandas add charm to the neat furnished rooms with attached bathrooms. Rs. 350 ($26.90) rents a cozy cottage for two.

Note: In cottages with cooking facilities you don't have to cook and clean. Food can be sent in à la carte from a nearby café. A "sweeper" is provided at no additional charge to tidy up each day. You would tip him at the end of your stay.

There are 33 four-bedded rooms at the **Tourist Lodge,** renting for Rs. 20 ($1.55) per person, with a Rs.-2.75 (21¢) charge for bed linens. Bring your own towel. Spartan but acceptable, and right on the bank of the River Beas.

The main recommendation for the **Hotel Beas** is the magnificent river view. Rates are Rs. 150 ($11.55) for a family suite, Rs. 75 ($5.75) to Rs. 125 ($9.60) for a double, depending on size; and Rs. 50 ($3.85) for a single.

The **reservation authority** for the HPTDC Travellers Lodge, Hotel Rohtang Manalsu, Tourist Cottages, Log Huts, Hamta and Birch View, Tourist Lodge, Hotel Beas, and Tourist Rest House is the Deputy General Manager, HPTDC, Manali (tel. 25).

The Banon family has been in the valley for over 100 years and some of them are now running guesthouses. **John Banon's** (tel. 35) is smack in the center of an orchard, and it offers 16 doubles with fragrant pine paneling (they also could use some sprucing up). All rooms have attached bathrooms, with hot and cold running water. They're popular with trekkers so you have to book at least a month in advance in season. Rates are Rs. 350 ($26.90) for singles and Rs. 500 ($38.45) for doubles, with meals included. Without meals, the flat room-only rate is Rs. 250 ($19.25). A 25% deposit is required on all confirmed bookings (and if you cancel with short notice, say good-bye to your deposit).

Another branch of the Banon clan runs **New Hope** (tel. 78). The lounge has seen better days. The 13 twin-bedded bedrooms have Himalayan views and fireplaces, and connecting bathrooms, but need some tender loving care. Rates range from Rs. 125 ($9.60) to Rs. 300 ($23.05) for double occupancy, and Rs. 250 ($19.25) single occupancy. The higher fee is for a wood-paneled room with better maintained furniture than the others. Two suites are Rs. 350 ($26.90).

The Banons again run **Sunshine** (tel. 20), with a pretty terraced garden. The main building of gray stones and green-painted accents has two sparsely furnished family suites with four beds each. These cost Rs. 100 ($7.70) single, plus Rs. 25 ($1.90) for each additional guest in the room. In the white annex are four doubles, and this is the best place to stay. Simply furnished, the annex rooms have fireplaces, dressing rooms, private bathrooms, and ample drawer space, at Rs. 200 ($15.40). All rooms have bathrooms attached, and hot water comes in buckets upon request. Meals are an additional Rs. 175 ($13.45), or can be taken à la carte.

Pinewood (tel. 118), another Banon-owned place, has nine rooms. All have attached bathrooms with hot and cold running water. It's a charming place with a typical wooden balcony and other local architectural touches. All the rooms have working fireplaces and sunny yellow walls. Rooms upstairs, overlooking the yard and garden, have stupendous views of the mountains. Rates throughout are Rs. 150 ($11.55) per day, but an increase was expected. Meals are à la carte and taken in the Victorian dining room, which has a large fireplace. Write to the manager for reservations and enclose a 50% deposit.

The **Highland** (tel. 99) is a stone building trimmed in white with eight thickly carpeted, pine-ceilinged bedrooms. The cheerful upstairs rooms have back balconies and look out on a veranda; main-floor rooms open at the garden level. The rooms have country stoves for heat, and it costs Rs. 25 ($1.90) to use them. Rates are Rs. 175 ($13.55) to Rs. 250 ($19.25), the higher prices for the larger rooms. Taking all meals here will cost an additional Rs. 175 ($13.55) per day.

Hilltop (tel. 140) is, appropriately enough, on a hilltop. It has very modest accommodations, with those upstairs preferred for view and quiet. Bathrooms are attached to rooms and have hot and cold running water. Rates are Rs. 150 ($11.55) double, Rs. 175 ($13.45) triple, without meals. The management was about to install TV (the last thing you need in Manali) and wall-to-wall carpeting. The restaurant serves tandoori dishes, at Rs. 30 ($2.30) for a tandoori entree, as well as Chinese and Indian foods.

Right in town is the renovated **Samrat** (tel. 56), located at the beginning of the market, has 18 adequately furnished rooms (with 18 more under construction). The rates are Rs. 150 ($11.55) without meals and Rs. 300 ($23.05) with meals. The restaurant has a wide range of dishes, and among them, tandooris at Rs. 20 ($1.55).

Low-Priced Cottages

Casual Western travelers with a taste for adventure rent cottages from local families and rough it in the hills. It makes sense if you're staying a month. But be prepared for basic, no-frills living. You'll need a sleeping bag. Rates run about Rs. 350 ($26.90) to Rs. 400 ($30.75) a month, if you're good at bargaining. Ask around town for local families interested in renting, or check with some of the Westerners who also call the Manali hills their home. You'll find them at the market in town when they come to stock up on provisions.

EATING OUT IN MANALI: Truly eating out here should mean eating outdoors in the glens and groves. Some hotels and guesthouses will pack a picnic lunch for you, or you can buy foods in the market.

As to restaurants, try the **Ardash,** across from the tourist information office. It's pleasant and pine paneled, and the food is good but the portions are small. A full Indian meal will run Rs. 25 ($1.90) to Rs. 30 ($2.30). Nearby is **Mona Lisa,** also recommended for a snack or meal.

SEEING THE SIGHTS FROM MANALI: Early in your visit, stop in at the **Tourist Information Office,** The Mall, the main street (tel. 25 or 116), and sign up for a tour to **Rohtang Pass,** about 32 mountainous miles (51 km) away over an old Tibetan trade route and 13,500 feet high. See the beautiful **Rahala Falls** on the way, and take a sweater—it can be cold at the top (and lonely too). The cost is Rs. 60 ($4.60) and the trip goes every day if there are ten or more people, which is the magic number that activates the following tours as well. And the Rohtang trip may not go at all in the rainy season when the road is not usable. The trek to Rohtang is a popular whole-day excursion. Check weather conditions before you start off.

Another tour goes to **Manikram,** an old village, and **Vashist Sulphur Springs,** costing Rs. 70 ($5.40) per person for the 25-mile (40-km) trip. Manikram is on the trekking route to Pulga and Pin Parbati Pass. It is a place of holy pilgrimage associated with Shiva and Parvati. Yet another tour goes to **Naggar,** which, as mentioned, is about the halfway point between Manali and Kulu, and site of the old Raja Sidh Singh Castle and Roerich museum, for Rs. 35 ($2.70).

On Your Own

Without a tour, take a hike through the piney woods to the **Hadimba Devi Temple** (ask at the Tourist Information Office for directions). Hung with antlers, the temple has ornate carvings outside and footprint-shaped humps of rock inside which are considered holy. When the bell isn't being used by fun-loving kids as a toy, it's rung to summon people to worship, around 8:45 a.m. and 5 p.m. A big celebration takes place at the temple on May 15 and 16.

Hiking and Climbing

Manali is headquarters for the H.P. Mountaineering Institute and Allied Sports. With a month's notice, a trek of 10 to 14 days can be arranged to peaks 16,000 to 19,000 feet or higher. Equipment and clothing can be rented, but it's best to come fully equipped with your own gear. Experienced guides accompany climbers. For details, write to the Director of the Department of Mountaineering and Allied Sports, or the HPTDC Ritz Annexe, Simla 171001 (tel. 3294), in Manali.

In addition, the HPTDC has prepared a pamphlet of suggested trekking routes, with rudimentary maps. You can get this pamphlet and more information from the Tourist Information Office in Manali.

GETTING TO THE KULU VALLEY: There are daily flights from Delhi for Rs.

525 ($40) to Bhuntar airport about six miles (ten kilometers) from Kulu. Simla is the end of the track when it comes to **trains,** and from there it's 143 miles (229 km) by bus or car. It's a spectacular scenic one-day round trip from Chandigarh 173 very curvaceous miles (277 km), on a road where frequent rockslides make detours common. A **car with a driver** is very pricey because the drive is in the hills, so figure that a round trip from Chandigarh should cost in the area of Rs. 700 ($54) to Rs. 1,000 ($77). It's best not to bargain with a cab driver for this trip, but to take a government-approved car, at a fixed rate, fit for the difficult journey.

The road trip can be made in **buses** equipped with video (showing Indian films) and air conditioning, traveling from Delhi to Manali at Rs. 250 ($19.25) per seat. The HPTDC operates luxury (by U.S. standards, in name only) buses costing Rs. 150 ($11.55) from Delhi and Rs. 100 ($7.70) from Simla. For information, contact the HPTDC, Chanderlok Building, Kanishka Shopping Plaza, 19 Ashok Road, New Delhi (tel. 345320); or the Ritz Annexe, Simla 171001 (tel. 3294). It's also possible to make bus reservations in Chandigarh, at SCO 1048-49, Sector 22-B (tel. 26494); in Calcutta, at 25 Carmac St. (tel. 446847); at Dharamasala's bus stand; and near the railway station at Pathankot.

Rules of the Road

If you decide to go by road, whether by bus or by private car, take some bottled water and fruit (remember a knife to peel it)—a good idea on any long India drive. On this particular mountainous drive, you can get stuck quite literally in the middle of nowhere, with no place to get food or hygienic water to drink, if there's a rockslide or road washout and you have to wait for help (which always turns up sooner or later in the form of a tractor or friendly hands). If you're splurging on a car and driver, perhaps from Chandigarh, getting an early start is always a good idea—you will want to arrive before dark. A few kilometers beyond the Simla turnoff is Bilsapur, where you can stop for a snack or meal at the clean **Lake View Café.** For instance, a continental breakfast is under $1, and you can use the clean (patrons only) bathroom. On the way back from Manali, the **Tourist Lodge** at Mandi is handy for food (slightly higher than the Lake View's prices) and a clean bathroom. Bus drivers also give passengers various rest stops.

Chapter VI

THE INCOMPARABLE VALE OF KASHMIR

1. Srinagar
2. Gulmarg and Pahalgam
3. Ladakh—Beyond the Vale

ABOUT ONE HOUR OUT OF DELHI, the airplane begins to climb and climb, and the jagged snow-topped peaks of the Himalayas ahead appear to bar entry to the other world. Then you are over the top and hovering above what seems to be a bowl of fluffy whipped cream—the clouds that spill around the edges of the mountains are but a topping to the gentle valley of Kashmir.

This is a vast area—only slightly smaller than Great Britain—surrounded by magnificent mountains, crammed so close it's surprising there's room for the many crystal lakes and cascades. It's filled with saffron-spangled meadows, fruit orchards, rice paddies, cattle; and populated by peasants in rough clothing and merchants swaggering in blouses, pantaloons, and fur caps. Some of the women cover their faces from strangers, others flash bold smiles along with bright jewelry.

For more than three centuries Kashmir has been the favorite resort of wealthy Indians, a respite from the heat of the plains. And for almost as long, Kashmiris have welcomed strangers and sold them their fine crafts (rugs, shawls, jewelry) but not their land. So Westerners took up residence on the water, building the ornate houseboats unique to Kashmir today.

People are always comparing Kashmir to some other place. If you set off believing it's an earthly Eden of perfection and abundance for all, you'll be disappointed. Kashmir is beautiful but broke. All is calm now, but it has been the scene of open conflict several times since the 1947 Partition. Srinagar is only 60 miles (100 km) from the Pakistan border.

There was civilization in Kashmir back in the 8th century, and ruins extant at Martand attest to this. But it was Akbar, the 16th-century Mughal emperor, and his successors who established it as a resort.

1. Srinagar

The town of Srinagar (pop. 585,000), at a height of 5,200 f
level, sprawls along the banks of a muddy river called the Jhelu
cuitous course necessitates nine bridges to bring the town toge

the inhabitants live in battered houseboats or barges on the river itself, but the majority cram into the box-like, unpainted homes that tumble one over another right up to the water's edge. The Srinagar skyline is one of endless fascination because of the occasional grass roofs and the variety of delicately carved and barn-like structures that mingle with the minarets and the bulbous towers that mark the mosques.

Frenetic activity, endless horn-blowing, wandering cows and geese, the jingle of horse-drawn carts characterize the streets. At first sight everybody seems to be in a hurry, even the youth between the shafts of a wagon which bears a tree trunk three times his size. But closer inspection reveals the static underpinning of patient souls who sit cross-legged on the sidewalk all day overseeing their piles of dried red peppers or sacks of apples.

Physically, the countless stores all look alike: a raised alcove with the owner sitting on the floor, sharing an occasional drag from his elegant hookah (water pipe) with the neighboring butcher whose clippers still hold the traces of a half-sheared sheep; or with the tailor whose hard work and experience is stitched into each wrinkle of his face. Local peasants in rough, sandy-colored clothes stop by to bargain. In the fall, their garments bulge with kangri (hot pots) strapped underneath to keep them warm.

A bewildering variety of goods sit or hang in the stalls—tea, incense, plastic bags, tin cooking utensils, piles of firewood, cheap radios, English candies—all for the homemaker. Other stores display woodwork, papier-mâché, shawls, pottery, semiprecious stones—an Ali Baba's assortment for tourists and locals too.

UPON ARRIVAL: Tourist buses from the airport take you at a stately crawl for the Rs.-10 (75¢) trip—or you can go by taxi for Rs. 57 ($4.40)—to the **Tourist Reception Centre** (tel. 72698), a stop most travelers make early in their trip no matter how they arrive in Kashmir. This huge complex of buildings in the heart of town houses a restaurant, post office, booking offices for tours and accommodation, Indian Airlines (tel. 73270; open from 10 a.m. to 5 p.m.), and the Jammu and Kashmir Road Transport Corporation (tel. 72698; open from 8 a.m. to 6 p.m.), and it's the place to get advice and information, and issue complaints.

There is also a modest 78-room hotel here, charging Rs. 80 ($6.15) to Rs. 100 ($7.70) for a suite and Rs. 130 ($10) for deluxe suite. Try to get a room facing the garden. For advance reservations, contact the manager, Reservations, J&K Tourist Development Corporation, Tourist Reception Centre, Srinagar 190001 (tel. 76107).

WHAT TO DO: On top of the list—and a major sight in Srinagar—is the series of symmetrical gardens spread around the fringes of **Dal Lake.** They were carefully created by Mughal emperors over 300 years ago, and were cool and relaxing places to contemplate the affairs of state. It is possible to take a city bus from one of the bridges in town and visit most of the gardens one after another. Buses run every few minutes in summer and cost Rs. 2 (15¢) or Rs. 3 (23¢). The most pleasant way to visit these gardens is by shikara, one of the small, curtained, cushioned boats plying Dal Lake. For about Rs. 100 ($7.70) to Rs. 130 ($10) A.B. (after bargaining), you can take an all-day tour of the gardens by shikara, having your boatman paddle you here and there and wait while you go off to look around. It's very nice to take a picnic lunch if you do this gardens-by-boat touring. For just a little paddling here and there figure on paying around Rs. 13 ($1) to Rs. 20 ($1.55) per hour, again A.B. You hire shikaras at any of the boating ghats from around 8 a.m. on.

The first garden, about five or six miles from town, is called **Chashma Shahi,** which means Royal Spring. Steps lead up the hillside to a series of flower-filled areas interlaced with fountains and waterfalls. The original garden was quite small, but it has been extended on each side. It is pleasant to sit quietly under the trees or in one of the old wooden tea houses and look across at the lake below. It's not available by shikara, but the others are.

Two other gardens are much bigger. The second one you'll come to, about eight miles from town, is called **Nishat** (meaning pleasure). It has ten terraces, two pavilions, many carefully laid-out flower beds and magnificent lawns. The trees here, and all around Srinagar, are the celebrated chenars, originally imported from Persia. To this day, they exist only in that country and Kashmir. In late summer and fall they turn a gorgeous reddish-golden color—and are invariably reproduced on tourist literature.

The biggest and most famous of the gardens is **Shalimar** (meaning garden of love), which was created in 1619 for Queen Nur Jahan by Emperor Jahangir and was extended in 1727 by Shah Jahan. It later became the inspiration for the famous song ("Pale hands I loved . . ."). A quartet of terraces—the fourth, once the private playground of court maidens—is bisected by a canal and resplendent with fountains and falls. At night, the romantic days when little lights glimmered in the garden and languid ladies lounged by the pools are recalled in a Son et Lumière performance, also tracing the history of the Mughals. It's presented from May to October, with the English show at around 8:30 p.m., and admission is Rs. 6 (45¢). There are Urdu and Hindi performances also.

A fourth garden, **Naseem Bagh** (meaning breezes), is rarely visited by tourists. It's on the west bank of Dal Lake and contains hundreds of handsome chenars which, it is said, were nurtured as saplings with milk and water. The engineering college is located here now.

After visiting the gardens, it's pleasant to paddle out to **Charchinari,** the island in the center of Dal Lake, named for the four chenar trees on it. This is the place to unpack your picnic and relax.

Or go by boat, car, or rented bike to **Hazratbal,** near Naseem Bagh on the west bank of Dal Lake, an important Muslim shrine. It is believed to house the hair of the Prophet, which is displayed on rare occasions. The hair came to India in 1634 via Medina and was in Bijapur and Lahore (now Pakistan) before winding up here.

You can also go on by car, bus, or bike around Dal Lake, through little villages where the local store serves as the focal point, just as in Old West days. Between the tiny hamlets, goats, lambs, ducks, and chickens amble across the road; orchards are abloom with ambri apple, cherry, pear, and peach trees; and terraced rice paddies are interspersed with vignettes of villagers threshing rice, chopping wood, or lazily lounging at the side of the road.

Towering above Dal Lake at one side, and dominating the entire town of Srinagar, is the 1,000-foot-high **Shankaracharya Hill,** atop which stands an ancient Temple to Shiva, holy to Hindus, and **Shahi-Handam Mosque,** venerated by Muslims. One way to climb is on foot—about a one-hour trek—which rewards the climber with a magnificent view of the surrounding area. The less energetic can go up by car and get the same view.

Some 5½ miles (9 km) away from town, **Nagin Lake** (jewel on the ring), less famous than neighboring Dal, features waterskiing at Rs. 10 (75¢) to Rs. 15 ($1.15) for one complete round; there's also motorboat rental for Rs. 250 ($19.25) for a full day, and the use of the bathing boat will cost Rs. 2 (15¢) to Rs. 7 (55¢). The trout fishing is said to be excellent here, but that seems doubtful in view of all the sporting activities on the water.

Above Nagin is **Hari Parbat Fort,** encircled by the remains of a wall Akbar built nearly 400 years ago. Nothing remains but the wall, but the spot is absolutely gorgeous in the spring when the almond trees bloom, and you can hike up there in half an hour.

Back in town, **Sri Pratap Singh Museum** (open from 10 a.m. to 5 p.m.; closed Wednesday and holidays) is appealing even to non-museum-lovers. It's a fine collection of miniature paintings, old weapons, tapestries, and sculpture. Admission is free, but a small donation is appreciated (you won't be hounded). The funds are to be used for improving this facility so the stunning array can be more suitably accommodated.

SHOPPING: A main occupation of many tourists in Kashmir is shopping (another is fending off persistent vendors). World-famous carpets are just one item to buy; shawls, silver, wood and papier-mâché, silks, and embroideries are among the other wares. Before setting off, be prepared to bargain like mad in all but the price-fixed government-run stores. Popular shopping areas are Polo View and Residency Roads, Hari Singh High Street, and Lambert Lane.

The best place to survey the many offerings is right down the street from the Tourist Reception Centre at the **Kashmir Government Arts Emporium,** in the old British Residency on Residency Road. It's more like a museum than a store, but all the items—rugs, textiles, and precious stones—are on sale to buy to take home. Other emporia around town have good selections in less historic surroundings, including the **National Handicrafts Emporium,** and the **Cottage Arts Emporium,** on Residency Road (tel. 73011 or 73012); the latter has hand-embroidered shawls for Rs. 600 ($46.15) and shirts for Rs. 250 ($19.25).

At the **Government Central Market** there are gardens and restaurants, as well as countless shops in a super-complex (intrepid shoppers allow half a day here). For sale are furs, crafts, and all the other items for which Kashmir is well known. In some of the shops you can see talented artisans making pretty objects. Hours are 10 a.m. to 9 p.m., except at festival time when it's open until midnight, and in March and April when closing time is 7 p.m.

In a number of shops around town you can see how the items are made: the papier-mâché process involves shredding and pulping the paper before coating it with gold leaf and painting it by hand with intricate designs inspired by local lore and scenery.

At other factories you see the way Kashmiri carpets have been made for more than 300 years: whole families of weavers—four to a loom—squat on low benches, weaving rugs that last more than a lifetime. One person in each team acts as "caller," chanting the pattern from a complex list of hieroglyphics on a strip of brown paper at eye level. While chanting, the caller makes a double loop of thread and brings it down almost faster than the eye can follow and chops it off with an S-shaped knife. So the carpet progresses, half an inch a day, for anywhere from 15 months to up to three years. Away from the cacophony of perhaps 100 rug-song instructions are the showrooms with finished products. Very fine rugs of silk with 900 knots per square inch, measuring 10 feet by 14 feet, with extraordinarily complex designs can cost $32,000 or more; fine quality 4- by 6-foot carpets, $2,500; and those 2 feet by 3 feet, $2,000.

The largest carpet showroom is the **Indo-Kashmiri Carpet Factory,** in Shah Mollah in the old part of Srinagar, where the helpful manager is Gulam Q. Butt. He will be glad to show you the rugs made with vegetable dyes, which are less frequently used than aniline dyes.

For furs, try **Shyam Brothers,** on Hotel Road, or **Darson's,** across from the Lhasa Restaurant, Boulevard Lane II. Make sure that the furs you buy have been properly treated so they won't crack and fall apart the minute you wear them. Right above Lhasa they have a large selection of handcrafts and jewelry, including quite a Tibetan selection. The pieces you buy here may look convincingly antique, but in actuality be brand-new. Here, however, they tell you the item's history or lack thereof before you buy it—which is quite a nice thing to do.

But in Kashmir you don't have to go to the shops—they'll come to you. **Shikaras** piled high with treasures go from houseboat to houseboat. When they get too pesty, houseboat servants are good at getting them to knock it off.

WHERE TO STAY: Most visitors to Kashmir want to stay in one of the famous houseboats, which happens to be a very wise choice. These throwbacks to the old British Victorian days are some of the fanciest and coziest homes afloat anywhere in the world, although some are not spanking new. Landlubbers will find a selection of hotels, including a once-grand palace turned into hotel.

Houseboats

The houseboats come equipped with a full staff of servants, including a cook and a boatman (for your shikara), who usually live in the adjoining "kitchen boat." The offered fare can often be bland British boarding school, but with insistence the cook will serve a variety of tasty Kashmiri dishes. Most houseboats will also provide packed picnic lunches.

A typical houseboat is about 80 to 125 feet long and 10 to 20 feet wide, and has at least six rooms to accommodate two or three families at a time. Visitors can book an entire boat at a premium price—full charges for their occupancy and 50% of the rest of charges for the unoccupied section of the boat.

The top deck is invariably devoted to sunbathing, and the boat itself is moored with many others in Nagin or Dal Lake or on the River Jhelum. Passing shikaras display handcrafts as well as such ordinary items as toiletries.

Houseboats are classified in Deluxe, A, B, C, and D or Doonga categories, according to their opulence or lack of same. Conditions aboard can vary within the same classification, depending on upkeep. Some houseboat owners embellish imaginatively on their ratings by adding "Super" to Deluxe or "Deluxe" to A, with no bearing on reality. Prices are supposedly fixed by the tourist officials, but expect to bargain (in Kashmir, it's like breathing—bargaining is a natural function of life). Almost without saying, you make your best deals off-season, in the early spring and late fall.

To move one of the smaller houseboats is possible, but a real production requiring four or five men to propel it with very long, sturdy poles. The end result of such a whimsical desire to change views would be more rupees and trouble than it's worth: mooring sites are the property of houseboat owners and rarely vacant. With no new place to park, you'll have to go right back to where you pushed off from.

The "Deluxe" category is, as the name implies, the classiest, with decors rooted in the days of the Raj, even if built yesterday, and others are quite modern (or rather, moderne). "A" is less luxurious and smaller, but quite pleasant; "B" and "C" continue down the line. A class apart, "doonga boats" have since the 1960s housed hippy communities. To be assured of the nicest accommodations, ask for a new boat.

For a stay during the peak season, roughly April through August, you are advised to make **houseboat reservations** well in advance by writing to: Manager, Reservations, J&K Tourist Development Corporation, Tourist Reception Centre, Srinagar 190001 (tel. 76107). You can also go directly to the Tourist Information Centre in Srinagar or the Kashmir and Jammu Information Centre in the Chanderlok Building, 36 Janpath, New Delhi (tel. 345373). Rates are fixed when you book through the government.

To make your own arrangements after arrival, you can take a shikara out to appealing-looking boats, meet the owner or manager, have him show you the rooms before making a decision, and bargain for what you consider is a fair price. As you might imagine, negotiating a lower rate is easier if it has been a slow season or if you are in town out-of-season.

Meals are included in houseboat rates as are service charges and shikara crossings. But when you leave, if your staff has performed well it's customary to tip a small amount above the service charge. Heaters from November to the end of March are Rs. 22 ($1.70) per day, one to a bedroom. Heating the drawing and dining rooms is the responsibility of management.

Official rates are quoted below. They are rates for rooms on boats, not entire boats. In *Deluxe:* Rs. 275 ($21.15) single, Rs. 405 ($31.15) double, and Rs. 135 ($10.40) for each additional person. In *Class A:* Rs. 172 ($13.25) single, Rs. 253 ($19.45) double, and Rs. 135 ($10.40) for each additional person. In *Class B:* Rs. 120 ($9.25) single, Rs. 204 ($15.70) double, and Rs. 80 ($6.15) for each additional person. In *Class C:* Rs. 78 ($6) single, Rs. 138 ($10.60) double, and Rs. 60 ($4.60) for each additional person. On *doonga boats,* full board is Rs. 54 ($4.15) single, Rs. 60 ($4.60) double, and Rs. 72 ($5.55) for each additional person. For lodging only in doongas, meaning a cotton mattress on the floor, you'll pay Rs. 48 ($3.70) daily to Rs. 780 ($60) for a month. All the boats special have rates for children.

Butt's Clermont Houseboats, Hasarad Bal Road, Budh Dal Lake, are off by themselves, at the uncluttered end of Dal Lake, about half an hour or more from Srinagar, depending on the traffic. The houseboats are old, but well kept, with magnificent views out over the lake to the mountains and, on the other side, of beautiful gardens Mr. Butt has created on the site of Akbar's (the Mughal emperor's) palace. Getting to and from Butt's boats may be a problem if you have no car, but if you stay there you can be assured of privacy. If you are assigned a two-bedroom houseboat, Mr. Butt will not rent the other bedroom while you are aboard. Butt housed the Beatles in their day and other luminaries. Rates for his three boats are the same as the official deluxe rate.

Bungalows

For a change of pace you might want to try a **Government Tourist Hutment,** a very unglamorous name for some very handsome, comfortable little houses. The stone, wood, and glass architecture is smart and in keeping with the area. Quality is high, but prices are right: Rs. 200 ($15.40) for a one-bedroom hut that accommodates two, Rs. 300 ($23.05) for a two-bedroom hut big enough for four, and Rs. 350 ($26.90) for a three-bedroom hut to hold six. All huts have gardens, patios, lawn furniture, full bathrooms with showers, and fully equipped kitchens. There's also a restaurant on the site where the view is staggering but the prices are not.

The huts are very popular in season. Be sure to reserve early by writing to Managing Director, Reservations J & K Tourist Development Corporation, Tourist Reception Centre, Srinagar 190001 (tel. 76107). There are two groups of hutments: at Parimahal Tourist Village you get a good view of the mountains and lake, but the best huts are those near Chahsma Shahi Gardens—but here's the drawback: they're a hefty six-mile (nine-kilometer) hike or costly car ride to the center of town.

Hotels

A number of hotels in Kashmir used to shut down in winter, while a few offered room heaters to guests braving the chill winds. Now more Kashmir hotels are centrally heated and comfortable year round. While most Westerners still visit in season, Indians from the temperate zone have started traveling to Kashmir in winter to see sights their palm-fringed landscapes can never offer: the famous snow-capped Himalayan peaks and downy snowfalls.

The rolling lawns, extensive gardens, and breathtaking lake view today remain the nicest features about the **Oberoi Palace,** Boulevard Road, Srinagar 190001 (tel. 71241), at one time the residence of the Maharaja of Kashmir. There's an outdoor restaurant, complete with umbrella-topped café tables, so if you don't stay here you can drop in for something to eat or drink and admire the scenery. In fair weather there's a buffet from noon to 2 p.m., served outdoors under the huge chenar trees (indoors if it's not nice). Bedrooms could use some sprucing up, and so could the dismal dining room. In the Harlequin Bar at night you can see the lights of houseboats on Dal Lake reflected in the mirror behind the bar. Room rates are splurge-high even with meals included: Rs. 960 ($73.85) for doubles, Rs. 705 ($54.25) for singles. Without meals, rates are Rs. 155 ($11.90) less per person.

The **Broadway,** Maulana Azad Road, Srinagar 190001 (tel. 71211), looks modern and expensive—and it is. Its exterior of textured concrete panels and wood give it a contemporary rustic look that carries through to the inside where the ceilings of the rooms are all of varnished slatted wood. Rooms on the second floor have balconies overlooking the swimming pool and small garden. Those slatted-wood ceilings are also in the lobby, right in the middle of which is a stone fireplace with a sunken conversation pit in front of it. There's also central heating. Several types of cuisines are served in the hotel: Kashmiri, Chinese, Indian, and continental. Rooms with breakfast cost Rs. 500 ($38.45) single and Rs. 680 ($52.30) double; suites cost Rs. 1,000 ($77) to Rs. 1,250 ($96).

Nedou's, Maulana Azad Road, Srinagar 190001 (tel. 73015), once grand, is in need of extensive repair, especially obvious in the run-down public rooms. The big bedrooms retain some old-fashioned Victorian charm and comforts, and the gardens are well kept. Despite the decline, the rates are high: Rs. 260 ($20) double and Rs. 200 ($15.40) single, with meals. Under the same management and at the same prices is the recently opened **Nedou's Lake View,** P.O. Box 15, Srinagar 190001 (tel. 72105), open from April to October. It's a Rs.-10 (75¢) ride to town in an auto-rickshaw.

A good buy is the **Hotel Zabarvan,** Boulevard Road, Srinagar 190001 (tel. 71441). Owned by carpet manufacturers/merchants, it is not only carpeted but also paneled with slatted wood. All the rooms are large doubles with adjoining big modern bathrooms. A smashing view from the rooftop restaurant (serving Kashmiri, Chinese, and continental dishes) and friendly management are pluses; plastic plants in garden-famous Kashmir are minuses. The premises are centrally heated. Rates are Rs. 470 ($36.15) double and Rs. 295 ($22.70) single, with meals; Rs. 260 ($20) double and Rs. 190 ($14.60) single, for room only.

Next door on Boulevard, the **Hotel Gulmarg** (tel. 75631) is so overdecorated with crewel-embroidered ceilings, mirrored archways, and blue-lit grottos that you can get indigestion of the eyes. It's a relief to get into one of the quietly decorated, large double bedrooms, all facing the lake, with big well-appointed bathrooms which cost Rs. 250 ($19.25) single and Rs. 350 ($26.90) double. There's a 10% service charge. Central heating is another amenity. The Shikara Restaurant (open from 7:30 a.m. to 2 a.m.) often has Kashmiri folk dancers performing, and features such local delicacies as gosthaba (lamb pounded to a paste and fried in ghee) and chaman (cheese-and-tomato curry), and North India's tandooris, costing Rs. 35 ($2.70) to Rs. 75 ($5.75) for most dishes. The Sapphire Restaurant (open from 7 a.m. to 3 a.m.) serves breakfast and snacks, plus there's a bar and a 35-shop shopping arcade.

Nearby, the **Shahenshah Palace,** Boulevard Road, Srinagar 190001 (tel. 71345), a handsome red-brick wood-trimmed hotel which juts above ground like an oversize houseboat overlooking the lake, also has a courtyard garden and cottages with comfortable accommodations. Wood stalagmites are prominent in the decor, as are wood-paneled walls and beautiful carved-wood chairs in the dining room. The grounds are lovely with chenar trees, floral areas, vines, and a heated swimming pool. The Mehfil restaurant features folk singers at night. Charges are Rs. 550 ($42.30) double and Rs. 450 single ($34.60) single in the main building, Rs. 300 ($23.05) single and Rs. 450 ($34.60) double in the cottages. The hotel is centrally heated and boasts of the biggest electrical generator in Kashmir.

Shah Abbas, Boulevard Road, Srinagar 190001 (tel. 77789), a relative newcomer to Kashmir's hotel row, has a papier-mâché ceiling in the lounge and central heating to take the chill off on crisp days. Real crewel-embroidered bedspreads are pretty accents in the rooms, all of which overlook Dal Lake and the Shankaracharya Mountains. Rates are Rs. 325 ($25) single and Rs. 425 ($32.70) double, Rs. 775 ($59.60) to Rs. 835 ($64.25) for suites. There is a coffeeshop and restaurant.

The **Mazda,** also on Boulevard Road, Srinagar 190001 (tel. 72842), is open from April 1 to the end of November and has a convenient location but is uninspired otherwise. Rates are Rs. 95 ($7.30) single, Rs. 145 ($11.15) double.

On Boulevard Road, Srinagar 190001, **The Boulevard** (tel. 77153) is open all year and charges Rs. 120 ($9.25) double and Rs. 66 ($5.05) single, without meals. It's a four-story walk-up, conveniently located. Rooms have full attached bathrooms with showers, and are clean and neat—which is something at these prices.

Another Boulevard Road choice is the **Hotel New Park,** Srinagar 190001 (tel. 74230), which has a deluxe block with rooms renting for Rs. 150 ($11.55) single and Rs. 190 ($14.60) double, and Rs. 250 ($19.25) for a suite; in the tourist block, rates are Rs. 100 ($7.70) single and Rs. 150 ($11.55) doubles, and Rs. 180 ($13.85) for a suite. There's a 10% service charge. If you want to stay on the American Plan, it will add about Rs. 70 ($5.40) per day per person. Each room has a private bathroom with hot and cold running water. It's a cut above so-so in all blocks.

Some new hotels have opened on Boulevard Road overlooking Dal Lake to the north of Dal Gate. They're neat, clean, and modern in all respects, with all the amenities to make you feel right at home.

Hotel Ornate Nehru's, Boulevard Road, Srinagar 190001 (tel. 73641), has 37 rooms at Rs. 250 ($19.25) single and Rs. 300 ($23.05) double. Add Rs. 100 ($7.70) for American Plan. The **Hotel Parimahal,** Boulevard Road, Srinagar 190001 (tel. 71235 or 71236), at the base of Shankaracharya Hill, has 35 rooms decorated with Kashmiri woodcarvings and crewelwork, with attached marble bathrooms. Rates are Rs. 180 ($13.85) to Rs. 300 ($23.05) for single occupancy, Rs. 250 ($19.25) to Rs. 375 ($28.85) for double. Add Rs. 60 ($4.60) a person for full American Plan.

The 70-room **Welcome Hotel,** Boulevard Road, Srinagar 190001 (tel. 73467), charges Rs. 260 ($20) double and Rs. 180 ($13.85) single. Deluxe rooms run Rs. 325 ($25) double. Nearby, the **Hotel Greenwald** (tel. 72028) has similar prices: Rs. 150 ($11.55) single to Rs. 225 ($17.30) double.

Next door, the Hotel Duke (tel. 73186), with 48 rooms, has different prices according to the view: the lake-view rate is Rs. 250 ($19.25) double; the hillside view costs Rs. 210 ($16.15) double; singles run Rs. 175 ($13.45). Heaters are Rs. 22 ($1.70) on cold nights. The owner of this hotel also manages some houseboats on Dal Lake.

Hotel Shangrila, Sonwar Bagh, Srinagar 190004 (tel. 75671), like many others, has a wood-paneled lobby and ceiling, and little homilies posted here and there such as "A house is built by hands, a home by heart." It doesn't matter how a hotel is built, but from the looks of the halls there are too few hands caring for this one. The rooms are fairly neat, however, and a pretty good buy: Rs. 110 ($8.45) for singles, Rs. 145 ($11.15) for doubles, with big beds and attached bathrooms. Service charge is 10%. Taking all your meals here will add Rs. 90 ($6.90) per person per day. There's a 20% discount from December to April 15.

Hotel Jehangir, Rajgarh Road, Srinagar 190001 (tel. 73013), is in a noisy part of town and overpriced for what it offers in the way of comfort and cleanliness: Rs. 95 ($7.30) to Rs. 110 ($8.45) single, Rs. 160 ($12.30) to Rs. 195 ($15) double. Add anywhere from Rs. 60 ($4.60) to Rs. 125 ($9.60) if you take your meals here.

On lush acreage jutting into Dal Lake is the **Centaur Lake View Hotel,** Chahsma Shahi, Srinagar 190001 (tel. 73175), part of the Air-India group of hotels, about five kilometers (three miles) from town and halfway to the Shalimar Gardens. The 254-room two-story rambling resort hotel is built of local gray stone in a design that blends the traditional and the modern. Big windows permit panoramic views of the lake and gardens. The rooms have modern furnishings and all the amenities you associate with luxury hotels. Accordingly, the rates are splurge-high: Rs. 500 ($38.45) single, Rs. 600 ($46.15) double; off-season they are Rs. 250 ($19.25) single and Rs. 350 ($26.90) double. A buffet is an attraction in one of the restaurants.

Budget Choices

Lack of maintenance and all the grubbiness that goes with it is a real problem when it comes to low-priced accommodation in Kashmir. When they get low-low, they're barely passable, so the hotels below are higher in price than my usual lowest-budget selections.

Many of the low-priced hotels are in busy Lal Chowk. Typical of these are **Budshah** (tel. 76063) and **Lalla Rukh** (tel. 72376). Rates in the Budshah start at Rs. 65 ($5) single and go to Rs. 90 ($6.90) double; it's Rs. 90 ($6.90) for two in the Lalla Rukh. Both are government-run and badly maintained. The other cheap hotels offer more of the same lack of fastidious conditions.

More pleasant are some of the little houseboat hotels moored on marshland in Dal Lake: **Heaven Canal,** Dal Lake (tel. 73943), charges Rs. 40 ($3.05) single and Rs. 90 ($6.90) double; the **Hotel Holynight,** Dal Lake (tel. 4608), charges similar rates.

There also are many guesthouses where accommodations vary greatly, but the rates are generally low: Rs. 30 ($2.30) to Rs. 100 ($7.70) double and half that for singles.

RESTAURANTS: The food in Kashmir goes way back to dishes favored by the Mughals, who put the place on the map as far as tourism goes. Some of the local specialties are biryanis (lamb or chicken cooked with rice, spices, and often topped with fruits and nuts), gustaba (a meatball curry), matar panir (a delicious mixture of cheese and peas in a rich gravy), gabargah (lamb cooked slowly in a sealed pan on a slow fire and seasoned with cloves, cinnamon, cardamom, and other spices), and kebabs (skewered lamb or chicken). In Kashmir, tea comes to the table sweet and perfumed with cardamom, adorned with almonds, colored by saffron and/or with milk. You can, of course, get it other ways.

The best-known restaurant in town, **Adhoo's,** Residency Road (tel. 2593 or 6588), is plain looking but serves good Kashmiri foods. It has a terrace in back and a phonograph to liven things up. The menu includes a score of local favorites—mutton dishes and vegetable concoctions—very few of which cost more than Rs. 16 ($1.25) or Rs. 17 ($1.30). You can get tandoori chicken here (that's the clay-oven specialty of North India) at Rs. 50 ($3.85) for a whole chicken, and about 16 other chicken dishes. Adhoo's has its own bakery and supplies bread and pastries to many other places around town. They'll even pack a picnic for you—chicken, eggs, sandwiches, pastries—about Rs. 15 ($1.15) to Rs. 20 ($1.55). Open daily from 9 a.m. to 11 p.m.

A slightly classy choice, but closed at this writing (right before the season), is the **Premier,** along the riverbank called the Bund, behind Residency Road (tel. 76595), has a tiny dance floor and a floor show at night. The restaurant, which also has a bar, describes itself as a "restaurant with a difference." One of the delights of eating here through the years, in addition to the good food, has been to enjoy the fractured English spellings (true in many places in India, but at some of their best here) on the menu. For instance, sundaes are on the menu as "sundaes, mondays, and schmumdaes"). "Chicken strongenough" (for Stroganoff, the classic sour-cream-sauce dish usually with beef) and "waffers" (for wafers) are just a few of the visual spelling treats. It's a place, however, where you can try gustaba (often part of a Kashmiri wedding meal). In the past very few entrees were more than Rs. 16 ($1.25), probably a bit more now. Open from 10 a.m. to midnight. The schmumdaes are in the ice-cream parlor downstairs, featuring 16 flavors and snacks and soft drinks. Minimum for the ice-cream parlor was Rs. 4 (30¢) and the hours are 10 a.m. to 9 p.m.

At the intersection of Residency and Polo View Roads is the **Alkasalka** (tel. 76559), highly recommended by Kashmiris. Trout is the house specialty, at Rs. 25 ($1.90); Chinese dishes range from Rs. 20 ($1.55) to Rs. 50 ($3.85); Indian, Rs. 18 ($1.40) to Rs. 23 ($1.75).

The **Capri,** up a flight of stairs on Polo View Road (tel. 73318), is a cozy place, offering food for a late snack or supper or dancing at any time, and it's popular with the younger set. Food is continental, including the Indian version of minestrone, pizza and pasta dishes, and there are Chinese and Indian choices as well. The average prices are Rs. 12 (90¢) to Rs. 25 ($1.90). There's rock music (not loud) in the background, plus a bar. Open from 10 a.m. to midnight every day.

Run by the government to promote delicious Indian-grown coffee, the **India Coffee House,** on Residency Road (tel. 77082), is popular with Kashmiris, who drop in for a cup of coffee and snacks on the balcony. Everything on the menu is about Rs. 1.25 (10¢) to Rs. 6.15 (45¢). Open from 10 a.m. to 7 p.m.; closed Sunday.

Lhasa, on Boulevard Lane (tel. 71438), is a candlelit restaurant serving Tibetan dishes such as gyathuk (noodle and meat soup), pishi, suchiao (both dumpling soups), and sha phali (minced meat and fried bread). Mo-mo (Tibetan dumplings) are available by special order, at Rs. 18 ($1.40) to Rs. 20

($1.55) a dozen. The restaurant also serves Chinese foods, including a special chow mein with black mushrooms, egg, and chicken; special prawns (done with black mushrooms); fried wonton; and many good rice and noodle dishes. Most of the dishes are Rs. 18 ($1.40) to Rs. 30 ($2.30). The propietor, A. R. Namgyal, will be glad to help you make Tibetan selections and explain to you what you're getting. The restaurant is open from noon to 11:30 p.m. or midnight all year.

Lunch **buffets** of Kashmiri and continental foods can be found at both the Oberoi-Palace (lunch only) and Centaur (lunch and dinner) hotels. Figure on Rs. 65 ($5) per person for either of the all-you-can-eat meals. Hours are 12:30 to 3 p.m.

TOURS: In addition to touring the Mughal gardens by shikara for about Rs. 100 ($7.70) to Rs. 130 ($10), there are coach tours and taxis to take you to see the sights.

The **Jammu and Kashmir Road Transport Corporation** runs two coach tours a day, at Rs. 22 ($1.70), from 8:30 a.m. to 1:30 p.m. and from 2 to 6:30 p.m. A special evening coach tour to Shankaracharya Hill and Chashmi Shahi Gardens costs Rs. 20 ($1.55). For information and tickets for the tours, check with the Tourist Reception Centre, which also is their departure place.

Taxi sightseeing rates are posted prominently in Srinagar at the taxi stand near the Tourist Reception Centre and other important taxi stands. But you'll probably have to engage in some Kashmiri bargaining rites before you're permitted passage to anywhere. Be sure to agree on where you're going and what it's going to cost before you get in. When this edition was researched, posted rates for sightseeing by taxi were: to ride around the Mughal Gardens, Rs. 110 ($8.45); around the city, Rs. 65 ($5); to the Shankaracharya Temple, Rs. 50 ($3.85); to the sound-and-light show, Rs. 80 ($6.15). These are round-trip fares. These are point-to-point fares to and from the Tourist Reception Centre.

TAXIS AND OTHER TRANSPORTATION: Taxis cost Rs. 3.55 (25¢) for the first two kilometers and 32.65 paise (2½¢) for each subsequent kilometer within the city. Some taxis don't have meters, so be sure to set rates before you get in. You might use a city map (get it at the Tourist Reception Centre) to show where you are going and distances. It's also advisable to read the odometer when you start and when you stop to check the distance covered. The above rates apply only within the municipal area and specified area limits.

Beyond these areas, if a taxi returns empty you must pay one-third of the normal rate. For instance, taxis from the airport to the Tourist Reception Centre cost Rs. 57 ($4.40), but going out to the airport runs about Rs. 100 ($7.70) —you pay for the return fare. (Coach fare to or from the airport is Rs. 10, 75¢.) Where taxi meters exist they may not have been properly calibrated, so ask for the tariff card to know what you should pay.

Auto-rickshaw rates are Rs. 1.40 (11¢) for the first kilometer or part thereof, and 65 paise (5¢) for each subsequent 150 meters, 40 paise (3¢) detention charges for each five minutes of waiting, 50 paise (3½¢) for each package or baggage exceeding 30 centimeters by 50 centimeters.

Bicycles can be rented near Dal Gate or Regal Chowk Square for Rs. 8 (60¢) for half a day off-season and Rs. 5 (40¢) an hour in season.

ENTERTAINMENT: The **Broadway Theatre**, Badami Bagh Road, features English, American, and Indian films. Admission is Rs. 7 (55¢) in the balcony,

Rs. 5.50 (42¢) in the dress circle, Rs. 4 (30¢) in second class and Rs. 2.50 (20¢) in third class. And would you believe separate lines for men and women?

GETTING TO SRINAGAR: You can fly from Delhi for Rs. 671 ($52), from Chandigarh for Rs. 571 ($44), from Amritsar for Rs. 388 ($30), and from Jammu for Rs. 223 ($17). Alternatively, you can take the **train** from Delhi to Jammu Tawi (the end of the line), a 590-km (360-mile) trip of 9 to 13 hours, for Rs. 200 ($15.40) in first class and Rs. 50 ($3.85) in second class. **Coaches** meet these trains to take you to Srinagar, for Rs. 68 ($5.25) deluxe, Rs. 43 ($3.30) for A Class, and Rs. 25 ($1.90) to Rs. 30 ($2.30) for B Class. **Taxis** are also at the Jammu station, and you can usually get a seat for Rs. 155 ($11.90); a full car, Rs. 621 ($47.75). There's also coach service from Delhi (a long trip), Kulu, Chandigarh, and Amritsar.

2. Gulmarg and Pahalgam

GETTING TO GULMARG: It's about 35 miles (56 km) from Srinagar to Gulmarg, through the rice paddies of the valley and the pine forests of the Himalayas. You can go directly by deluxe **sightseeing coach** run by the State Road Transport Corporation, for Rs. 45 ($3.45) round trip (leaving precious little time to see anything) or Rs. 26 ($2) one way, if you want to return after spending a few days. There is also **regular bus** service, which takes under three hours and costs less than half the above one-way prices. These buses leave about ten times a day.

By **taxi,** the trip is about Rs. 280 ($21.55) round trip, Rs. 230 ($17.70) one way. Despite the fact that these are fixed fares, you should make sure of the charges before you set off. Some drivers will try to get you to pay full round-trip charges for sending the cab back empty to Srinagar if you're only going one way. Alternatively, you can sometimes find an empty cab going back to Srinagar when you are, and can bargain down the fare. Split among three or four, the taxi isn't bad, and if you're just going for the day it gives you flexibility to sightsee as you choose. Your driver will stand by while you go off to admire the view or wander through a flower meadow, both of which are main attractions here.

Some people break the trip in **Tangmarg**—taxi fare this far is Rs. 172 ($13.25)—a village partway up into the mountains, only about 8 miles (13 km) from Gulmarg, and transfer to a pony or walk the remainder of the trip. You can hire a pony for Rs. 13 ($1) one way and a mazdur (porter with sling) to carry your bags for Rs. 9 (70¢), also one way. There's live entertainment however you go: lots of monkeys playing in the pine trees.

In Tangmarg, **Mahajan** is a sunny restaurant and bus stop where you can have coffee, soft drinks, snacks, or a complete meal before or after your trip to Gulmarg.

If you're there in the winter up to April 1, the road above Tangmarg may be snow-covered and you'll need a four-wheel-drive Jeep, at Rs. 150 ($11.55) one way). There is also a bus, costing Rs. 10 (75¢), but you may get awfully cold waiting for it and lose time. It comes only a few times a day in winter.

As an alternative in good weather, you might want to walk or take a pony from Tangmarg to Khilanmarg, famous for wildflowers, especially in spring, also for views of the mountains and lakes at all times. For this round trip, a pony will cost Rs. 30 ($2.30); a mazdur, Rs. 20 ($1.55). If you like, you can settle in at Gulmarg first and go to Khilanmarg from there for the same price, when the spirit moves you.

Now, when all is said and done, the easiest way to make arrangements for an excursion to Tangmarg and Gulmarg is to go to the booking counter in the Tourist Reception Centre in Srinagar and consider your options—a hurried day trip or a longer stay.

GULMARG: Gulmarg means "meadow of flowers." And in fact it's an earthly beauty spot, where pastoral pleasures are merged with the aforementioned diversions of long walks and pony rides, in addition to golf and trout fishing. From vantage points around Gulmarg you can see the entire valley of Kashmir set out like a doll's village below and admire the surrounding mountains: to the north is Nanga Parbat, at 26,000 feet, one of the highest mountains in the range.

A saucer-shaped valley, 8,700 feet high in the mountains, Gulmarg has elaborately carved wooden hotels and stores, aged dark brown by severe winter weather. Some of these buildings go back to bygone days when Gulmarg was the favorite haunt of the English establishment.

Skiing

In the summer, the days are mild, the mornings and nights cool and crisp; in winter, it's freezing cold and there's enough good snow to make Gulmarg attractive to skiers. Currently the area is being promoted as a ski resort. From about mid-December to mid-March five lifts operate: three T-bars, a rope tow, and a double-chair lift. They get you high enough for a pretty good run on superb slopes. But compared to Aspen or St. Moritz, skiing facilities are primitive. Though some of the hotels stay open, they are heated only by fireplaces and Bukhari stoves (small, wood-burning metal stoves). Moreover, flights from Delhi to Srinagar in winter are irregular at best, and roads to Tangmarg and Gulmarg are chancy. So skiing here will have most appeal to the adventurous. And to the budget-minded. Equipment (skis, poles, boots, and gloves) can be rented for Rs. 40 ($3.05) per day; an instructor is Rs. 20 ($1.55) per day; and a chair lift is Rs. 3 (23¢) per trip or Rs. 55 ($4.25) for a day ticket; other lifts, Rs. 1 (7½¢) per trip or Rs. 25 ($1.90) a day. If you want to ride the chair lift, up and back costs Rs. 6.5 (50¢). When it comes to skiing information, contact the Government of India Gulmarg Winter Sports Project, Suhk Niwas, Rajbagh, Srinagar; or Principal, Indian Institute of Mountaineering, Gulmarg; or Directorate of Tourism, Jammu and Kashmir Government, Srinagar 190001.

Golf

More on target for some visitors is the Golf Club, which adjoins what is purportedly the highest 18-hole course in the world. The golf course has recently been relaid by the famous Australian golfer Peter Thompson, and is a much greater challenge than before. Rates are Rs. 10 (75¢) to rent a full set of clubs, Rs. 20 ($1.55) for 18 holes, and Rs. 20 ($1.55) for a caddy. Membership costs Rs. 25 ($1.90) per day for one, and allows you to use the club's lounge and bar. You can also rent golf balls in various states of repair—used at Rs. 10 (75¢) or Rs. 15 ($1.15), and new at Rs. 25 ($1.90).

Trekking

From Gulmarg there are a variety of interesting treks requiring various degrees of fitness and expertise. True novices might want to take a walk rather than a multi-mile uphill hike. The **Outer Circle Walk** goes around Gulmarg through the piney woods, and provides panoramic valley views and glimpses of the great peaks. The 40-minute uphill hike to Khilanmarg is paved with posies (could it be the place the Mughal emperor Jahangir picked 21 different kinds of flowers?). From the top, you get a superlative view of Wular Lake, the largest freshwater lake in India and important to the hydrographic system of Kashmir. **Kantar Nag** is a three-day trip up to see a little lake on the mountain-top. For trekking maps and information, check with the tours counter at the **Tourist Reception Centre** in Srinagar, or **Kai Travels,** Tara Bhawan, Srinagar (tel. 74180), or another agent on the approved list available at the Tourist Reception Centre.

Getting Around Gulmarg

It should cost about Rs. 35 ($2.70) for a **pony trip** around Gulmarg. Should you want to go out for a day it's Rs. 70 ($5.40), and for Rs. 60 ($4.60) a guide will come along. On the trails you can see wild monkeys in the woods and beautiful birds and flowers. **Jeep taxis** also operate around the valley, which is only a couple of miles long. There are scenic walks to explore the valley, some of them described under "Trekking." In the winter you can also ski at Khilanmarg, a 40-minute uphill journey by foot or Jeep or a bus in fair weather.

Where to Stay and Eat

In Gulmarg, in season (May, June, September, and October) it's advised that you book rooms well in advance.

Excellent buys are the **Government Tourist Huts,** open all year with one, two-, three-, and four-bedroom accommodations. They're called huts, but that's somewhat of a misnomer for they have all the comforts of little homes: bathrooms, dressing rooms, kitchens, plus bedrooms. Rates for huts are Rs. 140 ($10.75) to Rs. 160 ($12.30) for a one-bedroom, Rs. 200 ($15.40) to Rs. 230 ($17.70) for a two-bedroom, Rs. 260 ($20) to Rs. 280 ($21.55) for a three-bedroom, and Rs. 285 ($21.90) to Rs. 300 ($23.05) for a four-bedroom. The foregoing rates are applicable May through June, and in August, September, and October. For the remaining months a concession of 25% will be made. During July there is a 50% concession for local occupants because it is vacation season.

You'll need to rent linens for bedrooms and bathrooms, at Rs. 4 (30¢) per day. Crockery and cutlery come with the some of the huts without a rental charge. You rent these items in the other huts. If you're interested, write at least two months in advance for reservations to: Deputy Director of Tourism Reservations, Tourist Reception Centre, Srinagar 190001.

A top choice for splurging, the **Highlands Park Hotel** (tel. 30 or 91), a chalet-style hotel whose pine-paneled rooms have bathrooms and phones. The hotel is heated in winter and is one of the few to remain open almost year round (it's closed only from November 1 to December 15). Rates are Rs. 525 ($40.40) for singles, Rs. 725 ($55.75) for doubles, including meals but not the 10% service charge. The dining room has a splendid view and is a combination of chalet and hunting lodge in decor: Indian instruments, weapons, and tiger skins on the walls. Shooting tigers is now prohibited in India, so presumably these skins are quite old. Hearty meals at lunch and dinner can include, soup, soufflé, meat curry, rice chapatis, vegetables, beverage, and dessert. This will cost you Rs. 45 ($3.45) if you just drop in. Breakfast for casual visitors—big and satisfying—runs Rs. 22 ($1.70).

Nedou's Hotel (tel. 28), open only from May until the end of October, claims to be the oldest hotel in India, and is the parent of the namesake Nedou's in Srinagar (but in far better condition here). The atmosphere is appropriately that of a mountain lodge, with a comfy lounge and bar. Rooms rent for Rs. 200 ($15.40) single and Rs. 260 ($20) double. There's a 10% service charge. The food at this hotel is good: breakfast costs Rs. 25 ($1.90); lunch and dinner, Rs. 45 ($3.45) each for nonresidents.

Set in pine trees on a hillside above Gulmarg's golf course, the **Hotel Woodland** (tel. 60) is a bit of a splurge. It's an inviting rustic place with main building and cottages of wood painted red, with corrugated metal roofs also painted red. Rooms and suites, some of which are in cottages, are nicely appointed, all with dressing rooms and bathrooms with geysers for hot water, some with fireplaces. Deep carpets cover the floors, and walls are of varnished wood, heightening the rustic atmosphere. It's open all year and is near an outdoor skating rink and beginner's ski slope. The dining room serves Indian, continental, and Chinese food. In the winter all the rooms are heated by fireplaces and Bhukari stoves, and you'll be charged Rs. 5 (40¢) per kilogram for extra wood when needed. With meals, rooms cost Rs. 275 ($21.15) singles and Rs. 375 ($28.85) double. Suites are Rs. 300 ($23.05) to Rs. 500 ($38.45). There is a 10% service charge.

The **Hotel Kingsley** (tel. 55) is a pretty spare place, and overpriced for what you get. But if everything's full up and you have to spend the night, singles are Rs. 100 ($7.70) and doubles cost Rs. 200 ($15.40). All rooms have bathrooms attached, all but one with a Western toilet; some rooms have geysers for hot water, while in others it's the bucket brigade, free of charge. Rooms are not well furnished or maintained. Those on the upper floors open off outside corridors and are bright and more cheerful than the others.

The **Gulmarg Inn** (tel. 57) is a charming chalet with double windows overlooking the golf course. There are only six rooms, all with bath attached. All have every amenity, but those in front have little balconies where you can stand outside and watch the golfers play—a great place to be during an important match. The rates are Rs. 225 ($17.30) single and Rs. 400 ($30.75) double, meals included.

A new hotel in town is the 14-room **Hotel Ornate Woodlands** (tel. 68), where singles with full board are Rs. 300 ($23.05) and doubles go for Rs. 500 ($38.45). This includes bedtime tea, breakfast, afternoon tea with cookies, and dinner. You can also stay for half board, which means breakfast and lunch or dinner. This hotel has a two price tiers for meals, the vegetarian being Rs. 10 (75¢) to Rs. 15 ($1.15) less than nonvegetarian. There is an 11-dish buffet, including soup and dessert, in case you want to drop in for lunch. Without meals, the room-only rate is about Rs. 100 ($7.70) to Rs. 200 ($15.40) less than full board.

Another newcomer is the **Hotel New** (where's the old one?) **Zum Zum** (tel. 15), with 20 double wood-paneled, carpeted rooms with bathrooms attached, plus running hot and cold water. They are heated with Bhukari stoves. Singles cost Rs. 175 ($13.45) and doubles go for Rs. 300 ($23.05).

New also is the **Pine Palace** (tel. 66), a clean place, but a bit high priced for accommodations which are not special: Rs. 210 ($16.15) for singles and Rs. 300 ($23.05) for doubles. If you're one of the rare tourists who comes to Kashmir to ski, this hotel is not far from the ski lift.

Scheduled to open soon were the Hotels Afferuat, Pashwan, and Welcome.

An old favorite with budgeteers, the government-run **Tourist Bungalow** is roomy and clean, with Indian-style toilets in the bathrooms, showers, and sinks. The bungalows are open year round, and are centrally heated. Rooms run Rs. 150 ($11.55). There's also the government-run **Tourist Hotel**, with similarly priced rooms. No meals are served at either the bungalow or the hotel. To reserve, write to: Reservations Manager, Jammu and Kashmir Tourist Development Corporation, Tourist Reception Centre, Srinagar, Kashmir 190001.

GETTING TO PAHALGAM: The best time to start from Srinagar is early in the morning so you can enjoy the interesting sights along this 60-mile (96-km) journey through villages and orchards. Take a snack, as you may have delays en route—tongas tangled in traffic with trucks, chickens crossing the road, that sort of thing.

You can take a sightseeing coach—Rs. 45 ($3.45) round trip or Rs. 26 ($2) one way—if you care to spend a few days. Regular **buses** also ply this route. A **taxi** to Pahalgam costs Rs. 287 ($22.05) one way and Rs. 345 ($26.55) round trip; if you go along the sightseeing route the round-trip fare to Pahalgam is Rs. 460 ($35.40). Like Gulmarg, a taxi is not too bad for the budget if you share, and it permits you the freedom to see the sights at your own pace. And below are the sights to see along the way.

Sights En Route

Pampore: Only 10 miles (16 km) from Srinagar are the famous saffron fields. They're fallow in summer but purple and pluckable in October. Kashmir produces, along with Spain, some of the world's finest saffron—highly prized and highly priced as a cooking spice. Then Sangam, noted for cricket bats.

Avantipura: Two ruined temples built by Avantivarmans in A.D. 855–883. The largest, dedicated to Vishnu, still has some carvings extant. Here also are what's left of a couple of ancient pleasure domes and palaces.

Anantag: A fairly large town and very busy, it has several mineral springs, the largest believed to be the home of Ananta, the serpent upon which Vishnu reclines—hence the town's name. Lots of people are milling about doing their daily chores.

Achabal: It's shortly beyond the Pahalgam turnoff, the site of a Mughal garden laid out by Jahanara, the daughter of Shah Jahan, builder of the Taj Mahal. She called this "Begumbad." To this day, bubbling springs from the hills send streams through the canal. There are three fountains and a pavilion. Nearby is the Government Trout Culture Farm, breeding baby fish to stock lakes around these parts. There's a **Tourist Bungalow,** at Rs. 50 ($3.89) double, and **Tourist Huts,** at Rs. 75 ($5.75) per two-bedroom hut. For reservations, contact the Director of Tourism, J&K Government Tourist Reception Centre, Srinagar 190001. You can get tea and snacks at the cafeteria on the site and at the Tourist Bungalow.

Kokarnag: Beyond Achabal, Kokarnag is famous for its rose gardens and natural springs gushing from a wooden hill. It's a restful little resort where there's a **Tourist Bungalow,** at Rs. 50 ($3.85) double per day, and **Tourist Huts,** at Rs. 105 ($8.05) a day. There's also a cafeteria for a rest break.

Mattan: Once again back on the Pahalgam route, Mattan is the site of a spring holy to Hindus.

Martand: On a plateau above Mattan are ruins of an ancient temple built by Lalitaditya Mukhtapida (A.D. 699–736). There's a pond as you enter, and you'll see women doing their laundry. Two other pools, Kamal and Vimal, are chock full of Kashmiri fish called chush. The fish are regarded as holy and must not be eaten.

PAHALGAM: Surrounded by mountains, garden-studded Pahalgam, on the Lidder River at 7,200 feet, is little more than a main street. Outside town the

Pahalgam Club (tel. 22), operated by the government tourist office, has table tennis, badminton, a card room, and a bar. Temporary membership is Rs. 3 (23¢) a day. The club is open all year from 9 a.m. to 10:30 p.m. There are three rooms available to nonmembers at Rs. 95 ($7.30).

Where to Stay

Right in town, the government-run **Tourist Bungalow and Cottages** are very nice. The "bungalow" has seven rooms renting for Rs. 50 ($3.85) to Rs. 75 ($5.75) a night. Meals are à la carte in the attractive wood-paneled dining room on the premises. The low-budgeteer's best best is to try to get into this tourist bungalow.

Like Gulmarg's, the "huts" or cottages in Pahalgam are quite nice. They cost Rs. 140 ($10.75) to Rs. 160 ($12.30) for one-bedroom "C"-class accommodations, Rs. 200 ($15.40) to Rs. 230 ($17.70) for two bedrooms, and Rs. 260 ($20) to Rs. 280 ($21.55) for three bedrooms. These rates are applicable during May, June, August, September, and October. Rates are 25% lower at other times, and for local occupants there is a 50% discount in July.

The **Hotel Woodstock** (tel. 27) looks like a gray fort from the road, but actually faces a beautiful site with a river and a garden to the rear. At this writing the hotel was under renovation but looked promising. The prerenovation rates in this centrally heated hotel are splurge-high and might be higher when all alterations are completed: Rs. 425 ($32.70) to Rs. 675 ($51.90) for singles and Rs. 500 ($38.45) to Rs. 750 ($57.70) for doubles.

The newly renovated **Pahalgam Hotel** (tel. 26) still looks the same from the outside—appropriately like a mountain lodge, with big windows and nice views. Lots of new additions—such as a covered heated swimming pool, color television, and a health club with a sauna—have made the rates splurge-high: Rs. 525 ($40.40) single and Rs. 700 ($53.85) double, with meals. The hotel is centrally heated. There is a 10% service charge, and taxes as applicable.

Less expensive, but still not cheap, the **Hotel Heaven** (tel. 17) is approached by a wooden bridge on the far side of the Aru River. This quiet spot is removed from the center and, indeed, guests are given free transportation to town from here. Rates are Rs. 375 ($28.85) single and Rs. 450 ($34.60) double, with meals; without meals, the rooms are Rs. 100 ($7.70) per person. However, in this out-of-the-way location you're probably better off including meals as you'll undoubtedly end up eating at least two of your daily meals here.

The **Natraj Hotel and Restaurant** (tel. 25) is lodge-like and cozy, in keeping with the area, and serves good food as well. Rooms are Rs. 190 ($14.60) single and Rs. 250 ($19.25) double. The rooms have telephones and piped-in music. There are cottages on the grounds, with kitchens and dining rooms, renting for Rs. 600 ($45.15).

The **Plaza Hotel** (tel. 39), open March 15 to November 15, has 30 rooms, and looks like it might have been a private home before it was a hotel. All rooms are doubles, with attached bath and hot and cold running water. Pleasant and breezy, the rooms have settees as well as beds and dressers; some look out on pasture, and others on a golf course. There's a charming garden surrounding the hotel. Rates are Rs. 325 ($25) for two; there are no single rooms, so you may have to pay the double rate. The price includes all meals, which in this case means bedtime tea, breakfast, lunch, afternoon tea, and dinner, with a choice of vegetarian and meat dishes. Lodging only is Rs. 200 ($15.40) double.

Three other places in the above price range are **Shepherd's Hotel** (tel. 74), **Pine View** (tel. 70), and **Mountain View** (tel. 21), the last under renovation as this edition was written.

Super Budget: Acceptable low-budget hotels are nearly impossible to find in Pahalgam; the following, therefore, are more in the moderate than the low price range.

Across the Lidder River from the posher hotels are some modest, less expensive places to stay. These include the **Windrush, Bente's,** and **Aksa Lodge.** Rates start at Rs. 80 ($6.15) and go up to about Rs. 150 ($11.55).

Others in this area are the **Hill Park,** high a top a hill in the woods. Farther out is the two-year-old **White House,** on Laripora Road, which stops just short of the hotel. The hotel provides Jeep transport into town. There are only eight rooms, with bathrooms attached. Rates are Rs. 40 ($3.05) to Rs. 100 ($7.70). A restaurant was to open shortly.

Finally, when you're talking cheap, you're talking a **tent.** The tourist office offers lodging in tents, five nights for Rs. 190 ($14.60). There are places in town to rent some of the items you need, such as cots and bedding, for a comfortable tent stay. For more information, contact the Srinagar tourist office.

Eating Out

The **Hotel Aspara,** in the center of town opposite the bus parking lot, is not much of a hotel, but the restaurant has good food, decently priced: a vegetarian lunch of alu gobi (curried cauliflower), palak paneer (spinach and cheese), chapatis, and a pot of tea is Rs. 18 ($1.40).

A Pilgrimage from Pahalgam

The magical time to visit Pahalgam is during the July-August full moon, when a five-day pilgrimage is conducted to the sacred cave of **Amarnath,** at 12,700 feet, where Hindus worship what they call the lingam of Lord Shiva. This is a stalagmite which shrinks and grows according to the full moon (and the varying, unseen water supply).

The pilgrimage, made on horseback, takes five days to cover the 27-mile (46.7-km) round trip and is accompanied by members of the tourist board who provide facilities such as medical van, cafeteria, and tents for sleeping. Although most Indians make the trip on foot, Westerners usually find it easier to rent a pack pony and riding pony for Rs. 375 ($28.85) and Rs. 385 ($29.60) respectively. No meat is served and none is supposed to be eaten during the pilgrimage.

The cave was discovered by a poor shepherd named Buta Malik who was searching for an Indian holy man, a sadhu who had given him a sack of coal. When Malik got home, he found that the sack contained gold and, rushing back to thank his benefactor, stumbled across the cave. The sadhu was never seen again, but the cave has been a holy place ever since. Part of the donations made on the pilgrimage go to Malik's descendants, who still live in the area, and the remainder to the Dharmardh Trust which cares for all Hindu religious places.

Trekking

On a little walk downstream or a multiday trek, you can best savor the beauties of the area. The popular three-day trek goes to **Kolahoi Glacier** (11,000 feet). **Kolahoi** is also a three-day pony trip, with pack and riding pony about Rs. 130 ($10) or more each by publication date. To **Sonamarg,** "meadow of gold" (9,000 feet) is a five-day trek through Kashmir's Sindh Valley, renowned for dense coniferous valleys where trees rise over 100 feet high. From Sonamarg, treks can be made to the distant white walls of the Himalayas bordering on Tibet.

For other routes and planning assistance, consult the tour desk at the Tourist Reception Centre in Srinagar, Kai Travels in Srinagar, or another approved travel agent.

Tours

You can take coach tours beyond Gulmarg and Pahalgam to **Wular Lake,** leaving at 9 a.m., for Rs. 38 ($2.90); to **Yusmarg,** in the Pir Panjal range, leaving at 9 a.m., for Rs. 38 ($2.90); and to **Sonamarg,** leaving at 8:30 a.m., for Rs. 43 ($3.30). All fares here are round trip, although there are one-way fares to some out-of-the-way places where rest houses offer overnighters a few rooms. Make sure you have a place to stay before you set off. All tours start and end at the Tourist Reception Centre. Some don't operate in the off-season, and the departure times vary seasonally, so check.

3. Ladakh—Beyond the Vale

Think of going someplace remote and Ladakh (pop. 120,000)—India's highest region, north of the Himalayas nudging into Tibet, closed by snow from November to May, open to tourists only since 1974—would seem to fill the bill.

Well, think again. With tour buses and taxis rumbling regularly in over the mountains from Srinagar and several jet flights, Ladakh, called the "rooftop of the world," is now high on the list of must-visit places for adventurous tourists. Such large numbers of Germans pass through these parts that a sign on an antique store in Leh, the main city, is written "Antiken" to attract Teutonic travelers.

Yet despite sizable inoculations of Westernism, Ladakh remains a place apart from all others. It is as rich a repository of Tibetan culture as you're apt to find in this day and age. In the towering mountains of Ladakh, Buddhists have meditated since three centuries before the birth of Christ, and in this country the purest form of Tibetan Buddhism is practiced to this day.

Long before Tibet was converted, Buddhism was introduced in Ladakh in the 3rd century B.C. by missionaries sent from India by the great Emperor Ashoka, ruler of the whole of non-Tamil India, Afghanistan, Kashmir, and Nepal. By A.D. 400 a Buddhist monk named Fa-hsein, traveling as a pilgrim from monastery to monastery, reported on Buddhist rites, and tooth and bowl relics of Buddha in Ladakh. Later came the Tibetan influence, dominant today. Now travelers make pilgrimages to marvel at gompas (monasteries) built on sheer rock faces and decorated with masterpieces of art hundreds of years old.

Since 1947 Ladakh has been part of Kashmir and Jammu—a not altogether happy arrangement. There are complaints that Kashmiris don't understand the Ladakhi's culture and that progress in farming and irrigation has been too slow. Now, as in centuries past, melting glaciers are the main source of irrigation for the patches of green that stand out against a background as barren as the moon.

Ladakh's scanty rainfall averages between five and nine inches a year. Where the sun shines brilliantly 320 days out of the year, there is little cloud cover and temperatures go up and down like bouncing balls—it can be extremely hot in the midday summer sun and downright cold by the middle of that same night. In the winter the temperatures drop to −60°F (−50°C) below. That's in a few parts of the warmer areas: up in the mountains it goes even lower.

The dazzling sun may be Ladakh's salvation: the use of solar energy for cooking and heating is getting under way in Leh. Presently so little of Ladakh is electrified that the lights in Leh come on for only three hours each night.

Ladakh today is a sensitive border area between India, China, and Pakistan, with the barest traces of the ancient splendor described by early silk traders. Yet this old land of gompas, apricot groves, and ancient rites still weaves a spell around visitors.

LEH: The main city, Leh (pop. 10,000), is virtually a main street at a spectacularly high 11,500 feet where Kashmiri merchants rent stores and pursue you relentlessly to buy merchandise you can get more cheaply in Srinagar, and numerous fascinating but untidy lanes where you can wander aimlessly poking into Tibetan shops.

In the long open market you can watch Ladakhis smoking, drinking butter tea, socializing, and haggling over bangles, prayer flags, beads, bells, mittens, and shawls. All day they come and go in the market—married women in their high hats and full skirts, and the unmarried, hatless, with simpler robes, men with deeply lined faces, ragged kids, stray dogs, and old men turning their prayer wheels round and round. Produce sellers turn up evenings with eggplants, peppers, and golden apricots (the last an acclaimed delicacy, to be eaten only after washing in treated water and peeled, or if dried, soaked in treated water before eating).

In the main bazaar is the mosque that was built in 1594. Islam was introduced in Ladakh more than 300 years ago. The Muslim religion is still prominent today.

Near Indian Airlines on the main road, the **Tourist Office** (open from 8 a.m. to 8 p.m. in summer and 10 a.m. to 4 p.m. in winter) provides maps and pamphlets on Ladakh. Next door is the environmental project, conducted by a German solar scientist, to teach Ladakhis how to use the sun as a source of fuel. Up the hill right next to the Tsemo-La Hotel is where they've built the solar-heated library. Across the road, little boys skinny-dip in the town tank and then stretch out along the retaining wall like chubby seals drying off in the sun.

Don't worry about getting lost in the labyrinth of old streets—you'll eventually reach the center again. And wherever you wander you'll find Ladakhis smiling, helpful, and willing to point you in the right direction.

Leh Palace

Leh Palace, looming above the town, is the main sightseeing attraction. Built around 1600 on a granite ledge shaped like an elephant's head, it's a smaller version of the Potala built around the same time by the fifth Dalai Lama in Lhasa, Tibet. A remnant of magnificence now, the decaying Leh Palace, dwarfed by the mountains, is dazzling by the morning sun and a ghostly guardian by moonlight. The palace was badly damaged during the Dogra Wars of the last century, when the royal family fled to Stok where their descendants live to this day. Centuries of abandonment and vandalism have further added to the deterioration of the once-grand Leh Palace, until the best thing about it is the view below. The palace is supposed to be open from 6 to 9 a.m. and again from 5 to 7 p.m. But don't be surprised if it doesn't open at the appointed hours, or any others for that matter, and you have to be contented only with the view below.

High above the palace are the even more ruined older **palace-fort** and what little remains of the **Temple of the Guardian Divinities,** which houses a big Buddha (sightseeing for those who dote on great views and long hikes). **Sankar Gompa** (monastery), a pleasant short walk from the town center (open from 6 to 8 a.m. and 5 to 7 p.m.), has a multi-armed and multi-handed Avalokiteshvara, or Buddha of Compassion.

Where to Stay in Leh

With tourism becoming a major factor in Ladakh, not surprisingly perhaps everyone in town seems to be going into the hotel and guesthouse business. Hotels are classified "A," "B," "C," and "D." "Class A" hotels cater to groups. Hotel rates include meals. Guesthouses are ranked "Upper," "Medium," and "Economy" class, and can be anything from a few rooms in a family's home to accommodations just for tourists. Meals are usually à la carte in guesthouses. Tariffs in both hotels and guesthouses are set by the district administration. They go lower in off-season, and occasionally you'll find someone trying to get more than the official rate. Prices quoted below for places to stay and throughout this chapter could well change by publication time.

Class "A" Hotels: Hotels in this class charge Rs. 350 ($26.90) to Rs. 450 ($34.60) doubles, Rs. 275 ($21.15) to Rs. 350 ($26.90) single.

Half-hidden by gigantic sunflowers and cosmos, the cheerful **Tsemo-La Hotel** (tel. 84) was once a private villa. Clean and neat, the rooms have bright patterned Indian spreads and attached tile bathrooms with hot and cold running water. Two upstairs rooms in the main building have little balconies with splendid views. There are also rooms in annexes looking out on the flower-filled garden. The glass-walled dining room is in a separate building in the garden. The hotel caters to tour groups and so the food to please them is often bland Western or Cantonese rather than favoring curry.

A young, friendly manager at the 22-room **Kangri Hotel** (tel. 51) was proud of the "Ladakhi-style" rooms with deep-pile Tibetan rugs and floor cushions for lounging at low-carved tables. Beds are the usual box springs. All rooms are doubles, with attached bathrooms with hot and cold running water. Three types of food—Ladakhi, Indian, and Chinese—are well prepared at the hotel. If you care to drop in for a meal, it will cost around Rs. 50 ($3.85) for two in Chinese or Ladakhi styles. The hotel is near the generator. It's turned off at 11 p.m. when you can turn in.

K-Sar (tel. 184) has fiery dragons on the reception walls. The generous-size rooms have clean white walls and red carpeting and bedspreads, with mountain views from the front, fields from the back. There are attractive carved wooden chairs in the dining room.

At **Lharimo** (tel. 101) there are 30 rooms, all double, all with bathrooms attached. The attractive lobby has a bright-red lacquered wooden beamed ceiling, and the dining hall is done up with decorative beams as well. The white-walled rooms are clean, and furnished in blond woods. All rooms have windows looking both over the mountains and the wheat fields, and verandas so you can step out and admire the views. The hotel has a spacious lobby, which is not usually the case in Leh.

Shambala (tel. 67), once run by the well-known Oberoi hotels, now is in local hands. Rooms and their attached bathrooms need a lot of tender loving care. The dining room has handsome cornices and pillars. There is also a big fireplace.

Kang La Chien Hotel (tel. 144) has a nice garden where you can sit out under the apple trees. Inside, the pleasant bedrooms have striped spreads and drapes. In the dining room are ornate painted wood pillars to divide up the space. Most of the 24 rooms have attached bathrooms.

You might also find out about the Indus and Lingzi Hotels, unchecked at this writing, but classified as "A."

Class "B" Hotels: Rates in this class are Rs. 300 ($23.05) double, Rs. 165 ($12.70) single.

Hotel Bijoo (tel. 131), behind an iron gate and surrounded by a high brick wall, is a two-story white building with brown-painted wood trim. The rooms, some with double exposures, are neat and have modern furniture, and attached bathrooms.

Very cushy quilts and attractive little dressing tables are interesting additions to the rooms at the **Ibex** (tel. 212), a pleasant hotel and a good buy. On site is a curio shop, travel agent, coffeeshop, and a nice terrace.

The **Hotel Ra-Rab** has clean, simple rooms with bathrooms attached. Away from the bazaar, the hotel's vegetable garden provides for guest meals in Tibetan, Chinese, and continental-style foods.

Himalayan Hotel (tel. 104) is tucked in a shady willow grove near a brook. The ramshackle building houses 16 simply furnished, fairly clean twin-bedded rooms—12 with attached Western-style bathrooms, four with a common bathroom—all overlooking a courtyard where young children play and the women do laundry in tubs. Travelers also camp out in the courtyard at Rs. 15 ($1.15) per tent, and eat their meals à la carte: Rs. 18 ($1.40) for breakfast, Rs. 30 ($2.30) to Rs. 35 ($2.70) for lunch and dinner. Rates for tents will increase to Rs. 15 ($1.15) when the hotel's rating is upped.

Through the red-and-green-trimmed doorway, the tidy **Hotel Omasila** has doubles with twin beds, webbed chairs, garden views, and attached bathrooms. **Hotel Dragon-Leh** (tel. 139) has 16 simply furnished doubles with bathrooms attached, and is almost always filled with trekking parties, whose cooks and porters pitch tents outside. In the lobby some Salvador Dali reproductions decorate the walls. The hotel is a cross between "B" and "C" classes when it comes to comforts.

Class "C": Rates are Rs. 250 ($19.25) double and Rs. 150 ($11.55) single. The **Choksar** is very modest.

In the "D" class, you might find some little uninvited guests living with you.

Guesthouses: Again rates vary by class of accommodation. In *Upper Class,* Rs. 880 ($6.75) double and Rs. 33 ($2.55) single. In *Medium Class,* Rs. 44 ($3.40) double and Rs. 22 ($1.70) single. In *Economy,* Rs. 27 ($2.05) double and Rs. 11 (85¢) single. Guesthouse rates do not include meals. Guesthouses open and close like wildflowers; what you see listed below may not be there when you are, but there will be others.

The best "Upper Class" guesthouse I found, the **New Antelope** (tel. 86), behind a white fence, is a white building trimmed in brown. It's a friendly place with 11 sparsely furnished clean rooms, six with bathrooms attached, the others with common bathrooms, all with Eastern fittings. While there are no single rooms, the rooms without a private bathroom rent at the single rate: Rs. 33 ($2.55). If you want to eat here it will cost Rs. 12 (90¢) for breakfast, Rs. 20 ($1.55) for lunch, and Rs. 50 ($3.85) for dinner.

Of the three "Medium Class" guesthouses I checked—the Toldan, Indus, and Moon Land—none had anything special to recommend it. In fact some in the economy class seemed far better.

Tops among the "Economy" accommodations is **Two Star,** around the bend from the Tsemo-La. Getting to the entrance is a feat, requiring you to wade on stones across a little brook and jump up to the bank before strolling to the door. Guests said the meals were tasty here and cost under $1. Another good "Economy" choice is the **Larchang Guest House,** offering six clean double rooms with cots. All the toilets are Ladakhi style (a hole in the mud floor) and have cold showers. You can get food for Rs. 5 (40¢) to Rs. 10 (75¢) per meal, if you order in advance—which can be an adventure as little if any English is spoken here.

Of the two "Economy Class" guesthouses next door to each other, the **Taj Guest House** (tel. 24), with 11 rooms and showers and toilets in an annex outdoors, is slightly better than the **Palace View,** also with 11 rooms.

The **Palace View Kidar,** another "Economy" accommodation, is near the Polo Grounds, off the main bazaar and down an untidy lane past a peanut seller—Rs. 4 (30¢) for a huge sack, Rs. 6 (45¢) for a bar of peanut candy. Rooms are in annexes on the grounds. A popular place to stay it is, but clean it is not.

Finally, there are the government-run **Tourist Bungalow,** charging Rs. 45 ($3.45) in the VIP room, plus Rs. 4 (30¢) for bedding; and **Dak Bungalow and Circuit House,** both charging Rs. 25 ($1.90). Each has a few double rooms: bathrooms attached, cold water on tap, hot water in buckets. You have to reserve in advance and send a 50% deposit to Assistant Manager of Tourism, Tourist Office, Leh 194001.

Check also the **Tourist Office** for the names places to stay if you arrive without a room. I've only skimmed the surface in this listing.

Eating Out

The best restaurant in town is **Dreamland,** run by Tsering Chodn, a friendly young Tibetan woman who enjoys wearing jeans. In clean surroundings, she serves mainly Tibetan and Chinese dishes. The water is said to be filtered, but the jasmine tea, at Re. 1 (7½¢) is safer and certainly more delicious. For breakfast you can get mango or orange juices at Rs. 6 (45¢) each, and butter pancakes also at Rs. 6. A specialty for dinner (requiring six hours' notice) is gagok (a variety pot of mutton, eggs, carrots, rice, and momos, which are dumplings). It costs Rs. 300 ($23.05) and serves six to ten people. But most main courses are around Rs. 5 (40¢) to Rs. 7 (55¢) with a few going up to Rs. 10 (75¢). Hours are 8:30 a.m. to 10:30 p.m. every day, at least in the tourist season. The restaurant closes in winter.

SEEING THE LADAKH SIGHTS: The main activity in Ladakh is to visit **gompas,** where you get a glimpse of Tantric Buddhism. To put centuries of tradition into a few descriptive lines: Tantric beliefs involve magical, mystical rites with mantras (chants) and yantras (drawings). When used in the right combination they are believed to evoke powers that lead to higher bliss.

One especially well-known mantra is the "Six Syllables," "Om mani padme hum" ("Praise be to the jewel in the heart of the lotus"). In Ladakh this phrase is everywhere—etched repeatedly on the prayer stones left by the pious at the sides of roads, banks of rivers, and especially on top of the many flat-topped walls called *manis.* There are countless manis all over Ladakh with all kinds of holy inscriptions and drawings—some are hundreds of years old and look like stone tapestries. Like the little prayer flags above the bridges, the stones are outdoors so the wind can sweep their blessings through the valley and beyond. Meditation and other techniques are also important to Tantric Buddhism.

Ladakhi Buddhists are united not only by what they believe, but by their powerful rinpoches, or head monks. Rinpoches are more than religious leaders; they cure ills, counsel those in trouble, and like Solomon, settle marital disputes.

Gompas are architectural marvels, built to conform to steep hillsides and blend with the rocks. You're more or less free to wander anywhere in the gompas, with occasional assistance from a monk who will appear from the shadows to show you special treasures such as scrolls or prayerbooks, or a row of jeweled deities with golden bowls in front of them holding something to drink. New offerings are brought by lamas—water in the morning and butter tea in the evening—to please the finicky gods who prefer their refreshments fresh and sanctified. Sometimes you'll be escorted by a lama to the monastery's smoky kitchen for some butter tea, the local favorite drink of mortals as well as gods. It's made, as the name implies, from tea, butter, and also soda and salt, all sloshed about in a big churn. So often have monks at Hemis monastery been photographed making this drink that they'll strike the pose, whether or not you have a camera, and expect a few rupees in return—rupees that go to refurbish the crumbling monastery.

Spitok

A good gompa for starters is **Spitok,** about five miles (eight kilometers) from Leh, and seen from the plane near the airport if you fly into Ladakh. On a small hill above the Indus River, the 500-year-old monastery has a main prayer hall hung with richly decorated tankas and walls with bejewelled gods and goddesses. All this you can see all of the time, but the main statue of the goddess Kali is demurely veiled and revealed only once a year, at festival time. The entry fee is Rs. 13 ($1).

Going beyond Spitok, the road beside the Indus River leads to monasteries at virtually every turnoff. As if to pave the way with prayers, mantra stones line the roadsides and riverbanks clear to Hemis, the largest gompa and farthest on this route from Leh.

Five miles (eight kilometers) from Leh, the first stop is **Choglamsar,** a Tibetan refugee camp, an important center for the study of Buddhism and the making and sale of handcrafts. Yak-wool carpets woven on the site cost Rs. 950 ($73) to Rs. 1,400 ($108), depending on size and the pattern.

Then a detour to **Sabu,** a sprawling village set in the midst of fertile marsh and farmland, where the springs are believed curative. Here's the famous Sabu headache cure: lie with your head between two rocks, face up, eyes shielded from the sun by a cap, and let someone pour thin streams of icy water from a tin can in the center of your forehead until the pain goes away. At another streamlet, people drink and then run around in circles to get sick and throw up their impurities. Having had no headache, I can't attest to the efficacy of the water-on-the-head cure. I can tell you that the mere thought of drinking water to throw up made me decidedly queasy.

Stok

Off the main road again, the suspension bridge to Stok Village is covered with brightly colored prayer flags flapping overhead and scattering blessings as freely as the dust over the route to the 200-year-old **Stok Palace** (entry fee of Rs. 20, $1.55; open from 8 a.m. to 6 p.m.). With few vestiges of its prestigious past, the palace is now home to the Queen of Ladakh (the king died in 1974). About four rooms are open to the public with tankas depicting various miracles of Buddha plus some other exploits. The most holy tanka is guarded by a lama who whisks aside the drapes to reveal it to you. From the summit of the twilight palace, it's a doll's world below of fields studded with chortens (stupas), relics of the saintly, and bright groves against the mountains.

Near the palace is another rug-weaving center where 18 to 20 women sit in two cramped rooms taking three months to make each intricate rug.

The splurgey **Ladakh Sarai** (named after the old tent villages on trader's routes) offers 15 comfortably furnished, tented bungalows in a cool and inviting willow grove below Stok Palace. Three tents share one of the five well-equipped bathrooms in separate cement "tents." There are also a lounge and two dining areas furnished Ladakhi style with low benches and tables a few inches off the floor. In the vegetable garden, foods are grown for the table. There's a Jeep to take you the slightly over 9 miles (15 km) to Leh, at Rs. 112 ($8.60) round trip, waiting charges included, or you can trek to town or around the surrounding areas to Stok and Shey. At the Sarai, rates are not set by the district administrator: Rs. 450 ($34.60), with meals, for a double. For reservations, contact Tiger Tops International, Inc., 2927 Lombard St., San Francisco, CA 94123 (tel. 415/346-3402); or Mountains Travel India Pvt. Ltd., 1/1 Rani Jhansi Rd., New Delhi 110055 (tel. 522004).

Shey and Thiksey

Shey Palace (open from 7 a.m. to 7 p.m. in summer), another six or seven miles farther along, in the 17th century was the sumptuous summer home of the kings of Ladakh and is now largely in ruins. Inside, there's a brightly colored bejewelled gold-gilded 40-foot-high Maitreya (Future) Buddha, and for Rs. 5 (40¢) a lama to show you a library with 1,000 more Buddhas on the walls. On the outside there's the largest victory stupa in the area, with a spire tipped in gold.

From the summit of Shey, the 12-story **Thiksey** gompa, about two miles away, is a breathtaking sight topping a hill overlooking the Indus. Built over centuries stretching back 800 years, Thiksey (entry fee of Rs. 10, 75¢) is a series of buildings constructed at various times and various heights. Some of the treasures include a pillar inscribed with Buddha's teachings, an impressive library, and Maitreya Buddha. You can often see religious ceremonies here. On some festival days the monks have spirited archery contests in the compound behind Skalzang Chamba, the tea shop below the gompa.

Adjacent to the tea shop near Thiksey (okay for tea and soft drinks only) are a few very spare and clean rooms at Rs. 15 ($1.15) per night, with separate shared toilets and showers for men and women—a handy place to stay if you want to catch the dawn ceremonies at Thiksey. But you should bring your own food. While water for tea is boiled and therefore safe to drink, the tea shop kitchen is not overly clean.

Hemis

From Thiksey, you can see **Stakna.** Off the main road, it's not often visited. One of the oldest monasteries in Ladakh, it has some notable 10th-century tankas. **Matho,** also off the beaten path in a side valley, dates from ancient times and is protected by oracles chosen every few years.

For many travelers, **Hemis,** 28 miles (45 km) from Leh, is the highlight of their visit to Ladakh. It's the largest gompa in Ladakh and probably the best known for its summer festival (June or July) held at the height of the tourist season. The three days of festival merriment include performances of masked dancers.

Even without festivities, 400-year-old Hemis (open from 7 a.m. to 7 p.m. in summer and 9 a.m. to 5 p.m. in winter) is an impressive sight: in the dimly lit halls are golden deities decorated with precious stones, their little golden bowls filled in front of them, a turquoise-encrusted stupa, and large library. There is also a big tanka that is shown only once in every 11 years (next time is 1991). The walls inside have paintings of Buddha and vengeful and peaceful deities of Tibetan Buddhism in fairly good condition. At this monastery, and some others, there were monks chanting their prayers and tourists watching and listening.

Below Hemis is a little **guesthouse** which was given by the head lama to Tsering Angchuk, who runs it (badly) now. The five double rooms are simply dreadful, at Rs. 45 ($3.45). Tents are Rs. 20 ($1.55), and just the ticket if you've taken the bus out (which requires overnighting). This is also a place to stop for a cool drink before and after the hefty climb to Hemis.

Other Monasteries

Off the Leh–Srinagar road are many other monasteries. Three of the most worthwhile are: **Lamayuru,** 84 miles (135 km) from Leh, the oldest of the trio, dates from the 10th century, and has caves in back and some artworks indoors; **Rizong,** 46 miles (74 km) from Leh near Khalsi, is the site of a Julichen nunnery and a monastery; and **Alchi,** 41 miles (67 km) from Leh, near Saspul, has remarkable paintings and a huge Buddha. Over ten centuries old, Alchi monastery is on the lowlands rather than on a hilltop. Not far away is **Likir,** which is a monastery and school.

TREKKING: No special permission is needed to trek in Ladakh's untamed mountain wilderness, alive with flowers and streams, and dotted with monasteries, mantra stones, and chortens. But be sure to take everything you need before you set off. While *latos* (shrines to the air and wind) will, according to ancient beliefs, protect you, and the landscape and friendly villagers will let you lodge with them, there won't be stores to provide supplies. Supplies are quite limited in Leh, so the best place to get provisions is the last major city you're in before Ladakh—Srinagar, for instance, or Delhi, if you're coming straight from the plains.

Special permission in writing is needed to climb mountains, and to get it you apply to the Indian Mountaineering Federation, New Delhi. You can rent boots, jackets, and sleeping bags through the tourist officer at the Tourist Office, but experienced trekkers and climbers bring their own.

The tourist officer is also the person to see for hiring ponies and porters.

Whatever you do, don't forget that you're in a sensitive border area and are not permitted to trek more than a mile north of the Leh–Srinagar road. You can visit the monasteries in the forbidden territory by obtaining formal permission from the district magistrate, who will provide the necessary papers and police escort for you.

GETTING AROUND LADAKH: Bus service is cheap, running from under Re. 1 (7½¢) for short rides to around Rs. 10 (75¢) to Rs. 15 ($1.15) for long hauls to stops near monasteries mentioned above. Service can be one, two, or three times daily depending on the route. Be sure to check bus schedules, and allow time to hike to the monasteries and look around. You may not be able to return the same day, so you'll want to be prepared to spend the night in a village home, or take your backpack. Jeeps can take you up and back from Leh to Hemis, stopping at Shey, Thiksey, Stakna, and Stok for Rs. 500 ($38.45), and for about the same price from Leh to Alchi, Rizong, or Likir—something to consider if you can round up a party of five or six.

SHOPPING: Like the rest of India, there are firm restrictions on the export of antiquities more than 100 years old. And it's doubtful that anything of this vintage will be easily found. However, you might locate something worthwhile down the little lane off the main bazaar in the Tibetan shops. **Tibetan Arts** and **Ladakhi Village Curios** had especially good selections of tankas, bowls inlaid with chips of turquoise, bangles, and beads. On the main street, **Imtaz,** Kashmiri merchants with shops in Srinagar, Agra, and Kovalam Beach, has some interesting ivory-chip bangles and bronzes, and a coral- and turquoise-encrusted chang vessel. There were also stores with some hand-knit mittens, shawls, and caps. Generally, the prices are high and the merchants reluctant to come down.

USEFUL INFORMATION: The altitude is 11,554 feet (3,522 meters). Take it easy until you're accustomed to the elevation: at least a day resting if you've flown straight from Delhi, half a day or more if you've come from a few days in Srinagar, at 5,200 feet (1,768 meters).

    Airport Taxis: Fare by Jeep taxi to your hotel or the tourist office is Rs. 25 ($1.90), but so many people usually cram in at once that Rs. 6 (45¢) is what you pay. There are only about 65 Jeep taxis in Leh, plus a few Ambassador cars. There's a mad scramble for Jeeps when at the airport. In town both Jeeps and cars are found at the taxi stand.

    Bag: Take a plastic sack when shopping for fresh apricots or apples (also good here) or you'll get them wrapped in a newspaper cone which falls apart, scattering fruit everywhere. Dried apricots are usually sold in plastic sacks.

    Change: Bring lots of small bills with you. No one ever seems to be able to make change in Ladakh. Not having change is common all over India, but in Ladakh it's difficult to cash traveler's checks.

    Clothing and Cosmetics: Dress in layers. When the sun's up, you'll want to strip down; in the shade, you'll reach for a sweater. You'll need sturdy shoes with nonskid soles for hiking up the steep trails to monasteries. You'll need a hat, sunglasses, sunblock, moisturizer, and lip protector. Take insect repellant. The gardens and groves are beautiful but buggy.

    Courtesies and Customs: "Jullay" is the all-purpose greeting used all the time; shoes are removed at monasteries.

    Electricity: Four hours each day in Leh, 7 to 11 p.m. (sometimes less).

    Flashlight: Don't leave your hotel without it if you want to see the works of art inside the gompas, where the lighting is minimal if at all. You'll also need your flashlight if you intend to prowl around at night.

    Food: There are almost no clean places to eat when you're out at the monasteries on day trips. Some hotels will pack box lunches for these outings. But if yours doesn't, be sure to buy something for the road. Fruit (take a knife to peel it) and Ladakhi bread (bakeries are behind the mosque) are always good munchies. Also remember to take lots of bottled or boiled water whenever you go on an outing. Thirst is almost a constant companion in Ladakh's extremely dry climate. Bottled water is expensive, Rs. 20 ($1.55) per liter in some places in Leh. But better to pay up than to be laid up. For general information, beer is Rs. 30 ($2.30) per liter in the better hotels. Sometime during your stay you might want to try chang, the local intoxicating drink. A local favorite food is thupka, a cereal.

    Passport: Take it with you. There are checkpoints on some routes.

    Taxis: There are about 65 Jeep taxis in all and a few Ambassador cars. The Jeeps are preferable for the unpaved side roads, which often turn into streamlets. You get taxis at the stand in Leh. The cost is Rs. 3 (23¢) to Rs. 5 (40¢) per kilometer around town, and various rates for sightseeing.

GETTING TO LADAKH: It's a two-day, 272-mile (434-km) trip (the road is open June through September, depending on the weather) from Srinagar to Leh, every mountainous moment fascinating, but not for the faint of heart or those who get car sick. The **bus** pulls out of Srinagar at 7:30 a.m., and with the exception of rest stops, comes to a halt 10 to 12 hours later each day. The first lunch stop is Sonamarg. The overnight stop is Kargil, second-largest city in Ladakh, largely Muslim, where the landscape begins to get barren and the hotels are overpriced—Rs. 300 ($23.05) to Rs. 25 ($1.90) double—at any price. There are some mosques to see in Kargil, and imamabaras (famous Turkish monuments), but hardly time to see them unless you break your journey. The highest point of the Srinagar–Leh road trip, quite literally, is Fotu La, at 13,432 feet.

Bus fares are by class. "Super Deluxe" costs Rs. 200 ($15.40), holds 22 people, has nonglare glass windows, and usually goes only on demand (when there is a full load). The Class "A" bus costs Rs. 92 ($7.05), take 24 people, and goes on Wednesday and Saturday, more often if there is a demand for it. The Class "B" costs Rs. 69 ($5.30), goes every day, and carries 52 people.

A seat in a **taxi** from Srinagar to Leh costs Rs. 452 ($34.75) one way or Rs. 905 ($69.60) in a Jeep seat, Rs. 520 ($40) for a single journey, and Rs. 1,041 ($80) round trip.

Indian Airlines flies 737s in three times a week from Srinagar for Rs. 334 ($26), and twice a week from Delhi via Chandigarh for Rs. 741 ($57). During the 30-minute flight from Srinagar, it's interesting to watch the landscape below change abruptly from fertile green fields to barren rockscapes as you approach dry Ladakh.

Aside from the price, there is one big drawback to flying: you may not get in or out as planned. The Leh flight goes only early in the morning and only when the weather is perfect, which isn't all the time. Even on a cloudless day, conditions over the Himalayas can disintegrate rapidly, so the flight is often delayed or cancelled altogether.

Since Ladakh is a sensitive border area and Leh is a major military post, airport security checks are very thorough. If you have sharp implements—scissors, Swiss army knife, whatever—put them in your check-through luggage. Don't attempt to carry them aboard. If they are in your hand baggage or pocket, they'll be taken from you and given to the pilot for you to retrieve from him upon arrival. The pilot is last off the plane and you'll have to wait and hunt him down. On a good day, he may have many Swiss army knives. Ever notice how they all look alike?

Chapter VII

HEADING EAST

1. Varanasi
2. Darjeeling

AT ABOUT SIX O'CLOCK every morning, just as the sun is beginning to rise, thousands of people can be found lining the banks of the muddy River Ganges. They are bathing in its sacred waters, washing their clothes or themselves; filling ornate brass jugs to take home; exercising, stripped to the waist, on the broad stone steps (ghats); or simply sitting, lotus-legged, gazing at the emerging sun with their hands clasped and their minds pure.

Most of them are older people, for Hindus (and others) come to Varanasi (pop. 1,000,000) to die, and to spend their last few years in religious works. But there are younger people too—certainly children, holding the strings of their flat, blue kites; always holy men; and innumerable goats, cows, pigs, pigeons, even an occasional camel.

1. Varanasi

The ghats of Varanasi (often called by its former name, Benares) have been described as the "roots of the city," and most Hindus would hope to visit the city during their lifetime. There are pilgrim houses all along the waterfront, and visitors can stay in them for up to four days with no charge. Then, if they can find the space, move from one to another for four days at a time. Countless pilgrims who have come for a visit have ended up dying and being cremated on one of the burning ghats (crematoriums) along the very same waterfront. The fires and smoke can be seen all day, as can the occasional body, wrapped in a shroud and lashed to a green bamboo stretcher.

Six o'clock in the morning is the magic hour to visit the waterfront, just as it is beginning to stir and the pilgrims, after a visit to one of the scores of priests who sit under rows of straw umbrellas, have their eager faces turned toward the eastern sun's watery rays.

You can take the tourist office's regular morning tour at that hour, or you can walk over to the main steps at the Dasaswamedh ghat and for about Rs. 8 (60¢) to Rs. 10 (75¢) per hour hire a small skiff to transport you up and down the waterfront. A steady creak of ancient oars, the slap of wet cotton garments on the rocks as professional laundrymen ply their trade (Re. 1—7½¢—per cotton piece), the shrill cries of bathers testing the tepid water and a tinkling of scattered temple bells disturb the morning calm. The clash of cymbals comes from a red house where widows sing hymns, their plain white saris unrelieved by any pattern.

Down the river, near the **Someshwar** ghat, a more or less permanent group of hippies share a brightly decorated houseboat; farther up is a Nepalese temple richly decorated with erotic carvings. And between these not dissimilar phenomena sits the elegant home of the "caretaker in charge of burning" at one of the major crematoria. Tigers flank the roof—a symbol that one is never far from death.

The broad and holy River Ganges, which generally flows southeast, in Varanasi reverses its course and flows north. People tell you that this is a tribute to the holiness of the city. But, alas, the scientific explanation is this: Like many old rivers on a flat flood plain, the Ganges is a meandering river and flows in huge U-shaped loops. Varanasi is in one of the loops, so on one side of the city the river flows south and on another it flows north. Despite its apparent pollution the river's sulfur-filled water is pure—some people drink nothing else—but it's not always harmless. White marks along the walls above the riverbank testify to the height of occasional floods.

INFORMATION AND ASSISTANCE: The **Tourist Office,** at 15B The Mall (tel. 43189), adjoining the Hotel de Paris, is very helpful and courteous. Help can be obtained there each day from 9 a.m. to 5:30 p.m. (closed Sunday), and they will happily assist you in hiring taxis or booking tours for sightseeing or give information on local activities.

WHERE TO STAY IN VARANASI: Fifty rooms, all centrally air conditioned, each with a good view and private balcony—these are the attractions of the **Varanasi Ashok Hotel,** The Mall, Varanasi Cantonment, Varanasi 221002 (tel. 42551 to 42559), run by India Tourism Development Corporation (ITDC). The hotel is well situated on the banks of the Varuna River, from which the city derives its name. The rooms are twin-bedded (some have settees that convert to a third bed), and have attached modern bathrooms and telephones. There's a restaurant and coffeeshop, nearly eight acres of landscaped grounds, and a swimming pool. All this can be at your disposal at prices suited to the top end of our budget for two, Rs. 380 ($29.25); Rs. 270 ($20.75) for one. These rates are without meals. Eating at the hotel is pricey. You might have breakfast in the coffeeshop and take your other meals outside at the inexpensive places to eat, mentioned later on.

The posh splurge in town, the **Taj Ganges,** Nadesar Palace Grounds, Varanasi 221002 (tel. 42480), is handsomely decorated with a lotus (symbol of cosmic creation, important to Jains, Hindus, and Buddhists) motif incorporated into the highly polished floors, staff uniforms, carpets, and around the lifts. There are interesting old and new works of art in the lobby. The rooms are comfortably furnished, with cool greens and soothing browns predominating. Bathrooms are brown and white. Cement canopies outdoors keep the sun from beating down and into the rooms, and reducing the air conditioning's effectiveness. Rates are Rs. 500 ($38.45) single and Rs. 550 ($42.30) double.

The most famous hotel in town is **Clark's,** The Mall, Cantonment, Varanasi 221002 (tel. 62021), a venerable, more than 100-year-old colonial-style place that has been considerably modernized. It has comfortable lounges, a long, cool, covered veranda overlooking the neatly kept garden, a spacious bar, and comfortable air-conditioned rooms (carpets, reading lamps, bedside radios). Rates, not including meals, are Rs. 450 ($34.60) single and Rs. 500 ($38.45) double.

Just down the street, the **Hotel de Paris** (tel. 42464, 42465, or 42466), still old colonial in style, but rather run-down, charges Rs. 175 ($13.46) single and Rs. 250 ($19.25) double. All rooms are air-conditioned. There's a pleasant garden dining room and bar.

An excellent, less expensive choice, the **Hotel Jai Ganges,** Maladhiya, Varanasi 221002 (tel. 62384), has nicely decorated rooms and well-appreciated warnings about the tap water in each bathroom: "Not Fit for Drinking." The hotel is walking distance from "everything": tourist office, Indian Airlines, railway station, the Ganges. The dining room has shiny marble floors and bamboo chairs. Air-conditioned singles cost Rs. 160 ($12.30); Rs. 110 ($8.45) air-cooled and Rs. 55 ($4.25) non-air-conditioned. Doubles run Rs. 225 ($17.30) air-conditioned, Rs. 130 ($10) air-cooled, and Rs. 70 ($5.40) with neither of the aforementioned coolers.

The **Diamond Hotel,** Bhelpura, Varanasi 221005 (tel. 56561 to 56565), is multifaceted when it comes to decor: there are bright abstract murals with Indian symbols, leatherette lounge chairs, and, appropriately, a diamond-patterned ceiling. It's a pleasant and colorful place to stay. However, reader Leonard Mehr of Milan, Italy, says that it's out-of-the-way; nor was he crazy about the food. The nicest rooms face the garden: Rs. 80 ($6.15) to Rs. 110 ($8.45) for singles, Rs. 150 ($11.55) to Rs. 210 ($16.15) for doubles, the highest prices for rooms with air conditioning. There's a coffeeshop and restaurant on the premises.

On the same street as the Hotel de Paris, and near it as well, but lower in price, the **Dak Bungalow** (tel. 42182), is owned and operated by the friendly Dr. Pram Asthana. It's actually two or three little bungalows, set in a not-too-well-tended garden. Simple, but fairly clean, the bungalows consist of a bedroom and a stone or tile bathroom. Suites in the main house also have sitting rooms and dressing rooms. Throughout there are drapes and carpeting. Rates are Rs. 45 ($3.45) to Rs. 75 ($5.75). Portable air coolers are Rs. 25 ($1.90) extra, and a bunk in the dorm costs Rs. 20 ($1.55). Breakfast is Rs. 20 ($1.55), and lunch and dinner go for Rs. 30 ($2.30) to Rs. 35 ($2.70). The restaurant is open from 7 a.m. to 10 p.m.

In Varanasi's Lohurabir section, about a mile and a half from the Ganges, are three hotels lined up as if for your inspection. They are a Rs.-3 (23¢) cycle-rickshaw ride from the Indian Airlines building where the buses stop, about a mile from the railroad station, and about 40 minutes from the airport. Though they are all much alike, the nicest is probably the **Ajaya Hotel** (tel. 43707). Its 33 rooms, four of which are air-conditioned and eight are air-cooled, are arranged around large central lounges on each of three upper floors. Although all the rooms are modest, only those with the higher prices are all right—the others should be avoided unless you are completely unfussy. All rooms have attached bathrooms with hot-water showers and cold running water. Room rates are Rs. 35 ($2.70) to Rs. 50 ($3.85) single, Rs. 50 ($3.85) to Rs. 70 ($5.40) double. Meals can be ordered à la carte and will run another Rs. 75 ($5.75) a day. Air-conditioned rooms cost Rs. 100 ($7.70) single, Rs. 150 ($11.55) double; air-cooled rooms, Rs. 75 ($5.75) to Rs. 90 ($6.90). There's a bar and a service charge of 10%.

Right next door, but not as clean, is the **Hotel Natraj** (tel. 65817). All 22 rooms have attached bathrooms and one room is air-conditioned. Singles cost Rs. 35 ($2.70) and doubles go for Rs. 45 ($3.45) to Rs. 55 ($4.25). No dining room: you can take your meals in a large central lounges on each floor.

Next in line is the **Pushpanjali** (tel. 54276). It's smaller than either of its neighbors with only 15 rooms, but it's under the same management as the Ajaya, and like it, could use some tender loving care. The rooms are not air-conditioned, but they have attached bathrooms with hot-water showers: Rs. 30 ($2.30) to Rs. 45 ($3.45) for singles, Rs. 40 ($3.70) to Rs. 55 ($4.25) for doubles. The higher the price, the lower the floor (less stair climbing). Price is the main recommendation.

The **Hotel International,** Lahurabir (tel. 57140), is not for the fussy, with rates from Rs. 33 ($2.55) single to Rs. 88 ($6.75) for an air-conditioned double, and prices between.

Near Lahurabir and the Sanskrit University, the **Hotel Pradeep,** Jagat Ganj, Varanasi (tel. 66362), is neat and clean with beds backed by leatherette headboards and dressing tables in the rooms, which also have carpets, telephones, and attached tile bathrooms. The lower-priced rooms are less well furnished; also, they have no air conditioning or air cooling, although they have overhead fans. Rates are Rs. 50 ($3.85) to Rs. 125 ($9.60) for singles, Rs. 80 ($6.15) to Rs. 175 ($13.45) for doubles. The highest prices are for air-conditioned rooms. Air-cooled rooms are Rs. 80 ($6.15) single and Rs. 110 ($8.45) double. The proprietor, Pradrep Narayan Singh, wrote me a note asking if I would mention that he also has a restaurant, the Poona, in the same building. He especially recommends the Chinese foods, in the Rs.-10 (75¢) to Rs.-15 ($1.15) range.

A suggestion from Marlin Roehl of Visalia, Calif.: Near the Pradeep is the **Gautam Hotel,** Ramkatora, Varanasi (tel. 44015), which this reader found to be "quite good," and "very good" service and food, with many selections. Rates are Rs. 100 ($7.70) to Rs. 150 ($11.55) single and Rs. 120 ($9.25) to Rs. 200 ($15.40) double, the higher prices for air conditioning. There are telephones in the rooms and attached bathrooms.

Of the Indian-style hotels downtown, a longtime favorite of budget travelers, the **Central,** Dasaswamedh Road (tel. 62776), was under renovation but is certainly worth investigating if you'd like a simple, traditional place to stay right in the center of things. For instance, the hotel's long, narrow dining room overlooks the endlessly fascinating street. The prerenovation rates made the hotel a find for low-budgeteers: Rs. 15 ($1.15) to Rs. 50 ($3.85); the lower-priced rooms were singles without private bathrooms.

Nearby, another centrally located choice, the **K. V. M. Hotel,** Godaulia (no phone), is a nice, fairly clean place to stay. All rooms have attached bathrooms with showers, and six have Western toilets. The rates creep up to moderate; singles are Rs. 35 ($2.70); doubles, Rs. 55 ($4.25) to Rs. 75 ($5.75); and triples, Rs. 80 ($6.15) to Rs. 100 ($7.70). Air-cooled rooms run Rs. 135 ($10.40) to Rs. 140 ($10.75) for doubles. There's no restaurant, but you can have room service or eat out.

Best bargain for low-budgeteers is probably the 39-room government-run **Tourist Bungalow,** just off Parade Kothi, Grand Trunk Road (tel. 43413), an efficiently operated two-story stone building, rather plain, in an H pattern around three sides of two small gardens. It has a shady veranda, minuscule restaurant, and plain clean rooms, with ceiling fans and stone bathrooms with hot and cold running water, some Western and some Indian style. Rates are Rs. 35 ($2.70) for an ordinary single sharing a bathroom, Rs. 40 ($3.05) for a single with attached bathroom; doubles run Rs. 75 ($5.75) and Rs. 45 ($3.45), the lower price for a room without an air-cooler. For rock-bottom budgeteers, the dorm is Rs. 15 ($1.15) per person, ten beds in all.

Nearby, the **Nur-Indira,** Parade Kothi (tel. 44686), is a good buy. All rooms are simply furnished and fairly clean, and 25 of the 30 rooms have Indian-style bathrooms. The price is Rs. 45 ($3.45) single and Rs. 60 ($4.60) double; with air conditioning, Rs. 150 ($11.55). You get air coolers for Rs. 60 ($4.60) single and Rs. 80 ($6.15) double.

Also on Parade Kothi is the **Hotel Amar** (tel. 43509), where price is the only attraction: rates begin at Rs. 15 ($1.15) for a single non-air-conditioned room and Rs. 30 ($2.30) for a double non-air-conditioned; with air conditioning, rooms cost Rs. 50 ($3.85) single and Rs. 65 ($5) double. The **Raj Kamal,** on Parade Kothi (tel. 44607), is also shabby. It has rooms starting at Rs. 20 ($1.55) and going up to an overpriced Rs. 60 ($4.60)—13 rooms in all, with attached bathrooms. The lowest price is for a single without air cooler; the higher rate, for an air-cooled double. The **Hotel Divan,** Parade Kothi, charges Rs. 15 ($1.15) for a single, going up to Rs. 80 ($6.15), and it's in the same down-at-the-heels class as the Amar.

The **Hotel Park Villa,** Rathayatra Crossing (tel. 55426), is a wonderful old red house with green gingerbread trim, and rose bushes and mango trees in the garden. Presently there are 12 doubles and two singles. It's too bad that it's not better kept because it's an atmospheric, interesting, and friendly place. As it is, the Park Villa is strictly for the least fastidious among us. Rates are Rs. 30 ($2.30) single, Rs. 40 ($3.05) to Rs. 100 ($7.70) double; the higher prices are for air cooling, available in doubles only. All rooms have attached bathrooms, with hot and cold water, and Indian toilets in the singles.

Back on the Mall near Clark's is the **Hotel Surya,** Varnasi 221001 (tel. 43014), once part of the Queen of Nepal's lavish palace. Now it offers simple, basic accommodations: for the two air-conditioned rooms, Rs. 125 ($9.60) double, Rs. 95 ($7.30) if occupied as a single; non-air-conditioned rooms cost Rs. 50 ($3.85) single and Rs. 70 ($5.40) double. There's a lovely garden left from the glory days, and a minuscule dining room open from 7 a.m. to 9 p.m.

Very primitive accommodations are available in some of the **houseboats** on the Ganges. These should cost Rs. 30 ($2.30) per person, after bargaining with the boatman.

EATING OUT IN VARANASI: A good restaurant is **Kwality,** Lahurabir Crossing, downtown, serving everything from soups to sundaes; the most elaborate of the latter, the "Killer Diller," has strawberries, nuts, two kinds of ice cream, and chocolate sauce, and costs about Rs. 14 ($1.05). Other dishes are sandwiches, around Rs. 9 (70¢) for chicken; soups, about Rs. 6 (45¢) to Rs. 7 (55¢); eight grills, of which the mixed is the most expensive at around Rs. 15 ($1.15); and various types of chicken, one stuffed with scrambled eggs, mint, and chiles, for about Rs. 16 ($1.25). Plain chops, lamb and pork, are less than that. Hours are noon to 10 p.m. daily.

In the center of Varanasi, near the K. V. M. and the Central Hotels, is the **Konamay Restaurant,** in the Deepak Cinema Building, Dasaswamedh Road. It's off to the left of the cinema entrance under an overhang, and locals say it's the best in town. Inside is a large, dimly lit room almost completely undecorated. The food is the attraction, and there is an extensive menu. You can have snacks, cold drinks, vegetarian and nonvegetarian dishes, and some continental offerings. Vegetarian dishes run Rs. 6 (45¢) to Rs. 14 ($1.05); nonvegetarian Indian curries, Rs. 12 (90¢) to Rs. 18 ($1.40). You might want to try tandoori chicken, at Rs. 17 ($1.30), or fish tikka, at Rs. 15 ($1.15). Or you might feel like a mutton hamburger steak. Open from noon to 10 p.m. every day. Air-conditioned.

Also on Dasaswamedh Road in the center of town is **Ayyar's Café,** which is totally vegetarian and serves real South Indian food. It is run by South Indians, and this is the place to try coffee as made in that region. It is served in a tiny pitcher, a dark syrupy liquid, distilled from coffee. You pour some into your cup, then add hot water until it reaches a consistency you like. Then drink it. It's delicious, Rs. 1.5 (12¢) a cup. Ayyar's has stone floors, is small, and has no decor. A complete vegetarian meal will come to Rs. 7 (55¢). Open from 8 a.m. to 9 p.m.

One step off University Road in the center of the city and you are practically in the middle of **The Restaurant.** It's a simple place with bare tables set on a stone floor, right across from the K. V. M. Hotel, serving only Indian food, vegetarian and nonvegetarian. What makes it worth a visit, besides the food, is that it is frequented by Varanasi intellectuals, writers, artists, and politicans, almost all of whom speak English. It's a good place to meet people. Vegetarian dishes cost about Rs. 5 (40¢). There are the usual curries; mutton dishes are Rs. 5 (40¢) to Rs. 8 (60¢). Open every day from 6 a.m. to 10:30 p.m.

Also across from K. V. M. is the **Gujarati Restaurant,** up one flight of stairs to the first floor. If you can't find it, ask someone to point the way— everyone knows this famous restaurant. It's so clean you can eat off the floor —and do, almost! Food is placed on wooden planks in front of you as you sit cross-legged on the floor on a carpet. The food is all vegetarian specialties of Gujarat, which is sweeter than some other Indian regional cuisines. A thali (all foods on a platter) with two vegetable dishes, dhapati, dahi, dal, chutneys, pickles, and papar, is Rs. 7 (55¢). Hours are 10 a.m. to 2 p.m. and 7 to 10:30 p.m. every day. No one speaks English at this restaurant, so ordering can be a bit of an adventure. Just smile and point to a thali—it works every time.

Down one flight of stairs off Dasaswamedh Road is the underground restaurant **Monga** (tel. 55443). It is no dimmer than those Indian restaurants above ground, and it has the same lack of decor, with stone floors and slowly turning overhead fans. Background music is soft. Dishes are Indian and Chinese, all in roughly the same budget-right price range. Vegetarian dishes are Rs. 7.50 (58¢) to Rs. 12 (90¢); nonvegetarian, Rs. 8 (80¢) to Rs. 25 ($1.90); and Chinese, Rs. 8 (60¢) to Rs. 13 ($1). Open from 9:30 a.m. to 9:30 p.m.

Authentically Chinese is the very popular **Win-Fa,** Prakash Cinema Building, Lahurabir, which has a Chinese chef. It has plain uncovered tables on a stone floor and Chinese and Western music in the background. The menu offers chow mein for about Rs. 13 ($1) to Rs. 15 ($1.15), chop suey for about Rs. 15 ($1.15), and prawns (in season), fish, pork, chicken, and egg dishes for Rs. 16 ($1.25) to Rs. 20 ($1.55). Open every day from 11 a.m. to 10 p.m.

Nearby **Tulsi** serves good vegetarian and nonvegetarian Indian foods in a moderate price range.

THINGS TO DO IN VARANASI: Visiting temples is the main occupation for Hindu visitors, and although you don't need to follow their example quite so slavishly, there are a few special places that are worth your attention.

Fairly new is the **Mother India Temple,** on the campus of Kashi Vidyapath University, one of three universities in the city. Started by followers of Mahatma Gandhi in 1921, it was inaugurated by Gandhi in 1936. The main reason to stop here is to see the marble relief map designed by Shiva Prasad Gupta, a noted freedom fighter.

The Mother India Temple lies en route to a temple tourists in particular enjoy—the **Durga Temple,** which looks something like a cluster of oversize brown asparagus tips clustered around a giant one in the center. Worshippers consider the smaller pointed spires to represent the individual soul, the larger one to be the universal soul. Monkeys clamber all over the spires and for this reason it has earned the nickname "the monkey temple."

Just a peanut's throw away is the new **Tulsi Manas Temple,** a pristine marble structure with the Hindu epic of *Ramayana* inscribed around its interior walls. This temple is open from 6:30 or 7 a.m. to 11:30 a.m. and again from 3 to 10 p.m.

All three temples can be reached by taxi, a short ride from downtown, and they are at least two-thirds of the way to the magnificent tree-lined campus of the famous Hindu University, among the largest in the world, where the impressive **Shiva temple** is located. This one, of beautiful white marble, rears its lofty head into the sky like a junior-league Chrysler Building. It's very eye-catching, both outside, where a rhinoceros fountain spouts water from its head, and inside, where water drips persistently onto a flower-decked lingam signifying that "every moment one should be conscious of God." The Hindu "God" is a basically formless one who nevertheless takes many different forms.

The walls of this Shiva temple, like many of its kind, are inscribed with basic tenets of the Hindu faith, for example: "There is no fire like lust, there is no grip like hatred, there is no net like delusion, there is no river like craving"; and "the senses are the horses, they say, the objects of the senses, their path, the man with mind well reined reaches the highest place of God."

One man whose mind was obviously well reined was the founder of the 1,100-acre **Benares Hindu University** (hours: 11 a.m. to 4:30 p.m., except Sunday and holidays), in which the temple sits. More than 20,000 students now attend the university, two-thirds of them living on campus in pleasant, tree-shaded buildings overlooking spacious playing fields. Madan Mohan Malaviya, the founder, was a barrister who left his profession to raise money for the university and once described himself as "the greatest beggar in the world." Among the donations he received was a loaf of bread from a beggar; it was later auctioned for 12,000 rupees and the beggar's name listed first among the donors.

Also on the university campus, and outstandingly worth a visit, is the **Art Gallery** (Bharat Kala Bhavan), which has an extensive collection of fascinating medieval miniatures, some on palm leaves, with such favorite themes as red, white, and blue cows, corporal punishment in the harem, peacocks in trees, and blue-faced Krishna in various guises. The pictures in the gallery deserve several hours of close scrutiny—there's a lot going on there.

Fourth and last of the not-to-be-missed temples is the holiest one of all, **the Viswanatha,** more commonly referred to as the Golden Temple for its gilded spires. It is particularly hard to find, being tucked away amid a maze of shops and homes in the crowded Chowk area near the river. A narrow shopping lane leads off the main street, Dasaswamedh, up to the temple; it's lined with tiny stores and knicknack stands, some selling holy Ganges water in tiny sealed brass pots (look into the **Cottage Industries** store, up to the left, for bargains in brass and ivory elephants). The view of the temple roof is up a sudden alley—there'll always be somebody who wants to guide you there and to hold candles to the narrow stone staircase so you won't get lost. You'll have to settle for views of golden spires on the rooftops—nonbelievers are not permitted in the temple.

A SIDE TRIP TO SARNATH:
In some ways Buddhism could be said to have started at Sarnath, a sleepy town five miles north of Varanasi. Here the young Buddha sat in the lotus position and gave a famous lecture, which seems to have been amply documented. An enormous brick-and-stone stupa, 100 feet high, built by King Ashoka in the 3rd century, marks the alleged spot of the lecture.

The impressive stupa dominates the grounds of the **Indian Buddhist Temple,** one of three—and the most ornate—in the town. Its interesting murals, painted by the Japanese artist Kosetsu Nosu in 1936, depict the life story of Buddha. The walk from the red sandstone temple to the stupa is lined with evergreen trees, the greenest things in an exceptionally green garden. Farther back are the excavated remains of a Buddhist monastery that once sat on the site (four pillars supposedly mark the room where Buddha stayed), as well as innumerable smaller stone stupas built by various pilgrims up to about the 4th century.

Across the street is a museum whose pride and joy is the glazed, mud-covered **Lion Capital,** the most valuable piece of sculpture in India and dating back to Ashoka's era. Wheels and elephants sit around the base, above which are four lions looking outward in every direction and joined at the center: the Lion Capital (which originally sat atop Ashoka's stupa) was long ago adopted as the Indian national symbol.

Other interesting exhibits include the earliest example of a swastika, considered auspicious since ancient times in India; a section of a wall from the 1st century B.C.; and a 5th-century A.D. statue of Buddha, sitting cross-legged on a lotus flower, which appears to smile only when you view it from the side, but then, oddly enough, continues to smile when you move around (do you recall those pictures of Jesus whose eyes follow you around the room?).

In recent years a deer park has been established adjoining the temple, replacing the one that existed on the site when the monastery was in existence.

There are two other Buddhist temples in Sarnath—a fairly austere Chinese one with a pleasant garden, and an extravangantly decorated Tibetan one with the Dalai Lama's portrait on the altar and hundreds of paintings of Buddha in different postures around the gaily decorated walls. The face on the big seated statue of Buddha bears a Tibetan cast, reflected in the faces of the maroon-robed Tibetan monks who live in rooms around the temple. Many old Tibetan manuscripts and scriptures are stored in the temple and more are constantly added by new arrivals, so that it has become a repository for keeping alive Tibetan culture.

The gates of each of the temples bear the deer and wheel emblems commonly associated with the Buddhist faith.

Since buses are jam-packed in Varanasi, scooters make a good alternative. You can go to Sarnath by scooter rickshaw in 45 minutes. You'll find scooters at Kacherhari Crossing, across from Varuna River or near the railway station in the center of town. Going back, get scooters in front of Deer Park. One way should cost about Rs. 12 (90¢), and round trip, Rs. 25 ($1.90). But you have to (forgive the expression in this holy city) bargain like the devil to get that rate! You can also visit Sarnath on a tour (no. 2; see below).

Sarnath has a **Government Tourist Bungalow,** set in a park a short stroll from the temples. It's in need of repair and care. Rooms are not air-conditioned, but they all have overhead fans. Rates are Rs. 50 ($3.85) single and Rs. 75 ($5.75) double, or Rs. 15 ($1.15) per person in the dorm. To reserve, write: Uttar Pradesh Tourist Development Corporation Tourist Bungalow, Sarnath 221007 (tel. 42515).

TOURS: Two tours round up the sights for you. Number 1 goes on a Ganges River trip, and to temples and Benares Hindu University, costing Rs. 10.75 (82¢). In summer it's 5:30 to 11:45 a.m.; in winter, 6 a.m. to 12:15 p.m. Number 2 goes to Sarnath and Ramnager Fort, costing Rs. 11.75 (90¢). Summer hours are 2:30 to 6:25 p.m., and winter, 2 to 5:55 p.m. The tours start from the UPTDC Tourist Bungalow, Parade Kothi (tel. 63233). You can also get the bus at the Government of India Tourist Office a few minutes after departure from the bungalow. Tickets are sold on the bus only. Another bus that stops at the bungalow goes to Kathmandu on Tuesday and Friday and costs Rs. 175 ($13.45) per person.

WHEN TO VISIT: The best time is from October to March; it's very hot and dry in summer. During the monsoon it's sometimes impossible to get around, especially the low-lying parts of the city.

GETTING TO VARANASI: There's daily **air** service from Delhi for Rs. 637 ($49), from Agra for Rs. 499 ($38), from Khajhuraho for Rs. 446 ($34), and daily flights also from Calcutta for Rs. 601 ($46), plus flights four times a week from Bombay for Rs. 1,282 ($98). By **train,** the *Upper India Express* from Delhi or Calcutta stops in Varanasi, as does the *Howrah Express* from Calcutta. From Delhi, 764 km (466 miles) away, the charge is Rs. 254 ($19.55) in first class and Rs. 62 ($4.75) in second; or from Calcutta, 700 km (425 miles), you pay Rs. 236 ($18.15) in first class and Rs. 58 ($4.45) in second. It's about a 13- to 15-hour train trip from either city. **Buses** ply the routes from Allahabad, Lucknow, Kathmandu, and other cities.

2. Darjeeling

Darjeeling (7,000 feet above sea level) is delightful. It's the mountain town par excellence, and like all mountain towns has a fresh clean air to it and happy, healthy-looking people. Physically, it's built in a series of steps hanging precariously onto the sides of the lower Himalayan Mountains. From the moment the old porter grabs your luggage from the taxi and, hanging it around his neck as if it were a bag of feathers, goes leaping up the hillside to the hotel, you know you're among a race of Sherpas. (There are also Bhuitas, Tibetans, Lepchas, Nepalese, and other tribes from mountain and plain.)

Darjeeling's population is listed at 56,857, many of whom work in the 140 tea estates of the district, picking and packing the tiny leaves that have made the town literally a household word all over the world. You're never far from nature in the lower Himalayas, and in addition to 4,000 species of plants and ferns, and 600 types of birds, there are all kinds of lovely animals— monkeys, leopards, civets, jackals, bears, otters, hares, deer, bears, and elephants, to name but a few—that have been charted.

The town's name comes from "Dorje-Ling"—place of the Dorje, or magnificent thunderbolt—a familiar term in the Lamaist religion. Because of the influx of Nepalese and refugees from Tibet, Buddhism is strong in the area, but Darjeeling also possesses Hindu temples, Muslim mosques, and Christian churches.

The British made Darjeeling their favorite hill station in 1835, and today it remains not only a popular choice of foreigners but also of Indians escaping the heat of the Bengali plains and Calcutta to the south. In the recent past an aggressive drive by some residents for a separate state—to be called Gurkhaland—had discouraged visitors to this ordinarily tranquil place.

The only reminder that there had been any trouble are typically Indian political slogans painted on every possible surface. Bright protest banners hung high everywhere give the entire area a festive look. There was nothing overt, however, to deter tourists from enjoying the many pleasures of this delightful resort.

WHEN TO GO: You may visit Darjeeling throughout the year. But the peak season is April to mid-June and mid-September to November. Winters can be damp and cold. In the summer, heavy rains cause landslides that sometimes cut off the highway as well as the famous "toy train" that winds its way up the mountain from Siliguri, 60 miles (100 km) away, and fog covers the famous peaks.

PERMITS: In recent years all foreigners have needed a permit to get into **Dar-**

jeeling because of its proximity to the Chinese border. Now this regulation has been relaxed slightly and you no longer need a permit if you arrive by air, bound for Darjeeling for under 15 days. You report to the Foreigners Registration Office at the airport at the time of arrival and departure and an endorsement is made in your passport. If, however, you plan to come by rail or road to Darjeeling, you must get a Restricted Area Permit. They are free and easy to get: you can get a permit upon request as an endorsement to your passport when you apply for a visa at any Indian embassy, high commission, or mission abroad.

Should you decide on Darjeeling when you're already in India, you can pick up your permit within 24 hours in India from the Deputy Commissioner of Police (Security Control), 237 Acharaya J. C. Bose Rd., Calcutta (tel. 443301); or the Under Secretary of the Government of West Bengal, Home (Political) Department, Writers' Building, B.B.D. Bagh, Calcutta (tel. 221681); or the Ministry of Home Affairs, North Block, New Delhi. There is a form to fill out, but no photograph is required.

If you go on to **Kalimpong**, a separate endorsement is required. For a stay of less than two days, you can get it on the spot from the Foreigners Registration Office, Laden La Road, Darjeeling (tel. 2261). There can be quite a crowd in the office during peak season, so plan accordingly. If you expect to visit for more than two days, you must apply for a permit when you get your visa or from the authorities above (as for Darjeeling) once in India.

Foreigners trekking to Sandakphu and Phalut do not need a special permit, but must inform the Foreigners Registration Office 24 hours in advance and also report their arrival at checkposts at Sandakphu and Phalut.

For **Sikkim**, foreign nationals require a permit which takes six weeks to get. You apply through the visa-issuing authorities abroad or the Ministry of Home Affairs, North Block, New Delhi 100001. It's free, but you need to fill out a form in triplicate and supply three photos.

WHERE TO STAY IN DARJEELING: Note that most hotels offer a discount of 30% to 50% off-season.

The **Oberoi Mt. Everest**, on Gandhi Road (tel. 2616), since the 1800s the top place in town, is closed for renovations. There was no word on when it would reopen, but you may wish to check up on the status if you're splurge-minded.

Tops today is the atmospheric **Windamere Hotel**, Bhanu Sarani, near Observatory Hill (tel. 2841), began in 1882 as a boarding house and has operated as a hotel since 1938. It's a charming place with comfortable rooms and big bathrooms, plus beautiful gardens with flowering vines, ferns, and well-trimmed shrubs, where you can sit out and admire the mountains. Afternoon tea is served outdoors when it's warm and indoors near the fireplace when it's cool. Rates are Rs. 400 ($30.75) single, Rs. 600 ($46.15) double, and Rs. 700 ($53.85) for suites, inclusive of meals. Service charge is 10%.

Hotel Sinclairs, 18/1 Gandhi Road (tel. 2930), billed as a top hotel, has little to offer except outrageously high rates: Rs. 400 ($30.75) to Rs. 500 ($38.45) for single occupancy, Rs. 680 ($52.30) to Rs. 760 ($58.45) for double, including meals and tea. There's a service charge of 5%.

New, the centrally heated **Hotel Valentino**, 6 Rock Ville Rd. (tel. 2228), is owned by the New Embassy Chinese Restaurant in Calcutta and here, too, has a well-appointed Chinese restaurant on the premises, open to outsiders as well as to guests. A sundeck and roof garden are other pleasant features. Rooms on the top floor are recommended for their view of the market below.

All rooms have deep carpeting, neat furnishings, and modern bathrooms attached, and rent for Rs. 350 ($26.90) double, Rs. 175 ($13.45) single.

The **New Elgin Hotel,** H. D. Lama Road (tel. 2182 or 2882), is in a white building strangely resembling a Methodist church. It has a cozy lounge with big windows, a small bar, and a dining room offering Chinese, Nepalese, Indian, and Western cuisines. All rooms are bright and sunny, and have bathrooms; most have fireplaces. Family antiques accent the entire place. There is a sensational view from the top floor. Rates, in season, are Rs. 475 ($36.55) double and Rs. 285 ($21.90) single, all meals included; off-season, Rs. 150 ($11.55) to Rs. 200 ($15.40) double and Rs. 100 ($7.70) to Rs. 150 ($7.69 to $11.55) single, for bed-and-breakfast only.

Also on H. D. Lama Road, **Pradhans Hotel Polynia** (tel. 2826) has spacious rooms, furnished simply and in a lot better condition than the run-down halls would lead you to expect. There are 34 rooms in all, some with Western-style toilets. Rates, in season, are Rs. 250 ($19.25) double and Rs. 125 ($9.60) single, Rs. 350 ($26.90) for a deluxe room, including breakfast. The dining room needs paint and polish.

Nearby, **Alice Villa,** H. D. Lama Road (tel. 2840), is one of those places with no frills—just simple, clean rooms. There is a long, pleasant lounge with striped seats along the front of the building. The brightly painted rooms have wooden floors, rugs, and fireplaces. Baths are attached, but have no tubs or showers. You can order hot water in buckets. With bed-and-breakfast, doubles are Rs. 150 ($11.55); triples, Rs. 185 ($14.25); quads, Rs. 220 ($16.90). Breakfast is Rs. 20 ($1.55) and lunch costs Rs. 30 ($2.30).

A good choice is the **Central Hotel,** Robertson Road (tel. 2033), in an 85-year-old building with a lot of charm which, we hope, will be retained as the owners plan to modernize. Presently, rooms in the main building are large and some have sitting rooms, bedrooms, and bathrooms with little dressing alcoves. All rooms have fireplaces. The rooms in the five-story annex are lighter than those in the main building. From the three-story main structure, there is a wonderful view of the middle and lower parts of town. Without meals, doubles rent for Rs. 300 ($23.05); singles, Rs. 200 ($15.40). Continental breakfast runs Rs. 19 ($1.45); an English breakfast, Rs. 30 ($2.30). Lunch and dinner will run Rs. 35 ($2.70) and Rs. 55 ($4.25) each, the lower price for vegetarian meals.

Right above the tourist bureau is the **Hotel Bellevue,** Nehru Road (tel. 2129), with 20 clean rooms, all with bathrooms attached and hot and cold running water 24 hours a day—a good buy at Rs. 300 ($23.05) for a large double, Rs. 400 ($30.75) for a suite. Some of the biggest rooms have couches, dressing tables, wardrobes, and chairs in addition to beds. There are also cushioned window seats on which to sit and admire the passing parade in the fascinating mall below. Rates don't include meals. Each floor has a rudimentary kitchen if you care to cook your own, or you can eat out locally.

The Bellevue also has an econo-block upstairs in an old Victorian cream-and-brown building. Clean bed/sitting rooms, with bathrooms attached, cost Rs. 120 ($9.25) in season, Rs. 75 ($5.75) off-season.

Nearby is the attractive Dragon Bar, which the Tibetan proprietors of the Bellevue, T. Lawangi Pulger and his wife, plan to restore as a restaurant and bar. Meanwhile, simple vegetarian meals are served for Rs. 20 ($1.55).

The West Bengal Tourist Development Corporation operates a number of lodges in the area. The **Tourist Lodge,** on Bhanu Sarani, formerly Mall Road (tel. 2611), needs some refurbishing, but offers rooms with spectacular views of the mountains at Rs. 241.15 ($18.55), Rs. 293.65 ($22.60), and Rs.

398.65 ($30.65) for small, standard, and large doubles respectively. All rooms have private attached bathrooms; there's a 50% discount off-season, from November 24. Meals cost Rs. 12 (90¢) at breakfast, and Rs. 25 ($1.90) and Rs. 35 ($2.70) at lunch and dinner, the higher price for Western meals. To reserve, write to the West Bengal Tourist Development Corporation in Darjeeling, or the Reservations Officer, West Bengal Tourism Development Corporation, Ltd., 3/2 B. B. D. Bagh East, Calcutta 700001.

The **Maple Tourist Lodge,** on old Kutchery Road (tel. 2092), was an army hostel during my recent visit; it is an old, pleasant but simple building, slightly run-down, and okay if you're not too fussy. Past rates had been moderate: Rs. 40 ($3.05) for a small single to Rs. 125 ($9.60) for a large room with a kitchen and dining area. You might check to see if the army is still occupying this lodge. The view is outstanding!

Tiffany's, Franklyn Prestige Road, (tel. 2850), has, alas!, declined over the years, and rates are high for the run-down state of the rooms, which have attached Western bathrooms and fireplaces: Rs. 250 ($19.25) single and Rs. 300 ($23.05) double, breakfast and dinner included.

Motel Magnolia-Deluxe, 25 Kutchery Road (tel. 3013), is anything but deluxe, except in price. Rs. 185 ($14.25) single and Rs. 400 ($30.75) double, inclusive of meals.

In addition, there are some 60 Indian-style hotels. Time did not permit checking all. A cursory check shows that rates ranged up to Rs. 100 ($7.70) and down to Rs. 10 (75¢), plus all prices in between. The degree of comfort and cleanliness also varied widely. If you're interested, the **Tourist Bureau,** Ajit Mansions, Nehru Road (tel. 2050), has a list and may be able to steer you in the right direction. The Tourist Bureau staff can also cue you into off-season rates. Check if in doubt about room charges.

A Youth Hostel

A pleasant place to stay, and one of the best youth hostels in India, Darjeeling's is on Dr. Zakir Hussain Road (tel. 2290), especially popular with trekkers. It's a three-story concrete building with wrap-around balconies at the very top of town, with views of both sides of the mountains. Dormitory rooms have large open fireplaces. Bathrooms are separate, shared, large, and with lots of showers. Rates are Rs. 8 (60¢) for nonmembers and Rs. 6 (45¢) for members. There's a big dining room with plenty of windows so you can see the view; breakfast costs Rs. 4 (30¢) or Rs. 5 (40¢). Reserve by writing to the warden, Youth Hostel, Darjeeling.

WHERE TO EAT: Most people who visit Darjeeling settle for the American Plan and take all their meals in their hotels—in the busiest season many hotels insist on this. But there are a few interesting places to eat in town, so try to be flexible enough to give one or two a try during your stay.

Famous **Glenary's,** on Nehru Road (tel. 2055), for many years a home-away-from-home for lots of young Western travelers who wrote postcards as they sipped soft drinks and met their friends here, was, alas, closed (except for the confectionery) during my most recent visit. The restaurant, also known for its Western dishes and tempting home-baked desserts, had a cheerful windowed main room. It was expected to reopen, so you'll want to pay a visit while in town. Hours are 9 a.m. to 9 p.m.

The restaurant with the best view is **Keventer's,** on Nehru Road opposite the Darjeeling Planter's Club (tel. 2026). You can sit outdoors and survey the entire valley while eating simple snacks and sandwiches. Try the delicious local cheddar-type cheese: Rs. 2 (15¢) to Rs. 3 (23¢). Sausage or bacon and eggs costs Rs. 12.50 (95¢) and ice creams run Rs. 5.50 (42¢). Hours: 9 a.m. to 9 p.m.

Penang, on Laden La Road near the main post office, has only four curtained booths and makes three dishes: moo-moos (dumplings) chow mein, and thupka (a Tibetan grain dish). Moo-moos are Rs. 3 (23¢) for four; chow mein, Rs. 12 (90¢); and thupka, Rs. 3 (23¢). No one speaks English, so just point to what you want. Open from noon to 8 or 9 p.m.

Chinese foods in the Rs.-30 ($2.30) range for entrees are well made and served at the splurge-priced restaurant in the **Hotel Valentino,** 6 Rock Ville Rd. (tel. 2228), open throughout the day and until 9 p.m.

Stardust, on Nehru Road beside the Tourist Bureau (tel. 3130), is a small outdoor café with blue-topped tables and South Indian vegetarian foods. Try the masala dosa for Rs. 5 (40¢), or pakoras or idli in the same price range. For something more substantial there's a mixed vegetable curry at Rs. 8 (60¢). If you've been craving a cup of coffee in this tea-plantation territory, you can find fresh-made espresso here.

You might also try the pleasant **Garden Café,** nearby on Chowrastra Road, for light meals and snacks.

WHAT TO DO: The big deal in Darjeeling, and the first item on most people's schedule, is to get up at four o'clock in the morning (that's right, 4 a.m.) to see the sun rise from **Tiger Hill.** The habit is so ingrained in the heads of the hotel porters that they'll probably wake you at 4 a.m. anyway on your first morning, unless you specifically ask them not to. Then, shivering under all the blankets you can wrap around you, there's a 40-minute ride in a Jeep through sleepy villages, climbing higher and higher until your vehicle struggles up the last quarter mile to the top of Tiger Hill (8,482 feet), about seven miles from the town.

There's a two-story concrete pavilion there, the roof and stairs already crowded with shawl-wrapped, barefoot natives, most of whom have walked up the mountain for the big moment. The ground floor is a small café, just as cold as outdoors, where you can sip some coffee, and the first floor is an unheated antechamber, doors and windows wide open, where VIPs (Western visitors) can sit and shiver.

At first the black sky is merely suffused with a dull red glow, but as time wears on the upper clouds begin to reflect a rust-colored incandescence, and this spreads and spreads until the entire eastern sky shines with reddish gold, the horizontal bands of color being gradually interspersed with streaks of lightening sky. To the northwest the snow-capped Kanchenjunga range is beginning to take on the glow. Suddenly the upper tip of the sun appears from the horizon, like a red-hot saucer pushing its way up out of the fire. Within five minutes it is over; the sun has risen and turned yellow, all traces of red have disappeared from the sky, and the chattering crowd atop Tiger Hill is dispersing.

If you want to overnight nearer to the area (and get a bit more sleep), **Tiger Hill Tourist Lodge** (tel. 2813) is two kilometers below the pavilion and has attracted foreigners ever since the 1900s when the British botanist H. C. Hooker stayed here and was struck by the awesome view. In fact, if you're too lazy to get up before dawn, you can see majestic peaks at sunrise from here. Or you can trek up from the lodge and beat the crowd to the observation tower. Built in 1915, the lodge is a simple place, clean with spartan furnishings. All rooms cost Rs. 100 ($7.70) and have private bathrooms. There's also a dorm, charging Rs. 12 (90¢) per person. Some renovations were under way, but will undoubtedly be completed by the time you arrive. Dinner is compulsory: Rs. 18.10 ($1.40) for nonvegetarian fare, Rs. 13.60 ($1.05) for vegetarian.

Most likely you'll return to your in-town hotel for breakfast (you'll pass Darjeeling's golf course—certainly one of the highest in the world), and make the customary two or three sightseeing stops en route: to beautiful **Senchal Lake,** a favorite picnic spot around the reservoir that provides Darjeeling's water supply; and to the **Ghoom Buddhist Monastery,** where half a dozen Tibetan monks faithfully preserve centuries-old manuscripts and the padded, silken cushion on which the Dalai Lama sat on one of his visits to the monastery. Heated air from candles in copper bowls keeps prayer wheels perpetually turning. Around the outside of the temples are 38 heavy brass prayer wheels, which everybody spins as they pass, and on the roof, in a small hut, are gilded Buddhas and ornate paintings of the type common to Buddhist temples. Star of the temple is the 15-foot image, gaudily painted, of the Maitreyee, or coming Buddha, its legs spread instead of in the more customary lotus position.

The narrow road that runs up to the monastery is as fascinating as the shrine itself: early-morning glimpses into homes, the community gathering beside the water pumps, shopkeepers setting out their wares, etc.

Your next major excursion is to the **Tibetan Refugee Self-Help Center,** about three miles out of town on the way to **Lebong** (where the world's smallest and fastest racetrack—mountain pony races in October—is situated). On the way you'll pass **St. Joseph's College** and, just adjoining, India's first ropeway—a cable car that takes you for a breathtaking 45-minute trip down the mountainside to **Barnesbeg Tea Estate,** open from 8 a.m. to 4 p.m. The ropeway costs Rs. 20 ($1.55), but isn't always running owing to occasional power shortages.

The Tibetan community is always ready to welcome visitors, and it's an inspiring place to visit. Essentially, it's a mountainside community, centered around a main courtyard in which everybody strolls, basks in the sun, or watches the children play. All around the yard are workshops—cobblers, painters, metalworkers, weavers, even a communal kitchen where all the food is prepared for the 560 or so Tibetan refugees who live here. There's a nursery in which numerous tiny babies with woolen caps snooze in individual cribs beneath brightly colored bedspreads; a weaving shop where the wool is woven into shawls, garments, and magnificent carpets; and a dyeing area in the rear where berries, tea leaves, and other natural products are used to make the lovely dyes. Raw wool sits drying on the roof of the sheds and new looms hang in the carpenter shop.

Most of the residents of this happy community (you never saw so many smiles in one place) fled from Tibet along with the Dalai Lama when the Chinese invaded in 1959 and finally found a home here when American Emergency Relief Committees joined with the Indian government to establish a community which one day would be self-sufficient.

Taking shortcuts across the hills, it's possible to walk to the community from Darjeeling in about 40 minutes; a taxi would charge about Rs. 120 ($9.25) round trip—but make sure before you get in.

Several times each year, Indians who want to study mountain climbing can attend a 40-day course at the **Himalayan Mountaineering Institute** just outside the town. For Westerners the only institute course available is a 21-day Adventure Course, open only to those 19 years old or younger. Institute advisor is Tenzing Norgay, the Sherpa guide who accompanied Sir Edmund Hillary on his conquest of Everest (29,028 feet) in 1953 and who is recorded to have reached the summit at 11:30 a.m. on May 29. One of the exhibits in the institute's museum—admission is Re. 1 (7½¢) at the gate and 50 paise (3½¢) for the museum—which is invariably visited by tourists, is the original manuscript of the expedition ("This is the story of how two men, both endowed with outstanding stamina and skill, inspired by unflinching resolve, reached the top of the world and came back to join us, their comrades . . .") written by Sir John Hunt.

The deputy director of the institute is Nawang Gombu, the only man to have been to the top of Everest twice, once with the British and once with the Americans.

Also on view in the museum are such fascinating pieces of memorabilia as electric socks, a high-altitude tent, Tenzing's reindeer-skin boots, ice clamps, clothes, equipment, and a glass case full of the interesting items of food carried by members of such an expedition.

The institute is open from 9 a.m. to 1 p.m. and 2 to 4:30 p.m. daily in season (closed Tuesday); check for off-season hours with tourist bureau. Admission is 50 paise (3½¢). It can be reached either by walking from town or by taxi, at Rs. 120 ($9.25) round trip. It's cheaper to take a tour.

Adjoining the institute is a very interesting **mountain zoo** which boasts all kinds of local black bears, yaks, pandas, civets, and leopards, as well as some magnificent tigers which were the gift of Russia's Khrushchev some years ago. The tigers, like the Indians themselves, have a meatless day once a week and watching them being fed the day afterward is a terrifying spectacle.

You can, if you wish, visit a tea estate and get a more intimate view of all this; the usual one that's visited is the **Happy Valley** tea estate, off the main Lebong road about one mile from Darjeeling. It's open every day except Sunday when it closes at noon, and Monday, when it's closed all day. Admission is free. Most of the tea processing goes on from May to October.

Various other local sightseeing spots are recommended by tourist guides for those who can't find enough satisfaction merely in walking aimlessly around town. The ones most commonly mentioned are the century-old **Lloyd Botanical Garden,** with its hothouses and collection of representative Himalayan plants and flowers, just below the main twin bazaar (market days are Saturday and Sunday); the **Natural History Museum,** closed a half day on Wednesday and all day Thursday, fee 40 paise (3¢); innumerable temples, especially **Shri Mandir** and **Dhirdham;** and the Nepalese shrine called **Temple of Mahakal** on Observatory Hill, from which there's a marvelous view of the surrounding mountains.

The Tourist Bureau, 1 Nehru Rd. (tel. 2050), can help with plans to visit any of these places and advise you on taxi rates, how to hire a car, etc.

TREKKING: M/S **Summit Tours,** at Hayden Hall (tel. 2710), and M/S **Tenzing Tours,** 1 D. B. Giri Rd. (tel. 3058), provide everything you need for a successful trek. But to ensure that things go smoothly, try to give them a month's notice, more if you can. Included are guides, porters, cooks, meals, fuel, cooking and table utensils, accommodations in Forest Bungalows, and when necessary such equipment as tents, sleeping bags, rucksacks, foam mattresses, air pillows, water flasks, hot-water bags, first-aid kits, etc. All you need bring is a pair of comfortable, well-broken-in hiking boots and clothing suitable for various climatic changes from tropical valleys to high-altitude passes. Take a lightweight rain parka for unpredictable showers. Most trekking routes go through Sherpa villages, across rivers and up high (11,000 to 12,000 feet) ridges north and west of Darjeeling on the Nepal and Sikkim borders. Remember that in June, July, August, and September the monsoons make it almost impossible to enjoy the experience, mid-October through December there will be frost and snow at the higher altitudes, February and March are misty, and April and May is the flowering season.

Should you decide to trek after you've arrived, you can rent just about anything but clothing and cooking utensils from the **Youth Hostel,** on Dr. Zakir Hussain Road (tel. 2290), at reasonable daily rates: two-person nylon tents, Rs. 6 (45¢); sleeping bag, Rs. 4.50 (35¢); rucksacks, Rs. 2 (15¢) to Rs. 2.50 (19¢)—a few examples only. Porters can also be arranged, costing around Rs. 25 ($1.90) for each stage of the trip. You have to leave a deposit for the equipment, which will be refunded, minus the charges for the gear, upon its return.

"**Himalayan Treks,**" a booklet published by the Directorate of Tourism, Government of West Bengal, and available at the Tourist Bureau, has everything you need to know about trekking in the area—it's free! Included are main routes, where to stay, what to take. Directions are given for one-day treks as well as much longer treks. Don't leave your Darjeeling home base without it.

SHOPPING: Look for tankas (scrolls), bold jewelry, bronze figures, beads, woven belts, shoulder bags, sweaters, gloves, and caps. Bargain everywhere except the **Manusha Bengal Emporium,** near Cart Road, and the **Tibetan Self-Help Center** (which are price-fixed), and the **main market,** also off Cart Road, where you haggle. At the Self-Help Centre shop are woven coin purses and belts for a few rupees and intricate carpets for a few thousand, plus many wares at prices in between.

Nehru and Chowrastra Roads are the main shopping centers. Among the stores in this group, **Nepal Curios** has an amazing assortment of wares—bronzes, tankas, jewelry—and honest owners who tell you when an antique-looking piece is not truly antique at all, but a convincingly made fake. Try **Sikkim Art Palace** on Gandhi Road for interesting bangles, from Rs. 15 ($1.15) and up, and interesting woven bags.

Habib Mullick, Chowrastra Road, is a 100-year-old shop with a remarkable assortment of curios: a Tibetan singing bell made of five metals, for instance, is Rs. 180 ($13.85); a precious old Diwali lamp, Rs. 2,500 ($2192.30); and countless little take-away gifts at reasonable prices. Health bracelets, at Rs. 15 ($1.15) always a good gift, are made of several metals to ward off disease. The proprietor enjoys talking about the items in the shop, and is well informed and honest about antiquities.

Should you want to buy tea in Darjeeling, go to **Dinesh Tea Stores,** Chowk Bazaar, Shop 26, where Gujmer Dinesh will give you a lesson in quality-testing and help you select something good to send home or take with you.

Descending the levels, the prices go down until you reach the main market in the lowest part of town, where items are most reasonable—and more so after bargaining.

TOURS: The **Tourist Bureau,** 1 Nehru Rd. (tel. 2050), operates Tiger Hill tours only during the season—March to mid-June and mid-September to November—and requires a minimum of eight participants at Rs. 20 ($1.55) per person; the trip includes Ghoom Monastery and the Loop. Or you can get up your own party of eight (a necessity, perhaps, out of season) and rent a Jeep for Rs. 20 ($1.55) per person; the entire Jeep-taxi would cost Rs. 160 ($12.30), inclusive of stops at Ghoom and the Loop. Intrepid tour-goers can go right on at 9:30 a.m. (to 12:30 p.m.) for a seven-points tour for Rs. 20 ($1.55) which includes the Mountaineering Institute, ropeway, zoo, Tibetan Centre, Happy Valley, Dhirdham Temple, and Art Gallery; this tour is also conducted from 1:30 to 4:30 p.m.

Travel agents conduct tours around town throughout the year, providing they can get a full car. The charge is generally Rs. 20 ($1.55).

You can rent **ponies** in town near the Tourist Bureau for Rs. 15 ($1.15) an hour for sightseeing.

Near the ropeway you can often find share taxis to popular places around town. For instance, from the ropeway to North Point costs Rs. 2 (15¢).

AN EXCURSION TO KALIMPONG: The most popular excursion from Darjeeling is to Kalimpong, 32 miles (52 km) east of Darjeeling and about half as high (4,100 feet, 1,250 meters), one-time part of the Rajah of Sikkim's domain, then a former headquarters of the Bhutan government until the British took over. Once the beginning point of the trade route to Tibet, Kalimpong still has flourishing Saturday and Wednesday markets where Bhutias and Tibetans come to trade as well as shop. Today there is little to see in Kalimpong but loads of quiet charm make it a relaxing place worth a day or two while in this part of India.

The 2½-hour drive down from Darjeeling to Kalimpong is a delightful ride through an Eden of japonica, cherry, teak, and magnolia trees, cardamom plants (the spice is exported from here), and terraced tea estates. On the way, there's a scenic viewing stop to admire the confluence of the Teesta and Rangeet Rivers, where river rafting is to be offered to tourists. In Kalimpong, there is little to detain you for long—monasteries and nurseries are the major sights—but it's a nice town with quiet charm.

Where to Stay and Eat:

Away from town, in a 1940s country home of a former British jute magnate, the **West Bengal Luxury Tourist Lodge** (tel. 384), is quite a place, built of stone with casement windows and a Burmese teak roof, overlooking a huge garden. A walk connects to Tashiding, the lodge annex. Less palatial, but still an impressive gray stone country house dating from 1935, the annex was formerly the summer hideaway of the prime minister of Bhutan.

You'll find some of the original furnishings in both houses. In the main lodge, standard doubles are Rs. 120 ($9.25); small doubles, Rs. 100 ($7.70); a large double with a balcony, Rs. 225 ($17.30); and singles, Rs. 50 ($3.85). In the annex, rates are Rs. 50 ($3.85) for singles and Rs. 100 ($7.70) for doubles. Throughout are private attached bathrooms. In both places, breakfast and dinner are compulsory: Rs. 37 ($2.85) per person.

Hotel Silver Oaks (tel. 296) is in town but has the ambience of a country estate and is filled with owner Diamond Oberoi's valuable collection of Daniels lithographs and Douglas paintings from the days of the Raj when this resort was the rage. Oberoi, owner also of the New Elgin in Darjeeling, has collected antiques for years and uses them as distinctive accents in the rooms so no two are exactly alike. Typically, each spacious room has chintz-covered chairs, bedspreads and drapes, but the colors vary and so do the old dressing tables, wardrobes, desks and chairs, and artworks. There are no silver oak trees (there were at one time, and they are to be planted again), but the big terraced garden out back has plenty of silver firs and many other lovely plants and flowers. Rates include meals: Rs. 285 ($21.90) single, Rs. 390 ($30) double, and Rs. 525 ($40.40) for a suite. The chef, who was with the Mount Everest in Darjeeling until it closed, now dishes up delicious dishes at Silver Oaks.

Kalimpong Park Hotel, Ringking Ring Road, Kalimpong 73430 (tel. 304), consists of an old British bungalow, which was the summer home of the Maharaja of West Dinajpur, and a modern annex on the grounds. The big rooms are simply furnished and better maintained than the lobby, which could use more care. Rooms, all with bathrooms attached, go for Rs. 240 ($18.45) single occupancy, with breakfast, and Rs. 360 ($27.70) double. There's a 10% service charge. A rock garden under construction should be flourishing by the time you arrive.

The **Himalayan Hotel** (tel. 248), originally the home of David MacDonald, who in 1924 turned it into a hotel, is now run by his daughter, Mrs. Victoria Williams, a lively octogenarian. Clean, simply furnished rooms are in the main building and a small annex on the grounds. All have bathrooms, but there is no running hot water because the walls are too old to support geysers; buckets of the hot stuff are delivered to the rooms. Rates are Rs. 250 ($19.25) for one, Rs. 380 ($29.25) for two, including meals. There's a 10% service charge. You'll find interesting tankas in the dining room.

There are also a number of lodges and Indian-style hotels in various states of disrepair. A cut above those I checked include the family-run **Munal Lodge,** Malli Road (tel. 404), with multicolored brick interior walls in the reception area and cement grills along the stairways. Rooms are reasonably clean and simple, and rent for Rs. 60 ($4.60) double, Rs. 15 ($1.15) per person in the five-bedded dorm. Dinner runs Rs. 9 (70¢) to Rs. 15 ($1.15), and breakfast, Rs. 5 (40¢). Bring a towel; one bedsheet is on each bed. Little English is spoken, but you can get by with a smile and sign language.

The Government of West Bengal's **Shangrila Tourist Lodge** (tel. 230), in an old British building, has three doubles at Rs. 50 ($3.85), two eight-bedded dorms at Rs. 11 (85¢) per person, and one three-bedded room at Rs. 75 ($5.75). Reasonably clean and basic. Breakfast costs Rs. 6 (45¢); tea, Re. 1 (7½¢) per cup.

What to Do

Main attractions are two monasteries: the 20th-century **Tharpa Choling Monastery,** a stroll away at Tirpal for the yellow-hat sect to which the Dali Lama belongs; and the **Buddhist** monastery, **Zang-dog-Palri-fro Brang,** from the 18th century, with a Buddhist scroll library and lively paintings. Prayer wheels surround the shrine and visitors are invited to turn each one chanting "Om Mani Padme Hum" to ensure long life, good health, and strength, as they go around the building. The view from here is a great attraction. The Wednesday/Saturday **market,** billed as big attraction, is nothing of the sort. It's for you if you're into housewares, fruit, Sly Stallone posters, chile peppers, yak cheese, and dense crowds—it's not the place to hunt arts and crafts to take home. You go to see it only because it's here and so are you. Kalimpong **nurseries** grow some of India's finest flowers and are enjoyable to visit. Among the best are Shri Ganesh Main Pradan Nursery, Standard Nursery, Shri L. D. Pradhan Nursery, and Twin Brothers.

Shopping

Kalimpong Arts and Crafts Centre is on Malli Road walking distance from the motor stand. Local hand-looms are used to make a variety of objects —coin purses, placemats, and wall hangings, in combination with paintings.

Store hours are 9 a.m. to 3 p.m. weekdays, to 1 p.m. on Saturday; closed Sunday.

Getting to Kalimpong

By road there is frequent service from Darjeeling by bus at Rs. 15 ($1.15) and by Jeep at Rs. 20 ($1.55) per seat; from New Jalpaiguri at Rs. 15 ($1.15) by bus and Rs. 30 ($2.30) per Jeep seat; from Siliguri at Rs. 15 ($1.15) by bus (five buses a day) and Rs. 20 ($1.55) to Rs. 30 ($2.30) by Jeep taxi; from Gangtok at Rs. 11.50 (85¢) by bus and Rs. 30 ($2.30) by Jeep. Full taxi to Kalimpong from Darjeeling will cost Rs. 350 ($26.90).

In season, the Tourist Bureau in Darjeeling runs day tours to Kalimpong, at Rs. 50 ($3.85).

Kurseong, 20 miles (32 km) from Darjeeling, 4,860 feet above sea level, is a low-key resort known primarily as a tea stop for taxis, buses, and the "toy train" going to Darjeeling. There's a pleasant Tourist Reception Centre (tel. 409), with a teak-paneled restaurant for transients. The centre is also a full-fledged little inn with four neatly furnished wood-paneled rooms, and an extension to be built. The cost is Rs. 75 ($5.75) for a double with attached bath. The bus to Darjeeling from here is Rs. 5 (40¢), and a Jeep-taxi seat, Rs. 15 ($1.15). The trip takes about one hour.

GETTING TO DARJEELING: Darjeeling is about 407 miles (555 km) from Calcutta. Many people fly from Calcutta, at Rs. 420 ($32) one way, or from Delhi via Patna, at Rs. 1,118 ($86), to Bagdogra, the nearest airport. From Bagdogra to Darjeeling, the scenic 3½-hour mountainous road trip costs Rs. 220 ($16.90) for a full taxi, Rs. 54 ($4.15) for a seat in a shared taxi, or Rs. 35 ($2.70) by government bus. Should you miss your connection, **taxis and buses** also go to Darjeeling from Siliguri, at Rs. 40 ($3.05) per taxi seat, Rs. 13 ($1) by bus; from New Jalpaiguri, a few kilometers away from Bagdogra, at Rs. 45 ($3.45) per taxi seat, Rs. 13.90 ($1.07) by bus; and from Kurseong, 36 miles (59 km) away from Bagdogra, at Rs. 15 ($1.15) by taxi and Rs. 5 (40¢) by bus.

The famous **"Toy Train"** started operating in the 1880s and is still the most interesting (and nowadays, crowded) way to get to Darjeeling. It starts from Siliguri and is a once-in-a-lifetime ride through the mountains. The trip takes about 7½ hours—twice as long as the drive up—of twisting and turning to climb the 48 miles (77 km) through steep passes, most of the way running not only parallel to the road but actually on it. It's a bargain when it comes to memorable experiences: Rs. 80 ($6.15) in first class, Rs. 10.65 (82¢) in second.

The best **regular train** from Calcutta is the *Darjeeling Mail,* which leaves Sealdah at 7:15 p.m. daily for an overnight journey and arrives at New Jaipalguri at 8:30 a.m., charging Rs. 198 ($15.25) in first class and Rs. 48 ($3.70) in second. Returning, it leaves New Jaipalguri at 7 p.m. and arrives in Calcutta at 8:45 a.m. In New Jaipalguri, you can grab a taxi or bus for Darjeeling or up to Siliguri for the train.

From Delhi, the super-fast *Northeast Express* takes 18 hours to cover the 1,582 km (965 miles) and leaves New Delhi at 8:25 p.m. and arrives at New Jalpaiguri at 3:40 p.m. the next day, at a cost of Rs. 837 ($64.40) in air-conditioned class, Rs. 420 ($32.30) in first class, and Rs. 162 ($12.45) in second class.

The best **bus** connection from and to Calcutta is the *Rocket Service,* departing Calcutta at 8 p.m. and arriving at 7 a.m. in Siliguri; on the return, departing Siliguri at 8 p.m. and arriving in Calcutta at 7 a.m. The fare is Rs. 91 ($7). Departures and information are from the North Bengal Transport Corporation booking offices, Esplanade Bus Stand, Calcutta (tel. 231854), and North Bengal State Transport Corporation's City Booking Office, Burdwan Road, Siliguri (tel. 20531). Another bus route via Bihar Transport connects Patna to Siliguri; it departs at 4 a.m., arrives at 4 p.m., and the fare is Rs. 57 ($4.40). From Siliguri, you can connect with the "Toy Train" or other transportation to Darjeeling.

Overnighting in Siliguri

If you want to break your journey in Siliguri, the **Mainak Tourist Lodge,** Hill Cart Road, Pradhannagar (tel. 20986), run by the WBTDC, is among the best (and most expensive) places in town. For air-conditioned rooms you pay Rs. 240 ($18.45) double and Rs. 175 ($13.45) single (three of the 38 rooms are air-conditioned); for non-air-conditioned rooms, rates are Rs. 110 ($8.45) to Rs. 170 ($13.05) double and Rs. 75 ($5.75) to Rs. 130 ($10) single. All rooms have connecting bathrooms. The noise in the halls could get a top prize, and the food in the restaurant will not win any awards.

Also on Hill Cart Road, **Siliguri Lodge,** Pradhannagar (tel. 21018), again government run, is less expensive: Rs. 45 ($3.45) to Rs. 50 ($3.85) with attached bathroom, Rs. 45 ($3.45) to Rs. 60 ($4.60) with a common bathroom. It's the next best place to stay.

Chapter VIII

CALCUTTA: THE EASTERN GATEWAY

1. Accommodations
2. Restaurants
3. Seeing the City
4. Useful Information

EVERYTHING YOU'VE EVER HEARD about Calcutta—its crowds, its poverty—is true. But despite it all, the city is one of the most fascinating on earth, and one of the largest. It's the heart of India's industry, its main port, and until just after the turn of the century, its capital. Then it got a little rough for the British, who made it what it is today, and administration shifted to Delhi. But Calcutta has never stopped growing and today its population is more than nine million—most of whom seem to be in the streets at the same time.

For what gives the city vigor and inimitable excitement is the outdoor life. It's as if somebody had built an enormous rambling city as a stage set and then invited the inhabitants of a thousand different villages to act out their lives on it.

What little space is left, in the center of the road, is contested for by aging cars, trucks, buses, taxis, horse-drawn surreys, bullock wagons, rickshaws, mangy dogs, the ubiquitous wandering cows, and the most motley collection of human carriers, men, women, and children, ever seen. It is impossible to conceive, before seeing Calcutta, of how many different loads can be carried by human beings, and the innumerable modes and methods by which they carry them. It's an unforgettable spectacle, so varied and kaleidoscopic that one hesitates to blink for fear of missing an important vista.

For more than 200 years Bengali and Bihari peasants have been migrating to Calcutta for economic opportunities, and additional enormous waves of refugees arrived from neighboring Bangladesh (formerly East Pakistan), both during the 1947 Partition and the 1972 Pakistan–Bangladesh war. Although the pace of refugee influx has slowed somewhat in recent years, the city is finding it hard to cope. Everything in Calcutta is overloaded. There is not enough housing, the traffic is snarled, the power-generating system produces outages so frequently that everyone has some alternative source of power—candlelight in private homes, backup generators in hotels and at other businesses—and perennial labor unrest shuts businesses periodically, doing further damage to the economy.

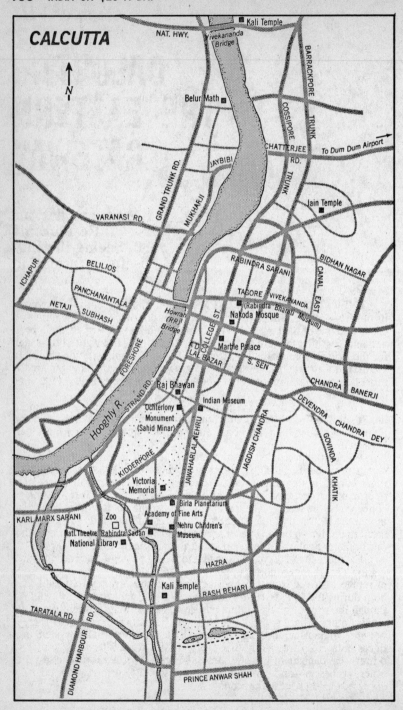

CALCUTTA

N

NAT. HWY.

Kali Temple

Vivekananda Bridge

BARRACKPORE TRUNK

Belur Math

COSSIPORE TRUNK

CHATTERJEE RD.

To Dum Dum Airport

GRAND TRUNK RD.

MUKHARJI

JAYBIBI

TRUNK

Jain Temple

VARANASI RD.

ICHAPUR

BELILIOS

PANCHANANTALA

NETAJI SUBHASH

RABINDRA SARANI

BIDHAN NAGAR

CANAL EAST

TAGORE VIVEKANANDA

(Rabindra Bharati Museum)

Nakoda Mosque

Howrah (R.R.) Bridge

FORESHORE

Hooghly R.

STRAND RD.

A.D. COLLEGE ST.

LAL BAZAR

Marble Palace

S. SEN

CHANDRA BANERJI

Raj Bhawan

Indian Museum

DEVENDRA CHANDRA DEY

Ochterlony Monument (Sahid Minar)

JAWAHARLAL NEHRU

JAGDISH CHANDRA

GOVINDA KHATIK

KIDDERPORE

Victoria Memorial

Birla Planetarium

KARL MARX SARANI

Zoo

Academy of Fine Arts

Nehru Children's Museum

Natl. Theatre

Rabindra Sadan

National Library

HAZRA

Kali Temple

RASH BEHARI

TARATALA RD.

DIAMOND HARBOUR RD.

PRINCE ANWAR SHAH

None of these problems need concern visitors, except to help explain what has made the capital of Bengal as it is and to instill in them a sense of admiration for the way life rumbles on with more than a degree of dignity despite all the difficulties.

Portions of the city are, of course, calmer than others. The areas around **B. B. D. Bagh (Dalhousie Square)**, with its crumbling old Victorian office buildings, and around **Chowringhee** (Jawaharlal Nehru Road), are more or less white-collar sections and their appearance is not all that different from what you've known before. But it's hardly necessary to go to the suburbs to see the panorama described above; about 90% of Calcutta is the suburbs, and any of the side streets in even the most "dignified" part of town will lead you to a different world.

For some observers the best way to get around is either by taxi or by **rickshaw**. And however you feel about rickshaws, they're an intimate way to see the action. (To socially conscious Westerners who complain about how rickshaws "exploit human dignity," one local editor replied succinctly, "Well, if everybody refuses to hire them the problem will solve itself: then they'll all starve to death.") Calcuttà is the last big city (apart from Hong Kong) to have human-pulled rickshaws, and when the local authorities tried to convert them to cycle rickshaws some years ago, the owners would have none of it. So, still on foot, they continue to negotiate the city's incredible traffic faster than most people can drive.

Of course, Calcutta has other distinctions. It has been the birthplace of the great reform religious movement started by Ramakrishna Paramanhansa. A Brahmin, he renounced his heritage to embrace all religions and preach unity of all mankind, and without regard to caste or color. Ramakrishna's disciple, Vivekananda, traveled widely to spread this message, and in 1897 founded the Ramakrishna Mission which now has 119 branches in India and abroad (his memorial is at Cape Comorin / Kanya Kumari).

In Calcutta, you can visit the **Ramakrishna Mission Institute of Culture**, Gol Park (tel. 46-3431), which seeks to promote international understanding with an emphasis on interpreting the cultural heritage of India. There you will be shown the 90,000-book library and universal prayer room. Also to be visited in north Calcutta is **Belur Math**, the mission's headquarters. This unusual structure resembles a temple, church, or mosque, depending on how you look at it, and is open from 6:30 a.m. to noon and again from 3:30 to 7:30 p.m. every day. Across the Hooghly is a group of 13 temples—in the one dedicated to Kali, Sri Ramakrishna had his vision of religious brotherhood.

The city has been home to two Nobel Prize winners. Most recently, in 1979 **Mother Teresa** received the Nobel Peace Prize. The other Nobel Prize winner, awarded in 1913 for literature, **Rabindranath Tagore** was a key figure in Calcutta's great cultural tradition.

To experience some of Mother Teresa's good endeavors, visitors can call at Mother House, 54A Lower Circular Rd., and attend prayers (from 6:30 to 7:30 p.m. on Monday, Tuesday, Wednesday, and Friday; from 6 to 7:30 p.m. on Thursday and Sunday). There you can get a list of Missionaries of Charity centers throughout the city, what they do, where they are, how to get to them, and when they are open for visitors.

As to Tagore, his house is a small museum, discussed later in this chapter. A poet, who was born in this city and died here in 1941, Tagore is credited with inspiring new forms of music, drama, dance, and prose.

Since Tagore's time the city's continuing literary tradition has expanded to include high-quality films which have won worldwide critical acclaim. Calcutta-made films deal realistically with life rather than take the escapist outlook of other Indian-made films. The filmmaker who first brought Bengali life to the attention of the world is Satayjit Ray, who still lives and works in the city today.

Recently, French author Dominique Lapièrre, inspired by Calcutta, wrote his now-famous account of life in a fictional Calcutta slum named in the title of the book, *City of Joy*. Now visitors regularly stop at the tourist office to ask where they can find this City of Joy. To which the staff replies, as many a Bengali might: "Here, it is here—everywhere in Calcutta." And while "joy" may be stretching it a bit when it comes to Calcutta, "City of Resiliency" is right on the mark.

1. Accommodations

Finding a good budget hotel in Calcutta isn't easy, and can be nearly impossible if you arrive without reservations during the peak season, roughly October to March, or during the Durga Puja, celebrated in September or October, the dates changing slightly from year to year. Many top-quality budget hotels are located on Sudder Street, which people will tell you is possibly not safe at night. You can, of course, hear this about many areas in the world's larger cities these days, but it's worth keeping in mind when staying at the Sudder Street hotels.

HOTELS: The West Bengal government levies a luxury tax of 10% on upper-priced hotel rooms, and sales taxes on food can add another 8% to 10%, so take this into account when budgeting in Calcutta.

Easily the liveliest and most colorful hotel in Calcutta, the very cozy **Fairlawn Hotel,** 13A Sudder St., Calcutta 700016 (tel. 24-4460), is owned and operated by Violet Smith, an Armenian woman whose family has had this hotel for about 50 years, and today it retains a lot of it's pre-Independence character. Entering through the garden and the open veranda full of red and green plants, it is quickly obvious that Mrs. S. has done everything possible to provide a bright, warm, and spotless home away from home. Plants abound, as do cozy lounges full of bright-painted furniture and cushions, patterned drapes, memorabilia, and many knickknacks. Rates include meals. With air conditioning, they are Rs. 280 ($21.55) single, Rs. 400 ($30.75) double; non-air-conditioned, Rs. 360 ($27.70) double. There's a 10% service charge.

A calm little oasis in this bustling city, the 110-room, **Hotel New Kenilworth,** 1 and 2 Little Russell St., Calcutta 700071 (tel. 44-8394), is well maintained, with an old and new wing, and a broad, green peaceful lawn. In the marble-walled reception and lounge are comfortable black leather armchairs and area rugs in shades of green on sparkling-clean marble floors which run throughout the hotel. The restaurant, also resplendent in marble, is called the Marble Room, and there's also cozy little Mikado Bar. The well-maintained rooms are airy and spacious, with tasteful furnishings and large windows. They are all air-conditioned, with telephones, color television, piped-in music, refrigerators, and attached bathrooms. Rates are creeping into the splurge range: Rs. 450 ($34.60) single, Rs. 550 ($42.30) double. There's a 10% service charge, a 10% luxury tax, and an 8% sales tax on food.

Just next door is the **Lytton Hotel,** 14 Sudder St., Calcutta 700016 (tel. 23-1875), less spectacular than the Fairlawn, but its renovated rooms—blond pine and clean, painted walls—are a cut above many others in this price range. All rooms are air-conditioned, and have attached bathrooms, hot water, telephones, and piped-in music. There is a pleasant dining room and balcony lounge. Singles in the new wing cost Rs. 330 ($25.40); doubles, Rs. 450 ($34.60), air-conditioned. In the old wing, the rooms are seedy and dark, and rates are a bit lower: Rs. 220 ($16.90) double, Rs. 170 ($13.05) single. There's a 10% service charge.

A striking-looking old red mansion is now the **Astor Hotel,** 15 Shakespeare Sarani, Calcutta 700071 (tel. 44-9957), with bright and cheerful rooms in the main building rated higher, and with higher rates, than those in the budget, but with a rather gloomy annex. All rooms are air-conditioned and have attached bathrooms. Annex rates are Rs. 325 ($25) to Rs. 425 ($32.70); in the main building, rates range from Rs. 390 ($30) to Rs. 550 ($42.30). There is no service charge.

Rutt-Deen, 21-B Dr. U. N. Brahmachari Sarani, formerly Loudon Street (off Park Street), Calcutta 700016 (tel. 44-2884), is run-down and overpriced. Rates are Rs. 400 ($30.75) single, Rs. 480 ($36.90) to Rs. 500 ($38.45) double, for air-conditioned rooms with bathrooms attached.

In the bustling, B. B. D. Bagh (Dalhousie Square) area, location of the main post office and American Express, is the **Shalimar Hotel,** 3 S. N. Banerjee Rd., Calcutta 700013 (tel. 28-5030). This hotel, in south B. B. D. Bagh, near the Cottage Industries Emporium, is fairly new, with a hi-tech lobby, done up in orange and white with stainless-steel trim. All 22 rooms are air-conditioned, with modern bathrooms. Singles are Rs. 265 ($20.40) to Rs. 290 ($22.30), and doubles run Rs. 325 ($25). Rooms are neat and compact, but hardly serene as the street is noisy. There is a restaurant for residents only, and you can eat at any number of restaurants nearby.

In South Calcutta—but away from the main tourist area—are two **Hotels Bliss,** 5 Jatin Das Rd., Calcutta 700029 (tel. 42-4695), near Lake Market; and 193/2 Rash Behari Ave., Calcutta 700019 (tel. 41-1941), near Gariahat Bazaar. The no-frills rooms cost Rs. 110 ($8.45) to Rs. 160 ($12.30) single, Rs. 170 ($13.05) to Rs. 220 ($16.90) double, and Rs. 200 ($15.40) to Rs. 250 ($19.25) for deluxe doubles. The higher rates are for air-conditioned rooms. All rooms have attached bathrooms with hot and cold running water.

You can get an extremely modest room with bathroom attached at the **Minerva Hotel,** 11 Ganesh Chandra Ave., Calcutta 700013 (tel. 26-3365). The Minerva charges Rs. 195 ($15) to Rs. 215 ($16.55) for non-air-conditioned singles, Rs. 295 ($22.70) to Rs. 325 ($25) for non-air-conditioned doubles, and Rs. 420 ($32.30) to Rs. 450 ($34.60) for air-conditioned doubles. It's an Rs.-8 (60¢) taxi ride to Park Street from here.

If every other place is full, try the well-located, but run-down **Astoria Hotel,** 6/2/3 Sudder St., Calcutta 700016 (tel. 24-1359). It has 21 doubles and 6 singles; nine rooms are air-conditioned. However, the rooms are in better condition than the halls in this shabby old house turned into a makeshift hotel. Rates are Rs. 60 ($4.60) for non-air-conditioned singles, Rs. 200 ($15.40) for non-air-conditioned doubles, and Rs. 250 ($19.25) for air-conditioned doubles. There's a 10% service charge. Not for the fastidious at any price.

CHEAPIES ON SUDDER STREET AND STUART LANE: Although **Uncle Chowbey's Most Welcome Tourist Inn,** 4/1 Sudder St., Calcutta 700016 (tel. 24-3732), has slipped over the years, it still offers fairly clean, basic accommodations. The small rooms—four doubles and two singles—are divided by very thin wooden partitions, painted light blue. Uncle Chowbey, who is 83 years old, has been practicing yoga most of his life, and now, despite failing eyesight, will give guests a free yoga lesson if they ask him. For rooms, he charges Rs. 35 ($2.70) single and Rs. 75 ($5.75) double. You share bathrooms in all but the one four-bedded room, which has its own.

Off Sudder Street on Stuart Lane are two well-known cheap hotels. The

Modern Lodge, 1 Stuart Lane, Calcutta 700016 (tel. 24-4960), charges Rs. 25 ($1.90) for doubles, Rs. 8 (60¢) per person in the dorm. The **Paragon,** 2 Stuart Lane, Calcutta 700016 (tel. 24-2445), has rooms upstairs that are light and airy facing a roof terrace which always seem full of travelers doing laundry. Rooms on the ground floor are dark little cells. Rates are Rs. 50 ($3.85) double, Rs. 20 ($1.55) single. At the Paragon, rent is collected every day. At both Modern Lodge and Paragon, foreign guests at suspected of using drugs—whether it's true or not.

Back on Sudder Street, the **Hotel Maria,** 5/1 Sudder St., Calcutta 700016 (tel. 24-3311), is always crowded with budget travelers—indeed, among them are workers for Mother Teresa. The rooms are plain, fairly clean, but not for the fussy. The rates are Rs. 30 ($2.30) single and Rs. 70 ($5.40) double with private bathrooms, Rs. 40 ($3.05) double with a common bathroom. Dorm beds are Rs. 15 ($1.15) per person. The pleasant proprietor, Ismail Abbasbhai, puts guests on the roof under a tent when all 21 rooms and the 11-bed dorm are full. Renovations have been planned for the hotel, which could use fixing up. No meals are served at the Maria.

GUESTHOUSES: Tops in guesthouses, **Bengal Chambers,** 60 Queens Mansions, 12 Park St. or 12 Russell St., Calcutta 700016 (tel. 29-7953), on the fourth floor of a quiet residential building, often puts up guests from various embassies. The lounge has a neat, well-kept look with Picasso and Dubuffet prints on the walls, and a nicely upholstered settee and chairs. Cleanliness throughout adds to its attractiveness. The 15 rooms have a vaguely 1930s feeling in their decor, which includes highly polished dressing tables, desks, and wardrobes among the well-kept furniture; many have balconies. Rates are at the top of our budget and beyond, and they include all meals. Room 1 is especially spacious, with its own balcony, no air conditioning but an overhead fan, at Rs. 220 ($16.90) per person for a double, Rs. 240 ($18.45) single. Other non-air-conditioned rooms are all singles, at Rs. 240 ($18.45). The remaining rooms are large doubles, renting for Rs. 280 ($21.55) to Rs. 350 ($26.90) per person. There's a 10% service charge. Building entrances are on both Park and Russell Streets, and the halls going up are enough to scare you away. The Bengal Chambers' halls are clean, swept, painted, and well maintained.

Camar Guest House, 25 Camar St. (tel. 43-3127), in a residential building, offers modest overpriced accommodations in three rooms, one of them air-conditioned. Rates are Rs. 150 ($11.55) single and Rs. 175 ($13.45) double, non-air-conditioned; with air conditioning, Rs. 200 ($15.40) single and Rs. 225 ($17.30) double. Breakfast will add an additional Rs. 10 (75¢).

Look for the Jamuna Cinema, where English-language films play, and across the street you'll find the **Woodland Guest House,** up a flight of decrepit stairs at 5 Mushtaq Ahmed St. (formerly Old Marquis Street), Calcutta 700016 (tel. 24-4729), tucked away in an office building. Five neat rooms await—none with air conditioning, but there are fans. Only two doubles have private bathrooms and they cost Rs. 100 ($7.70); doubles with a common bathroom, Rs. 70 ($5.40). Breakfast can be sent in for a few extra rupees.

Lindsay Guest House and Hotel, 8B Lindsay St., Calcutta 700087 (tel. 24-8639), is, as far as I know, the only guesthouse with a star rating—one star, in this case. The halls could certainly use a coat of paint, but the rooms are nice, simple, and clean enough. Numbers 901, 902, and 903 have fantastic city views. Rates are Rs. 240 ($18.45) double and Rs. 180 ($13.84) single, air-conditioned; Rs. 160 ($12.30) double and Rs. 125 ($9.60) single, without air conditioning. Rooms have bathrooms attached. There's a 10% service charge. The Lindsay is popular with Indian men traveling on business.

A bit off the beaten tourist path in South Calcutta, Mrs. Krishna Banerjee has turned her pleasant ten-bedroom home into **Saroj Deep Guest House,** 16/1 Hindustan Rd., Calcutta 700029 (tel. 46-3895), ideal for someone seeking a family atmosphere. All the neat and clean rooms have private bathrooms, but the light and airy upstairs rooms are nicest. Rates run Rs. 200 ($15.40) a day for an air-conditioned single, Rs. 250 ($19.25) a day for an air-conditioned double; non-air-conditioned rooms run Rs. 80 ($6.15) to Rs. 200 ($15.40) single and Rs. 200 ($15.40) to Rs. 260 ($20) double. All rooms have attached bathrooms. Monthly rates are available. Home-cooked Bengali meals are another attraction. Breakfast and tea cost Rs. 5 (40¢); lunch and dinner, Rs. 30 ($2.30) each. Mrs. Banerjee was considering increases in the rates. The taxi fare to Park Street from here is Rs. 10 (75¢); the Gariahat Market, with bargains galore, is nearby.

OTHER BUDGET CHOICES: Just across the street from the Fairlawn and Lytton Hotels is the **Red Shield Guest House,** 2 Sudder St., Calcutta 700016 (tel. 29-7033), run by the Salvation Army, with 70 beds (a few double rooms, but mainly dorm style). The gate is locked at midnight; to get in after that you have to inform the gatekeeper in advance. Breakfast is the only meal served here. For Re. 1 (7½¢) per day, you can rent a locker for your valuables. The superior double rooms cost Rs. 70 ($5.40); other doubles are Rs. 40 ($3.05). Dorm rates are Rs. 15 ($1.15). There is a seven-day limit. Lights out at 10 p.m. Popular with young travelers.

The **YMCA,** 25 J. Nehru Rd., Chowringhee, Calcutta 700016 (tel. 29-2192), takes transients in its 26 rooms. This Y takes in men, women, families, and groups; it's the oldest YMCA in Asia. A single room with bath attached costs Rs. 150 ($11.55); a double, Rs. 200 ($15.40). A dorm bed is Rs. 80 ($6.15). Temporary membership runs Rs. 10 (75¢) for seven days; on the eighth day you renew by paying another Rs. 10. Tariff includes bed, bedtime tea, breakfast, and dinner. Some travelers I met liked it a lot; others complained that it wasn't clean enough. It's nearly always full.

The 75-room **YWCA Gallaway House,** 1 Middleton Row, Calcutta 700071 (tel. 29-7033), takes in single travelers, married couples, and sometimes a family with children under 12. There are 38 rooms in all available for transients. Most of the rooms are off a veranda, and all have attached baths (some shared with an adjoining room) with big tubs or showers. There is a large lounge and a utilitarian dining room. The front door is locked at 10 p.m., but there's a man on duty to let you in up to 1 a.m. A few single rooms are available for Rs. 50 ($3.85); mostly you share a room, at Rs. 30 ($2.30) per person. These rates include breakfast. To reserve write: Secretary, YWCA, 1 Middleton Row, Calcutta 700071.

The Government of West Bengal runs a **Tourist Hostel** in northeast Calcutta, D.G. Block, Sector 2, Salt Lake City, Calcutta 700091 (no telephone), named after a long-ago salt lake nearby. It's a good 20 km (12 miles) from the center and a taxi runs Rs. 25 ($1.90) to B.B.D. Bagh or Park Street from here. Rates are Rs. 15.75 ($1.20) for dorm beds, Rs. 63 ($4.85) for a four-bedded room, and Rs. 42 ($3.25) for a double. It's frequently full and not overly well cared for. Some rooms have common baths.

SPLURGES: The top place in town for big spenders is the venerable old **Oberoi Grand,** 15 J. Nehru Rd., Calcutta 700013 (tel. 29-2333), right across from the maidan (grassy central park), with its elegant shops, lovely garden, swimming pool, and some of the most gracious service in all of India. The 250 rooms are big and comfortable, with attached bathrooms and ample space to spread out and move around. Everything's air-conditioned. Rates are Rs. 1,075 ($82.70) single and Rs. 1,175 ($90.40) double, but suites run Rs. 2,050 ($157.75) to Rs. 3,250 ($250).

The modern **Hotel Hindustan International,** 235/1 Acharya Jagdish Bose Rd., Calcutta 700020 (tel. 44-2394), with its 212 centrally air-conditioned rooms with tubs, showers, and four-channel music. There's a 24-hour coffeeshop, as well as a restaurant-nightclub, a swimming pool, and a shopping arcade. Rates are Rs. 550 ($42.25) to Rs. 605 ($46.50) for singles, Rs. 660 ($50.75) to Rs. 715 ($55) for doubles; suites cost Rs. 935 ($72) to Rs. 1,650 ($127).

The **Park,** 17 Park St., Calcutta 700016 (tel. 29-7336), a splurge hotel, has central air conditioning, plus an around-the-clock coffeeshop, swimming pool, and a couple of good restaurants, and is adding color television to every room. Rates are Rs. 600 ($46.15) to Rs. 700 ($53.85) single, Rs. 700 ($53.85) to Rs. 800 ($61.55) double.

Finally, the **Great Eastern Hotel,** 1–3 Old Court House St., Calcutta 700069 (tel. 23-2311), once an elegant establishment of the moneyed traveler in the old days, is getting all spruced up again. Indeed a massive restoration project has been going on for some years since the government of West Bengal's Tourism Department started to run it. Although government-run, the hotel is not institutional, having retained its warmth and personal feeling. It is, however, popular with government officials, and is often fully booked. Most of the rooms are spacious, with big attached bathrooms. Air-conditioned rooms are Rs. 450 ($34.60) single and Rs. 525 ($40.40) double; non-air-conditioned rooms cost Rs. 180 ($13.85) to Rs. 225 ($17.30) single and Rs. 230 ($17.70) to Rs. 275 ($21.15) double. One of the suites has a dining room, bar room, bedroom, living room, and bathroom about as big as the living room itself, and is really quite a buy as suites go: Rs. 775 ($59.60). Some past readers of this guidebook have been disappointed in the hotel's maintenance and service, as well as the Chinese restaurant (mentioned later). The food, however, is still good.

At the Airport

The **Hotel Airport Ashok,** Calcutta Airport, Calcutta 700052 (tel. 57-5111), an India Tourist Development Corporation hotel, is a splurge, and convenient only in transit. Singles cost Rs. 660 ($50.75), and doubles, Rs. 760 ($58.50). Of the 156 rooms, 12 are suites, and these rent for Rs. 1,125 ($86.50). There is a swimming pool, restaurant, coffeeshop, and bar.

A Posh Old Club

Fashionable playground of the British, the 200-year-old **Tollygunge Club,** 120 Deshapran Sasmal Road, Calcutta 700033 (tel. 46-3106), is still attracting the rich and famous. The neatly furnished rooms in bungalows cost Rs. 400 ($30.75) to Rs. 450 ($34.60). There's a golf course, pool, and grand gardens. Of course, you're away from it all—nine kilometers (5½ miles) from Park Street, a Rs.15 ($1.15) taxi ride. Buses and the new Metro Railway come out this way in case you want to look around. Guest memberships cost Rs. 15 ($1.15) per day.

2. Restaurants

Before listing notable Calcutta restaurants, here's a little trivia: Calcutta claims to have more bars outside of hotels than any other Indian city. From all appearances this could be true. Certainly you see a lot more bars around this town than around others, and in the evenings they're filled with men hoisting a few with their buddies. But Westerners wonder why there are rarely any women on the scene, and here's the explanation. Generally, Indian women are nondrinkers. Often when they go out, it's a family affair with the kids along and they'll head to a vegetarian restaurant where no liquor is served. Only very modern women go out to eat with each other in India, and then it's likely to be for lunch.

Running diagonally off J. Nehru Road just below the Oberoi Grand Hotel is Park Street, one of the places to head when you're hungry. There are a dozen or more restaurants—most air-conditioned—all near each other, and one or more has music at night. A number of these and other restaurants in Calcutta are closed on Thursday, which is both a meatless and a dry day. When they are closed, hotel restaurants are always open. Chinese and vegetarian restaurants are also likely to be open when the others are closed. Wherever you chose to eat, at least once during your stay be sure to try hilsa, a local white fish. It's bony, but delicious! Chingri malai, a local prawn curry, also rates a taste.

PARK STREET CHOICES: Mocambo, 25B Park St. (tel. 29-4152); **Trinca's,** 17B Park St. (tel. 29-8977); **Magnolia,** 12K–N Park St. (tel. 29-7701); **Blue Fox,** Park Street (tel. 29-7993); and **Moulin Rouge** (closed because of labor problems, but planning to reopen)—all are dimly lit, open similar hours (from around 10 a.m. to midnight; closed Thursday), and what's more, similar menus. They all feature Indian, continental, and a smattering of Chinese foods in about the same price ranges: Rs. 22 ($1.70) to Rs. 30 ($2.30) for entrees. At Trinca's, a number of the Chinese dishes are Szechuan style, rather than the usual Cantonese-style dishes found elsewhere. Adjacent to Trinca's is the **Tavern,** with the same menu, but its Arthurian decor and swords and shields makes it look different from the other restaurants. On top of the Tavern is the **Other Room,** with the same owners and serving the same foods at slightly higher prices. Trinca's also runs the **Ming Room,** in the same complex, for its Chinese menu.

Continuing along Park Street, the **Sky Room,** 57 Park St., Park Mansions (tel. 29-4362), open from 10:30 a.m. to 11:30 p.m. (closed Tuesday), again serves a similar menu, but in a tonier ambience and at slightly higher prices. Residents say the food here is tops, which has made it very popular at the moment. Here you dine on familiar Indian or continental foods at an average main-course price of Rs. 35 ($2.70), while stars twinkle overhead in the sky-blue ceiling, lamps covered with paisley shades cast a soft glow on the snowy-white linen tablecloths and red chairs.

Peter Cat, 18 Park St. (tel. 29-8841), open from 10 a.m. to midnight (closed Thursday), has two levels joined by a teak staircase rimmed in copper. Upstairs the walls have a soft metallic finish and red and beige banquettes are lit by copper lanterns. Downstairs there are stained-glass lampshades contrasting with the textured stucco walls. Specialties here include delicious Iranian and Afghani dishes—among these, a delicious Afghani chicken marinated in fruit juice and herbs, and Iranian kebabs, both Rs. 23.50 ($1.80). With a rice pulao at Rs. 15 ($1.15) to Rs. 20 ($1.55), either dish makes a satisfying meal. The continental specialties are "sizzlers"—foods served sizzling on hot platters, such as hamburger steak, or grilled dishes with mushrooms and liver, in the Rs. 21 ($1.60) to Rs. 24 ($1.85) range. Beer is Rs. 21 ($1.60), a bit lower than at similar restaurants. Sappy off-color cartoons decorate the bar menu. Rich desserts include ice creams and soufflés, at Rs. 10 (75¢) to Rs. 14 ($1.05).

Tandoor, 55 Park St. (tel. 29-8006), open from noon to midnight every day but Wednesday, is a cheerful white-walled place divided by whitewashed brick archways with green chairs and orange- and yellow-topped tables.

Chicken butter masala, at Rs. 17 ($1.30), is among the well-prepared tandoori dishes here, as are a host of others that go into the clay oven and come out tinted red and tasting fine. Unfortunately, this restaurant is frequently closed due to labor–management disputes.

There are two **Kwality** restaurants in Calcutta, at 17 Park St. (tel. 29-7849), open from 10:30 a.m. to midnight; and at 2A Gariahat Rd. (tel. 47-7372), open from 10 a.m. to 10:30 p.m. Both are popular family places. A dinner for two with dishes like biryani with vegetables, accompanied by a chicken or fish dish, will cost about Rs. 112 ($8.60)—not cheap to be sure. Or you might enjoy kebabs or chicken tandoori for Rs. 20 ($1.55) each.

Two is also the number of **Oasis Restaurants,** at 33 Park St. (tel. 29-9033), open from 11 a.m. to 11 p.m. (closed Thursday); and at 3 Madge Lane, open from 10 a.m. to 10 p.m. (closed Sunday). The tidy Park Street branch is decorated with paintings of Calcutta, and Indian foods are highlighted. Especially popular dishes include vegetables navratan, a mixture of vegetables and fruits, at Rs. 16 ($1.25), vegetables jhalfrazy made with chilis at Rs. 15 ($1.15), and fish Punjabi, made with butter and spices, for Rs. 19 ($1.45). It's a family outing place on weekends.

Olympia, 21 Park St., practices old-fashioned separation of sexes—women eat upstairs only. Deep-fried prawns and chicken kebab are both Rs. 19 ($1.45). Hours are 11 a.m. to 11 p.m., on Sunday to 10:30 p.m. This place has seen better days.

AWAY FROM PARK STREET: Two of the best-known restaurants in Calcutta are **Amber,** on two floors at 11 Waterloo St. (tel. 28-6768), open from 10 a.m. to 11 p.m.; and **Sagar,** 1 Meredith St. (tel. 27-7979), open from 10 a.m. to 10 p.m. Both have the same menu: snacks and meals. Tasty specialties include tikka kebab (skewered and tandooried) at Rs. 24 ($1.85), chicken sag (spinach-like vegetable) at Rs. 15.50 ($1.20), and kulcha (bread) at Rs. 8 (60¢). Closed Thursday.

Elfin Restaurant and Bar, 5 Meredith St. (tel. 27-4199), is open from 11 a.m. to midnight every day but Thursday. It's dark and cozy with some stone decorations and paintings of early English merrymakers on slatted-wood walls and tile floors. The cuisine is Indian and Chinese. Vegetarian dishes range from Rs. 3 (23¢) to Rs. 15 ($1.15); nonvegetarian meals are somewhat higher, Rs. 12 (90¢) to Rs. 15 ($1.15), with tandooris slightly more. Chinese dishes average Rs. 10 (75¢). Elfin serves a nonvegetarian thali with chicken, nan, rice, and condiments for about Rs. 18 ($1.40). You can get a Chinese lunch for the same price.

On Middleton Row, adjacent to the YWCA, **Shenaz** (tel. 29-8385) has dancing figures made of wire along one wall and usually a group waiting to get in at the door. Reservations are a must in this small, cozy place where the Indian food is delicious. Among the highest-priced specialties is chicken Baghdadi (stuffed with minced mutton, eggs, and cream sauce), at Rs. 45 ($3.45). Less pricey, and delicious, the fish tandoor kebab is Rs. 18 ($1.40), and mutton kebab, Rs. 12 (90¢); both dishes are a good meal for two along with plain rice pulao, at Rs. 9 (70¢). Open from 11 a.m. to midnight every day but Thursday.

Kabab-E-Que, located on the spacious lawn of the Astor Hotel at 15 Shakespeare Sarani (tel. 44-9950), is a popular snack stop after work. Several kinds of kebabs (chicken, mutton, fish, and vegetable) are featured at Rs. 12 (90¢) to Rs. 30 ($2.30), and an assortment of seven kinds of tandoori breads to eat with or wrap around them is Rs. 2 (15¢) to Rs. 6 (45¢). Beer is served, a bargain at Rs. 23 ($1.75) to Rs. 26 ($2) when you know it's half the price of most other hotels. Inside, the **Sarai Restaurant** serves Indian dishes, with entrees costing Rs. 23 ($1.75) to Rs. 25 ($1.90) explained in English for foreign guests. Some of the dishes in both Kabab-E-Que and Sarai were researched from historical texts. The delicious anecdotes about them are unfortunately not on the menu. For example, the story is that murgh kasturi so delighted a former maharaja that to express his compliments, he gave the chef his weight in pearls.

CHINESE: The Chinese restaurants in Calcutta are some of the best in India. Here are some, among many, worth trying.

The **Waldorf,** 24B Park St. (tel. 29-7514), has red-lacquered pillars, dragon motifs, lanterns, and delicious Cantonese foods. It's a bit higher in price than some other Chinese restaurants around town, but consistently good. Highest-priced entrees are around Rs. 26 ($2) for such tasty items as prawns in tomato sauce or garlic, sweet-and-sour chicken, and an un-Cantonese, Indian-Chinese chili chicken. These dishes are very good with special fried rice, Rs. 14 ($1.05). The Waldorf's menu offers both large and small portions, the latter about one-third less. This restaurant is not air-conditioned, but big, whirling overhead fans and breezes from the open windows keep it comfortable. Open from 11 a.m. to 11:30 p.m.; closed Tuesday.

The lantern-lit **Jade Garden,** in the Park Hotel, 17 Park St. (tel. 29-7336), has Szechuan food, in the splurge range. The range of dishes is broader, and the prices higher, here than in most local Chinese restaurants. Entrees average Rs. 30 ($2.30) to Rs. 40 ($3.05). Dishes include drums of heaven chicken (wings), lime chicken with garlic, and "stick in the pan" (dumplings). Open from noon to 3 p.m. for lunch and 8 to 11 p.m. for dinner every day.

Ask many Calcuttans where to eat the best Chinese food in town and they'll send you straight to **Dragon in Sherry's,** in the Great Eastern Hotel, 1, 2, and 3 Old Court House Rd. (tel. 28-2311). Such delicacies as crab, shark's-fin soup, and chicken with cashews run around Rs. 13 ($1); vegetarian dishes run Rs. 8 (60¢) to Rs. 13 ($1); and various rice preparations are around Rs. 6 (45¢) to Rs. 14 ($1.05). Open every day from 12:30 to 3 p.m. for lunch and 7:30 to 11 p.m. for dinner.

New Embassy Restaurant, 53-A J. Nehru Rd. (tel. 44-0670), open from 10 a.m. to 10 p.m. (closed Tuesday), is air-conditioned and has the same owners as Valentino's in Darjeeling and the Sunflower Beauty Parlor in Calcutta. It's a vest-pocket-size restaurant, dimly lit and pleasant, with shiny blue-and-green striped walls, blue plastic upholstered chairs, all under a Chinese-design and polka-dotted ceiling. The menu is Cantonese, with many familiar dishes in the Rs.-20 ($1.55) range. At this price, and a house specialty—not found all over town—are duck dishes, and the management also recommends the special chow mein made with pork, prawns, chicken, and chicken liver.

VEGETARIAN: Neat and clean **Junior Brothers,** above Gupta Confectionery at 18B Park St., serves thali that's a bit higher in price than some, but also ample and delicious, with three curries, dahi (yogurt), dahl (gravy-like), salad, pappadam (cracker bread), a choice of breads (such as naan, roti, or parantha), pulao, and a sweet for Rs. 20 ($1.55). Coffee or tea is Rs. 4 (30¢) to Rs. 5 (40¢). Open from 12:30 to 3 p.m. for lunch, from 3 to 7 p.m. for snacks, and from 7 to 10 p.m. for dinner; closed Wednesday.

Maple Restaurant, 15 Park St. (tel. 29-9192), is an attractive, calm, neat trilevel restaurant with wood-trimmed balcony and a maple-leaf-shaped doorknob. Offerings include such Western dishes as vegetarian hamburgers (on the menu as "humburgers") and Indian dishes such as pakoras (fritters), each Rs. 16 ($1.25). Another house special is "Temptation"; two slices of toasted bread, filled with mixed vegetables and topped with a slice of fresh pineapple and a cherry, for Rs. 25 ($1.90). Open from 10 a.m. to 10 p.m. (closed Tuesday). A high price to pay for vegetarian food, but good-tasting, however.

Vineet, 1 Shakespeare Sarani (tel. 44-0788), opposite the Tourist Office in the Air-Conditioned Market, is open from 11 a.m. to 3 p.m. and 7 to 11 p.m. serving mini-meals such as nan and curry of the day for Rs. 25 ($1.90); Western sandwiches, such as cottage cheese with pineapple for Rs. 14 ($1.05); and a host of Indian sweets for Rs. 5 (40¢). It's neat, clean, unfancy, and a place for a refreshment break if you're shopping in the Air-Conditioned Market.

For shoppers at the Gariahat Junction Market, **Ideal Vegetarian Refreshment,** 26/4 Hindustan Park Rd., is a clean place for South Indian foods. Rs. 5 (40¢) to Rs. 6 (45¢) will get you a meal. Hours are 11 a.m. to 9 p.m.

CALCUTTA BUFFETS: At **Polynesia Restaurant** in the Oberoi-Grand Hotel, 15 J. Nehru Rd. (tel. 29-8947), the all-you-can-eat buffet features both Chinese and Polynesian foods. The price is Rs. 80 ($6.15), and it's on from 12:30 to 2 p.m.

At **Trinca's,** 17-B Park St. (tel. 24-0205), there's a buffet of Indian, Western, and Chinese foods every day but Sunday when only the menu is offered, and Thursday when the restaurant is closed. The cost is Rs. 35 ($2.70) and the hours are 1 to 2:30 p.m.

Every Tuesday and Thursday there are Chinese dishes at the **Jade Room buffet,** in the Park Hotel, 17 Park St. (tel. 24-8301), for Rs. 50 ($3.85).

SWEETS AND SNACKS: When Indians visit Calcutta, they eat sweets and take some back home, for these are well-known specialties of this bustling business and industrial center. Famous for some 60 years for Western sweets is **Flury's,** 18 Park St. (tel. 29-7664), where chocolate and assorted pastries run about Rs. 3 (23¢) to Rs. 7 (55¢) apiece. Flury's serves excellent tea, at Rs. 6 (45¢) per small pot. It's pleasant to drop in at 11 a.m. when everyone from chief executives to clerks stop in for a break. Sunday is fun as well, when families turn out for treats. Open from 7:30 a.m. to 7 p.m.; closed Monday.

At the spotlessly clean **Gupta Brothers Confectionery,** 18-B Park St., under Juniors (tel. 29-9687), famous for more than 100 years for their delicious Indian sweets, you can buy by the piece or get an assortment to take out and nosh as you please. Expect to pay a price for some of these famous Bengali treats—roshgullas (cottage cheese balls, flavored with saffron and simmered in rosewater syrup) are Rs. 26 ($2) for 875 grams, or almost two pounds (probably about eight pieces). Pista (pistachio) barfi, a fudge-like sweet covered in a thin layer of edible silver, surely must be the Tiffany-priced sweet at Rs. 300 ($23) per kilogram (a little over two pounds). Special sandesh (a milk sweet) is more modest, Rs. 2.50 (20¢) per piece. If you're invited to visit someone at home, a sweet box from Gupta's will be an appreciated gift that will undoubtedly get you invited again. It's interesting to know that around festival times treats like these are sometimes rationed, not only to make sure there are enough to go around to satisfy the enormous Bengali sweet tooth, but also to ensure enough milk for more nutritious uses. Open from 7 a.m. to 10 p.m.; closed Wednesday.

For a snack and a spectacular view of the Hooghly, go to **Gay Rendezvous,** Man-o-War Jetty, where nothing runs higher than about Rs. 14 ($1.05). You can have fish and chips or chicken cutlets if you're feeling hungry, or a dish of ice cream just to tide you over while watching the drifting river tides. The partly covered country boats below can be rented—around Rs. 30 ($2.30) or less per hour after bargaining—and often are by young lovers in a mood for romance. Gay is open seven days a week from 10:30 a.m. to 8:30 p.m. It's a Rs.14 ($1.05) taxi trip from Park Street.

Some 70 years ago an Iranian immigrant founded **Nahum's,** F-20, in New Market, off Lindsay Street, a confectionery shop which has become an institution in Calcutta. Few shoppers in New Market can pass by without buying a pastry to nibble or a selection to take home. For Rs. 50 ($3.85) you can get quite an assortment of rich cream-filled, fruit-stuffed, or chocolate-covered pastries, tarts, and cakes. They can also be bought by the piece for around Rs. 3.50 (25¢) and up to Rs. 6 (45¢).

Newer, but also known for rich sweets and pastries, **Kathleen Confectioners,** 12 Free School St., charges Rs. 3.50 (25¢) for chocolate pastries, a bit less for others.

3. Seeing the City

The best possible thing to do in Calcutta is to walk around aimlessly and watch the life around you. If this is too rich for your blood, try sitting on a streetcar (sit on the side nearest the sidewalk) and ride as far as it goes. Sooner or later it will get hopelessly stuck in a traffic jam, but meanwhile you'll get a superlative closeup view of the streets. A rickshaw—if your conscience can stand this example of imperialist exploitation—is marvelous for even closer viewing. Bargain with the rickshaw driver *before* you get in, and remember that a fair fare is Rs. 4 (30¢) to Rs. 5 (40¢) per kilometer. Or try a ride in one of those stately, horse-drawn hansom carriages. Don't worry about getting lost; when you're tired of looking around, hop into a taxi and head back to your hotel. Make sure that the taxi has a meter and the driver turns it all the way back to Rs. 2.50 (19¢), the regular starting price. (The fare should be Rs. 3.50, or 27¢), for the first two kilometers, and 25 paise, about 2¢, every 500 meters thereafter. However, you must add 40% to reflect an increase not shown on the meters—or ask for the rate card.)

THE TOP SIGHTS: Among the things to see in Calcutta is the **Victoria Memorial,** which sits in majestic splendor at the bottom end of the big green space called the maidan, and should certainly be looked at even if not visited. An immense palace of white marble, it's a fitting reminder of the days when pomp and ceremony were more important than money. The 25 galleries inside are chock-a-block with lithographs, furniture, firearms, portraits, statues, manuscripts, and other historical evidence of Britain's reign in India. Outside the ornamental gate, you'll most assuredly see ice-cream vendors and performing monkeys.

The Memorial, which cost around a million dollars to build back in 1920, is open daily except Monday from 10 a.m. to 3:30 p.m. Admission is Re. 1 (7½¢) for adults, 50 paise (4¢) for children.

In the complex just across the greensward from the Memorial are other places of interest: the **National Theatre Rabindra Sadan** (outside is a lovely fountain whose jets constantly change color), which presents plays and musical and dance concerts almost every evening at 6:30 p.m.; the **Birla Planetarium** (biggest in the world after the one in Russia), which has two shows in English daily; admission is Rs. 4 (30¢) (check the *Statesman* for a schedule of this and other events); and the **Academy of Fine Arts** (open from 3 to 8 p.m.; closed Monday), built in 1847 in the Indo-Gothic style, with its fine selection of miniatures, Kashmiri shawls and carpets, old engravings, mica paintings, Bengali and Varanasi saris, and Tagore paintings. The ground floor usually shelters a temporary show of contemporary art. It's on Cathedral Road next to St. Paul's Cathedral.

On the western side of the maidan is the **Ochterlony Monument** (now **Sahid Minar**), a 158-foot tower honoring Sir David Ochterlony who won the Nepalese war (1812–1814) for the British. The monument, built in 1828, is a strange mixture of Turkish, Syrian, and Egyptian architectural styles. Supposedly you can climb it to view the city, but first you have to get permission from the chief of police.

Behind the Victoria Memorial in the other direction is the **race course** (admission is Rs. 10, 75¢), and behind that to the left down Belvedere Road are the **Zoological Gardens**, covering 41 acres. The zoo (open from 6 a.m. to 5 p.m.) is worth a visit in any case, partly because it's extremely attractive with flower bed and pools, it's easy to walk around, and has lots of distractions, and partly because it owns some rare white tigers, descendants of Neeladri and Himadri, who were born on the premises in 1963 from an ordinary-colored mother and a valuable white tiger caught and donated to the zoo in 1951 by the Maharaja of Rewa. Admission to the zoo is Re. 1 (7½¢) for adults and 50 paise (4¢) for children, and it costs another Re. 1 to get into this special tiger enclosure.

Be sure to buy peanuts before you enter the zoo; you'll have lots of opportunities to give them away, if not to the ostrich, deer, chicks, or peacocks, then to the ubiquitous black crows that line the fences of every cage awaiting such a generous gesture.

Opposite the zoo is the rather elegant former **Residence of the Governor of Bengal,** with an enormous banyan tree entirely sheltering its rear garden. Sharing the same grounds is the **National Library,** with an extensive card index file on European authors and subjects.

The biggest banyan tree in the area, and probably in the world, is the more famous one in the **Botanical Gardens** (open from dawn to dusk), on the other side of the River Hooghly (merely a continuation of the Ganges, which, 80 miles to the east, finally empties into the Bay of Bengal). You can also take a bus (no. 54, 55, or 57A from Esplanade bus stand and jam-packed with people) or taxi across the massive **Howrah Bridge (Rabindra Setu),** third largest in the world.

At the other side of the bridge is one of India's most famous landmarks, the **Howrah Railroad Station,** where any hour of the day or night you'll see families virtually living (sleeping and cooking) on mats spread on the station's stone floor. As many as 210 trains arrive or depart from here every day.

Calcutta, as mentioned, is the birthplace of Rabindranath Tagore, one of India's greatest poets, who was born and died (1941) in Calcutta in a lovely old house known colloquially as **Thakur Bari.** With its cupolas and balconies, it's a little like old New Orleans in style and was at one time "the nerve center of Bengal's cultural life." Located at K. K. Tagore Street, off Rabindra Sarani, it is today part museum and part university, and gentle doe-eyed beauties flit about its corridors and relax on the flower-fringed lawn. The museum, **Rabindra Bharati Museum** (open from 10 a.m. to 5 p.m., on Saturday until 1:30 p.m.), is an invaluable trove of photos, letters, and portraits pertaining to the Nobel Prize winner (who subsequently turned his hand to plays, drama, short stories, and a poem called "Morning Song," which later became the Indian National Anthem).

Up a nearby little alley, Muktaram Babu Street, Chorebagan, is the **Marble Palace,** once a private collection of art and now open to the public from 10 a.m. to 4 p.m. (closed Monday and Thursday). It houses a mixed bag of artworks, paintings by Rubens and Reynolds, Roman fountains and Grecian clocks. Admission is free, but you must get a visitors permit from the Indian Tourist Office.

Over at 94/1 J. Nehru Rd., the **Nehru Children's Museum** (tel. 44-3516), has, among other things, delightful displays of the *Ramayana* and *Mahabharata*—an easy way for adults to bone up on these epic poems. Admission is Re. 1 (7½¢) for adults, 50 paise (4¢) for children; open from 11:30 a.m. to 6:30 p.m.; closed Monday.

At 27 J. Nehru Rd., the **Indian Museum** is one of the oldest and most comprehensive in the country; it's also said to be the largest museum in Asia. Especially fascinating are the archeological relics located on the southern side of the main floor; upstairs on the second floor is a small, interesting Mammal Gallery. Open from 10 a.m. to 5 p.m.; 25 paise (2¢) for adults.

In northeast Calcutta, the **Jain Temple,** on Budree Das Temple Street, is open from 6 a.m. to noon and 3 to 7 p.m. You wouldn't call it beautiful, but nobody could deny that it's extraordinary. How to start describing it? It's like a combination of New England rococo, with Victorian gingerbread plus the entire contents of your grandmother's attic tossed in for good measure. Silver statues of men on horseback, flower-inlaid marble tiles, cut-glass chandeliers, stained-glass windows, mirrors and walls encrusted with semiprecious stones —these are but a handful of the things the tourist has to contend with on first inspection. As you walk around the temple—built in 1867 by the court jeweler—things seem to fall more into place. The temple belongs to the Jain sect, a Buddhist extremist faction founded by Mahavira, an ascetic noted for austerity. It is dedicated to Sri Sheetalnathji, the 10th of the 14 Jain reformers. One wonders what these men would have made of this osentatious display. It's set in a formal garden.

TOURS: The **India Tourism Development Corporation** operates a coach tour daily (except Monday) with a guide, from 8 a.m. to 5:15 p.m., costing Rs. 30 ($2.30), and covering the commercial area, Jain temple, botanical gardens, the Victoria Memorial, the zoo, and other points. Departure is from the Government of India Tourist Office, 4 Shakespeare Sarani (tel. 44-1402). You book at the tourist office counter.

The **West Bengal Tourist Bureau,** 3/2 B. B. D. Bagh East (tel. 28-8271), also operates daily full-day coach tours: Rs. 45 ($3.45) air-conditioned, Rs. 30 ($2.30) non-air-conditioned.

SHOPPING: The main place to bargain for assorted wares is the **New Market** (formerly Hogg Market), now in two locations; off Lindsay Street and opposite the Oberoi Grand on J. Nehru Road (the latter stalls are temporary and a result of a fire at their original location; they will be moved back to the old New Market as soon as renovations are completed). This is a huge market of more than 2,000 stalls where you can find everything you need to sustain life and then some, arranged according to merchandise category. Still, if you get lost meandering around, don't worry—there is always someone to tell you how to find the shop you want or how to get out to the street again.

Serious shoppers in search of more bargains galore should investigate farther south in **Gariahat Junction Market** where there are also stalls selling diverse merchandise, from arts and crafts and gowns for home deities to ready-to-wear for all of us. For example, in this market, **Kimbadanti,** 196/11 Rash Behari Ave., has a good selection of traditional salwar kamiz from Lucknow in cotton pastels and dark colors, with white embroidery, at Rs. 85 ($6.55), price-fixed.

Back in Chowringhee, at 7/1 Lindsay St., the **West Bengal Emporium** is, as the name implies, devoted to items made in West Bengal such as the famous terracotta toys and hand-looms in cottons and silks. Among the prettiest textiles are from Murshidabad. At **Central Cottage Industries Emporium, 7 J. Nehru Rd.** (tel. 28-4139), open weekdays from 10 a.m. to 6:30 p.m. and on Saturday to 2 p.m. (closed Sunday), there is merchandise from West Bengal and a number of other states. Several other Indian states also have emporia in Calcutta for their merchandise.

Not far from B.B.D. Bagh, there's **Bentinck Street,** renowned for its roughly 100 Chinese shoemaker shops. Custom-made shoes for men cost Rs. 200 ($15.40), and copies cost a little less. Ready-made sandals are Rs. 60 ($4.60)—not cheap, but it's good-quality merchandise. Looking for a book? On **College Street** there are more than 200 secondhand bookshops.

NIGHTLIFE: Calcutta, like the other major Indian cities, has little in the way of traditional nightlife. But in this cultural capital, there is an evening life. Around 6 or 6:30 p.m. you can almost always find a cultural event somewhere in town—a dance recital or music recital, or other discipline. They are listed in "Calcutta This Fortnight," a free pamphlet available from the tourist office. The office sometimes has a limited number of free tickets for these events, so be sure to ask when you're there. Also at 6:30 p.m. every evening, there's *Dances of India,* an introduction to various styles, with commentary, in the Moghul Room of the Oberoi Grand Hotel, 15 J. Nehru Rd., for Rs. 25 ($1.90).

Otherwise, you're more or less stuck with having a quiet dinner in a nice restaurant and calling it a day, unless you're in the mood for dinner-dancing to standard Western pop tunes, in which case you should head for any of the top hotels or Trinca's on Park Street. This kind of entertainment gets going around 8 or 9 p.m. and winds down around midnight. For disco devotees, there's the **Pink Elephant** in the Oberoi Grand Hotel, 15 J. Nehru Rd., at the moment the city's only discothèque. The entry fee for foreign tourists is Rs. 50 ($3.85), free to hotel guests. It's open from 9:30 p.m. to 3 a.m. Places with dancing are closed on Thursday.

You might also catch a **movie.** Elite, Lighthouse, Metro, Minerva, New Empire, Tiger, and Jamuna cinemas show English-language films, censored to remove the steamy parts; Satyajit Ray's films are shown here, as might be expected, in Bengali.

4. Useful Information

TOURIST INFORMATION: The **Government of India Tourist Office,** 4 Shakespeare Sarani, Calcutta 700001 (tel. 44-1402), is open from 8 a.m. to 6 p.m. daily (in winter from 9 a.m.), except Sundays, alternate Saturdays, and national holidays (open other holidays from 8 a.m. to 1 p.m.) to answer all questions tourists may have. Tourist office also maintains a counter at the airport, open when flights depart and come in.

The **West Bengal Tourist Bureau** is located at 3/2 B.B.D. Bagh East, Calcutta 700001 (tel. 28-8271), and also has a counter at the airport.

GETTING AROUND: New, efficient, cheap, fast, clean—just what the budget tourist and Calcuttans need—this is the **Metro,** which runs from the Esplanade to Tollygunge, with eight stops en route, a trip that takes 16 minutes. The Metro operates every day except Sunday from 8 a.m. to 9:15 p.m. It gives easy access to south Calcutta, site of most hotels, restaurants, bars, and many top tourist attractions. The fare is Re. 1 (7½¢) or Rs. 1.50 (12¢) per sector. Timetables are available free at stations. The next link, to Dum Dum in northeast Calcutta, may be in service as well by the time you arrive.

Yellow **cabs** can make suburban journeys; black-and-yellow taxis cannot. Taxi meters start at Rs. 2.50 (20¢) and you add 40% to the meter reading at the end of your journey (the meters have not been reset since 1981). On **auto-rickshaws,** meters start at Rs. 1.25 (9½¢) per kilometer, but they, too, are out-of-date, and you will pay about 25% over the meter reading. When in doubt about any metered fare, ask to see the rate card before paying up. There's no fixed rate for manually operated **rickshaws,** but the asking rate for foreigners is about Rs. 4 (30¢) to Rs. 5 (40¢) per kilometer. You must bargain and set a fare before you get in.

Minibuses operate from B.B.D. Bagh and the Esplanade, north to Dunlop, south to Gariahat, southwest to Thakurpukur, and east to Tangra. These are clean and not so crowded as the usual Calcutta buses (no one is supposed to hang outside, for instance), but the fare is slightly higher. There is a minimum of 80 paise (6¢) and you can spend as much as Rs. 3 (23¢) depending on where you're going.

MONEY CHANGING: Banks are open Monday to Friday from 10 a.m. to 2 p.m., until noon on Saturday. **American Express,** located on Old Court House Street opposite the Great Eastern Hotel, is open for money changing only from 10 a.m. to 2 p.m.; for all other business, from 10 a.m. to 2 p.m. and 2:30 to 5 p.m. Monday through Friday, to 2 p.m. on Saturday. Calcutta International Airport's bank is open 24 hours a day. Top hotels will change money for guests.

SEASONS: Best time to visit Calcutta is October to March; the rainy season is June to early September. Special time to visit is during Dusshera (in September/October) when the entire area is festive with displays everywhere depicting the forces of good and evil represented by deities and demons.

SIDE TRIPS: The terracotta-paneled temples at **Vishnupur,** 95 miles (155 km) away, are worthy of inspection. **Santiniketan,** 133 miles (218 km), is an open-air university founded by Rabindranath Tagore.

ARRIVALS AND DEPARTURES: Trains arrive and leave from two stations, Howrah and Sealdah. Be sure to check which station your train will depart from. Eastern Railway reservations are made at 6 Fairlie Pl. (tel. 22-4356 for first-class, or 22-6811 for other information). Southeastern Railway is at Esplanade Mansions (tel. 23-9580). The Indian Airlines city office is Airlines House, 39 Chittaranjan (tel. 44-2396); Vayudoot, 53/F J. Nehru Rd., Chowringhee (tel. 447062); and Air-India, 50 J. Nehru Rd., Chowringhee (tel. 44-2356).

GETTING TO CALCUTTA: Calcutta is connected by **air** to all of India's major cities, and is the gateway to the northeastern region. Some sample airplane fares to Calcutta are: from Delhi, Rs. 1,142 ($87.85); from Bombay, Rs. 1,370 ($105.40); from Madras, Rs. 1,201 ($92.40); from Bagdogra, gateway to Darjeeling, Rs. 420 ($32.30). The coach between the city and the airport costs Rs. 15 ($1.15); taxis will charge what they think the traffic will bear, so don't bargain—haggle!

There are many **trains** serving either Howrah or Sealdah stations. The best train from Delhi is the *Rajdhani Express,* which makes the trip overnight from Delhi (leaving at 5 p.m. and arriving at 11 a.m.) five days a week, at Rs. 330 ($25.40) for an air-conditioned chair and Rs. 615 ($47.30) in two-tier air-conditioned. From Bombay, the *Gitanjali Express* takes 30 hours and costs Rs. 522 ($40.15) in first class, Rs. 126 ($9.70) in second. From Madras, the best train is the *Coramandel Express,* costing Rs. 335 ($25.75) in first class and Rs. 80 ($6.15) in second class. If you're coming from Darjeeling, try to catch the *Darjeeling Mail* at New Jaipalguri, which makes the trip to Calcutta as an overnight journey: Rs. 235 ($18.05) in first class, Rs. 105 ($8.05) in second.

Chapter IX

THE ANDAMAN ADVENTURE

IF YOU THINK you've gotten away from it all before, you haven't really until you've been to the little-known Andaman and Nicobar Islands. This distant strip of land in the Bay of Bengal is over 1,000 km (610 miles) east of the coast of India. The northern tip of the Andamans is in fact 192 km (117 miles) off the south coast of Burma, and the southern tip of the Great Nicobar Island is only about 145 km (88 miles) from Sumatra in Indonesia. It's almost like not being in India at all! Of the 293 islands stretching 500 miles into the sea, 274 are in the Andamans and 19 are in the Nicobars. Only 26 of the Andamans and 12 of the Nicobars are inhabited. Very few of these islands are open for tourism because of various restrictions.

In ancient mythology the islands were the monkey-god Hanuman's stepping stones over the ocean, and they bore his name. Historically, the islands were split off from India by the Marathas in the latter part of the 17th century. They were a base for the indomitable 18th-century Admiral Angre, noted for skirmishes against Europeans. During the British colonial period these peaceful islands were a penal colony for Indian freedom fighters.

From the plane, the Andaman and Nicobar Islands are a vast ribbon of greenery stretching as far as the eye can see into the sea. Over 90% of the area is covered with evergreen species and tropical rain forests of incredible beauty, filled with some of the most rare flora in the world. The capital of this lush archipelago, **Port Blair,** the tourist's entry point, is little more than a main street, with houses scattered about the hillsides and a couple of good hotels (one on the beach, the other up on a cliff overlooking the sea).

Less than a quarter of a century ago these islands had about 50,000 inhabitants—aborigines, Burmese settlers, and convicts and their keepers. The population has swelled since then to 180,000 largely due to central government's encouragement of immigration and the offer of land as repatriation for property losses by Bangladesh refugees. Obviously with this kind of growth and a push to attract tourists, the sooner you visit, the better your chance of seeing the Andamans and Nicobars at their most beautiful and unspoiled.

One-fifth of the current inhabitants are tribal. They are divided into two main groups: the first are of Negreto stock (the Andamanese, Onges, Sentinelese, and the Jharawas) who live in the Andamans; the second group are Mongoloid in origin, and includes the inhabitants of the Nicobar Islands (the Shompens and Nicobarese). Except for the Nicobarese, the others live in "Special Primitive Tribal Reserve Areas," described in the fact sheets as a means of encouraging development while protecting their way of life.

The closest the average tourist comes to seeing tribals living traditionally is in photos in the small Anthropological Museum in Port Blair, one of the sightseeing attractions. Otherwise, you stand little chance of firsthand observation, as the government does not permit visits to restricted areas. Rare exceptions are made to this rule for those who get permission from the Indian Ministry of Home Affairs in New Delhi. You would be well advised to make any special request six to eight weeks in advance of your trip and have some credentials warranting such a visit. Before making an application, check with your nearest Indian embassy or consulate to get the necessary forms. You can also file for your permit through these authorities, who will forward your application to New Delhi.

Permission to visit areas open to tourists is given upon arrival at the airport in Port Blair. The airport is, in reality, only slightly larger than an airstrip. Ask the duty officer to stamp your passport with the necessary permit otherwise you'll waste a lot of time trying to get one later. At present, you can roam freely in Port Blair and the islands of Grub, Snob, Jolly Buoy, Boat, Redskin, and Cinque. These islands fall within a radius of 40 nautical miles (70 km), and are accessible by boats and launches.

WHERE TO STAY IN PORT BLAIR: There is not a great selection of budget-priced accommodations, but new hotels and lodges keep opening all the time. Lack of maintenance is a big problem in the budget hotels.

Presently the only hotel on the beach is the pricey **Andaman Beach Resort,** Corbyn's Cove, Port Blair 744101 (tel. 2599), a concrete structure painted cream and rose with 32 double rooms (but hoping to have 56 rooms by the time you use this book). All rooms overlook a beautiful natural beach and an 18-acre garden planted by the hotel's manager, Captain Prasada, a former naval officer, and his wife. This gorgeous garden displays oversize crotons in a whole range of colors, huge daisy-like gerberas, magnificent hibiscus, and cascading bougainvillea among the many plants. The clean, cheerful hotel is in ship-shape condition. All rooms have bamboo furniture, bright drapes and bedspreads, and private bathrooms. Rates are splurge-high: Rs. 330 ($25.40) single and Rs. 385 ($29.60) double, air-conditioned; Rs. 265 ($20.40) single and Rs. 315 ($24.25) double, non-air-conditioned. Flowered chintz cushions on bamboo settees carry the garden look into the lobby, which has a bold black-and-white geometric-patterned granite floor, overhead lights covered with straw-basket shades, and plants here and there. Food is à la carte in the restaurant and should add another Rs. 100 ($7.70) per person per day to your bill, not including drinks.

Another high-priced hotel is the Welcomgroup's **Bay Island,** Marine Hill, Port Blair 744101 (tel. 2881), a striking white stucco structure with a deep sloping dark-wood roof, designed by prize-winning architect Charles Correa of Bombay to blend into the natural environment. The multilevel hotel built into a cliff overlooking the sea has a huge open lounge furnished with log-cut furniture upholstered in brown and beige hand-woven cotton, and low tables stencilled with ink designs and inlays. The big wooden bar in the lounge is a popular meeting place. Loud taped Western music in all public rooms strikes a sour note in these otherwise serene surroundings. The hotel offers two types of accommodation: Western style, with beds, chairs, and dressing tables; or Indian style, with sleeping platforms topped with bedding, floor cushions, as well as dressing tables. Each room has an attached modern bathroom. At varying levels are a dining terrace and an outdoor swimming pool. Buffet meals at lunch and dinner run Rs. 70 ($5.40) per person. Rates for air-conditioned rooms are Rs. 425 ($32.70) single, Rs. 525 ($40.40) double; non-air-conditioned rooms cost Rs. 360 ($27.70) for singles, Rs. 400 ($30.75) for doubles. From April to September, the rainy season, there's a 20% to 25% discount.

Under construction for some time and taking guests into surreal half-finished surroundings is the **Hotel Aasiana** ("nest"), South Point, Port Blair 744101 (tel. 2937), where unfinished halls go off into nowhere and construction materials fill the lounge, but guests don't seem to mind the confusion. When completed (and maybe it is by now), the five-story hotel will have 48 rooms and a natural pool for swimming. I saw it with 23 rooms, all facing the sea with balconies and basic furniture. Under the circumstances the prices seemed too high: Rs. 200 ($15.40) single, Rs. 300 ($23.05), non-air-conditioned throughout.

Now, some in-town choices. The new **Hotel Dhan Lakshmi**, Aberdeen Bazaar, Port Blair 744101 (tel. 3306), has 16 double rooms, clean and cheerfully painted either blue, cream, green, or pink. Overpriced, however, the rates are Rs. 125 ($9.60) double, Rs. 110 ($8.45) single, not air-conditioned, but all rooms have attached bathrooms. The restaurant should be open by now, and serving Indian and Chinese foods. From here, a taxi to the Corbyn Cove beach costs about Rs. 25 ($1.90).

Sampat Lodge, Aberdeen Bazaar, Port Blair 744101 (no phone), has six rooms, all doubles; two have attached bathrooms, and four with common bathrooms. It's very basic and for the unfussy. Rates are Rs. 60 ($4.60) double, Rs. 40 ($3.05) in rooms with common baths. This hotel has a view of the city coconut-shell dump to one side and a building (under construction when I was there) is sure to block its windows on another side.

Ram Niwas Lodge, Aberdeen Bazaar, Port Blair 744101 (tel. 3026), has 16 simple rooms, four doubles with attached bathrooms at Rs. 50 ($3.85), ten singles at Rs. 25 ($1.90), and two four-bedded rooms with common bathrooms at Rs. 80 ($6.15). Strictly for the unfussy among us.

The following government-run accommodations will take in tourists if they are not occupied by officials: **Tourist Home,** Marine Hill, Port Blair 744101 (tel. 2365), has six rooms; two four-bedded rooms and four doubles, split between old and new wings, and renting for Rs. 25 ($1.90) per person. Try to get in the new wing, which has a terrace overlooking the bay and a nice bathroom. **Tourist Home,** Haddo, Port Blair 744101 (tel. 2380), has 18 basic rooms at Rs. 25 ($1.90) per person. **Megapode Nest,** Haddo, Port Blair 744101, is a cut above the others, with ten rooms adequately furnished and carpeted. Rooms without air conditioning cost Rs. 40 ($3.05) single and Rs. 80 ($6.15) double; those with air conditioning increase to Rs. 55 ($4.25) single and Rs. 110 ($8.45) double. Nearby are the **Nicobarese Cottages** (tel. 2207), with palm-thatched rooms, charging Rs. 130 ($10) for a non-air-conditioned cottage, to Rs. 160 ($12.30) with air conditioning. They may go up to Rs. 200 ($15.40) to Rs. 300 ($23.05) per cottage. Simple meals are available in the government-run accommodations, and should add another Rs. 10 (75¢) to Rs. 15 ($1.15) per day, depending on whether you order vegetarian or nonvegetarian.

WHAT TO DO AND SEE, AND HOW TO DO IT: The main reason for visiting Port Blair is for some R&R. Unless you are one of the very rare few who get to visit the tribes, sightseeing is limited to the following attractions.

The **Cellular Jail,** which once housed freedom fighters now houses interesting exhibits and memorabilia (open from 9 a.m. to noon and 2 to 5 p.m.). Then there are **Chatham Saw Mill,** one of the largest in Asia; **Corbyn's Cove beach;** the **Anthropological Museum** (open from 9 a.m. to noon and 1 to 4 p.m.; closed Saturday and public holidays); the Marine Museum (open from 8:30 a.m. to 4 p.m.); a **mini-zoo** (open from 7 a.m. to noon and 1 to 5 p.m.; closed Monday); the **Cottage Industries Emporium** (open from 9 a.m. to 1 p.m. and 1:30 to 5 p.m.; closed Monday and Friday); and the **Botanical Survey of India** (open from 8:30 a.m. to 4:30 p.m.), which has a rich collection of flora found in the islands.

TOURS AND INFORMATION: The **Government of India Tourist Office,** Middle Point, Port Blair 744101 (tel. 3006), open from 8:30 a.m. to 5 p.m. Monday through Friday and 8:30 a.m. to 12:30 p.m. on Saturday, can provide basic information on sights and tours.

The **Tourist Information Center,** in the Tourist Home, Haddo (tel. 2300), is the place to book tours and buy tickets on the day of departure: the city tour and beach tour each cost Rs. 4.50 (35¢); the Wandoor (National Park) tour and Chidiya Tapu tour each cost Rs. 10 (75¢).

The **Marine Department,** Marine Building, conducts a harbour cruise for Rs. 20 ($1.55) and a full-day cruise to Jolly Buoy Island for Rs. 50 ($3.85) from Wandoor. For Jolly Buoy, you make reservations a day in advance, arrive at Wandoor promptly at 10 a.m., and bring lunch, snacks, and bottled water. There's nothing to buy and noplace to buy it on the island.

You can also arrange a Jolly Buoy trip through the travel agents in top hotels, and M/S **Island Travels,** Aberdeen Bazaar (tel. 3350). They should include transportation to and from Wandoor and a box lunch, the latter to be ordered at your hotel when you make your reservation for pickup the day of departure. These arrangements, inclusive of lunch, add about Rs. 50 ($3.85) to the cost of the cruise, bringing the total to Rs. 100 ($7.70). The Jolly Buoy trip is limited to about 20 people, so it's not a mob scene.

A DAY AT JOLLY BUOY: An excursion to Jolly Buoy Island is a full day's outing—starting with a ferry cruise through the tropical forest-fringed backwaters. The leisurely trip gives everyone a chance to get acquainted, and soon delicious snacks are being exchanged between the passengers. On the island, settled into secluded coves, everyone spends a lazy day swimming, picnicking, snorkeling, hunting shells. The Indian women go in the sea wearing their saris, which billow up around them like fluffy clouds. Later they duck behind the bushes and change, reappearing in fresh dry saris, thus providing an improvised fashion show.

Small groups climb into the makeshift glass-bottom boat—a rowboat with a glass window installed, complete with sash—until everyone has a chance to see the reefs. The boatman's assistant constantly wipes off the droplets of moisture that collect like perspiration on the glass as passengers peer at the myriad of neon-bright fish darting through delicate-looking flower-like corals.

On the return trip, although everyone is stuffed from a huge picnic, it's snack time again—the Bengalis aboard have a seemingly endless supply of tantalizing foods. Arrival is just before tea time and everyone heads off to Port Blair rested, well fed, and ready for more.

SHOPPING: Next to the Tourist Office, **Cottage Industries** is open from 8:30 a.m. to 5 p.m., selling local crafts including textile hangings and shell work. Shops in Aberdeen Bazaar also have shell-studded items.

GETTING AROUND: Bikes can be rented for Rs. 10 (75¢) a day in the Aberdeen Bazaar at the cycle shop between Sapna Photos Studios and M. Permual General Merchants. Be prepared for some very hilly pedaling. At this writing, this is the only cycle shop in town that rents bikes. There is a ferry around South Andaman Island offering service from the Fisheries Jetty in Port Blair to Haddo wharf, Jungleghat Jetty, Bamboo Flat, and Dandus Point. Buses go throughout Port Blair.

GETTING TO PORT BLAIR: From Madras, flights covering the 1,191 km (727 miles) to Port Blair operate twice a week (on Tuesday and Friday), and from Calcutta, 1,255 km (765 miles) away, once a week (on Sunday). The one-way fare from Madras is Rs. 1,178 ($90.60); from Calcutta, Rs. 1,168 ($89.85). These flights take two hours. Flights were under consideration from Bhubaneswar and could be in operation by now.

In 2½ days you can reach Port Blair on passenger ships sailing every 10 to 12 days from either Madras or Calcutta. The cost of the journey ranges from Rs. 558 ($43) for the deluxe fare, down to Rs. 110 ($8.45) for an air-conditioned bunk and Rs. 70 ($5.40) for a non-air-conditioned bunk. The Shipping Corporation of India, 13 Strand Rd., Calcutta 700001, and K.P.V. Sheikh Mohammed Rowther Co., Madras 600001, will have information on how to book. Arranging passage can be complicated and time-consuming.

Chapter X

THE ROUTE TO THE SOUTH

1. Orissa's Sacred Seashore: Konarak and Puri
2. Hyderabad

THE JOURNEY RUNS SOUTHWARD now, through country and city celebrated for attractions God-given and man-made: flourishing wildlife, sparkling lakes . . . ancient temples, immense mosque, sturdy bastion, triumphal arch . . . delicate glasswork, heady perfumes, golden filigree. Join us.

1. Orissa's Sacred Seashore: Konarak and Puri

ON THE WAY—BHUBANESWAR: The beautiful east-coast state of Orissa has as its capital Bhubaneswar (pop. 350,000)—a city with a split personality —an old town of crowded, narrow streets and ancient temples surrounded on three sides by a newer settlement of modern architecture and California-style habitations. Many of the buildings are composed of the reddish lavastone blocks that are characteristic of the region.

Most tourists give it one night en route to Konarak and Puri, and, in truth, this pleasant capital doesn't have much to detain you longer. The area around **Rajmahal Square** (intersection of the main roads to Calcutta and Puri) contains a few stores and some restaurants and hotels. Not far away is the bus station. From here, buses leave frequently for Puri, costing about Rs. 5 (50¢), and less frequently for Konarak, at Rs. 5 (50¢).

A trip to **old town,** many of its mud homes decorated with white lacy paintings as a tribute to Lakshmi, the goddess of wealth, by cycle rickshaw is Rs. 15 ($1.59) per hour (that's supposedly the rate, but it's not fixed so discuss it downward before you get in). Touring by taxi can be pricey—supposedly there's a minimum of four hours for Rs. 100 ($13), but you can probably negotiate a better rate. For more advice on getting around, call the tourist officer (tel. 50079) or the OTDC, Orissa Tourism Development Corporation (tel. 54515).

Orissa is well known for its filigree silver and gaily colored hand-woven cottons. Also widely sold are soapstone reproductions of erotic scenes from the temples, often inset neatly into matchboxes. The state government maintains an excellent low-cost store for local handcrafts at Bhubaneswar airport and in Bhubaneswar and Puri.

Where to Stay in Bhubaneswar

Best bet for the budget traveler is the OTDC's **Panthanivas Tourist Bungalow,** Lewis Road (tel. 54515), right across from the state government tourist office, about three miles from the airport, a mile from the railway station, and walking distance from some of the temples. There are 14 rooms in the old block and 62 in the new block (the new block is recommended). All rooms have attached bathrooms, with hot and cold running water; big overhead fans swirl the air in the non-air-conditioned rooms. There are no single-occupancy rates: rooms cost Rs. 100 ($7.70) non-air-conditioned, Rs. 150 ($11.55) air-conditioned. There's a no-frills bar and restaurant, where you can get a complete Indian vegetarian thali meal for Rs. 12 (90¢) and nonvegetarian for Rs. 28 ($2.15) to Rs. 30 ($2.30).

Indian-Style Hotels: As always, these are the cheapest. If those below are full or don't appeal, check others on Station Square, Cuttack Road, or Kalpana Square. Don't expect much in the way of cleanliness.

Modest, but a cut above the others, the **Hotel Anarkali,** Station Square, Bhubaneswar 751001 (tel. 54031), near the railway station, is often all booked. A newly renovated reception looks neater than the rooms, which need a paint job. Some rooms have balconies. Rates are Rs. 60 ($4.60) single, Rs. 70 ($5.40) double; family rooms with three beds run Rs. 90 $6.90).

The **Puspak,** Kalpana Chowk, Bhubaneswar 751014 (tel. 50545), is fairly clean, well lit, and pleasant. The floors are tiled with mosaic patterns. There are 21 doubles and two singles, all with attached bathrooms, some with Western fittings. Rates for air-conditioned doubles are Rs. 120 ($9.25); non-air-conditioned rooms rent for Rs. 60 ($4.60) single and Rs. 75 ($5.75) double.

You have to climb a flight of stairs off a dirty street to get to the **Rajmahal,** Bapujinagar (tel. 52448), where rooms are off a veranda, and not for the fussy. Price would be the main reason for recommending this hotel: Rs. 40 ($3.05) double and Rs. 30 ($2.30) single without air conditioning; Rs. 85 ($6.55) double, air-conditioned. The same recommendation can be made for the **Hotel Swapnapur,** B52 Saheed Nagar (tel. 53241), with rooms for Rs. 45 ($3.45) double and Rs. 25 ($1.90) single.

The **Hotel Jajati,** Station Square, was still under construction, but the run-downs had already set in. Guests in half-finished premises pay quite a price too: non-air-conditioned rooms cost Rs. 80 ($6.15) to Rs. 100 ($7.70) single and Rs. 115 ($8.85) to Rs. 135 ($10.40) double; air-conditioned singles are Rs. 165 ($12.70) and doubles go for Rs. 200 ($15.40). Some have Western-style bathrooms; there's running hot water from 5 to 9:30 a.m.

Western-Style Hotels: Across from Jajati, the centrally air-conditioned **Hotel Swosti,** 103 Janpath, Bhubaneswar 751001 (tel. 54178), has a lobby with few pieces of furniture except red settees, dominated by huge Puri murals of gods and goddesses. The 48 double rooms are efficiently, rather than imaginatively, done up. Each has an attached bathroom. Rs. 350 ($26.90) double and Rs. 275 ($21.15) single includes a television set and other amenities such as piped-in music and telephones; Rs. 250 ($19.25) single and Rs. 325 ($25) double brings all the conveniences but no television sets. A dimly lit restaurant and cozy wallpapered bar are on the premises; swimming pool and roof garden, under construction, are undoubtedly completed now.

Nearby is the **Poonam Hotel,** 225 Bapujinagar, Bhubaneswar 751009 (tel. 55476), with 21 rooms and central air conditioning. This place needs a paint job to shape it up. All rooms have balconies overlooking nothing very inspiring—alleys, roofs. Dimly lit hallways give the hotel a sinister look, but it's not half bad at Rs. 150 ($11.55) double, Rs. 100 ($7.70) single, and Rs. 300 ($23.05) for suites.

New and fairly clean, the **Hotel Kamala,** Old Station Bazaar, near the railway station (tel. 56132) is budget priced at Rs. 40 ($3.05) single and Rs. 60 ($4.60). All rooms have attached bathrooms, some Western style. There's a ten-bedded dorm charging Rs. 15 ($1.15) per person, and three- and four-bedded rooms go for Rs. 80 ($6.15) to Rs. 100 ($7.70).

Under construction when I visited, the **Safari International,** 721 Rasulgarh, Bhubaneswar 751010 (tel. 53443), is a high-priced holiday resort spread over a big garden, with ten cottages and a tower hotel. Only a few cottages could be seen: air-conditioned rooms in them cost Rs. 250 ($19.25) single and Rs. 325 ($25) double, with bathrooms attached. The plans call for a pool, jogging path, health club, indoor and open-air restaurants, and rose garden.

Hotel Meghdoot, 5B Saheed Nagar (tel. 55802), has large rooms with bright flowered bedspreads and drapes, and a marble-floored restaurant and coffeeshop. It's overpriced at Rs. 240 ($18.45) to Rs. 300 ($23.05) single, and Rs. 325 ($25) to Rs. 400 ($30.75) double. Non-air-conditioned rooms cost Rs. 100 ($7.70) single and Rs. 150 ($11.55) double. All rooms have attached bathrooms.

The ITDC's **Hotel Kalinga Ashok,** Gautam Nagar, Bhubaneswar 751014 (tel. 53318), started out many years ago as 12 simple rooms off a courtyard and now has 64 rooms furnished in motel-modern with attached bathrooms and air conditioning. Rates are Rs. 425 ($32.70) double and Rs. 350 ($26.90) single. Having all your meals here will add about Rs. 100 ($7.70) per day to the room charges.

Lower in price is the **Hotel Prachi,** 6 Janpath, Bhubaneswar 751001 (tel. 52689), with 48 clean but worn rooms. The 19 plainer-than-plain non-air-conditioned rooms cost Rs. 125 ($9.60) single and Rs. 175 ($13.45) double; the 29 air-conditioned rooms, slightly more dressed up, go for Rs. 250 ($19.25) single and Rs. 350 ($26.90) double. All have modern bathrooms. There's a restaurant where Indian music is played on Sunday, and a swimming pool and outdoor terrace where barbecues are held in fair weather.

A top-priced place to stay, the **Hotel Konarak,** Gautam Nagar, Bhubaneswar 751014 (tel. 53330), has a replica of the famous Sun Temple wheels outdoors. Inside, the spacious marble lobby is dominated by a bold Puri-style mural of Lord Krishna done in ceramic tile prominently displayed on the landing of the staircase up to the air-conditioned modern rooms. Rates are splurge-high: Rs. 400 ($30.75) single, Rs. 525 ($40.40) double, Rs. 800 ($61.55) for suites. The lively looking 24-hour coffeeshop has a Pipli-made shamiana (canopy) overhead and Puri paintings.

The top hotel is the **Oberoi Bhubaneswar,** Nayapalli, Bhubaneswar 751013 (tel. 56116), on 14 acres of land away from the center. A striking modern structure, the work of architect Sathesh Grover, it was designed as a harmonious blend of old and new, as is the city. The spacious creamy-white lobby with red granite floors is accented with red sandstone pillars and hanging lamps. Handsome paisley hangings and Tanjore paintings decorate the public halls; rooms are hung with subtle architectural renderings of local landmarks. Orissa-woven textiles in earth tones have been used in the drapes, bedspreads, and upholstered settees and chairs in the rooms. The hotel's unusual swimming pool, like its Delhi Oberoi counterpart, looks as if the water is a sleek surface level with the ground, rather than the usual step-down-into-pool. The centerpiece of an interior courtyard, the pool is surrounded by a garden with a terrace for drinks and snacks. All rooms are doubles; Rs. 500 ($38.45) single occupancy, Rs. 600 ($46.15) double occupancy, with attached marble bathrooms.

Eating Out

Orissan curries with fish and prawns are delicious, and at some point you should try chhenapodapitha, a long name for what, in short, is a delicious local delicacy, baked cheesecake.

Best suggestion is the **Oberoi Bhubaneswar** if you're in the mood for a splurge meal of well-prepared foods in elegant surroundings. Especially recommended are the Indian dishes on the menu.

For simple South Indian foods, **Oasis,** Plot 367, Saheed Nagar, a neat, popular all-vegetarian restaurant, is open from 7:30 a.m. to 10:30 p.m. every day. Fresh coconut paratha (bread) at Rs. 3 (23¢) is delicious and different; around the same price is the familiar masala dosa. Highest-priced dish is Kashmiri pulao, at Rs. 12 (90¢).

Vineeth, Plot 109, in the Master Canteen area, another popular gathering place near the railway station, charges Rs. 7 (55¢) for a thali. It's open from 7:30 a.m. to 9 p.m.

For sweets, it's **Dama Maharaja,** Satya Nagar, near Ram Mandir.

The Sights

Despite the ravages of time—and deliberate destruction—over the years, there are still several hundred ancient temples in the region of Bhubaneswar. Most visitors content themselves with visiting a cluster of the older ones, which happen, conveniently, to be fairly close together. Oldest of all is the one called **Parasurameswar,** built in the 7th century and dedicated to Lord Shiva. It is elaborately carved on the exterior with hundreds of figures: natives catching wild elephants, gods sitting on lotus flowers, a lingam being draped with garlands of flowers. Nearby, sticking out of the ground, is a similar stone lingam that present-day worshippers have decorated with real flowers.

The magnificent temple called **Mukteswar,** built in the 9th century, shows both Buddhist and Hindu influences in its carvings. The interior has a beautifully carved ceiling, including a fully open lotus flower; on the exterior walls, numerous examples of the mythical animal Gajasimha—half lion, half elephant—identifies the architecture as Kalingan in period. A famous legend, illustrated in numerous carved panels, is of the frolicking monkey who lived in a tree beside a river and ate blackberries all day. His friend, the crocodile, shared his daily feasts until one day, taking some blackberries home for his wife, he was urged by the latter to bring the monkey home for dinner. The wife, apparently, had conceived the idea of having tender monkey heart for dinner. On the way home, the crocodile asked the monkey, who was riding on his back, if he'd donate his heart to Mrs. Crocodile for dinner. Thinking fast, the monkey replied, "Why, if you'd only told me before, I would have brought it with me instead of leaving it in the tree trunk." And back he went to get it.

A third temple nearby is **Raja Rani,** built of red sandstone in the 9th century.

To the east of Rajrani is another temple jewel, **Brahmeswar,** from the 10th century, frequently overlooked and not on any tour. You can only peer in the incense-filled hall at the lingam. But the big show's on the outside for everyone to see in the intricately carved friezes of slender-waisted beauties and their handsome lovers, noble warriors, a nursing mother, parading pachyderms, prancing monkeys, and watchful birds.

The other temple that should be seen—but that cannot be visited by non-Hindus—is the 10th-century **Lingaraj Temple,** built successively by three kings. Surrounded by a high wall, it comprises a 170-foot-high main shrine with the traditional four separate chambers, plus 20 smaller temples in the grounds. The numerous stone lions peering pensively from among the moss-covered stones are representative of the Keshari (lion) dynasty. As mentioned, the temple cannot be entered, but can be observed from a stone platform nearby. Unlike the other temples mentioned, it is not away from the town but right in the center of the old city, not far from the sacred tank—**Bindu Sagar**—which is supposed to contain water from all the holy rivers and tanks throughout India.

The other main sightseeing activity is to visit the caves cut into the twin hills of **Udayagiri** and **Khandagiri,** about four miles away. The caves were excavated about 2,000 years ago as a Jain monastery and are impressively decorated outside with numerous carvings. The caves are a series of hollowed-out living cells with a stone ridge on the floor of most to act as a pillow. Despite the fact that the overhanging stone roof has survived for 20 centuries, the Indian government has recently added stone pillars for additional support.

Farther up the hill is the **Hatigumpha** cave, with its famous rock on which is inscribed the year-by-year diary of events during the reign of King Kharavela, who ruled the area, then known as Kalinga, in the 2nd century B.C.

A little over 18 miles (30 km) from town, **Nandankanan** (named for "Nandan Van," the pleasure garden of the gods) is indeed a pleasurable experience. This vast tract is part zoological and biological park, divided by a big lake, and carved out of a generous swath of jungle. Rare even here among the many exotic beasts such as panthers, lions, rhinoceros, pangolin, barking deer, and sambar—all in their natural settings—are five white tigers, the unusual offspring of tiger parents of the usual brilliant stripes. There is also a lion safari park (African lions, as there are not enough Indian lions to stock a park).

In the botanical garden are more than 100 species of trees and plants. The huge lake is a sanctuary for dozens of birds, including cranes, storks, pelicans, pea fowls, parakeets, and wild ducks.

To go around the park by car costs Rs. 2 (15¢); by cycle rickshaw, 20 paise (1½¢). There's also a 75-paise (6¢) entry fee. Rides on the toy train and elephants are 50 paise (4¢) each.

Should spending a few hours in this interesting park not be enough, there are four cottages available for the whole day (not night). They're nice if you want to bring a picnic and relax a while, at Rs. 15 ($1.15) for the one-room cottages and Rs. 25 ($1.90) for the one two-room cottage. To reserve, write: Director, Wildlife Park, Orissa, 145 Saheed Nagar, Bhubaneswar. The zoo is open every day from 7 a.m. to 6 p.m. in summer, 8 a.m. to 5 p.m. in winter; closed Monday.

The local **museum,** opposite the Hotel Kalinga Ashok, is open from 10 a.m. to 1 p.m. and 2 to 5 p.m. every day but Monday. It's worthwhile for its local and statewide exhibits and artifacts. There is interesting information on Orissan tribes, and the museum houses the Tribal Research Bureau.

About five miles (eight kilometers) south of Bhubaneswar at **Dhauli,** off the Puri Road to the right, are edicts carved into a rock slab in the 3rd century by Emperor Ashoka. In these, Ashoka describes the horrors of the Kalinga war from which he emerged the victor and his conversion to the peaceful beliefs of Buddhism. So well have they withstood the ravages of time that you can read them clearly today.

The well-preserved rock edicts stand below a **Peace Pagoda** built in 1972. It's a popular place at sunset for its beautiful view of the surrounding countryside.

Getting Around

A frequent choice of penny-watchers are **cycle rickshaws,** charging Rs. 2 (15¢) for the first kilometer and Re. 1 (7½¢) thereafter, but set the fare before you get in. Metered taxis are virtually nonexistent. **Tourist taxis** can be booked from the OTDC, Panthanivas, Lewis Road (tel. 55515). They cost about Rs. 30 ($2.30) an hour, or Rs. 145 ($11.15) for four hours of sightseeing, supposedly a minimum.

As in other cities in India, **buses** are very crowded. Before busing it, be sure to check timings and routes. For instance, you can grab a bus in town at the bus stand around 9 a.m. and go to Khandatri Traffic (where four roads converge), then walk 300 yards to the caves, for Re. 1 (7½¢). Return to the circle to get another bus around 11 a.m. on to Nandankanan, also for Re. 1, and later on to Puri, if you wish. Or you can take a 7 a.m. bus from Puri, near the hospital, go to Bhubaneswar for Rs. 6 (45¢) to see the caves and the park, and return to Puri on the late-afternoon bus. Trains take you to Barang Railway Station, which is a short walk from Nandankanan Park. There are also city buses to take you directly to Nandankanan.

Far more leisurely, and a bit more costly, is taking a cycle-rickshaw tour of the temples in town and going out to the caves, which comes to about Rs. 45 ($3.45), or less after bargaining. Alternatively, a car and driver can be hired for four hours, as mentioned, at Rs. 145 ($11.15).

From Bhubaneswar's bus stand, a bus leaves about every ten minutes for Puri at Rs. 6 (45¢) from 5:30 a.m. to 9:30 p.m. Buses to Konarak leave Bhubaneswar about every hour, from 5:30 a.m. to 9 p.m.

State buses going to Konarak, Puri, and elsewhere often have signs in Oriya, so ask before you get in. Town buses usually have English signs. You can board town buses at the bus stand, where they are apt to be less crowded, and at main roads, although the latter are not marked bus stops.

Tours

The easiest way to round up all the Bhubaneswar sights and the park as well is on the OTDC's tour, operating every day but Monday from 9 a.m. to 5 p.m. for Rs. 30 ($2.30) per person. The tour goes to the temples, cave, park, and Dhauli. Another daily OTDC tour, lasting from 8 a.m. to 6:30 p.m. goes to Konarak and Puri for Rs. 40 ($3.05). Both tours leave from Panthanivas, Lewis Road. There's also a tour from Bhubaneswar to Rourkela, the site of a major steel plant, for Rs. 65 ($5). Bookings are made through the manager, OTDC Transport Unit, at Panthanivas (tcl. 55515).

From Puri, a tour operates from 6:30 a.m. to 6:30 p.m. every day but Monday to Bhubaneswar, taking in Konarak, the caves, and the temples, for Rs. 35 ($2.70). Book it through Manager, Transport Unit, OTDC, Puri, in the Panthanivas (tel. 2562). From Puri, tours go on Monday, Wednesday, and Friday to Chilika Lake, with islets that are havens for exotic birds, from 6:30 a.m. to 6:30 p.m. for Rs. 50 ($3.85); book through the OTDC.

Tours go from Cuttack, the old capital, about 35 miles (57 km) north of Bhubaneswar, to Puri and include Konarak, for Rs. 45 ($3.45); book this tour through the Manager, Panthanivas, Cuttack (tel. 2367).

Tourist Information

The **Government of India Tourist Office,** B-21 Kalpana Area, Bhubaneswar 751014 (tel. 54203), is open from 9:30 a.m. to 5 p.m. weekdays. The **Orissa Tourist Information Office,** near Panthanivas (tel. 50099), is open from 10 a.m. to 5 p.m. There's an Orissa Tourist Information Counter at Bhubaneswar Railway Station, open around the clock (on holidays from 6 a.m. to 10 p.m.) and at the airport, open during flight hours.

KONARAK: Virtually in the middle of nowhere, Konarak is a shrine built in the 13th century by King Narasimha. According to legend, 1,200 architects took 12 years to build the temple under the direction of a master architect named Bishnu Maharana, who had left his native village to stay at the site and work. When the temple was almost ready for completion, calculations proved that the tower could not be added until corrections were made, and about that time Bishnu's son arrived in search of him, made some adjustments, and finished off the job. However, to atone for his father's shame, he jumped off the newly completed tower into an adjoining river and died.

Whatever the truth of the story, the tower no longer exists. Speculation is that it fell in an earthquake several centuries ago. But even without it, the temple rises almost 100 feet high and can be seen from five miles away. It is ornately decorated with thousands of carved animals, larger-than-life erotic groupings, statues, and honeycombed rock.

At ground level on each side are 12 immense stone chariot wheels, each spoke of which is intricately inset with sculpted scenes of animals and people, and on the top level are various statues of Surya, the Sun God, to whom the temple is dedicated. In the morning sun the statue of Surya looks peaceful; in the evening he looks tired (he's on horseback).

This shrine to the Sun God, a 24-wheeled chariot pulled by seven stone horses, is sometimes known as the **Black Pagoda** and sits majestically in a semi-wooded area about a mile from the coast. It's a beautifully peaceful spot, with cattle grazing beside the ruins, the ideal place to get away from everything for a day.

There are almost always archeological teams restoring parts of the temple, working as they might have centuries ago. They carry cement in metal pans one by one, passing it along a human conveyor belt. Skilled workers make about Rs. 35 ($2.70) a day, and helpers get Rs. 10 (75¢) to Rs. 12 (90¢) a day.

The Sun Temple is open from 6 a.m. to 5 p.m. It is illuminated with floodlights from 5:30 to 9:30 p.m. in summer, 6 to 10 p.m. in winter.

For Refreshment: Fresh coconut juice is a delightful thirst-quencher on a hot day. Try it and see. Buy a coconut for Re. 1 (7½¢) from a vendor near the temple. He'll slice off the top and insert a straw so you can sip with ease. When you've enjoyed all the juice, there's another treat inside—the sweet, tender coconut cream. The vendor will crack the coconut and return the meaty part to you with a small sliver of shell to use as a scoop to get the delicious cream and pop it into your mouth. Some shells have no cream, but usually they do not disappoint.

Where to Stay at Konarak

There are three tourist accommodations adjoining the site. The OTDC's **Travellers Lodge** (tel. 23), which is rarely used and very run-down, charges Rs.

50 ($3.85) for a double room. Meals will run an extra Rs. 20 ($1.55) to Rs. 30 ($2.30) a day. The **Panthanivas** (tel. 31) is cleaner than the lodge, and charges Rs. 60 ($4.60) for a large double, Rs. 50 ($3.85) for a small double, and Rs. 60 ($4.60) for a four-bedded room. For reservations, contact the manager, Panthanivas and Travellers Lodge, Puri District, Orissa.

The **Inspection Bungalow** (tel. 34) is for you if no government officials are booked in; if they show up, you'll be asked to move on. The charge is Rs. 51.50 ($3.95) for each person, or Rs. 106 ($8.15) for an air-conditioned room. You can take your meals at the Panthanivas. For reservations, contact: Superintending Engineer, P.W.D. (near Heads of Department Building), Bhubaneswar; or Executive Engineer, P.W.D. (near the Court), Puri. You must reserve: no drop-ins.

If you plan to stay, take along some bottled water, fruit, and cookies, and also something to read because, aside from shopping at souvenir stalls, there are no diversions and nowhere to buy things you need in the "village" nearby. There are plenty of coconuts available though.

What to Do

Konarak is only about two miles from a beautiful stretch of deserted beach along the Bay of Bengal. You might want to walk there early in the morning to see the sunrise and watch men from the fishing villages launch their boats. About a kilometer from the Temple, right next to the Travellers Lodge, is a **museum** operated by the Archaeological Survey of India, containing statues and carvings from the Black Pagoda, images of the Sun God, animals, celestial musicians, nymphs, etc. It is open, free, from 10 a.m. to 5 p.m. every day but Friday.

Getting There and Around

The bus from Bhubaneswar takes 1½ hours to cover 41 miles (64 km) and costs Rs. 6 (45¢) each way. Alternatively, you can take the OTDC Tour every day (at least in season) which goes all the way to Puri and covers Konarak on the way, 9 a.m. to 6:30 p.m., costing Rs. 40 ($3.05). Reservations and information at the OTDC Transport Counter, Panthanivas, Bhubaneswar.

PURI: Sitting comfortably on the coast of the Bay of Bengal is the town of Puri (pop. 101,000), a sleepy place in between the numerous holy pilgrimages and festivals that, especially in June and July, draw visitors from all over India.

Although the region is rich in temples, the **Sri Jagannath** is one of the most visited in India. Built in the 12th century by a king of Orissa, it celebrates the cult of Jagannath, a reincarnation of Vishnu, and entry is barred to non-Hindus. The traditional thing for tourists to do is climb onto the roof of the **library** (which, by the way, contains interesting ancient palm-leaf paintings), at one end of the big square beside the temple. From there, just outside the 34-foot-high pillar **Aruna Stambhe** (brought from Konarak), you can see through the main gates of the gaudily decorated temple.

It's a distinctive structure, with a cone-shaped tower, 192 feet high, surrounded by several buildings that seem to go up in steps. According to legend, the unfinished wooden images that stand on the altar inside (unseen from outside) were carved by God himself, in the guise of an old carpenter, after many other carpenters had broken their chisels on a holy log fished out of the sea.

From your rooftop perch you can see acolytes and helpers at work outside the temple's enormous kitchens—at festival times they feed 10,000 people—steaming rice and curries for thousands of temple servants who traditionally are fed on the premises.

Library hours are from 9 a.m. to noon and from 4 to 8 p.m.; closed Sunday and holidays. If you ask, the librarian will show you some of this private library's treasures, manuscripts written on palm leaves, centuries old, many in Sanskrit. He will also ask for a small donation for the library. This donation is, of course, not compulsory.

Where to Stay and Eat In and Around Puri

At various scenic spots along the 22-mile (35-km) Marine Drive connecting Konarak and Puri are resorts and camping grounds, in addition to the accommodations in town.

On Marine Drive, **Toshali Sands,** Mohinipur, Puri–Konarak 752002 (tel. 2888), is 7 km from Puri and 23 km from the Sun Temple at Konarak. A 12-acre garden is the vivid centerpiece for this attractive resort surrounded by a coconut and casuarina grove. The big open reception/lounge is dominated by a huge red Ganesha; big clay horses and other clay figures accent the garden. Guests are accommodated in seven four-room and 13 two-room simply furnished garden cottages, all with little patios overlooking the well-kept grounds. Entire cottages cost Rs. 475 ($36.55) air-conditioned, Rs. 410 ($31.55) non-air-conditioned. You can also rent rooms in cottages: a non-air-conditioned double is Rs. 250 ($19.25), Rs. 325 ($25) air-conditioned. There's a swimming pool. The restaurant has deep brown walls decorated with white graffiti, supposedly reminiscent of a village hut, where entrees run Rs. 20 ($1.55) for nonvegetarian dishes and Rs. 8 (60¢) to Rs. 18 ($1.40) for vegetarian. Often there is a buffet lunch, at Rs. 50 ($3.85). There are plans to expand this place to 30 acres, and a minibus will taxi guests to a secluded beach.

L. G. Patra or his brother is always around to see to guests' comforts at their **Hotel Holiday Resort Sandy Village,** Chakratirtha Road, Puri 751002 (tel. 2440). The Patras are well-known exporters of Orissan lobsters and prawns to European markets, and new hands at hotelkeeping. By the looks of things they seem to have the hang of it, offering warm hospitality to guests at their well-located moderate splurge resort. A neat garden frames a five-story 100-room hotel and 26 rooms in trim white cottages. All rooms face the sea, a few steps from the beach. Dark-wood furniture, with taupe spreads and a rose-colored ceiling, was the decor in the cottage I checked. Similar looks prevailed in the main-wing rooms. The potted plants around the hotel are changed with the seasons, and the foods offer variety as well—dishes from all over India are served in the restaurant at the hotel. Rooms in the main wing rent for Rs. 150 ($11.55) double with TV, Rs. 120 ($9.25) without TV; VIP cottage rooms run Rs. 250 ($19.25), with air conditioning, TV, and private lawn; and a double in a non-air-conditioned cottage is Rs. 200 ($1540). All rooms have modern attached bathrooms. From the hotel, it's a Rs. 4 (30¢) cycle-rickshaw ride to the Temple of Lord Jagannathan, Rs. 2 (15¢) to the railway station, and Rs. 4 (30¢) to the bus stand.

A swimming pool was to be added to the **Hotel Vijoya International,** Chakratirtha Road, Puri 752002 (tel. 2702), which has 44 rooms with bathrooms attached. Furniture in the rooms is modern and looks like a lot of other hotel decors, but the view is nice: all rooms face the sea. Rates for non-air-conditioned rooms are Rs. 250 ($19.25) double and Rs. 200 ($15.40) single; for air-conditioned rooms, Rs. 300 ($23.05) double and Rs. 250 ($19.25) single. Modern bathrooms are attached to the rooms. There's a nice terrace with a view of the sea.

The **Hotel Prachi**, Puri 752001 (tel. 2685), is the beach version of the hotel bearing its name in Bhubaneswar. In a desolate location and in need of care, the rooms rent for Rs. 200 ($15.40) single, Rs. 300 ($23.05) double, and Rs. 450 ($34.60) for suites, all with attached bathrooms and air conditioning.

The Southeastern Railway Hotel (tel. 2063) was posh when it was built in 1925 in a lovely location—across from the beautiful beach and in a garden. The hotel's 32 rooms, all facing a shady veranda, are clean but in need of repair (the upstairs rooms are especially unkempt). Attached to some rooms are *two* bathrooms—one with a bathtub and the other with a shower. There are big overhead fans to stir the breezes in all the rooms. Single rooms range in price from Rs. 185 ($14.25) to Rs. 310 ($23.85), depending on whether or not you have air conditioning, and inclusive of bedtime tea and breakfast. Double rates run Rs. 320 ($24.60) to Rs. 435 ($33.45), including bedtime tea and breakfast, and depending on where you're located and if you have air conditioning. There's a billiard room, bar, lounge, and library. The food is good at this hotel, and outsiders are welcome to eat in the dining room, but are advised to phone to make arrangements before doing so. Lunch and dinner are Rs. 55 ($4.25) each.

Moderately priced, and the best buy for budgeteers, the OTDC's **Panthanivas Tourist Bungalow** (tel. 2562) is right on the beach. This is a simple, clean, and pleasant place. In the 27-room new wing—the best, so ask for it—there's wicker furniture, sea views, and room rates of Rs. 100 ($7.70) double, Rs. 120 ($9.25) four-bedded, and Rs. 80 ($6.15) for a small double. A Western-style lunch or dinner is Rs. 15 ($1.15), Rs. 12 (90¢) for Indian food.

Below the Panthanivas, the yellow stucco building with brown trim and turrets overlooking the sea was a former palace and is now the very unpalatial **Panthabhawan** (tel. 2507), offering nine rooms in all. It's a cut below the Panthanivas in every way, though the rates are slightly higher; Rs. 120 ($9.25). Meals are extra. The bar upstairs has a wonderful sea view, especially striking at sunset. There's a nice small garden out back.

Indian-Style Hotels: Of the many Indian-style hotels along the beach, the best is the **Puri Hotel,** Swargadwar (meaning "gateway to heaven") (tel. 114). Opened in 1947, it has expanded slowly until it now has 150 rooms in five connected buildings. Those in the newest building are nicest, and you pay a slight premium for them. Though undecorated except for a fairly fresh paint job and an occasional tile floor, the special rooms look right out over the ocean across 50 yards of beach. You can lie in bed and watch the sunrise hit the sea. Attached bathrooms are all Indian style; you can have hot water in buckets if you want it. If you ask in advance, the dining room will serve you Western-style vegetarian food, but the Indian food is a far better bet. Outsiders can also eat here. Rates are higher for sea-facing rooms: Rs. 70 ($5.40) to Rs. 80 ($6.15); Rs. 160 ($12.30) air-conditioned. Other rooms, renting for Rs. 35 ($2.70) to Rs. 45 ($3.45) do not face sea. There is a 10% service charge.

Of the Grand Road Indian-style hotels, **Subhadra,** Puri 752001 (tel. 2960), offers simple, none-too-clean rooms for Rs. 60 ($4.60), Rs. 75 ($5.75), and Rs. 130 ($10). The location, above the main bazaar, is noisy but never boring, as the action below suggests a set for an extravagant opera with a huge cast in bright saris, loincloths, blue jeans, dhotis, and turbans. In the crescendo of activity are hawkers selling their wares, sadhus looking for handouts, carriages, rickshaws, and automobiles tangling with bullock carts.

A cut above the Subhadra and some others is the **Hotel Paradise,** Grand

Road, Puri 752001 (tel. 2711), where rooms run Rs. 35 ($2.70) single and Rs. 50 ($3.85) double in the back of the hotel, and Rs. 60 ($4.60) facing the busy road. One room has an air cooler and costs Rs. 150 ($11.55).

Low Budget: Very popular and fairly clean, the **Youth Hostel** (tel. 424) charges members Rs. 5 (40¢), and nonmembers, Rs. 8 (60¢). There are 49 beds in all; 31 for men and 18 for women. In the hostel's restaurant you can get a Rs.-8 (60¢) vegetarian thali.

Shopping

There are more than 30 different handcrafts from Orissa and half a dozen or so hand-looms from the area. Among the best-known craft items is silver filigree jewelry from Cuttack, paintings on silk panels, painted palm-leaf items such as book marks and wall hangings, soap stone carvings of deities, many of these originating in Puri. But the most famous Puri crafts are the charming primary-colored paintings of gods and goddesses, animals and birds, from playing-card size to huge and custom-designed, and the papier-mâché statues of Jagannathan, his brother Balbhadram, and his sister Subhadra. From Pipli come handsome appliqués made into large items such as garden umbrellas and small packable coin purses and fans. The bold designs with animal and floral motifs distinguish many of the local saris from those of other regions. Some hand-looms can be subtle as well.

You can get an overview of handcrafts at **Utkalika**, Market Building (open from 9 a.m. to noon and 4 to 9 p.m.; closed Sunday), or try the **Arts and Crafts Complex,** on Station Road. In Puri, there's the **Arts and Craft Emporium,** Mochisahi Chawk. These resources are price-fixed; elsewhere, bargain.

A favorite bargaining place for everyone is the **daily market** on Rajpath, Unit 2, near Utkalika, in Bhubaneswar, where you can find everything from household items to silk saris. The market is especially diverting in the evenings when there's little else to do.

GETTING TO BHUBANESWAR AND PURI: There are **Indian Airlines** flights to Bhubaneswar from Hyderabad for Rs. 829 ($63.75), from Calcutta for Rs. 365 ($28.05), from Nagpur for Rs. 637 ($49), and also from Delhi and Bombay. **Vayudoot** links Bhubaneswar with Calcutta, Visakhapatnam, and other places. There's airport coach service to the Indian Airlines office for Rs. 10 (75¢); taxis to town cost Rs. 30 ($2.30) to Rs. 45 ($3.45); a cycle rickshaw, Rs. 15 ($1.15).

From Hyderabad, a 1,154-km (704-mile) **train** journey takes 19 hours on the super-fast *Konarak Express* and costs Rs. 335 ($25.75) in first class, Rs. 81 ($6.25) in second. From Calcutta, the distance covered is 437 km (266 miles) and the best train is the *Coromandel Express,* leaving Howrah at 3 p.m. and arriving Bhubaneswar at 10:15 p.m., for Rs. 168 ($12.90) in first class, Rs. 42 ($3.25) in second. This train does not stop at Puri, but goes all the way to Madras, as do a number of others which are slower. From Madras, the *Coromandel Express* covers 1,226 km (748 miles) in 19 hours, for Rs. 358 ($27.55) in first class, Rs. 87 ($6.70) in second. The fastest train from Delhi, the *Kalinga Express,* goes to Bhubaneswar and on to Puri, a distance of 2,136 km (1,302 miles) in 37 hours, for Rs. 543 ($41.75) in first class and Rs. 130 ($10) in second. The *Puri–New Delhi Express* takes 48 hours, as do other Delhi trains. From Bhubaneswar, there are numerous trains to Puri, 62 km (38 miles), a two-hour trip, for Rs. 38 ($2.90) in first class, Rs. 8 (60¢) in second.

Orissa State Transport operates interstate **bus** services between Calcutta and Puri via Bhubaneswar.

The **OTDC** offers a five-day economy trip to Bhubaneswar, Puri, Konarak, and Chilika, by second-class reserved train for Rs. 385 ($29.60). Departure point is Howrah Station, Calcutta; the cost includes accommodation at Panthanivas, an English-speaking guide, and all major sightseeing attractions in the area.

BEST TIME TO VISIT: The season is September through March. But many people come in June or July for the important festival, Rath Yatra (Cart Festival) at Puri, when Lord Jagannathan and his brother and sister are taken from the temple, placed on carts, and pulled down the main street to their summer garden. Jagganath's cart is about five stories high with 16 enormous wheels. The other carts are only slightly smaller. It takes 4,000 professional draggers to drag the deities one mile to their summer house, where they spend seven days before being dragged back to their home shrine again. Other festivals and fairs take place throughout the year.

2. Hyderabad

What the late Pandit Nehru described as the "meeting place between north and south" is Hyderabad (pop. more than 3,000,000), capital of Andhra Pradesh and India's seventh-largest city. It is actually twin cities—**Old Hyderabad,** founded by Mohammad Quli Qutb Shah in the late 16th century, and modern **Secunderabad,** which owes its origin to the British, in the early days of occupation. The two cities, usually regarded as one, sprawl for a considerable distance over relatively flat, rocky countryside about 1,200 feet above sea level.

The climate is pleasant, except for the overly humid spring months, and the city is luxuriant in trees, plants, and flowers.

It really is a meeting place in a sense, for 16 languages are spoken by the natives of the region (the major ones are Telugu and Urdu). Minarets and beautifully graceful spires and towers form the skyline, and combined with the Musi River, which winds through the old city, the panorama makes for one of the most attractive cities in India. There are thousands of bicycles and motorbikes in the city, which is apparent to anybody trying to negotiate rush-hour traffic.

HOTELS: Among Western-style hotels are a former palace up in the hills overlooking the twin cities as well as hostelries with pushbutton modernity. Whichever your choice, be sure to book in advance. There are a limited number of hotels in Hyderabad and Secunderabad.

Indian-style hotels in Hyderabad (they get much better farther south) are simple places, cheap by Western standards but catering to fairly affluent Indians. Their kitchens are usually vegetarian and the plumbing generally Indian style (sans commode).

Note that most tourists stay in Hyderabad to be near the main attractions. If you stay in Secunderabad, be prepared to spend 20 minutes or more, depending on the traffic, and many rupees going by bus, auto-rickshaw, or taxi to and from Hyderabad. Aside from the inconvenience, the acceptable Secunderabad Hotels tend to be expensive.

Indian-Style Hotels in Hyderabad

The **Hotel Dawarka,** Lakdi ka Pul Rajbhavan Road, Khairatabad (tel. 237971), represents one of the best bargains in town. The 165-room hotel has a small circular reception area, and each room opens onto a wide gallery and has a private balcony. The air-conditioned singles rent for Rs. 90 ($6.90); air-conditioned doubles, Rs. 120 ($9.25). A non-air-conditioned single is Rs. 65 ($5); a double without air conditioning, Rs. 90 ($6.90). Deluxe rooms run Rs. 100 ($7.70) single and Rs. 160 ($12.30) double. Only some of the rooms have Western plumbing. In the neat dining room, a vegetarian lunch or dinner costs Rs. 5 (40¢). Eating is done with the hands (the right one only, please), and the trick is to take a bit of rice, mix it with your curry, and down it all neatly.

Hotel Taj Mahal, on King Kothi Road (tel. 237988), is a pleasant place with wicker chairs, shade trees, and a porch to sit out on. There are 70 rooms, split between the old and new annexes. Of these, 34 rooms are air-conditioned and a few have Western-style plumbing: Rs. 60 ($4.60) single and Rs. 80 ($6.15) double, non-air-conditioned; Rs. 95 ($7.30) single and Rs. 175 ($13.45) double, with air conditioning. In the Taj Mahal's big, popular, noisy dining hall (open from 6:30 to 9 a.m. for breakfast, 9 a.m. to 3 p.m. for lunch, and 7 to 9:30 p.m. for dinner) you can get snacks and plate meals, South Indian style, for Rs. 1.25 (10¢) to Rs. 4 (30¢).

The busy 72-room **Hotel Brindavan,** Station Road (between the main post office and the railway station), Hyderadbad 500001 (tel. 2397970), has an entry that looks as if it's recovering from a disaster, but the rooms I saw were neat and clean. All of them open onto verandas where you can sit out and relax. Rates are Rs. 80 ($6.15) double, Rs. 60 ($4.60) single. All have attached Indian-style bathrooms. You may have to assert yourself at the reception to get a harried clerk to pay attention to you as a steady stream of guests check in and out and get their keys.

A place where both Eastern and Western travelers meet is the **Hotel Kakatiya,** Nampally Station Road, Hyderabad 500001 (tel. 553767). The air-conditioned rooms—at Rs. 150 ($11.55), Rs. 160 ($12.30), and Rs. 200 ($15.40)—are in better shape than the non-air-conditioned rooms. This is probably because they are higher in price, and therefore less frequently occupied. Non-air-conditioned rooms run Rs. 75 ($5.75) single and Rs. 100 ($7.70) double. Going to see the air-conditioned Chandrala Restaurant, I was taken via the kitchen and I can vouch for the hygienic food preparation as well as the excellence of the idlies, having tasted them fresh from the steamer (see my restaurants recommendations for details).

Surely one of the nicest Indian-style hotels in town is **Annapurna,** Nampally Station Road, Hyderabad (tel. 557931), with a glass mural of goddesses and lotus blossoms in lobby. There are orchid-colored halls with orchid and ochre color schemes in some rooms. Rooms are tidy and nearly always full, at Rs. 95 ($7.30) single and Rs. 120 ($9.25) double, non-air-conditioned; Rs. 140 ($10.75) single and Rs. 180 ($13.85) double, air-conditioned. One drawback: the flush systems frequently don't function because of lack of water pressure—the management supplies guests with buckets of water to create the pressure necessary for carrying out the task.

Hotel Sarovar, 5-9-22 Secretariat Rd., Hyderabad 500004 (tel. 237638), is next to the British Library. It's an eight-story cream-colored concrete building with 77 rooms, not far from Hussain Sagar. Rooms have attached bathrooms, some Indian style, others Western. Singles rent for Rs. 120 ($9.25) non-air-conditioned, Rs. 200 ($15.40) air-conditioned. Double rooms go for Rs. 150 ($11.55) without air conditioning, Rs. 250 ($19.25) with. The rooms are modern and roomy, but need a paint job. If you can overlook the scruffy walls, then this hotel isn't too bad.

A marble reception area and latticework screens and ceilings add decorative touches to the **Hotel Jaya International,** Abids Circle, Hyderabad 500001 (tel. 232929), situated in a little lane right in the center of town. The rooms are large, with adequate furnishings but uninspired decor. South and North Indian vegetarian foods are served at this hotel's restaurant. Singles cost Rs. 110 ($8.45) air-conditioned, Rs. 70 ($5.40) non-air-conditioned; doubles run Rs. 140 ($10.75) air-conditioned, Rs. 90 ($6.90) non-air-conditioned.

A photo mural and Indian artworks hang in the lobby of the **Hotel Siddartha,** 4-1-465 Troop Bazar, Hyderabad 500001 (tel. 557421). The rooms are bright, but not too clean, with large windows and the mostly Indian-style bathrooms are not in good condition. A coat of paint would help the entire hotel. Air-conditioned rooms are Rs. 125 ($9.60) single and Rs. 145 ($11.15) double; non-air-conditioned rooms go for Rs. 80 ($6.15) single and Rs. 100 ($7.70) double.

The **Hotel Minerva,** 3-6-199 Himayat Nagar, Hyderabad 500029 (tel. 38015), has 30 new rooms to recommend over the old. None of the rooms has any special decor, but they're okay for a short stay. Rates are Rs. 40 ($3.05) single and Rs. 60 ($4.60) double, non-air-conditioned; Rs. 100 ($7.70) air-conditioned.

You can get nonvegetarian food at the **Hotel Suhail,** 527 Troop Bazar (behind the main post office), Hyderabad 500001 (tel. 41286), but the hotel is classified as Indian style. There are 28 fairly clean rooms in all, each with an Indian-style bathroom attached; Rs. 65 ($5) single and Rs. 85 ($6.55) double, non-air-conditioned; Rs. 100 ($7.70) single and Rs. 130 ($10) double, air-conditioned. Deluxe rooms with air conditioning run Rs. 130 ($10) single and Rs. 160 ($12.30) double. Two additional floors, with Western-style bathrooms, were in the planning stages and may be completed by the time you arrive.

High vaulted ceilings make the reception area look spacious at the **Hotel President,** Mozzamshahi Market (tel. 44444). The non-air-conditioned rooms are stuffy and dark, but clean. The air-conditioned rooms throughout are a bit better than the others. The location (on a very noisy street) may be a drawback if you're a light sleeper. There are both Indian- and Western-style bathrooms in the hotel. Rates are high for what you get: Rs. 150 ($11.55) single and Rs. 200 ($15.40) double, non-air-conditioned; Rs. 225 ($17.30) single and Rs. 275 ($21.15) double, air-conditioned.

Hotel Emerald, Abid Road, Chirag Ali Lane, Hyderabad 500001 (tel. 237835), is a five-minute drive from the Hyderabad Railway Station and 20 minutes from the airport. The hotel is okay for those who aren't fussy. The air-conditioned deluxe rooms, at Rs. 175 ($13.45) single and Rs. 225 ($17.30) double, are a bit better than the non-air-conditioned rooms, which run Rs. 100 ($7.70) single and Rs. 120 ($9.25) double.

Low-Budget Choices: Rock-bottom-rated hotels are clustered in a compound near the railway station at Nompally. These are the Royal Hotel, Neo Royal, Gee Royal Lodge, Royal Home—deposed royalty, when you see their down-at-the-heels condition. However, a spot check of each shows that if you look at a few rooms, you're apt to find some rooms that are cleaner than the others. If you want to stay in any of these places, you should ask to see more than one vacant room before settling in. The rates range from Rs. 40 ($3.05) to Rs. 75 ($5.75)—a bit high for what they offer in the way of comfort and cleanliness. Bathrooms are shared. If you're backpacking, you'll undoubtedly have what you need to be comfortable. If not, bring a sheet and towel.

Nearby, but slightly higher in price, the **Aspara Hotel,** Nompally (tel.

45663), charges Rs. 50 ($3.85) single, Rs. 70 ($5.40) to Rs. 80 ($6.15) double. All rooms were occupied and could not be inspected, but the lobby looked clean and cared for.

Another trove of rock-bottom accommodations can be found on Kachiguda Road near Kachiguda Railway Station, Hyderabad 500027. Two of these are the **Tourist Hotel** (tel. 68691) and the **Tourist Home** (tel. 68611). At the first there are 41 singles costing Rs. 35 ($2.70) and 37 doubles at Rs. 50 ($3.85). Meals in the dining room run about Rs. 4 (30¢) per plate. Rates at the Tourist Home are slightly higher, but the accommodations are an infinitesimal bit better: Rs. 40 ($3.05) single, Rs. 65 ($5) double. Indian-style plumbing predominates at both.

Western-Style Hotels in Hyderabad

The **Hyd-Inn,** Lake Hills Road, Hyderabad 500483 (tel. 237573), is a simple place where all rooms have balconies. Non-air-conditioned rooms cost Rs. 75 ($5.75) single and Rs. 110 ($8.45) double; rooms with air conditioning run Rs. 100 ($7.70) single and Rs. 175 ($13.45) double. Just so-so.

The **Nagarjuna,** Basheerbagh, Hyderabad 500029 (tel. 37201), looked run-down when I stopped in. The management said that renovation was planned throughout the hotel. Meanwhile, it was open for business. Rates are Rs. 225 ($17.30) single and Rs. 250 ($19.25) double. All rooms have air conditioning, private bathrooms, and telephones. The rooftop Ming Restaurant, open from 3 to 11 p.m., was better cared for than the hotel and offers a fine view. Foods are Indian, Chinese, and continental, and entrees run Rs. 15 ($1.15) to Rs. 20 ($1.55). Gulmohar, the wood-paneled, silk-accented ground-floor restaurant has nearly the same menu as Ming's, but its hours are 7 a.m. to 3 p.m. and 7 to 11 p.m.

The **Hotel Sampurna International,** Mukramjahi Road, Hyderabad 500001 (tel. 40165), has a mirrored Indian pageant mural in the lobby, black bucket armchairs, and a marble floor. Centrally air-conditioned, the sleekly modern rooms look like those in Western motels with twin beds, dressing tables, and attached bathrooms. Rates are Rs. 250 ($19.25) to Rs. 300 ($23.05) single and Rs. 300 ($23.05) to Rs. 350 ($26.90) double. The restaurant serves the usual Indian, Chinese, and continental dishes.

Splurge Hotels in Hyderabad

High in the hills and high in price—indeed a splurge for budget travelers on their own, but okay for two—is the **Ritz,** Hill Fort Palace, Hyderabad 500463 (tel. 233571), once the palace of the Nizam's second son. There are little outdoor passages by which to go from one part of the hotel to another, and a roof garden from which the guests gaze at the sunset on nearby Hussain Sagar. Off the open courtyard, with tropical plants out of a Rousseau painting, is the dining room, lounge, and bar. The hotel has a swimming pool, pretty enough for royalty, and there are tennis courts. Prince's, the restaurant, welcomes outside guests as well as residents. Single occupancy costs Rs. 315 ($24.25), and doubles run Rs. 360 ($27.70), all with air conditioning, wallpapered walls, and loads of old-fashioned charm. Meals will add about Rs. 70 ($5.40) to Rs. 80 ($6.15) a day.

If you feel like a big splurge, there's the expensive **Hotel Banjara,** Banjara Hills, Hyderabad 500034 (tel. 222222), with a little lake to look out on. The rooms, which needed renovating, rent for Rs. 660 ($50.75) to Rs. 760 ($58.45) single and Rs. 760 ($58.45) to Rs. 860 ($66.15) double. There's a swimming pool and a patio restaurant. Indoor restaurants serve various Chinese, Mughali, and Western foods. A pastry bar is adjacent to the lobby.

Two splurge hotels—the Bhaskar Palace and Krishna Oberoi—were under construction during my visit. They are undoubtedly functioning now for those living it up in Hyderabad.

Indian-Style Hotels in Secunderabad

The best Indian-style hotel in Secunderabad is the **Hotel Taj Mahal,** Sarojini Devi Road (tel. 70105), a branch of the Hyderabad Taj, with similar neat accommodations and low prices. Most rooms have a private bath, though some of the lowest-priced share common baths. These cost Rs. 35 ($2.70) and Rs. 45 ($3.45). Otherwise, non-air-conditioned singles cost Rs. 60 ($4.60) and doubles run Rs. 80 ($6.15); air-conditioned rooms are Rs. 95 ($7.30) single and Rs. 150 ($11.55) double. A plate meal of rice, vegetable curry, sambar, and rasam runs Rs. 2.60 (20¢) in the immensely popular dining room.

Western-Style Hotels in Secunderabad

The door at **Baseraa,** 9-1-167/168 Sarojini Devi Rd., Secunderabad 500003 (tel. 823200), is a replica of a wheel from the Sun Temple at Konarak in Orissa, headquarters of the owners, Hotel Kamal Pvt. Ltd. There are elaborate brass designs to brighten the reception area. Behind the modern main building is an older mini-palace which has a few rooms (including a honeymoon suite) all done up in red—a red flower-petal-shaped headboard on a king-size bed, a spangled velvet wall hanging of lovers. This room costs Rs. 600 ($46.15). Less elaborate rooms, in more subdued colors, also have petal-shaped headboards, wicker furniture, velvet stylized murals on the walls, and nice private attached tiled bathrooms, for Rs. 350 ($26.90) single and Rs. 450 ($34.60) double. All the rooms have telephones, TV, and piped-in music. There is air conditioning throughout the hotel. Daawat restaurant serves South Indian vegetarian dishes and snacks, while Mehfil serves Mughali, Indian, continental, and Chinese dishes (see the restaurant listings for Hyderabad and Secunderabad).

The **Hotel Deccan Continental,** Sir Ronald Ross Road, Secunderabad, 500003 (tel. 70981), has a panoramic view of Hussain Sagar, and a nice view of the city as well. It's a splurge. The non-air-conditioned deluxe rooms are spacious with modern furniture and balconies, and rent for Rs. 225 ($17.30) single and Rs. 300 ($23.05) double. The other rooms are more compact: with air conditioning rates are Rs. 280 ($21.55) for a single in a double room, and Rs. 375 ($28.85) as a double; non-air-conditioned rooms cost Rs. 250 ($19.25) single and Rs. 280 ($21.55) double. There's a swimming pool and shopping arcade, restaurant, and coffeeshop.

Not far from the main shopping area is the **Hotel Parklane,** 115 Park Lane, Secunderabad 500003 (tel. 70148), with a copper mural above the reception desk. The centrally air-conditioned hotel's 50 rooms have all the amenities—attached bathrooms, piped-in music, telephones. Low ceilings make them seem cramped. They also could use some tender loving care. There are vegetarian and nonvegetarian restaurants, a coffee parlor, swimming pool, and garden. Standard rooms cost Rs. 250 ($19.25) single and Rs. 330 ($25.40) double; deluxe rooms go for Rs. 350 ($26.90) single and Rs. 400 ($30.75) double. Suites cost Rs. 500 ($38.45).

The **Asrani International Hotel,** 1-7-179 Mahatma Gandhi Road, Secunderabad 500003 (tel. 822287), has sleek, modern rooms with beds covered with satin spreads, and little refrigerators in each room. At these prices the maintenance should be much better: Rs. 275 ($21.15) single and Rs. 400 ($30.75) double. There are both vegetarian and nonvegetarian restaurants.

A Youth Hostel

Jutting into the lake is the **Youth Hostel,** behind the Boat Club (tel. 70087), with 51 beds in five dorms. Members and students pay Rs. 5 (40¢); others, Rs. 8 (60¢) per day. It's run-down and you might want to use a sleeping bag rather than the shabby bedding at the hostel. It's nearly always full, so you must reserve well in advance by writing to the warden.

Out of Town

About 14 miles (22.5 km) from Hyderabad is Osmansagar Lake (Gandipet) with a four-room **guesthouse,** charging Rs. 50 ($3.85) per room and nearly always full. There's another bungalow with rooms for government VIPs. It's truly not worth the effort to stay out here. However, if you want to inquire, write or phone: Managing Director, AP Travel and Tourism Development Corporation, B-3/3 Diamond House, Second Floor, Himayat Nagar, 500029 (tel. 556493).

RESTAURANTS: Geographically, this is South India, but typical foods have Muslim overtones. Be sure to try the local biryani and baghara baigan, with eggplant. Many dishes of South India are served as well. A typical local dish, haleem, is made with wheat and mutton.

For a special meal, there's the elegant **Palace Heights,** eighth floor in the Triveni Complex, Abids, Hyderabad (tel. 232898), offering a splendid city view. Just inside the entrance there's a clubby little alcove with velvet-tufted Victorian chairs and love seats, and a gleaming dark-wood bar where you can sit and have an apéritif. Inside the oblong dining room the white walls are hung with paintings of former nizams and harem dancers, and there are handsome antique sideboards and other furniture.

The Palace Heights menu has a number of Mughlai dishes not usually encountered, such as a special boneless chicken with herbs and spices at Rs. 38 ($2.90) and sabzi bahan, a mixed vegetable curry with red sauce, at Rs. 24 ($1.85), plus many others. If you're in doubt, the maître d' will gladly help you order. The average price for entrees is Rs. 48 ($3.70) to Rs. 50 ($3.85), so it's a splurge. Reservations are suggested, especially if you want a window table. Hours are 11 a.m. to 11 p.m.

On Abid Road in Hyderabad the quiet, refined-looking splurge-priced **Golden Deer** (tel. 236081), open from 11 a.m. to 11 p.m., is dimly lit, with crystal lighting fixtures, mirrored pillars and arches decorated with golden vines, and black-wood chairs upholstered in green leather. Specialties are chicken aashiana (with tomatoes and a white cream sauce), at Rs. 50 ($3.85); and mutton Golden Deer (with fruits, nuts, and coconut gravy), at Rs. 20 ($1.55). Nearby on Abid Road, **Golden Gate** (tel. 230019), open from 11 a.m. to 11 p.m., has a sophisticated decor combining a dark wood-paneled ceiling and walls with light metal murals. It serves such well-known North Indian dishes as kebabs and tandooris, at Rs. 24 ($1.85) to Rs. 26 ($2) for the average entree.

On Abid Road you can get freedom of choice at **Liberty,** an immensely popular fast-food cafeteria with a Statue of Liberty logo. It's neat and colorful with tile walls, and self-service. The foods include burgers made with mutton, chicken, or vegetables for Rs. 40 ($3.05) to Rs. 50 ($3.85); pizzas for Rs. 7.50 (60¢) to Rs. 10 (75¢); and many Indian dishes in this same price range. Popular for ice cream, at Rs. 7 (55¢) or less, depending on the flavor. Hours are 11 a.m. to 10:30 p.m. every day.

Some Hyderabad hotels have restaurants worth trying. Among these is

Prince's, in the Ritz Hotel, Hill Fort Palace (tel. 233571), where the average price of an entree at lunch or dinner is Rs. 20 ($1.55). You can order an Indo-Western meal with such dishes as subtly spiced mulligatawny soup followed by a mild baked pomfret (fish) for Rs. 20 ($1.55), and finish off with chocolate soufflé for Rs. 15 ($1.15) or fresh fruit at Rs. 11 (85¢). Open for breakfast from 6:30 to 10:30 a.m. A full English breakfast is Rs. 20 ($1.55); a continental breakfast, Rs. 12 (90¢). Lunch is served from 1 to 2:30 p.m., and dinner from 8 to 10:30 p.m.

Dark, dimly lit, the **Blue Fox,** in the Hotel Minerva, 3-6-199 Himayat Nagar, Hyderabad (tel. 38015), is owned by the Palace Heights and is the older of the two. The menu is the more or less predictable Indian, Chinese, and continental, with main dishes as high as Rs. 38 ($2.90). It's open from 11 a.m. to 11 p.m., and only two kilometers (1¼ miles) from the Salar Jung Museum.

For vegetarian food, the dining room at the **Hotel Annapurna,** Nampally Station Road, Hyderabad (tel. 557931), is a good bet for budget travelers. Full thali meals run from Rs. 7 (55¢) to Rs. 22 ($1.70), depending on the number of dishes on your platter. Hours: breakfast, 6:30 to 10 a.m.; lunch, 11 a.m. to 2:30 p.m.; snacks (try the snacks with cashews), 2:30 to 7:30 p.m.; dinner, 7:30 to 10 p.m.

Opposite the Birla temple, on Secretariat Road, Saifaibad, the restaurant in the **Kamat Hotel** (tel. 232225), is open from 7 to 10 a.m., 11 a.m. to 2 p.m., and 7 to 9 p.m. There's another Kamat on Station Road, Nampally, and in Secunderabad. By government order, some items in this restaurant and a few others are especially cheap at certain times. These items are posted on a board outside, and you must get coupons for them inside. Even without the coupons, the Kamat's prices are reasonable for thali meals: Rs. 6.60 (50¢) for rice, puri, curds, two curries, rasam, and sambar; a sweet is extra.

Next door is the **Hotel Indu,** whose very plain-looking nonvegetarian restaurant, charges Rs. 12 (90¢) to Rs. 25 ($1.90) as the average price for entrees. Hours are noon to 3 p.m. and 5 to 10 p.m. Opposite is the **Gopi,** another popular vegetarian restaurant with similar foods in a similar price range to Kamat.

Clean and cheerful, the **Chandrala Restaurant,** in the Hotel Kakatiya, Nampally Station Road in Hyderabad (tel. 533767), famous for idlis, serves more than 1,000 of these light and fluffy dumplings each day. The restaurant offers other South Indian dishes, and a filling vegetarian thali for Rs. 10 (75¢) with rice, condiments, and curry.

Up and down Mahatma Gandhi Road, the main thoroughfare, and all over the twin cities are **snack shops** with such names as Olympia, Berry's, Grand, and Alpha. They all look somewhat alike, but vary greatly when it comes to cleanliness. Many of these shops are run by Iranians who, over the years, have settled in Hyderabad. They don't always have menus, but serve such foods as biryani (rice, lamb, and spices) or omelets with toast and butter for Rs. 10 (75¢) to Rs. 15 ($1.15). Like small grocery stores in the States, the shops also sell toiletries, tinned goods, and candies, as well as fast meals and snacks.

Famous for sweets in the twin cities is **Pullardy,** on Station Road near the Brindavan Hotel. Treating yourself can be costly: the Hyderabadi delicacy kalakahn runs Rs. 48 ($3.70) per kilogram, and sweets with cashews are Rs. 100 ($7.70) per kilogram. You can sample a sweet in the spotless shop before you make a purchase—but no samples without a purchase.

For a buffet in Hyderabad, try the **Banjara Hotel,** Banjara Hills (tel. 222222), at Rs. 50 ($3.85).

In Secunderabad, **Daawat,** in the Baseraa Hotel, on Sarojini Devi Road (tel. 823200), South Indian specialties are served from 7:30 a.m. to 10 p.m. every day in a pretty setting combining mosaic walls with mirrored archways, marble floors, and bamboo accents. Idlis, "the best in the twin cities," I was told by the maître d', cost Rs. 3 (23¢); crispy, delicious masala dosa is Rs. 4.50 (35¢), and thalis with a variety of dishes are Rs. 10 (75¢) to Rs. 15 ($1.15). In the same hotel, the mirrored and brass-muraled **Mehfil** serves well-prepared Mughlai foods. A meal ordered à la carte consisting of soup, boneless tandoori chicken, and pulao will cost about Rs. 150 ($11.55) for two, including beer or cocktails—a nice place for a splurge meal. The Baseraa Hotel often has buffets on weekends and holidays for Rs. 50 ($3.85) from 12:30 to 3 p.m.; and barbecues are held in the garden at peak times. To check, telephone the hotel at the number above. Pastries and ice creams are available at all times in the hotel's Havmor ice cream parlor.

Kwality and **Kwality-Sechuan,** next door to each other at 103 Park Lane, Secunderabad (tel. 77735), serves Mughlai and continental-Chinese dishes in the Rs. -20 ($1.55) to Rs. -40 ($3.05) range for entrees. The Sechuan is Szechuan in name only, the menu is so similar to Kwality's. Hours are noon to 3 p.m. for lunch and 6 p.m. to midnight for dinner. Also in Secunderabad on Park Lane is **Nanking,** open from 11 a.m. to 3:30 p.m. and 6 to 10:30 p.m., serving Chinese dishes and curries, none too expensive. Specialties are chicken with cashews and sweet-and-sour prawns.

GETTING AROUND HYDERABAD AND SECUNDERABAD: Auto-rickshaws start at Rs. 2 (15¢) and add 60 paise (4½¢) per kilometer thereafter; from 11 p.m. the charges are double. Black-and-yellow taxis, of which there is a shortage, cost Rs. 2.50 (20¢) minimum and Rs. 2 (15¢) thereafter. The drivers will invariably try to get more from tourists by demanding a return fare. Bicycle rickshaws have a Rs. 3 (23¢) minimum and cost Rs. 5 (40¢) to Rs. 6 (45¢) for an average ride of three to four kilometers.

Renting a tourist taxi for half a day costs Rs. 150 ($11.55) for 50 km (30 miles) or Rs. 250 ($19.25) for a full day or 100 km (61 miles). Be sure to check the kilometer reading before setting off and when you return. If you're going out of town by taxi, bargain for the best fare before setting off.

Local buses are best boarded at the terminus, otherwise they are so crowded you probably won't be able to squeeze in. You might, however, try to board no. 95 near the Char Minar, which goes to the zoo. But I'm willing to bet you'll give up and take an auto-rickshaw.

BEST TIME TO VISIT: From October to March. Summer can be in the 90s or higher; winter averages a pleasant 70°, but can get higher. The rainy season is June to September.

LOOKING AROUND HYDERABAD: Visiting Hyderabad without taking a look at the bangles in the **Lad Bazaar** would be like traveling to Agra and not looking around the Taj Mahal: it just isn't done. The bazaar is the street that leads down from the famous Char Minar, and the numerous stores with which it is lined contain enough brightly colored bangles to line the wrist of virtually every woman in the world. For a handful of rupees—maybe a dollar's worth—you can festoon your arm with a dozen or more delicately spun glass circles.

Down another street of this bazaar you'll find heady perfume oils, jasmine soaps, multiflavored incenses, and oil lamps—indeed, clusters of stalls selling everything from the frivolous to the practical.

Hyderabad is also renowned for its pearls and gold filigrees. Almost as famous is Hyderabad bidriware, which is silver inlaid in zinc-copper alloys, and you can see it being made at the **Mumtaz Bidri Works,** 22-1-1042 Daru Shifa. This is a cooperative society where artisans are at work fashioning a myriad of such things as boxes, ashtrays, letter openers, pen holders, etc., and where the finished items are displayed for sale. Visit between 10 a.m. and 5:30 p.m.

More bidriware can be found at **Lepakshi Handicrafts Emporium** (Gun Foundry; tel. 35028), starting at about Rs. 10 (75¢) for small ashtrays, and ascending to the Rs.-300 ($23) range for elegant carafes. Rugs inspired by Persian motifs begin as low as Rs. 50 ($3.85) per square foot, and some of the attractive translucent decorations carved from animal horns can be bought for under Rs. 50 ($3.85). For the budget-souvenir hunters, there are brightly painted and lacquered animal toys costing Rs. 10 (75¢) to Rs. 25 ($1.90) apiece.

The place consists of two gigantic floors crammed with all the above, plus silver filigree, yard-long sticks of incense, saris, Nirmalware (hand-painted teak trays from the village of the same name)—most of the best handcrafts produced in Andhra Pradesh State. Open till 8 p.m.; closed Sunday. Everything is price-fixed.

The heart of ancient Hyderabad—and an absolute must for the first-time visitor—is the immense arch called **Char Minar** (building with four minarets) —something referred to as the Arc de Triomphe of the East. It is so closely associated with the city that it is also the name of a local brand of cigarettes that displays the monument on its yellow packet. The arch is illuminated from 7 to 9 p.m. daily; entry is 50 paise (3½¢).

Almost 200 feet high, the Char Minar was built to celebrate the ending of a plague in 1591 by Quili Qutb Shah, the fifth of seven kings whose dynasty ruled the region during most of the 16th and 17th centuries. All around it are the streets of the bazaar, including the famous "Street of Bangles."

Traffic of all kinds—vehicular, human, and animal—flows around the Char Minar from all these streets and alleys into a perpetually busy area in front of the **Mecca Masjid,** one of the biggest mosques in Asia, which reputedly can accommodate 10,000 worshippers at one time. As with most mosques, there are impressive historical statistics to recite to newcomers: the immense door arches are made from solid slabs of granite, mined in a stone quarry seven miles to the north and brought here with the pulling power of 1,400 sweating oxen. It was started in 1614 and completed in 1657.

Buses leave for various places from the general area around the Char Minar, the first destination being the **Nehru Zoological Park** (bus 95 from outside the Madina Hotel, three blocks from Char Minar), which is one of the biggest—and certainly among the nicest—in the world. Covering 300 acres of seemingly undeveloped land, the zoo houses about 1,800 animals, most roaming in their natural habitat. Open from 9 a.m. to 6 p.m.; closed Monday.

Inside the zoo grounds is a **Natural History Museum** (with the same hours as the zoo) guarded by a stuffed bear whose paws hold the sign "Please Do Not Touch the Exhibits." Most of the exhibits are life-size reproductions in glass cases of incidents in the life of a tiger. ("To see a tiger striding on velvety paws across a meadow of grass with the fading rays of the setting sun harmonizing with its tawny black-striped coat, the very symbol of physical beauty, strength and dignity, is surely one of the greatest aesthetic experiences in nature.")

There is also a ten-acre prehistoric animal park with creatures 25 feet high and 50 feet long, and a rare chance to see the Asian lion in 30 acres of hills and forests. A minibus takes you to lion territory. Charge: Rs. 2 (15¢).

To most people Hyderabad's outstanding possession would be the **Salar Jung Museum** (tel. 523211), surely one of the world's most amazing collections of art treasures. What adds to its fascination is the fact that the museum's contents were the collection of one man, Mir Yusuf Ali Khan Salar Jung III, who, prior to his death in 1949, had briefly acted as the nizam, or prime minister, of Hyderabad. He was a bachelor and seems to have been single-mindedly devoted to acquiring representative treasures from all cultures of the world, ancient and modern. There are 35,000 exhibits in 35 rooms, ranging from junk to great treasures. Hours: 10 a.m. to 5 p.m.; closed Friday. Entry fee: Rs. 2 (15¢).

Also worth visiting are the **Birla Archeological Museum** in Asman Ghad Palace (tel. 558347), a small collection of objects excavated from nearby sites; and **Birla Planetarium,** one of the most modern in India, near the Birla Temple (Naubat Prahad), which has shows daily. Entry fee is Rs. 5 (40¢). Both the planetarium and temple stand on a hill overlooking the city and Hussain Sagar. The white temple is modern and interesting for its carvings and decorations. Non-Hindus are allowed inside.

SIGHTS OUTSIDE THE CITY: A little over seven miles (11.5 km) west of the city, the remains of the almost-impregnable **Golconda Fort** sprawl over a hillside about 1,000 feet above the surrounding countryside. Built originally of mud, it was converted into a stone bastion by the seven kings of the aforementioned Qutb Shahi dynasty, each of whom added to and strengthened it during the years of his reign (1518–1687). The three walls enclosing the fort are still intact, the fort having fallen but once—when Aurangzeb, after an eight-month seige, bribed a traitor to open what is now called the **Victory Gate.** The conqueror, believing rumors about hidden gold, ripped the roofs from the palaces on the grounds, but otherwise the structures are substantially as they were almost 300 years ago.

Once out of the fort, a visit to the **tombs,** distinctively designed with sensuously shaped domes, is recommended. There are seven altogether, all with accompanying little "tomblets" to house their queens—but the seventh is unfinished because the seventh king, Abul Hassan, was conquered and captured by Aurangzeb and imprisoned in Daulatabad before he had a chance to complete his own tomb.

Nagarjunakonda and Nagarjunasagar

Almost 94 miles (150 km) southeast of Hyderabad is **Nagarjunakonda,** which in the 2nd and 3rd centuries A.D. was an important Buddhist center in South India. Archeological finds over the years have been the remains of stupas, monasteries, carvings and sculptures, and Hindu temples. Unearthed here also have been some paleolithic and neolithic tools attesting to prehistoric civilization in these parts.

The finds at Nagarjunakonda are in a museum that looks like a vihar (Buddhist monastery). They were moved so **Nagarjunasagar** could be built to flood and thereby irrigate the arid areas of Andra Pradesh. It's been called "India's Aswan Dam," but is by no means as ambitious as its namesake Egyptian project. The museum is open from 9 a.m. to 5 p.m.; closed Friday. It's free.

TOURS: The **Andhra Pradesh Travel and Tourism Development Corporation** (APTTDC), first floor, Gagan Vihar, M. I. Road, Hyderabad 500001 (tel. 556493), conducts a daily tour covering the Public Gardens, Budhapurnima boating complex, Qutub Shahi, Golconda Fort, Gandipet (Osmansagar),

Safarjung Museum, Char Minar, Mecca Masjid, Zoological Park, and Birla Mandir. The tour, including an English-speaking guide, starts at 9 a.m., finishes at 5:50 p.m., and costs Rs. 30 ($2.30), which covers the guide fee but not entrance fees. A lunch break takes place at Gandipet. Pickup starts at 8 a.m. at the Youth Hostel in Secunderabad, then the Secunderabad Railway Station at 8:10 a.m., and finally the head office (address above) at 9 a.m. This tour allots 60 minutes to Golconda Fort, and 90 to the Salarjung Museum.

In addition to the APTTDC office (open from 6:30 a.m. to 8 p.m.), bookings can be made at the tourist information counters at the airport and railway stations in Hyderabad and Secunderabad, and the Youth Hostel in Secunderabad. It's best to book in person the day before the tour of your choice. The APTTDC offers a daily tour to Nagarjuna Sagar Dam, covering 360 km (220 miles) and lasting 16 hours (it leaves at 6 a.m. and returns at 10:30 p.m.). The round-trip fare is Rs. 48 ($3.70) and the local sightseeing charges are Rs. 10 (75¢).

The APTTDC also runs a series of weekend tours to more distant points in Andhra Pradesh; get details at the M. J. Road office.

Among the travel agents running daily Hyderabad tours is **Bharat Tourist Travels,** opposite the Tourist Hotel, Kachiguda (tel. 550079). The tour starts at 7:30 a.m. and finishes at 5:30 p.m., covers the main sights, and stops an hour at Golconda Fort and two hours at the Salarjung Museum. This tour picks tourists up at various hotels, and costs Rs. 25 ($1.90), including the guide fee but not entry fees. The lunch break is at the Tourist Hotel. A similar tour, also for Rs. 25 ($1.90), is offered by another travel agent, **Amar Travels,** inside Gee Royal Lodge (tel. 234511). Lunch break is at Nampally. Lunch is not included in the price of tours.

All tours are rushed, especially at Golconda. The two private tours offer two hours at the Salar Jung Museum rather than the APTTDC's 90 minutes, but they drive through the Charminar and Mecca Masjid while the APTTDC's halts for ten minutes at each of these places.

Bharat and Amar Travels offer tours to Nagarjuna Sagar Dam. They leave Hyderabad at 7:30 a.m., return at 9 p.m., and cost Rs. 60 ($4.60).

USEFUL INFORMATION: The **Government of India Tourist Office** is located in the Sandozi Building, Himaynatnagar (tel. 66877). . . . The **APTTDC** address for information is First Floor, Gagan Vihar, M. J. Road (tel. 556493); information counters are also at the airport and railway stations in Secunderabad and Hyderabad. . . . Both **Indian Airlines** (tel. 36902) and **Vayudoot Airlines** (tel. 72910) are located at Safaibad. . . . There are over 80 **cinemas** in the twin cities, some showing English-language movies. . . . Higginbothams, the leading South Indian **book** chain, is at Lal Bahadur Stadium, as is Vidyarthi Book Store. . . . When it comes to reading, you can't miss the dramatic political slogans that cover huge surfaces throughout the city. . . . **Banking hours** are Monday to Friday from 10 a.m. to 2 p.m., and on Saturday from 10 a.m. to noon. . . . **Swimming** is permitted for a fee in the pools at the Hotel Nagarjunga (tel. 37201); Parklane, Secunderabad (tel. 70148); Ritz (tel. 33571); and Deccan Continental (tel. 70981). Telephone each hotel for more information before plunging in.

GETTING TO HYDERABAD: By **air** from Delhi costs Rs. 1,085 ($83.45); from Bombay, Rs. 717 ($55.15); from Madras, Rs. 502 ($38.60); from Calcutta, Rs. 1,166 ($89.70); from Bhubaneswar, Rs. 829 ($63.75); from Bangalore, Rs. 552 ($42.45); and from Aurangabad, Rs. 446 ($34.30).

Hyderabad/Secunderabad is a major rail center, and some express **train** connections are: from Delhi (24 hours), for Rs. 481 ($37) in first class, Rs. 111 ($8.55) in second class; from Madras (17 hours), Rs. 179 ($13.75) in first class, Rs. 44 ($3.40) in second; from Bombay (15 hours), Rs. 264 ($20.30) in first class, Rs. 69 ($5.30) in second. The *Bangalore–Hyderabad Express* takes 20 hours and costs Rs. 144 ($11.05) in first class, Rs. 36 ($2.75) in second.

Interstate **buses** connect Hyderabad with Aurangabad, Bangalore, Bombay, Goa, Madras, and Mysore. Within Andhra Pradesh, buses available to and from such sites as Bidar (home of bidriware), Nagarjuna Sagar Dam (museum housing finds at Nagarjunakonda), Tripupathi (ancient temple), and Vijayawada (former Buddhist site now noted for toys). For information on super-deluxe video coach service to some of these places, contact Bharat Tourist Travels (tel. 550079), Amar Travels (tel. 234511), or other travel agents.

Chapter XI

MADRAS: WHERE THE SOUTH BEGINS

1. Hotels
2. Restaurants
3. Shopping
4. Seeing the City
5. Nightlife
6. Useful Information
7. An Excursion to Kanchipuram and Mamallapuram (Mahabalipuram)

THE CAPITAL OF TAMIL NADU, and its largest city (pop. 4,500,000), Madras is regarded as the gateway to South India. Unlike the rushed atmosphere in the north, the pace is slower here, as is characteristic of southern climes; the climate is invariably humid and conducive to leisurely living.

The British were here fairly early in their occupation of India and have left traces military (**Fort St. George**), commercial (banks), and religious—the oldest Anglican church in India.

One of the curiosities of this spacious city—it is India's fourth largest—is that despite its vast population there always seems to be room to spare. The large, wide beach known as **Marina** is almost always deserted (except in late afternoon) and the streets and stores are never as crowded as could be expected.

There are not many things to disturb the compulsive sightseer. A climb up the new lighthouse at the end of Marina Beach will give a good perspective of the city, dotted with open green spaces and lush palmy vegetation; Fort St. George has an interesting museum, and the official **Government Museum** is worth a couple of interesting hours.

Try to see some of the lovely, big houses in the suburbs (probably on a visit to **Elliot's Beach**) and drop by the enormous grounds of the **Theosophical Society** to stand under the gigantic banyan tree.

The state of Tamil Nadu and city of Madras are, above all, places to take it easy and savor the delights of the south slowly. When your stay is over, you'll find it harder to move on than you thought.

1. Hotels

India's fourth-largest city is her least Westernized and so it's an ideal place for staying in an Indian-style hotel, where the prices are fine for budget travelers. These hotels are among the best in the south, and the prices are lower simply because the style of life on the premises is not imported, as it is in a hotel catering to Western visitors. Be prepared, therefore, for granite floors, and rooms that are rather bare in appearance. You will have all the necessities of life, but may lack such Western frills as wall-to-wall carpeting, a well-appointed lounge, and central air conditioning (some Indian-style hotels have window units). The service in these South Indian hotels is generally very good, however, and the standard of cleanliness is high.

Above all, there are wonderful touches of personal luxury: in the Hindu religion cleanliness is next to godliness, and bathing several times a day is so much a part of life that almost every room in a South Indian–style hotel has an attached bath and toilet. There are two styles of plumbing in these places: Western, with a commode; and Eastern, without. Some Indian-style hotels have Western fixtures, but always specify when you make your reservations to be sure of getting just what you want. Also, do book in advance, for while some of the Western-style hotels in Madras may have an occasional vacancy if you just drop in, these Indian-style places are enormously popular and booked throughout the year.

The one big difference at these Indian-style hotels is the food. In accordance with orthodox Hindu beliefs, not one shred of meat can cross the threshold—so the food is vegetarian, but so deliciously prepared as to make you forget all that nonsense about the plainness of any such diet.

On the other hand, beach buffs might prefer relaxing in a well-appointed cottage by the sea at Mamallapuram (Mahabalipuram), 40 miles to the south and 1½ to 2 hours away by car, coming into Madras to sightsee. The beach accommodations are described in Section 7 of this chapter. So, take a look before deciding.

Also, keep in mind that luxury taxes can add to your hotel bill in Madras, 10% to 20% or perhaps more.

INDIAN-STYLE HOTELS IN MADRAS: Altogether delightful, the **Dasaprakash,** 100 Poonamallee High Rd., Madras 600084 (tel. 661111), has nine landscaped roof gardens, each one different from the other and interspersed with eating spots. Copies of the *Bhagavadgita* (the "bible" of Hinduism) instead of the Gideon Bible are in the rooms; a statue of Lord Krishna stands in the garden where there is also a playground for the children beneath a huge acacia tree. Rooms are very attractive with highly polished wood walls and wardrobes, and small sitting rooms. There are 52 singles, 48 doubles and suites, with connecting baths and mostly Western toilets. Standard rooms cost Rs. 55 ($4.25) to Rs. 100 ($7.70) single and Rs. 150 ($11.55) double. Air-conditioned rooms cost Rs. 120 ($9.25) single and Rs. 175 ($13.45) double. The hotel will pack a picnic lunch of soup, vegetarian sandwiches, fruit, and barfi (a rich fudge-like sweet).

If you want to take an unusual sightseeing tour, ask the caterer for a tour through the kitchen of the **Hotel Madras Ashoka,** 33 Pantheon Rd., Egmore, Madras 600008 (tel. 568977). You'll see five or six electrified stone mortars and pestles grinding away at a number of chunky coconuts (the base of many South Indian foods), a cook flipping dosas (pancakes) on the hot griddle, a special room for sweets, and everything and everyone spotlessly clean. Architecturally, the Ashoka is unusual because its main building is circular. Rooms cost Rs. 90 ($6.90) single and Rs. 160 ($12.30) double, non-air-conditioned;

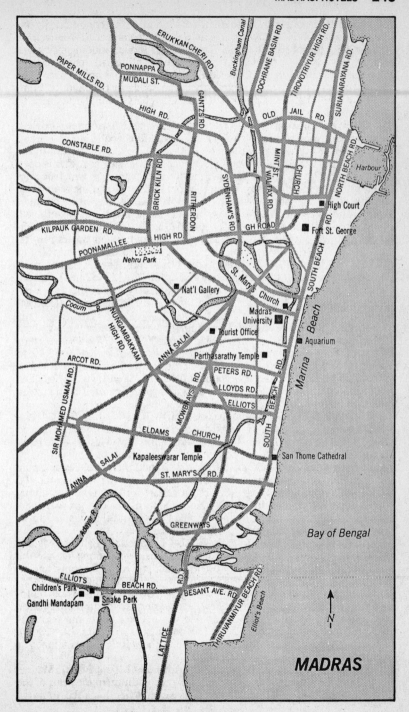

MADRAS

Rs. 140 ($10.75) single and Rs. 200 ($15.40) double, air-conditioned. Cottages cost Rs. 200 ($15.40). There's an 8% service charge. All rooms have Western-style plumbing. The hotel is popular for Indian wedding receptions and, as Indians are extremely hospitable, they will usually enjoy sharing the occasion with a foreigner. Speak to the hotel manager first, though. The dining room at the Ashoka serves vegetarian foods in the Madras, Bombay, and Andhra styles. There's a 10% service charge and taxes of 10% to 20%.

The **New Woodlands**, 72-75 Dr. Radhakrishnan Rd. (formerly Edward Elliot's Road), Madras 600004 (tel. 473111), is another good hotel choice and another Indian wedding favorite. You can play table tennis or swim in the small pool, set in a lovely flower-filled garden. A pool-side snackbar is open from 7 a.m. to 7 p.m. The hotel has 75 singles and 89 doubles, with balconies and Western-style bathrooms. When I looked in there was some renovation under way, but the lobby was intact and looked handsome with a mural of dancers and elephants. This is a very nice hotel, clean and well maintained. Non-air-conditioned singles rent for Rs. 70 ($5.40) to Rs. 100 ($7.70); non-air-conditioned doubles, Rs. 135 ($10.40). Air-conditioned singles run Rs. 115 ($8.85) to Rs. 140 ($10.75), and air-conditioned doubles are Rs. 170 ($13.05) to Rs. 230 ($17.70). There are 11 air-conditioned, pleasant, well-equipped cottages on the grounds, available for Rs. 375 ($28.85). Service charge is 5%, and to that you must add the luxury tax. If there's a wedding going on, ask the manager, V. Satyanarayana, and he'll see that you get in.

Plastic walls divide the bedrooms from the sitting rooms at the fairly neat **Udipi Home,** 1 Hall's Rd., Egmore, Madras 600008 (tel. 567911), a vegetarian hotel with 80 rooms. Non-air-conditioned rooms rent for Rs. 70 ($5.40) to Rs. 75 ($5.75); air-conditioned rooms cost Rs. 115 ($8.85) to Rs. 135 ($10.40). The food here is very good, and Rs. 18 ($1.40) will buy a filling South Indian thali meal. If this hotel had a new coat of paint, it would look a lot better.

Hotel Palmgrove, 5 Kodambakkam High Rd., Madras 600034 (tel. 471881), despite its name, has no garden and no decor. But it's very neat and clean. Although it's an Indian-style hotel, all rooms have Western-style bathrooms and the more expensive double rooms have bathtubs. Some of the 82 rooms have small balconies and sitting rooms, and there are, besides, nine cottages. All rooms are doubles. Rates range from Rs. 110 ($8.45) to Rs. 400 ($30.75) in rooms and cottages (highest prices are for cottages). Two dining rooms serve vegetarian foods. Of these, Oorvasi, on the top with air-conditioning, is most pleasant; open from 11 a.m. to 2:30 p.m. and 7 to 11 p.m. There's a Permit Room (euphemism for bar) also.

All rooms at the **Hotel Swagath,** 243-244 Royapettah High Rd., Madras 600014 (tel. 82176), open off polished marble balcony-corridors. Actually the hotel is two buildings: a five-story original building, with 47 rooms, and an eight-story annex, with 63 rooms that are newer and nicer, and where the hotel's dining room and restaurant are located. Some of the rooms in both buildings are air-conditioned, and only a few have Western-style bathrooms. Rates: Rs. 75 ($5.75) single, Rs. 85 ($6.55) double, without air conditioning; doubles with air conditioning run Rs. 125 ($9.60) and singles go for Rs. 105 ($8.05). Meals in the dining room are also budget right, about Rs. 8 (60¢) for lunch or dinner, vegetarian.

The **Hotel Shrilekha,** 49 Anna Salai (formerly Mount Road), Madras 600002 (tel. 840082), is a cast-concrete box on a podium, in the heart of the city. The podium is the lobby, where two glass chandeliers hang above an area crowded with plastic-covered couches and potted plants. On the eight-story exterior, balcony panels are painted brown and orange against a yellow building. All rooms have small balconies and wooden cabinets. Deluxe rooms have wallpaper. Bathrooms are Indian style, except in the suites, and have decorative tile up to shoulder height. Rooms are clean, pleasant, but undistinguished: singles run Rs. 95 ($7.30), and doubles go for Rs. 145 ($11.15) without air conditioning. An air-conditioned double costs Rs. 185 ($14.25). In the vegetarian dining room, you can get a Madras meal for Rs. 10 (75¢). In addition, a restaurant in the building is open from 6 a.m. to 10 p.m.

A six-foot-high woodcarving of Shiva dances at one end of an otherwise undistinguished lobby at the **Hotel Maris,** 9 Cathedral Rd., Madras 600080 (tel. 470541). You can find touches like this throughout the hotel. On the exterior, for instance, an ordinary yellow concrete building is given some life by extending support beams at every other floor and painting these extensions in bright colors. All rooms have small balconies, and some of the railings and panels on these balconies are painted bright colors too. Inside the rooms there is occasional wood paneling and wallpaper above the beds. Each room has a phone, music, and attached Western-style bath. All are clean and pleasant, but could use a coat of paint. Non-air-conditioned singles cost Rs. 70 ($5.40); doubles run Rs. 110 ($8.45). Rates with air conditioning are Rs. 100 ($7.70) single and Rs. 150 ($11.55) double. In the dining room, open from 6 a.m. to 10 p.m., you can get fixed-price vegetarian meals for Rs. 8 (60¢) at breakfast; other meals are à la carte.

Though it is called a hotel, the **Vishram Hotel,** at 308 Walltax Rd. (tel. 38725), is really a lodge, simpler than a hotel and, accordingly, less expensive. There are many lodges in this area, right by the railway station, but the Vishram is probably the best. It is fairly clean. Most of the double rooms have attached Western-style bathrooms. These baths are tiny but have showers. Rooms cost Rs. 25 ($1.90) single, Rs. 40 ($3.05) double.

The **Hotel Ramprasad,** 22 Gandhi Irwin Rd., Egmore, Madras 600008 (tel. 567875), with 32 fairly neat rooms, is conveniently near the Egmore Railway Station. It faces a busy street so the rooms get a lot of traffic noise. Some singles share a common bath. Rates are Rs. 55 ($4.25) single and Rs. 80 ($6.15) double, non-air-conditioned; Rs. 125 ($9.60) single and Rs. 145 ($11.15) double, air-conditioned.

On this same road, clean, simple rooms with floral wallpapered walls can be found at the **Vaigai Hotel,** 39 Gandhi Irwin Rd., Egmore, Madras 600008 (tel. 567373), near the Egmore station. Some rooms have glazed glass partitions between them and the halls are always light—a drawback. There's hot running water only in the morning. Rooms are overpriced—even more of a drawback—Rs. 95 ($7.30) and Rs. 150 ($11.55), the higher rate for air conditioning. The restaurant is run by Ramprasad nearby.

Near the Air-India and Indian Airlines offices, the **Hotel Guru,** 69 Marshalls Rd., Egmore, Madras 600008 (tel. 82001), has wallpapered rooms with spare furnishings. Prices are moderate: Rs. 60 ($4.60) single and Rs. 80 ($6.15) double, non-air-conditioned; Rs. 100 ($7.70) single and Rs. 125 ($9.60) double, air-conditioned. There's hot and cold running water in the attached bathrooms. A thali meal costs Rs. 7 (55¢) in the Sreedevi restaurant.

The **Hotel Ganpat,** 103 Nungambakkam High Rd., Madras 600034 (tel. 471889), has 13 air-conditioned rooms, all doubles, and 24 without air conditioning, occupying the fourth and fifth floors of a commercial building. Not for the fussy, the rooms are big and functional, with attached bathrooms. Rates for non-air-conditioned rooms are Rs. 90 ($6.90) single and Rs. 136 ($10.45) double; with air conditioning, Rs. 185 ($14.25) double. There's a rooftop restaurant dotted with plants and offering a good view of the city. You'll pay Rs. 10 (75¢) for a vegetarian thali.

WESTERN-STYLE HOTELS IN MADRAS: The **Hotel Atlantic,** 2 Montieth Rd., Egmore, Madras 600008 (tel. 810561), is a simple, clean place with 60 rooms. There are no carpets in the corridors (only in the deluxe rooms), and absolutely no frills. Without air conditioning, singles are Rs. 85 ($6.55) and doubles are Rs. 140 ($10.75). Air conditioning boosts the price of a single to Rs. 110 ($8.45), and a double to Rs. 165 ($12.70). An air-conditioned suite is Rs. 250 ($19.25). There's a coffeeshop and dining room. They have a stage in the garden for weddings and performances by groups. An annex is to be built.

The **Hotel New Victoria,** 3 Kennet Lane, Madras 600008 (tel. 567738), is a pleasant place with gleaming-white marble floors grand enough for a palace, a roof garden, and ornate grillwork. There are 35 air-conditioned singles costing Rs. 145 ($11.15), and 15 doubles, mostly air-conditioned, at Rs. 250 ($19.25). All rooms need paint jobs and come with private bathrooms, and front rooms have balconies. There's a 20% service charge. The dining room has grillwork doors and a glass wall. A complete meal will cost around Rs. 40 ($3.05) to Rs. 45 ($3.45) at lunch and dinner.

The modern, fully air-conditioned, 63-room **Madras International** is at 693 Anna Salai (formerly Mount Road), Madras 600006 (tel. 811811), which is an excellent location. Rooms are compact and have radios, phones, and bathrooms with showers. The best rooms are in the new wing. Singles rent for Rs. 190 ($14.60) to Rs. 275 ($21.15), and doubles cost Rs. 275 ($21.15) to Rs. 330 ($25.40). The Regal Room Restaurant is open from 10 a.m. to midnight, serving Chinese, continental, and Indian cuisines.

The **Admiralty Hotel,** Norton Road, Mandauallipakkam, Madras 600028 (tel. 71121), is a complex of three white three-story buildings set in small gardens and surrounded by a wall. Only a ten-minute walk from the beach, the Admiralty is an ideal place for an extended stay, and indeed many guests linger three or four months at a time. Some of the rooms have kitchens, some have dining rooms, and all are clean. In non-air-conditioned rooms you'll pay Rs. 100 ($7.70) single and Rs. 120 ($9.25) double; air-conditioned rooms cost Rs. 200 ($15.40) single and Rs. 273 ($21) double. Deluxe suites go for Rs. 450 ($34.60). Renovation was under way when I visited, and rates may increase when it is completed.

At the **Imperial Hotel,** Gandhi-Irwin Road, Egmore, Madras 600008 (tel. 566176), the lounge and dining room are set apart from the rooms, all of which face a court. The rooms are carpeted, and have radios and private bathrooms. The upstairs rooms are best—adequate if uninspired. Non-air-conditioned singles run Rs. 75 ($5.75); doubles, Rs. 150 ($11.55). With air conditioning, rates are Rs. 150 ($11.55) single and Rs. 195 ($15) double.

Hotel Peacock, 1089 Poonamallee High Rd., Madras, 600084 (tel. 39081), is a cross between Eastern and Western styles: 18 of the 73 rooms have Indian-style toilets in the attached bathrooms, and both vegetarian and nonvegetarian meals are served in the restaurant. Rooms are neat and adequately furnished, and 43 are air-conditioned, renting for Rs. 150 ($11.55) to Rs. 200 ($15.40) single, and Rs. 200 ($15.40) to Rs. 275 ($21.15) double. Non-air-conditioned rooms cost Rs. 95 ($7.30) to Rs. 105 ($8.05) single, and Rs. 125 ($9.60) to Rs. 150 ($11.55) double.

Between mid and low price is the **Hotel Broadlands,** 16 Vallabha Agraharam St., Madras 600005 (tel. 845573), a rambling old pastel-painted Victorian building with pink gingerbread trim. The hotel caters to budget-conscious Westerners, and the proprietor, A. P. Kumar, takes a personal interest in their comfort. The basic rooms will do for true penny-watchers. Rates are Rs. 30 ($2.30) and Rs. 35 ($2.70) for singles, Rs. 60 ($4.60) and Rs. 65 ($5) for doubles; there's a "penthouse" for Rs. 75 ($5.75). Bring a towel. Tea and coffee are available, but no meals served. It's a 10- to 15-minute walk from all the activity on Anna Salai, or rent one of the seven bikes for Rs. 5 (40¢) per day. Also, buses 30, 31, and 32 at Esplanade Road outside the express bus terminus or 29D, 22, and 27B at Egmore Station can take you to and from the hotel.

SPLURGE HOTELS: Above the reception desk of the high-priced **Hotel Chola Sheraton,** 10 Cathedral Rd., Madras 600086 (tel. 473347), is a large mural by the contemporary artist Krishan Khanna. It shows the voyages of the Chola kings, the difficulties they met, and their thanksgiving when they reached their destination. The message is clear for any traveler, and indeed the Hotel Chola is a haven even a king would give thanks for. Singles cost Rs. 600 ($46.25) to Rs. 750 ($57.75), and doubles run Rs. 700 ($53.75) to Rs. 850 ($65.50). Suites go as high as Rs. 3,200 ($246).

The lobby of the splurge-rated **Taj Coromandel,** 17 Nungambakkam High Rd., Madras 600034 (tel. 474849), is vast, filled with overstuffed couches, huge octagonal rugs in shades of blue and purple, glass-topped coffee tables, and tour groups. Overhead are brass lamps suspended in metal frames. And throughout the rest of the hotel are touches reflecting the rich South Indian heritage. The carpeted rooms have every amenity and tile baths. There are 220 rooms and 28 suites. Rates are Rs. 650 ($50) single and Rs. 750 ($57.75) double; a deluxe double is Rs. 900 ($69.25).

At the **Savera Hotel,** 69 Dr. Radhakrishnan Rd., Madras 600004 (tel. 474700), the severity of the lobby is relieved by stone statues of deities. In the halls are full-length mirrors with baroque frames. Rooms, modern in style, have such appointments as two phones (one in the bathroom) and piped-in music, and the rooms on higher floors have terrific city views. Beside the swimming pool, and visible in a palm grove through a glass wall in the living room, there is a statue of Buddha said to be 2,000 years old. Rates are Rs. 320 ($24.60) for ordinary singles and Rs. 385 ($29.60) for superior singles; doubles are Rs. 440 ($33.85); various suites go for Rs. 550 ($42.30) to Rs. 900 ($69.25). There are two restaurants, the Minar on the 11th floor serving Mughali foods, and the Chakra, site of the lunch buffet (see "Restaurants"), plus the Chariot coffeeshop.

The **Ambassador Pallava,** 53 Montieth Rd., Madras 600008 (tel. 812061), is owned by the Ambassador, a Bombay hotel long known for its antique appointments. The tradition continues here with a handsome antique mirror in the lobby where there is a stone grotto to one side and an ornate lotus-patterned ceiling overhead. Renovations, under way by the new owners, should be completed by the time you arrive. Rooms I saw were neat and well maintained, renting for Rs. 450 ($34.60) single and Rs. 500 ($38.45) double; suites cost Rs. 700 ($53.85) to Rs. 1,400 ($108). Rates are scheduled to go up when all renovations are completed. There's a lavish daily buffet (see "Restaurants") in the Other Room restaurant.

With glass chandeliers shaped like stalactites, fountains, a console organ player, and white wicker furniture, the lobby of the **Adayar Park,** 132 T. T. K. Rd. (formerly Mowbrays Road), Madras 600018 (tel. 452525), has a happy, unsophisticated ambience which pervades the entire hotel. Imagine a "Jungle Evening" promoted as "groovy" in this day and age! It's run by the Welcomgroup. Rates are Rs. 650 ($50) to Rs. 750 ($57.75) single and Rs. 750 ($57.75) to Rs. 850 ($65.50) double; suites go up to Rs. 2,000 ($154). There are buffets on weekdays and Sunday. It's a Rs.-12 (90¢) auto-rickshaw ride to the tourist center of town on Anna Salai.

The style of the 1930s is still echoed in the atmosphere of the **Connemara,** Binny Road, Madras 600002 (tel. 810051), which dates from 1936. The lounge blends the earlier era with contemporary furniture, beautiful stone carvings, and oil lamps, and a plant-filled indoor court has a pleasant ornamental pool. The outdoor swimming pool is bordered by vine-entwined trellises. At one time owned by Spencer's, the South Indian department store chain, Connemara is now part of the Taj Group. The new owners had plans for renovations when I stopped in, so the look (as well as the rates) could change. Presently, rates are Rs. 500 ($38.45) to Rs. 600 ($46.25) for doubles; other rooms and suites run Rs. 700 ($53.75) to Rs. 1,600 ($123). The 20% tax is added to be these charges.

The big red Victorian building next door to the hotel is a Spencer's Department Store, dating back to the Raj days and flourishing today. Across the main road is the India Tourist Office on Anna Salai.

LOWEST BUDGET CHOICES: It's almost impossible to find an acceptable room under Rs. 35 ($2.70) these days. If you care to try, head north on Anna Salai (Mount Road) to the area around Parry's Corner and the surrounding streets. Good luck!

Clean, but 30 minutes from town, the **Tourist Hostel** (Andra Mahila Sabha), 12 Dr. Durgabai Deshmukh Rd., Raja Annamalaipuram, Madras 600028 (tel. 416001), is run by an organization engaged in welfare services. The hostel, built in 1964, has the comforts of a private home and is popular with budgeteers craving peace and quiet. There are six singles, 14 doubles, and some larger rooms that can accommodate three or four. In the new wing are Western toilets, if you care about such things. Singles run Rs. 40 ($3.05); doubles, Rs. 80 ($6.15). It's Rs. 7 (55¢) for a cot, Rs. 4 (30¢) for floor space in the mammoth dorm. Some air-conditioned doubles are available Rs. 150 ($11.55). Breakfast will run Rs. 5 (40¢) and a vegetarian lunch is Rs. 6 (45¢). Buses from town to the hostel (no. 19M from High Court to Thiruvanmiyur, no. 5 from Parry's to Adayar B.S., and others) cost 60 paise (4½¢) to 75 paise (5½¢); taxis cost around Rs. 30 ($2.30), and auto-rickshaws, about Rs. 15 ($1.15), for a 30-minute or more ride, depending on the traffic.

The **YWCA,** 1086 Poonamalle High Rd. (tel. 34945) is pleasantly situated in a garden compound, and the building itself is full of green plants. In the main lobby is a small lounge, and an attractive dining room opens off the veranda. There are 199 rooms, three of them singles at Rs. 35 ($2.70); doubles range from Rs. 35 ($2.70) per person to Rs. 55 ($4.25). The rates include breakfast, but not the Rs.10 (75¢) temporary membership fee. All rooms are spotlessly clean, and have attached bathrooms and mosquito netting for the beds. Other meals run Rs. 15 ($1.15) for lunch, Rs. 20 ($1.55) for dinner. Preference is given to women and families, but men can stay for a minimum of three days.

The **Laharry Transient Youth Hostel,** in the same compound, accepts low-budget female students and teachers for 15-day stays. There are two dorms with eight beds and two two-bedded rooms. A bed costs Rs. 6 (45¢).

2. Restaurants

The state of Tamil Nadu is famous for spicy South Indian vegetarian dishes and the capital, Madras, is a great place to taste them. (In the south, food tends to be hotter, less rich, and includes more rice and coconut, which are abundant locally.) There are more orthodox Hindus in this area too, and therefore a greater proportion of strictly vegetarian restaurants (not even eggs served on the premises) to cater to them. The best cooks, by repute, come from a small town called **Udipi,** and many eating places incorporate this word into their names.

Traditional South Indian meals are served on banana leaves, and before you leave the south you'll undoubtedly acquire the technique of eating from them with your fingers, using the dry rice as a base to handle the more liquid dishes such as curry.

Hot spicy foods are supposed to cool you by making your body temperature rise and thus more susceptible to balmy breezes. It is true, at any rate, that spices perk up the appetite, which tends to get sluggish in the tropics.

While you can eat all kinds of dishes, from East and West, served with great élan in elegant surroundings at any of the top hotels, it would be a shame to come to Madras and not eat in some of the plain places, favored by Madrasis, where the food is simply delicious. Contrary to what you've heard, not all South Indian foods are fiery—but that's not to say that they're mild as morning porridge either. Taste them and see for yourself. This is coffee—not tea—country. South Indian coffee made with steaming milk is a rich delicious drink.

Excellent vegetarian dishes are served at **Woodland's Drive-In,** 29/30 Cathedral Rd. (tel. 471981), where they bring trays to cars as they did in the '50s in the States. Better than eating in a car is nibbling your dosa under the beautiful trees in what was once a botanical garden. There is no set menu, but apart from daily specialties in the Rs.-4 (30¢) to Rs.-6 (45¢) range, there are 45 to 60 standard items such as sambhar (zesty soup), idlis (rice-and-lentil pancake), and various chutneys, all decently priced. The indoor section is air-conditioned and has a menu. A self-service counter is open for breakfast, lunch, and dinner. On Sunday, Woodland's is full of families eating and keeping a watchful eye on their kids riding ponies in the children's park. Open from 6 a.m. to 9 p.m. every day.

At 83 Anna Salai on the ground floor, **Buhari's** (tel. 840391) is worth checking out if only for the magnificent candies, butter cakes, and pastries, at Re. 1 (7½¢) for a small pastry. Ice cream is available, as are such snacks as vegetable cutlets or omelets, both Rs. 4 (30¢); toast is Rs. 1.25 (9½¢), and tea, 75 paise (5½¢). Upstairs, under the same owners, at the **Moghul** the atmosphere is air-conditioned and more serene with dim lighting and comfortable booths. Here are Chinese dishes and Mughlai food, as the name implies, plus Western lamb chops and vegetarian foods, with the highest-priced items about Rs. 22 ($1.70) for non-vegetarian entrees. There is also a place to sit outdoors. Hours are 8 a.m. to 4 a.m. downstairs; 11:30 a.m. to 1:30 a.m. upstairs.

Buhari's, in business for 35 years, has seven restaurants around town and surrounding area. Some of these locations are 14 Beach Rd., N.S.C. Bose Rd., Poonamalee High Road, the Imperial Hotel, and the Blue Lagoon Resort.

The **Fiesta Café,** inside Spencer's Department Store, 769 Anna Salai (tel. 041525), is a haven for anyone looking for familiar Western foods. Pizza is Rs. 9 (70¢), and there are ice creams for Rs. 7 (55¢) for plain flavors, large glasses of fresh juice for Rs. 9 (70¢), and a menu full of reasonably priced dishes, soft drinks, coffee, and tea. Hours: 8 a.m. to midnight.

Eskimo, at 827 Anna Salai (tel. 827840), is a funny name for a restaurant in perpetually warm, warmer, warmest Madras. But this air-conditioned little place is as cool as an igloo and serves good, inexpensive food. Right near the movies and shops, it's popular for meals and snacks, from 9 a.m. to 10 p.m. Snacks, sandwiches, kebabs, and such are Rs. 7 (55¢) and Rs. 8 (60¢). More substantial dishes are also offered, such as tandoori chicken at Rs. 24 ($1.85) or chicken do piaza (a curry with onions) at Rs. 14 ($1.05)—quality food at a fair price.

South India goes south-of-the-border at **Taco Tavern**, 24 Commander-in-Chief Rd. (no phone), open from 11 a.m. to 11 p.m., and this is the place for you to head for taco Azteca (made with beans and green peppers), gazpacho, and a very un-Mexican vegetable whopper. Murari, the owner, lived in South Carolina for a while where, he says, he learned about Mexican food. (Whatever happened to hominy and black eyed peas?) Everything here is in the Rs.11 (85¢) to Rs.13 ($1) range. The Madrasis are eating Mexican and loving it!

Next door is the expensive **Mahal**, with North Indian foods, open from noon to 3 p.m. and 7 to midnight.

Eating outdoors at **Tick Tac**, 123 Nungambakkam High Rd. (tel. 472674), offers two North Indian possibilities—tandoori foods, like a full chicken for Rs. 36 ($2.75), and less expensive kebabs—and Chinese foods. Or you can just stop in for a soft drink or ice cream. Hours are 12:30 to 2 p.m. and 5 to 9 p.m. Near the Taj Coromandel Hotel, Tick Tac is very popular at night.

For Indian sweets, go to the clean **Bombay Halwa House**, on Anna Salai to the left of the Khadi Gramodyog Bhavan, where halwa is Rs. 4 (30¢) per portion and other sweets are around Rs. 8 (60¢). Delicious South Indian coffee served here.

BUFFETS: Like the other major tourist centers in India, the top hotels in Madras serve bountiful buffets at lunch, featuring Indian and Western foods, salads, and desserts, all for a fixed price, no matter how full your plate the first time or how often you go back for more.

At the **Connemara**, on Binny Road (tel. 810051), the daily buffet at Rs. 55 ($4.25) is in the Binny Room (tel. 810051), served from 12:30 to 3:30 p.m.

At the **Taj Coromandel**, 17 Nungambakkam High Rd. (tel. 474849), the buffet is served for lunch (from noon to 3 p.m.) and for dinner (from 8:30 p.m. to midnight), at Rs. 75 ($5.75) per person.

The **Adayar Park**, 132 T.T.K. Rd. (tel. 452525), has a buffet from 1 to 3 p.m. during the week in the Residency for Rs. 75 ($5.75) and a Sunday-night vegetarian buffet from 8 p.m. to midnight for Rs. 45 ($3.45).

At the **Hotel Savera**, 69 Dr. Radhakrishnan Rd. (tel. 474700), the buffet is in the Chakra from 12:30 to 3 p.m. for Rs. 56 ($4.30).

The **Ambassador Pallava**, 55 Monteith Rd. (tel. 812061), has a lunch buffet from 12:30 to 3 p.m. featuring 39 dishes in the Other Room, for Rs. 49 ($3.75). The pastry chef at the Ambassador is one of the best in town, so be sure to save room for dessert. A tea lounge is planned for this hotel, so if you miss the buffet, drop in at tea time and try the biscuits.

THALIS: Notable thalis can be found in many Madras restaurants. Here are just two such places.

The **New Woodlands Hotel**, 72-75 Dr. Radhakrishnan Rd. (tel. 473111), charges Rs. 20 ($1.55), and is open from 11:30 a.m. to 2 p.m. and 7:30 to 9:30 p.m.

At the **Chariot**, Hotel Savera, 69 Dr. Radhakrishnan Rd. (tel. 474700), the Rs.-25 ($1.90) thali includes sambhar, pappadams, two curries, rice, pickles, fruit salad, and paan. Hours are 11 a.m. to 3 p.m. and 7 to 11 p.m.

3. Shopping

Silks woven in the temple city of Kanchipuram, not far from Madras, are good buys at many stores, including **India Silk House**, 846 Mount Rd. (Anna

Salai; tel. 845512), open from 9 a.m. to 8 p.m., and at **Radha Silk Emporium,** 1 Sannadhi St., Mylapore, near the main Madras temple, where tourists get a brochure on how to wrap, wear, and care for a sari. This store has Western items as well, such as shirts in famous Madras plaid crêpe cotton for Rs. 20 ($1.55) and scarves that make easy-to-pack gifts. Ready-mades also include salwar kamiz for women. Hours are 10 a.m. to 8 p.m. Monday through Saturday; closed Sunday.

The famous cotton plaids of Madras are well represented at **Handloom House,** 8 Rattan Bazaar, and **Khadi Gramodyag Bhavan,** 844 Anna Salai, where there are also tailors to make your fabrics into fashionable clothing. Hours are 9:30 a.m. to 7:30 p.m.; closed Sunday.

For handcrafts, try the **Cottage Industries Exposition** (not to be confused with the government-run Cottage Industries Emporia in other cities; this one is privately owned), 118 N. H. Rd., across from the Taj Coromandel (tel. 473438), where you'll find items in rosewood and sandalwood, ivory, bronze, silver, and leather, as well as textiles, carpets, and precious jewelry. Open from 10 a.m. to 1 p.m. and 4 to 9 p.m.

The 100-year-old **Victoria Technical Institute,** 765 Anna Salai (tel. 812131), open from 9:30 a.m. to 7:30 p.m. weekdays and on Saturday from 9:30 a.m. to 2 p.m., has a special room for antiquities and unusual items made especially to be sold here. It's the place to look for a one-of-a-kind souvenir. Less special, but very nice, are the VTI's rosewood elephants dangling from a key chain for Rs. 3 (23¢), and hand-embroidered easy-to-pack linens.

Hand-woven textiles, brassware, pottery, and sandalwood beads can be found in a good selection at **Khadi Krafts Emporium,** N. S. C. Bose Rd. (tel. 20461), open from 10 a.m. to 1 p.m. and 3 to 7 p.m. There are similar items and hours at **Mini Khadi Kraft,** 172 Anna Salai (tel. 81954).

Before visiting any of the many **jewelers** in town, drop in at the India Tourist Office, 154 Anna Salai, for an approved list to make sure you get the real thing.

Spencer's Department Store, 769 Anna Salai (tel. 041525), is the most famous department store in Madras. It's a positive delight for travelers weary of trying to find many different necessities under one roof, for here, gathered together, is everything from gifts to pharmaceuticals and clothes to cooking utensils. Hours: 8:30 a.m. to 7:30 p.m.

To be enveloped by the sweet scent of jasmine, visit the **Fruit and Flower Bazaar** on N. S. C. Bose Road. This is where Madras women buy single blossoms for their hair and devotees select garlands for worship. Nearby stalls display bananas, custard apples (they look somewhat like artichokes), and other luscious fruits. Wash and/or peel before you eat.

4. Seeing the City

A preliminary exploration of Madras might start in the northern area along Poonamallee High Road, near the majestic civic buildings of the **Municipal Corporation** and the Madras Central Railway Station. Just past there, taking the right fork of the road, you'll come to what's left of old **Fort St. George,** major cog in the city's defenses when the British were in power two centuries ago, its buildings now used for various administrative and garrison purposes. This was the home of legendary British Empire builders such as Robert Clive (originally an obscure clerk in the East India Company, later in the 1750s a governor of Bengal), and Colonel Wellesley, later Duke of Wellington (of the Battle of Waterloo fame).

Part of the fort itself is now a **museum** (open from 9 a.m. to 5 p.m. every day but Friday) containing portraits of these famous figures as well as those of various governors and such English kings and queens as could be said to have ruled India. The signatures of King George V and his wife, Mary, written when they visited here in 1906, are still preserved in the visitors' book. In glass cases downstairs are stamps from that period bearing the heads of British sovereigns, and—by contrast—the infinitely more interesting stamps issued when India became independent (Aug. 15, 1947); when Gandhi was murdered (Jan. 30, 1948), and on the inauguration of the Republic of India (Jan. 26, 1950). A scale model of the fort as it was centuries ago demonstrates that the sea used to lap at the walls where now the road runs past. Also in the grounds is **St. Mary's Church,** built by the East India Company in 1680, with its near-copy of Leonardo da Vinci's *Last Supper,* done by some unknown French artist early in the 18th century. One of St. Mary's generous benefactors was Elihu Yale, a former governor, and yes, donor to the university of the same name.

You're now on South Beach Road, parallel with the sea but separated from it by dockyards. Up to your left are the stalls of the **Burma bazaar**—lots of bargains here—but we'll head south, past the stately **government buildings** and campus of the **University of Madras,** past the thatched mud huts of the fishermen displaced years ago by a hurricane (they've been offered better homes but prefer to stay near the sea) and past the **aquarium** and almost-deserted sandy beaches. It's quite a lengthy walk, this stretch along the **Marina,** and maybe you'd prefer to get a taxi or cycle rickshaw. Our destination is the **Cathedral of San Thomé,** a small gray church where Thomas, one of the 12 apostles, is alleged to be buried (there is some skepticism about the legend locally). It's a pleasant church, patches of color from the stained-glass windows casting patterns on the shiny wooden pews.

Just around the corner, so to speak, life is busier near the incredible **Kapaliswarar Temple,** its wedge-shaped **gopuram,** or tower, composed of tier after tier of exceptional carvings. The centuries-old temple is dedicated to Lord Shiva and the palm-fringed tank at its rear is the scene of an annual festival (early spring), when the temple images are taken out and floated upon the water.

Your next destination is about a mile to the south: **Elliot's Beach** has developed into one of the poshest areas of Madras. Though not as secluded as it once was, it's still worth a visit. Bus 5E from Vadapalani to Besant Nagar or 5M from Parry's to Adyar B.S. will take you there.

Inshore from the beach, we're now in the suburbs, as a glance at the surrounding houses and gardens will prove. On the way you'll see the elegant mansion and extensive grounds of the Theosophical Society, with its enormous banyan tree. There are two other landmarks on the highway out here: a delightful **Children's Park** ("Children—please don't leave anything behind but your footprints; the animal pets look to you for kindness and protection, do not tease and provoke them") with playground, midget railway, deer, cranes, monkeys, bears, panthers, and an elephant; and a simple, attractive park, **Gandhi Mandap,** where some of the ashes of the great pacifist are enshrined.

The Children's Park is located on the vast grounds of **Raj Bhavan,** the governor's estate, itself at the edge of **Guindy National Park,** the only national park in India within city limits. There are two other parks within this park: A deer park houses rare black buck and spotted deer in their natural habitat, and a snake park, home to some 500 snakes, including cobras and pythons, their friends and relatives slinking around in natural-looking surroundings. The animals and reptiles make good photographic subjects. City buses 18E from Parry's Corner, 45 from Periyar Bridge, and 46 from Anna Square go to Guindy. Or grab a commuter train from Egmore or Beach Station.

Going back to the midtown area in Egmore, you'll find the **National Gallery of Art** (open from 10 a.m. to 5 p.m.; closed Friday, Republic Day, Independence Day, and Mahatma Gandhi's birthday), with an interesting collection of both ancient and contemporary works, housed in a pleasant, red stone building on Pantheon Road, between the two midtown areas represented by Anna Salai (Mount Road) and General Hospital Road.

Adjoining the art gallery is the infinitely more time-consuming **Government Museum** (open from 10 a.m. to 5 p.m.; closed Friday, Republic Day, and Independence Day), with its collection of bronze statues (a repetitious set of god images dating back to the 4th and 5th centuries) but also much more absorbing galleries devoted to anthropology and natural history.

Some attention should also be given to the armory in another of the galleries, devoted not only to ancient weapons but also to relics from old Indian tribes: bamboo and coconut utensils, pipes, bows and arrows, equipment for igniting fires, and musical instruments.

TOURS: City sightseeing tours are conducted daily by the **Tamil Nadu Tourism Development Corporation (TTDC)** from either 8:30 a.m. to 1:30 p.m. or 2 to 6:30 p.m. The fare is Rs. 25 ($1.90). Places covered are Fort St. George, Government Museum, Valluvar Kottam (memorial to poet Saint Tiruvallar, fashioned after a temple cart and engraved with couplets), Snake Park, Kapaleeswarar Temple, Elliot's Beach, and a drive along Marina Beach (Government Museum closed on Friday). Pickup points are the Central Railway parking area, the express bus stand (I.T.C. Esplanade), the TTDC office at 143 Anna Salai, and the India Tourist Office at 154 Anna Salai. Seats are confirmed on a first-come, first-served basis, upon payment. For information, call the TTDC (tel. 849803, 849115, or 846825) or the Government of India Tourist Office (tel. 88685 or 88686), or drop in at the addresses above.

The **India Tourism Development Corporation (IDTC)** also conducts a daily city sightseeing tour of Madras from 2 to 6 p.m. for Rs. 25 ($1.90) per person. All the sights mentioned above are covered. On Friday the Government Museum and National Gallery are closed, so the tour goes instead to the Botanical Garden and Parthasarathi Temple. For reservations, contact the IDTC at the Government of India Tourist Office, 154 Anna Salai (Mount Road; tel. 88685 or 88686), or ITDC's Reservation Counter, Express Bus Stand, Esplanade (tel. 561830).

5. Nightlife

Every day the two local papers, the *Hindu Express* and the *Indian Express* (mornings) carry a list of local entertainment. There are dozens of movie theaters—at least four or five showing English and American films regularly (movie timings are usually 3:30, 6:30, and 9:30 p.m.). Like Bombay, Madras is a filmmaking center and local Tamil-language films are, like most India-made films, romantic boy-meets-girl-loses-girl-gets-her-back or religious-theme stories. It is advisable to book movie seats in advance. In addition to films, quite often there are dance concerts of the South's beautiful classical dance, Bharata Natyam, and singing and music, most especially from mid-December into January when there city is the site of a music/dance festival. This event attracts renowned artists from all over India. Two Indian instruments, the stringed veena and the drum-like mridangam, are popular locally. Check with the Government of India Tourist Office, 154 Anna Salai, about the arts festival in season.

Hallo Madras, a monthly magazine available free at most hotels and the tourist office, contains information on current events of all kinds.

The top hotels have **bars.** And such **rooftop hotel restaurants** as the Minar at the Savera (where ghazals, North Indian songs, are sung), the Oorvasi at the Palmgrove, the Sagari at the Chola Sheraton, and the Regal at Madras International provide pretty views as well as dinners, and music too.

At the **Taj Coromandel,** in the Mysore Room there is Indian and classical music and dance in the evenings. Shows are at 8:45, 9:45, and 10:45 p.m., but double-check by telephoning 810051. At the Connemara there's a **poolside barbecue** from 7 to 11:30 p.m., with a sitar player and classical Indian music as well in the Kolam Restaurant.

Maxim's in the Hotel Imperial is one of the last remaining places in town to see **girlie shows**—the Folies-Bergère need lose no sleep over this weak imitation of Middle Eastern belly dancing, with a singer and band. There's a Rs.-30 ($2.30) entrance fee, and shows at 7:30, 9:30, and 11 p.m.

6. Useful Information

The best overall view of the city and harbor is from the 150-foot-high new **lighthouse** at the southern end of Marina Beach. Admission is Re. 1 (7½¢).

The **General Post Office,** on Anna Salai, is open from 8 a.m. to 8:30 p.m.

Best **bookstore** in town is **Higginbothams Ltd.,** 814 Anna Salai (tel. 81184), open from 8 a.m. to 7 p.m.; a branch is located in the Varsa Arcade, Fe-39 Anna Nagar East, near Chintamani Market, open the same hours. Other bookstores on Anna Salai are Kennedy Book House, Pai and Co., and M/S Krishnamurthy in Spencer's. Most of the top hotels have bookstores as well.

The **Government of India Tourist Office,** 154 Anna Salai (tel. 88685 or 88686), is open from 9 a.m. to 5 p.m. Guides can be hired from the office for about Rs. 48 ($3.70) for half a day and Rs. 72 ($5.55) for a full day. The tourist office staff is very helpful and has a good supply of booklets and maps. The tourist office maintains counters at the international airport, open according to flight timings; and at the domestic airport, open from 8 a.m. to 1 a.m.

The **Tamil Nadu Government Tourist Office,** 143 Anna Salai (tel. 840752), is open from 10 a.m. to 5 p.m., and has airport counters (open from 8:30 a.m. to 9:30 p.m.) and a Central Railway Station counter (open from 6 a.m. to 8 p.m.).

Indian Airlines is at 19 Marshalls Rd. (tel. 477977), open from 8 a.m. to 7 p.m.; **Air-India** is at the same address (tel. 47477), but open from 8:30 a.m. to 5:30 p.m. Other Indian Airlines booking offices are located in the Mena Building, 57 Dr. Radhakrishnan Rd. Mylapore (tel. 478333); 7 Umpherson St. (tel. 23321); and 57 Venkatanarayana Rd., T. Nagar (tel. 447555).

S.S. Day & Night Chemists, 106 D Block, First Main Road, Anna Nagar (tel. 615263), is a drugstore open as the name implies—day and night.

Opposite the Presidency College, at Marina, is an aquarium and **public swimming pool.**

Traveler's checks can be cashed at **Thomas Cook & Co.,** Eldorado Building, G/4-112 N. H. Road (tel. 473092), from 9:30 a.m. to 4:30 p.m., although the office stays open until 6:30 p.m.

For studying yoga or getting your horoscope cast or visiting a classical dance school, check with the tourist office. Like Florida, it's always summer in most of Tamil Nadu, with the exception of the hill resorts where it's comfortably cool.

Visa extensions are made at the Foreigners Registration Office, 9 Village Rd., Madras; Superintendent of Police, Chengaipattu (West), Kanchipuram; or S. P. Chengaipattu (East), St. Thomas Mount, Madras.

To take a break from temple splendor, make a visit to **Vedanthangal Bird**

Sanctuary, 85 km (50 miles) south of Madras, where herons and other exotic birds can be seen. It's especially fine from November to January.

The **temperature** in Madras and other lowlands never goes below 70°F and often rises to the 90s even in the winter months, which are, by the way, the most pleasant. The rainy season is June to September.

GETTING AROUND AND TO/FROM THE AIRPORTS:
P.T.C.'s **mini-coach service** plies the route between the Meenambakkam (International) Airport, Egmore Railway Station, and Indian Airlines office, for Rs. 15 ($1.15). Departures from the airport run from 5 a.m. until 10 p.m.; from Madras, departures start at 3:30 a.m. and run until 8 p.m. The mini-coach will call at hotels if informed by hoteliers well in advance (tel. 841284). The trip takes between 40 and 60 minutes. The bus for the national airport costs Rs. 15 ($1.15) to and from the airport, calling at the Indian Airlines office and various hotels.

If you're traveling light, for less than the coach you can take a **commuter train** from Egmore or Beach Station to Ninambakkan Station and walk ten minutes from there to Meenambakkam. Figure on the rates below for taxis from the airports to Madras city, but also add a flat Rs. 5 (40¢) for luggage and parking fees.

Taxis—the black-and-yellow ones—are metered and have a minimum fare of Rs. 3 (23¢) for the first 0.8 or 0.9 km or any part thereof, and go up 10 paise (1¢) for every 0.1 km thereafter, and they may charge 10 paise for every five minutes of waiting time. **Auto-rickshaws** are metered and start at Rs. 2 (15¢) per kilometer. A full day of gadding about town with a private **car and driver** costs Rs. 240 ($18.45) for up to 90 km. Check with the India Tourism Development Corporation (ITDC) at the booking counters at either Government of India Tourist Office, 154 Anna Salai, Madras (tel. 88685 or 88686) or the Express Bus Stand, Esplanade (Parry's Corner; tel. 23830).

Both state **buses** and Tiruvalluvar Transport Corporation buses run in Madras. State buses are cheaper. Schedules at the bus stand are most frequently in Tamil, but there's always someone around to translate for you. For a telescopic view of local and express bus routes within Tamil Nadu and to other states, and train timings, check the monthly *Hallo Madras* (see "Nightlife") or the Tuesday and Friday *The Hindu* and *Indian Express* newspapers, or for more extensive information, buy the *Madras City Tourist Guide*.

GETTING TO MADRAS:
Madras is served by international **flights** of Air-India, Air Lanka, and the Malaysian Airlines System. In fact, there is a gateway discount on Indian Airlines of 30% for Madras (as well as Tiruchirappalli and Trivandrum) passengers originating in Sri Lanka or the Maldives. Be sure to inquire about this if you are booking your flight from either place. Flights from all points in India fly to the domestic terminal: from Delhi, it costs Rs. 1,428 ($110); from Bangalore Rs. 285 ($22); from Bombay, Rs. 949 ($73); from Calcutta, Rs. 1,201 ($92.40).

From Delhi, the best **train** is the *Tamil Nadu Express,* departing three times a week for a 30-hour trip of 2,195 km (1,340 miles) to Madras Central, at Rs. 563 ($43.30) in first class and Rs. 126 ($9.70) in second class; the daily train from Delhi is the *Grand Trunk Express,* also to Madras Central. From Bombay, the *Dadar Madras Express* takes about 26 hours to cover 1,279 km (780 miles), for Rs. 380 ($29.25) in first-class and Rs. 91 ($7) in second. From Ernakulam, on the *West Coast Express* and other trains it's a 700-km (425-mile) trip, made in about 13 hours, for Rs. 236 ($18.15) in first class and Rs. 58 ($4.45) in second. From Bangalore, the *Brindavan Express* covers the distance of 362 km (220 miles) in about six hours, as do the *Bangalore Express* and other trains, for Rs. 141 ($10.85) in first class and Rs. 35 ($2.70) in second.

At Madras Central Station there's a general inquiry telephone number for train information other than arrival times (tel. 563535) and to make current reservations (tel. 567585); there are also special numbers to make reservations for broad-gauge (BG) and meter-gauge (MG) first-class seats (tel. 566545); for second class, BG (tel. 564455); and for MG (tel. 563344). Egmore Station also has numbers for general inquiries and current reservations (tel. 566565), MG first-class inquiries and reservations (tel. 564010), second-class reservations (tel. 566555, 566556, or 566557). For inquiries from Madras Beach, phone 25034.

Interstate express **buses** operate frequently from Bangalore, taking 8¼ hours, for Rs. 33.50 ($2.60); from Ernakulam (Cochin), nine hours, for Rs. 76.30 ($5.85); from Trivandrum, 12½ hours, for Rs. 80 ($6.15). Within Tamil Nadu, bus connections can be made from Madurai, about nine hours, for Rs. 38 ($2.90); from Ooty, about 14 hours, for Rs. 40.20 ($3.10); from Tanjore, about ten hours, Rs. 29.70 ($2.30). From Trichy, there are buses nearly every half hour starting at 3 a.m. until 11:30 p.m. for the ten-hour trip, for Rs. 27.20 ($2.10) or Rs. 27.70 ($2.15), depending on the route. These are only a few of the bus routes to Madras.

7. An Excursion to Kanchipuram and Mamallapuram (Mahabalipuram)

The major—and virtually indispensable—excursion from Madras is to the coastal village of Mamallapuram (Mahabalipuram) and the small town of Kanchipuram, which are famous for their memories of the Pallavas, a dynasty that ruled this part of India more than 1,000 years ago. The latter town, which is still filled with well-preserved temples, was their capital, while the fishing village of Mamallapuram (Mahabalipuram) was their port and today is visited to see the ancient monuments of the Pallavas and as a relaxing resort.

There are two trains a day to Kanchi (as it is called for short), and buses from Madras almost every half hour, the trip taking two hours. There are several buses each day to the Mamallapuram (Mahabalipuram) port too. For the visitor on a leisurely schedule, it might be very pleasant to spend a quiet night there, returning to Madras after a day or so.

It is also possible to join the daily ITDC or a TTDC conducted tour for Rs. 70 ($5.40) in an air-conditioned coach, Rs. 50 ($3.85) non-air-conditioned. The ITDC tour leaves at 7:30 a.m. and returns at 6 p.m. TTDC leaves at 6:30 a.m. and returns at 6 p.m.

KANCHIPURAM: Kanchi is a typically rural town of southern India. The mud streets are dotted with groups of people winding and sorting colored thread—this is a big weaving center—amid a kaleidoscope of animals, women carrying brass pots to the well, cycle rickshaws, and holy men with ash-covered faces.

It's a very holy town, in fact one of the group of seven holy places that an ardent Indian pilgrim will try to cover on his crusade around India. Most of the temples were built by the Pallavas in the 8th century and, although time and the weather have chipped away their ancient carvings, they are still spendidly decorated with, as in the case of the **Kailasanatha Temple**, some traces of the ancient colorings. At this place in particular (but also at many others) you'll encounter a self-appointed priestly guardian who'll suggest a donation for temple funds in return for illuminating the interior sculptures.

The most interesting temple is **Ekambareswara,** dating from a later period, with its 188-foot-high gopuram, or ornamental tower. This is decorated in steps with excellently carved blue and yellow figures and stands beside a small stone pool in which the neighborhood women wash their clothes. A larger tank, however, behind the main hall of the compound, is much more the center of action. Here, half a dozen small boys carrying buckets of puffed rice will urge their attentions on you. For 10 paise (½¢) they'll tip a measure of the rice into your hands and accompany you down the steps of the tank to feed the fish. Beside the bottom step the water is so thick with these small fish that it seems all you need to do is reach in a hand to pick one out. They're too fast for the average visitor, but easy for the boys to catch barehanded. They're always tossed back into the water, though. The building flanking the tank is held up by scores of stone pillars, all intricately carved.

Visitors usually include a third temple in their tour, the one dedicated to **Varadarajaswamy,** scene of an annual pilgrimage. Built in the 12th century, its main hall, also adjoining a holy tank, is supported by enormous pillars, each carved from a separate rock. The pillars are covered with a wealth of tableaux: horsemen, lions, and even a man carrying what must have been one of the earliest-known rifles. The extreme right-hand pillar nearest the tank does have one especial curiosity: a tableau of three men with four legs between them but carved in such a way that it seems each man has two legs.

Most of the weaving in Kanchi is of the cottage-industry type, with several looms in one house operated as a family business. If you visit one of the homes (and this can be arranged either through the Madras Tourist Office or by asking at one of Kanchi's sari stores), you're likely to see two barefoot boys sitting at a small loom with such an intricate array of threads, strings, wooden bars, slats, and metal weights that it takes several days to set it up for production of the particular design. Working almost as fast as the eye can see, the boys dexterously pass the shuttle under and over the taut threads, the bare toes of the operator manipulating the strands. Working together, a pair of weavers can complete a sari in about 15 days, including the time for setting up. For this, the retail price in the stores is Rs. 500 ($38.46) or more. You're better off buying in Madras.

Very few tourists stay in Kanchipuram overnight, but if you'd like to, there's the TTDC's **Hotel Tamil Nadu** (tel. 2561) in a pleasant little garden. It has only a few rooms, with attached bathrooms. Single occupancy costs Rs. 75 ($5.75) to Rs. 100 ($7.70); double occupancy is Rs. 100 ($7.70) to Rs. 125 ($9.60). For reservations, go through the TTDC in Madras.

Those deeply interested in South India's glorious heritage will want to continue on 70 miles (115 km) west of Kanchipuram to **Vellore,** site of a well-preserved 16th-century Vijaynagar Fort housing a handsome temple from the same period. Both state buses and expresses run by Tiruavallur Transport Corporation from Madras to Kanchipuram go on to Vellore.

En route from Madras to Mamallapuram (Mahabalipuram), or as an excursion itself, on the Muttukkadu Road, beyond Thirumanuyar, lies the **Cholamandal Artists' Village and Work Center,** a short distance from Adayar, developed by artists for artists. A large number of sculptors and painters live here today, and their works are on display and for sale.

You may, however, be wise to make your sculpture purchases in Mamallapuram (Mahalbalipuram). There you will find numerous artisans, chipping and hammering away at stone blocks to create souvenirs inspired by the local landmarks, and hoping that you will want to buy their wares.

MAMALLAPURAM (MAHABALIPURAM): At Mamallapuram (Mahabalipuram), the sights to be seen are a famous temple on the beach, a group of enormous carved monuments called rathas, some rock-cut cave temples, and what is said to be the largest bas-relief in the world.

Entering the village, the first thing that catches the newcomer's eye is a bunch of enormous rocks casually strewn around the landscape. One of them, often referred to as **Krishna's Butterball,** is a tremendous egg-shaped rock which at first appears to be balanced precariously on the hillside but has actually been stationary there for several hundred years. At least a thousand years ago there was a big tidal wave in these parts, which may account for the random position of some of these stones. It's known that the wave washed away several of the seashore temples, but one attractive temple remains right on the beach, the waves lapping against its surrounding walls. This **Shore Temple,** surrounded by about a score of big stone bulls, contains a few stone carvings, but the walls of the temple itself are also sculpted, and its charm lies more in its location than its content.

Up until recent years, Mamallapuram (Mahabalipuram) was isolated and almost unvisited, its temples and monuments forgotten or ignored. It had once been a busy port but was now merely a small fishing village so remote that visitors could get there only by boat or on foot from the nearest road. Then the town was "rediscovered" and now tourists not only come to sightsee but also to stay. It's a charming little place with a vast unused beach and attractive accommodations right beside the sea.

The major attraction is the group of five blocks of stone called **rathas.** They were carved in the form of temple chariots by the Pallavas and named after five Pandava princes' wives (Yudhishtira, Bhima, Arjuna, Nakula, and Sahadeva). Each of the rathas is carved, decorated, sculpted, and hollowed out so that it seems more like a decorated building than a work of art carved from solid rock. Adjoining the group are three life-size animals—a lion facing north, an elephant south, and a bull on the eastern side.

Back inside the town is a **lighthouse** (not open for climbing), but behind it on the hill is a much older lighthouse which was once a Shiva temple and is heavily carved. Naturally, from the ledge surrounding it there is a panoramic view of the town and the beach.

Down a few steps, around and under the lighthouse, is what's known as the **Mahishasuramardini Mandapam** (cave), in which is carved the legendary story of the fight between the goddess Durga, mounted on a lion, and the evil buffalo-headed demon.

Down below, at the side of the main road, is another cave, the **Krishna Mandapam,** in which is carved a lovely pastoral scene of a man milking a cow plus other aspects of rural life.

Not far away from this is the famous bas-relief known as **Arjuna's Penance.** This is a huge boulder—part of the cliff face—that is 90 feet long and 30 feet high. Carved on it are more than 400 beautiful figures, including an old hermit, arms outstretched, doing penance; a standing cat, paws outstretched, mimicking the old man; a deer scratching its face with its hind leg; elephants sheltering baby elephants; and a host of gods, snakes, lions, leopards, monkeys, and mice. Down through the center of the panel is a natural gap representing the Ganges and through which, it is believed, water once flowed.

To wind up your Mamallapuram (Mahabalipuram) sightseeing, stop at the **Government College of Architecture and Sculpture,** near the Youth Hostel, where you can see how students are trained in the various aspects of temple art and architecture, according to ancient traditional methods. On display is an exhibit of student sculpture.

For a worthwhile side trip, accessible by bus from Mamallapuram (Mahabalipuram) and about 17 km (10 miles) inland, there is calm and peaceful **Thirukkazhukundram (Thirukalikunram).** The name means "hill of the sacred kites" (in this case birds, not playthings), and sights include a hilltop temple where around noon every day two sacred kites come to get lunch from the hands of the temple priest. This practice is believed to have been started ages ago, and according to legend the two birds are saints in disguise and on their way south to Rameswaram from Varanasi.

Back on the road to Madras, about four kilometers from the main monuments is **Tiger's Cave,** an ancient open-air theater where performances were held for Pallava royalty. Farther on a few kilometers you'll see a big sign for the **Crocodile Bank,** where there are endangered species of Indian crocodile. More accurately, it's a savings bank, for it was set to breed and restore rare crocodile species. Entry fee is Re. 1 (7½¢); hours are 8:30 a.m. to 5:30 p.m. daily. Buses to and from Madras drop you near both the Tiger's Cave and the Crocodile Bank.

Where to Stay Around Mamallapuram (Mahabalipuram)

About 12 miles (19 km) south of Madras on the Bay of Bengal is **VGP Golden Beach Resort,** East Coast Road, Enjambakkam Village, Madras 600041 (tel. 412893), a vast resort-park attended by some 300 staff. The 60 landscaped acres are dotted with fantasy pavilions, sculptures, and a 60-foot waterfall. For casual visitors who want to look around, there's an Rs. 10 (75¢) to Rs. 15 ($1.15) entry fee, deductible from charges for any food purchased on the premises. Both the lounge, which has handsomely carved support beams, and the restaurant are separate from the accommodations. These are mainly in cottages raised on stilts of concrete or bamboo nestled in groves of casuarina trees. Another design is fanciful—a well-appointed landlocked yacht, surrounded by a canal. Inside the yacht, you look out portholes at the sea as if you were on a voyage. Rates for the ship cottage are Rs. 750 ($57.70); other accommodations start at Rs. 85 ($6.55) non-air-conditioned, and include cottages for Rs. 150 ($11.55) up to Rs. 650 ($50), and a range of prices between.

Cultural performances are presented in an open auditorium which is flanked by torch-shaped pillars; there is a meditation hall, health club, and shops. About a kilometer away is Cholamandal Artists' Village, mentioned earlier. From Madras city buses (route 19) go out here every 15 minutes, in case you just want to look around.

The elegant and pricey place to stay is the **Fisherman's Cove,** on Covelong Beach, Chingleput District, (tel. 474849) a Taj Group hotel. The tasteful decor features vegetable-dye prints of mythological figures. In the main building are 42 rooms with all the amenities and South Indian decor. Beyond the main building are 28 cottages on the beach, 10 of them nestled right in the dunes. A band plays on Saturday nights in the Tropicana Restaurant, which has woven tapestries with ferns on them on the walls; barbecues are held on Saturday and Sunday. There's a freshwater swimming pool, and bicycle and walking tours are organized to the nearby sights such as the Crocodile Bank and village. Rates are Rs. 450 ($34.60) to Rs. 500 ($38.45) for single occupancy of a room, Rs. 525 ($40.40) to Rs. 575 ($44.25) for double. Cottages cost Rs. 500 ($38.45) to Rs. 550 ($42.30) single, and Rs. 575 ($44.25) to Rs. 625 ($48.05) double. In Christmas season, December 15 to February 28, it's Rs.

650 ($50) for rooms and cottages, single or double. Catamaran rides are offered for refreshing recreation.

Yeshwant Veecumsee, the jovial and hospitable owner of **Silversands,** Mamallapuram (Mahabalipuram), Madras, 603104 (tel. 04-113-228, 282, or 284; or 477444 in Madras), was a pioneer, opening this, the first resort out this way, in 1968 with six simple thatched-roof cottages. Now greatly expanded, it includes 55 circular huts and Silverinn, an economy-priced annex for budgeteers. The huts, topped with thatched roofs, are rather primitive in appearance outside, but charming. Inside they have such sophisticated amenities as attached bathrooms, refrigerators, radios, and in some, air conditioning and television. The rates read like a short novella, with several different prices for various rooms and times of year—off-season, low, high, and peak. They can run anywhere from Rs. 35 ($2.70) to Rs. 110 ($8.45) for a basic clean economy-block room in off- to peak seasons, and from a low of Rs. 80 ($6.15) for a non-air-conditioned cottage in off-season to a high of Rs. 620 ($47.70) for a beach villa seafront suite in peak season, December and January. There's a delightful waterfront restaurant serving delicious seafood and a separate vegetarian kitchen.

On Monday and Friday there are classical Indian dance concerts for Rs. 25 ($1.90); on Wednesday there are free music concerts, and open-air barefoot dancing every night. Airport transfers are free of charge for a minimum of a three-day stay. Free transportation is also offered between Silversands and other resorts, as well as to Mamallapuram and the village. For those wishing to make this their base, there are tours of Madras for Rs. 80 ($6.15) and various other places, such as Pondicherry, at Rs. 150 ($11.55), available to guests.

For those in transit, in Madras there's Transit House, 26 Venkataraman St., T. Naggar, Madras 600017 (tel. 441346). From Madras, buses plying routes 119A and 19C go to Silversands.

The swimming pool setting at **Ideal Beach Resort** (tel. 240 or 243), with its gazebo to one end and statues here and there, could be an Indian film set—and indeed it is often used as a location by Madras filmmakers. The Ideal itself is a pleasant, friendly family-run resort with the cheerful, friendly P. M. Dharmalingam and his wife, son, and daughter-in-law seeing that guests are happy and well looked after. When I stopped in there were 16 clean, simple rooms and the owner was about to add 10 more, to make 26 and his limit. He wants his hotel to remain small and cozy so guests get personal attention. Rates for non-air-conditioned rooms are Rs. 125 ($9.60) single and Rs. 143 ($11) double; air-conditioned rooms cost Rs. 200 ($15.40) single and Rs. 225 ($17.30) double. Each has a bathroom attached. The hotel serves both vegetarian and nonvegetarian foods.

Golden Sun Hotel and Beach Resort (tel. 245 or 246) has an open reception hall supported by pillars and archways covered with trailing bougainvillea. This is a simple place, favored by Russian tour groups. The hotel rooms are cheerful, with basic furniture, attached bathrooms, and straw matting on the floors. The stone cottages tend to be dark inside and have an unattractive dump behind them. Rates are Rs. 210 ($16.15) single and Rs. 260 ($20) double.

Only a kilometer from the ancient shore temple, the air-conditioned **Temple Bay Ashok Beach Resort,** ITDC Shore Cottages, Mamallapuram 603104 (tel. 251 to 257), has well-appointed stone cottages equipped with sundecks, refrigerators, and kitchenettes, and also nicely appointed rooms with simple modern furniture in the central building. The dining room is in the main building. There's a swimming pool and an extensive garden. Rates run Rs. 375 ($28.85) single and Rs. 465 ($35.75) double in the hotel; in the cottages, Rs. 330 ($25.40) single and Rs. 425 ($32.70) double.

Nearby is the **Shore Temple Beach Resort** (tel. 235), a group of cottages, some bearing a resemblance to a modern version of old English rowhouses and the others with the look of American Indian tepees. The newest cottages are the best, and good value for the price: Rs. 80 ($6.15) single and Rs. 100 ($7.70) double in the older cottages, non-air-conditioned; Rs. 115 ($8.85) to Rs. 125 ($9.60) in the new cottages without air conditioning, and Rs. 200 ($15.40) to Rs. 250 ($19.25) with air conditioning. A vegetarian thali buffet costs Rs. 8 (60¢).

Clean, basic, and a bargain right in Mamallapuram are the spartan rooms at **Mamalla Bhavan** (tel. 250), at Rs. 30 ($2.30) for a double. Rooms have bathrooms attached and face the sea so you get the cool breezes. The one hitch is that this place is often booked up. Delicious South Indian meals in the restaurant run Rs. 3.50 (27¢) to Rs. 7 (55¢). Cheerful bearer Raju enjoys serving guests the best South Indian coffee in the village.

The **Youth Hostel,** near the Sculpture Training Institute, offers 40 beds for Rs. 10 (75¢) per, cottages for Rs. 50 ($3.85), and a deluxe cottage for Rs. 70 ($5.40). Bare and spare but clean and a good buy.

There are a few lodges—Royal and Pallava are two of them—to be tried if everything else is full. After seeing some of them, I believe you'd be better off camping out at the Temple Bay Ashok Beach camping grounds—provided you're properly equipped. But first check with Temple Bay's reception. Don't just plunk your gear down. Hotel security does not welcome uninvited guests.

Eating Out

Try the Mammala Bhavan's delicious South Indian thali for Rs. 8 (60¢), or the Shore Temple Resort's similarly priced thali buffet.

Tours

From Madras, the **TTDC** (tel. 848803) offers a daily tour, from 6:30 a.m. to 6:30 p.m., which includes Kanchipuram and Mamallapuram as well as Tirukazhukundram and the Crocodile Bank, for Rs. 70 ($5.40) air-conditioned and Rs. 50 ($3.85) non-air-conditioned. The **ITDC** (tel. 88685) offers a similar daily tour from 7:30 a.m. to 6 p.m. for the same price. For splurgers, a trip from Madras to the points above, returning on the same day, in a small non-air-conditioned car with a driver will run about Rs. 480 ($36.90).

Information

The **Government of Tamil Nadu** has a tourist office on East Raja Street (tel. 32), near the post office and bus stand.

Getting to Mamallapuram

The Tamil Nadu State Transport bus 19A takes off about every 30 minutes from 6:30 a.m. to 8:30 p.m. from the Central Bus Stand; the trip takes 2½ hours.

Chapter XII

SOUTHERN INDIA: TAMIL NADU

1. Pondicherry and the City of the Future
2. Towering Temples from Chidambaram to Tiruchirapalli
3. Madurai
4. Kanya Kumari (Cape Comorin)
5. Udhagamandalam (Ootacamund)

BEYOND THE UNION TERRITORY of Pondicherry lies the Dravidian southland of Tamil Nadu which remained relatively unaffected by foreign incursions. A pleasant place with a leisurely pace, its land is green-spangled with rice paddies cooled by palms. But the memory that remains most vividly about this part of India are the templed cities of long past dynasties whose rulers were undoubtedly among the world's greatest temple builders. Like much of India, the splendid temples present the visitor with a surfeit of riches. It is necessary, therefore, to be selective to see even some of them. Now to cover these centuries, let's start with French-accented Pondicherry, then dig deeper into the past and end with the ghost of the Raj in the hill station of Udhagamandalam (Ootacamund).

Pondicherry (pop. 444,000), a union territory, was developed by the French who relinquished their rule in the 1950s, but it still bears the unmistakable stamp of a sleepy French colonial town.

The coconut palms of the Coromandel coast fringe the community right up to the seafront and the roar of the waves is a perpetual accompaniment to all who stay or pass by the eastern side of the town.

1. Pondicherry and the City of the Future

Except during the winter monsoon season, Pondicherry slumbers under an almost constant sun, its streets tranquil but humid. There are few cars, so cycle rickshaws are the major means of getting around. The famous Tamil poet Bharathiar lived here, and later came Sri Aurobindo, a young revolutionary turned yogi, whose ashram is now the town's major attraction.

WHERE TO STAY: Many people who visit Pondicherry want to stay in the two guest accommodations run by the Aurobindo Ashram. The first is the **Park Guest House,** on Goubert Salai, (tel. 4412), with 75 small, neat, monastic rooms and dorms next to the town beach. These rent for Rs. 100 ($7.70) with attached bath and Rs. 15 ($1.15) per person in the dorm. Vegetarian meals are served. The **International Guest House,** Gingy Salai (tel. 6699), is a pretty, three-story modern building with a profusion of potted plants and 57 clean, simple rooms with attached Western-style bathrooms and fans overhead to stir the breezes. Rates are Rs. 30 ($2.30) to Rs. 50 ($3.85) double.

Other places to stay include the **Aristo Guest House,** 50-A Mission St., Pondicherry 605001 (tel. 6728). It's clean, has a friendly management, and is one flight up off the street. Rooms cost Rs. 40 ($3.05) for singles and Rs. 50 ($3.85) for doubles without air conditioning, Rs. 100 ($7.70) single and Rs. 125 ($9.60) double with air conditioning. All have bathrooms attached.

For old French atmosphere, there's the **Grand Hotel d'Europe,** which has no phone or air conditioning and was opened in 1891 by the current owner's father. There are six rooms with private bathrooms costing Rs. 160 ($12.30) to Rs. 200 ($15.40), plus a 10% service charge. In the bar/dining room, made-to-order French food is served; lunch or dinner costs Rs. 65 ($5). Transients can eat these meals here also, but must order at least two hours in advance.

The new **Hotel Ajanta,** 15 Zamidar Gardens, Pondicherry 605001 (tel. 5727), has eight air-conditioned and eight non-air-conditioned rooms, all with attached bathrooms, and four with Indian-style toilets in them. There's a 24-hour coffeeshop, an air-conditioned restaurant, and an open-air roof garden. Rooms cost Rs. 60 ($4.60) non-air-conditioned, Rs. 100 ($7.70) air-conditioned.

Wallpapered and linoleum walls are to be seen at the **Ram International,** 212 West Blvd. (tel. 7230), where rooms have attached bathrooms with either Western- or Indian-style toilets. No-frills, non-air-conditioned rooms are Rs. 45 ($3.45) single and Rs. 70 ($5.40) double; air-conditioned rooms go for Rs. 90 ($6.90) single Rs. 110 ($8.45) double.

Hotel Mass, Maraimalai Adigal Salai, Pondicherry 605001 (tel. 7067), is centrally air-conditioned, and could use a paint job to spruce up the walls. Rooms have modern furniture and rent for Rs. 120 ($9.25) single, Rs. 160 ($12.30) double; a mirrored honeymoon suite costs Rs. 180 ($13.85). A so-called disco operates in the restaurant at night (see below).

The **Government Tourist Home,** Uppalam Road (tel. 3376), is right behind the railroad station (turn right, then right again, and walk across the tracks). It's a modern three-story building in its own small compound, with airy balconies and eight single and six double rooms, two air-conditioned—and all fairly clean and simple. There's a dining room. Rooms, complete with fans and bathrooms, cost Rs. 25 ($1.90) single and Rs. 50 ($3.85) double; air-conditioned rooms go for Rs. 80 ($6.15).

The same rates apply at the **Tourist Home Annex,** Indra Nagar (tel. 6145), in the suburbs near the hospital, with balconies overlooking a palm grove. There are 12 doubles (one air-conditioned, one air-conditioned deluxe) and 26 singles, fairly clean, with a small canteen for simple meals.

The most dramatic sea views and sunsets can be seen from the roof of the **Youth Hostel,** Solaithandavankuppan (tel. 3495), north of the city, five kilometers from bus stand and railway station. There are 45 beds in six dorms for Rs. 8 (60¢) per person, Rs. 5 (40¢) for Indian students and members. Sheets are provided, and there are kitchens for food preparation. For Rs. 50 ($3.85) you can hire a stove and cooking implements.

WHERE TO EAT AND A BIT OF NIGHTLIFE: Very pleasant and popular is the **Hotel** (meaning restaurant) **Aristo,** 36/E Nehru St. (tel. 6728), run by the Aristo Guest House. Both the roof garden and indoor restaurant serve well-prepared, decently priced food in Indian, Chinese, and Western styles. Rs. 15 ($1.15) is a top-priced entree; vegetarian meals, Rs. 8 (60¢). The softly lit **Bon Ami Restaurant,** 22 Rue St. Louis (tel. 4457), is closed on Tuesday, but otherwise serves an array of nonvegetarian foods in the same price range as the Aristo.

Spencer's runs the **Fiesta Seaside Café,** off Goubert Avenue, near the Park Guest House and overlooking the new pier. The terrace is pleasant, the indoors stuffy, and the prices a bit steep for Pondicherry: Rs. 20 ($1.55) for entrees in the usual Western, Indian, and Chinese styles; Rs. 10 (75¢) for a dish of vegetarian curry. Hours are 10 a.m. to 10 p.m.

For cheap snacks and coffee, there are two Indian **coffeehouses,** one across from the Aristo and the other on Beach Road, where hot coffee is 80 paise (6¢), and toast and jam or masala dosa are Rs. 1.40 (11¢).

At the **Hotel Mass,** Maraimalai Adigal Salai (tel. 7067), there's a buffet from 7 p.m. to midnight—Rs. 35 ($2.70) vegetarian and Rs. 65 ($5) to Rs. 70 ($5.40) nonvegetarian—and a disco-dancing floor show, at Rs. 30 ($2.30) including a complimentary soft drink, where you see belly dancing and disco dancing performed on a wood floor with glass-lighted panels. There are two shows nightly, 7 to 8:30 p.m. and 9 to 10:30 p.m. Despite the town's French background, this show has no savoir-faire.

Ratna Talkies show English-language **films,** as do some other theaters. There are **bars** at the Grand Hotel d'Europe and the Rama International.

FOR SOME HELP AND A TOUR: Before you begin your visit, you'll want to stop in at the **Tourist Information Bureau,** Rue de la Compagnie, Secretariat Building (tel. 4575), open from 8:45 a.m. to 1 p.m. and 2 to 5:45 p.m., to get pamphlets and a map. The bureau also runs a minibus tour to the ashram and around town, from 9 a.m. to noon or from 2 to 5 p.m. for Rs. 10 (75¢), providing a minimum of five people show up. You will also want to call at **La Boutique d'Auroville,** 12 J. Nehru St., Pondicherry, for information on visiting Auroville.

SEEING THE TOWN: The heart and soul of Pondicherry is the **Sri Aurobindo Ashram,** focal point for pilgrims not only from India but from all parts of the world. It is an unusual ashram in the sense that its buildings are spread all over the town, and some of its businesses provide employment and services for other residents of Pondicherry. It includes, for example, its own laundry, perfumery, printing press, and travel agency, as well as bakery, tailors, furniture factory, oil mill, and handmade paper workshop. The ashram also sponsors cultural and educational activities in the community.

While few dispute the worthwhile contributions made to the community by the ashram, many believe it has become too powerful and ingrown, and urge more outside participation in the group's affairs.

In the Education Centre of the ashram, almost every evening you can go to a film, slide presentation, or lecture. Tourists, residents at the ashram, and local people can attend these programs, which are usually without charge. You might be asked for a donation, but you won't be hounded.

The founder of this movement, which combines the two disciplines of yoga and science, Sri Aurobindo, was born August 15, 1872, in Calcutta. Educated at Cambridge, England, he became a writer and revolutionary in the extremist wing of the Indian Independence Movement early in the century. Jailed by the British in 1908 for his involvement in a bomb plot, he studied yoga and meditation during his year in prison and by 1910 was in Pondicherry continuing his silent divinations and rejecting political overtures from the increasingly active independence parties. He died on December 5, 1950, but his philosophical essays, translated into many languages, influence and inspire many people today.

On the other hand, the woman who became known as the Mother of the Sri Aurobindo Religious Movement was born Mira Alfassa, in Paris, to wealthy parents of Egyptian ancestry. From her earliest days she was exposed to different spiritual and religious systems.

In 1914 she accompanied her second husband, Paul Richard, a French diplomat, on a journey to India and had an audience with Sri Aurobindo. The meeting changed the course of Mira Richard's life.

She left India when World War I broke out, but returned, alone, six years later. When Sri Aurobindo went into seclusion in 1926, the Mother, as she was then called by all, took complete charge of the ashram and all activities, encouraging its economic independence. She remained as head of the ashram until her death, at age 95, on November 17, 1973. Nolini Kant Gupta, oldest disciple of Sri Aurobindo, succeeded the Mother.

All during the late Mother's life, everyone connected with the ashram in any way, and many of the people in the town, regarded her with reverence. When problems or doubts arose, it was automatically assumed by all that the late Mother could solve them. Also a prolific writer, her widely translated essays have influenced people throughout the world. At her death, thousands of mourners streamed into the ashram to pay their final respects to this remarkable woman.

The Samadhi (Meditation Place) of Sri Aurobindo and the Mother (in which their bodies are now entombed) is open to all visitors between 8 a.m. and 6 p.m. daily.

If there are enough visitors, the Reception Service in the main building will arrange a conducted tour of the ashram, any day but Sunday, "darshan days" (blessing), and other special days. The tour starts at 8 a.m. and in two hours covers the highlights. The Mother's meditation chamber can be seen at 11:30 a.m. for 15 minutes, but only by appointment.

AUROVILLE: To carry its experiment in international harmony further, during the Mother's lifetime there was conceived the idea of an international city in which people from all races and nationalities could live and work together. The new city, Auroville ("City of Dawn"), was greatly hailed in 1968 at its ground-breaking: the president of India and dignitaries from around the world attended and brought soil for an urn to symbolize the city's high ideals of harmony. From the initial dedication ceremony, you can see today the crater-shaped amphitheater with a lotus center containing the earth from the 125 countries participating in the inauguration festivities.

In the original design (seen at the settlement's Auromodel) by French architect Roger Anger, the 800-acre city spirals out from a center core into five main zones: work, dwelling, education, society, and the world. While there was to be light industry, Auroville has remained as envisioned—in close contact with nature, with plentiful planting of fruit orchards and other food crops, now to be seen along with a blend of modern architectural styles.

As the first settlers came from France, England, the Netherlands, and North America, funds were contributed to the community by the central and state governments and by UNESCO. Work then began on the "soul of Auroville," the golden spherical Matri Mandir ("concentration" hall—beyond the usual meditation and symbolizing the birth of the new consciousness) and continues today, along with agriculture, energy, and other developmental projects.

From the beginning, the settlers faced considerable challenges, lack of energy resources and soil erosion major among them. To solve the most formidable problems, they constructed windmills and a solar reflector for energy, and planted more than a million trees on 2,000 acres as a land-reclamation project. Giant steps since then have been taken to set up such essential services as schools and a health center to satisfy the needs of the residents living in the settlement. Contributing to further self-sufficiency are successful income-producing ventures in computer sciences and handcrafts. The well-designed handcrafts are sold in La Boutiques in Auroville and Pondicherry, and shops in the major cities of India. La Boutique d'Auroville in Bhara Nivas is open from 9 a.m. to 1 p.m. and 3 to 5:30 p.m.

Presently, the city which was to have housed 50,000 has about 1,000 residents living in 14 settlements, and remains in a largely unfinished state. Much of the delay in development can be traced to the long conflict which began soon after the Mother's death in 1973, and pitted the Sri Aurobindo Society and Auroville's residents against each other in a battle for control of the new community. The society claimed it owned the land and therefore the town on it; and indeed it did control the funds, which it often delayed and eventually refused to transfer to Auroville. Thus work had to be severely curtailed and ultimately stopped for a while. It has been resumed again.

The people in Auroville, recalling the Mother's word, insisted that Auroville was a "city of the world, belonging to everyone." The society continued its attack by charging that drug abuse (actually, drugs and alcohol are not permitted) and promiscuous sex at Auroville vilified the Mother's ideals. To this the Aurovillians counterattacked by accusing the society of misusing funds intended for the new city. When word of the wrangling spread around, fundraising efforts, and therefore outside funds, greatly declined.

Despite the conflict's escalation, the Aurovillians managed to get by for a time by pooling their resources and doing some successful outside fundraising. But ultimately the situation between the two factions grew so grave that in 1976, the ambassadors of the United States, France, and Germany stepped in to provide food and supplies to the residents. Soon after this occurrence the central government took over Auroville temporarily, and today it is governed out of Pondicherry. When this ends, no one is certain who will be next in command, but the residents seem determined on the success of their idealistic experiment, whatever the future holds.

Staying at Auroville

Some residents will take in guests for fees of Rs. 30 ($2.30) to Rs. 50 ($3.85) per day per person. Reservations should be made in advance by writing the Secretariat, Auroville Trust, Auroville 605104, Kottakuppam, India. Mention if you require staying with someone who speaks English. Student housing located in Aspiration is simple, pleasant, and clean, with a bed mat and mosquito netting, for Rs. 20 ($1.55). A French student said that he enjoyed the good meals for Rs. 5 (40¢) and the Bharata Natyam performance he saw during his visit.

Snacking at Auroville

There's a food store (open from 10 a.m. to noon) at Auroville where you can buy cardamom-scented tea, lassi, lemon juice for lemonade sweetened as you wish, homemade macaroons, and other biscuits. The kitchen, open from 1 to 2 p.m., feeds residents primarily, and occasionally five or six visitors—but don't count on it. If you plan to be out here a while, you might want to bring some fruit or another foods to nibble on.

Getting Around Auroville

The first thing to do is to stop at La Boutique d'Auroville, on J. Nehru

Street, to get advice on visiting. You can also set up a tour and get information on where to rent bikes or hire taxis or rickshaws. Whatever transport you arrange to get there, keep it while you're looking around; the distances are too great to cover on foot and you'll need some way to return.

As to biking, keep in mind that there are miles of unpaved roads that can be hard to navigate over the beautiful rural setting—hard-going unless you're a good biker in good shape.

For bike rentals, several shops on Gingy Salai in Pondicherry, including **Jaypal Cycle Store,** Gingy Salai, ask Rs. 4 (30¢) to Rs. 5 (40¢) for a day (plus a refundable deposit of Rs. 200, $15.40). Store hours are 9 a.m. to 9:15 p.m. For the highly experienced, some shops have **mopeds,** at Rs. 14 ($1.05) to Rs. 20 ($1.55) for a day. The asking price by **auto-rickshaw** is usually Rs. 30 ($2.30) round trip, but bargain—you can probably settle for Rs. 20 ($1.55).

GETTING TO PONDICHERRY: From Madras, express **buses** leave about every 45 minutes to an hour apart (starting at 4:20 a.m. until about 10:20 p.m.) from the Central Bus Stand. The fare for the four-hour journey is Rs. 13.90 ($1.07), and if you book in advance, there's a Rs. 10 (8½¢) reservation fee. As close as you'll get by **train** is to Villupuram, but it's 38 miles (62 km) away. A car and driver will cost a minimum of about Rs. 500 ($38.45) round trip from Madras, not including the driver's overnight fee.

2. Towering Temples from Chidambaram to Tiruchirapalli

CHIDAMBARAM: From Pondicherry, a 40-mile (65-km) coastline drive south takes you back in time to the 9th-century temple at Chidambaram. This huge temple has enormous impact on visitors. It covers 32 acres of land stretching between two rivers, and has a tank measuring 315 feet by 170 feet. Two of the temple's four 160-feet-high gopurams are covered with carved figures showing the 108 poses of Indian classical dance. Indeed, the temple is dedicated to Shiva as the Cosmic Dancer.

Surrounded by high walls, within the temple are five halls. Two of these are roofed with a total of 21,600 golden tiles, each tile said to be worth Rs. 2,500 ($192.25) today, and make up the main sanctum. In this there is a statue, cast of five metals, depicting Shiva as the Cosmic Dancer. In two of his hands are the insignia of his diverse powers: the drum of creation and the flame of destruction. His left leg is raised and his right foot rests on a dwarf-like figure to represent stamping out illusions.

Of the other halls, most memorable are Rajah Sabah, the hall of 1,000 pillars, 340 feet long and 190 feet wide. This was the site of victory ceremonies held by the Pandyas, Cholas, and other rulers who helped build the temple. The other hall, Nritta Sabah, resembles a chariot and continues the dance motif on the 56 pillars covered with what some art historians believe are the most elegant and graceful dance figures in all South India. Lately this hall has been used again as in ancient times for dancing during Natyanjali, the February-March festival dedicated the Cosmic Dancer. Ask about it if your visit is during these months.

In the temple are shrines to Parvarti, Subramanian, and Ganesh. There's a temple to Vishnu as well, where he reclines on a bed of snakes.

The temple hours vary with holidays and other celebrations, but generally the main shrine is open from 5 a.m. to noon and 4 to 10 p.m. Subshrines are open from 5 to 8 p.m. The best time to visit is during any of the six daily pujas, when the temple reverberates with drums and chanting and smells sweetly of sandalwood paste and floral offerings.

Another interesting sight is the tiny Thillai Kali temple at the northern end of town, built in the 13th century by a Chola king, Kopperunjingan. The best time to visit is for the 4 p.m. puja, in which you will be allowed to participate. Hours are 9 a.m. to 1 p.m. and 3 to 6 p.m.

For an escape from temples, there's **Pichavaram,** 16 km (10 miles) east of the city—3,000 acres of backwater laced with mangrove trees. There's a snack pavilion and a government-run place to stay.

Where to Stay and Eat

The nicest place is the clean, well-run government-operated **Hotel Tamilnadu,** Station Road, Chidambaram 608001 (tel. 2323), where non-air-conditioned singles and doubles cost Rs. 30 ($2.30) to Rs. 50 ($3.85) and air-conditioned rooms go for Rs. 100 ($7.70). All have Western bathrooms attached. There's a restaurant serving simple but adequate meals.

Three other places for your consideration include the **Hotel Raja Rajan,** 162 W. Car St. (tel. 2690), which is simple, clean, and boasts of air-conditioned rooms for Rs. 100 ($7.70). Without air conditioning, singles cost Rs. 30 ($2.30) and doubles are Rs. 45 ($3.45).

P.M. Lodge, 15 S. Sanathi (tel. 2663), is fairly clean. Some top-floor rooms have good view of the temple; others are dark. Rooms cost Rs. 25 ($1.90) to Rs. 45 ($3.45) with Indian-style bathrooms.

The **Star Lodging Complex,** 101-102 S. Car St. (tel. 2743), is made up of both a lodge and a restaurant. The lodge has simple, no-nonsense rooms for Rs. 25 ($1.90) single and Rs. 35 ($2.70) double, both basic and clean. The cheerful, crowded **Star Restaurant,** with striped walls and pink marble table-tops, serves excellent vegetarian food—worth a visit while you're in town. It's Rs. 3 (23¢) for an ordinary thali, Rs. 6 (45¢) with a sweet and soft drink.

Getting to Chidambaram

Private and government **buses** operate frequently from the Central Bus Stand in Pondicherry for a 1½-hour ride, costing around Rs. 7.50 (58¢). There are also buses from Madras, Cuddalore, and elsewhere. **Trains** to the south connect with Tiruchirapalli, Madurai, and other cities, and to the north to Madras and Bangalore, to name only two.

Getting Around the Town

Auto-rickshaws are available, but you must bargain. From the Hotel Tamilnadu, expect to pay about Rs. 3 (23¢) to the bus station and Rs. 4 (30¢) to the temple. Bikes can be rented from the Hotel Tamilnadu or shops in town for Rs. 5 (40¢) a day.

Tourist Information

The **Tamil Nadu Tourist Office** is next to the Tamilnadu Hotel on Station Road (tel. 2939). It is open from 10 a.m. to 1:30 p.m. and 2 to 5:30 p.m.; closed Saturday and Sunday.

KUMBAKONAM: A temple elephant lumbers along the road as we near the next destination, Kumbakonam, 46 miles (75 km) from Chidambaram. This peaceful town at the juncture of the Cauvery and Asarlar Rivers in Tanjore district is one of the oldest in South India. A modern commercial center as well, the town has also held fast to its traditional side, as seen in the lovely copies of old jewelry displayed in shop windows.

Kumbakonam is known for its 18 temples. Four are immense and of the most importance: Kumbheswara Swamy, Sarangapani, Chakrapani, and Ramaswamy. The largest gopuram, at Sarangapani, soars 147 feet high. Look closely at the intricate jewelry on the handsomely carved figures and you'll see that it provides the inspiration for the pieces seen in the jewelry-shop windows.

The approach to Kumbheswara Temple is a wide avenue of shops thronged with shoppers and devotees. I was greeted by a great procession: everything stopped when the temple gods, dressed in silks and jeweled finery, and comfortably propped up on cushioned palanquins, were escorted by musicians sounding horns and drums as they took their charges out to call on gods at another temple.

This is a routine event. Much more excitement occurs every 12 years (last time was March 1, 1980) at the Mahamaham Tank festival. On these occasions, it is believed that the Ganges flows into the tank and thousands of devotees flock here to bear witness. The next festival will be in March 1992.

Where to Stay

The best place in town is the pleasant **Hotel A.R.R.,** no. 21 T. S. R. (Big Street), Kumbakonam 612001 (tel. 21234), with string lanterns and Diwali lamps in the lounge and a wood-paneled reception area. There are 46 rooms in all. Air-conditioned rooms are wallpapered and rent for Rs. 80 ($6.15) single and Rs. 120 ($9.25) double. Non-air-conditioned rooms are clean and basic with painted walls, and cost Rs. 50 ($3.85) single and Rs. 75 ($5.75) double. All have bathrooms attached. There are two restaurants, vegetarian and nonvegetarian, as well as a bar.

Two other accommodations barely sneak by my lowest standards. The **V.P.R. Lodge** (tel. 21949) has 45 rooms for Rs. 22 ($1.70) single, Rs. 35 ($2.70) double, and Rs. 85 ($6.55) with air conditioning (there are two). All have bathrooms attached. The rooms, while not for the fastidious, look better than might be expected from the condition of the dirty hall walls. The **Hotel New Karpagam**, T. H. S. Road (tel. 21255), has dirty walls, but clean floors in the rooms. Rates start at Rs. 10 (75¢) per person in a rudimentary dorm. Singles cost Rs. 14 ($1.05) without air conditioning to Rs. 50 ($3.85) with air conditioning; doubles run from Rs. 22 ($1.70) to Rs. 24 ($1.85) non-air-conditioned to Rs. 60 ($4.60) with air conditioning. The furniture consists of steel cots and steel folding chairs.

Eating Out

The **Hotel A.R.R.** non-air-conditioned vegetarian restaurant charges Rs. 5.50 (42¢) to Rs. 16 ($1.25) for a thali meal. Its air-conditioned nonvegetarian restaurant serves tandooris and biryanis as well as some Western dishes. The highest-priced nonvegetarian entree is about Rs. 22 ($1.70). The hotel will pack a box lunch for Rs. 20 ($1.55) vegetarian and Rs. 30 ($2.30) nonvegetarian.

Getting to Kumbakonam

There are buses and trains from both Chidambaram and from Tanjore. Kubakonam is also connected by road and rail to Trichurapalli and Madras.

Some Interesting Temples Nearby

The best way to enjoy these temples is to pack a picnic and some bottled water, strike a bargain with a taxi driver, and make a day's outing of it. Alternatively, you can base in Tanjore and visit these temples, taking into account that the drives will be longer from there.

Dharasuram is in a silk-weavers village three kilometers (1¾ miles) west of Kumbakonam. This Chola temple, now protected by the Department of Archeology, has beautiful sculptures. If you can find the caretaker, he'll show you how the granite slabs on the temple sound like the seven different tones of Karnatic music.

Swamimalai lies six kilometers (3½ miles) west of Kumbakonam and is dedicated to Lord Subramanian. The temple is at a slight elevation. Villagers here make metal statues of the deities.

Thirubuvanam, a Chola temple at Kampahareswara, eight kilometers (five miles) from Kumbakonam, is dedicated to Shiva and dates from the 13th century.

Gangaikonda Cholapuram, 32 km (19½ miles) away, was constructed in the 13th century by Rajendra Chola, a grandson of Raja Raja Chola, builder of the Brihadeshwara temple at Tanjore, and strived to be a copy of it. Its tower is visible for miles around. There are beautiful sculptures to be seen.

THANJAVUR (TANJORE):
A quiet romantic refuge almost at the delta of the Cauvery River, the pleasant town of Thanjuvar (Tanjore; pop. 184,000), in its glory days during the reign of the late Chola kings from the 10th to the 14th centuries, was a noted center of learning and culture. In the Thanajavur district are some of South India's most celebrated temples built by the Cholas, including the foregoing and others.

Tanjore is known today as the "rice bowl" of Tamil Nadu, and historically income from Tanjore's fertile paddies financed the initial Chola building sprees. They were later supplemented with funds derived through carrying on a flourishing trade with China. Later dynasties, the Nayaks and Marathas, ruled from the vast palace, which today is a library and museum, and a playground for birds enjoying games of hide and seek in the vaulted halls.

Not only rice, but fertile fields of sugarcane and bananas surround Tanjore, filling the entire district, which is best visited in winter. In January, throngs arrive for the music festival in the village of Tiruvarur, seven miles way, which celebrates the anniversary of one of South India's greatest composers, Saint Thygaraja, at the Thyagarajaswami Temple, a place of great importance for devotees of Karnatic music.

Hotels in Thanjavur

The best place to stay is the **Hotel Tamilnadu,** on Gandhi Road, Thanjavur 613001 (tel. 21421), set in a small garden and surrounded by big trees, with 32 clean rooms; bathrooms are attached to all rooms, Indian style downstairs and Western style upstairs. Most of the rooms have balconies and all have big ceiling fans. Rates for non-air-conditioned rooms are Rs. 40 ($3.05) single and Rs. 50 ($3.85) double. Air-conditioned rooms cost Rs. 80 ($6.15) single and Rs. 120 ($9.25) double. There's a restaurant for both vegetarian and nonvegetarian meals.

Tamil Nadu Tourism is now also running what was the ITDC's Ashok Travellers Lodge, renamed the **Hotel Tamilnadu II,** Vallam Road, Thanjavur 613001 (tel. 20365), out of town. In truth it needs work, and few people stay here these days. Rates are Rs. 50 ($3.85) single, Rs. 70 ($5.40) double, Rs. 120 ($9.25) if air-conditioned.

In town, the **Hotel Karthik,** 73 S. Rampart St., Thanjavur 613001 (tel. 21116), in the main market, is fairly new and offers a few air-conditioned doubles for Rs. 125 ($9.60) and ordinary singles and doubles for Rs. 30 ($2.30) to Rs. 58 ($4.45), with Indian-style bathrooms attached. Loud music is played throughout the hotel, and on top of that there's traffic noise from the street. But the rooms are a slight cut above the others in this price range.

Ashoka Lodge, 93 Abraham Pandithar St., Thanjavur 613001 (tel. 20021), in a pink, ochre, green, and blue building, has very helpful management and 76 rooms—some clean and some not too well kept. Upstairs rooms are airy and light, and so preferable; ask to see a room or two before settling in.

Rates are Rs. 20 ($1.55) single, Rs. 40 ($3.05) double, Rs. 49 ($3.75) for a deluxe double, and Rs. 15 ($1.15) per person in the dorm. It's a very busy place.

New and most expensive is the **Hotel Parisuthan,** 55 G. A. Canal Rd., Thanjavur 603001 (tel. 21456), with a waterfall at the entrance and gleaming marble floors. Everything is neat and efficient looking. Non-air-conditioned rooms are Rs. 55 ($4.25) single and Rs. 95 ($7.30) double; Rs. 110 ($8.45) single and Rs. 160 ($12.30) double, air-conditioned. A 15% increase in rates have been announced for the near future. The air-conditioned vegetarian restaurant looked pleasant (open from 7 a.m. to 11 p.m.); a nonvegetarian restaurant is planned, and should be open from noon to 2:45 p.m. for lunch and 7 to 11:45 p.m. for dinner.

Eating Out

The restaurants in the new **Hotel Parisuthan** (see above) seemed to hold promise for a splurge meal. The simple **Padma Hotel,** Ananda Bhavan, Gandhi Road opposite the Hotel Tamilnadu, is clean and cheap for tasty vegetarian foods. The same holds true for the main-floor restaurant in the **Hotel Karthik,** which makes an excellent South Indian coffee, as well as meals and snacks.

What to See Around Town

Soaring from the flat South Indian plains is the 13-tiered tower of the **Brihadeshwara Temple** (also spelled Brahadeeswara), built by the Chola emperor Rajaraja the Great in the first decade of the 11th century. Polychromed brightly in the 16th century, the temple has now been restored to its natural reddish color (thanks to sun, rain, extreme age, and loving care on the part of archeological experts). The temple is open from 6 a.m. to noon and 4 to 9 p.m. Without special permission from the archeological department in Madras, no one may enter the inner shrine, housing a huge lingam and some ancient sculptures and frescoes. These Chola wall paintings were uncovered only around 300 years ago when layers of paint the Nayaks applied were stripped away. But you can get close enough to see the 13-foot-high lingam, measuring 54 feet around its massive base and 26 feet around the top, covered with silver and floral offerings—Rs. 2 (15¢) is usually given to the priest. The doors on each side of the sanctum lead to the forbidden frescoes. However, their reproductions can be viewed in the museum adjoining the temple.

To get the full impact of the Brihadeshwara Temple, take a few minutes to sit outdoors on a stone ledge at one of the entrances. Then let the breezes restore you as you take time to contemplate the great glory of this remarkable architectural work.

Note: Should you want to try to get rare permission to see the frescoes, write to the Archeological Survey of India, Fort St. George, Madras 600001, far in advance of your visit with an excellent reason for wanting to see them. No groups are allowed.

You can wander freely (barefooted, please) in the courtyard after entering through a 90-foot-high gopuram guarded by two huge striking statues of dwarapalakas (doorkeepers).

Commanding the courtyard, facing the shrine, sits a huge image of Nandi, Shiva's sacred mount, almost 13 feet high and 16 feet long, all carved from a single block of granite. Anointed daily for centuries by the pious, the effigy now gleams as if it were made of bronze. The figures in the friezes on the pavilion are believed to be from the 16th century.

Shiva's bull sits patiently in front of the vimana, its 216-foot-high, geometric-shaped tower crowned with an invisible tympanic plate of granite (80 tons) under the dome. The Cholas, inventive engineers, had their workmen push this huge plate and dome slowly into place along an inclined ramp (as the Egyptians did with the Pyramids) which started in a village four miles away—a distance four times the length of the Golden Gate Bridge.

Northeast of the temple is the **Palace,** on a street that used to run through the **Great Fort.** It is a vast structure built mainly by the Nayaks in 1550. One of the buildings, the former armory, is 190 feet high and was used until 1885 as a military lookout. In the palace is a research and reference library (closed Wednesday), with a working library where there are more than 30,000 valuable painted palm-leaf and paper manuscripts in Indian and European languages. The expansive **Darbar Hall** (closed Thursday) is acoustically perfect.

But all other palace sights pale in comparison with the small **Art Gallery** (open daily, except national holidays), full of choice sculptures—113 in granite and 250 in bronze, dating from the 9th to the 12th centuries. Some of the best pieces in the collection were salvaged from village fields where they were abandoned when old temples fell to ruin. An excellent, if expensive, book written by the gallery's most knowledgeable staff member can give you details; it costs Rs. 270 ($20.75).

East of the palace is **Schwartz Church,** honoring Danish missionary C. V. Schwartz, and built in 1779 by Rajah Serfoji to commemorate their friendship. A fine relief of marble figures depicts the missionary's death.

Tourist Information

The **Tamil Nadu Tourist Bureau** is in Shop 3 adjacent to the Tamilnadu Hotel, open from 8 to 11 a.m. and 4 to 8 p.m. A limited supply of brochures is available, but you might want to drop in and see for yourself.

Shopping

Tanjore craftsmen excel in unusual metalwork that combines burnished copper, brass, and gleaming silver into all kinds of objects—trays, plates, bowls, and boxes. Bellmetal is another process for making figures and small decorative objects. Tanjore paintings (the genuine antiques are rare, but there are some convincing copies) make heavy use of gold leaf and fake or real gems while depicting various deities in a stylized way. Local silks are lovely, lustrous, and heavy—six yards would be enough for a long dress or sari. Other items are papier-mâché dolls, objects made from unhusked paddy, sandalwood paste, and musical instruments such as the veena, the latter quite a challenge to get home. For a survey, see **Poompuhar,** the government emporium on Gandhiji Road a few steps from the Hotel Tamilnadu.

Getting Around

Taxis are not metered and are few and far between; the same goes for auto-rickshaws. You must bargain for your fare before you get in. Also, if you do find a taxi, keep it while sightseeing as you may not get another. A tourist taxi charges about Rs. 1.25 (9½¢) per kilometer, but they're not easy to find here either. Buses can take you to most points of interest.

Getting to Tanjore

Plans for an airport have been announced and it may be built by the time you arrive. As to **trains,** there are 13 a day between Tiruchirapalli and Tanjore, from 4 a.m. to 10:30 p.m., for Rs. 34 ($2.60) in first class and Rs. 6 (45¢) in second. Trains also connect Tanjore with Madurai, Nagore, and Madras; the last takes about 8½ hours, and costs Rs. 139 ($10.70) in first class, Rs. 35 ($2.70) in second.

Buses leave about every ten minutes from Tiruchirapalli to Tanjore, costing Rs. 4.95 (38¢) for a trip of about an hour through the famous southern rice paddies. Buses also depart every ten minutes from Kumbakonam for the hour-long trip. You can also go from Madras via Pondicherry, for an eight-hour trip costing Rs. 29.70 ($2.30); from Madras via Villapuram takes nine hours, for Rs. 28.90 ($2.22).

A **tourist taxi** from Tiruchirapalli to Madras and return will cost about Rs. 125 ($9.60) for the splurge-minded.

TIRUCHIRAPALLI (TRICHY):
The overwhelming thing about Trichy (pop. 361,000) is the centuries-old **Rock Fort** that looms almost 300 feet overhead and completely dominates the city. Characteristic views of Trichy show the fort with the Cauvery River in the foreground, but actually most of the city sprawls over the crowded streets behind.

Artificial diamonds are manufactured locally, and the region is also known for its cigars, glass bangles, hand-loomed cloth, and toys made from wood and clay.

Winter is the best time to visit, especially during the three-day harvest festival in January when cows and bullocks are painted and decorated, and the interesting pilgrimage in December when visitors from all over India stream to the temple on Srirangam Island, three miles upriver.

Where to Stay

It's hard to find a clean budget hotel in Trichy charging less than Rs. 35 ($2.70) for a single and Rs. 60 ($4.60) for a double. Here are some recommendations in various price ranges.

The 40-room **Hotel Sangam,** Collectors Office Road, Tiruchirapalli 620001 (tel. 25202), needs better maintenance and management to justify its prices—Rs. 240 ($18.45) single and Rs. 340 ($26.15) double, with modern furniture, wallpapered rooms, and baths attached.

Attractive, with pretty flowered chintz-covered rattan furniture in the reception area and cheerful botanical and bird prints on the walls throughout, the fairly new **Rajali Hotel Privated Ltd.,** 3 / 14 MacDonald's Rd., Tiruchirapalli 620001 (tel. 31302), has a swimming pool among its amenities. There are 78 rooms in all. Singles run Rs. 130 ($10) to Rs. 195 ($15), and doubles go for Rs. 180 ($13.85) to Rs. 280 ($21.55), the higher rates for air conditioning. The hotel's vegetarian and Chinese restaurants are covered under "Where to Eat."

A pleasant garden hidden from the street, with tables where you can sit and sip a cool drink, is an appealing feature at the intimate, 11-room **Ashby Hotel,** 17-A Junction Rd., Tiruchirapalli 620001 (tel. 23652 or 23653), dating from the Raj days. Rooms open onto the garden and have no frills (but all the essentials), and are clean, neat, and comfortable. Non-air-conditioned rooms cost Rs. 50 ($3.85) single and Rs. 60 ($4.60) double. Air-conditioned singles run Rs. 90 ($6.90), and air-conditioned doubles, Rs. 110 ($8.45). There's no hot water on tap—it's delivered in buckets, upon request. There's a cozy restaurant.

Run by the Tamil Nadu Travel Development Corporation, the **Hotel Tamilnadu,** Cantonment, Tiruchirapalli 620001 (tel. 25383), is pleasant and a good buy, and would rate higher if better maintained. There are 35 rooms, functionally furnished with attached bathrooms: singles cost Rs. 35 ($2.70) non-air-conditioned, Rs. 75 ($5.75) air-conditioned; doubles are Rs. 50 ($3.85) non-air-conditioned, Rs. 110 ($8.45) air-conditioned.

Also run by the TTDC as the **Hotel Tamilnadu II** is the former Ashok Travellers Lodge, on Race Course Road (tel. 23498), away from the town. The four double rooms are run-down and there had been no guests here for more than a year. Rates are Rs. 60 ($4.60) for a double, Rs. 40 ($3.05) single—unless it's renovated, go here only if everyplace else is booked.

Painted in lemon, beige, pink, and green pastels like some of the South Indian temples, the **Hotel Aristo**, 2 Dindigul Rd., Tiruchirapalli 620001 (tel. 26565), is a modern Western-style hotel with 31 rooms (5 singles and 26 doubles) in the main building and in stone cottages in the garden. Each cottage has a slightly different decor; the honeymoon suite has a round bed surrounded by mirrors. Other rooms are conventional, and all are clean, with attached bathrooms. Room rates are Rs. 50 ($3.85) single and Rs. 70 ($5.40) double, non-air-conditioned; Rs. 85 ($6.55) single and Rs. 120 ($9.25) double, air-conditioned. Air-conditioned cottages cost Rs. 180 ($13.85) single and Rs. 260 ($20) double. You can have your meals in the garden, a more pleasant choice than the indoor restaurant.

New, clean, with a streamlined modern look, the 66-room **Hotel Gajapriya**, 2 Royal Rd., Cantonment, Tiruchirapalli 620001 (tel. 23220), has non-air-conditioned singles for Rs. 49 ($3.75) and non-air-conditioned doubles for Rs. 75 ($5.75) to Rs. 85 ($6.55); with air conditioning, rooms are Rs. 125 ($9.60). A restaurant was under construction when I visited.

Indian-Style Hotels: The **Hotel Vigneesh**, 1-A Dindigul Rd., Tiruchirapalli 620001 (tel. 32432), has 45 rooms, and in the reception is a statue of Ganesha, garlanded with flowers. Rooms cost Rs. 40 ($3.05) to Rs. 175 ($13.45), the latter for a deluxe double. The halls are murky and the rooms need some care; there are some Western commodes in the doubles.

Guru Hotel, 13-A Royal Rd., Cantonment, Tiruchirapalli 620001 (tel. 33881), has rooms that vary greatly in comfort and cleanliness; some of the doubles are clean and well maintained. Overall, price would be the main reason for staying here: Rs. 30 ($2.30) single, Rs. 49 ($3.75) double, Rs. 60 ($4.60) for a deluxe double.

The **Hotel Rajasugam**, 13-B / 1 Royal Rd., Tiruchirapalli 621001, can be passed by unless everything else is full. Rates are Rs. 30 ($2.30) to Rs. 60 ($4.60).

Fairly clean singles are Rs. 35 ($2.70) and doubles are Rs. 50 ($3.85) to Rs. 120 ($9.25) at the **Hotel Anand**, 1 Racquet Court Lane, Tiruchirapalli 621001 (tel. 26545).

Where to Eat

The Rajali Hotel's **Chogori Restaurant** has Chinese dragons, red tablecloths to contrast with blue walls, and black wrought-iron furniture. It specializes in Chinese dishes, but also serves some continental dishes. Rs. 25 ($1.90) is the average entree price. Hours are 12:15 to 2:30 p.m. and 7:15 to 11:30 p.m. In the same hotel, **Silent Spring** (no reference to the Rachel Carson book intended) is a bright, cheerful garden-like vegetarian restaurant with pretty bird prints. Here a special lunch is Rs. 36 ($2.75) and consists of soup, five vegetarian dishes, chapatis, pappadams, rice, and a sweet.

Many of the Indian-style hotels have clean, cheap restaurants attached to them, and among the best of these is the **New Kurunch** at the Guru Hotel. Near the Rock Fort, **Vasanta Bhavan Sweet Stall and Vegetarian Restaurant,** next door to the big sari store, also has a branch in town, and at both offers a wide range of such South Indian snacks as dosas (rice-and-lentil pancakes) for Rs. 3 (23¢). In town, and also at near the Rock Fort, is **Summerhouse,** another pleasant all-vegetarian restaurant.

A thali lunch is Rs. 7 (55¢) at the Tamilnadu Hotel.

What to Do and See

Artificial diamonds made locally, bangles, and other souvenirs are best sought in the **Big Bazaar,** around the section called **Woriyar,** or at stalls near the **Sirirangam Island Temple.** The Tourist Office can probably arrange for you to visit a local cigar factory (there are several) or an artificial diamond factory.

The major sightseeing attraction, of course, is the **Rock Fort** (open from 6 a.m. to 9 p.m.). You must climb barefoot (434 steps) and it is advisable to make the climb early in the day. The view from the top is worth the climb even though the various shrines are barred to non-Hindus.

Local historians are somewhat vague as to the fort's origin, although it is believed the Pallavas first built a temple at the rock's base more than 1200 years ago. Until 1772, when it was almost destroyed by an explosion, there was a hall containing 1,000 pillars near the main entrance.

Once at the top you'll be asked for 10 paise (1¢) before you can step out and see the view: to the north, **Srirangam Temple** and the Cauvery River, a mere trickle except during the rainy season; the modern suburb of **Golden Rock,** where the French were defeated in a celebrated 18th-century battle, to the south; and to the east and north, respectively, the **Green Hills** and the 4,000-foot mountain called **Kollimalai.** At the base, be sure to see the cave temples constructed by the Pallavas 1,200 years ago.

Near the foot of the fort is the **Teppakulam,** or sacred tank, with a pavilion in the center of it. Southeast is a house in which Clive is supposed to have stayed, now part of **St. Joseph's College;** northwest is **Christ Church,** built by a Danish missionary in the 18th century.

Srirangam Island, three miles upriver, is attached to the mainland by a bridge with 32 arches. The water surrounding the island is considered holy. The 11th-cenutry Chola kings built a great stone dam, 1,000 feet long and 60 feet wide, which still sends sacred streams through a series of canals to irrigate the fields.

About one mile from the bridge is the 17th-century **Ranganathaswamy Temple** (open 7 a.m. to noon and 4 to 8 p.m.), dedicated to Vishnu.

The temple is almost a town in itself, with most of the houses tucked within the mile-long walls. The main entrance gateway, 48 feet high, is tall enough to admit a multistoried temple cart. Buy a ticket at the temple office (10 a.m. to noon) for 50 paise (5¢), and climb on the roof of one of the buildings to survey the entire scene.

Getting Help and Going Sightseeing in Trichy

After stopping at the **TTDC Tourist Information Centre,** next to the Hotel Tamilnadu, Cantonment, for pamphlets and a map, step across the street to the bus stand and grab bus 1, which goes frequently to stops near the main monuments. You can also board this bus at the railway station.

For confirming ongoing plane tickets, **Indian Airlines** is on Dindigul Road (tel. 23116).

As to **taxis,** there was some talk of metering then, and this may be a reality by the time you arrive. If not, as elsewhere in unmetered taxi-land, you have to bargain to get a fare fair; figure on Rs. 1.25 (9½¢) per kilometer, less for auto-rickshaws. Tourist taxis get Rs. 1.30 (10¢) to 1.50 (11½¢) per kilometer.

Shopping

Try **Khadi Kraft** for brassware and silks, and the shops in **Big Bazaar Street** near the fort for brass and other items. Shopping for your future? There are many palm-readers in Trichy to help you; their English may be limited, however.

Getting to Trichy

You can go **by air** from Trivandrum for Rs. 296 ($22.75); from Madras also for Rs. 296 ($22.75); from Colombo for Rs. 502 ($38.60); and from some other cities. There's a 30% discount on passengers originating in Sri Lanka (Colombo) or the Maldives. Bus transfer between the airport and the Indian Airlines office costs Rs. 8 (60¢).

From Madras, **buses** take about three hours and go via Villapuram, Sivaganga, or Eral for fares under Rs. 40 ($3.05).

Trichy is a major junction on the Southern Railway. Meter-gauge **trains** connect Trichy to Madras, Thanjavur, and Madurai as well as Rameswarum. Broad-gauge trains connect Trichy with Bangalore, Coimbatore, Udhagamandalam (Ooty), Cochin, and Kanya Kumari. From Madras, the *Tiruchirapalli Express* takes about six hours to cover the 337 km (205 miles) for Rs. 134 ($10.30) in first class and Rs. 35 ($2.70) in second. Train service from Madurai takes about three hours for the 155 km (94 miles), at Rs. 71 ($5.45) in first class, Rs. 19 ($1.45) in second. From Pudukkottai, it takes about an hour to cover the 55 km (33 miles), for Rs. 36 ($2.75) in first class and Rs. 6 (45¢) in second. These are only a few examples.

There are also the many trains and buses that ply the roads between Thanjavur and Trichy, mentioned previously.

Excursions from Trichy

The byways between Trichy and Madurai are an archeological treasure trove. I have space here for only a few highlights.

Kodumbalur is about 67 miles (110 km) south of Trichy. At the 38-km stone go left, and left again at a huge figure of Nandi, to the Muchukundeswara Temple, from an early Chola period. You are a short walk from Muvacoil, where there are two Chola shrines with magnificent sculptured figures in fairly good condition, although time and the weather have taken their toll. Adjacent is a small museum of recently excavated objects, which you can see if the attendant is on duty—unfortunately a rare occurrence.

Continuing the journey south of Trichy, about 20 miles (33 km) north of Pudukkottai is **Sittannavasal,** a fascinating Jain hideout from the 2nd century B.C. The attendant is near the trees below the monument, and he'll accompany you to the caves, which are up 245 steps and over the rocky terrain, tufted with lemon grass, but otherwise as barren as the moon. Once at the caves, sit in their shade, enjoy the view, and see what remains of some ancient wall paintings.

Pudukkottai is a town with a long history interwoven with the usual South Indian cast of characters—the Pandayas, Cholas, and Pallavas, to name a few leading players. The modern town, originally a fort, has some old buildings such as the palace, but most interesting to you will be the small museum housing displays about the area. On sale in the museum is a "Guide to the Important Monuments in and Around Pudukkottai," at Rs. 30 ($2.30) an indispensable reference for any travelers interested in South India's long history as chronicled in temple architecture.

Tirumayam is 13 miles (21 km) from Pudukkottai toward Madurai, a fort-temple dating from the 12th and 13th centuries with many interesting shrines and an adjoining fort, part of which is well preserved.

Getting to any of the above is not the easiest thing in the world (unless you splurge on a taxi), but the truly dedicated can manage by taking the bus from Trichy to see Kodumbalur and Muvacoil; then doubling back to Trichy and getting a bus to Pudukkottai. From Pudukkottai, a bus can take you close to Sittannavasal, but you must ask the driver to make the stop. From here you can get buses to Muvacoil that go back to Trichy, or you can return to Pudukkottai and get a bus either to Trichy or farther south to Madurai, making a stop en route to see Tirumayam. Be sure to ask for directions about taking the buses, and make note of their numbers, as the schedules are in Tamil. Bus connections may keep you waiting around, but I discovered no clean lodges or hotels en route for overnighting.

While in Pudukkottai, there's a clean little café near the Vashanta Lodge (itself not worth bothering about) for coffee and dosa, no higher than Rs. 3 (23¢).

3. Madurai

The second-largest city in Tamil Nadu, Madurai (pop. 905,000) is at an inland location almost equidistant between the east and west coasts and the southern tip of India.

It is an important textile center and an interesting city in its own right, with several special attractions including a museum devoted to Gandhi, and one of the most incredible—and probably the largest—temples in India.

WHERE TO STAY: The pleasant **Madurai Ashok,** Alagarkoil Road, Madurai 625002 (tel. 42531), surrounded by gardens, has 43 well-appointed, functionally furnished rooms. At Rs. 310 ($23.85) single and Rs. 410 ($31.55) double, without meals, it's a bit of a splurge for those on their own. Meals will set you back another Rs. 100 ($7.70) or so per person, if eaten here. Both Indian and continental cuisines are served. The restaurant is also open to outsiders.

There are two **Hotel Tamilnadus,** one on Alagarkoil Road (tel. 42461), rated two stars, and the other on West Veli Street, Madurai (tel. 31435), both run by the Tamil Nadu Tourism Development Corporation (TTDC). The former is fairly new, well appointed, well kept, and rather reasonably priced: Rs. 90 ($6.90) single and Rs. 125 ($9.60) double, without air conditioning. A single with air conditioning is Rs. 125 ($9.60) and a double runs Rs. 150 ($11.55)—a good buy overall for budget travelers. Multiroom suites cost Rs. 250 ($19.25). Some 21 of the 50 rooms are air-conditioned. The bathrooms have Western-style plumbing, and there are balconies on the rooms. The dining room serves Indian and Western foods, at about Rs. 10 (75¢) for vegetarian meals and Rs. 20 ($1.55) for nonvegetarian entrees.

At the **Hotel Tamilnadu,** on West Veli, Madurai (tel. 31435), there are lower rates to match the less distinctive decor. Here, non-air-conditioned single rooms are Rs. 40 ($3.05) and doubles go for Rs. 60 ($4.60); rooms with air conditioning cost Rs. 75 ($5.75) single and Rs. 120 ($9.25) double. The restaurant serves both vegetarian and nonvegetarian foods. The average price of a nonvegetarian entree is Rs. 13 ($1) for something like ginger chicken. The Hotel Tamilnadu is near the bus station and a ten-minute walk from Meenakshi Temple.

The **Pandyan Hotel,** Race Course, Madurai 625002 (tel. 26671), is modern architecturally. Each room has its own Western-style marble bathroom, and a "pamper panel" near the bed for calling room service or tuning in the radio. All rooms are air-conditioned. There are 57 rooms and suites. The cost? Without meals, rates are Rs. 300 ($23.05) single and Rs. 350 ($26.90) double. Suites run into the thousands of rupees. There's a distant view of the Meenakshi Temple from some of the rooms. Like the Ashok and the posher of the two Tamilnadus, this hotel is away from the center, three miles (five kilometers) from the railway station and about the same distance from the shopping area.

Another choice for budget travelers, the **Hotel Prem Nivas,** 102 W. Perumal Maistry St. (tel. 31521), has a small lobby with a dome-shaped ceiling, crystal light fixtures, and light-wood reception counter. Rooms are smallish, but nicely done up with clean wallpaper and bed lamps. The tile bathrooms have dark-green fixtures. Half the toilets are Western, half Indian. Rooms open off a breezy hall. Rates are moderate: the 20 singles cost Rs. 40 ($3.05); the 32 doubles, Rs. 66 ($5.05); the eight air-conditioned doubles run Rs. 109 ($8.40). It's fairly clean. In the hotel's air-conditioned restaurant, a simple thali costs Rs. 8 (6¢), and a Bombay thali, Rs. 12 (90¢). There's no thali at dinner.

Across the street is the **Hotel Gangai** (tel. 36211), where the beds take up most of the space in the clean, tiny rooms. Rates are Rs. 30 ($2.30) single and Rs. 40 ($3.05) double. This hotel may win the prize for the loudest piped-in lobby music in Madurai, a city where every small hotel has blaring music.

Here are some more budget hotels, all centrally located, simply furnished places, mainly with Indian-style toilets, for your consideration.

The none-too-clean **Arima,** 4 Tourist Bungalow Rd., Madurai 625010 (tel. 23261), charges Rs. 20 ($1.55) to Rs. 23 ($1.75) single and Rs. 35 ($2.70) to Rs. 38 ($2.90) double, the higher rate for a phone in the room. Two air-conditioned doubles cost Rs. 65 ($5).

TM Lodge, 50 W. Perumal Maistry St., Madurai 625001 (tel. 31481), has 57 small, fairly clean rooms on four floors. Singles cost Rs. 30 ($2.30); doubles, Rs. 50 ($3.85). Eight air-conditioned doubles run Rs. 77 ($5.90), with attached Western-style bathrooms.

The **Hotel International,** 46 W. Perumal Maistry St., Madurai 625001 (tel. 31552), has 35 rooms opening off balcony corridors, simple accommodations in rooms that could use a paint job but are all right. Four deluxe doubles, at Rs. 55 ($4.25), have tile floors, Western-style bathrooms, and small balconies overlooking the street. These are the nicest. Ordinary doubles cost Rs. 40 ($3.05); singles, Rs. 22 ($1.70). It's close to the bus and railway station and the Meenakshi Temple.

The Indian-style **New College House,** Town Hall Road, Madurai 625001 (tel. 24311), was originally built as housing for Madurai College students. Rooms now rent at Rs. 24 ($1.85) to Rs. 32 ($2.45) for singles and Rs. 48 ($3.70) to Rs. 60 ($4.60) for doubles, depending on size and if there's a phone. Air-conditioned doubles cost Rs. 95 ($7.30), and these have Western-style plumbing in the attached bathrooms. The building faces a cheery, bustling courtyard and is covered with vines. Vegetarian food is available: Rs. 4 (30¢) to Rs. 6 (40¢) for curry, rice, and the trimmings. The place is very popular with Western and Indian travelers, but also very untidy—price is the main reason to stay here.

A great view of the Meenakshi Temple from the upper floors is an attraction at the pleasant, friendly **Hotel Aarathy,** 9 Perumalkol West Mada St., Madurai 625001 (tel. 31571). There's also a small temple across the street. Upstairs, where the view's the best, there's no air conditioning. But there are overhead fans and breezy little balconies off the neatly furnished rooms with attached bathrooms. Singles rent for Rs. 45 ($3.45), and doubles, Rs. 70 ($5.40), non-air-conditioned. Lower down, you lose the view but gain air conditioning: Rs. 80 ($6.15) single and Rs. 120 ($9.25) double. In the small dining room, a thali (meal on a platter) is Rs. 10 (75¢). There's also an outdoor self-service cafeteria where you have a meal with a show—a large cage of love-birds to watch as you eat.

The **Hotel Sangam,** 20 Kakkathoppu St., Madurai 625001 (tel. 22842), needs a lot of tender loving care. Price is the main recommendation for the small rooms in this six-story hotel: singles run Rs. 25 ($1.90) without air conditioning, Rs. 68 ($5.25) with. Doubles go for Rs. 43 ($3.30) non-air-conditioned and Rs. 88 ($6.75) air-conditioned.

The **Sentosh,** 7 Town Hall Rd., Madurai 625001 (tel. 26693), is over-priced and not terribly clean, with hot water in buckets. Rates are Rs. 30 ($2.30) for singles, Rs. 35 ($2.70) for doubles. There are 69 rooms in all, including some triples at Rs. 50 ($3.85) and family rooms at Rs. 60 ($4.60).

Possibly one of the lowest-priced places in town is the **Santhanam Lodge,** with 26 rooms at Rs. 15 ($1.15) single, Rs. 25 ($1.90) to Rs. 27 ($2.05) double. At these prices you can't expect fancy decor—but I wish it were a lot cleaner.

WHERE TO EAT IN MADURAI: One of the least expensive and tastiest meals in town can be found at the clean, simple **Ashok Bhavan,** near the railway station, where there's a fish tank in the front room and a South Indian thali will cost Rs. 7 (55¢), and a North Indian thali, Rs. 8 (60¢). Or drop in for a cup of delicious South Indian coffee at Rs. 1 (7½¢) and a snack at Rs. 2 (15¢) to Rs. 3 (23¢) for dosas and other delights. Hours are 5:30 a.m. to 11 p.m. Under the same ownership, with similar prices and foods, is the little outdoor cafeteria at the pleasant **Hotel Aarathy,** 9 Perumalkoil West Mada St. (tel. 31571).

For a delicious vegetarian meal in a comfortable air-conditioned setting, try **Hill King,** the dimly lit restaurant in the Hotel Prem Nivas, 102 W. Perumal Maistry St., where you'll pay Rs. 8 (60¢) for a standard South Indian thali, Rs. 12 (90¢) for the more elaborate Bombay thali. Thalis are not served at dinner, but there are host of decently priced à la carte dishes. Hours: breakfast, 7 to 10 a.m.; lunch, noon to 3 p.m.; dinner, 7 to 10:30 p.m.

Appropriately, there are North Indian dishes at the **Taj Restaurant,** 10 Town Hall Rd. (tel. 22250), named for the famous Agra monument. The friendly manager, S. A. Abdul Gaffar, recommends chicken Madurai, sautéed in coconut oil, for Rs. 7 (55¢), or the more elaborate and slightly more expensive chicken Kumar, cooked with coconut and cashews in a subtly spiced sauce, for Rs. 8 (60¢); add Rs. 1.50 (11¢) for paratha. These prices are for a quarter of a chicken; a half or a whole chicken would be higher. Other house specialties are roast chicken with vegetables and tandoori chicken tikka, both Rs. 15 ($1.15), served with either chapati or nan, at Rs. 1.50 (11¢) and Rs. 3 (23¢) respectively. Desserts include fresh fruit salad or pêche Melba for around Rs. 6 (45¢) each. Open from 7 a.m. (with a breakfast / snack menu) until 11 p.m. every day. There are two sections (air-conditioned is downstairs).

Similar foods are offered at the **Little Taj,** under the same ownership, at 1 Thiruvenkadapuram Rd., Goripalayam (tel. 43633), a distance from all the tourist attractions so it's rarely visited by foreigners. Near the Little Taj is the **Guru** (tel. 42251), serving similar foods but at slightly lower prices—again inconveniently located for most tourists.

Finally, for splurging, the **Jasmine Restaurant,** in the Pandyan Hotel, Race Course (tel. 26671), serves a tasty Malabar fish curry for Rs. 30 ($2.30) in surprisingly plain surroundings. A number of other dishes on the menu run Rs. 40 ($3.05) or more. There is both Western and Indian music on Sunday from 6 to 11 p.m.; lunch is also served here, as is breakfast, from 6 a.m. on.

At the **Hotel Madurai Ashok,** on Alagarkoil Road (tel. 42531), a well-prepared but expensive thali with many different dishes, puris, and rice, for Rs. 20 ($1.55), is served at lunch from noon to 3 p.m. and at dinner from 7 to 11 p.m.

GETTING HELP AND GETTING AROUND: Whether you arrive by plane or train or bus, you will find a government **Tourist Information Centre** ready and willing to serve you—at the airport; the railway station (tel. 24535), open from 7 a.m. to 8 p.m., but on government holidays from 7 to 10:30 a.m. and 5 to 8 p.m.; and near the Central Bus Stand in the Hotel Tamilnadu complex on West Veli Street (tel. 22957), the main office, which is open from 10 a.m. to 5 p.m. (closed Saturday, Sunday, and government holidays). The offices have a useful brochure incorporating a map.

If you're staying in the center of town, you can walk to Meenakshi Temple and Thirumalai Palace. Otherwise, buses 3 and 4 go to the Gandhi Museum and Mariamman Theppakulam, and bus 44 runs out Alagarkoil Road where the top hotels are located. Black-and-yellow taxis are scarce and unmetered—you must bargain. Bargain also for cycle rickshaws. Auto-rickshaws are metered; Rs. 2 (15¢) minimum and Rs. 1.20 (9¢) for each subsequent kilometer; waiting charge is 10 paise (1¢) for each five minutes. You may end up having to take a tourist taxi (usually dark green), and again bargaining is not out of the question. Prices generally amount to Rs. 130 ($10) for five hours and 50 km, and Rs. 240 ($18.45) for ten hours and 100 km.

SIGHTS AROUND TOWN: Despite its size, Madurai is in some ways a small town, as are almost all cities in southern India, with most of the action in the streets. Here and there you'll see men and women stretching the brightly dyed threads that eventually go into some of Madurai's beautiful saris (this industry supports almost half the local population), and judging by the bright colors seen on the local women, many of these saris never leave the town where they are made.

The city was founded more than 2,500 years ago and is by far the most famous and most ancient home of the Tamil culture. To Hindus it is a holy place and thousands of them flock from all over India to visit the fantastic **Meenakshi Temple,** whose present form dates back to the reign of the Nayak kings, in the early 16th century. The temple occupies a vast plot of land in the center of the old part of town, south of the River Vaigai. Its major masterpieces are four vast terraced gopurams, or towers, each of them more than 150 feet high and ornately decorated all the way to the top with stair after stair of brightly colored statues and carvings. There are many smaller gopurams dotted around the temple grounds, but the tallest one, the south gopuram (160 feet), can be climbed by a series of interior stairs that open into smaller and smaller chambers, all leading eventually to a narrow trap door on the roof—and a fantastic, dizzying view of the surrounding countryside.

Down below, in the center of the temple, a shallow tank is the magnet for pilgrims bent on immersing themselves in the holy water. All around are worshippers carrying bowls of coconuts and flowers; a ceaseless chatter ascends to the recently repainted psychedelic ceilings aglow with eye-popping mandalas and those historical / mythical scenes of which Hindus are so fond. Many of the visitors, their foreheads caked with white ash, gather excitedly around what looks like a cashier's cage, waiting to participate in the numerous weddings that are always taking place under the immense stone pillars. A cage full of green parrots adds to the clamor. Demure young girls in gold-threaded saris restrain their younger sisters who gaze curiously at the random non-Hindu strangers, who must stop short at the entrance to the inner temple. The entrance hall leading to the tank bears brightly painted murals of age-old scenes, beside which ever-enterprising vendors offer bangles and cheap toys. There are flower vendors and incense peddlers—a bustling bazaar inside the temple itself.

To the rear of the temple is what is known as **One Thousand Pillar Hall,** now turned into a museum open from 7 a.m. to 7:30 p.m. for an entry fee of 50 paise (3½¢). Originally the perspective, looking past the pillars, was one of geometrical intrigue, but today cases of photos and relics interrupt the natural lines. On closer inspection, however, many of the exhibits turn out to be quite fascinating—for example, the colored pictures of goddesses, each with full breasts and four hands holding symbolic objects. There are paintings of old Tamilian ships with animal-shaped prows; elephant-headed figures (Lord Ganesh) sitting on dragon-type lions; delicate wire sculptures demonstrating lotus postures; and intriguing charts explaining "Life in Colors" (black equals malice; lilac stands for fear; pure blue indicates pure religious feeling; orange means pride; fuschia, pure affection; light violet equals love for humanity; light green stands for sympathy). Another display is devoted to rituals. The consecration of a temple, it explains, requires 64 different rites, the first of which is to pour—into the first hole that is dug—liquid from the seven seas (symbolized by brine, water, milk, curd, ghee, cane juice, and honey).

One particular section emphasizes the contribution the Tamil race has made to the world. There are samples of spices (smell), pepper (taste), peacock feathers and pearls (sight), and hand-looms (touch).

Despite the hall's name, it is alleged, there are only 997 pillars, but all are different and the ones just to the left of the museum exit are even more so. If tapped with a stick they respond with musical notes.

The temple is open (entry fee: 50 paise, 3½¢) every day from dawn to 1 p.m., when it closes to everyone but photographers, who may enter by purchasing a Rs. 5 (40¢) ticket for each camera they carry inside. At 4 p.m. the temple reopens and stays open until 9:30 p.m., on Friday until 10:30 p.m. To climb the South Tower (the only one you can climb), open from 6 a.m. to 5:30 p.m., you must pay an entrance fee of Re. 1 (7½¢). Note that while climbing was not permitted when I was there, it may be by the time you arrive.

In the One Thousand Pillar Hall you must pay a 50-paise (3½¢) entrance fee and an extra Rs. 5 (40¢) photography fee if you plan to take a camera inside. You'll need a flash for inside photography here.

You should also return to the temple at night between 9 and 10 p.m. for the centuries-old ceremony that gives Westerners a rare glimpse of Indian religious life. This rite signals the time when Shiva leaves his chamber to spend the night with his wife, Parvati, in her chamber. It happens almost every night, although it's not confirmed in advance. Get there about 8:30 p.m. You'll see other people near Shiva's sanctum waiting for the ceremony to begin.

A crash of cymbals and blaring of horns announces the procession that forms around the concealed Shiva held aloft in a jewel-encrusted silver litter on the shoulders of dhoti-draped priests. Other priests stir the incense-filled air with giant peacock-feather fans. A stop is made to anoint the litter's step with sandalwood paste in preparation for Shiva's feet. Then the cortège passes by to music that seems loud enough to wake all the gods in the world before it disappears through the shadowy corridors leading to Parvati's room.

Don't wait for Shiva's return. Not even the temple priests know when he leaves. All they know is that they will find Shiva in his chamber again in the morning when it's time for them to bathe and dress him—and Parvati alone in her room. If Shiva doesn't go out, the temple is always abuzz with fascinating activity to make your evening visit worthwhile.

A few blocks southeast of the Meenakshi Temple is what remains of the 17th-century **Palace of Tirumala,** one of the Nayak kings who ruled Madurai for almost 200 years, and built a succession of fortifications, dams, aqueducts, and the celebrated Meenakshi Temple itself.

European writers of that era compared Tirumala's palace with the ancient monument of Thebes. Although much of it was destroyed late in the 17th century, there still survives today an enormous roofed arcade supported by 40-foot-high stone pillars elaborately carved and painted. Griffins, lions, and other monster gargoyles are to be seen everywhere. The covered arcade encloses an enormous sandy courtyard, in the center of which is a grove of trees. Today the palace is a protected monument and museum. It's open from 8 a.m. to noon and 1 to 4 p.m.; the entry fee is 40 paise (3¢) per person.

There are many traces of the late Mahatma Gandhi all over India, but here in Madurai, at the **Gandhi Memorial Museum,** it is possible to study Gandhi's life in all its facets. Opened by India's late great prime minister Nehru in 1959, the museum, ensconced in a 300-year-old palace, is open every day except Wednesday from 10 a.m. to 1 p.m. and 2 to 6 p.m. (take bus 3 or 4 from the station—they run every 15 minutes—or a taxi, about a Rs.10, 75¢, ride from anywhere in town). The museum contains room after room of touching mementos of Gandhi's life—a white woolen shawl, a pair of rimless glasses, an eating bowl—as well as innumerable letters he wrote to world-famous figures who influenced him (Tolstoy) or whom he hoped to influence (Hitler, FDR). He was never averse to trying to fight for anybody who needed help, even to the extent of sending letters to schoolteachers pleading for mercy for students who had been barred from school for taking part in the fight for independence. "In my opinion non-cooperation with evil is as much a duty as is cooperation with good" is one of his famous sayings.

SPECIAL EVENTS AND SPECIAL OCCASIONS: There's a one-hour Sound and Light Show at the Palace of Tirumala at 6:30 p.m. in English and at 8 p.m. in Tamil, every day. Tickets cost Rs. 1 (7½¢) to Rs. 3 (23¢).

Pongal, a January harvest festival, is marked in various places throughout the South, but unique in Madurai at this time is the **Jallikatu**—a bullfight with a big difference. For this contest the bulls get all primped up, their horns polished and painted and pointed, to be pursued by bullfighters who catch the animal, tame it, and claim the cash reward tied to its razor-sharp horns.

Serene is the **float festival,** at the Teppakulam Tank, in January or February when the deities are treated to a trip around the tank on a raft decorated with flowers and little lights. The most important festival is **Chitirai,** celebrated for ten days in March and April, and marking with many processions the marriage of the goddess Meenakshi to Lord Sundereswarar.

SHOPPING: You can get small souvenirs around the Meenakshi Temple, and beautiful hand-loomed textiles at several stores, including **Co-optex,** on South Chithirai Street and also on West Tower Street. For Tamil Nadu handcrafts, there's **Poompuhar,** West Veli Street, and for a wider selection from other states, try **All-India Handicrafts,** on Town Hall Road. New to town is **Cottage Industries Exposition,** a privately owned company, with high-priced, good-quality merchandise, at 142-44 Netaji Rd., near the temple. Handcrafts, churidars, jewelry, and small statues are a few of the items sold here. From the shop's roof you can get a terrific view of the temple, whether you buy or not—ask permission before going up. Open from 9 a.m. to 10 p.m. including Sunday. The shop will change traveler's checks if you make a purchase.

GETTING TO MADURAI: Daily nonstop flights from Madras take about 50 minutes and cost Rs. 398 ($30.60). Flights also connect to Cochin and Bangalore.

There are several **trains** from Madras. One of the best is the *Pandyan Express,* leaving Egmore Station at 7:25 p.m. and arriving in Madurai at 7:45 a.m., for Rs. 182 ($14) in first class and Rs. 45 ($3.45) in second. This train also stops in Trichy, where it leaves at 3:20 a.m. and arrives in Madurai at 6:35 a.m. Another possibility is the *Nellai Express,* departing Trichy at 1:45 p.m. and arriving in Madurai at 5 p.m. First class from Trichy costs Rs. 71 ($5.45); second class, Rs. 19 ($1.45).

From Madras, luxury **buses** with 35 pushback seats depart from Egmore daily at 8:30 p.m. and arrive in Madurai at 6:30 a.m. The fare is Rs. 45 ($3.45) for the nine- to ten-hour trip. Other Madras-to-Madurai buses from Egmore and Esplanade cost Rs. 38 ($2.90) and leave from 3:30 a.m. to 11:45 p.m. daily. Madras buses go through Trichy, where you can board as well. Buses from Kanya Kumari go to Madurai for under Rs. 70 ($5.40) and then on to Madras.

EXCURSIONS FROM MADURAI: At **Kochadai,** a few kilometers south of the city, the fat ferocious-looking village deity lives in a park surrounded by smaller deities and a rearing horse. The more famous **Thirupparankundram** is eight kilometers (five miles) south of Madurai and the site of a temple to Subramanian. Behind it is an ancient rock-cut temple, particularly beautiful at sunset when peacocks strut their stuff. (Take bus 5 to these sights, or take an auto-rickshaw and keep it for the return.) In the River Vagai, west of Madurai near Vandiyoor, is the oft-overlooked Nayak-era mandapam, supported by 24 pillars, in rather dilapidated condition, but looking pretty good for its 400 years.

4. Kanya Kumari (Cape Comorin)

The multicolored sands of Kanya Kumari (Cape Comorin), according to Hindu legend, were formed when Parvati, daughter of the king of the Himalayas, stood up at the altar by Lord Shiva, angrily tossed the uneaten wedding feast into the waters where it was transformed forever into the sands of brown, yellow, silver, orange, blue, purple, and russet. The sands aren't the only mind-blowing natural phenomena of the cape: wait until you see the unforgettable sunrises and sunsets!

Three bodies of water meet here at India's southernmost point—the Arabian Sea, the Indian Ocean, and the Bay of Bengal—and the tip of land has been famous among navigators for centuries. Ptolemy's maps mention it ("Comaria Akron") and Marco Polo also marked it on his charts.

Today it is revered by Hindus for its **Kanya Kumari Shrine** and by all Indians, and many others, for its **Gandhi Memorial,** a yellow structure trimmed with green and encircled by a walkway which you can climb to gaze into the waters into which the great statesman's ashes were cast after his cremation 37 years ago. Inside the memorial is a simple chamber, a black marble marker indicating the spot where the ashes rested. Above this marker is a minute hole in the ceiling, cleverly designed so that once a year, on Gandhi's birthday (Oct. 2), the sun casts one long beam on the marker.

Offshore, almost directly opposite the Gandhi Mandir, are the two rocks on which the 19th-century philosopher Vivekananda sat in meditation before he set sail to preach love and brotherhood to Americans. It took 500 workmen to build the memorial dedicated to Vivekananda that stands on the site and is a structure of ancient and modern inspiration. A boat trip permits closer inspection.

WHERE TO STAY AND EAT: There are simple, neat and clean accommodations at all the following:

The **Hotel Tamilnadu** (tel. 57), under the direction of the Tamil Nadu Tourism Development Corporation (TTDC), has rooms with attached bathrooms and balconies overlooking the beach. All the rooms are double, but are rented as singles for Rs. 50 ($3.85) and as doubles for Rs. 70 ($5.40). There's a cafeteria where you can get Kerala- or Tamil Nadu–style Indian meals for around Rs. 10 (75¢).

The cafeteria also serves the nine-room **Cape Hotel** (tel. 22), again under the direction of the TTDC. Its simple accommodations have attached bathrooms and rent for Rs. 110 ($8.45) double with air conditioning, Rs. 70 ($5.40) without.

Reader Beatrix Ouwerkerk of Switzerland recommends the **D.K.V. Lodge**, in the main part of the city facing the Bay of Bengal, charging Rs. 40 ($3.05) for two. She says: "There are many lodges at that price, but not all are so nice. Some of them don't have showers."

Neat and new and nicely furnished is the **Hotel Sangam,** Main Road (tel. 62), where all rooms have balconies facing the sea and bathrooms are Western style. Doubles cost Rs. 100 ($13), Rs. 75 ($5.75) for single occupancy of a double. Suites run Rs. 150 ($11.55).

Also on Main Road and a little less expensive is the totally acceptable **Sankar's Guest House** (tel. 60), which has breezy balconies on its rooms. A double is Rs. 65 ($5); a single, Rs. 40 ($3.10). There are a few air-conditioned doubles, at Rs. 110 ($10.98). There's a dining room but you must order your meals in advance. A vegetarian meal will cost about Rs. 4.50 (45¢).

A nice old low-budget standby, **Kerala House** (tel. 29) is a cream-colored building with a bright-red roof and a wonderful sea view from its dozen rooms. All the rooms have bathrooms attached and almost all have Western-style toilets. Rates are Rs. 16 ($1.25) single, Rs. 22 ($1.70) double, with three air-conditioned rooms at Rs. 20 ($1.55) extra. Meals run an additional Rs. 13.50 ($1.35) to Rs. 23 ($2.30), the higher rate for Western food. Even if you don't plan to stay overnight, Kerala House is a good place to stop for lunch (which you reserve as soon as you arrive); a simple Western lunch costs Rs. 10 (75¢), a vegetarian lunch about half that. Ask the manager if you can drop back and see the sunset from the roof terrace.

GETTING TO KANYA KUMARI: Although in Tamil Nadu, Kanya Kumari is only 55 miles (86 km) from Trivandrum, and so is most easily approached from Kerala's capital. The journey can be made pleasantly and inexpensively by **train** from Trivandrum. There are three trains a day each way, taking 2½ hours in either direction and costing Rs. 48 ($3.70) in first class and Rs. 11 (85¢) in second class, one way. There are also five buses a day from the terminal near the railway station in Trivandrum, from 4:30 a.m. to 6:30 p.m., or the stand near the Ashok Beach Resort in Kovalam four times a day, at 6:45 and 9:50 a.m., and 1:45 and 6:40 p.m. Going by train or bus means you bypass the Pandmanabhapuram Palace and Suchidam Temple.

The easiest way to see these sights and take in Kanya Kumari is on the daily **tour** run by the Kerala Tourist Development Corporation. It departs Trivandrum at 7:30 a.m., returns at 9 p.m., and costs Rs. 60 ($4.60) per person, not including meals. For information and reservations, contact: KTDC Tourist Reception Centre, Thampanoor, Trivandrum 695001 (tel. 2643). You can get information on their tours to Thekkady and Punmudi here as well.

You can also rent a four-passenger, non-air-conditioned **car** (larger, air-conditioned cars are available, but more expensive) for around Rs. 400 ($30.75) to Rs. 500 ($38.45) for the round trip, perhaps sharing expenses with others from your hotel and stopping to sightsee as you wish. **Taxis** will be willing to take you to and from Kanya Kumari from Trivandrum or Kovalam, but set the rate before you get in and make sure your driver has a permit to cross into Tamil Nadu.

Finally, since the completion of Vivekananda's memorial, Kanya Kumari is often bursting at the seams with visitors. So if you plan to stay overnight, reserve well in advance and expect not to get on the first bus you try from Trivandrum. You should also book train seats in advance.

5. Udhagamandalam (Ootacamund)

Ootacamund (in Tamil, Udhagamandalam) or "Ooty" for short—by any name, this town will be the fading remains of a 19th-century English community in the flower-strewn hills of Tamil Nadu's Nilgiris ("Blue Hills"). The hills were so named for the distinctive bluish halo that surrounds them (similar to that seen in the U.S.A.'s Great Smokies).

Ooty (elevation 7,500 feet) today has old gabled manor houses and vast gardens that rival Kew, flower shows, and a town center called Charing Cross. Yet it's quite a different place from what it was when the Duke of Buckingham made his summer headquarters here: tucked in one little corner of Wenlock Downs, a massive tract of grassy lawns, hills, and dales, is Hindustan Photo Films, India's only manufacturer of sensitized photographic materials. You can visit the factory. Fortunately the downs extend for some 50 miles, so despite the light industry there is still plenty of room for picturesque beauty and outdoor activities.

Beyond, the roads climb through forests of teak and eucalyptus and the terraced slopes of the south's renowned tea and coffee estates set into this junction of Western and Eastern ghats. Indeed, eucalyptus oils and other extracts from cinchona trees, introduced in 1842, have become a thriving local industry. Pungent wintergreen and geranium and other oils are for sale in the marketplace.

Though Ooty's past may seem rooted mainly in England, it truly goes deeper, back to the aboriginal tribes that once roamed the walnut and teak groves. Their descendants can be seen today herding their cattle along the roads, as can their animist shrines in the fields nearby.

Light industry aside, Ooty hasn't changed in one respect since the days when the Madras government moved here for the summer. Now as then it is a delightful place where the average temperature, between 50° and 60° makes it an ideal escape from the heat of the plains. As with other hill stations, taking a trip to Ooty is to step away from the rigors of travel and relax before digging more deeply into other treasures and pleasures of India.

WHERE TO STAY IN OOTY: Budget hotels are mainly in the Charing Cross area and around the eastern end of Ooty Lake; the better hotels are scattered here and there. Some visitors prefer to stay in Coonoor and commute to Ooty (see below).

Despite the fact that Ooty has many hotels, the maintenance is lax in all but a few of those that I saw.

The prices are high in season (generally April 1 to June 30), even in modest places; however, they dip as much as 50% off-season, July through March 31. There was virtually no place in the lowest price ranges I could wholeheartedly recommend, but when the off-season prices are in effect, some of the moderate hotels fall in the category for low budgeteers. Budget travelers should keep in mind that luxury taxes add from 10% to 20% to hotel bills.

The top hotel in town, dating from the Raj heyday (1877), is the charming old **Savoy Hotel,** on Club Road a Taj Group Hotel (tel. 2572), with cozy, old-fashioned rooms, suites, and cottages set around a spacious garden. The hotel was undergoing a massive facelift—new bathrooms, new paint job, and new decor, which should be completed by the time of your arrival. In season, rates are Rs. 600 ($46.15) for single occupancy and Rs. 800 ($61.55) for double, including bedtime tea, breakfast, and two main meals commencing on the day of arrival (breakfast only on the day of departure). Off-season, you'll pay Rs. 350 ($26.90) single and Rs. 400 ($31.75) double, with meals as mentioned.

If Stephen King wrote a novel about India, he might set it at **Fernhill Palace** on Fern Hill (tel. 2056), once a summer palace of the former Maharaja of Mysore, where there are ghosts of grander days everywhere. Still run by the maharaja's family, the rambling white building in a 50-acre garden would be delightful if better maintained. Sadly, the walls, drapes, and old furniture greatly need repair—when replacements are made I hope that some feeling for the period prevails. Alas, this seems not to be the case: new lamps, seen here and there, are bazaar quality brassware that would be at home in a budget production of *The Arabian Nights,* rather than a Raj-period palace. Breakfasts are served on the bright, cheerful glassed-in sun porch; other meals, in the huge, gloomy ballroom, which in its heyday must have been attractively lit and often filled with glittering merry-makers. The rooms, with connecting old-fashioned bathrooms, cost Rs. 250 ($19.25) single, Rs. 300 ($23.05) to Rs. 650 ($50) double, and suites much higher, in season; off season, Rs. 150 ($11.55) single and Rs. 150 ($11.55) to Rs. 300 ($23.05) double (again, suites at higher rates). Meals are à la carte, and food prices are high. For instance, Rs. 24 ($1.85) is the average price of a vegetarian entree, the same price as the usually more expensive nonvegetarian foods. The season at this hotel is March 15 to June 15.

The **Palace Hotel** (tel. 2170) needs care as well, has 22 rooms with connecting bathrooms, and charges Rs. 300 ($23.05) for a double and Rs. 450 ($34.60) to Rs. 600 ($46.15) for suites, European Plan. There's a 50% discount off-season.

The new splurge hotel in town, the sleek **Southern Star,** 32 Havelock Rd. (tel. 3601), had 14 rooms when I saw it, but should have 62 by now. This is a branch of its namesake hotel in Mysore. The lounge has parquet flooring and white walls with comfortable tub-shaped chairs in intimate groupings. Rooms have modern dark-wood furniture, deep-pile carpeting, and club chairs covered in print. Each has an attached tile bathroom. Rates are Rs. 500 ($38.45) single and Rs. 650 ($50) double, with all meals, in season; off-season, Rs. 250 ($19.25) and Rs. 300 ($23.05). The hotel is located on a hill about two kilometers (1¼ miles) above the town and has a nice view.

Nearby is the intimate **Snowdon Inn,** Snowdon Road (tel. 3686), an old cottage with 12 neat, comfortable rooms and shiny wooden floors. Rates are Rs. 240 ($18.45) single and Rs. 340 ($26.15) to Rs. 425 ($32.70) double in season, Rs. 100 ($7.70) single and Rs. 150 ($11.55) to Rs. 200 ($15.40) double off-season, without meals. All rooms have bathrooms attached, and there were plans to update them with new tile.

Now for more moderate budgets: Across from the Tourist Office is **Nahar Tourist Home,** Charing Cross Road 643001 (tel. 2173), fairly clean, Indian style, with 86 rooms. Singles cost Rs. 60 ($4.60) to Rs. 90 ($6.90) and doubles go for Rs. 90 ($6.90) to Rs. 150 ($11.55) in season. Deluxe rooms rent for Rs. 125 ($9.60) single and Rs. 250 ($19.25) double in season. There are wallpapered walls in the bedrooms and some Western toilets in the bathrooms. A thali meal is Rs. 10 (75¢) here.

With a lake view, the rambling yellow-painted red-accented Indian-style **Hotel Dasaprakash** (tel. 2434), a member of the famous South Indian chain, has 100 rooms, making it the largest hotel in the city. Unfortunately, it is not as well maintained as the other Dasaprakash hotels in this book, and some of the rooms painted dark green are glum-looking. Still, it's one of the most popular hotels in town, run by pleasant staff and priced modestly: Rs. 90 ($6.90) for doubles and Rs. 150 ($11.55) for deluxe doubles, with a discount of nearly 50% off-season. Meals are vegetarian, at Rs. 15 ($1.15) for a thali, and there's a nice outdoor snackbar with a good view of the lake.

The government-run **Hotel Tamilnadu,** behind the supermarket and tourist office, and near Charing Cross Road (tel. 2544), clean and a good buy, has these in-season rates: singles are Rs. 100 ($7.70); doubles and suites, Rs. 175 ($13.45); and cottages, Rs. 250 ($19.25). They are discounted almost 50% off-season. All rooms have connecting bathrooms. There are steep penalties (up to 50% or loosing your whole deposit) for not canceling in-season reservations more than three days in advance.

Also centrally located is the Indian-style **Hotel Natraj** (tel. 2772), which needs a paint job and charges Rs. 70 ($5.40) single, Rs. 100 ($7.70) double, and Rs. 225 ($17.30) for suites, in season; Rs. 40 ($3.05) single, Rs. 60 ($4.60) double, and Rs. 120 ($9.25) for suites off-season.

A good bet is the **YWCA Guest House,** Anandagiri (tel. 2218), which takes both men and women and is posher than you'd expect a Y to be, and has rates to match: Rs. 140 ($10.75) to Rs. 160 ($12.30) with attached bathroom, Rs. 160 ($12.30) to Rs. 180 ($13.85) for cottages. A dorm bed costs Rs. 15 ($1.15), and is one of the best low-priced places to stay. Off-season, the rates go down to Rs. 35 ($2.70) for a double and Rs. 50 ($3.85) for a cottage.

Hotel Blue Hills, Commercial Road (tel. 2034), and **Hotel Sanjay,** Charing Cross (tel. 6103), both in Ooty, are owned and operated by the pleasant Hotel Blue Hills in nearby Coonoor. Time did not permit checking the Ooty branches, but if they are anything like their Coonoor cousin, they are clean and friendly places to stay. Prices are moderate as well.

You might try to get in the pleasantly located **P.W.D. Bungalow** by making a reservation in advance to make sure. There was no one around to tell me the rates for certain, but they should be about Rs. 20 ($1.55) per person. From here, it's a delightful 15- to 20-minute walk to Charing Cross Road. For reservations write: Sub-Divisional Officer, P.W.D., Udhagamandalam.

The **Youth Hostel,** Charing Cross Road (tel. 235), is in run-down condition but cheap: Rs. 10 (75¢) for nonmembers.

WHERE TO EAT: Most of the hotels welcome outside visitors to their restaurants, though some, like the Savoy, require an hour's advance notice for the preparation of meals. In town, the vegetarian thali at the **Nahar Tourist Hotel** is well prepared, but pricey at Rs. 10 (75¢).

WHAT TO DO: Strolling around town is the best way to soak up the atmosphere and see the few sights.

The main attraction in Ooty is the **Botanical Gardens,** which were started in 1847 by an English marquis. They are laid out in spacious terraces, graded one on top of the other, almost like a tea estate. The gardens' dramatic backdrop is Doddabetta Peak. In the pretty 50-acre park are huge shade trees, 650 species of plants, and near the little lake, a fossil tree trunk dating back some 20 million years. A fairly late addition is a world map in plants, made from contributions sent from many nations.

From the garden, Ooty's man-made lake, two miles wide and 45 feet deep, is a little over a mile away. It was created by John Sullivan, the first European to have a summer house here, in 1819. Rowboats, renting for Rs. 10 (75¢) to Rs. 15 ($1.15) for a four-seater, are available, as are ponies for about the same price for a 10- to 15-minute ride. Beyond the lake is a train that runs a few kilometers—a great favorite of children.

Doddabetta Peak is ten kilometers (six miles) away. It's a Rs.-2 (15¢) bus ride from the Central Bus Stand (the bus stays about 20 minutes before returning). At 8,650 feet this is the highest peak in Tamil Nadu and offers a spectacular panoramic view of the surroundings. It is only one of several viewing points, some named for illustrious English citizens, scattered between Ooty and Coonoor, 18 miles (30 km) away.

USEFUL INFORMATION: There's a **tourist office** on Charing Cross Road in the Supermarket Building, Charing Cross (tel. 2416), with limited supply of brochures, one of them with a little map. . . . There's a branch of **Spencer's Department Store** in the center of town; Poompuhar and Kairali have emporia as well. . . . The **Municipal Market** is the main place to bargain, and worth a visit. . . . To book an **elephant ride** at Mudumalai (Rs. 40, $3.05, for four people), check with the District Forest Office on Coonoor Road. Rides should be reserved two days in advance of your sanctuary visit.

MUDUMALAI WILDLIFE SANCTUARY: Most people plan to spend a day in Mudumalai, the 114-square-mile wildlife sanctuary 40 miles (65 km) from Ooty, nudged up against both Karnataka (see Chapter XIV) and Kerala. Elephants are most frequently seen, and there are also bison, tigers, panthers, and hyenas, plus a number of snakes and rare birds. In addition, a main attraction for visitors takes place at 6:15 p.m.—the elephant puja, when a trained elephant actually lumbers through a puja (prayer ceremony) in honor of the evening. Late afternoon is also the best time to visit the elephant-feeding camp. The park itself is open from 6:30 to 10 a.m. and 4 to 6 p.m. The elephant puja and elephant feeding are at 6:15 p.m. Elephant riding hours are 6 to 8 a.m. and 4:30 to 6 p.m.

Accommodations in Mudumalai

Seeing the sanctuary properly takes overnighting. However, there are so few accommodations that you absolutely *must* reserve in advance, especially in season.

Bamboo Banks Farm Guest House, Musinigudi, P.O. & T.O., Nilgiris 643223 (tel. 22), is, as its name implies, a working farm as well as a small family-run guesthouse. Owners Siasp T. and Zerene Kothavala are always around to see to guests' comforts. Bearing some resemblance to a U.S. southwestern hacienda, the rose-colored main building with red-tile roof houses the lounge/dining room and two of the seven guest rooms. The other five rooms are in cottages in the well-tended garden. All rooms are clean and tastefully furnished in a simple, homey style. Rates are Rs. 95 ($7.30) single and Rs. 180 ($13.85) double. Meals will run an additional Rs. 120 ($9.25) per day per person. For Rs. 20 ($1.55) per hour you can go by Jeep to see the animals.

Elephant rides, birdwatching, horseback riding, and hiking are also offered to guests.

Clean and colorful as a rainbow is **Mountania Rest House,** Masinagudi P.O., Nilgiris 643223 (tel. 37). The ten simply furnished rooms containing nothing much more than tables, chairs, and beds have such uninhibited color schemes as lemon-yellow doors and lavender walls or aqua, peach, and avocado combined with a ruby carpet and red clay floors—all as neat and as cheerful as can be. The price ranges from Rs. 90 ($6.90) to Rs. 120 ($9.25) per person. There's cold running water, hot water in buckets, and some Indian-style toilets.

The TTDC runs a **Youth Hostel** (tel. 49) in Mudumalai. The walls are in need of washing and/or painting. The charge is Rs. 10 (75¢) per person. There are two rooms with 12 beds and one room with 6 beds. Meals are served here, and will cost about Rs. 60 ($4.60) per day. To make reservations, check with the tourist office on Charing Cross Road in Ooty (tel. 2416) in the Supermarket Building; or contact the manager at the hostel.

Last, you might try to get a **Forest Rest House** accommodation by calling at the District Forest Office on Coonoor Road in Ooty.

If everything is booked at Mudumalai, you might try **Belvedere Hotel-Lodge,** Gudalur (tel. 262), about 20 miles from the sanctuary. Fairly clean rooms with bathrooms attached cost Rs. 66 ($5.05) in season. You can get a meal here as well.

COONOOR: Coonoor, another hill station, is 18 miles (30 km) from Ooty, at an altitude of 5,600 feet. Here are Sim's Park and a number of view points. It's much quieter than Ooty, and some travelers prefer it for that reason. Buses go from Ooty to Coonoor, for Rs. 2 (15¢), from 7:20 a.m. to 7 p.m.

Accommodations in Coonoor

The top place to stay is the **Hampton Manor Hotel,** on Church Road, Coonoor, Nilgiris 643101 (tel. 6244). This 31-room, 108-year-old hotel has a main lounge and dining room, and accommodations in white stucco cottages topped with red-tile roofs and set on a well-manicured lawn surrounded by neatly trimmed hedges. Each well-cared-for bedroom has an individual decor and an attached bathroom, and many also have both sitting and dressing rooms. Though much of the furniture is old, it is well cared for throughout. There are inviting overstuffed chintz-covered armchairs and gleaming dark-wood tables and chests. In season, rates are Rs. 240 ($18.45) for a single, Rs. 500 ($38.45) for two, inclusive of meals. You can eat outdoors in the garden or indoors in the brick-and-beamed dining room.

The '40s-style, 20-room **Ritz Hotel,** Orange Grove Road, Coonoor 643101 (tel. 6242), right near Sim's Park, is also very nice. It is neat and newly renovated. The bedrooms' yellow walls are as cheerful as sunshine, and highly polished dark-wood furniture shines in the rooms as well. All rooms have balconies above the well-cared-for garden. Prices are Rs. 175 ($13.45) to Rs. 230 ($17.70) for singles and Rs. 210 ($16.15) to Rs. 300 ($23.05) for doubles in season, which is April 15 to June 15 here. Off-season is just about half price.

The new **Hotel Blue Hills,** Mount Road Coonoor (tel. 6103), has motel-modern furniture in the clean rooms and a nice view from the terrace. There's a small garden with a topiary, and the management is eager to please visitors. Doubles cost Rs. 150 ($11.55) to Rs. 200 ($15.40); singles go for Rs. 80 ($6.15) to Rs. 160 ($12.30). Rates go down out of season. Indian vegetarian and nonvegetarian foods are served in the dining room, in the Rs.-10 (75¢) to Rs.-15 ($1.15) range for entrees.

The cement-block and red-brick façade of the **Vivek Tourist Home,** Figure of Eight Road, near Upasi, Coonoor (tel. 6658), is back to basics. The walls in the simply furnished rooms need painting. The obliging manager said they might renovate. A new annex was under construction and should be finished in early 1988. High-season rates are Rs. 60 ($4.60) single occupancy and Rs. 90 ($6.90) double; off-season, Rs. 30 ($2.30) single and Rs. 50 ($3.85) double.

What to See

Sim's Park, started in 1874, has many rare roses and a 180-year-old eucalyptus. A new attraction is a map of the world made from plants sent by various countries, much like Ooty's. The third week in May there's a fruit fair when growers come from everywhere to exhibit their produce. You'll want to tour the various view points, such as Dolphin's Nose, Lamb's Rock, and Lady Canning's Seat (for a view?). You can also visit tea estates, and Ketty Valley View toward Ooty.

At **Kotagiri,** another small hill station 12 miles (19 km) from Ooty, even quieter than Coonoor, and a bit higher at 6,500 feet, there's Kodanad View Point, St. Catherine Falls, and Rangaswamy Pillar and Park. Buses from Ooty run on the half hour from 7:30 to 6:30 p.m. and cost Rs. 3 (23¢).

TOURS: The **TTDC** conducts daily tours of Ooty, including the Botanical Gardens, lake, Doddabetta, and the Mudumalai Sanctuary. It starts at 9 a.m. from the Hotel Tamilnadu and returns at 8:30 p.m.; the price, Rs. 60 ($4.60), includes vegetarian snacks, lunch, and entry fees. The tour picks up and drops off at your hotel. Reservations must be made in advance at Hotel Tamilnadu, the Youth Hostel, or any leading hotel in the city.

Cheran Transport Corporation also offers a Rs.-60 ($4.60) one-day tour, from 8:30 a.m. to 7:45 p.m., leaving from the Central Bus Stand. **Sri Saravana Travels,** in the Nahar Shopping Center, Charing Cross (tel. 3022), offers daily tours of Ooty and Coonoor, Ooty and Mudumalai, Kodanad and Coonoor, and Ooty and Kodaikanal. For more information and rates, call or visit the office.

GETTING TO OOTY: Many people **fly** from Madras to Coimbatore ($53) and then go by road (bus fare is Rs. 6.50, 50¢) to Ooty some 50 miles (82 km) away. Buses leave every half hour, 6:30 a.m. to 8:30 p.m., from Coimbatore's Central Bus Stand at Gandhipuram. They also meet the express trains from Madras.

More interesting is the little black-and-yellow **mountain railway train** that goes to Ooty from Mettupalayam, north of Coimbatore. While this train does not traverse the road like Darjeeling's "toy train," it chugs along the tracks cut into steep slopes to offer a fascinating ride with plenty of heart-stopping views into deep wooded valleys. This little train connects with **express trains** from Madras, one of the best being the *Nilgiris Express.* The express-train fare from Madras to Mettupalayam, 538 km (328 miles), is Rs. 195 ($15) in first class, Rs. 46 ($3.55) in second; the fare from there for the nearly five-hour trip to Ooty on the mountain railway is Rs. 40 ($3.05) in first class and Rs. 5 (40¢) in second. The mountain railway goes through Coonoor, so you can forgo the long ride and board at Coonoor and chug along for about an hour to Ooty for around Rs. 20 ($1.55) in first class.

The government-run Cheran Transport **buses** ply the roads between Bangalore and Ooty for Rs. 41.60 ($3.20); these buses leave Ooty for Bangalore at 6:30 a.m., 10:30 a.m., noon, and 8 p.m. The Mysore–Ooty bus ride costs Rs. 19.40 ($1.50), and these buses leave Ooty for Mysore at 8, 9, and 11:30 a.m., and 1:30 and 3:30 p.m. Ooty departure is from the Central Bus Stand (tel. 2770). Some Mysore–Ooty buses go to Bandipur, the wildlife sanctuary.

A Stop in Coimbatore En Route

Coimbatore, the third-largest city in Tamil Nadu (pop. 704,514), has so many textile mills that it has been nicknamed the "Manchester of South India." Sometimes people call it "The Detroit of the South" because some pumps used in Indian-made automobiles are made here, but that's truly stretching it. Coimbatore's main interest to tourists is as a stopover connection with Ooty. If you arrive by plane and have to connect to an Ooty train or bus in Coimbatore, the airport bus costs Rs. 20 ($1.55) to town. If you are truly a temple glutton and have some time, there's an old temple about six miles from Coimbatore with some fairly good sculptures.

Should you spend the night in Coimbatore or have a meal en route to Ooty, here are some choices:

Hotel Surya International, 105 Race Course Rd., Coimbatore 641018 (tel. 37751 to 37755), has modern rooms renting for Rs. 150 ($11.55) single and Rs. 225 ($17.30) double, without air conditioning; Rs. 275 ($21.15) air-conditioned. A continental breakfast costs Rs. 10 (75¢).

The TTDC's **Hotel Tamilnadu,** Dr. Nanjappa Road, Coimbatore 641018 (tel. 36311), has singles for Rs. 60 ($4.60) to Rs. 120 ($9.25), and doubles for Rs. 90 ($6.90) to Rs. 150 ($11.55), the higher prices for air-conditioned and/or deluxe accommodations.

At the **Hotel Guru,** 996 Raja St., Coimbatore 641001 (tel. 30341), the rooms are nothing to rave about, but rates are Rs. 45 ($3.45) single and Rs. 75 ($5.75) double, non-air-conditioned; Rs. 100 ($7.70) for an air-conditioned double. Both Indian and Western food is served in the restaurant.

Hotel Sree Annapoorna, 47 E. Arokiaswamy Rd., Coimbatore 641002 (tel. 37621), a cut above the Guru, is an Indian vegetarian hotel charging Rs. 100 ($7.70) to Rs. 130 ($10) for non-air-conditioned rooms, and Rs. 130 ($10) to Rs. 160 ($12.30) air-conditioned. The lower rates are for singles.

Chapter XIII

KERALA: CITY
LIFE AND WILDLIFE

1. Trivandrum
2. Cochin
3. Periyar Wildlife Sanctuary

THE SOUTHERN TIP of India can make a strong claim for being its most attractive and interesting part. Certainly it is one of the least-visited areas, which in itself makes it especially enjoyable for the tourists who do get there. The lush and lovely state of Kerala has always gone about its business pretty well undisturbed by the rest of the world. In its capital city of Trivandrum visitors do not need conducted tours. They can discover their own treasures, perhaps with the aid of the local tourist office or a couple of quaintly printed local guidebooks. Conducted tours are available however, and they can be a helpful orientation to the city and budget-stretchers in outlying areas.

1. Trivandrum

Trivandrum (pop. 520,000) is a delightful city, tropical and sleepy, as southern communities are apt to be, yet with some modern buildings, wide avenues, and the inevitable liveliness of a state capital. It's not quite on the water, although the Arabian Sea is only a mile or two away, and seven miles (11.5 km) to the south, at **Kovalam,** is one of the best-known beaches in all of India—its fame spread far and wide by Chester Bowles, a former U.S. ambassador to India, who used to vacation annually in the century-old palace nearby.

Trivandrum, like the rest of Kerala state, is best avoided during the monsoon season (June-July, and to a lesser extent in October) and is at its coolest in November and December. Its busiest season is November-January and during the festivals at the local temple in March to mid-May, exact dates varying from year to year (the hottest time of the year), when temple deities are paraded through the streets and exotically dressed performers re-create ancient Hindu legends via kathakali, the dance-drama for which Kerala is famous. If you plan to visit Trivandrum at festival time, make sure you have advance reservations.

WHERE TO STAY IN TRIVANDRUM: Many tourists don't stay in town at all, but at beautiful Kovalam Beach, seven miles (11.5 km) and a 20-minute taxi ride from town. The beach is an especially good choice for low-budget travelers who will find less pricey places out there than in town. No matter where you stay, remember that service charges at some hotels are 10% and luxury taxes at all hotels run from 5% for the lowest budget rooms to 10% at the upper end.

An old standby, the 41-room **Mascot Hotel,** Mascot Junction, Trivandrum 695033 (tel. 68990) is about two kilometers (1¼ miles) from the downtown area. The old wing of this rambling structure was originally constructed as an office building more than a century ago. Rumor has it that one of the leading luxury hotel chains may soon take it over, which surely means a rate increase. All rooms share a pleasant shady veranda. Presently, non-air-conditioned singles are Rs. 90 ($6.90); doubles, Rs. 120 ($9.25). Air-conditioned singles cost Rs. 200 ($15.40); doubles, Rs. 250 ($19.25). Add to these rates a 10% service charge and 10% luxury tax. The hotel has a 24-hour coffeeshop, and an open-air restaurant in the evenings where barbecue is served as long as the weather permits. The indoor restaurant features some good Kerala curries. Yoga and meditation instruction are available at the hotel.

Hotel Luciya Continental, East Fort, Trivandrum 695023 (tel. 73443), with 104 rooms. There's television and video in all 55-air conditioned rooms. Rates are Rs. 235 ($18.05) single and Rs. 300 double ($23.05) air-conditioned; rooms without air conditioning are Rs. 125 ($9.60) single and Rs. 180 ($13.85) double. Add 10% for the luxury tax.

Another in-town choice is the **Hotel Horizon,** Aristo Road, Trivandrum 695014 (tel. 66888), with 47 rooms going for Rs. 220 ($16.90) single and Rs. 275 ($21.15) double with air conditioning, and Rs. 120 ($9.25) single and Rs. 150 ($11.55) double without. Luxury tax is 10%.

In the heart of town, the 52-room **Hotel Pankaj,** M. G. Road (opposite the Secretariat), Trivandrum 695001 (tel. 66557), is modern with a terrific view from the top-floor coffeeshop. Non-air-conditioned rooms are Rs. 125 ($9.60) single and Rs. 175 ($13.45) double; with air conditioning, they're Rs. 225 ($17.30) single and Rs. 300 ($23.05) to Rs. 350 ($26.90). There are luxury taxes of 10% and a service charge on food of 10%.

The atmosphere of a private home prevails at the **Magnet,** Thycaud, Trivandrum 695014 (tel. 63301), with a pleasant garden dotted with shady mango trees. You'll find the essentials here, but no frills. All rooms have attached bathrooms, but hot water in buckets. Non-air-conditioned rooms are Rs. 47 ($3.60); air-conditioned rooms, Rs. 92 ($7.05). Inexpensive meals, both vegetarian and nonvegetarian, are available. The service charge is 10% and the luxury tax is 10%.

At the **Jas Hotel,** P.B. no. 431, Thycaud, Trivandrum 695014 (tel. 64881), rooms run Rs. 150 ($11.55) single and Rs. 180 ($13.85) double, air-conditioned; without air conditioning, Rs. 100 ($7.70) for singles and Rs. 120 ($9.25) for doubles. There's a service charge of 10% on food and a 10% luxury tax.

A plant-filled lobby and modern functional furnishings are features at the **Hotel Geeth,** near the main post office, Pulimoodu Junction, Trivandrum 695001 (tel. 71987), one kilometer (about half a mile) from downtown Trivandrum. Rooms are overpriced at Rs. 110 ($8.45) to Rs. 165 ($12.70) without air conditioning, and Rs. 275 ($21.15) and Rs. 385 ($29.60) air-conditioned. There's a rooftop restaurant where a full meal will run under Rs. 30 ($2.30), either Western or Kerala style.

A good choice among the Indian-style hotels is **Woodlands,** Thycaud, Trivandrum 695014 (tel. 67129), where everything is fairly neat and clean. Doubles are Rs. 120 ($9.25) without air conditioning, Rs. 160 ($12.30) with; suites run Rs. 300 ($23.05) single and Rs. 375 ($28.85) double. It's near the railway station and bus stand.

The non-air-conditioned rooms at the modern, fairly neat, 27-room **Hotel Amritha,** Thycaud, Trivandrum 695014 (tel. 63091), run Rs. 40 ($3.05) single and Rs. 60 ($4.60) double; for Rs. 65 ($5) single and Rs. 100 ($7.70) double you get one of the ten air-conditioned rooms. All rooms have attached bathrooms with tubs or showers. Luxury charge is 5% at the low end and 10% at the high end.

About six kilometers (3½ miles) from Kovalam Beach is the **Hotel Belair,** Agricultural College Road, Vellayani Post Office (tel. 3402 or 3403), has an abundance of rosewood in the attractive decor because the owner has some connection with the rosewood business. The pleasant hotel has a pool and cottages; the current tariff sheet was not available at press time but should be in the upper price range.

Budget

The Indian-style **Baba Tourist Hotel,** Pulimoodu (tel. 77099), a five-minute walk from the bus station, is not for the overly fussy. It's back from the street so it enjoys some quiet. Rates are Rs. 14 ($1.05) to Rs. 28 ($2.15).

Rock-bottom travelers here should follow one of the basic rules of finding cheap accommodation in India: Check out the Indian-style hotels near the bus and railway station, where you'll spend around Rs. 25 ($1.90) to Rs. 45 ($3.45) a night, but don't expect anything more than bare essentials and little in the way of cleanliness.

Another choice, seven miles (11.5 km) from town is the **Youth Hostel,** pleasantly situated on a canal but inconvenient to nearly everything. Another drawback is that no meals are served unless there are 15 or more guests, and then the warden will hire a cook. There are men's and women's dorms accommodating eight to ten travelers each at Rs. 5 (40¢) per person for members, Rs. 8 (60¢) for nonmembers.

WHERE TO EAT IN TRIVANDRUM: Kerala House Restaurant, Statue Junction, approached through a narrow alley, has four rooms each with four tables. This is the place to try delicious, inexpensive, and spicy Kerala curries: six vegetable and one fish curry arrayed on a banana leaf with rice, Indian breads, and condiments. Even less without the fish. You eat with your right hand. Banana leaves are considered cleaner than plates: they're plucked fresh, right before the meal is served, used once, and tossed out, while plates, although washed, are usually stacked where they can gather dust. Use the right hand for eating. Washed right as you sit down to table, it's cleaner than the much-washed, dust-gathering flatware.

The simple **Indian Coffee House** on the Main Road, is where, as the name implies, coffee (locally grown in South India) is outstanding. South Indian snacks are available to go with it. Indeed, you'll rarely find anything over Rs. 5 (40¢) here, so lowest-budget travelers should make a beeline for this place. Open from 8:30 a.m. to 8:30 p.m.

At the non-atmospheric **Azad Hotel,** Mahatma Gandhi Road ("hotel" meaning "restaurant" in this case), there's no printed menu, but a waiter will serve you some North Indian specialties such as biryani (rice, meat, and spices) or a southern vegetable curry, or fried chicken, none of which should cost more than Rs. 10 (75¢) to Rs. 12 (90¢). Coffee and tea are also available. When Westerners drop in, they are given what silverware there is (usually big spoons of the serving type) out of courtesy. Everyone else eats with the hands, as is the local custom. Try it, especially if you want to encourage some amused glances from the locals. The Azad has a branch at Statue Junction with a similar range of foods and prices.

Arya Bhavan, near the railway station and across from the bus depot, has vegetarian meals for Rs. 5 (40¢).

If you crave nappery and service, head to any of the top hotels.

TOURS: One tour conducted by the **Kerala Tourism Development Corporation (KTDC)** is the Trivandrum city tour. It operates daily except Monday from 8 a.m. to 7 p.m., costs Rs. 40 ($3.05), and covers Padmanabhapuram Palace, Shankumugham Beach, the aquarium, SMSM Institute, Aruivkkara Dam, Neyyar Dam, Kovalam Beach, museum and art gallery, and zoo. The tour to Kanya Kumari (Cape Comorin) takes in Kovalam Beach, Padmanabhapuram Palace, Suchindram Temple, Kanya Kumari, and the Vivekananda Memorial. It operates daily from 7:30 a.m. to 9 p.m. and costs Rs. 60 ($4.60). The tour to Ponmudi, a hill station, runs daily from 8:30 a.m. to 7 p.m. for Rs. 40 ($3.05). The tour to Thekkady and the Periyar Wildlife Sanctuary costs Rs. 100 ($7.70), runs every Saturday from 6:30 a.m. to 9 p.m., and includes boating at Thekkady; food and accommodation are extra. All tours are by coach. They all start at, and can be booked through, the KTDC Tourist Reception Centre, near the KSRTC Bus Stand, Thampanoor, Trivandrum. Check whether there's an English-speaking guide; if not, you may have to pay extra for one.

To book a backwater trip by country boat, contact Tourindia, Mahatma Gandhi Road (P.B. Box 163), Trivandrum 695001 (tel. 79407).

GETTING HELP AND GETTING AROUND: Maps, pamphlets, and people to answer questions or assist with hotel reservations can be found at the **Tourist Information Centres** at the airport, the railway station, and in town at the office between the railway station and Mahatma Gandhi Road. The office in town is where you book city sightseeing tours as well as tours to Kanya Kumari and the Periyar Wildlife Sanctuary (Thekkady). The Kerala State Tourism Development Corporation is located in the Secretariat Building.

WHAT TO SEE: The list of more or less mandatory tourist attractions is small indeed: the famous **Sri Padmanabhaswamy Temple** and the **Public Gardens,** the latter containing the **Napier and Sri Chitralayam museums.** Of passing interest are the **Kaudiyar Palace,** once the residence of the local maharaja; the ancient **observatory;** and the **Oriental Library,** with its historic palm-leaf manuscripts.

The **Padmanabhaswamy Temple** was probably built during the 18th-century reign of Raja Marthanda, although legends say there was some sort of temple on the site as far back as 3000 B.C. At any rate, its 300 pillars and imposing seven-story tower make it by far the most impressive landmark around town, and it's not hard to believe the story that 4,000 stonecutters, 6,000 other workers, and a few hundred elephants were employed in its construction. Non-Hindus aren't allowed inside the gates but will find it most interesting to peek in through them between 6 and 8 a.m. and 5 and 7 p.m. when most of the worshippers gather inside.

Trivandrum's **Public Gardens** will consume most of your time, partly because it's pleasant to meander among the tropical plants and flowers and visit the moderate-size zoo (the animals are housed as much as possible in their natural habitat), and second, because it contains the town's two museums. The **Napier Museum,** a monumental piece of Victorian architecture, with a striking red-and-white exterior, is devoted mainly to stone sculptures, bronzes, and woodcarvings, the oldest relics dating back to between the 2nd and 9th centuries. There are ancient musical instruments, a reconstructed family dwelling, and a natural history section with the usual showcases of everything from stuffed owls to whale skeletons. Entrance to the museum (closed Monday and on Wednesday mornings) is free and it is open, like the zoo and the park itself, from 8 a.m. to 6 p.m. There's a token charge for admission to the zoo, which can also be toured without getting out of your car upon payment of a few rupees. There is a range of fees for cameras, depending on their type.

Also in the gardens, not far from the Napier, is the smaller **Sri Chitralayam Museum,** which is renowned for its varied collection of art from China, Japan, and Tibet; miniatures from northern India; gold-leaf pictures from Tanjore; works from Bali and Java; copies of Ajanta frescoes; and contemporary works by local artists. Admission free; the same hours as the Napier: 8 a.m. to 6 p.m.; closed Monday and on Wednesday mornings.

To wrap up all these sights and then some there's a Kerala Tourism Development Corporation (KTDC) **tour** every day but Monday. It leaves at 8 a.m. and returns at 7 p.m. after covering the Padmanabhaswamy Temple, Sankumugham Beach, museum, zoo, art gallery, handcrafts emporium, waterworks, Neyyar Dam, and gardens. The fare is Rs. 40 ($3.05) per person, excluding food. For details and reservations, check with the KTDC Tourist Reception Centre, Thampanoor, Trivandrum (tel. 2643). The KTDC also runs tours to Thekkady (described later in this chapter under Periyar) and to Kanya Kumari (described in Chapter XII). The Tourindia travel agency (tel. 79407) arranges backwater trips by country boat.

SHOPPING: Once you've covered the obvious sights, then you'll turn to every tourist's favorite pastime: shopping. Trivandrum's most rewarding spots are the **Chalai Bazaar,** where you can haggle to your hearts' content, and the state-run **S.M.S.M.** (Central Handicrafts Emporium), where the prices are fixed.

BEST TIME TO VISIT: Ulsavom (March/April and October/November) is celebrated at Padmanasbhaswamy Temple for ten days. The temple elephants go out in processions around the town and there are folk music and dancing performances. Best season is November to March; the rainy season is May to November. Summer's usually above 90°F., and winter's rarely below the high 60s.

KOVALAM BEACH: About seven miles (11.5 km) south of Trivandrum is Kovalam Beach, so fabulous it's almost a cliché: age-old black rocks, towering palms, pale sands, and gentle surf (take care—there can be an undertow!). It has remained peaceful as it develops into a popular resort. Below are only a few hotels in various price ranges, but by the time you get there new hotels undoubtedly will have opened. A number of hotels offer off-season rates or will negotiate in season if they're not fully occupied. It literally pays rupees to ask about special rates.

Where to Stay in Kovalam

Top choice for beauty and a moderate splurge is the **Rockholm Seaside Hotel,** Lighthouse Road, Vizhinjam (tel. 695521), perched on a rocky ledge overhanging the sea. The large attractively decorated rooms have big connecting bathrooms and balconies to catch the soft sea breezes. The feeling overall is that of a gracious, well-cared-for private home. Steps lead down to the beach, from which it's a pleasant 15-minute walk to a string of outdoor cafés. Rates: Rs. 150 ($11.55) double, Rs. 120 ($9.25) single. Lunch and dinner cost about Rs. 25 ($1.90) to Rs. 35 ($2.70), less for breakfast.

Also on Lighthouse Road is the much simpler **Sea Weed** (tel. 391), charging Rs. 40 ($3.05) single and Rs. 60 ($4.60) double. Nearby is the **Hotel Neelakanda** (tel. 321), with simple doubles for Rs. 80 ($6.15) to Rs. 100 ($7.70). Another Lighthouse Road hotel is the **Paradise Rock,** truly modest at Rs. 25 ($1.90). **Green Valley Cottages,** near Lighthouse Road, charges Rs. 30 ($2.30).

Next to the expensive Ashok (see "Splurging," below) is the moderate **Raja Hotel** (tel. 55), with neat, pleasant rooms suitable for a simple beach holiday; rates are Rs. 250 ($19.25) double and Rs. 120 ($9.25) single. Nearby is the **Neela** (tel. 377), less nice than its neighbor and with lower rates: Rs. 30 ($2.30) to Rs. 40 ($3.05). Another neighboring choice is the **Hotel Palm Gardens** (tel. 333), charging Rs. 25 ($1.90) to Rs. 30 ($2.30).

Away from it all is **Sun and Waves** (tel. 361), asking Rs. 100 ($7.70) for the one double air-conditioned, and Rs. 25 ($1.90) single and Rs. 40 ($3.05) double, non-air-conditioned. It's a hike to the beach from here.

On the beach are the **Hotel Sea Rock,** charging Rs. 75 ($5.75) to Rs. 175 ($13.45) a day; and the lower-priced **Velvet Dawn,** at Rs. 30 ($2.30) per day.

You'll find higher prices at KTDC's **Samudra,** G. V. Raja Road (tel. 3605 or 4024), for acceptable cottage accommodations: Rs. 150 ($11.55) single and Rs. 175 ($13.45) double, air conditioned; Rs. 100 ($7.70) single and Rs. 125 ($9.60) double, non-air-conditioned.

And that's a mere sampling. Stroll along the beach and you'll find many hotels (some strangely enough called "restaurants," which makes some kind of cockeyed sense since restaurants in these parts are often called "hotels"). Some of these little places will give you a room for Rs. 15 ($1.15) or Rs. 20 ($1.55), but prices like these are rare nowadays—unless it's off-season.

Splurging at Kovalam

Kovalam Ashok Beach Resort, Trivandrum 695522 (tel. 68010), is a splurge-priced India Tourism Development Corporation resort. It's composed of cottages, a hotel, and a curious old Victorian castle, now a convention meeting hall, but in its heyday a favorite hotel of former U.S. ambassador Chester Bowles. In the cottages, rooms make wide use of colorful local motifs and contain little kitchenettes with refrigerators; plus, they have private sundecks and piped-in music to sunbathe by. The air-conditioned hotel has well-appointed rooms as well. There are swimming pools, bars, restaurants, and a shopping arcade. But everything else is just a mundane pleasure when compared to the extraordinary enjoyment of the oil massages at the Yoga Centre, where the body and soul are restored according to ancient Ayurvedic methods. Rooms in the hotel are Rs. 600 ($46.15) single and Rs. 675 ($51.90) double; in the cottages, Rs. 550 ($42.30) single and Rs. 605 ($46.55) double. Suites go for Rs. 1,110 ($85.40). Meals will add another Rs. 125 ($9.60) to Rs.

150 ($11.55) per day per person. There's a 10% luxury tax and taxes as applicable.

Eating Out

There's a string of cafés along the beach with names like Pussycat, Place International, and Velvet Dawn that are open mainly in season, or when there's a large enough number of visitors to make it worthwhile. While they all serve light meals such as omelets and Indian snacks, your best bets are Kerala vegetarian curries and rice or seafood dishes. Some of the cafés have Western music on tape and sometimes there's live entertainment at night. Along the beach during the day, vendors hawk fruits and drinks for the sunbathers, much as they do at many other beaches the world over. The main difference at Kovalam is even a papaya is not price-fixed—you bargain for your snack.

Getting to Kovalam

The bus from Trivandrum runs frequently from around 6 a.m. to 9 p.m. You get it at the Fort Bus Depot. Early and later buses are the least crowded, although all of them become less crowded as you make stops along the way to the beach. Coming back from Kovalam, buses run often, from around 6 a.m. to 10 p.m. The bus stand is near the Kovalam Ashok Beach Resort.

PADMANABHURPAM PALACE: Usually visited en route to Kanya Kumari (Cape Comorin; see Chapter XII) and part of the Kanya Kumari Tour, Padmanabhurpam Palace can also be an interesting excursion from Trivandrum or Kovalam.

The palace, dating mainly from the 17th century, looks like one structure. But it's actually a series of buildings with peaked pagoda roofs blending as one. Dark teak from the local forests was the basic building material. The mirror-shiny floors look like highly polished stone, but are actually a stone-hard compound of pulverized coconut shells and raw egg whites. The rooms and their accoutrements are impressive—a dining hall that could hold 1,000 guests at a time, a stone dancing hall with delicately carved stone screens at one end, behind which the ladies of the court used to watch discreetly, and vivid orange, green, and brown murals depicting epic poems.

A century or two ago the palace served as the ancient capital of the rulers of southern India. The maharaja's old bed, composed of 64 different kinds of medicated wood and given to him by Portuguese visitors, can still be admired, as can the ivory-inlaid bed of his queen.

The palace, about 33 miles (53 km) south of Trivandrum, and about 20 miles (12 km) from Kovalam, is open daily except Monday from 9 a.m. to 5 p.m.

Ten miles farther south, another landmark is the **Suchindram Temple,** but non-Hindus are not allowed inside.

GETTING TO TRIVANDRUM: Daily Indian Airlines flights from Madras take two hours and cost Rs. 568 ($43.70). From Cochin, flights operate on Monday and cost Rs. 191 ($14.70). Between Bombay and Trivandrum the air fare is Rs. 1,085 ($83.45).

Trains originating in Delhi or Bombay take 48 and 45 hours respectively to reach Trivandrum. More practically suited to many travelers' schedules are trains from Madras, such as the *Trivandrum Mail,* which takes 18 hours and costs Rs. 576 ($44.30) in air-conditioned class, Rs. 291 ($22.40) in first class, and Rs. 70 ($5.40) in second. Or you might consider the scenic coastal route on one of the express trains to Trivandrum that also stop at Cochin/ Ernakulam and Quilon. A good choice from Cochin is the *Ernakulam– Trivandrum Express,* covering a distance of 221 km (135 miles), which departs around 6 a.m. and arrives around 10 a.m. so you can see the sunrise and sights along the way. The fare is Rs. 97 ($7.45) in first class and Rs. 23 ($1.75) in second.

Bus routes go from Ernakulam/Cochin via Alleppey, Kottayam, and other Kerala cities such as Kozhikode in the north. KSRTC buses ply these routes. The best bus from Ernakulam is the KSTRC's deluxe daily service aboard a 29-seat Mitsubishi bus at 3 p.m. (time should be double-checked when you reserve your seat; tel. 352033) to Trivandrum via Kayamkulam; it takes four hours and costs Rs. 40 ($3.05). There are also several express buses between 1 to 9:30 p.m. from Ernakulam to Trivandrum, via Alleppey, for Rs. 27 ($2.05); the 221-km (135-mile) journey lasts a little over five hours. Fast passenger buses from Ernakulam cost Rs. 25 ($1.90) for a journey of about 6½ hours. From north Kerala, buses leave Kozhikode at 9:30 p.m. The KSTDC's telephone number in Ernakulam is 352033.

2. Cochin

If Kerala is India's most beautiful state, which many tourists believe, then the lovely port of Cochin is its jewel. It's heard its share of superlatives—Queen of the Arabian Sea, Venice of the Orient, etc., etc.—but earns most of them simply by being inimitably its unspoiled, relatively unvisited self.

Yet Cochin has everything the average tourist usually seeks—true tropical, palm-studded surroundings, constant sunshine, a harbor that rivals that of Hong Kong, hotels with swimming pools and good food, endless backwater boat trips to eavesdrop on life and work that has not changed for centuries, and cheerful, good-natured people as yet uncorrupted by the corroding tide of tourism.

Kerala is a luxuriant garden state, the fabled land of incense and myrrh —"to which King Solomon's ships sailed a thousand years before Christ"— and Cochin is the port from which such exotic cargoes as pepper, spices, ivory, and coir are still exported. When the Portuguese established the first European colony in India here in the early 16th century, it had already known the Romans, the Greeks, and the Chinese.

Cochin owes its modern status as an important port to a British admiralty engineer, Sir Robert Bristow, who opened up its backwaters in 1929 by cutting a long, deep channel in the ocean bed.

ORIENTATION: Cochin (pop. 600,000) is not just a town but a complex of islands grouped off the mainland town called **Ernakulam.** One of the islands, **Willingdon,** named after Viscount Willingdon (a former governor), 12 square miles, was created in 1900 by a dredge and is where most of the port facilities are centered, also the airport and Cochin Harbor Railway Terminus.

If you arrive by air or some trains, Willingdon will be your debarkation point, and it also contains the main Tourist Office, and two top hotels, Malabar and Casino; the third top hotel is Abad Plaza, in Ernakulam.

Also in the harbor are **Gundu Island,** site of the coir factory, and

Bolghatty Island with one hotel. To the south are **Mattancheri,** with such attractions as the 16th-century synagogue and Dutch palace and Fort Cochin, site of what is supposed to be the oldest European settlement on the Indian subcontinent. Even from the briefest of descriptions you can see that Cochin has a fascinating blend of cultures. To the north is Vypeen, of little interest to tourists. On the mainland are many hotels, the Ernakulam Junction Railway Station, the Cochin Cultural Centre, main post office, Indian Airlines office, and Kerala State Transportation bus station and Tourist Reception Centre, where you can book sightseeing tours.

All the locations are connected by ferries, easily the most pleasant way to go from island to island. A good road and bridges also link Willingdon and Fort Cochin/Mattancheri and Ernakulam.

GETTING AROUND THE ISLANDS AND TOWN: Willingdon is connected by **ferry** to the mainland town of Ernakulam (65 paise, 5¢; 25 times a day in either direction). The first ferry from Ernakulum leaves at 6:30 a.m. and the last at 9:40 p.m.; from Mattancheri, the first ferry leaves at 6 a.m. and the last at 9 p.m. After the last ferry, the trip to and from Ernakulam can be made by taxi or auto-rickshaw—all the way down the island, across the bridge, and back up the mainland on the other side—costing about Rs. 50 ($3.85) by taxi. The Perumanoor ferry also goes to Willingdon for Rs. 30 ($2.30), but is not conveniently located for tourists; it's handy if you're going to or from Air India, which is near the Perumanoor jetty.

Willingdon and Mattancheri are also connected by ferry, running on the hour and half hour from 6 a.m. to 9 p.m. The ten-minute trip costs Rs. 40 ($3.05). There is no ferry service between Fort Cochin and Willingdon. You can hire a rowboat for this trip, which should cost Rs. 2 (15¢) or Rs. 3 (23¢), but invariably the boatowners ask more from foreigners.

Fort Cochin is connected with Ernakulam by ferry service (65 paise, 5¢ one way; 20-minute crossing, 18 times a day in either direction): from Ernakulam beginning at 6:30 a.m. until 9:40 p.m., and from Fort Cochin beginning at 6:50 a.m. until 9 p.m.

Ernakulam and Vypeen Island ferries operate all day: beginning at 5:30 a.m. from Ernakulam until 10:30 p.m.; from Vypeen, beginning at 6 a.m. to 10 p.m. The cost is 65 paise (5¢). Between Fort Cochin and Vypeen, there is service about every ten minutes from 6 a.m. to 9 p.m. at 25 paise (2¢) for the five-minute trip. You can change at Vypeen for the ferry to Fort Cochin.

There is no ferry service to Gundu, which can be seen on the sightseeing tour.

Private boats operate between Ernakulam and Varapuzha, from 7:40 a.m. to 7:40 p.m. You take this ferry for Rs. 1.50 (11¢) if you wish to cruise leisurely for two hours to get a superb close-up look at village life. (Skip Varapuzha if you plan to do the backwater cruise between Alleppey and Quilon, described later.)

Taxis in Cochin don't always have meters, so drivers try to charge what they think the traffic will bear. You must bargain to get a fair fare—about Rs. 2 (15¢) to Rs. 2.20 (17¢) per kilometer—and set the rate before you get in. Tourist taxis—those with white license plates and black letters—will probably charge Rs. 2.20 (17¢) per kilometer or Rs. 24 ($1.85) per hour, whichever is higher. Waiting charges are an extra Rs. 30 ($2.30) per day, but it's a good idea to check the odometer at the beginning and end of your trip. Yellow-topped metered taxis charge Rs. 2 (15¢) per kilometer or Rs. 20 ($1.55) per hour, whichever is higher. Waiting charges are an extra Rs. 28 ($2.15) per day.

Auto-rickshaw drivers in Ernakulam use their meters, but often try to get a bit more from tourists; in Fort Cochin, forget the meters (the drivers' do) and just bargain to set a fare before you get in, based on the metered rate of 80 paise (6¢) per kilometer and a minimum of Rs. 2 (15¢). Waiting charges are extra.

WHERE TO STAY IN COCHIN: Luxury taxes add 5% to 10% to most room tariffs quoted below. Some hotels also add a 10% service charge.

On Willingdon Island

On Willingdon are two top hotels, the famous Malabar and the newer Casino, and next to it the Maruthi Tourist Home, for budget travelers.

The splurge-priced **Hotel Malabar,** Willingdon Island, Cochin 682003 (tel. 6811) was adding 18 rooms to its former total of 37 rooms when I stopped in. This old favorite, right on the waterfront overlooking the harbor, is the best situated, with spacious lawns, a swimming pool, bar, and restaurants. Dating back to colonial days, it has been refurbished, and has all the modern amenities such as air conditioning, but still retains its old-fashioned charm. Rates for rooms are Rs. 500 ($38.45) single and Rs. 600 ($46.15) double, with special deluxe doubles at Rs. 650 ($50); an Indian-decor suite costs Rs. 1,750 ($134.60). A Government of India Tourist Office is on the grounds.

Set back from the street, the elegant **Casino Hotel,** Willingdon Island, Cochin 682003 (tel. 6821), is situated only a couple of hundred yards from the Cochin Harbor Railway Terminus. It's light and airy, with colored coir carpeting and other local furnishings. There's a swimming pool, an attractive restaurant in an adjoining building (the hotel began from this restaurant), an outdoor seafood café, and a bookstore. Rooms are attractively and comfortably furnished, with refrigerators and air conditioning among their amenities. Singles cost Rs. 300 ($23.05); doubles, Rs. 350 ($26.90); and suites, Rs. 600 ($45.16)—plus the expected 10% luxury tax.

Next to the Casino Hotel, the **Maruthi Tourist Home,** Willingdon Island, Cochin 682003 (tel. 6365), has 26 rooms that are almost always full of business travelers who congregate in the bar. The rooms are simple, clean, and pleasant, with attached Western-style bathrooms. Rates without air conditioning run Rs. 30 ($2.30) single and Rs. 50 ($3.85) to Rs. 55 ($4.25); air-conditioned doubles go for Rs. 100 ($7.70). You can get a good meal in the vegetarian restaurant for Rs. 6 (45¢).

In Ernakulam

One of the most outstanding buys are the non-air-conditioned rooms at the **Hotel Luciya,** Stadium Road (near the state bus stand), Ernakulam, Cochin 682011 (tel. 354433), which cost only Rs. 25 ($1.90) for a single and Rs. 50 ($3.85) for a double. Here as elsewhere, if rooms are not air-conditioned, they have ceiling fans. Air-conditioned singles are moderately high at Rs. 60 ($4.60); doubles cost Rs. 100 ($7.70). You get such higher-priced touches as attractive furnishings, private modern bathrooms, and piped-in music. It is also clean, with a bar and restaurant on the premises which serves both vegetarian and nonvegetarian food. There are 104 rooms, including two suites costing Rs. 85 ($6.55) to Rs. 125 ($9.60), accommodating quite a few budget travelers.

A 10% discount to travelers who have this book to show at the reception is offered by E. K. Paul, managing director of two hotels popular with Westerners. These are the **Sangeetha,** Chittor Road, Ernakulam, Cochin 682016 (tel. 368736), and the **Gaanam Hotel** (tel. 367123), in the same compound. At the all-vegetarian Sangeetha there are 48 functionally furnished rooms, all with bathrooms attached and hot and cold running water. Rates are Rs. 40 ($3.05) to Rs. 43 ($3.30) for non-air-conditioned singles, and Rs. 65 ($5) to Rs. 75 ($5.75) for doubles without air conditioning; also without air conditioning, a deluxe double is Rs. 95 ($7.30) and a deluxe single is Rs. 70 ($5.40). Air-conditioned rooms rent for Rs. 100 ($7.70) to Rs. 110 ($8.45) single, and doubles are Rs. 130 ($10) to Rs. 150 ($11.55).

Recently refurbished, the 40-room Gaanam has also been upgraded to three stars. All rooms have phones, piped-in music, and modern attached bathrooms with marble flooring. Deluxe rooms have closed-circuit TV. For 40 pleasant, comfortable rooms, singles without air conditioning cost Rs. 70 ($5.40), and doubles Rs. 125 ($9.60); air-conditioned rooms go for Rs. 100 ($7.70) single and Rs. 130 ($10) to Rs. 180 ($13.85) double. Single occupancy of a deluxe double is Rs. 150 ($11.55). The Gaanam serves both vegetarian and nonvegetarian food, and has a pleasant rooftop restaurant open in the evenings.

Near the bus terminal, the 95-room **Bharat Tourist Home,** on Durbar Hall Road, Ernakulam, Cochin 682016 (tel. 353501), is also next door to Indian airlines and a two-minute stroll to the east to the Cochin Cultural Centre where Kathakali dances are performed at night. Bharat is a vegetarian hotel with a pretty little garden and a mural featuring a five-headed snake in the reception area, which is decorated in a red-and-gray color scheme. The two restaurants (covered later in "Where to Eat") serve both South and North Indian vegetarian foods. There is also a 24-hour coffeeshop for drinks and snacks. The rooms overall are nice, especially those with sea views, although some need paint jobs. There are 31 singles at Rs. 50 ($3.85), 51 doubles rooms for Rs. 90 ($6.90) to Rs. 110 ($8.45), and 14 air-conditioned double suites for Rs. 150 ($11.55) to Rs. 275 ($21.15).

On Mahatma Gandhi Road, where there are many hotels, the **International Hotel,** P.B. 3563, Ernakulam, Cochin 682035 (tel. 358911), is spacious and fairly clean, with a big upstairs lounge, Persian carpets on the stairs, and most rooms with radios, balconies, and big bathtubs. There is a bar, dining room, and roof garden. Rates are two-tiered: singles rent for Rs. 80 ($6.15) without air conditioning and Rs. 105 ($8.05) with; single occupancy of a double room runs Rs. 100 ($7.70) to Rs. 235 ($18.05), the higher rate for a special deluxe room with air conditioning. Doubles start at Rs. 100 ($7.70) without air conditioning, Rs. 160 ($12.30) with, and Rs. 295 ($22.70) for a special deluxe double room. Other singles and doubles range between these prices. The Coq d'Or Restaurant serves both vegetarian and nonvegetarian meals in the Indian, continental, and Chinese styles, from 7 a.m. to 12:30 a.m. The Belle Bar, with leatherette booths and a "jug of wine, loaf of bread" theme mural is open from 10:30 a.m. to 10:30 p.m.

Also on Mahatma Gandhi Road, the **Grand Hotel,** Ernakulam, Cochin 682001 (tel. 353211), is in a pleasant tropical-style building whose 24 doubles (8 non-air-conditioned and 18 air-conditioned) have Western-style bathrooms and showers. There are also two suites. Large and clean, the non-air-conditioned rooms run Rs. 80 ($6.15) single and Rs. 100 ($7.70) double. Air-conditioned rooms cost Rs. 120 ($9.25) single and Rs. 140 ($10.75) double. The deluxe rooms, with Persian carpets and balconies, go for Rs. 200 ($15.40) to Rs. 225 ($17.30). The 12 new rooms on two fully air-conditioned floors should be ready by the time you arrive. Meals are served in the large, airy dining room. There is also an air-conditioned restaurant, the Peacock (see "Where to Eat"). A tiny, cozy little round bar room with wood-slatted walls, booths, and marble-topped bar is open from 10 a.m. to 11 p.m.

The **Hotel Seaking,** Mahatma Gandhi Road, Ernakulam, Cochin 682035 (tel. 355341), is a four-story building set back in a lane off the street. All 50 rooms have small balconies overlooking the neighborhood. They also have attached bathrooms, but only ten have running hot water; in the others, hot water is provided in buckets, upon request. Unfortunately, the hotel is not well maintained, but the fairly low rates in the non-air-conditioned rooms will be appealing to the unfussy: Rs. 30 ($2.30) to Rs. 35 ($2.70) single, and Rs. 45 ($3.45) to Rs. 55 ($4.25) for doubles (the higher rates for rooms with telephones), and Rs. 70 ($5.40) triple (without a telephone). The air-conditioned rooms, with a telephone, cost Rs. 75 ($5.75) single, Rs. 100 ($7.70) double, and Rs. 125 ($9.60) triple. In the Hong Kong Room, open from 11 a.m. to 11 p.m., you can get Indian and Chinese foods for Rs. 14 ($1.05) to Rs. 33 ($2.55). The very dark, ground-floor bar, open from 10 a.m. to 11 p.m., has erotic plaster wall sculpture and round tables.

Mahatma Gandhi Road is also the location of the tidy and pleasant Indian-style **Dwaraka Hotel,** Ernakulam, Cochin 682016 (tel. 352706), with 42 rooms. Singles run Rs. 55 ($4.25) without air conditioning, Rs. 135 ($10.40) with; single occupancy of larger and deluxe rooms, and suites ranges from Rs. 125 ($9.60) to Rs. 175 ($13.45). Doubles cost Rs. 100 ($7.70) non-air-conditioned and Rs. 150 ($11.55) air-conditioned; for larger and deluxe doubles and suites, prices range from Rs. 175 ($13.45) to Rs. 200 ($15.40). Luxury tax is 10%. There's a pretty roof garden with potted plants galore, and the rooms are clean, big, and nicely furnished, with music, television, refrigerator, phone, and modern bathrooms. In Dwaraka's two vegetarian restaurants serving South and North Indian dishes, you can get a meal for Rs. 10 (75¢) to Rs. 15 ($1.15), depending on what you order and whether you eat in the non-air-conditioned or air-conditioned dining room.

Simpler but also pleasant, another Indian-style hotel, the **Woodlands,** Mahatma Gandhi Road, Ernakulam, Cochin 682011 (tel. 351372), has 65 rooms—spacious, not elaborate, but with such amenities as attached bathrooms with either Western- or Indian-style toilets, phones, piped-in music, and television. Some rooms have balconies. Rates for non-air-conditioned singles are Rs. 65 ($5), Rs. 100 ($7.70) air-conditioned; doubles without air conditioning are Rs. 100 ($7.70) and Rs. 130 ($10) air-conditioned. Suites run Rs. 120 ($9.25) and Rs. 185 ($14.25), with and without air conditioning respectively.

Sleek modern rooms at the multistoried **Hotel Blue Diamond,** Market Road, Ernakulam, Cochin 682031 (tel. 353221), feature all the amenities—television in both air-conditioned and non-air-conditioned rooms, and bathrooms with hot and cold running water throughout the premises. Rates are Rs. 46 ($3.55) single and Rs. 110 ($8.45) double; with air conditioning, rates are Rs. 99.50 ($7.65) single and Rs. 144 ($11.05) double.

Splurge priced, the attractive centrally air-conditioned, **Abad Plaza,** Mahatma Gandhi Road, Ernakulam, Cochin, 682035 (tel. 361636), is the posh new addition to Ernakulam's hotels. Through the glass-framed doorway you step onto gleaming marble floors in the small, understated lobby and reception, with an imposing chandelier. The tastefully furnished spacious rooms have varied color schemes—soft earth tones or crisp white, green, and blue, among other combinations. Coir matting covers the floors in the standard rooms, which are somewhat smaller than deluxe rooms and suites (which also have wall-to-wall carpeting). In all rooms are television, telephones, and piped-in music. Single rooms rent for Rs. 160 ($12.30) and Rs. 240 ($18.45); doubles, Rs. 200 ($15.40) and Rs. 300 ($23.05). Suites cost Rs. 500 ($38.45). The handsome Regency Room (see "Where to Eat") is open for lunch from 12:30 to 3 p.m. and for dinner from 7:30 p.m. to midnight.

Over on Shanmugham Road, the splurge-priced 40-room **Sealord Hotel,** Ernakulam, Cochin 682031 (tel. 362682), has all kinds of amenities, a pleasant rooftop Chinese restaurant, and a sunbathing terrace in the shape of a ship's deck. The Princess Room restaurant serves well-prepared food on the first floor (see "Where to Eat"). The Sealord's rooms are modern and functional, and have music and TV. All are doubles or suites. Single occupancy costs Rs. 155 ($11.90) and Rs. 220 ($16.90); double, Rs. 210 ($16.15) and Rs. 275 ($21.15). Suites go for Rs. 500 ($38.45).

The lower-priced **Hotel Seashell,** Shanmugham Road, Ernakulam, Cochin 682031 (tel. 353807), has nine sparsely furnished rooms, two of them air-conditioned with both hot and cold running water in the attached bathrooms, and seven rooms where hot water is supplied in buckets to the private bathrooms. A friendly staff compensates for lack of decoration, as do the moderate rates: the two air-conditioned rooms are Rs. 65 ($5) double and Rs. 85 ($6.55) triple; six standard doubles cost Rs. 42 ($3.25), and one deluxe double, Rs. 48 ($3.70). The Seashell has a bar and small dining room serving vegetarian and nonvegetarian dishes, at prices averaging around Rs. 3 (23¢) to Rs. 10 (75¢).

Almost as simple as the Seashell, and nearby, is a budget traveler's favorite, the **Hotel Hakoba,** Shanmugham Road, Ernakulam, Cochin 682031 (tel. 33933), with its 12 double rooms. Five of these are air-conditioned, and from three of them (preferred) you look out toward the sea from huge windows. Besides this, the attached bathrooms have Western-style plumbing and running hot water. The halls could be a lot tidier, but the rooms are clean and the service is friendly and efficient. Rates are Rs. 81 ($6.25) for air-conditioned doubles and Rs. 50 ($3.85) for standard doubles; single occupancy of a double room costs Rs. 32.25 ($2.50). All these rates include tax. The ferry dock is nearby.

Budget Accommodations in Ernakulam: At the **Cochin Home,** Ernakulam South, 682016 (tel. 35182), rates are Rs. 20 ($1.55) and Rs. 35 ($2.70-), non-air-conditioned. There are similar rates also at the better-located **Broadway Lodge,** Broadway, Ernakulam, Cochin 682031 (tel. 368679), with singles for Rs. 20 ($1.55) and doubles for Rs. 30 ($2.30); and the **Hotel Deepak,** with non-air-conditioned rooms for Rs. 15 ($1.15) single and Rs. 20 ($1.55) double, Rs. 50 ($3.85) with air conditioning—but don't expect much in the way of comforts or cleanliness.

In Fort Cochin and Mattancheri

The **Hotel Seagull,** Calvery Road, Fort Cochin, set back from the street and right on the water, has six non-air-conditioned rooms for Rs. 50 ($3.85), where the attached bathrooms have cold running water and hot water can be ordered by the bucket. The two air-conditioned rooms (the only choice if you're fussy) cost Rs. 100 ($7.70), with attached bathrooms with hot and cold running water. The rooms are modern and the views from them are not spectacular, but the entire front of the hotel is a dining room lounge and it faces the sea. The restaurant's fish curry at Rs. 10 (75¢) is considered some of the best in town. There's an air-conditioned bar.

Higher in price, the **Hotel Abad,** Chullikal Junction, Cochin 682005 (tel. 28211), is on the main highway between Fort Cochin and Ernakulam. This pleasant hotel is under the same ownership at the splurgey Abad Plaza but not nearly as posh. This Abad's rooms are done up with printed spreads and drapes, and have neat attached modern bathrooms. Rates are Rs. 60 ($4.60) single and Rs. 95 ($7.30) double, non-air-conditioned; Rs. 110 ($8.45) single and Rs. 165 ($12.70) double, air-conditioned. Suites run Rs. 300 ($23.05). The Pavilion Restaurant, open from noon to 3:30 p.m. and 7:30 to 11:30 p.m., serves some notable Indian and international cuisine (see "Where to Eat"), and South Indian dishes are featured in the Caravan Coffee Shop, open from 7:30 a.m. to 11:30 p.m.

A very nice roof garden crowns the modest **Hotel Geo,** Thoppumpady, Mattancheri, Cochin 682005 (tel. 28303). The ten rooms are fairly clean. The seven non-air-conditioned rooms rent for Rs. 32.25 ($2.50) single and Rs. 48.40 ($3.70) double. The three air-conditioned rooms cost Rs. 73.40 ($5.65), and all these rates include tax.

La Bella Hotel, Kappalandi Mukku, Mattancheri (tel. 26313), is neither bella nor for the fastidious, but the rooms are attractively priced: Rs. 52.50 ($4.05) double and Rs. 32.25 ($2.50) for single occupancy of a double room. Hot water is provided in buckets, although there are cold-water showers in the bathrooms. "Beautiful" is an apt description of the hotel restaurant's Kerala-style vegetarian meal: five vegetarian curries and rice for Rs. 7.50 (58¢). The nonvegetarian foods run as high as Rs. 54 ($4.15) for a full chicken cooked with tomatoes; other snacks range around Rs. 7 (55¢) to Rs. 15 ($1.15). There is a bar. Both bar and restaurant are open from 9:30 a.m. to 11:30 p.m.

On Bolghatty Island

On the island of Bolghatty, the **Bolghatty Palace Hotel,** Cochin 682504 (tel. 355003), has a commanding position, facing the outlet to the open sea to one side and the High Court Jetty in Ernakulam, but a brief ferry boat ride away, to the other. The building was once a governor's palace, soundly built by the Dutch in 1744, and later the home of British governors. It has timbered ceilings, polished plank floors, and teakwood staircases to enchant the tourist snowed by history, and each of its enormous rooms and vast bathrooms could accommodate a cricket team. Unfortunately, much of this is seedy now. There are cottages on the grounds which bear no relationship to the architectural grandeur of the main building. Rooms in them are as small and compact as train compartments; their nicest feature is verandas overlooking the water. In the main building, non-air-conditioned rooms cost Rs. 90 ($6.90) double, Rs. 65 ($5) single, Rs. 100 ($7.70) for a suite. The air-conditioned honeymoon cottage (with a round bed) goes for Rs. 120 ($9.25) single (single on a honeymoon?), Rs. 160 ($12.30) double; the air-conditioned twin cottage has the same rates. An air-conditioned suite in the main building runs Rs. 175 ($13.45) single, Rs. 250 ($19.25) double. There is a 10% service charge. There's ferry service between the island and the mainland, or you can hire a rowboat for the journey.

The palace has been managed by the Kerala Tourism Development Corporation, but change seemed imminent when I was there. During my past visit, there was a staff slowdown to protest the hotel's takeover by the Taj Group, which planned to restore it and run it as one of its luxury hotels. The Taj management had promised to keep the old staff, but that was not the source of their discontent. The hotel personnel told me that the staff feared that if Taj took over, the Bolghatty Palace would be too high-priced for Indian tourists and the gardens, long favorite picnic spots for local residents, would be declared off-limits as well. Thus a delightful haven for penny-watching tourists may soon disappear.

Budget Choices

The **PWD Inspection Bungalow** at Fort Cochin (tel. 25797) has two rooms for occupancy by tourists when they are not in use by government inspectors on tour. The building has a terrific sea-facing location and huge rooms with adequate if basic furniture, but no running hot water in bathrooms (it comes in buckets). The price is basic also: Rs. 10 (75¢) single and Rs. 15 ($1.15) double. For reservations, write the Executive Engineer, PWD (Buildings and Roads) Ernakulam, Cochin, or write in charge of the PWD Inspection Bungalow, Fort Cochin.

The **YWCA,** Chittor Road, Ernakulam, Cochin (tel. 36520), has five rooms for male guests only: two singles for Rs. 15 ($1.15) and three doubles for Rs. 25 ($1.90), all with attached bathrooms. Meals are served in the big dining hall where you get inexpensive vegetarian and nonvegetarian fare.

WHERE TO EAT: Budget-stretching buffets, served from 12:30 to 3 p.m. and featuring a wide array of Eastern and continental foods, cool salads, and rich desserts, are to be found on Willingdon Island at the **Malabar Hotel** (tel. 6811) in the Rice Boats restaurant, off the lobby with a distinctive boat decor with a great water view, for Rs. 45 ($3.45); and at the **Casino Hotel, in** Tharavadu, meaning "Ancestral Home" (tel. 6821), and appropriately decorated in locally made arts and crafts, for Rs. 40 ($3.05).

In Ernakulam, the **Hotel Abad Plaza,** Mahatma Gandhi Road (tel. 361636), sets its Rs.-40 ($3.05) buffet in the Regency Room, aglow with mirrors and rosewood pillars, lacy drapes, and stucco walls. At the **Sealord Hotel,** on Shanmugham Road (tel. 32682), the buffet is on Saturday night from 8 to 11 p.m. for Rs. 45 ($3.45).

To the starvation-budget traveler this might seem a great deal of money for one meal, but as you can eat as much as you like, a buffet can be filling and economical. They are very popular, so it's advisable to call in advance for a reservation and go early for the best selection.

Thalis

My best advice to the low-budgeter traveler is to eat the vegetarian thalis at the **Bharat Tourist Home** in its plain but clean South Indian restaurant. Here a filling Bombay thali meal is Rs. 14 ($1.05) in the air-conditioned section, Rs.-2 (15¢) less in the non-air-conditioned section. In the Bharat's dressier, quietly decorated Subhisksha, (meaning "satisfaction"), open from 11:15 a.m. to 3 p.m. and 7 to 11 p.m., a North Indian vegetarian meal will run Rs. 24 ($1.85), and there are South Indian foods as well as a 24-hour coffeeshop for snacks and drinks.

Good bets also are the restaurants in the other Indian-style hotels mentioned, which average Rs. 7 (55¢) to Rs. 14 ($1.05) for a healthful delicious meal.

Also try the **Indian Coffee Houses** around town for inexpensive snacks and South India's famous coffee. Nothing runs over Rs. 5 (40¢) or Rs. 6 (45¢).

Moderate to Splurge Choices

For a panoramic water view with Chinese fishing nets and the mainland thrown in, it's hard to beat the down-to-earth-priced rooftop restaurant at the

Seagull Hotel, Fort Cochin (tel. 28128), open from 8:30 a.m. to 10:30 p.m. A three-course meal of soup, curry, and a sweet runs about Rs. 25 ($1.90). Or go for just tea and to see the sunset: Rs. 4 (30¢) for tea and Rs. 5 (40¢) for toast—the sunset is free.

In Ernakulam, for your eating pleasure, the busy, plain **Malaya Restaurant,** Banerji Road (tel. 361029), features Peking-style cooking. It's a bright and cheerful place, up a flight of stairs above a row of shops. Chinese lanterns and fans hang from the ceiling. Family rooms are partitioned off from the main restaurant. The extensive menu lists about 240 Chinese dishes and about 50 Western dishes. Specialties include prawns with cashews and vegetables, a dish that is among the most expensive, at Rs. 24 ($1.85). Other specialties are prawns with bamboo shoots and vegetables, at Rs. 22 ($1.70), and sliced duck with pineapple and vegetables, also Rs. 22. Most dishes run about Rs. 20 ($1.55). Open every day from 11:30 a.m. to 3 p.m. and 6:30 to 10:30 p.m.

At the well-designed moderate-to-splurge **Pandhal,** Mahatma Gandhi Road, Ernakulam (tel. 367759), open from noon to midnight, owned by the Casino Hotel, the dark-wood ceiling and white walls serve as backdrops to the orange upholstered chairs and an abundance of potted palms. The total effect is sophisticated, inviting, and cool. Continental dishes are tops here, especially those made with locally famous fish and seafood: try the fish Bercy, prepared with shallots and spinach at Rs. 19 ($1.45), or the grilled shrimp or crab at Rs. 21 ($1.60). There are also Indian and Chinese dishes, as per most other places. For dessert at table or at the stand-up bar downstairs adjoining the bakery, there are delicious cakes and pastries. At the stand-up bar, one of the rich chocolate pastries, made from the highest quality chocolate, runs Rs. 4 (30¢), and coffee or tea, Rs. 3 (23¢).

Now that you're in the South, you may crave some good North Indian cooking, and you can get it at the **Oberoi Restaurant,** 60 Mahatma Gandhi Road, Ernakulam (tel. 31609). It's a favorite spot for Indian navy personnel stationed in Cochin, many of whom are from the North, and indeed Mr. Dhannapadrai, who is usually on hand running things from a desk in the front, is from Delhi and so are his chefs. The room itself is simple, with plain Formica tables standing beneath a baroque plaster ceiling, but the menu is complex. It lists no fewer than 286 North Indian dishes and 71 Chinese dishes in the Rs.-20 ($1.55) to Rs.-30 ($2.30) range. The ginger prawns are tender and very spicy; you can also get a full tandoori chicken, or half. There are rich concoctions such as chicken tikka makanwalla (boneless in butter), murgh mussallam (with eggs, spices, cashews, and raisins), and a host of other Indian and Chinese dishes. You can get Indian sweets as well—rasgullas (boiled milk sweet) and halwa (made with carrots and sugar) for around Rs. 5 (40¢). There are snacks as well, suitable for breakfast as well as other times of day. Air-conditioned, the Oberoi is open daily from 9 a.m. to 11:30 p.m.

Nice looking and mid-priced is the **Peacock Restaurant,** in the Grand Hotel, Mahatma Gandhi Road, Ernakulam (tel. 33211). It has a fancy floral-patterned ceiling, teak and leather booths, gold drapes, and wood paneling—all this and air conditioning too. The chicken Afghani (made with nuts and white sauce) at Rs. 18 ($1.40) and poached prawns for the same price are two of the specialties. Open for lunch and dinner: from 11 a.m. to 3 p.m. and 5 to 10 p.m.

For a splurge in Ernakulam, try the **Princess Room** of the Sealord Hotel, Shanmugham Road (tel. 32682), where there's delicious seafood for Rs. 35 ($2.70) to Rs. 40 ($3.05) or fish Véronique (with grapes) for Rs. 30 ($2.30), which are among the highest-priced dishes on the menu. There's also steak, grilled prawns, and for an unusual dessert, there's fried ice cream—coconut-coated ice cream which is deep-fried and dished up on a bed of sweet vermicelli. There's a band and dancing at night. Open from 7 a.m. (for the breakfast menu) to midnight every day. Another possibility at the Sealord is the barbecue, every Sunday on the rooftop, from 7:30 p.m. to midnight.

Another Ernakulam splurge spot is the **Regency Room** at the Hotel Abad Plaza, where in addition to the aforementioned buffet at lunch, there is an á la carte menu where main dishes average Rs. 35 ($2.70) but can go higher. Seafood is a specialty. Dinner is served from 7:30 p.m. to midnight.

Between Fort Cochin and Ernakulam, you'll find one of the more varied menus around town in the **Pavilion Restaurant**, a splurge at the Abad Hotel (tel. 28211), done up with wood trellis dividers and red draped windows. Instead of the usual Indian, continental, and Chinese fare, there is tempura for Rs. 22 ($1.70) and well-prepared seafood. Lobsters in season (January, February, and March) are sold by the kilogram. For a one-kilo lobster that looks big enough to ride, the price is around Rs. 100 ($7.70) and can easily serve two. Heavier lobsters can run $30 and feed you and some friends. Another less pricey specialty is black tiger prawns, cooked in the tandoor, at Rs. 40 ($3.05), and for about the same price, crabs and squid.

On Willingdon Island, the **Casino Hotel**, Fort Cochin (tel. 6821), has a high-priced outdoor café specializing in well-prepared seafood, such as lobster masala (a tandoor dish with spicy sauce), tissue-thin romali roti ("handkerchief" bread), and Chinese fried prawns. Meals can run Rs. 250 ($19.25) without wine. Here lobsters are priced by weight and one can easily serve two people.

For high-priced Chinese foods in inviting surroundings, there's the **Jade Pavilion** at the Malabar Hotel (tel. 6811).

SIGHTS AROUND TOWN: The island known as **Fort Cochin,** with its settlement named **Mattancheri,** probably has the most to intrigue the tourist. Supposedly it was the first place in India to be settled by Europeans (Portuguese) and in numerous landmarks their memory remains. Not far from the ferry dock is the **Mattancheri Palace** (open from 8:30 a.m. to 12:30 p.m. and 2 to 5 p.m.; closed Monday), which was built by the Portuguese in 1555, later taken over and altered by the Dutch, and finally handed over to the local maharajas, who added the ambitious *Ramayana* murals that cover the walls of the royal bedchamber. The building itself, low slung and with gently sloping red-tile roofs, is quite incongruous in Indian surroundings and therefore all the more interesting to see. Its carved teak ceilings could have come from any wooden warship of the period. Apart from the brightly colored Shiva and Vishnu scenes and some stray weapons hung on the walls, the chief interest centers on some elegant ivory palanquins (the family motto "Honor is our family treasure" painted on the side) with gold-embroidered coverlets, and that celebrated piece of Indian furniture, the howdah, for riding on the back of elephants. Referred to locally as the "Dutch Palace," the building was never used as a residence, only for a coronation. It is really four buildings in one, arranged around a central courtyard. Two of the buildings are Hindu temples, one dedicated to Vishnu and one to Shiva. A high wall, with entrances to the east and to the west, surrounds the complex.

Not far away is the area where still live the surviving remnants of a centuries-old colony of Jewish refugees from Roman-dominated Jerusalem. There were a lot of them originally, once protected by one of the local kings (who gave them a charter to the land, inscribed on copper plates), persecuted later by the Portuguese, and finally once again allowed peace under Dutch, British, and Indian rule. In December 1968 they celebrated the 400th anniversary of the founding of their lovely Chinese-tiled **synagogue**; the ceremonies were attended by Indira Gandhi, who stood amid the silken drapes and under the colored lanterns and chandeliers and wished the community—now under 100—long life. The synagogue is open to visitors from 9 a.m. to noon and 2 to 5 p.m. every day but Saturday.

Another religious shrine is Fort Cochin's **St. Francis Church,** built by the Portuguese in 1503, converted into a Dutch Reform and then later an Anglican church. Tombstones of members of all three faiths line the aisles, the most famous of which is the Portuguese explorer Vasco da Gama who died here in 1534, his remains later being removed to Lisbon. Locked up in the church office are Dutch baptism and marriage records dating back to the 1730s.

Even if you stay on Willingdon Island you'll be making at least one trip to the mainland of Ernakulam. One of your stops should certainly be at **Pai & Co.,** the best bookstore in Cochin, very well stocked with magazines as well as books. It's on Broadway where the narrow shopping street begins (ten minutes from the ferry dock, toward the towering Sealord Hotel). Another recommended stop: the **Kerala Government Handicrafts Store Kairali,** on Mahatma Gandhi Road, Ernakulam, open every day but Sunday from 10 a.m. to 1 p.m. and from 3 to 8 p.m. Though small, it has a varied collection of carved rosewood, buffalo horns, ivory sculptures, cigarette cases and elephants of sweet-smelling sandalwood, incense, beads, saris, shawls, and some unique coconut-shell spoons, egg cups, etc., all of which are amazingly cheap. **Kerala State Handicrafts, Apex Society, Handloom and Handicrafts Emporium,** all on Mahatma Gandhi Road, also have beautiful buys!

A boat ride euphemistically tagged "round the backwaters" will ease you gently around some of the nearby islands, calling at the coir factory on **Gundu Island** and exploring an occasional backwater channel where little boys beg from the shore and everybody waves as the boat passes. Until about 50 years ago it was a local custom for the women to go topless, but today only the men are bare-chested and all of them are busy working, drying prawns, chopping open coconuts, and packing and loading the exotic local crops of coir, cashews, lobster, pepper, and spices.

A pleasant Kerala Tourism Development Corporation (KTDC) **tour** takes in the major landmarks—synagogue, Dutch Palace, etc., plus Gundu Island—for Rs. 15 ($1.15) per person. Usually there are two tours a day, at 9 a.m. and 2 p.m., lasting 3½ hours each. Departures are from the Sealord Hotel's jetty. Reservations can be made through the KTDC Tourist Reception Centre, Shanmugham Road, Ernakulam (tel. 353234), open from 8 a.m. to 6 p.m.

Should the tour timings not suit you, it's also possible (and expensive) to rent a boat for about Rs. 65 ($5) per hour, with room for up to a score of people, so you can round up your own party to cruise the lagoons to the sights. Only a brief outline need be given to the captain, who has covered the route many times before. The boat rental can be arranged through the tourist office in the Malabar Hotel, which might also find you a smaller, less expensive boat if your party is a small one.

Keep in mind when booking your tour that the Dutch Palace is closed on Friday, the synagogue on Saturday, and St. Francis Church and Gundu Island are closed on Sunday and major holidays. But even if some part of the tour is not possible, it is worthwhile, relaxing, and interesting.

FOR YOUR ENTERTAINMENT: There are nightly performances of
Kathakali (kath=story, kali=play) in Cochin at the Cochin Cultural Centre,
Durbar Hall Ground, D. H. Road (near the Shiva Temple and opposite
T.D.M. Hall), from 6:30 to 8:30 p.m. usually for Rs. 25 ($1.90), but the price
is subject to change. This two-hour performance of Kathakali in the theater
for visitors is a mere teaser compared to the traditional performance of
Kathakali for local audiences. It is a light educational overview, introduced
by E. M. Sukumavan, the knowledgeable director of the Cultural Centre. A
real performance of Kathakali often lasts all night and is usually done outdoors. It's not unusual for members of the audience to come equipped with
cots for the occasion.

It's also a long time back to the origins of Kathakali, which dates from
early temple worship. The performers dip into an endless supply of story materials from the nearly 3,000-year-old tales in the *Ramayana* and *Mahabharata*. It even takes a long time to train an actor (no women) for
Kathakali—about eight years, in fact. Starting at age 12, he's ready to go on
stage by age 20. He's been trained to be both flexible and strong enough to leap
about nimbly under excessively heavy makeup and costumes for many hours.

Four or five hours are needed to apply makeup on the actors. They lie flat
on the floor while their faces are covered with rice-flour paste and then
painted in bright colors in stylized representations of the gods, goddesses, demons, and kings they portray. Even the whites of their eyes must be part of
their makeup—they are irritated especially for the performance by placing
eggplant seeds under the lids and blinking the eyes until the whites are red.

You can see some of this makeup artistry and learn more about
Kathakali prior to performances at 6 p.m. Bring your camera. Double-check
timing when you book your seat through the Cochin Cultural Centre, Mahatma Gandhi Road (tel. 33732 for the office, 37866 for the theater).

This unusual art form takes patience to understand. In spite of my own
dance background and my continuing genuine love of dance, the first time I
saw Kathakali in the long version, I found myself wishing for a "digest"
(which is what the visitor sees today). At any rate, I've always been happy that
somehow I got to see very great theater in any form, and I'm sure you'll find it
provocative as well.

For other entertainment, several **movie theaters**—among them the
Sreedmar on Shanmugham Road and Shenoy's on Mahatama Gandhi Road
—show English-language movies, usually at 3:30, 6:30, and 9:30 p.m.

There's music every night in the Jade Pavilion of the **Malabar Hotel.**

A good crowd is usually on hand every night in the restaurant of the **Casino Hotel,** where a band plays for dancing or listening from 8:30 to 11:30 p.m.

BEST TIME TO VISIT: Onam (August / September) is a statewide harvest
festival, but particularly colorful in the lagoon communities such as Cochin,
and especially Alleppey, where "snake boats" (carved, decorated boats) compete in races for the prime minister's trophy. Also, much cymbal and drum
beating, lots of gorgeous floral decorations on the homes, and many graceful
dancing girls in white saris make this festival memorable.

The heavy visitor season is October to March. The rainy season is June to
October.

MISCELLANY: Kerala State Handicrafts, Apex Society, Handloom, Handicrafts Emporium, Khadi Bhavan, Khadi, Village Industries, and Kairali, all on

Mahatma Gandhi Road, Ernakulam, are places to head if you want to shop price-fixed. Look for Kerala's beautiful white cotton, gold-trimmed saris that make up into lovely summer dresses or skirts, sandalwood carvings of gods and goddesses that take months to make; bookmarks in these woods (easy-to-carry, inexpensive gifts), and many coconut-fiber items.

Indian Airlines is on Durbar Hall Road, near the Bharat Tourist Home, in Ernakulam (tel. 353907). . . . For **railroad** service, go to the Cochin Harbour Railway Terminus, Willingdon Island (tel. 32465) or Ernakulam Junction Railway Station, Ernakulam South (tel. 33100). For **bus information and reservations,** use the Kerala State Road Transport Corporation, in the Bus Station, Stadium Road, Ernakulam (tel. 32033). . . . Many **travel agents** offer luxury video coaches to distant points. The videos will be in a local language; the ride, more comfortable than ordinary buses. . . . The Indian Airlines coach between the **airport** and Ernakulam costs Rs. 15 ($1.15).

An absolutely indispensable aid to the traveler in Cochin is the *Jaico Time Table and Travel and Tourist Guide,* available for Rs. 2 (15¢) at book-stalls. It lists the latest bus, train, and air timings, entertainment, and dozens of other facts of interest to your plans.

SIGHTS OUT OF TOWN: Put sightseeing to landmarks aside and take a trip on the backwater for lifeseeing by boat, all along the Kerala waterways scalloped with beaches and villages of whitewashed houses where graceful women go about their chores. It's said that in the fishing communities one of the essential attributes expected in a prospective bride is her dexterity at cutting and cleaning fish. Sometimes on the sparkling waters other boats glide by with whole families and their animals, off to market for the day.

Varapuzho

A short trip by boat to Varapuzho, two hours from Cochin, costs Rs. 1.50 (11¢), and you can return the same day. Ferries run 17 times a day, from 7:40 a.m. to 7:30 p.m.

Alleppey

Or in under two hours, at a cost of Rs. 10 (75¢), you can be in Alleppey, a center for boat traffic in Kerala and a scene of great activity during the festival of Onam (August / September) when "snake" boat races take place on the canals.

For overnighting in Alleppey, some budget choices include the **PWD Rest House,** on Beach Road, charging Rs. 10 (75¢) single and Rs. 20 ($1.55) double. For reservations, contact the District Collector, Municipal Sathrom, on SDV Road, near the boat jetty. Tarriff, Rs. 5 (40¢) single and Rs. 10 (75¢) double.

Higher in price is the **Alleppey Prince Hotel,** A.S. Road, Alleppey 688007 (tel. 3752), recommended by reader Barbara Masters of Norwich, Conn. She describes the air-conditioned rooms as clean and adequate, with baths attached, renting for Rs. 120 ($9.25) single and Rs. 150 ($11.55) to Rs. 200 ($15.40) double, and the restaurant as "excellent." Peak rates during the colorful Nehru Trophy Snake Boat Race the second Saturday of August each year go up to Rs. 250 ($19.25) for both singles and doubles.

Other hotels to investigate are the **Bhima Garden** (tel. 24177), **Hotel**

Komala (tel. 3117), **Karthika Tourist Home** (tel. 2554), and **Narasimhapuram Lodge** (tel. 3698).

Wherever your accommodation, remember that rates go up and reservations are hard to get during the Nehru Trophy Snake Boat Race mentioned above.

Kottayam

Alleppey's bus stand is near the jetty from which boats sail to Kottayam 14 times a day, about every hour from 5 a.m. until 10:30 p.m., for Rs. 5 (40¢) for the 2½-hour trip. In Kottayam you can see old Syrian Christian churches and rubber, tea, pepper, and cardamom plantations.

Kottayam's accommodations include the **Anjali Hotel,** K. K. Road, Kottayam 686001 (tel. 3661), near downtown. The centrally air-conditioned rooms cost Rs. 140 ($10.75) single and Rs. 180 ($13.85) double. The slightly lower-priced **Hotel Ambassador** is also on K. K. Road, Kottayam 686001 (tel. 3293). The **Hotel Aida,** on M. C. Road, Kottayam 686039 (tel. 3691), five kilometers (three miles) from downtown, has singles for Rs. 40 ($3.05) to Rs. 60 ($4.60) and doubles for Rs. 70 ($5.40) to Rs. 90 ($6.90), the higher rate for air conditioning. The **Hotel Triveny,** T. B. Road, Kottayam 688001 (tel. 3393), is right in town and partly air-conditioned. Rates are Rs. 35 ($2.70) single and Rs. 65 ($5) double, non-air-conditioned; with air-conditioning, Rs. 100 ($7.70) single and Rs. 170 ($13.05) double.

Kottayam is the place to get the bus to the Periyar (Thekkady) Wildlife Sanctuary, 71 miles (114 km) away. The bus to Thekkady costs less than Rs. 20 ($1.55) for a four-hour trip. Once there, you can make arrangements for a boat tour, at Rs. 7 (55¢) per person for two hours. You should book your accommodations in advance during the peak season (see Section 3 in this chapter).

Or you can leave for Periyar from Cochin on the conducted tour operated by the KTDC every Saturday from 7:30 a.m., returning the next day after lunch and reaching Ernakulam at 8 p.m. Cost is Rs. 100 ($7.70), food and room extra. Make reservations at the KTDC Tourist Reception Centre, Shanmugham Road, Ernakulam (tel. 353234), open from 8 a.m. to 7 p.m.

Quilon

But when people refer to *the* backwaters trip, they mean the scenic seven-hour stretch between Alleppey and Quilon, an experience you won't want to miss. In Alleppey, grab the daily 10 a.m. passenger ferry to Quilon for Rs. 5 (40¢) and you are headed south through waterways shaded by palms. Conversely, the passenger boat going north leaves Quilon for Alleppey at 10 a.m. and arrives at 7 p.m.

En route the boat calls at many little villages. Sailing along you past slow-moving wallams (flat-bottom cargo boats with thatched roofs). Introduced centuries ago by the Chinese, they carry two-person crews and cargos weighing some 20 tons.

At Quilon, you have arrived at one of the oldest ports in these parts and well known for **Ashtamudi Lake,** rimmed with palms and promontories, where, if you haven't had enough boating, you can go rowing. The town itself is still a market center, but not the important port it was when the ancient Phoenicians, Greeks, Persians, and Romans called here for spices, sandalwood, and ivory. The Chinese also traded here from the 7th to the 14th centuries, and so did the later-arriving Dutch, Portuguese, and British. Two miles from town you will also want to explore the ruined fort, old lighthouse, and European graveyards.

Should you wish to overnight in Quilon, try the **Hotel Karthika,** Paikada Road, Quilon 690001 (tel. 76240), charging Rs. 38 ($2.90) single and Rs. 75 ($5.75) to Rs. 125 ($9.60) double, with air conditioning; non-air-conditioned rooms are all singles, at Rs. 23 ($1.75). The **Hotel Sea Bee,** Jetty Road, Quilon 691001 (tel. 3631), has air-conditioned rooms for Rs. 60 ($4.60) single and Rs. 75 ($5.75) double. **Hotel Sudarsan,** Parameswar Road, Quilon 690001 (tel. 3755), and the **Hotel Neela,** Quilon Cantonment (tel. 3616), with rates similar to the Sea Bee's. At the **Government Guest House,** accommodation is Rs. 25 ($1.90), and even less at the **Government Rest House.**

Alwaye

Another excursion takes you 13 miles to the northwest of Ernakulam to the town of Alwaye, with its big fertilizer and aluminum plants, to get a glimpse of modern Kerala. There's nothing much to do here, although there's a nice ten-room **Tourist Bungalow** (once the maharaja's palace) with a lovely view of the wide River Periyar whose waters lap the steps at the foot of a pleasant garden. There are peacock-decorated screens in the dining room and other occasional bits of former affluence, and the spacious rooms are fairly clean and comfortable. Rates are Rs. 25 ($1.90).

GETTING TO COCHIN: By **plane,** Indian Airlines flights from Madras, with stops in Tiruchirapalli and Trivandrum, take about three hours and cost Rs. 605 ($46.55); from Trivandrum, the flying time is 40 minutes at Rs. 191 ($14.70); from Bombay, daily flights take 1¾ hours at Rs. 937 ($72.10); from Goa, the flight costs Rs. 597 ($45.90). Flights also operate between Cochin and Bangalore for Rs. 520 ($40); between Cochin and Delhi, Rs. 2,600 ($200).

Vayudoot Airlines operates three flights a week from Madras to Cochin, at Rs. 575 ($44.25). This flight also connects Cochin with Bangalore, at Rs. 410 ($31.55), and Coimbatore, at Rs. 165 ($12.70). Vayudoot's schedule changes frequently.

One of the **trains** to Cochin is the *Cochin Express,* leaving from Madras Central at 7:40 p.m. and arriving at Cochin Ernakulam Junction at 9:17 a.m., at Rs. 236 ($18.15) in first class and Rs. 58 ($4.45) in second. This train pulls into Cochin at 9:50, should Willingdon Island be your destination. Another train, from Trivandrum, the *Kerala Express,* leaves at 1 p.m. and arrives in Ernakulam at 5:05 p.m. for Rs. 97 ($7.45) in first class and Rs. 25 ($1.90) in second. For a most scenic ride, local trains connect Trivandrum, Quilon, Kottayam, and Cochin.

Express **buses** from Trivandrum take 6½ hours to cover the 221 miles (362 km) for Rs. 27 ($2.05); from Bangalore, 565 km (345 miles) and 15 hours away, for Rs. 64.30 ($4.95); from Madras, Rs. 76.90 ($5.90) for the 16¼-hour trip. The bus from Kanya Kumari, via Alleppey, Quilon, and Trivandrum, costs Rs. 36 ($2.75) for a trip lasting 8¾ hours and covering 302 km (184 miles), and many more buses ply this route as well.

3. Periyar Wildlife Sanctuary

Roughly halfway between Madurai and Cochin, just inside the borders of Kerala State, is the Periyar Wildlife Sanctuary—a large artificial lake filling a series of related valleys and all surrounded by dense forest—where many varieties of Indian beasties roam.

It's not very accessible, the last stage being reachable only by car or bus, but worth the trip for those who seek a quiet rest.

A popular spot to head for is **Aranya Nivas** (tel. Kumily 23), right beside one end of the lake, about two miles past **Kumili** village. A solidly built stone pavilion on the hillside, it is clean and comfortable with a rather old world air to it. Meals and service are very good. Air-conditioned deluxe suites rent for Rs. 270 ($20.75) to Rs. 360 ($27.70) single and Rs. 360 to Rs. 480 ($27.70) ($36.90) double; deluxe rooms, air-conditioned, cost Rs. 240 ($18.45) single and Rs. 300 ($23.05) double; standard air-conditioned rooms go for Rs. 120 ($9.25) single and Rs. 180 ($13.85) double. These rates do not include meals or the 10% service charge. If you want to stop merely for lunch or dinner on the way through, Western-style meals cost about Rs. 50 ($3.85).

By paying Rs. 350 ($26.90) single and Rs. 520 ($40) double, you can stay at the **Lake Palace** (tel. Kumily 24), once a palace of the Maharaja of Travancore. It is on an island in the lake and still has some old furnishings. You can get there by ferry from the Aranya Nivas Hotel for Rs. 10 (75¢).

Another possibility is **Periyar House** (tel. Kumily 26), a short walk through the woods from the boat landing, modern and two-storied. Double rooms, at Rs. 56 ($4.30), have attached bathrooms with a choice of Western- or Indian-style toilets; singles, sharing a bathroom, cost Rs. 33.50 ($2.55).

Four other places—all very modest—are the **Hotel Ambadi,** near the forest check-post, Thekkady 685536 (tel. Kumily 11), with doubles for Rs. 50 ($3.85); the **Holiday Home** (tel. 16), with singles for Rs. 20 ($1.55) and doubles for Rs. 30 ($2.30); the **Hotel Vanarani,** with doubles for Rs. 30 ($2.30); and the **Lake Queen Tourist Home,** charging Rs. 20 ($1.55) single and Rs. 45 ($3.45) double.

BOAT TOURS: A small motor-powered vessel, looking a bit like a houseboat, sets off around the lake nosing its way past the tips of lifeless trees that protrude above the surface and into quiet backwaters. It is always hoped that a herd of elephants will be found drinking at water's edge, but more usually three or four of the great gray beasts are seen on a hillside in the distance. An occasional wild pig can be spotted snuffling in the foilage, and gaur (Indian bison) are not uncommon. Cutting the motors and gliding quietly up to the water's edge, the boat is sometimes lucky enough to come within sight of a pack of red foxes that have killed an elk, and are drinking unsuspectingly, and trying to drag its body out of the water.

Tours operate from 7 a.m. to noon and 2 to 4 p.m. for Rs. 7 (55¢) per person. Reservations are made through the manager at the Aranya Nivas and other hotels.

The season for Periyar is September to May, when it's dry and the animals come out to look for water. Be sure to take your binoculars to view the animals too shy to come close. There's a machan (viewing tower) for a long-distance look around. Dawn and dusk are the best times to see the animals.

GETTING TO PERIYAR: From Cochin, take the bus to Kottayam, where you can pick up another bus to Periyar, at a cost of less than Rs. 20 ($1.55) for the more than four-hour, 71-miles (114-km) trip.

Alternatively, from Cochin you can take a bus to Alleppey and ferry the canals to Kottyam, then connect with a bus for Periyar.

Or from Cochin / Ernakulam you can take the KTDC's conducted **tour.** It departs every Saturday at 7:30 a.m. and returns the next day after lunch, arriving in Ernakulam at 8 p.m. The cost is Rs. 100 ($7.70), food and room extra. For reservations, contact the KTDC Tourist Reception Centre, Shanmugham Road, Ernakulam (tel. 353234), open from 8 a.m. to 7 p.m.

Chapter XIV

THE STATE OF KARNATAKA

1. Bangalore and Environs
2. Mysore City and Onward

FROM BANDIPUR, a wildlife sanctuary at the southern tip, to Bijapur in the north, and including the capital, Bangalore, the entire state of Karnataka (formerly Mysore) is a delight. There are temples so amazingly decorated that they appear to be lace or carved ivory (Somnathpur, Belur, and Halebid); distinctive Muslim tombs (Gumbaz and Gol Gumbaz); and an impressive palace in Mysore City itself.

For a rest from such man-made riches, there are forests of teak, ebony, and sandalwood. Abundant flowers make the entire state seem to be one huge garden; indeed the name Karnataka, taken in 1973, means plateau land or rich black soil.

At Bandipur and Nagarhole you can see bison, elephants, deer, and black-faced monkeys; at Ranganathittu (a bird sanctuary) there are ibis, storks, and egrets. Dams and waterfalls are refreshing sights in Karnataka and the unusual rock formations are purported to be among the oldest in the world. Chandragupta, the emperor who adopted Jainism 300 years before Christ, spent his last years here. Ashoka, the grandson of Chandragupta, once ruled part of this state. It was the Hoysalas (11th to 14th centuries) who put all of what is now Karnataka State under one ruling house and left some of the most memorable monuments. The Hoysalas' capital was destroyed in 1327, and four centuries of Hindu-Muslim struggles followed, until Hyder Ali became victorious over all in 1761. He and his son, Tipu Sultan, whose former capital we will visit, ruled until 1799 when the British defeated Tipu and restored an old Hindu dynasty.

The best starting point from which to see the state is the capital, Bangalore. October through February are the finest months to visit, although March is still quite bearable. April to June is very hot, and July to end of September is rainy. In general, though, Bangalore's climate is salubrious, so many Indians choose to retire here. And since there are economic opportunities in Bangalore, many others come here to work. All this migration is one of the reasons why Bangalore is now India's fifth-largest city, the position once held by Hyderabad, and according to some sources, the second-fastest-growing city in the world.

1. Bangalore and Environs

The name Bangalore (pop. 4,000,000) means "baked beans," but, of course, it's as different from Boston as you can possibly imagine. Bangalore is quite modern, having been built mainly in the 18th century, and it's spacious, well planned, dotted with graceful parks, and surrounded by pretty suburbs. There's nothing here to detain you for very long, but it's a good place for a brief visit.

HOTELS: Accommodations in Bangalore are of a fairly high standard, as even many budget hotels boast of lovely gardens abloom with luscious tropical plants and posies. However, sales and luxury taxes can add as much as 5% to 20% to your room bill and another 5% to 10% to the cost of food. There is good news as well: during my last visit, the state tourism authorities were considering reducing these taxes to encourage tourism—a benefit you might enjoy during your visit.

Indian-Style Hotels

Woodlands Hotel, 5 Sampangi Tank Rd., Bangalore 560025 (tel. 225590), with its approach through a narrow tree-lined lane, gives the impression of entering a private estate. Once inside the well-kept grounds of the hotel, all ablaze with fresh roses and frangipani, you will see a series of buildings that look almost like a small village. In these various buildings are the rooms and dining salon, spread out over five well-manicured acres. All the rooms are neatly furnished and extremely clean. The food in the large, pleasant dining room is vegetarian only, and the cook will go easy on the spices for Western visitors who request this. All rooms have attached bathrooms and many have Western plumbing—be sure to specify when you reserve, if this is important to you. There is also a single-block seven-story annex housing more elegantly furnished rooms with carved wooden headboards and a bar called The French Connection. The lobby in the annex is subdued, but dramatically highlighted by two huge murals with scenes from the *Bhagavadgita* and Krishna's life. In all there are 245 rooms, but this is a popular place and if you want to stay here, reserve far in advance. Rates are Rs. 70 ($5.40) single and Rs. 90 ($6.90) double, non-air-conditioned; Rs. 195 ($15) single and Rs. 225 ($17.30) double, non-air-conditioned but with TV. Deluxe rooms without air conditioning run Rs. 170 ($13.05) single and Rs. 195 ($15) double. Air-conditioned rooms cost Rs. 245 ($18.85) to Rs. 275 ($21.15); the higher rates have TV. Victorian-looking cottages run Rs. 245 ($18.85) to Rs. 300 ($23.05).

In the restaurant in the annex, open from 11 a.m. to 3 p.m. and 7 to 11 p.m., a delicious vegetarian meal will run about Rs. 20 ($1.55) à la carte.

Monkeys sometimes bound through the grounds of the **Hotel Kamadhenu,** Trinity Circle, Mahatma Gandhi Road, Bangalore 560008 (tel. 574451). This is a hotel without much personality and a bit seedy, but good old-fashioned comfortable rates make it of interest here: Rs. 35 ($2.70) single and Rs. 63 ($4.85) to Rs. 77 ($5.90) double. All rooms have running hot and cold water, and some have Western-style plumbing. There are phones and music in all 100 rooms. Plate meals in the dining room cost Rs. 5 (40¢).

The **Brindavan Hotel,** 40 Mahatma Gandhi Rd., Bangalore 560007 (tel. 53271), looks a little like an American-style motel: the ground-floor rooms all have private entrances. All rooms have attached bathrooms, some with Indian- and some with Western-style toilets. Some of the rooms are quite large, with separate little sitting rooms and dining tables. It's very popular with Indian business travelers. Rates are Rs. 35 ($2.70) to Rs. 55 ($4.25) single and Rs. 75 ($5.75) to Rs. 90 ($6.90) double. The ground-floor rooms, being the most convenient, are the highest in price: Rs. 175 ($13.45). Vegetarian foods are served in the dining room, where a thali costs Rs. 8 (60¢).

Hotel Mayura, 16 Tank Bund Rd., Subash Nagar, Bangalore 580009 (tel. 74819), has a black-and-white mural of horses in the lobby and basic, clean, non-air-conditioned accommodations where you can be cooled by ceiling fans. The Mayura is better than many others in this price range: Rs. 40 ($3.05) single and Rs. 60 ($4.60) double, with attached bathrooms where the hot water is on from 6 to 8:30 a.m. (at other times, cold water is on tap, hot is in buckets).

At Rs. 40 ($3.05) single, Rs. 60 ($4.60) for single occupancy of a double, and Rs. 80 ($6.15) for a double, each room with a private attached bathroom (mostly Indian style), the **Hotel Amar,** 5-6 Ayurvedic Hospital Road (tel. 29208), is really a good buy. There's no air conditioning, but fans are provided and there's piped-in music on three channels and phones in all 100 fairly clean, pastel-painted rooms.

Nearby, the pleasant, friendly **Hotel Rajmahal,** 33-34 Seshadri Rd., Bangalore 560009 (tel. 27304), has a lobby decorated with a pastoral mural depicting peacocks and Krishna, red settees, and shining granite floors. The 250 rooms are usually full, but I managed to see a rare vacancy on the fifth floor, a double in the new wing—bright, clean, and freshly painted with modern furniture, air conditioning, a small refrigerator, and a phone, renting for Rs. 300 ($23.05). The non-air-conditioned rooms have ceiling fans. In the new wing, they cost Rs. 125 ($9.60), Rs. 150 ($11.55), and Rs. 200 ($15.40); in the old wing, these rooms, with little in the way of decor, are Rs. 60 ($4.60) and Rs. 70 ($5.40), and none has Western-style fittings. The hotel's halls were clean and nicely cared for—even the hall walls were dirt free, not often the case with Indian budget hotels. The Rajmahal's outdoor restaurant, serving both vegetarian and nonvegetarian food, is in a delightful garden; the indoor all-vegetarian restaurant, dark and slightly sinister, is not altogether appealing and totally out of keeping with the hotel's overall cheerfulness. Main dishes at both are in the Rs. 7 (55¢) to Rs. 15 ($1.15) range, with a few nonvegetarian dishes higher. A special vegetarian thali with several curries and a sweet will run Rs. 14 ($1.05); a less elaborate thali goes for Rs. 6 (45¢).

The Rajmahal's management also runs the popular, economy-priced **Hotel Prashanth,** 21 E. Tank Bund Road (tel. 74041), a flight of stairs above street level in the busy, noisy City Market area. Clean, simple no-frills rooms with Indian-style bathrooms attached cost Rs. 40 ($3.05), Rs. 60 ($4.60), and Rs. 75 ($5.75).

In the center of the entrance drive of the **Hotel Broadway,** 19 Kempegowda Rd., Bangalore 650009 (tel. 27166), is a large circle of pots filled with bright, welcoming flowers. These are the Broadway's most decorative touch. But its 88 rooms—at Rs. 35 ($2.70) single, Rs. 55 ($4.25) double, Rs. 65 ($5) for a special double, and Rs. 85 ($6.55) for a family room, all with private attached bathrooms (some with Western-style toilets) with hot and cold running water and private telephones—are a good buy. A vegetarian plate meal (no refills, no seconds) costs Rs. 5 (40¢).

A bit higher in price, and a good moderate splurge, the 64-room **Janardhana Hotel,** Kumara Krupa Road, High Grounds, Bangalore 560001 (tel. 24444), has functional, clean, and when I saw them, freshly painted rust-and-blue rooms with various amenities. In addition to beds, ordinary doubles had chairs, coffee tables, bathrooms with little dressing rooms, and telephones, and cost Rs. 110 ($8.45); deluxe rooms, at Rs. 150 ($11.55), have wood paneling but are no better than the ordinary rooms, so save your rupees. Small, compact neat singles go for Rs. 70 ($5.40). All rooms have little balconies and private attached bathrooms with either Indian or Western fittings. There's a vegetarian restaurant.

There are 219 very simple rooms at **Sri Ramakrishna Lodge,** Subedar Chatram Road (tel. 73041). Rates are Rs. 30 ($2.30) to Rs. 32 ($2.45) for singles, and Rs. 50 ($3.85), Rs. 55 ($4.25), and Rs. 60 ($4.60) for doubles. For this you get hot and cold water in an attached bathroom, with a shower and an Indian-style toilet. There's a vegetarian dining room where you can get a plate meal for Rs. 7 (55¢), or you can eat at one of the restaurants nearby.

Two hotels that are more Indian than Western, although they have bathroom fittings in Western style, are the **Ajantha,** 22A Mahatma Gandhi Rd., 560001 (tel. 57322), and the Hotel Cauvery Continental.

At the Ajantha, the 63 rooms are simple, clean, and suitable for those on a moderate budget: Rs. 42.50 ($3.25) single and Rs. 82.50 ($6.35) double; five air-conditioned doubles go for Rs. 121 ($9.30) each. There are fans and mosquito nets. If your attached bathroom doesn't have a shower, the management will provide a plastic tub to splash in.

Several cuts above this is the **Hotel Cauvery Continental,** 11-37 Cunningham Rd., Bangalore 560052 (tel. 29358), whose neat, efficient, and modern rooms have attached bathrooms with hot and cold running water, telephones, and piped-in music. There are two restaurants for South Indian vegetarian and nonvegetarian foods. Rates are up there in the splurge range: Rs. 165 ($12.70) single, Rs. 220 ($16.90) double, and Rs. 275 ($21.15) for a suite, all non-air-conditioned. Rates with air conditioning are Rs. 220 ($16.90) single, Rs. 300 ($23.05) double, Rs. 330 ($25.40) for a suite, and Rs. 600 ($46.15) for an air-conditioned cottage.

They were fully occupied (generally the case) at the **Airlines Hotel,** 4 Madras Bank Rd., Bangalore 560001 (tel. 573783), so I couldn't inspect the rooms. But in the past I have found them okay and I believe this to be the case now as well. Certainly the rates have remained in line: Rs. 48 ($3.70) single, Rs. 70 ($5.40) and Rs. 85 ($6.55) double; and an air-conditioned cottage costs Rs. 250 ($19.25). The 44 spacious rooms all have attached bathrooms with Western-style toilets.

A Splurge: For a splurge Indian style, try the new **Ashraya International Hotel,** 149 Infantry Rd., Bangalore 560001 (tel. 71921), convenient to Vidhana Soudha (housing the state legislature and secretariat), the race course, golf club, and Cubbon Park, and currently a favorite of visiting Arabs. The low-ceilinged marble-lined lobby has a mural depicting Krishna and Arjuna from the epic *Mahabharata*. Deluxe double rooms have dark-wood furnishings and beds topped with chenille spreads, carpeted floors, and big tile bathrooms with tub and showers, for Rs. 250 ($19.25); ordinary doubles are smaller, with the dark-wood furniture, attached tile bathrooms, and uncarpeted granite floors topped with area rugs, for Rs. 200 ($15.40). Suites run Rs. 300 ($23.05). The Shanbhag restaurant offers vegetarian Indian cuisine and some interesting vegetarian Chinese dishes (see "Restaurants and Nightlife in Bangalore"). The restaurant is open from 5:30 to 6 a.m. for coffee and tea, and 7:30 a.m. to 10:30 p.m. for breakfast, lunch, dinner, and snacks. A nonvegetarian restaurant was planned, and will no doubt be open by your arrival.

Low Budget—Indian Style: The **Hotel Tourist,** Race Course Road, Ananda Rao Circle (tel. 72381), has 50 singles at Rs. 20 ($1.55), 50 doubles at Rs. 35

($2.70), ten three-bedded rooms at Rs. 45 ($3.45), and ten four-bedded rooms at Rs. 50 ($3.85). They are very unfancy, though fairly clean, with Indian-style toilets in the bathrooms and cold water on tap.

Many hotels around the City Market offer rock-bottom prices. Among these, the **Hotel King** (tel. 70364) is passable.

Western-Style Hotels

For 90 years or so the **West End Hotel,** High Grounds, 41 Race Course Rd., Bangalore 560001 (tel. 29281), has earned its reputation as a gracious, well-run establishment with personalized service, and this continues now that the hotel is part of the Taj Group. As this type of gracious old hotel is fast disappearing from the face of the earth, and just as quickly being replaced with sleek, pushbutton-modern hotels, I am leading off with it here. Although the rates are too high for the budget traveler's pocketbook, if you're in the mood for a splurge with a bit of history to it, this could be the place. The old wing (preferred) houses guests in comfortable rooms with lofty peaked-beamed ceilings, comfortable furnishings, and big old-fashioned bathtubs in the bathrooms. (When I dropped in, I found that these rooms were about to be renovated, so describing the new decor is not possible. They should be all spruced up when you visit.) The new wing, in contrast, resembles an American-style motel. The rambling two-story structure is modern with compact rooms, each with its own balcony or patio. Rates are Rs. 450 ($34.60) to Rs. 550 ($42.30) for singles and Rs. 550 ($42.30) to Rs. 650 ($50) for doubles, the higher rates in the modern wing (but this may change when the old wing is redone).

The gardens at the West End are extensive, and it's pleasant to stroll along the paths through the rose arbors and under the huge shade trees. The Crazy Horse Bar at the West End, open from 11 a.m. to 11 p.m., is a favorite local meeting place—so if you don't stay here, you might drop in for a drink. The Supper Room also serves a daily buffet (see "Restaurants and Nightlife in Bangalore"). The swimming pool is in the garden, and every day you can be served a poolside barbecue from 11 a.m. to 2:30 p.m. and again from 6:30 to 10:30 p.m. when tiny lights illuminate the trees. There's a shopping arcade, travel agent, three tennis courts, and a post office on the premises.

For two travelers on $25 a day, a wise choice is the **Hotel Harsha,** 11 Venkateswamy Naidu Rd., Shivajinagar, Bangalore 560051 (tel. 565566), a clean, cheerful hotel with an imaginative, caring management at the helm. The rooms have attractive cane headboards on the beds and coordinating cane-backed chairs with comfy cushions. Some of the older rooms had heavier, less attractive furniture, but they were about to be renovated. Air-conditioned rooms cost Rs. 300 ($23.05) for doubles, Rs. 250 ($19.25) for singles, making the air-conditioned rooms at this hotel a bit of a splurge for loners. Non-air-conditioned accommodations—35 rooms in all—run Rs. 150 ($11.55) to Rs. 200 ($15.40) single (in the bracket of a traveler going it alone on $25 a day), and Rs. 250 ($19.25) double. There's a 10% service charge, 5% sales tax, and luxury tax as applicable.

Outside, a pagoda-style arch leads to the Jade Garden, a Chinese restaurant near the pool, with main dishes in the Rs.-15 ($1.15) to Rs.-30 ($2.30) range. Chaupal (meaning "village meeting place") is the indoor Indian restaurant (described fully in "Restaurants and Nightlife in Bangalore").

Bedtime tea and continental breakfast are served at the centrally located **Barton Court,** Mahatma Gandhi Road, Bangalore 650001 (tel. 575631 to 575635), but other meals must be taken out at one of the many delightful nearby restaurants. There's a glass mosaic peacock behind the reception counter in the simple lobby. Rooms are very clean, and larger rooms are called studios. All have air conditioning, TV sets, mini-refrigerators stocked with sodas, and attached Western-style bathrooms. Rates are Rs. 225 ($17.30) for single occupancy of a double room, Rs. 310 ($23.85) for two; Rs. 275 ($21.15) for single occupancy of a studio, Rs. 350 ($26.90) for two.

The **Shilton Hotel,** St. Mark's Road, Bangalore 560001 (tel. 568185), always a good bet for budget travelers—with high-ceilinged rooms and quality furniture, private tile bathrooms with tubs and showers—was on strike during my visit. The rates were said to be Rs. 265 ($20.40) for singles, Rs. 330 ($25.40) for double, air-conditioned; in non-air-conditioned rooms, Rs. 145 ($11.15) to Rs. 190 ($14.60) for singles, and Rs. 230 ($17.70) for doubles. Strikes often drag on endlessly in India, but if the Shilton has reopened it should be worthy of consideration.

The halls were getting a much-needed paint job when I stopped in at the **Hotel Rama,** 40/2 Lavelle Rd., Bangalore 560001 (tel. 53381), an unimposing three-story concrete-block building near a main shopping area and next to beautiful Cubbon Park. Rooms are clean and comfortable, with carpeting, built-in desk-vanities, and wardrobes. They all have attached bathrooms. Singles are Rs. 140 ($10.75); doubles, Rs. 175 ($13.45); deluxe singles, Rs. 180 ($13.85); deluxe doubles, Rs. 215 ($16.55). Suites go for Rs. 250 ($19.25) and Rs. 300 ($23.05). There are 20 air-conditioned rooms out of a total 40, and they have the higher prices. Although the Shilpa Bar and Restaurant has no decor, it is modern and clean, with booths and tables. You can order continental, Indian, or Chinese foods, all in about the same price range: Rs. 15 ($1.15) to Rs. 23 ($1.75) for main dishes. Hours are 7 a.m. to 11 p.m.

The rust-and-beige **Hotel Bangalore International,** Crescent Road, High Grounds, Bangalore 560001 (tel. 298011 to 298017), has 57 clean and adequately furnished rooms off verandas. The tile bathrooms are big and clean. From the roof terrace, there's a fine view of the city. The Amber Bar and Restaurant has brick walls and mirrored pillars, and is open from 7 a.m. to 3 p.m. and 7 p.m. to midnight. Non-air-conditioned rooms rent for Rs. 140 ($10.75) single, Rs. 210 ($16.15) double; air-conditioned rooms, Rs. 190 ($14.60) single and Rs. 265 ($20.40) double. Deluxe air-conditioned rooms cost Rs. 220 ($16.90) single and Rs. 330 ($25.40) double. There's only one single room, so single-occupancy rates are charged for the doubles.

The **Curzon Court,** 10 Brigade Rd., Bangalore 560001 (tel. 569997), is a cozy, tastefully furnished air-conditioned find in the heart of the main commercial district. The rooms have cane-backed furniture, printed drapes and spreads, and attached tile bathrooms. A studio goes for Rs. 245 ($18.85); a double, Rs. 290 ($22.30); a deluxe double, Rs. 400 ($30.75); and a suite, Rs. 450 ($34.60). The more expensive rooms are larger and have bigger bathrooms, but are not worth the extra rupees. There's no restaurant in the hotel. You can have food delivered to your room or eat in one of the many restaurants nearby.

A small palace of the former Maharaja of Gujarat, set in 20 acres of gone-to-seed garden, and now the **Jayamahal Palace Hotel,** Jayamahal Road (tel. 575561), was once an interesting, offbeat place to stay. Now it's too run-down to recommend. The manager told me that renovations were planned. If they're completed by the time you visit, this would be a place worthy of consideration.

Splurge Choices: The splurge-priced **Taj Residency,** 14 Mahatma Gandhi Rd., Bangalore 560001 (tel. 56888), has a nice garden and looks a whole lot more gracious inside than its concrete-and-brick exterior would lead you to believe. In the handsome marble-pillared lobby are splashing fountains and comfortable rust and brown settees. The tastefully decorated rooms have all the comforts—chaises longues in addition to beds, cane-backed chairs, and attached small but well-appointed bathrooms. Rates are Rs. 425 ($32.70) single and Rs. 525 ($40.40) double. No expense has been spared in the decor of the restaurants and bar, and they are among the highest priced in India (see "Restaurants and Nightlife in Bangalore"). Plus there's a swimming pool and other five-star amenities for guests.

At the luxurious **Holiday Inn Bangalore,** 28 Sankey Rd., Bangalore 560052 (tel. 73554), a glass-walled elevator whisks guests to rooms off a glass-topped atrium which has the effect of making the lobby seem a greenhouse pampering both guests and potted plants. The Regency-inspired decor throughout shows up in the printed drapes and spreads and the dark woods used in the guest rooms. Bathrooms feature pulsating shower heads to soothe the weary traveler. All rooms are doubles: Rs. 600 ($46.15) for single occupancy, Rs. 700 ($53.85) double, and Rs. 750 ($57.70) to Rs. 850 ($65.40) for larger executive rooms and suites. Ambrosia, the lobby coffeeshop, accented with plants, has a soothing indoor-outdoor feeling. This is a delightful place for a delicious tea, with biscuits made by one of the best pastry chefs in the city. There's a swimming pool in the garden and a health club inside.

Also on Sankey Road, what looks like a beautiful old royal residency is the **Windsor Manor,** 25 Sankey Rd., Bangalore 560052 (tel. 28031), with gleaming marble floors, sweeping staircases, and a comfortable lobby lounge with an antique bar and velvet banquettes—a place to have a drink, tea, or coffee even if you don't stay here. It's very splurgey, but you may feel you owe it to yourself after some hard traveling. Ordinary (small) singles cost Rs. 575 ($44.25); doubles, Rs. 675 ($51.90). Somewhat larger rooms called "executive" are Rs. 750 ($57.70); "manor" rooms, Rs. 750 ($57.70) to Rs. 850 ($65.40). Suites run Rs. 2,100 ($161.50) to Rs. 2,800 ($215.50). A swimming pool and health club are among the amenities.

The pleasant IDTC **Hotel Ashok,** Kumara Krupa, High Grounds, Bangalore, 560001 (tel. 79411), is another hotel for those with plenty of rupees. Air-conditioned, surrounded by lovely gardens with a swimming pool, the hotel's spacious marble lobby is broken up by intimate conversational groupings. The newly decorated guest rooms are nicest with printed textiles and dark woods (others were to be renovated). Rates are Rs. 500 ($38.45) single and Rs. 600 ($46.15) double. Deluxe doubles cost Rs. 700 ($53.85), and suites go for Rs. 1,000 ($77) to Rs. 2,500 ($192.25). There's a fine view from the elegant, expensive Mandarin Restaurant on the rooftop—a good choice to enjoy a special meal. There's a daily buffet elsewhere in the hotel (see "Restaurants and Nightlife in Bangalore").

Low-Budget Places: The **YMCA,** Bourdillon, 65 Infantry Road (tel. 572681), offers rudimentary accommodations for men only at Rs. 15 ($1.15) to Rs. 20 ($1.55). Mattresses and pillows are provided for the cots, as are one bed sheet and a pillow case, but no towel. From the looks of things, you might be more comfortable, and far wiser, using a sleeping bag rather than the bedding provided.

Also basic, the **YMCA,** 57 Millers Road (tel. 55885), takes families as well as men and women, for Rs. 50 ($3.85).

The **YMCA Guest House,** on Infantry Road (tel. 570997), founded in 1823 and still in the same building, takes families as well as women, at Rs. 25 ($1.90) single and Rs. 40 double ($3.05), for bed and breakfast.

RESTAURANTS AND NIGHTLIFE IN BANGALORE: Best overall bet for budget stretching are the eat-all-you-like buffets in the high-priced Western-style hotels. They're not cheap, to be sure, but they allow you to come back for seconds so you can indeed eat hearty and make this your main meal of the day.

Buffets Around Town

There are buffets in the Lotus Room of the **Hotel Ashok** (tel. 79411), served from 12:30 to 3 p.m. daily, at Rs. 50 ($3.85); the Wellington Room at the **Windsor Manor** (tel. 28031), at Rs. 60 ($4.60); and the Supper Room of the **West End Hotel** (tel. 29281), at Rs. 55 ($4.25), tax included.

The Southern Comfort at the **Taj Residency** (tel. 568888), charges Rs. 45 ($3.45) for its weekday buffet, Rs. 50 ($3.85) on Saturday when the buffet becomes a Regional Food Festival saluting the country's highly diverse cooking styles. The Taj also has a Sunday buffet in its Memories of China restaurant, at Rs. 50 ($3.85), which is quite a buy when you know that main dishes in this expensive restaurant can run Rs. 34 ($2.60) or more.

In the planning stages, and probably a reality by now, is the buffet at the Ambrosia at the **Holiday Inn Bangalore.**

Unless otherwise noted, taxes must be added to the above prices, and the timings are 12:30 to 3 p.m. at all locations.

Vegetarian Meals and Snacks

Not to be missed for South Indian vegetarian foods is **Mavalli Tiffin Room,** 2-C Lalbagh Rd. (tel. 220022), near the Main Gate, recommended by the Jayadevas of Bangalore. This famous 50-year-old restaurant lives up to its acclaimed reputation. Billed as "the world headquarters of the Indian dosa" —they may well also be the most delicious—the restaurant also features a host of other well-prepared South Indian dishes, idlis and wadas (melt-in-the-mouth mini-doughnuts made from ground lentils and bathed in spiced curds) to name but two. The specialty, in addition to delicious foods, is a high regard for good hygiene: everything is served on sterilized dishes and plates by waiters in spotless uniforms. They offer coffee and tea in silver services. Most dishes are moderate: Rs. 3 (23¢) for superb dosa. One more thing: So popular is the Mavalli Tiffin Room that there is usually a line. You leave your name, wait and wait, and then, when called, take a seat wherever there's a vacancy. Hours are 7 to 11 a.m. and 4 to 7 p.m. (closed Monday and holidays).

You'll find vegetarian foods in a pleasant setting at the **Swathi,** a drive-in restaurant on Infantry Road. There is no menu, but typical south Indian dishes are served outdoors under spreading trees, like a dosa for Rs. 2 (15¢). There's an indoor restaurant with air conditioning as well. Open daily.

For a change of pace, try the Chinese-style vegetarian dishes at the **Shanbhag,** in the Hotel Ashraya International (tel. 719211), a restful-looking place with a beige-and-brown color scheme. To start, there are such typical soups as sweet corn and hot-and-sour soup, for Rs. 8 (60¢) to Rs. 10 (75¢). A number of dishes made with vegetables and either cashews or almonds are also Rs. 8 (60¢) to Rs. 10 (75¢). Hours: 7:30 a.m. to 10:30 p.m. daily.

Nonvegetarian Indian, Continental, and Chinese

Charming Warli folk paintings, each with a tale of men and tigers, dancers, and other matters, decorate the walls of the **Chaupal** (meaning "village meeting place"), a restaurant in the Harsha Hotel (tel. 565566). There are white-brick pillars to break up the space, and satin-finish cotton-bunting hangings and electrified oil lamps add festive notes. This innovative decor is a good backdrop for unusual Indian dishes not found everywhere else. A special recommendation is matka chicken (cooked with spices in a tightly sealed clay pot) for Rs. 24 ($1.85), kaibai paneer (cheese in freshly ground spices) at Rs. 15 ($1.15), Shah Jahani kebab (chicken) for Rs. 22 ($1.70), and beer to wash it down at Rs. 18 ($1.40) to Rs. 20 ($1.55). Desserts include mango kulfi at Rs. 12 (90¢) or phirni (custard) for Rs. 10 (75¢). Each dish on the menu is explained so you know just what you're getting. The restaurant is open all day, but the Indian foods are featured at lunch (from 12:30 to 3 p.m.) and dinner (from 7 p.m. to midnight). There's disco dancing at night on a postage-stamp-size floor to taped music and special lighting effects.

The **Napoli,** Kempegowda Road (tel. 79021), is an air-conditioned, upstairs seedy hideaway with a cabaret featuring live music and scantily clad, not especially talented disco-type dancers. Rs. 35 ($2.70) is the exorbitant entry fee. Shows go on from 8 to 9 p.m., 9:45 to 10:15 p.m., and 10:15 to 11:40. From 7:30 to 8 p.m. there's live music and the entry fee is Rs. 30 ($2.30). The menu features a few Indian dishes, for Rs. 16 ($1.25) and up. Most of the clientele is not here for the food. Hours are 6 to 11:40 p.m. every day.

Tiffany's, 23 Grant Rd. (tel. 50377), has long offered good food in attractive surroundings for moderate prices. Alas, it was on strike during my last visit. You might want to try it if it's open again when you're in town.

Cool, comfortable, and dimly lit, the **Kwality Restaurant,** Brigade Road (tel. 571633), has a high beamed ceiling, green velvet banquettes, ceramic-tile walls, and tables covered with snowy-white cloths. Specialties are tandoori foods and kebabs, ranging from Rs. 24 ($1.85) to Rs. 40 ($3.05). Well known for its rich desserts, the menu features a selection of ice cream and other sweets, for Rs. 9 (70¢) to Rs. 14 ($1.05). Upstairs is the Chinese Room, featuring, appropriately enough, Chinese foods much like others around town. Hours are 1:30 to 3 p.m. and 7 p.m. to midnight every day.

Like Siamese twins, **Koshy's Parade Café** and the **Jewel Box Restaurant** on St. Marks Road (tel. 573793), are joined—by the same kitchen. Koshy's is on the plain side and the once-glittering Jewel Box, with a gem-studded mermaid mural, has lost its luster. Both have almost the same menu, but the prices are lower at Koshy's. Chinese, Indian, and continental specialties range from Rs. 18 ($1.40) to Rs. 28 ($2.15). Both have good food and are much liked by Bangalorans. Jewel Box is open from 11:30 a.m. to 3:30 p.m. and 6:30 to 11:30 p.m., and Koshy's, from 9 a.m. to 11:30 p.m. every day. You can get a light breakfast and snacks at Koshy's.

Stone arches set off the tables at **Blue Fox,** 80 Mahatma Gandhi Rd. (tel. 570608), long a local favorite for food and dancing to recorded Western music at night on a dance floor bathed in strobe lights. The menu features a host of continental dishes, such as fish à la Blue Fox (filet of fish with mushroom-cream sauce, baked with cheese, and garnished with vegetables) for Rs. 28 ($2.15) and chateaubriand (steak) for Rs. 32 ($2.45). For Indian food, try chicken kalme kebab (special drumsticks), at Rs. 24 ($1.85), or other Indian entrees for Rs. 24 ($1.85) to Rs. 43 ($3.30); most continental entrees cost Rs. 32 ($2.45). There are also many rich desserts, appetizers, and soups to round out your meal. Open from 11 a.m. to 3 p.m. and 7:30 p.m. to midnight every day.

The coir-carpeted **Oasis,** 1 Church St., Bangalore 560001 (tel. 561981), is a dark hideaway with coir-inlaid wood-paneled walls where seafood is the main attraction, from 11 a.m. to 11 p.m. daily. It is specially recommended for curries with seafood such as prawns, as well as fish, for Rs. 12 (90¢) to Rs. 14 ($1.05). Most dishes run no higher than Rs. 20 ($1.55).

Next door, the cozy, dark **Pub** serves only snacks and drinks, should you care for quick refreshment. Hours are 11 a.m. to 10:30 p.m.

Lawrence DiSouza, owner of **Caesar's,** 9/1 Mahatma Gandhi Rd. (tel. 565644), has won international tourism awards for his restaurant expertise in India and Kuwait. He had plans for restaurants in Orlando, Fla., and Baltimore, Md., which may by now be open. Meanwhile, Caesar's in Bangalore is Roman in name only, and, to some extent, its decor. The foods are the usual array of Indian, Chinese, and continental dishes found many other places—but here, however, well prepared and pleasantly served. Cantonese dishes include sweet-corn chicken soup, fried ginger chicken (a specialty), and sweet-and-sour fish, and cost about Rs. 20 ($1.55) to Rs. 22 ($1.70); some Chinese fish dishes are more. If you want Western foods, steaks, and veal chops run Rs. 25 ($1.90) to Rs. 28 ($2.15). Tandoori chicken, at Rs. 34 ($2.60), is about the highest-priced dish on the menu. Open from noon to 3 p.m. and 7 p.m. to midnight every day.

Blue Heaven, 22 Church St. (tel. 56176), open from 10:30 a.m. to 3 p.m. and 7 to 11 p.m. every day, is a huge, cheerful Chinese restaurant with a lavender (not blue) ceiling, shiny white pillars, and bright-red Chinese characters on cream-colored walls. Specialties include a number of spiced Szechuan dishes for Rs. 22 ($1.70) to Rs. 26 ($2), familiar Cantonese dishes for Rs. 19 ($1.45) to Rs. 22 ($1.70), delicious noodle concoctions for Rs. 14 ($1.05) to Rs. 16 ($1.25), and beer at Rs. 17 ($1.30), Rs. 18 ($1.40), and Rs. 23 ($1.75).

Another large, pleasant Chinese restaurant with an inappropriate name is **Continental,** 4 Brigade Rd. (tel. 570263), open from 11 a.m. to 11 p.m., serves good fried chicken Chinese style, and rice dishes at roughly the same prices as at Blue Heaven. The attractively decorated **Nanking,** 3 Grant Rd. (tel. 54301), has a Cantonese menu and makes some Japanese foods, on special request.

Splurges and Views

At the hushed and elegant wood-paneled **Jockey Club,** in the Taj Residency (tel. 568888), a well-prepared and attentively served continental-style three-course meal will run about Rs. 200 ($15.40) per person, without wine. Indian wine costs Rs. 140 ($10.75) per bottle, and French wines, from Rs. 500 ($38.45)—and not the best quality at that. In the same hotel, the sumptuous **Memories of China,** with hand-painted peach silk wall panels and Regency-period Chinese furniture, has beautifully presented Chinese dishes you're not apt to find elsewhere, deftly prepared by a chef from Canton, China: grape cluster fish is fish filet, cut and rolled to resemble grapes and cooked in a grape sauce, at Rs. 30 ($2.30); jade chicken is minced and cooked in a spiced cream sauce, for Rs. 34 ($2.60); homemade noodles, especially good with prawns and chicken, for Rs. 22 ($1.70). A thick soup with minced chicken and prawns is Rs. 18 ($1.40). Beer costs Rs. 24 ($1.85) and Rs. 26 ($2).

You'll find more Chinese elegance—this with a splendid view—at the rooftop **Mandarin Room,** in the Hotel Ashok (tel. 79411), where specialties include crisp lamb Peking style at Rs. 38 ($2.90), mixed fried noodles at Rs. 20 ($1.55), and vegetarian wonton for Rs. 20 ($1.55). Most entrees at the Mandarin range from Rs. 18 ($1.40) to Rs. 38 ($2.90). It's open for lunch and dinner every day; there's a dance band at night.

Splurge-priced frontier foods are delicious at the **Aghan,** in the Windsor Manor (tel. 28033).

At night from **Topkapi,** on the top floor of the Utility Building, Mahatma Gandhi Road (tel. 578040), open from 11 a.m. to 12:30 p.m., the twinkling lights of the city below are indeed spread out like jewels in a sultan's palace. Except for the name, there's nothing Turkish about this restaurant, owned by the Hotel Harsha and so named because it's a "top cap" on the building. Rose and gray upholstery on the chairs, little domes in the ceiling, and windows all around make it possible to relax in comfort and enjoy the view while eating well-prepared Indian foods, such as a delicious murgh (chicken) saffron for Rs. 32 ($2.45), vegetable biryani for Rs. 32 ($2.45), and nan for Rs. 4 (30¢). There are other Indian breads costing up to Rs. 10 (75¢) and a host of Indian dishes in addition to those mentioned. Continental foods are said to be good here as well. Taped music, a bit too loud at times, adds a jarring note to otherwise serene surroundings.

Every night but Tuesday there's a poolside barbecue at the **Hotel Ashok,** with dance music too. The barbecue at the **West End** is in the garden with trees lit with tiny lights.

Sweets

Notable Benagli sweets can be found at **K. C. Das, Private Ltd.,** 48 St. Marks Rd., at Rs. 60 ($4.60) and Rs. 90 ($6.90) per kilo. Also highly recommended for Indian sweets is **Kanti Sweets,** Kempegowda Circle, K.G. Road, and **Arya Bhavan Sweets,** Santosh Shopping Center, Kempegowda Road, open from 9 a.m. to 10 p.m.

GETTING HELP AND GOING SIGHTSEEING: The **Government of India Tourist Office,** KFC Building, 48 Church St., Bangalore 560001 (tel. 579517), is eager to help with pamphlets, maps, and advice. You can book guides from the tourist office at Rs. 48 ($3.70) for a half day (four hours), Rs. 72 ($5.55) for a full day (eight hours), for a party of one to four persons. There's a lunch break of Rs. 20 ($1.55) for full-day sightseeing. If you take a guide out of the city, there's a Rs. 75 ($5.75) overnight, outstation charge.

Be sure to stock up in Bangalore on pamphlets for Mysore and other places you're going in Karnataka. There's no comparable tourist office in the state.

Sightseeing tours operated by the **Karnataka State Tourism Development Corporation (KSTDC)** are the most economical ways of seeing the sights.

The **Bangalore Tour** operates twice a day, except Sunday, from 7:30 a.m. to 1:30 p.m. and from 2 to 7:30 p.m. for Rs. 30 ($2.30) per person. It covers Lalbagh (beautiful botanical gardens, designed by Tipu Sultan and now the Government Botanical Gardens, a splendid display of 1,000 varieties of trees covering 1,240 acres), Bull Temple (Dravidian style, built by Kempegowda, founder of Bangalore), Tipu Palace (begun by Tipu's father and completed by Tipu himself in 1791, and also on the Mysore City tour), Cauvery Arts and Crafts Emporium, Anjaneya Temple, Ulsoor Lake (a popular boating spot), and Vidhana Soudha (the town's most imposing structure, housing the legislature, secretariat, and other government offices).

A full day (eight hours) or 80 km (48 miles) with a **private car and driver** in Bangalore costs Rs. 220 ($16.90); a half day (4 hours) or 40 km (24 miles) is Rs. 120 ($9.25). It's Rs. 1.90 (14½¢) per extra kilometer; for overtime, Rs. 10 (75¢) per hour. **Auto-rickshaws** in Bangalore and Mysore charge a minimum of Rs. 2 (15¢) and Re. 1 (7½¢) per kilometer for subsequent kilometers.

If you hire a car and driver for an outstation trip, the charge is Rs. 1.90

(14½¢) per kilometer (minimum of 250 km); Rs. 30 ($2.30) is also charged for the driver's overnight.

The following **conducted coach tours** go outside Bangalore: to Mysore City, departing daily at 7:15 a.m. and returning at 10:30 p.m., for Rs. 100 ($7.70); to Belur, Halebid, and Sravanabelagola, departing daily at 7:15 a.m. and returning at 10:30 p.m., for Rs. 120 ($9.25); and to Ootacamund ("Ooty"), departing daily in season (April 15 to June 15; off-season, on Friday only) at 7:15 a.m. and returning three days later at 10:30 p.m., including Mysore, Bandipur Sanctuary, one night halt at Brindavan Gardens, and a second-night halt at Ooty, for Rs. 400 ($30.75), inclusive of accommodation.

A two-day tour on Friday only departing at 10 p.m. and returning on Sunday at 10:30 p.m., goes to Mantralaya, Tungabhadra Dam, and Hampi, ruins of the once-powerful royal city of Vijayanagar, which made foreign visitors gasp at its brilliance as far back as the 14th century, for Rs. 250 ($19.25), inclusive of accommodation. On Wednesday a tour departs at 10:30 p.m. to Tirupathi-Mangapura, an important pilgrimage place, and returns the third night at 9:30 p.m., for Rs. 180 ($13.85), including accommodation and darshan (offering).

To **book tours** or get further information about them, contact the Karnataka State Tourism Development Corporation (KSTDC), 10/4 Kasturba Rd., Queen's Circle, Bangalore (tel. 578901); the KSTDC Booking Counter, Badami House (opposite the corporation's offices), N.R. Square (tel. 221299); the KSTDC Bangalore Airport Counter (tel. 571467); or the KSTDC Tourist Information Counter at the city railway station (tel. 70068). All of these tours begin from the KSTDC Booking Counter, Badami House.

The **India Tourism Development Corporation (ITDC)** also conducts a daily tour to Mysore by deluxe coach for Rs. 100 ($7.70) starting at 7:30 a.m. and returning to Bangalore at 10:45 p.m., taking in all the highlights along the way. Reservations can be made at ITDC's Ashok Bangalore and other leading hotels, travel agents, and tour operators. Pickup points are Tank Bund Road opposite the Sangam Theatre, the City Railway Station, and the Hotel Ashok.

SHOPPING: Look for handcrafts in sandalwood, rosewood, and ivory; elegant silks and hand-looms in saris or by the meter or as ready-made or made-to-order fashionable salwar kamiz sets (pajamas and tunics) for women; and kamiz and tailored shirts for men.

Main **shopping centers** are Mahatma Gandhi Road, Commercial Street, Kempegowda Road, Chickpet City Market, Russel Market, Brigade Road, and Residency Road. As elsewhere, many hotels have shopping arcades where prices tend to be much higher than in the markets. A number of states, in addition to Karnataka, have boutiques in Bangalore. Among the shops are:

Cauvery, Karnataka State Arts and Crafts Emporium, is at 23 Mahatma Gandhi Rd. (tel. 571418), open from 10 a.m. to 1:30 p.m. and 3 to 7 p.m. every day but Sunday. Among the packable items are sandalwood letter openers with hand-carved motifs along the handle or edge, for Rs. 13 ($1); silk scarves for Rs. 30 ($2.30) and up; and sandalwood and rosewood beads for Rs. 23 ($1.75) and up. Toys in wood, such as charming giraffes on wheels at Rs. 17.50 ($1.35), are just a few of the many made-in-Karnataka souvenirs found in this shop.

The oldest silk store in Bangalore, and one of the best in India, **Vijayalaskshmi Silks and Saris,** 20 J/61 Mahatma Gandhi Road (tel. 570937), has opulent temple saris woven with real gold from the temple-sari-weaving town of Dharmavaram, 110 miles (180 km) from Bangalore on the way to Bombay. The store's literature describes having one of these saris as "possessing a precious jewel," and indeed they're gem-high in price—Rs. 15,000 ($1,154), for example. Less costly, but absolutely lovely georgette saris heavily embroidered in silver or gold wirework—works of fabric art—range from Rs. 350 ($26.90) up to the highest realms as well. Lovely silks in vivid colors from Kanchipuram cost Rs. 90 ($6.90) per meter without gold and Rs. 150 ($11.55) per meter with gold. Brocade stoles run Rs. 80 ($6.15) to Rs. 160 ($12.30). These are just a sampling of the store's gorgeous silks. Open from 10 a.m. to 1:30 p.m. and 3 to 8 p.m.; closed Sunday.

Luxurious silks are also found at the two-level **Deempam Silk International,** Mahatma Gandhi Road (tel. 578560), open from 10 a.m. to 9 p.m. (on Sunday to 2 p.m.). Here are elegant ready-made silk salwar kamiz, from Rs. 600 ($46.15) to Rs. 1,500 ($115.40); some of the highest-priced have hand-brush-painted designs on the finest quality silk. Cotton salwar kamiz cost Rs. 400 ($30.75), with some hand embroidery on them. The salwar kamiz are upstairs, as are cotton saris; silks and silk saris, downstairs.

Near the Blue Fox restaurant, **Ashok Silks,** Shrungar Shopping Centre, Mahatma Gandhi Road (tel. 571523), will copy your favorite fashions or work from patterns in one day, for Rs. 125 ($9.60) and up, depending on design and type of fabric. Elegant silk shirts for men, ready-made, cost Rs. 265 ($20.40) to Rs. 350 ($26.90); silk-cotton blends and cotton and polyblend shirts are also available, as are made-to-order shirts. Ready-made salwar kamiz for women also in stock. Men's ties were to be introduced and are probably in stock by now. Hours are 10 a.m. to 8 p.m. (to 2 p.m. on Sunday).

One of Bangalore's best bookstores, **Gangaram Book Bureau,** is on Mahatma Gandhi Road, as is **Spencer's,** the South Indian department store chain.

On Commercial Street, several jewelers have inexpensive silver chokers and earrings as well as precious things. **C. Krishniah Chetty & Sons** has one of the best selections of jewelry. Sandals are good buys in Bangalore and again on Commercial Street you'll find them in many stores. You have to keep trying on pair after pair until you find your size. Good-quality leather thongs should cost about Rs. 20 ($1.55) to Rs. 50 ($3.85).

At the **Regional Design Center,** 8 Church St., you can watch artisans carving ivory, inlaying wood, sculpting stone. It's very interesting and gives you great appreciation of what goes into even the tiniest article. Nothing is for sale —but you can place orders for display items. Open from 9:30 a.m. to 6 p.m.; closed Saturday and Sunday.

GETTING TO BANGALORE:

Bangalore is easily accessible by air, train, and bus. **Train** connections are available from all major locations including Cochin, Mangalore, and smaller cities in the South. **Bus** services are available from Cochin and Madras. Flights from Madras, 1 hour, Rs. 285 ($22); Bombay, 1½ hours, Rs. 770 ($59.25); Hyderabad, 1 hour, Rs. 490 ($37.70).

GOING BEYOND BANGALORE:

Every three hours from 7 a.m. to 10 p.m. there are express trains between Bangalore and **Mysore** from the City Railway Station, for a three-hour journey of 87 miles (140 km), for Rs. 66 ($5.05) in first class, Rs. 16 ($1.25) in second class. Passenger trains cover the Bangalore–Mysore distance in six hours for Rs. 11 (85¢) and are obviously best avoided.

There are express buses from Bangalore to Mysore every ten minutes from around 5:40 a.m. to 9:20 p.m., from the City Bus Stand in front of the City Railway Station, for Rs. 20 ($1.55). They leave from Mysore's Central Bus Stand to Bangalore with similar frequency. A car and driver between Bangalore and Mysore will cost Rs. 1.90 (14½¢) per kilometer plus the driver's overnight charges. Private operators run video buses between Bangalore and Mysore for Rs. 30 ($2.30); get them at the Private Bus Stand. Near the City Bus Stand are private taxi operators who will sell seats to Bangalore; in Mysore, try the Metropole Hotel Circle for the same kind of deal.

Splurgers might consider the Bangalore–Mysore Vayudoot 35-minute flight on Monday, Wednesday, and Friday for Rs. 150 ($21). You won't see the sights from here to there, however.

Srirangapatna can be reached by the Bangalore–Mysore–Bangalore express trains, for Rs. 65 ($5) in first class and Rs. 15 ($1.15) in second. Passenger trains cost Rs. 4 (30¢) or Rs. 5 (40¢) less and take hours more than the express. Buses go all day long to Srirangapatna from either Bangalore or Mysore.

There is one direct bus a day between Srirangapatna and Somnathpur.

One bus a day leaves Bangalore at 9 a.m. for **Nagarhole,** costing Rs. 27 ($2.05), arriving at 4 p.m. Two buses daily from Bangalore to **Ootacamund** (**"Ooty"**) go via Mysore and Bandipur Sanctuary, for Rs. 35 ($2.70). You can stop at the **Bandipur Sanctuary** (you'll get there about 11:30 a.m.), spend the day sightseeing, and catch the evening bus from Gundlupet, about 15 km (9 miles) from Bandipur, at 6 p.m. and go on to Ooty. Two other Bangalore buses go to Ooty direct, at 9:30 a.m. and 8 a.m.

For **Bijapur,** you can fly from Bangalore to Billary on Vayudoot for Rs. 335 ($46), and take an express train from Billary to Bijapur for Rs. 90 ($6.90) in first class, Rs. 24 ($1.85) in second. Or you can take an express train from Bangalore to Hubli and change to the *Gol Gumbaz Express* to Bijapur, for Rs. 209 ($16.05) in first class, Rs. 50 ($3.85) in second. There are also express buses between Hubli and Bijapur.

BETWEEN BANGALORE AND MYSORE CITY:
The landscape is dotted with rocky hills, paddy fields, huge trees, and farmers plowing their fields. Here are some sights to see and stops to make between Bangalore and Mysore City:

About 30 km (18 miles) from Bangalore, you can get a glimpse from the bus of the **caves** used in the film *Passage to India,* up in the hills. If you're driving, this is a good place to stretch your legs. Then about seven kilometers (4½ miles) before Srirangapatna, there's the **Mayura Highway Restaurant,** with clean toilets, a restaurant, and rooms.

Srirangapatna, 77 miles (140 km) from Bangalore, an island in the Cauvery River where the Tipu Sultan died in battle in 1799, is full of historic sites, among them the remains of the **Old Fort** and dungeons. In a much better state of preservation is the 500-year-old **Sri Ranganatha Temple,** where (after taking your shoes off) you can wander in the cool halls and peer in at gods and goddesses in splendid adornments. Nearby, you can climb to the top of the former sultan's **mosque** and get a glimpse of Mysore's gleaming domes in the distance.

Also on the island is Tipu Sultan's **summer palace,** outside the fort. This is a pavilion of graceful arabesques and pillars, richly decorated in ornamental paintings. The gold-accented walls are covered with murals in a dizzying and dazzling profusion, depicting scenes of court life and battle from the days of Tipu Sultan and his father, Hyder Ali. On the west wall is a realistic rendition of the battle at which Hyder Ali beat the British at Pollilore. This painting was whitewashed in the 19th century but restored by an artist who knew the original. The summer palace also contains a museum with portraits, maps, gleaming silver cups, and other artifacts. Admission is 50 paise (3½¢), and it's open from 9 a.m. to 5 p.m. At the eastern end of the island is **Gumbaz,** Tipu's elegant, square-shaped, cream-colored mausoleum, with a graceful dome, surrounded by black pillars as shiny as mirrors. Each of the four corners of the tomb has a tall minaret. Double doors of rosewood inlaid with ivory lead to the interior. Inside you will see the tiger-stripe insignia of **Tipu.**

About 1½ miles beyond Srirangapatna is the **Ranganathittu Bird Sanctuary,** best seen June through October when a variety of feathered friends are in residence. The sanctuary is included in the KSTDC Mysore City sightseeing tour, mentioned earlier. If you go by car, the entry fee for each car is 50 paise (3½¢); bikes, 10 paise (1¢)—plus Rs. 2 (15¢) for each person. Boating fee is Re. 1 (7½¢). Camera fees run from Rs. 3 (23¢) for a still camera to Rs. 10 (75¢) for a movie camera; telelens, Rs. 3 (23¢). Open from 8:30 a.m. to 6 p.m. Prime time is sunset, when the Cauvery, birds, and colorful sky are a beautiful sound and sight.

A Pretty Place to Stay

Should you want to spend time in and about Srirangapatna examining the fascinating sights, there's the small, simple **Hotel Mayura River View** (tel. 114), run by the KSTDC, in a splendid setting overlooking the Cauvery. Neat little rooms with nice verandas are Rs. 80 ($6.15) double, with private attached bathroom. A restaurant on the premises serves meals and snacks.

2. Mysore City and Onward

Mysore City (pop. 1,000,000) is chock full of gardens, the streets are wide, there are many grand dwellings and even some of the more mundane buildings (railway offices, Maternity Hospital, and Technical Institute) look very elegant. Most of the buildings in Mysore are painted creamy yellow, and the **Palace** is by far the most outstanding structure in town. It's open from 10:30 a.m. to 5 p.m., and admission is Rs. 2 (15¢).

Built in 1897, the Palace is a mixture of the Hindu and Saracenic styles and also shows some influence of the Hoysalas, who built some temples nearby. Inside you can visit the rooms. Some big paintings depict **Dussehra** (the fall festival), showing the maharaja leading the procession and the handsomely costumed members of his retinue. In the Palace museum is the golden howdah (elephant "saddle") upon which he used to sit on this occasion. In November 1973, the late Maharaja Sri Jaya Chamarajendra Wadiyar Bahadur, member of the ruling dynasty from the 18th to the 20th century, announced he was preparing to turn his elaborate palace over to the government to become "somewhat like Versailles." His descendants live in a few rooms.

Across from the Palace grounds is **Statue Square,** where a statue of the grandfather of the present maharaja sits under a golden canopy.

The conducted tour bypasses the Palace but goes up **Chamundi Hill,** at whose summit you will be greeted by a grotesque, brightly painted statue of the terrifying demon King Mahishasura, who was slaughtered by the goddess Chamundi after whom the hill is named.

The top of the hill is crowned by the **Shri Chamundeswari Temple,** whose tower is a mere 300 years old, whereas the foundation dates from 2,000 years ago.

About halfway up the hill is the huge 17th-century statue of Nandi, Shiva's mount, 16 feet high and carved out of one rock from tail to tinkling rock bell and stone-cut garland. The bull has been anointed over and over again and shines like metal.

Another highlight in Mysore is the **Shri Chamarajendra Art Gallery, Jagan Mohan Palace** (open from 8:30 a.m. to 5:30 p.m. every day). Look for paintings from the Mughal and Rajput schools, gem-like miniatures, each one a jewel.

Mysore's **zoo** (open from 9 a.m. to 2 p.m. and 3 to 6 p.m.) is one of the best in India. Admission is Re. 1 (7½¢).

HOTELS IN MYSORE: As a major Indian city, Mysore has hotels for everyone, from the super-splurge for jet-setters to the following, which fit our budget.

Indian-Style Hotels

Especially good in Mysore are two well-run hotels in the Dasaprakash chain. In the older **Dasaprakash,** on Gandhi Square, Mysore 570001 (tel. 24444), two worlds blend: tongas draw up and park alongside cars; guests in white dhotis and brilliant saris shot with gold threads mingle with those in dungarees and dresses. From the hotel's top floor there's a superb view of Mysore's distinctive domed skyline. Inside, all 145 rooms are spotlessly clean: 50 of them have Western-style toilets in attached bathrooms; the others are outfitted Indian style. Single rooms cost Rs. 45 ($3.45); doubles, Rs. 80 ($6.15). Deluxe (meaning larger) singles run Rs. 70 ($5.40); deluxe doubles, Rs. 110 ($8.45). Air-conditioned doubles are Rs. 125 ($9.60). As in other traditional hotels, the food is vegetarian and Rs. 10 (75¢) will get you a satisfying thali meal.

In the sleek octagonal **Dasaprakash Paradise,** 105 Vivekananda Rd., Yadavagiri, Mysore 570020 (tel. 26666), there is a plant-filled lobby and 90 spacious rooms, neatly furnished in modern style, many with lovely views. An attraction at this hotel is the Vishala restaurant, serving superb vegetarian cuisine (covered under "Where to Eat"), and there's a cozy bar. Rates are Rs. 195 ($15) to Rs. 245 ($18.85) for singles and Rs. 245 ($18.85) to Rs. 295 ($22.70), the higher rates for air conditioning.

The Indian-style **Hotel Dasharath** is a good place to stay, opposite the Mysore Zoo, Mysore 570010 (tel. 32068), is in the same complex as the Yatrick restaurant (see "Where to Eat"). It has small, clean, and simple rooms with such frills as telephones, piped-in music, and attached bathrooms. Doubles cost Rs. 50 ($3.85), and four deluxe rooms have Western-style bathrooms, TV in the rooms, and go for Rs. 100 ($7.70). Air-conditioned rooms, at Rs. 88 ($6.75), are under construction.

The **Indra Bhavan,** Dhavantri Road, Mysore 570001 (tel. 23933), is rundown, but rates are only Rs. 30 ($2.30) single, Rs. 35 ($2.70) to Rs. 40 ($3.05) double, and Rs. 55 ($4.25) with air conditioning.

A lush flower garden greets you at the **Sujatha,** Tilak Nagar (tel. 22211), a modest 22-room hotel with spacious rooms showing off pink tile floors, green walls, and purplish-blue bathroom and wardrobe doors. Rooms cost Rs. 45 ($3.45) single and Rs. 65 ($5) double, with private bathrooms and showers. Vegetarian food is served, a full meal costing Rs. 8 (60¢). A good buy.

Small, with only 12 rooms (two with Western-style bathrooms), the **Hotel Parag,** 200 Garden Rd. (tel. 26514), is less than a mile from the bus station. You can get snacks and drinks in the Chirag Bar (open from 10:30 a.m. to 11:30 p.m. every day), which with its lacquered bamboo ceiling and walls and rattan chairs is the fanciest part of the hotel. Doubles cost Rs. 65 ($5). There's a vegetarian restaurant open from 6:30 a.m. to 8:30 p.m.

The **Hotel Brindavan,** Bangalore-Nilgiri Road (tel. 24550), opposite St. Philomena's Church, needs a coat of paint but otherwise is fairly clean. Rooms cost Rs. 45 ($3.45) double and Rs. 75 ($5.75) triple. Vegetarian meals are served.

And if you're really bargain hunting, there are many low-priced Indian-style hotels and lodges all around Gandhi Square and along Dhanavantri Road, charging Rs. 20 ($1.55) to Rs. 40 ($3.05). They're in various states of repair, so check them out before checking in.

Western-Style Hotels

One of the roads to Chamundi Hill goes to the **Lalitha Mahal** (meaning "beautiful building"), Mysore 570011 (tel. 27650), once owned by the maharaja and now a delightful 54-room hotel run by the India Tourism Development Corporation. Inside the 22-room old wing there are big bedrooms and marble baths, a sweeping marble staircase, and a glittering ballroom with a stained-glass dome; the 32 rooms in the new wing are less spectacular. The dining hall has three stained-glass domes, large pillars, and potted palms. You can sit in splendor while you savor something simple like a bowl of soup for Rs. 17 ($1.30) or dine more graciously on chicken tikka masala for Rs. 45 ($3.45) and nan for Rs. 6 (45¢). There are also continental dishes. The conference room chairs are inlaid with the maharaja's crest. All this opulence understandably comes at splurge prices: singles cost Rs. 400 ($30.75); doubles, Rs. 550 ($42.30). Suites go for Rs. 825 ($63.50), Rs. 1,650 ($127), and Rs. 2,500 ($192). There are terrace rooms for Rs. 330 ($25.40) single and Rs. 400 ($30.75) double.

Like a jewel box, the **Hotel Rajendravilas Imperial,** Chamundi Hills, Mysore 570018 (tel. 22050), sits high atop Chamundi Hill, 14 km (8½ miles) from town overlooking Mysore City. It was once a weekend getaway for the Maharaja of Mysore and is now a sumptuous, intimate 28-room hotel. Many of the palace furnishings—Oriental rugs, canopied beds, antique mirrors, and highly polished wood furniture—have been kept. Rates are Rs. 250 ($19.25) single, Rs. 300 ($23.05) double, and Rs. 400 ($30.75) to Rs. 600 ($46.15) for a suite. A few downstairs rooms without air conditioning go for Rs. 100 ($7.70) to Rs. 150 ($11.55). The hotel is about a half-hour drive up a narrow winding road from Mysore City. Many of the rooms have balconies or terraces overlooking the town and the countryside, and each room is individually furnished and individually shaped. The ground-floor Canopy Restaurant has walls and ceilings covered with red velvet, and crossed lances and spears on display. The Chariot Bar has a splendid view of the city.

The **Hotel Metropole,** Jhansi Lakshmi Bai Road, Mysore 570005 (tel. 20871), once a maharaja's guest house, is under the same management as the Krishnara-jasagar outside the city. From the reception desk, in a small open area on the ground floor, you go up a circular staircase to the rooms, all of which open onto a shady veranda overhung with scarlet, fuchsia, and orange bougainvillea. The big rooms are comfortably furnished and clean—many handsome rosewood pieces are still in use—and the spreads, rugs, and drapes are tasteful. Some of the rooms have two huge bathrooms and four beds, specifically for families traveling together. High ceilings in all the rooms make even those without air conditioning cool. All rooms have ceiling fans, dressing tables, nightstands with reading lamps, comfortable chairs, beds with mosquito netting, and attached bathrooms. Singles cost Rs. 135 ($10.40) and doubles go for Rs. 200 ($15.40), without air conditioning. Air conditioning will make the room rates Rs. 200 ($15.40) single and Rs. 250 ($19.25) double. There's a 10% service charge and 10% luxury tax on the rooms. Should you care to drop in for dinner, the charge is about Rs. 40 ($3.05) to Rs. 45 ($3.45) for a full meal from soup to dessert, including coffee or tea. Various food taxes will add another 21%.

The motel-like **Kings Court,** Jhansi Lakshmi Road, Mysore 570001 (tel. 25250), is clean with wallpapered rooms and rubber tile flooring and charges

Rs. 145 ($11.15) single and Rs. 180 ($13.85) double without air conditioning, Rs. 245 ($18.85) with air conditioning. In the restaurant, you eat surrounded by mirrors and pillars from a menu offering the by-now-familiar array of Chinese, Indian, and Western dishes in the Rs.-9 (70¢) to Rs.-14 ($1.05) for the average entree.

Brightly colored marbles are inset in the lobby floor of the **Hotel Highway,** New Bannimantap Extension, Mysore 570015 (tel. 21117). There are 32 rooms with rugs, overhead fans, small balconies, and attached tile baths with showers. Baths in the suites have tubs, and half the rooms are air-conditioned. But what may please you more are the rates: rooms cost Rs. 135 ($10.40) without air conditioning and Rs. 195 ($15) with air conditioning; suites run Rs. 250 ($19.25). There's an airy, attractive enclosed rooftop restaurant, open from 11 a.m. to 11 p.m. Most main dishes are Rs. 18 ($1.40), with Chinese fried chicken at Rs. 22 ($1.70) one of the highest priced on the menu.

A blend of India and the West is the **Hotel Mayura Hoysala,** 2 Jhansi Lakshmi Bai Rd., Mysore 570001 (tel. 25349), run by the KSTDC. There are neatly furnished, clean rooms off breezy balconies for Rs. 120 ($9.25) double and Rs. 90 ($6.90) to Rs. 95 ($7.30) single. Suites cost Rs. 145 ($11.15). Every room has an attached bathroom with both Indian- and Western-style toilets. There are two restaurants (tour buses stop), one for vegetarian food the other for nonvegetarian.

New splurge in town, the **Hotel Southern Star,** Vinobha Road, Mysore 570005 (tel. 27217), has a spacious lobby decorated with beautiful plants in red-clay planters, and tapestry-upholstered cane and rattan furniture, placed in intimate groupings. The tasteful rooms have quiet, pleasant color schemes, rosewood headboards and furniture, and all the amenities—television, music, telephones, and private tile bathrooms. Rates are Rs. 300 ($23.05) single and Rs. 360 ($27.70) double. Deluxe rooms cost Rs. 650 ($50), and suites, Rs. 1,200 ($92.30), plus 10% taxes on food and beverages and 20% on room. Angoor (meaning "grape") is the 24-hour coffeeshop, which appropriately displays a grape motif and trellises that give it an arbor-like look. Jyothi ("lamp"), the restaurant, is a place for a special meal (see "Where to Eat"). There's a swimming pool and health club.

Less expensive and bright as a new penny, the pleasant **Hotel Park Lane,** Sri Harsha Road (formerly Curzon Park Road), next to the K.E.B. Building, Mysore 570001 (tel. 30400), has six pristine white rooms with dressing rooms and private bathrooms for Rs. 48 ($3.70) single and Rs. 82 ($6.30) double. The indoor restaurant is all white with fern paintings; nestled in the courtyard, a rustic outdoor café is topped with a red-tile roof. Both restaurants serve the usual Indian, continental, and Chinese dishes, but the pleasant ambience (especially outdoors) gives them special flavor. Prices for meals are in the Rs.-14 ($1.05) to Rs.-24 ($1.85) range.

Run by the same family as the Park Lane, the **Dewdrop Inn,** on Hunsur Road (at the 17-km milestone from Mysore), (tel. Yelwal 77), a delightful place to have a meal en route to or from Nagarhole, Hunsur, or Mercara, or to spend a few days relaxing away from the city. The rustic red brick-and-tile roof architecture adapts the local village style. Each simple, clean room has basic furniture and attached bathrooms with hot and cold running water. Rates are Rs. 48 ($3.70) single and Rs. 60 ($4.60) to Rs. 70 ($5.40) double. Focal point of the garden restaurant is a huge tree; the well is surrounded by a dance floor. Innkeeper C. P. Muthanna does the cooking and serves delicious dishes reflecting his Coorgy origins that you rarely find on menus. Try the light and delicate papyttii, a rice-and-coconut pancake, served with a vegetable or meat curry for Rs. 10 (75¢). Start your meals with the fresh-made tomato juice. An adventurous cook, Muthanna improvises from his large cookbook collection and produces such innovative dishes as nan pizza: Rs. 9 (70¢) for vegetarian and Rs. 11 (85¢) nonvegetarian.

Getting to the Dewdrop is a breeze: city buses 106 and 74 from the City Bus Stand ply the roads to and from Yelwal every 20 minutes for Rs. 1.50 (11½¢); the inn is only a 1.5-km walk (less than a mile) from the terminus. In addition, at the Metropole Hotel Circle, there are countless privately owned vehicles—taxis and tempos (oversize auto-ricksahws)—making regular runs to Hunsur. They will gladly drop you, for Rs. 2.50 (20¢), and your luggage, for Rs. 4 (30¢), at the inn's gate.

Staying Outside Town at Brindavan Gardens

Outside of Mysore City by 12 miles (19 km) to the northwest is the **Krishnarajasagar Hotel** (tel. Belgola 22). This old-fashioned hotel is beautifully situated in the Brindavan Gardens, huge and handsomely terraced with symmetrical floral designs, accented boldly with red and yellow flowers, where countless fountains send glistening sprays of water into pools and channels. The gardens are part of the huge irrigation dam that was built between 1911 and 1927, and the landscaping took six years to create. From the dining room of the hotel you can see the waters, harnessed by the dam, gushing forth through the riverbed. Matching the floral display, the hotel's exterior is yellow, trimmed with aquamarine, and there are spacious rotundas from which you can see the gardens and fountains. At night, colored lights play on the fountains and flowers, transforming this setting into an enchantment of shapes and colors. The gardens are open from 6:30 a.m. to 10 p.m., and there is an entrance charge of Rs. 2 (15¢) per person or Rs. 20 ($1.55) per carload (maximum of six). If you're planning to use a camera, there's a camera charge of Rs. 20 ($1.55) to Rs. 100 ($7.70), depending on the type of camera. There's a light and fountain show at sunset every night: from 7 to 8 p.m. on weekdays, to 9 p.m. weekends and holidays, depending on the time of sunset.

In the hotel, rooms have wardrobes, night stands, desks, comfortable chairs, and balconies. Each room has a private bathroom and ceiling fan. Rates are: Rs. 135 ($10.40) to Rs. 170 ($13.05) single and Rs. 200 ($15.40) to Rs. 235 ($18.05) double, higher rate for air conditioning. There's a service charge of 10%, a luxury tax of 10% on room, a sales tax of 11% on board, and a state tax of 10% on food. À la carte meals should run an additional Rs. 60 ($4.60) to Rs. 70 ($5.40) a day.

Even if you don't stay here, make it a point to see the gardens; conducted tours of Mysore generally include them.

Adjacent to the Krishnarajasagar is the **Hotel Mayura Cauvery** (tel. Belgola 52), run by the government of Karnataka, where for Rs. 60 ($4.60) single and Rs. 90 ($6.90) double you can admire the elaborate gardens while living in the simplest surroundings. The rooms have balconies, from some of which you can see the river. All rooms have attached baths, and five rooms have Western-style toilets. There's a restaurant for guests.

You can stay at the Mayura Cauvery Hotel and eat at the Krishnarajasagar Hotel, where the à la carte menu is extensive.

WHERE TO EAT IN MYSORE: Delicious vegetarian foods, such as tender idlis for Rs. 4 (30¢) and cutlets at Rs. 3 (23¢), with some of the best coffee in South India, are served at the clean and spacious **Akshaya Restaurant,** in the Dasaprakash Hotel, Gandhi Square (tel. 24444), open from 6 a.m. to 10 p.m.

daily. As an Indian friend and I enjoyed Bombay thalis for Rs. 12 (90¢)—comprising a more elaborate array of foods than the South Indian–style thali, which costs Rs. 10 (75¢)—one of the managers overheard me remarking how much I liked the food and offered to show me the preparation in the kitchen. There I saw coconuts grinding in machines, idlis steaming in steamers, piles of pappadams (wafer-thin breads), mounds of rice, and bags of spices. While the kitchen tour taught little more now than I already knew about making this kind of food, I did learn one important thing: happily, it is that the food preparation at this restaurant is truly hygienic.

The classier **Dasaprakash Paradise,** on Vivekananda Road (tel. 26666), serves notable vegetarian food in Vishala, decorated in earth tones. It's open from 6:30 a.m. to 11 p.m., with Indian classical music from 8 to 10 p.m. The accent is regional here, and so you can eat specialties from various parts of the country, such as the north's matter paneer (peas in a cheese sauce), kofta curry (ground vegetable balls in a sauce thickened with yogurt and nuts), and elaborate pulaos (rice dishes), as well as South Indian idlis, dosas, puris, and coconut-milk-based curries. These dishes, à la carte, run Rs. 9 (70¢) to Rs. 15 ($1.15); thali meals cost Rs. 17.50 ($1.35). Recommended desserts are the rich ice creams; Rs. 6 (45¢) for something as mundane as vanilla to Rs. 12.50 (95¢) to some exotic flavor like mango topped with sauces and fruits.

For a bargain-priced well-prepared thali in clean, cheerful surroundings, try the **Yatrik,** in the Hotel Dasharath complex, opposite the zoo (tel. 30892), run by the genial brothers, V. M. and V. S. Rao. The South Indian thali with rice, chapati, sambhar (tamarind, spices, and vegetables), rasam (thin, peppery lentil-based soup), curds, pappadams, pickle, and two vegetable curries will run Rs. 5 (40¢). You can also get dosas, idlis, and other South Indian snacks, and an array of North Indian foods. Those who wish Western food will be made an omelet or vegetable sandwich. Hours are 6 a.m. to 10 p.m. The Raos suggest making a reservation for dinner, when it can be very crowded.

Samrat, on Dhavantri Road, run by the Hotel Indra Bhavan, is somewhat of a pleasant surprise. While the hotel (as mentioned) has gone down hill, the restaurant is clean, neat, and simple, offering vegetarian plate meals for Rs. 6 (45¢) and à la carte dishes, with the highest price around Rs. 10 (75¢) for a vegetarian shish kebab. Lassi (yogurt drink) is Rs. 5 (40¢).

An old favorite, the once very plain Indra Café, has been renovated, redecorated, and air-conditioned, and is now called **Indra / Paras Café,** Sayaji Rao Road (tel. 20236). Hours are 7:30 to 11:30 a.m. for snacks and breakfast, noon to 3:30 p.m. for lunch, and 5 to 8 p.m. for tea, snacks, and dinner; a special North Indian dinner is served from 7:30 to 10 p.m. (closed Thursday). Remaining unchanged are the wide range of delicious vegetarian dishes, like Rs. 10 (75¢) for a South Indian thali and Rs. 22 ($1.70) for North Indian thali. Average price for other à la carte dishes is Rs. 8 (60¢). Clean, sparkling Indra Sweets adjoins the restaurant.

Across from Indra / Paras is what may be the town's most famous sweet stall, **Guru Sweets,** owned by a sweets cook to a former maharaja. But past connections are not the only reason for high regard—the Mysore pak (a paste made with pure ghee or clarified butter) here is truly a royal treat, at Rs. 60 ($4.60) per kilo. A little goes a long way because it's a very rich dish.

Back on Gandhi Square, **Shailpashtri** (tel. 25979), open from 9:30 a.m. to 11 p.m., is jammed on fair evenings and a fun place to have a bite. There's nothing special about the indoor restaurant, which is in operation throughout the day and evening. Indian foods, both vegetarian and nonvegetarian, run Rs. 10 (75¢) to Rs. 12 (90¢), and there are also some Chinese selections.

When sightseeing at the Palace, the nearby **Gun House Restaurant and Bar** (tel. 20608) is a convenient place to eat. Indeed, this building used to house the former maharaja's gun collection and ammunition. Now the walls are red, there's green carpeting, and the gunpowder kegs have been enamelled, cut in half, and mounted on the walls alongside cannon wheels. Especially good dishes are the tandooris; Rs. 15 ($1.15) for half a chicken, with nan (oven-baked bread) at Rs. 3 (23¢) more. Many other dishes also available. Hours are 11 a.m. to midnight.

There is a dimly lit **Kwality** on Dhavantri Road with the by now-predictable menu of Indian, Chinese, and Western dishes, ranging from Rs. 15 ($1.15) to Rs. 25 ($1.90).

For a splurge, there's **Jyothi,** with tapestry-covered banquettes and little Indian lamps (*jyothi* means lamp) in niches. Painted on velvet panels are portraits of the royalty of old, and a lively mural shows Radha and Krishna. There's a band and dancing at night. Chicken chetena, a mildly spicy dish costs Rs. 20 ($1.55), about average for the entrees. There are continental foods and Chinese dishes. Hours are 12:30 to 2:45 p.m. and 7:30 to 11:30 p.m.

When there are tour groups in residence, which is frequent between October and March, the **Lalita Mahal** (tel. 27650) serves a buffet lunch from 1 to 2:30 p.m. for Rs. 65 ($5). It's a filling meal and will give you a chance to feast your eyes on the lavish former palace.

TOURS: Tours run by the Karnataka State Tourism Development Corporation (KSTDC) include the following:

Mysore Sightseeing is a rushed daily tour that turns the sights into a shifting kaleidoscope of exotic forms. Included are St. Philomena's Church, Jananmohan Art Gallery, the zoo, Maharaja's Palace and Chamundi Hill; outside of town, it visits Somnathpur (site of the Kesava Temple), Sriranagatpatna, and in season, the Ranganathittu Bird Sanctuary, polished off by the Brindavan Gardens' light show. All these attractions barely swim into focus from 7:30 a.m. to 8:30 p.m. But if you're short on both time and money, for Rs. 40 ($3.05) it's the really unbeatable answer.

The **Belur, Halebid, and Sravanabelagola** tour goes every Wednesday and Friday from 7 a.m. to 9 p.m., for Rs. 70 ($5.40). Also rushed, it's not leisurely enough for those who wish to savor the temples and also climb to the Gomateswara statue.

The **Ootacamund Tour** is daily in season and costs Rs. 70 ($5.40), including lunch, and takes in the botanical garden, lake, and dam.

To book, contact the **KSTDC Transport Wing,** Hotel Mayura Hoysala, 2 Jhansi Lakshmi Bai Rd., Mysore 570005 (tel. 23652). Bookings and information are also possible through some hotels.

GETTING AROUND MYSORE: As in Bangladore, auto-rickshaws cost Rs. 2 (15¢) minimum and Rs. 1 (7½¢) per subsequent kilometer. Tourist taxis in Mysore charge Rs. 2 (15¢) per kilometer; the driver's overnight charges are Rs. 25 ($1.90) to Rs. 35 ($2.70).

TRAVELING OUTSIDE MYSORE CITY: To get to Somnathpur, take the bus from the Suburban Bus Stand in Gandhi Square to Tirarasipura, and change there for the bus to Somnathpur.

For touring Belur, Halebid, and Sranabelagola, the most popular base is

Hassan 120 km (73 miles) from Mysore, reached by passenger train at Rs. 59 ($4.55) in first class, Rs. 8 (60¢) in second class. Buses from Hassan go to Belur in 1½ hours, and from Belur to Hassan in half an hour. It's necessary to go back to Hassan to get a bus to Sravanabelagola.

For Bandipur Wildlife Sanctuary, buses leave three times a day from Mysore's Central Bus Station. Or you can take one of the seven buses that go to Ootacamund each day.

From the Central Bus station you can also get a bus to Arsikere from which, instead of Hassan, you can visit Belur, Halebid, and Sravanabelagola before going to Bijapur.

Alternatively, you can pick up an express train in Arsikere to Hubli, where you change for the *Gol Gumbza Express* to Bijapur, at Rs. 139 ($10.70) in first class, Rs. 35 ($2.70) in second.

From the Central Bus Stand you can get buses to Nagarhole Game Sanctuary, at Rs. 15 ($1.15) for the trip. Two or three of these buses go via Mercara, site of an important old fort and the Omareswara Temple. If you break your journey in Mercara, you can overnight at the Tourist Home or look around and get the bus to Nagarhole. From Mysore to Karapur (near the Kabini River Lodge; see below) costs Rs. 9 (70¢) by bus. Some of the buses from Mysore to Nagarhole are express, so ask for these when you buy your tickets.

SEEING THE ENVIRONS: There are a number of places in the general area of Mysore City, many of which offer accommodations in case you want to spend a longer time visiting the temples and other major sights.

Somnathpur

About 21 miles (35 km) east of Mysore City, accessible by bus, is the modest village of Somnathpur, with its extravagant 13th-century **Kesava Temple.** The temple stands on a star-shaped platform. Eye-level sculptures depict some of the great Hindu epics and elaborate friezes are bursting with elephants, swans, scrolls, horsemen, and mythical beasts.

Near the temple are the government-run **Tourist Cottages** (tel. 82), with two usually unoccupied clean rooms with adjoining bathrooms, at Rs. 20 ($1.55) single and Rs. $35 ($2.70) double. To reserve, write or telephone the caretaker, Tourist Cottages, Somnathpur, Bannur, Mysore District.

Hassan

North of Mysore are three of South India's major sights, the sculptures and statues at Sravanbelagola, Belur, and Halebid, relatively near the town of Hassan.

In Hassan, the best place to stay is the **Hotel Hassan Ashok,** on Bangalore-Mangalore Road, Hassan 573201 (tel. 8731), under the direction of the India Tourism Development Corporation (ITDC), a three-story structure with functionally modern rooms and attached bathrooms. About half the rooms are air-conditioned, which usually isn't necessary in these parts, but does drive up the bill. Air-conditioned rooms cost Rs. 275 ($21.15) single and Rs. 360 ($27.70) double. Non-air-conditioned rooms run Rs. 120 ($9.25) single and Rs. 180 ($13.45) double.

There are also a number of Indian-style hotels in Hassan. The **Karnataka Tourist Bureau** in Hassan (tel. 8862) can give you leads on vacancies. Expect to pay Rs. 20 ($1.55) to Rs. 40 ($3.05) per person for a room—and don't expect much in the way of comforts.

Sravanabelagola

This is the site of the huge statue of **Gomateswara** (57 feet high), an important saint in the Jain religion. It was at Sravanabelagola that the Emperor Chandragupta was supposed to have lived his final days, after scorning all worldly wealth and possession. To see the statue you remove your shoes and climb barefoot up 614 steep, smooth rock stairs that run to the top of the 470-foot high **Indragiri Hill,** as pilgrims have done for centuries.

The statue, carved in A.D. 983 from one immense rock, is a stylized nude gazing serenely into the idyllic valley below. Creeping vines entwine the arms and thighs. They symbolize that the saint meditated so long and deeply that vines grew unnoticed around him. The nudity represents denial of worldly wealth. According to legend, the statue commemorates a young man who exemplified unselfish denial. He fought his older brother and won their father's kingdom. But he turned his prize back to his brother and went into the woods to follow the aesthetic life.

You can park your gear at the Karnataka Tourist Bureau when you climb up.

There's a government-run **Tourist Bungalow** (tel. 54) at Sravanabelagola, charging Rs. 20 ($1.55) single and Rs. 35 ($2.70) double. For reservations, contact the manager, Tourist Cottage, Sravanabelagola, Hassan District. But even with 50 rooms it's almost always full of Jain pilgrims visiting one of their most important religious sites, so you're advised to book well in advance. You'd be wise to stay in Hassan instead, since your chances of getting in here are mighty slim.

Belur

It's a pretty ride through wooded groves and grassy plains to Hassan; from there the countryside looks more tropical, as you head some 21 miles (35 km) farther on to Belur, almost 900 years ago the prosperous capital city of the Hoysala kings. Nothing matters here except the **Chennakasva Temple**—but that matters a lot. Built in the 12th century, this Hindu contemporary of such great European cathedrals as Chartres and Rheims represents medieval architecture at its most exalted level. It is star-shaped in plan, as is Somnathpur. The sculptures are easy to see, most on a level with the eyes. Remove your shoes to inspect more closely the carvings: rows of graceful goddesses bedecked with jewels and surrounded by lacy stone canopies, handsome gods with stone-cut crowns and garlands. You also find a sculptured "novella" of royal life—hunters, dancers, musicians. There are elephants, demons, trees, flowers, and scrolls to delight the eye and to fascinate.

Belur's temple has three entrances—at the east, south, and north—each worth close inspection. The north doorway is decorated with full-bosomed female statues and nearby is a stone-cut "filmstrip" of the evils of destruction —involving such diverse participants as an eagle, attacking a beast, which is trying to get a lion, which in turn is going after an elephant, which is preying on a snake about to down a rat. The south doorway is resplendent with a myriad of gods and goddesses, beasts and evil demons. The eastern doorway is unusually fine, with eight elaborate friezes. On the right are small musicians. Above are 28 windows carved with star patterns and leafy designs. Be sure to note the 30 or more bracket figures that support the eaves of the temple. These are well-endowed women, striking various poses with a lyrical grace.

There is usually a government-approved guide at Belur to offer help.

The KSTDC's modest **Hotel Mayura Velapuri** (tel. 9), charges Rs. 45 ($3.45) for singles and Rs. 65 ($5) for doubles. Contact the manager for reservations. Here you'll be near the temple, main market, and local restaurants (called "hotels") where you can get simple South Indian foods and soft drinks and coffee.

Halebid

Fergusson, who documented so much of India's architecture, placed Halebid's **Hoysaleswara Temple** at the extreme opposite pole from the Parthenon. Here there is nothing austere. The sculptors seemed convinced that to leave any surface uncovered would be a lavish waste of space. So—almost 900 years ago—they created a rococo structure which looks as if it might be intricately carved ivory with lacy trims, declaring the adoration of their gods in a series of photographically realistic statues. About ten miles from Belur, and built ten years after the other temple, Hoysaleswara was never completed. It took 80 years to create what you see now. The material used was soapstone, which hardens with age, but is soft enough at the onset to permit these intricate designs. The Hoysaleswara Temple has two shrines, one to Shiva and the other to Parvati. You must remove your shoes before looking around.

The friezes that surround the building are painstakingly executed and arranged to play off the horizontal elements against the verticals. Time and time again, elephants, symbolizing stability, march in procession on the bottom tier. On top of them are lions, then horses, oxen, and birds. Scrolls curl to set off scenes of religious epics, and there are legendary beasts and swans.

The most outstanding of the friezes show curvaceous, heavenly maidens lavishly adorned with gorgeous jewels and posed arrestingly under sculptured awnings that have provided eight centuries of shade for them. You can also see the entire roster of Hindu gods and goddesses. Be sure to look for Ganesh, the elephant-headed god of good luck, who is especially well turned out in a huge headdress.

Inside there are cool, black marble pillars rising like dark stone trees and more carvings; in the courtyard opposite the temple is a small museum of sculpture.

Not far from Halebid's Hoysaleswara Temple is an early Jain temple, eloquent in its simplicity. The pillars inside gleam like mirrors, as an attendant will demonstrate. Tip him 50 paise (3½¢).

At Halebid, the **Tourist Cottage** (tel. 24), right across the road from the temple, charges Rs. 20 ($1.55) single and Rs. 35 ($2.70) double in its two rooms. Contact the receptionist for reservations; the cottage is rarely occupied so you can probably get in without too much advance notice. There are one or two simple places to eat nearby.

Bandipur

Only 50 miles (80 km) from Mysore City is Bandipur, a wildlife sanctuary where you can see such animals as black panthers, wild elephants, deer, bison, black-faced monkeys, sloth bears, and chital, and many rare birds.

Game-viewing is a matter of luck. You may spend a day going about with a guide in a Land Rover and see only one or two animals, or you may see them all on a two-hour trip. The Bandipur setting is pretty, and even if you do not see an abundance of game, it provides a relaxation from Karnataka's extraordinary temples.

The 689-square-kilometer tract is actually part of the larger Venugopal Wildlife Park, which takes in Mudumalai Forest in Tamil Nadu and Wynad in Kerala.

In Bandipur, Jeeps are available for game viewing at Rs. 5 (40¢) per kilometer, or you can make your expedition on a tame elephant. The best time for viewing is between October and May.

There's a modest **Forest Rest House,** charging Rs. 50 ($3.85) per overnight.

Both accommodations and Jeeps have to be booked in advance to make sure of getting them. For information and reservations, write to: Assistant Director, Project Tiger, Government House Complex, Mysore (tel. 20901).

Bandipur is also a day's excursion from Mysore. If you're on the 6:15 a.m. Ootacamund bus, you can take the last Bandipur bus back at 3:15 p.m. It'll be rushed, but if you're short of time you might try it.

Nagarhole National Park

From Mysore there's a good road to Nagarhole National Park. Beyond the city you pass a number of electronics industries, a joint U.S.-India Jeep venture, Mahendra and Mahendra, and manufacturers of shovels, dumpers, and bulldozers. But soon the scene is pastoral as you go through villages and paddy fields and near the 572-square-mile game sanctuary, south of Coorg and bordering on Kerala.

The 80-km (48-mile) trip from Mysore to Nagarhole can be made by express bus from Mysore for Rs. 15 ($1.15) in approximately three hours; or from Bangalore, 215 km (130 miles) away, for Rs. 27 ($2.05), a full day's trip. The Mysore–Nagarhole road turns south at Hunsur. Continuing straight west for 34 km (20 miles), however, takes you to **Mercara,** the capital of the scenic Western ghats, noted for orange groves, coffee plantations, and dense woods. Main attractions are an interesting fort, the terrific view from Rajah's Seat, Omkareswara Temple, and palace. There's a modest Rest House at Rajah's Seat.

Going south, the Nagarhole road deteriorates as it winds through dense untamed jungles of the lush wild terrain. The name Nagarhole means "Snake River" in Kanwada, the local language, and the namesake river winds through the beautiful park where there are also lakes, swamps, and bamboo groves, and towering rosewood and flowering trees.

One of India's most beautiful sanctuaries now, ruins indicate that years ago it was a thriving settlement. More recently, part of the vast park was the exclusive hunting preserve of the Maharajas of Mysore and famous as the site of the kheddas—elephant roundups. They led to the capture of 1,536 wild elephants between 1890 and 1971.

Today the park is a sanctuary for elephants, gaur (among the world's largest oxen), sambar, chital (spotted deer), bison, leopards, and tigers, a few of the species roaming this protected area. Peacocks and storks are among the 250 birds nesting in the park.

A daily **game-watching tour** at 5:15 p.m., lasting about an hour and costing Rs. 10 (75¢) per person, goes in an old green bus which lurches along the dusty tracks with forest rangers as driver, spotters, and guides. Although the bus rattled and wheezed, the animals did not run and hide. We saw a whole congress of elephants, as well as a few smaller family groups with babies protected by females bringing up the rear, plus gaur, sambar, and black-faced monkeys all within a few yards of the vehicle—much to the delight of everyone, but especially the children on our bus. Once we climbed to the top of a machan to see if we could see a tiger, but all we saw were bits of bones—the only remains that a tiger had not carried away from a recent feast.

The fee per person for a tour goes up if the bus is not full. There are also Jeeps for hire at Rs. 5 (40¢) per kilometer for a private tour. In addition, you pay Rs. 3 (23¢) per person for park admission, and Rs. 2 (15¢) to Rs. 300 ($23.05) for cameras, depending on type—the highest fee is for 35-mm movie cameras. All fees quoted here are for "others"; Indians pay less.

Best bet for accommodation is at one of the **Forest Lodges** right in the park. Mine, Gangotri Lodge, had four double rooms, two on the upper floor and two on the ground floor, and all the comforts of home (bedrooms, attached bathrooms, living room cum dining room) and more—a bearer to clean, cook, and serve. The charge is Rs. 50 ($3.85) per person, plus another Rs. 15 ($1.15) to Rs. 20 ($1.55) for vegetarian lunch, dinner, and several teas. There are no desserts with the meals, but a special treat at sunset was seeing from my forest lodge herds of deer and elephants roaming and grazing around the compound. Another lodge, Cauvery, with two double rooms, costs Rs. 100 ($7.70) a day.

To book a lodge, at least one-week in advance contact Chief Wildlife Warden, Aranya Bhavan 18th Cross, Malleswaram, Bangalore 560003 (tel. 361193); or Assistant Conservator of Forests, Wildlife Sub-Division, Vanivlas Road, Mysore (tel. 21159).

Adjacent to Nagarhole at Karapur is the expensive **Kabini River Lodge,** on the banks of the Kabini Reservoir. The 180-year-old main building, once the former maharaja's game lodge, still sports his crest, but now is the reception and administrative area. Two new buildings, built to look like the old one, have 20 twin-bedded rooms usually occupied by tour groups. The cost is Rs. 660 ($50.75) per person, including accommodation, meals, game drives, coracle rides for birdwatching, visits to villages and an elephant-training camp, sailing, lectures, slide and film shows, services of a resident naturalist, taxes, and fees. These rates are for foreign nationals only; Indians pay less. For reservations and information, Jungle Lodges and Resorts Ltd., 13th Main Rd., Rajmahal Vilas Extension, Bangalore 560080 (tel. 31020).

Bijapur—Mughal Architectural Masterpieces

The last stop, at Karnataka's northern end, is Bijapur, "City of Victory." The leading sight is **Gol Gumbaz** (open from sunrise to sunset), the vast tomb of Mohammed Adil Shah, who ruled here in the 17th century. The dome is remarkable, 124 feet in diameter and second in size only to St. Peter's in Rome, which surpasses it by 15 feet. It is famous for its acoustical marvel, the Whispering Gallery. A whisper carries hundreds of feet here, so . . . shhh! Nearby is an archeological museum (mainly stone carvings), open every day from 9 a.m. to 5:30 p.m.

The **Jama Masjid** is renowned for its architectural perfection, and old palaces and gardens make Bijapur a grand sight today. There are other monuments to see here: over 100 Muslim tombs, palaces, and mosques in various stages of repair. Emperor Aurangzeb desecrated some of these structures, and sadly time has taken its toll. Still beautiful, Bijapur is South India's treasury of Mughal architecture.

The KSTDC's **Hotel Mayura Adil Shahi,** Anand Mahal Rd., Bijapur 586101 (tel. 934), charges Rs. 80 ($6.15) single and Rs. 160 ($12.30) double. Other, more modestly priced hotels offering basic accommodation are mainly on Station Road, with rates from Rs. 25 ($1.90) to Rs. 35 ($2.70).

From Bijapur you can take a bus to Aurangabad or a train to Hubli, and from there go on to Vasco da Gama (Goa) or Bombay, with a change in Miraj. Or you can retrace your steps, taking the train to Bellaryd and going back to Bangalore.

BEST TIME TO VISIT: For most of Karnataka, visit during October through

March. You might want to time your visit to Mysore during Dussehra (the all-India ten-day festival in October and November) and see this holiday marking the triumph of good over evil celebrated as it was in bygone days.

For the game sanctuaries, visit Bandipur between May and November, Nagarhole between October and May, and Ranganathittu from June through October.

GETTING TO KARNATAKA: Bangalore is well connected **by air** with all major cities. For example, there are flights from Delhi, at Rs. 1,417 ($109); from Bombay, at Rs. 870 ($66.92); from Calcutta, at Rs. 352 ($27); from Madras, at Rs. 283 ($21.76); from Cochin, at Rs. 352 ($27); from Hyderabad, at Rs. 552 ($42.46); and from Dabolim (Goa), at Rs. 455 ($35)—to name only a few.

At Bangalore airport, there is an Indian Airlines bus to take you to various top hotels in town, for Rs. 10 (75¢). There is also a sign at the airport telling how much it costs to go by taxi to various hotels. The porterage fee at the airport is Rs. 2 (15¢) per piece of luggage, paid to the employee at the airport in charge of the porters. Don't cave in and give more rupees to the porter, who will continue to follow you after you've paid up and have your receipt in hand.

Direct express **train** service connects major cities in the south and central regions with Bangalore. From Bombay, a distance of 1,121 km (683 miles), direct express trains go through Pune (famous as the former site of Bhagwan Sri Rajneesh's ashram) and Hubli (where you can pick up the train to Bijapur) to break the journey en route. Fare from Bombay is Rs. 358 ($27.55) in first class, Rs. 87 ($6.70) in second.

BOMBAY: INDIA'S MOST "WESTERN" CITY

BOMBAY (pop. over 9,000,000), with 1.3% of the country's population, is India's second-biggest city and the one nearest to Western tastes. It's Hollywood, New York, and Chicago rolled into one, and almost every visitor has a friend or contact there or can find one. The Indian movie industry, devoted to those ephemeral Indian films full of coy boy-and-girl chasing around pillars, bursting into song and dance below an ever-blue sky, is the biggest in the world, churning out an estimated 900 movies a year. Bombay makes about 150 of these films, all in Hindi. Every day dozens of films are in production in Bombay studios. New releases come out two to three times a week. Other filmmaking states are Tamil Nadu, Bengal, Andhra Pradesh, Gujarat, Karnataka, and Kerala, each working in the language of the region.

Bombay is also India's richest and busiest industrial center; more than 3,000 factories, on immense estates, ring the city for miles. Visits to all kinds of different firms and businesses can be arranged; one offbeat trip, for example, is to the world-famous **Mysore Sugandhi Dhoop Factory** whose 130 different brands of incense are a major export item to the U.S. and elsewhere.

Check with the Government of India Tourist Office (tel. 293144) about touring almost any enterprise. The plant owners will usually greet you warmly and show you around with pride. Even the film companies welcome you to their sets during shooting.

It was Britain's East India Company that managed to link the seven islands of the Bombay area, but nobody has managed to merge the various sects and creeds—the Punjabis, Parsis, Muslims, Gujaratis, South Indians, and Maharashtrans—who give the city its rich diversity and business acumen.

1. Hotels

If you can easily locate some good inexpensive hotels with vacancies in Bombay, let me know and I'll celebrate. A severe shortage of hotels keeps Bombay accommodation prices high and rooms in short supply. Be prepared to spend plenty of rupees for rooms, and book them in advance if you want a place to stay.

At one time it was only necessary to reserve your Bombay hotel rooms during the peak season, October to February. Now it's becoming essential even during the rainy season, June to September, when the Arabs and their harems by the charter-planeload make trips to Bombay on package tours to see the monsoon. Not all Arabs are as rich as the old Mughals. Some hang out with you and me at the budget hotels.

Business executives from all over the world grab the best Bombay accommodations, and so do the well-to-do tourists. This leaves few rooms for penny-conscious travelers.

An alternative might be to head for Juhu Beach or suburban hotels. But they're not cheap, nor are taxis to town.

Good food can be cheap in some Bombay restaurants. So what you must spend on rooms, you can save on your meals.

If for Brahma knows what reason you arrive in Bombay without a place to stay, check the **Tourist Office** at the airport or in town at 123 M. Karve Rd., Churchgate (tel. 293144). The tourist office has a list of paying guest accommodations that may just provide the answer to your predicament.

IN TOWN: Looking on the sea is the **Bentley Hotel,** Krishna Mahal, Third Floor, Netaji Subhash and D. Watcha Roads, Bombay 400020 (tel. 250639), with a nice-looking reception area. The Bentley's rooms are very basic, though clean enough, however. No visitors are allowed in the rooms; all company must be entertained in the reception/lounge. Tea and coffee are available on request, but no meals are served; there are many restaurants nearby. Rates for rooms are Rs. 110 ($8.45) single and Rs. 140 ($10.75) double. Tax is 3% on each of these rates.

You're paying mainly for location at the **Hotel Delamar,** 141 Sunder Mahal, Netaji Subhash Road, Bombay (tel. 2042848), where air-conditioned singles cost Rs. 250 ($19.25), and doubles run Rs. 400 ($30.75).

Just behind the Prince of Wales Museum is the **Hotel Lawrence,** Ashok Kumar House, 28 K. Dubash Marg, Bombay (tel. 243618), in a neighborhood of bookstores. The hotel is on the third floor. There are three common bathrooms, only one with hot water. But you can always get some hot water boiled. This simple place has one of the nicest proprietors in Bombay in the person of Alvito Abreo, who is cheerful and helpful, and speaks flawless English. He's an ocean liner enthusiast, and there are books on liners and pictures of them too. You might wish the place was a bit better maintained, but it's nice anyway. Doubles cost Rs. 60 ($4.60) to Rs. 90 ($6.90), and triples are Rs. 150 ($11.55), including breakfast.

The **Hotel Diplomat,** 24–26 Mereweather Rd., Bombay 400001 (tel. 2021661), has 25 double rooms in need of some tender loving care. Singles cost Rs. 325 ($25); doubles, Rs. 400 ($30.75). All rooms have attached bathrooms.

Back on what used to be Marine Drive but is now Netaji Subhash Road, the **Sea Green Hotel,** 145 Netaji Subhash Rd., Bombay 400020 (tel. 249828), has very simply furnished rooms with attached baths, many with sweeping sea views. Renovations were underway when I looked in and all should be in order by the time you arrive. There are 21 air-conditioned rooms for Rs. 210 ($16.15) single and Rs. 300 ($23.05) double; without air conditioning, Rs. 150 ($11.55) single and Rs. 240 ($18.45) double. At these prices and with such views, this hotel is nearly always full. Rates include tea and breakfast, but not the 10% service charge or luxury taxes. There are also suites for two, at Rs. 320 ($24.60).

The **Sea Green South,** 145-A Netaji Subhash Rd., Bombay 400020 (tel. 221613), is a modest hotel with a marvelous location. If you don't expect anything lavish in the way of decor (you will have a phone, radio, and private bathroom), you'll be happy. There are 36 rooms (11 air-conditioned), 24 with private bathrooms and eight with shared facilities, but the price is not lower for sharing. This hotel also was being renovated when I stopped in, and again everything should be in order by now. Rates are Rs. 150 ($11.55) to Rs. 210 ($16.15) single and Rs. 240 ($18.45) to Rs. 300 ($23.05) double, the higher prices for air conditioning. Tea and breakfast are included, but there is no reduction if you don't take these meals. There is a 10% service charge and state taxes of 3% to 7%. It's a popular place.

Facing the sea on Ramachandani Marg (formerly Strand Road) are three reasonably priced hotels. At **Shelleys,** Ramachandani Marg, Bombay 400039 (tel. 240229), the rooms are comfortably appointed with leatherette couches among the furnishings. Each room has an attached bathroom and phone. Non-air-conditioned, singles cost Rs. 121 ($9.30) and doubles run Rs. 162 ($14.45); air-conditioned singles are Rs. 190 ($14.60), and doubles, Rs. 265 ($20.40), breakfast included.

The **Strand Apollo Bunder,** Ramachandani Marg, Bombay 400039 (tel. 241624), has a minimum of furniture and atmosphere, needs a coat of paint, and will do for those who require absolutely no frills. A single room sharing a bathroom costs Rs. 100 ($7.70); a single with a balcony, Rs. 120 ($9.25); a single with attached bath and air conditioning, Rs. 160 ($12.30). A double with bathroom and air conditioning costs Rs. 210 ($16.15), and a suite facing the sea with an attached bathroom and air conditioning, Rs. 290 ($22.30). The flush system sometimes doesn't work well in this hotel (it could have been repaired by now), so guests are given buckets of water to give the flush a bit of help.

To the right is the home-like and cheery **Sea Palace,** Ramachandani Marg, Bombay 400039 (tel. 241828), with cool balconies allowing panoramic views of harbor activity. The furnishings are okay—you'll be comfortable and have a phone, radio, complete attached bathroom, and air conditioning. Non-air-conditioned singles are Rs. 155 ($11.90), Rs. 198 ($15.25) with air conditioning. Doubles are all air-conditioned and rent for Rs. 327 ($25.15); suites cost Rs. 500 ($38.45). A very pleasant reception/manager is in charge.

Fernandes Guest House, 5 J. N. Heredia Marg, Ballard Estate, Bombay 400038 (tel. 260554), on the third floor of the Balmer Lawrie Building, resembles a partitioned loft. Only 16 guests can be accommodated, two to three to a room. There are iron bedsteads, absolutely no frills, but everything is clean and spacious. There are two showers and three toilets. Some rooms have little balconies, with a splendid harbor view. Rates include breakfast; Rs. 60 ($4.60) single and Rs. 80 ($6.15) double. They lock up at midnight, so you must be tucked in by then. You get one sheet and a cover, but most guests use their bedrolls (the mattresses are not so neat).

The **Grand Hotel,** Ballard Estate, Bombay 400038 (tel. 268211), on Ballard Pier was receiving visitors in 1927 when Katherine Mayo's book *Mother India* described this country as a mere three-week voyage from New

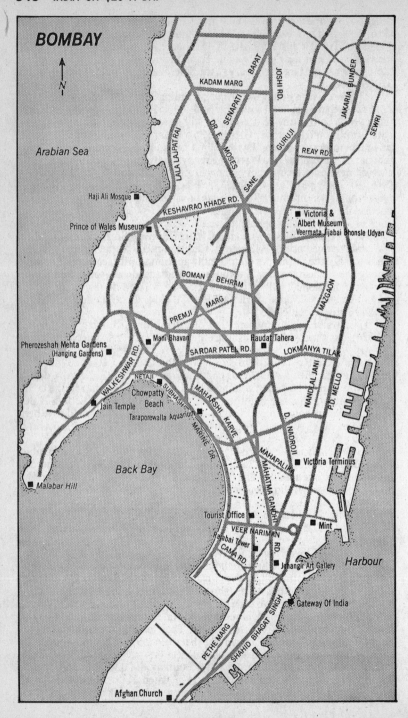

BOMBAY

N

Arabian Sea

KADAM MARG

BAPAT

JOSHI RD.

SENAPATI

DR. E. MOSES

LALA LAJPAT RAI

SANE

GURUJI

JAKARIA BUNDER

SEWRI

REAY RD.

Haji Ali Mosque

KESHAVRAO KHADE RD.

Prince of Wales Museum

Victoria & Albert Museum

Veermata Jijabai Bhonsle Udyan

MAZGAON

BOMAN BEHRAM

PREMJI MARG

Pherozeshah Mehta Gardens
(Hanging Gardens)

Mani Bhavan

Raudat Tahera

SARDAR PATEL RD.

LOKMANYA TILAK

WALKESHWAR RD.

NETAJI

SUBHASH

Chowpatty
Beach

MAHARSHI KARVE

NANDLAL JANI

P.D. MELLO

Jain Temple

Taraporewalla Aquarium

MARINE DR.

D. NADROJI

Back Bay

MAHAPALIKA

MAHATMA GANDHI

Victoria Terminus

Malabar Hill

Tourist Office

VEER NARIMAN RD.

Mint

Rajabai Tower

CAMA RD.

Harbour

Jehangir Art Gallery

Gateway Of India

PETHE MARG

SHAHID BHAGAT SINGH

Afghan Church

York. Even in these jet-paced days, the hotel has—despite the modernization of its lobby—lots of character. Old-fashioned touches of luxury include spacious rooms, some with separate little dressing chambers and big, clean bathrooms. All rooms have balconies. Singles cost Rs. 370 ($28.45); doubles are Rs. 425 ($32.70) air-conditioned, Rs. 280 ($21.55) non-air-conditioned.

Ballard Estate is not far from the Prince of Wales Museum, walking distance from Flora Fountain, and convenient to Victoria Terminus. But it's dead after 5 p.m. and taxis can be hard to get from then on.

Hotel Cowies, 15 Walton Rd. (near Electric House), Bombay 400039 (tel. 240232), has little to recommend it aside from location. But if everything else is full, then you might try here. The rates are high for what you get: Rs. 136 ($10.45) single and Rs. 195 ($15) double, with an attached bathroom; without air conditioning, Rs. 115 ($8.85) single and Rs. 186 ($14.30) double, with common bath; with air conditioning, Rs. 181 ($13.90) single and Rs. 240 ($18.45) double.

At the **Hotel Apollo,** Landsdowne Road, Apollo Bunder, Bombay 400039 (tel. 2020223), the gloomy halls won't please you but the pleasant rooms will. While small, they're clean and have such amenities as air conditioning, small refrigerators, TV, telephones, and clean private tile bathrooms. Rates are Rs. 285 ($21.90) single and Rs. 360 ($27.70) double. An off-season discount is offered in March, April, and May. The hotel is well located, behind the Taj and off Colaba Causeway.

Under Apollo management is the **Garden Hotel,** Park View Building, 42 Garden Rd., Colaba, Bombay 400039 (tel. 240895), once a grand mansion. Again there are drab halls that give no clue to the clean and cheerful rooms with modern furniture and tiled bathrooms. There are telephones, two-channel music, and TV in the rooms, and refrigerators, the last for a surcharge of Rs. 20 ($1.55). Rates are Rs. 345 ($26.55) double and Rs. 275 ($21.15) single, air-conditioned. Suites are Rs. 380 ($29.25) to Rs. 450 ($34.60). There's a 5% service charge and 7% government luxury tax. A sundeck is at guests' disposal. An off-season discount of 10% to 15% is offered in March, April, and May.

The **Hotel Godwin,** Jasmine Building, 41 Garden Rd., Colaba Reclamation, Bombay 400039 (tel. 241226), another Apollo-managed hotel, has small, tidy, comfortable rooms with attached tile bathrooms. Air-conditioned rooms rent for Rs. 290 ($22.30) to Rs. 330 ($25.40) single, and Rs. 360 ($27.70) to Rs. 425 ($32.70) double. Non-air-conditioned rooms cost Rs. 240 ($18.45) single to Rs. 425 ($32.70) double. An off-season discount of 10% to 15% is offered in March, April, and May. There's a terrace with a harbor and city view. Both guests and outsiders can eat in the Godwin's restaurant, which is all done up with red-velvet walls and crystal chandeliers, and open for breakfast, lunch, and tea. Average entree prices run Rs. 12 (90¢) to Rs. 30 ($2.30).

The **Ascot Hotel,** at 38 Garden Rd., Bombay 400039 (tel. 211067), could use sprucing up. Rates are Rs. 368 ($28.30) single and Rs. 440 ($33.85) double, air-conditioned, for bed and breakfast. At times there are so many Arabs in the lobby here you might be near the Persian Gulf instead of the Arabian Sea.

Cozy, clean accommodations await you at **Château Windsor Guest House,** 86 V. Nariman Rd., Churchgate, Bombay 400020 (tel. 2043378), in 35 pleasant rooms. With shared bathrooms, rates are Rs. 150 ($11.55) to Rs. 180 ($13.85) single and Rs. 200 ($15.40) to Rs. 235 ($18.05) double; with bathrooms attached, singles are Rs. 225 ($17.30), and doubles, Rs. 415 ($31.90). Some large family rooms have air conditioning and attached baths, for Rs. 415 ($31.90) to Rs. 555 ($42.70). Service charge is 10%; government tax, 7%. Rates include morning tea. There is hot and cold running water, and 24-hour room service for light refreshments.

The **West End Hotel,** 45 V. Thackersey Marg, Bombay 400020 (tel. 299121), has well-kept old-fashioned rooms with boxey '40s furniture and new tile bathrooms. All rooms are air-conditioned and have balconies; Rs. 350 ($26.90) to Rs. 420 ($32.30) for singles, Rs. 450 ($34.60) to Rs. 460 ($35.40) for doubles, Rs. 550 ($42.30) to Rs. 650 ($50) for suites. There's a 10% service charge.

Hotel Premier, 32-38 Vishnu Mahal (opposite Metro Cinema), A. P. Marg, Dhobi Talao, Bombay 400002 (tel. 314843), has a minuscule lobby/reception area and a *Playboy* bunny on the door leading to the restaurant which is, despite the tacky entrance, surprisingly tasteful and quietly decorated with mirrors, an abstract mural, and red carpeting. Wood paneling is used on the halls leading to the 24 compact air-conditioned rooms, reminiscent of motels in the West. They have those by-now-familiar built-in headboards and vanities, and small attached bathrooms, and rent for Rs. 275 ($21.15) single and Rs. 325 ($25) double.

In a superb location, opposite the Gateway to India, the **Gateway Hotel,** Villar Ville, 16 P. J. Ramchandani Marg, Bombay 400039 (tel. 235114), once a private home, is now a nine-room hotel facing the sea. All but one room has an attached bathroom; they're clean, neat, and basic, with some lovely sea views. Virtually every square inch of the hotel is wallpapered, except the ceilings. Rates run Rs. 220 ($16.90) to Rs. 250 ($19.25)—a real find for the budget traveler who's not hung up on atmosphere and decor.

Sharing the Villar Vihar, and right above Gateway but a bit below its neighbor's comfort-cleanliness level, is the **Samsons Hotel** (tel. 230707), with its own entrance. There are eight air-conditioned rooms, all doubles and all but two with common bathrooms renting for Rs. 150 ($11.55) single and Rs. 200 ($15.40) double. Two rooms with attached bathrooms have verandas overlooking the sea. An okay place if you're casual about accommodations.

In this same area, and popular since the hippie days of the 1960s, **Rex and Stiffles,** both in the Mehra Building at 80 Ormiston Rd., Apollo Bunder, Bombay 400001, have the same surly manager. In this double-decker hotel arrangement, the Stiffles (tel. 20220306) is under the Rex (tel. 2021518). The Rex has mostly private bathrooms. Both have cheerless little rooms, rundown and overpriced. Rates run Rs. 100 ($7.70) to Rs. 185 ($14.25). Whether founded in fact or not, the hotels are rumored to be druggie hangouts.

Outside the Center

Opposite the Central Station and next to the State Transport Depot, the **Hotel Sahil,** 292 J. B. Behram Marg (tel. 391421), has a lavish marble lobby and small, cozy rooms with low ceilings. They are clean, and so are the attached bathrooms, and rent for Rs. 375 ($28.85) to Rs. 440 ($33.85). The hotel's proximity to train and bus depots makes it popular with Indian business travelers. You're about a Rs.-15 ($1.15) taxi ride from Hutatma Chowk (formerly Flora Fountain) or the Fort.

In a residential area near the American Consulate and within walking distance of the Hanging Gardens (S. P. Mehta), the **Regency Hotel,** 73 L. Jagmohandas Marg (formerly Nepean Sea Road), Bombay 400006 (tel. 8220765), opposite Petit Hall, is a pleasant, quiet place with an attractive restaurant off the reception area. Rooms cost Rs. 330 ($25.40) to Rs. 350 ($26.90) for singles, Rs. 370 ($28.45) to Rs. 390 ($30) for doubles, all with air conditioning and private attached bathrooms. A taxi (there are rarely any auto-rickshaws around here) will cost about Rs. 15 ($1.15) to Rs. 20 ($1.55) to Hutatma Chowk or the Fort.

Near the fashionable Cumballa Hills section is **Shalimar,** August Kranti Marg, Bombay 400036 (tel. 821311), a modern place with wood-paneled lobby and air conditioning. Some of the 74 rooms are so tiny it's hard to believe they contain so many comforts. It's not lavish but clean. Singles run Rs. 190 ($14.60) to Rs. 345 ($26.55), and doubles go for Rs. 395 ($30.40)—all with private bathrooms attached. There's a 10% service charge, a bar, and good North Indian, Chinese, and continental foods in the Gulmarg Restaurant. The famous Hanging Gardens (now S. P. Mehta Garden) are ten minutes away.

Also on August Kranti Marg is **Kemp's Corner Hotel,** 131 August Kranti Marg, Bombay 400036 (tel. 8224646), with 35 clean, air-conditioned rooms, with television, telephones, and attached bathrooms. Rates are Rs. 245 ($18.85) single and Rs. 285 ($21.90) double.

In a bustling neighborhood opposite the Gloria Church, the **Heritage Hotel,** Sant Savita Marg, Byculla, Bombay 400027 (tel. 851485), is popular with Indian businessmen. The wallpapered rooms are clean and simply, but adequately furnished, with attached bathrooms. Non-air-conditioned singles run Rs. 150 ($11.55) to Rs. 170 ($13.05); air-conditioned singles, Rs. 240 ($18.45) to Rs. 270 ($20.75). Doubles without air conditioning cost Rs. 260 ($20) to Rs. 290 ($22.30); with air conditioning, Rs. 350 ($26.90) to Rs. 390 ($30). The Parsi-owned hotel has a restaurant appropriately named Parsiana where you can eat Parsi dishes not easily found outside of private homes. (see "Restaurants").

LOW-BUDGET CHOICES: The **Jones Lodging House,** Abbas Building, 35 Mereweather Rd., Bombay 400039 (tel. 240031), is recommended only because of its low prices in the high-priced district: Rs. 30 ($2.30) single and Rs. 60 ($4.60) double, or Rs. 25 ($1.90) in the dorm. Very basic—not for the fussy. You get lockers for your valuables. The door is locked at midnight, but if you make arrangements someone will let you in. A sign above the reception counter expresses the management's view: "Come as a guest and go as a friend." Jones is hard to find; it's not really on Mereweather, but in a courtyard off the road.

TWO Y'S AND A HOSTEL: Living up to the slogan on its tariff sheet, "a clean, decent, and safe accommodation for individuals and families," is the **YMCA International House & Programme Centre,** 18 YMCA Rd., Bombay Central, Bombay 400008 (tel. 891191), where single occupancy costs Rs. 115 ($8.85), and double, Rs. 210 ($16.15), both with a common bath; with attached bathrooms, Rs. 124 ($9.55) single and Rs. 240 ($18.45) double. An air-conditioned double goes for Rs. 248 ($19.05). All tariffs include bedtime tea, breakfast, and dinner. In addition there's a Rs.-40 ($3.05) charge for transient membership. Service charge is 10% on the total bill.

The well-located **YWCA International Guest House,** 18 Madame Cama Rd., Fort, Bombay 400039 (tel. 2020445), has 33 cheerful rooms, at this writing restricted to single women, or married couples alone and with their children (no single men) and charges Rs. 10 (75¢) per person as transient membership fees, which are valid for one month. Rooms are nicely furnished, and charges include linens, attached bathroom, continental breakfast, 10% service charge, and telephone extension charge: Rs. 70.30 ($5.40) for singles,

Rs. 138.40 ($10.65) for doubles, and Rs. 246 ($18.90) for family rooms. You'll be expected to give a deposit for an advance reservation. Meals other than breakfast and tea/soft drinks are taken out at one of the many restaurants nearby.

Right behind the expensive Taj Mahal Hotel, the **Salvation Army Hostel** (also known as the **Red Shield Hostel**), 30 Mereweather Rd. (tel. 241824), is clean and reasonably priced. This popular place accommodates only 60 guests in 20 dorm-style and double rooms: Rs. 50 ($3.85) per day in the dorm, Rs. 200 ($15.40) double. Bed linens and meals—bland Western-style cooking—are included in the rates. You must reserve well in advance or show up at the crack of dawn and wait to see if you can get a room or dorm bed when a guest checks out. Visitors are not permitted in the rooms and a sign in the entry says "Drugs, alcohol, hashish smokers strictly prohibited."

SPLURGE HOTELS: At these prices and in this day and age, it will come as no surprise that the following hotels are air-conditioned. All have attached bathrooms, and television in the rooms, along with telephones and multichannel music, and many have individual refrigerators in each room as well.

A moderate splurge, the **Ritz Hotel**, J. Tata Road, Bombay 400020 (tel. 220141), has a quiet, old-fashioned charm. The clean, spacious rooms have white-painted furniture, cream-colored walls, printed spreads and drapes, and big tiled attached bathrooms. Rates are Rs. 500 ($38.45) single and Rs. 625 ($48.05) double.

At the 127-room **Ambassador Hotel,** V. Nariman Road, Bombay 400020 (tel. 291131), the revolving rooftop restaurant isn't the only thing that's high-priced—there are valuable works of Indian art throughout the hotel, and the rates are high as well. Indeed, there is such a wide assortment of high-priced rates that I mention only the basics here: single, Rs. 761 ($58.50); single occupancy of a double, Rs. 878 ($67.50); double, Rs. 995 ($76.50). Suites, including duplexes, run Rs. 1,170 ($90) to Rs. 2,925 ($225).

Right off Arthur Bunder Road, Colaba, Bombay 400005, the ten-story **Fariyas** (tel. 2042911) is a pleasant place with modern functional furniture in the bedrooms. The ornate dining room has a Hyderabadi feeling. Rates are Rs. 550 ($47.30) single, Rs. 670 ($51.55) double. There's a swimming pool.

The **Natraj,** 135 Netaji Subhas Rd., Bombay 400020 (tel. 294160), recently renovated, boasts of a lobby with Gujarati-style wooden chairs upholstered in purple reflected under a glittering mirrored ceiling. Pretty botanical and bird prints on silk panels are in the halls. Some of the fresh and cheerful rooms have white cane furniture and others are more tailored, with dark woods. Corner rooms have balconies and beautiful sea views. Singles cost Rs. 636 ($48.90); single occupancy of a double, Rs. 760 ($58.45); doubles, Rs. 830 ($63.85); suites, Rs. 1,498 ($115.25) to Rs. 1,802 ($138.60). These rates include service charges, tax, TV charges, and local telephone calls.

At the 35-story **Oberoi Towers**, Nariman Point, Bombay 420021 (tel. 2024343), there are fountains splashing gently against marble walls in the lobby and 700 well-appointed guest rooms above. Rates are Rs. 1,300 ($100) single, Rs. 1,400 ($107.70) double; suites cost Rs. 2,900 ($223) to Rs. 5,500 ($4.23). The hotel has six restaurants, two bars, a three-level shopping center, and a swimming pool.

Next to the Oberoi Towers and connected by an indoor walkway, is the **Oberoi,** Nariman Point, Bombay 420021 (tel. 2025757), an elegant, chic, sleek marble-lined hotel with black and white predominating in the lounge, and a sophisticated international look throughout. The 375 rooms, many with sweeping sea views, have modern furniture with lovely textiles used as bedspreads and draperies. There are three restaurants, a bar, and swimming pool. Rooms rent for Rs. 1,500 ($115.50) single and Rs. 1,600 ($123) double. Suites cost Rs. 3,250 ($250) to Rs. 7,500 ($577).

The suburban-located Welcomgroup **SeaRock,** Land's End, Bandra, Bombay 400050 (tel. 6425454), juts into the sea with 450 rooms, many commanding views of the sea or city. There's a swimming pool beside the sea, shops, five restaurants, a bar, and a discothèque. Basic rates are Rs. 750 ($57.70) single and Rs. 850 ($65.40) double. Executive chambers (larger rooms) run as high as Rs. 1,010 ($77.75) and suites go up to Rs. 4,000 ($308).

Back in town, the **President Hotel,** 90 Cuffe Parade, Bombay 400005 (tel. 4950808), a member of the Taj Group of hotels, is an 18-story, 300-room hotel in a residential area but a stone's throw from shops and other amusements. The pillared lobby is hung with elaborate glass-tiered chandeliers and the rooms have modern, functional furnishings. There's a swimming pool, three restaurants, a bar, and shops. Rates are Rs. 935 ($72) single and Rs. 1,045 ($80.50) double. A special attraction at the President is Delores Periera, a renowned card reader who divides her time between this city and Bangalore. To see what the cards say in a 30-minute reading costs Rs. 100 ($7.70). Her hours are 10:30 a.m. to 1 p.m. and 4 to 7 p.m., by appointment only.

The most famous hotel in Bombay is the more than century-old **Taj Mahal,** Apollo Bunder, Bombay 400039 (tel. 2023366), an impressive hunk of Indo-Saracenic and Gothic architecture with elegant old-world charm and a modern wing, called the Taj Mahal Inter-Continental. There are 650 rooms —all with every amenity—and some suites that are truly inspired in decor. Single occupancy costs Rs. 1,200 ($92.25) to Rs. 1,400 ($107.75), and doubles go for Rs. 1,350 ($103.75) to Rs. 1,500 ($115.50). Suites run Rs. 3,000 ($230.75) to Rs. 7,000 ($538.50). There is a swimming pool, shopping arcade, four restaurants, a dining room, two bars (the Harbour Bar is the oldest in the city), a snack lounge, and a discothèque. Even if you don't stay here, you'll probably end up spending time in the lobby—a popular meeting place which bustles with activity day and night—or in the 24-hour coffeeshop where you can get delicious snacks and light meals.

SUBURBAN HOTELS: Keep in mind that taxis cost Rs. 40 ($3.05) to Rs. 45 ($3.45) one way from some of these hotels to the center of town. Buses, costing only about Rs. 1.50 (11¢), run regularly to the center, and here and there you can get cheap train service. However, public transportation is so crowded in this populous city that during peak times passengers ooze out of the vehicles and sometimes hang onto the sides of trains for dear life.

On the Way to Juhu Beach

The **Oriental Palace,** 746 Khar Pali Rd., Khar, Bombay 400052 (tel. 547381), has 50 air-conditioned rooms with lots of wood paneling. It was under renovation, but looked promising when I stopped by.

Caesar's Palace, 313 Vithal Bhai Patel Rd. (formerly Linking Road), Khar, Bombay 400052 (tel. 542311, 542312, or 542313), is as unlike any residence the emperor might have had, or the hotel in Las Vegas, as you can possibly imagine, but the rooms do have air conditioning, telephones, and carpeting, in addition to the furnishings you need. Rooms are Rs. 250 ($19.25); suites, Rs. 350 ($26.90).

Off Vithal Bhai Patel, (Linking) Road, Bombay 400052, the **Royal Inn,** opposite the Khar Telephone Exchange (tel. 539888), has 19 ordinary rooms and four deluxe, all air-conditioned, at Rs. 300 ($23.05) single and Rs. 360 ($27.70) double. It's overpriced for small, not well-lit and not too clean rooms.

Many Westerners who follow Radha Swami Satsang stay near his religious center, especially during the winter, at the **Hotel Mayura,** 352 Vithal Bhai Patel Rd. (Linking Road), Bombay 400052 (tel. 535416, 535417, or 535418), which has small, clean, adequately furnished rooms at upscale prices (so what else is new?), all with air conditioning and television: Rs. 280 ($21.55) single and Rs. 350 ($26.90) double. There's a restaurant and coffeeshop on the premises.

The **Hotel Linkway,** 519A Vithal Bhai Patel Rd. (Linking Rd.), Khar, Bombay 400032 (tel. 535431, 535432, or 535433), has 27 neat, clean moderately priced air-conditioned rooms for Rs. 150 ($11.55) single, Rs. 175 ($13.45) double; and suites for Rs. 250 ($19.25).

The nearby **Hotel Sunshine,** 538 Vithal Bhai Patel Rd. (Linking Road), Bombay 400052 (tel. 533081), could be cleaner. Rates are high: Rs. 355 ($27.30). There's air conditioning, attached bathrooms, a bar, and a restaurant.

At Juhu Beach

From here, you can count on about a Rs.-50 ($3.85) taxi fare to Warden Road, Rs. 80 ($6.15) to Colaba. You can also take bus 231 to Santa Cruz (50 paise, 3½¢) and local train (Rs. 2, 15¢) from there to Churchgate Station, opposite the Tourist Office. Be sure to avoid rush hours and take precautions against pickpockets. While there are hotels even closer to the airports for those in transit, you can also stay at Juhu Beach and easily make your early-morning plane. Some hotels have transfer service to the airports; if not, taxis to the domestic airport will run about Rs. 27 ($2.05), and to the international airport, Rs. 42 ($3.25).

A cubist exterior makes the **Hotel Ajanta,** 8 Juhu Tara Rd., Bombay 400049 (tel. 6124890), stand out under the towering palms. Additional rooms to bring the total up to 64 were under way when I stopped in, and a rate increase was a distinct possibility. The accommodations are already overpriced because they need better care: Rs. 321 ($24.70) single, Rs. 375 ($28.85) double, including tax, air conditioning and such other amenities as private attached bathrooms, two-channel piped-in music, and airport greeting service.

Right next door, the 38-room **South End Hotel,** 11 Juhu Tara Rd., Bombay 400049 (tel. 6125213), makes no pretense about being anything more than a modest beach place, with prices to match: Rs. 75 ($5.75) single and Rs. 125 ($9.60) double. Air conditioning costs Rs. 25 ($1.90) more, but only three rooms are air-conditioned. There's a 10% service charge and taxes as they apply. You pay in advance.

The Krishna Consciousness Movement runs the red-and-pink sandstone double-towered **Iskcon Hotel,** Juhu Beach, Bombay 400049 (tel. 626860), with an adjoining temple (open from 4 a.m. to 1 p.m. and 4 to 10 p.m.) decorated with dioramas of Hindu mythology. Of the hotel's 43 rooms, 20 are for members and the remainder are for tourists seeking a clean, quiet, affordable place to stay. Krishna is seen in tapestries in the halls, as well as in paintings on the walls of the rooms, which have Gujarati lacquered wood furniture and print drapes, balconies, attached tile bathrooms, and shiny marble floors. The rates are Rs. 295 ($22.70) for air-conditioned rooms, Rs. 245 ($18.85) for non-air-conditioned; deduct Rs. 54 ($4.15) to get the single-occupancy rate. There are also six dorms with common bathrooms and only two to three beds per dorm, at Rs. 50 ($3.85) per person—they're heavily in demand, so book well in advance. There's no smoking or drinking on the premises.

The **Sea View Hotel,** Juhu Beach, Bombay 400049 (tel. 6123244), has, as its name implies, a grand view of the sea from the reception, which is also the indoor restaurant adjacent to an even more pleasant outdoor terrace. The 13 simple, basic, affordable rooms—Rs. 150 ($11.55) double—are arranged motel-like around a court. They have attached bathrooms with cold water only, but you can order hot water by the bucket. The restaurant serves many Goan specialties (see my restaurant recommendations at Juhu).

Up a notch or two in price is the **Golden Manor,** opposite Juhu Church, Juhu, Bombay 400049 (tel. 6149287), with a pool and garden. The hotel is air-conditioned, and while some of the doubles are small, big mirrors above the vanities make them seem larger. They have white walls (some needed scraping and painting, others were in fine shape), printed bedspreads and drapes, and tile bathrooms with hot and cold running water. Rates are Rs. 300 ($23.05) to Rs. 350 ($26.90) single, Rs. 350 ($26.90) to Rs. 400 ($30.75) double. A small restaurant off the pool is done up in blue tweed and open for lunch and dinner; breakfast is delivered to your room.

In the same price range, but not worth it, is the simple **Sea Side Hotel,** 38/2 Juhu Beach, Bombay 400048 (tel. 572986). All rooms are air-conditioned with bath attached, and run Rs. 308 ($23.70) for single occupancy, Rs. 364 ($28) double.

Splurges at Juhu: Next to the Golden Manor, the **Hotel Horizon,** 27 Juhu Beach, Bombay 400049 (tel. 571411), is a favorite with Russian tour groups. Rooms with every modern amenity run Rs. 575 ($44.25) for a single, Rs. 650 ($50) for a double. There's a pool, shops, and an attractive restaurant called Legends hung with portraits of legendary heroes and past rulers of various periods, where Indian foods are accompanied by Indian music at night. There's a 24-hour coffeeshop, and an outdoor restaurant with a village atmosphere (the current "in" look in Bombay) serving regional cuisines, and Xanadu, a laser-lit discothèque.

Sun-n-Sand, 39 Juhu Beach, Bombay 400054 (tel. 571481), one of the first hotels to be built out this way, was undergoing some renovations when I looked in. It's air-conditioned and has modern furnishings, shops, a swimming pool, a bar, and the Sunset Restaurant with music in the evenings. Rooms cost Rs. 500 ($38.45) single and Rs. 600 ($46.15) double; suites run Rs. 900 ($69.25) to Rs. 1,400 ($107.70).

A newcomer to Juhu, next to the Sun-n-Sand, is the **Sands Hotel,** 39/2 Juhu Beach, Bombay 400049 (tel. 571451). The elaborately decorated lobby has glass chains instead of conventional window shades, highly polished granite floors in shades of brown and gray, lots of planters full of greenery, and big, brown-leather club chairs to relax in—more a city than beach look. Some rooms have textured walls contrasted with smooth walls, distressed-wood dressing tables, and headboards. Other rooms have marble tiles in the walls, little café tables and chairs, as well as easy chairs, beds, desks, and dressing tables. All rooms have attached tile bathrooms, and rent for Rs. 526.50 ($40.50) single and Rs. 643.50 ($49.50) double, tax included. In the Mehman Restaurant, on Friday and Saturday you can hear a singer perform ghazals (Urdu love songs); during the week, there's Indian classical music. There is coach service to the airport from this hotel.

Tailored, tasteful decor can be found at the high-priced **Palm Grove Hotel,** Main Point Beach, Juhu, Bombay 400049 (tel. 6149361), where rates are Rs. 550 ($42.30) single, Rs. 660 ($50.75) double, and Rs. 1,500 ($115.40) for suites; some rooms have beautiful sea views. The service charge is 10%. There's a glassed-in coffeeshop, swimming pool, and dimly lit grill room.

The **Holiday Inn,** Balraj Sahani Marg, Juhu Beach, Bombay 400049 (tel. 571425), has 201 guest rooms overlooking the sea, four restaurants, a bar, a confectionery, and swimming pools for adults and children. The rooms are modern and well appointed, with all the amenities expected in a five-star hotel. Rates are Rs. 825 ($63.45) for singles and Rs. 925 ($71.15) for doubles. There's coach service to town twice a day.

The **Centaur Hotel,** Juhu Tara Road, Bombay 400049 (tel. 6143040), in the Air-India chain, blends modern architecture with five acres of Mughal-inspired gardens. This new/old theme continues indoors with the sleek marble reception and contemporary lobby-lounge contrasting with a traditional wood-paneled club-like Regency-period Mahogany lounge/bar. The coffeeshop has a garden setting, and the 370 guest rooms and suites are functional and modern, with all the amenities. They rent for Rs. 700 ($53.85) single and Rs. 800 ($61.55) double. Including the coffeeshop there are five restaurants, plus a swimming pool and courtesy coaches to the airports.

Near the Airports

International flights, and some domestic ones too, depart and arrive at Bombay at very early morning hours. So staying close to the airports saves you a trip from town if you're taking off for good or merely passing through to another town. It won't save you money—rates are high at the airport area hotels. They cater not only to transiting travelers, but to well-heeled executives doing business at the nearby industrial estates.

The **Imperial Palace,** 45 Telly Park Rd., Andheri East, Bombay 400069 (tel. 6345234), is not palatial. Rates are Rs. 210 ($16.15) single and Rs. 250 ($19.25) double. Suites run Rs. 350 ($26.90) to Rs. 450 ($34.60).

Nearby is the 24-room **Hotel Ras International,** 26 Telli Galli, Andheri (East), Bombay 400069 (tel. 6340438), charging Rs. 250 ($19.25) single, Rs. 300 ($23.05) double, and Rs. 330 ($25.40) for suites. All are air-conditioned with attached bathrooms. A restaurant and bar are in an adjoining building.

Hotel Transit, off Nehru Road, Vile Parle East, Bombay 400099 (tel. 6129325), offers very simple air-conditioned accommodations, decent enough for an overnight stay or a "day room" if your plane leaves in the middle of the night. The hotel stations a representative at the airport (ask at the Information Desk), and he or she will see that you are given free transportation to the hotel and back again to make your flight. All rooms are doubles and rates are Rs. 365 ($28.05) for single occupancy, Rs. 495 ($38.05) double, plus a 10% service charge.

The **Avion,** Nehru Road, Vile Parle East, Bombay 400099 (tel. 6123902), with a two-story glass front and white interior, air conditioning, and high rates: Rs. 314 ($24.15) single and Rs. 385 ($29.60) double. Similar rates apply next door at the strictly vegetarian **Hotel Jal,** Nehru Road, Vile Parle East (tel. 6123820)· Rs. 275 ($21.15) single and Rs. 350 ($26.90) double.

Near the Avion, the **Hotel Aircraft International,** Plot 179, Dayaldas Road (off Western Express Highway), Vile Parle (East), Bombay 400057 (tel. 6123667), is a four-story establishment without a restaurant. The 20 doubles rent for Rs. 250 ($19.25) single, Rs. 290 ($22.30) double, and Rs. 350 ($26.90) for a super-deluxe.

In a higher price range is the **Hotel Airport Plaza,** 70-C Nehru Rd., Vile Parle East, Santa Cruz Airport, Bombay 400099 (tel. 6123390), with 81 double rooms, all soundproofed—a fine feature for a hotel near the airport. The rooms are also air-conditioned, with attached baths, telephones, four-channel piped-in music, and a restaurant that stays open around the clock. Tariff is Rs. 445 ($34.25) single, Rs. 535 ($41.15) double. The Airport Plaza has a hotline: at the airport right near Egypt Air's check-in counter—so you can call in for free bus service when your flight arrives. They take you back to make your departure too. The hotel has a swimming pool, and discothèque.

And topping them all in terms of price and grandeur at the airport is the lavishly decorated marble-walled **Centaur,** Bombay Airport (tel. 6126660). The unusual circular design features all rooms facing an inner courtyard centered on a swimming pool and garden. There are courtesy coaches to take you to and from the airport, plus coaches twice a day to the city. All rooms and public areas are soundproofed as well as nicely furnished. Three restaurants, room service, shopping arcade, and many rupees per room: Rs. 700 ($53.85) single, Rs. 800 ($61.55) double.

2. Restaurants

Bombay provides the rare chance to sample some of the delicacies of the Parsis, the Zoroastrians who fled Persia in the 7th and 8th centuries and settled in and about the city. One of these dishes is the unusual **dhansak,** literally meaning wide mouth, a curry made with countless different ingredients. Other Parsi specialties include **patrani machli** (fish stuffed with chutney and steamed in banana leaves), and Bombay duck, which is not duck, but a whitefish served curried or sautéed. Bombay also boasts Goan specialties like **vindaloos,** spiced meat or chicken in a special sauce, and **foogaths,** vegetables made with coconut sauce.

Other local foods, of the vegetarian variety, are influenced by Maharashtra, Bombay's state, or by the neighboring state of Gujarat. What is interesting here are the subtle differences in the styles of eating. The Maharashtran takes a bit of rice to begin his meal and ends with a taste of rice. The Gujarati eats his wheat-based foods first, such as puri (also spelled poori, a fried bread shaped like a disc), and ends his feast with his rice. In both cases, dessert usually accompanies the main course.

A traditional Bombay meal will be served on a thali, a round plate made of brass, silver, or (more recently) stainless steel. In the center will be a little hill of rice and around the edges will be vegetables, lentils, and curds. There will also be dabs of chutney (a fruit-and-vegetable relish), pickles, your personal piece of salt, and your dessert. The idea is to eat what you want in the order you prefer.

Puris, steaming hot flat discs of wheat bread, will be served along with the meal, and the food is eaten with the fingers. Eating with the hands (please use only your right hand) is considered cleaner than with a fork or spoon because you can wash your hands seconds before you eat, whereas a regular utensil might have been washed many hours previous to the meal.

The technique is to tear off a little bit of the puri and to use the small piece to help you pick up your other foods. Rice can be used in the same way, by gathering some grains into a little ball and mixing it with a bit of curry, some dhal (the lentil preparation almost like soup), and chutney, then popping it all in your mouth. No more than the first knuckles of your fingers are ever supposed to get dirty and this is a standard by which Bombay thali manners are judged. At the end of the meal, you wash your hands.

Incidentally, should you want seconds, never help yourself, even if the serving dish is right in front of you, because your right hand would get the handle of the service spoon messy. Always ask for the assistance of the waiter. He will serve you and also bring piping hot puris when needed.

By the way, if you are invited to eat "trash" in Bombay, be sure to say yes immediately. This is no insult, but rather an invitation to share a great local pleasure, known as **bhel-puri.** This is a delicious concoction of cereals, chutneys, and sauces. Other variations are pani-puri, a puff of fried dough filled with tamarind water, and bhelpuri, which is made of raisins, puffed rice, saffron, lentils, nuts, and other spices.

Outside of bhel-puri, made best in Bombay, there is no local cuisine identified with the city. Instead, you find an amalgam of different regional foods, and Western and Chinese as well. However, Bombay has an unusual food service that creates one of the great sights in the city's never-dull streets.

Throughout Bombay, on work days before noon you will see many messengers negotiating the congested streets with large wooden platforms holding foot-high tin cylinders balanced on their heads, or pushing carts full of these receptacles. In the cylinders are hot lunches for clerks in offices, bazaar wallahs, executives, and factory hands all over Bombay. But they are not from local caterers.

The lunches known as **dabbas** were made earlier that morning in kitchens at the recipients' homes all over the outlying areas, spooned into the cylinders which have several interlocking dishes, sealed tight, and identified with a written code standing for a person's name. With countless other identical cylinders, they then are loaded by these same messengers on trains to make extensive journeys from the suburbs to Victoria Terminus and Central Station, two main pickup points in Bombay. By now, I am speaking of 100,000 of these cylinders, all alike except for their codes, all lined up, ready and waiting for delivery in an hour or so somewhere specific in the huge city of Bombay.

Picked up by the messengers, who can decipher the codes but can't read otherwise remarkably, the cylinders are taken to the right place to give the right person the right hot lunch at the right time. When the lunch break is over, the messengers pick up the cylinders, retrace their steps, and are themselves back home before 4 p.m. Another shift of messengers serves the night workers.

Aside from providing a hot meal at midday and being a lot cheaper than going out, these lunches do something else. They permit a melting pot of people working in Bombay to observe many different regional and religious customs which are not easily abandoned anywhere in India.

Now go and enjoy the attentive service in Bombay's restaurants. Below are a handful only. Most of them are air-conditioned; if not, it's been noted.

GOOD CHEAP MEALS: Modest South Indian vegetarian and Iranian nonvegetarian restaurants, located on the side streets behind the Taj Mahal Hotel, offer some of the best possibilities for good cheap meals. These places are so similar in terms of their menus and appearance that they are not described separately in the following section. Great favorites of the people who work in this part of Bombay, they all offer spicy foods to please local palates. Most are not air-conditioned; whirling fans and open windows cool their interiors.

Typical of the South Indian places is **New Laxmi Vilas,** Nawroji Furounji Road (tel. 231447), where a complete vegetarian meal runs Rs. 5 (40¢) to Rs. 6 (45¢). A number of other vegetarian restaurants in this price range can be identified by the use of the word "Udipi" (meaning the cooks come from a small South Indian town famous for its chefs) in their names or on their signboards. Like New Laxmi Vilas, most of these places are open as early as 7:30 a.m., when patrons drop in for dosas (rice-and-lentil pancakes stuffed with potato) for Rs. 3 (23¢) and South Indian coffee (made with steaming milk) for Rs. 2 (15¢). They stay open until 10 p.m.

The nonvegetarian places are a cross between the simplest French brasseries and American delicatessens, with clean, bare floors, tables without cloths, floor-to-ceiling doors opening onto the streets, and shelves of tinned goods as well as prepared foods. **Café Leopold,** 39-41 S. Bhagat Singh Rd. (tel. 21122), is a good example. On the menu is mutton curry with rice, vegetable cutlets, and omelets, all under Rs. 13 ($1), plus a host of other main dishes, and sweets, soft drinks, and coffee and tea. **Sun Rise** and **Royal** are two of the other Iranian cafés. They too are open early, around 7 a.m., and remain open until 10 p.m. or later.

A cross between one of the cheap Iranian cafés, a bistro pub, and an Indian snackbar is **Paradise,** Sindh Chambers, Colabar (tel. 4932434), somewhat more pricey—Rs. 50 ($3.85) for two—than the aforementioned, and run by the friendly J. M. Irani, who takes pride in serving a good dhansak (Parsi dish made of mutton, vegetables, spices, and more). It's the Wednesday special. Another special is Tuesday's chicken vindaloo, from Goa. You can always get spaghetti, sandwiches, and samosas (turnovers), ice creams, and soft drinks. Hours: 10 a.m. to 11:30 p.m. Cleanliness is another attraction here. Not air-conditioned.

And since the British days in India there's been the **Wayside Inn,** K. Dubash Marg (tel. 244324), now, however, with a New York skyline mural as well as old Toby mugs kept safe in a cabinet. Served even now are the old English-type foods in very plain surroundings: liver and onions for Rs. 15 ($1.15), and a whole meal of soup, fish, and dessert for about Rs. 13 ($1). Hours are 9 a.m. to 5:30 p.m.; closed Sunday and bank holidays. By the way, in the Raj days, if you personally knew five diners in this restaurant, you were considered among the city's social elite. Not air-conditioned.

BOMBAY'S BUFFETS: The following is a sampling of Bombay's notable buffets. The hours are usually 12:30 to 3 p.m., or as noted below. It's also a good idea to call in advance to double-check timings and to reserve a place.

At the **Taj Mahal,** Apollo Bunder (tel. 2023366), where the idea originated some years back, the meal is served in the Ballroom daily from 12:30 to 3 p.m. and costs Rs. 85 ($6.55). It begins with soup served by waiters in crisp uniforms, and is followed by a host of serve-yourself main dishes, hot and cold, vegetarian and nonvegetarian, Indian and Western styles, plus salads, relishes, assorted breads and rolls, sweets, fruits, and cheeses. Coffee, tea, and other drinks are not included in the tab at "The Taj" or any of the buffets. At all of the buffets, you can eat all you want, taste all the dishes, and return to the table as often as you like. Light classical music at "The Taj" provides a pleasant backdrop. Reservations are advised here, and at all other buffets, and so is eating early for the best selection. There's a breakfast buffet in the Taj's Shamiana every day—Monday through Saturday from 7 to 10 a.m. and on Sunday from 7 to 10:30 a.m.—for Rs. 58 ($4.45).

At the **Oberoi Towers,** Nariman Point (tel. 2024343), you can have Polynesian foods at the buffet in the Outrigger for a pricey Rs. 150 ($11.55), or Indian foods in the hotel's Moghal Room for Rs. 130 ($10), both buffets served Monday through Saturday only.

At the **West End Hotel,** 45 Thackersey Marg (tel. 299121), there's a 16-course buffet, and every day there's a different selection in the Gourmet, for Rs. 60 ($4.60).

At **Rangoli,** on Nariman Point in the handsome Performing Arts Complex (tel. 234678), the buffet is Rs. 58 ($4.45), every day.

In the **President Hotel,** 90 Cuffe Parade (tel. 4950808), there are two buffets: Monday through Saturday in the Real McCoy, and Italian foods in the rustic-looking Trattoria on Sunday: Timings for both are 12:30 to 3 p.m., and the price is Rs. 70 ($5.40) each.

In the dining room of the **Grand Hotel,** Ballard Estate (tel. 268211), the buffet is served Monday through Saturday for Rs. 45 ($3.45).

At the **Ambassador,** V. Nariman Rd. (tel. 291131), there are two buffets: at The Top, the revolving restaurant, for Rs. 99 ($7.60) from 12:30 to 3 p.m., and also the Late-Late buffet in the Salt and Pepper Coffee Shop, for Rs. 48 ($3.70), until around 2 a.m.

The newly decorated **Natraj,** 135 Netaji Subhash Rd. (tel. 2044161), was planning a buffet as well, which could be a reality by the time you're in Bombay.

Some restaurants outside the hotels also feature buffets. There are Chinese dishes at **Chopsticks,** 90 V. Nariman Rd. (tel. 2049284), for Rs. 60 ($4.60), and at the restaurant's branch at Seven Bungalows, Versova (tel. 625750), for Rs. 50 ($3.85). And **Talk of the Town,** 143 N. Subhash Rd. (tel. 2230883), serves Indian and continental foods at its buffet, for Rs. 48 ($3.70).

In the **Dasaprakash,** Sir P.M. Road, Lakshmi Building (tel. 2861753), the Bristol Grill has South Indian vegetarian foods, for Rs. 35 ($2.70), from noon to 3:30 p.m. Monday through Saturday.

At Bandra, the Welcomgroup **SeaRock,** Land's End (tel. 6425454, ext. 270), in the revolving restaurant Palace of the West Empress, dishes up a splurge-priced Chinese buffet, with a great view, on Sunday only for Rs. 110 ($8.45).

At Juhu, the **Holiday Inn,** Balraj Sahani Marg (tel. 571425), serves a poolside buffet every Sunday, at Rs. 65 ($5) for adults and Rs. 35 ($2.70) for children. **Sun-n-Sand,** 39 Juhu Beach (tel. 571481), in the Sunset Room, the Sunday-only buffet is Rs. 70 ($5.40). The **Centaur,** at the airport (tel. 6126660), has a poolside brunch buffet on Sunday for Rs. 75 ($5.75); during the monsoon it's moved to the Oriental Room. At **Iskcon,** Juhu Beach (tel. 626860), in the wood-trimmed marble-pillared dining room, a delicious Gujarati vegetarian-style buffet is served from noon to 3 p.m. for Rs. 25 ($1.90) weekdays and Rs. 30 ($2.30) on weekends.

By the time you use this book there may be many more buffets, and many I did not discover, so let me know what you find in the way of buffets, prices, and how you liked them.

PARSI FOODS: As mentioned, Bombay is the place in India to try the delicious dishes associated with the Parsis, whose ancestors settled in this city when they fled Persia in the 7th and 8th centuries. Few restaurants serve these foods, so when I came across them, I made notes to pass on to you.

At the unpretentious 40-seat **Piccolo Café,** 11-A Sir Homi Mody St. (tel. 274537), patrons pamper themselves on pastries and cakes for around Rs. 5 (40¢) to Rs. 6 (45¢) apiece, on patrani fish, stuffed with chutney and cooked in banana leaves and a special roti (bread) to scoop it up with, for Rs. 12 (90¢), and on many other Indian and some Western items. Two can get by for Rs. 50 ($3.85) for a delicious meal here. Hours are 9 a.m. to 6 p.m.; closed Sunday. Run by Ratan Tata Institute which donates profits to charity.

Profits also go to charity at the **Landmark,** 35 S. Patkar Marg (tel. 8226077), a full-fledged restaurant run by the Ratan Tata Institute (RTI). It's a pretty place: rose-pink and gray marble floors, two levels with tables set with snowy cloths contrasting with dark woods, rose tweed upholstery picking up the rose tone in the marble. Open from 10:30 a.m. to 11:30 p.m. While most of the foods are continental, such as the house special chicken à la Landmark (with sausage and bacon) at Rs. 42 ($3.25), there are also some Parsi dishes on the menu (RTI is Parsi in origin). So you might be able to taste the famous Parsi fish stuffed to the gills with chutney and cooked in banana leaves, for Rs. 24 ($1.85), or javdaloo sale boti (mutton with apricots), at Rs. 41 ($3.15). Whatever you do, don't miss the dessert, chocolate sin, a house secret—Rs. 19 ($1.45) and worth every caloric bite. A carry-out food shop adjoins.

Probably the most extensive menu of Parsi foods is found in the Parsi-owned **Hotel Heritage,** Sant Savta Marg, Byculla (tel. 8514891), where these entrees rarely cost more than Rs. 12 (90¢) to Rs. 15 ($1.15). They are served in Parsiana, a white-walled restaurant hung with floral prints and divided by garden trellises. Fish patrani (the banana-leaf-wrapped dish), prawns patia (made with tomatoes, garlic, onion, and sauce), and sale boti (meat, spicy gravy, poppyseeds, and cashew nuts) are on the daily menu, as is a Parsi custard for dessert. Other Parsi dishes like roast kid (made with cashews) are generally available. Dhansak is the most famous Parsi dish. "Dhan" means wealth, and aptly describes this rich dish made of chicken or lamb in a rich purée of a seven or eight kinds of lentils and many different vegetables. Hours are 7 a.m. to midnight every day. For 7-a.m.'ers and other breakfast and brunch eaters, there are ekuri, scrambled eggs Parsi style.

THALIS—INEXPENSIVE VEGETARIAN FEASTS: Excellent vegetarian

restaurants abound in Bombay. One of the oldest and most renowned is in the **Purohits Hotel,** V. Nariman Road (tel. 2046241), where connoisseurs convene. Here you can test your skill in eating off a thali (gleaming metal platter with little cups) and with your fingers. There is a set menu, but I've never used it, preferring instead to let the waiters rattle off the specialties as if they were reciting the alphabet. If you order a complete Purohit's Special, your thali will appear with rice, a variety of specially cooked vegetables, curds (to cool down your spicy foods), condiments, raita (a combination of yogurt and vegetables used to clear the palate after heavier foods), and a sweet. About Rs. 21 ($1.60) is the charge for this bountiful Bombay feast. Or Rs. 18 ($1.40) for a plain thali; a two-sweet thali is Rs. 30 ($2.30). Open daily from 10:30 a.m. to 11 p.m.

Highly recommended also are the thalis served at **Thacker's,** 116 / 118 First Marine St., Marine Lines (tel. 296603). There's a main floor and mezzanine. The front room has dark woods and beige walls, mirrors, and lanterns, and in the back is a staircase leading to the upper level. An ordinary thali, including two vegetarian preparations, dal (a gravy-like mixture), curds, rice, puris (the wheat-based disc bread), papad, pickles, and a sweet, will run about Rs. 22 ($1.70). Deluxe thalis, at Rs. 38 ($2.90), have two sweets and other additions. Open 11:30 a.m. to 2:30 p.m. and 7 p.m. to 10:45 p.m. daily.

Not far from main hotel area is **Satkar,** in the Indian Express Building, Churchgate Station (tel. 293259), which is absolutely jammed with business people eating lunch between 1 and 2 p.m. There's no thali here, but numerous delicious vegetarian dishes to order by themselves or with rice and breads. A good choice is the vegetarian curry, served with rice for Rs. 5.75 (45¢), or the masala dosa at Rs. 5 (40¢). In the air-conditioned section prices are about Rs. 2 (15¢) to Rs. 5 (40¢) more. Hours are 8:30 a.m. to 10 p.m. in the non-air-conditioned section, 11 a.m. to 10 p.m. in the air-conditioned; open Sunday until 10:30 p.m.

Samarambh (Kamat) Restaurant, next to B.E.S.T. House on Bhagat Singh Road (tel. 2874734), is famous for well-prepared vegetarian dishes in Bombay (as well as in Bangalore, Goa, Belgum, Hubli, and Hyderabad). A special thali, for Rs. 15 ($1.15), has a variety of vegetarian dishes and rice, as well as soup, salad, and a sweet; the Rs.-7.50 (60¢) thali has no soup, salad, or sweet. If you're not in a thali mood, an interesting dish is chola battura, a puffy puri crowned with spiced chickpeas for Rs. 7 (55¢), or the ravi idli, made with semolina, and served with sambhar on the side, at Rs. 3.50 (25¢). Open every day from 8 a.m. to 10 p.m. with both air-conditioned and non-air-conditioned sections. There's a buffet on Sunday (see the buffet section).

Also good for inexpensive to moderate vegetarian meals is **Mathura,** V. Nariman Road, where the highest-priced items are Rs. 6 (45¢). A bit higher in price is **Rasna,** J. Tata Road, Churchgate (tel. 220995), where a thali runs Rs. 22 ($1.70) in the non-air-conditioned section and Rs. 25 ($1.90) in the air-conditioned; closed Sunday.

Two more vegetarian suggestions in town: the copper-muraled, mirrored **Samrat,** Prem Court, J. Tata Road, Churchgate (tel. 220942), open from noon to 10:30 p.m. (on Sunday from noon to 3 p.m. and 6 to 10:30 p.m.), is very popular and a bit noisy. An abundantly full Gujarati thali runs Rs. 18 ($1.40) without a sweet and Rs. 23 ($1.75) with a sweet. **Shilpa,** 112/A Panchratna, on the first floor in the Opera Building (tel. 388427), open from 11 a.m. to 10:45 p.m. (on Sunday and holidays from 11 a.m. to 2:45 p.m. and 6 to 10:45 p.m.), has an attractive carved-wood entrance and a filling Gujarati thali for Rs. 18 ($1.40). Both Samrat and Shilpa are fully air-conditioned, and like the other vegetarian restaurants, serve à la carte dishes as well as thali meals.

Among the most attractive places to have a thali, away from the center, is the Juhu branch of the famous South Indian **Woodlands' Garden Café,** Juhu Scheme, Vaikuntial Mehta Road (tel. 6145886), where the surroundings are definitely sunny looking—a red-tiled entry, filled with potted plants, shiny green walls, yellow tables, and a windowed veranda where the sun streams in, but covered by a tin roof so you can hear the rain on a monsoon day. Woodlands' thali is Madras style, at Rs. 27 ($2.05). You can also get idly (steamed rice cakes) and special rice dishes and sweets—all with a southern accent. In town there's a Woodlands at Nariman Point, so popular you may have to wait in line to get in. The Juhu Woodland's Garden Café is open from 6 a.m. to 11 p.m. weekdays, noon to 3 p.m. and 6 to 11 p.m. on Sunday and bank holidays; the Nariman Point Woodlands (tel. 2023499), from 11 a.m. to 11 p.m. Monday through Saturday, and on Sunday from 8 a.m. to 11 p.m.

For a thali with talent, try the **Tanjore Room** in the Taj Mahal Hotel, Apollo Bunder (tel. 2023366). Here, at dinner, you are graciously served on a gleaming brass platter more fancy in design than in the simple vegetarian restaurants, with a vast array, including rice, three different vegetables, condiments, puris (wheat bread discs), roti, papads, and a sweet, while being entertained by graceful classical Indian dancers accompanied by live music. As a finale to your meal, you might try paan (an Indian digestive of spices, betel nuts, enclosed in a betel leaf), which is served from an antique silver paandaan (special chest). All this—cuisine and concert—costs Rs. 75 ($5.75) and should be your vegetarian splurge in Bombay. The classical dance and music is on at regular intervals, about 15 minutes apart, from 8:15 to 11 p.m. The Tanjore Room serves lunch from 12:30 to 3 p.m. and dinner from 7:30 p.m. to midnight, every day.

CHINESE DINING AROUND TOWN: An unexpected find with delicious food and friendly atmosphere is **Flora,** Worli Seaface, A. Gaffar Khan Road, near Hiltop Hotel (tel. 4936602), where over 200 Chinese dishes run from Rs. 12 (90¢) to Rs. 47 ($3.60). Open every day except Chinese New Year, from 11:30 a.m. to 11:30 p.m. Other Chinese restaurants with reasonably priced menus and recommended foods are **The Chinese Room,** Kemp's Corners (tel. 8225068), open from noon to 3 p.m. and 5 to 7 p.m.; and the **Nanking,** C.S.

Maharaj Road (tel. 211825), open daily from 12:15 to 3 p.m. and 6:15 to 10:30 p.m. They both serve shark's-fin soup, fried rice, fish or chicken, and an assortment of sweet-and-sour dishes made with prawns, pork, and crispy vegetables. Often, one portion will serve two, so you can order different dishes and share. Lichees and other fruits are offered for dessert. Main-dish prices are about Rs. 25 ($1.90) to Rs. 30 ($2.30).

Try the **Kamling,** where the Chinese sign for happiness decorates the entry and the interior is accented in red. Located on V. Nariman Road (tel. 2042618), this restaurant offers you 209 choices, including the wonderful ye fu (stewed noodles with vegetables and crab) at Rs. 25 ($1.90) and chicken Canton at Rs. 35 ($3.70). There are about 21 ice cream treats also. Open from noon to 11:30 p.m. daily.

In the residential district of Cumballa Hills is **Chinatown,** 99 August Kranti Marg, Kemps Corner (tel. 8227147), which has one menu and two levels for dining—upstairs made slightly more attractive than downstairs with straw mats on the wall and Chinese lantern lighting. Recommended are shrimp in garlic sauce at Rs. 35 ($2.70) and spring rolls (a version of eggroll) at Rs. 18 ($1.40). There are also many other dishes in the Cantonese, Szechuan, and Mandarin styles, with 27 varieties of soup (some nearly meals in themselves) from which to choose your appetizer. Open daily from noon to 3 p.m. and 7 to 10 p.m.

Bombay is a wonderful place to eat seafood, and a fine place to try it prepared Szechuan style is the very splurgey velvet-walled **Golden Dragon** at the Taj Mahal Hotel (tel. 2023366), where dinner for two can run Rs. 500 ($38.45) and up if you eat modestly and stick to beer. For such a big tab, you could start with golden fried prawns, or have some crabs in black-bean sauce (not on the menu, but a specialty and made if requested), then chicken in garlic sauce or lamb with peppers, some noodles or rice, sweets, and tea. Open for lunch from 12:30 to 3 p.m., and from 7:30 p.m. to midnight for dinner.

The moderately priced **Chopsticks,** 90-A V. Nariman Rd., Churchgate (tel. 2049284), serves Haka foods (which are very highly seasoned) as well as other styles of Chinese cooking. The restaurant makes an effort to offer items not often on other menus: for instance, taro nest (diced boneless chicken cooked in chilis, herbs, and celery leaves, in a nest of potato sticks) for Rs. 65 ($5), and steamed noodle chicken for Rs. 30 ($2.30). Desserts include date pancakes and toffee bananas. Entrees range from Rs. 40 ($3.05) to Rs. 60 ($4.60), and hours are 12:30 to 3 p.m. and 7:30 p.m. to midnight. The Churchgate branch is nicely decorated with wood-carvings, wood and brick walls, and lantern lighting. Other branches are at 354 Vithal Bhai Patel Rd. (Linking Road; tel. 537789); Jewel Mahal A.C. Shopping Complex, and Seven Bungalows, Versova (tel. 625750). All have the same hours as Churchgate and all are open every day.

Across from Chopsticks in the Pheroz Building is **Nanking,** Apollo Pier Road (tel. 2020594), where the Ling brothers dish up some interesting seafood entrees in the Rs.-30 ($2.30) range. Try the pickled fish with a rice side dish, or let the Lings recommend something for you. Figure on Rs. 100 ($7.70) for two. Hours: 12:30 to 3 p.m. and 7:30 p.m. to midnight.

Finally, the new splurge Chinese spot in Bombay is the white-walled **China Garden,** Om Chambers, 23 August Kranti Marg, Kemp's Corner (tel. 8280841). Except for the phony plants and fast-food-quality table mats with horoscopes on them, this is a handsome restaurant. The bar, with big leather chairs and a waterfall, is an inviting place to sip a drink. In the dining room, walls are hung with modern drawings and semicircular mirrors which make the oblong room seem deeper than it is. Regal-looking white wooden

Regency Chinese chairs and banquettes, upholstered in muted Madras plaids, complete the pleasant decor. The restaurant seems overpopulated with people to serve you, but service can be very slow. While waiting, you can nibble on the give-away hot Chinese pickle on each table. Master Chef Nelson Wang tries hard—and succeeds at not being trite with his dishes. All 124 selections on the menu are listed with their Chinese names and explained in English. The entrees are mainly Rs. 65 ($5) to Rs. 80 ($6.15), although some vegetarian dishes are less. Interesting among them are chew has (no. 71), white prawns in ginger wine sauce; and moo goo mun fan (no. 97), a mild steamed rice in an earthen pot. Other choices include Chinese black beans with meat and baby vegetables, and the interesting no. 89, mun faan— fortune rice with oyster sauce and chicken and mushrooms. Iced lichees for dessert were crisp and refreshing. Originality, high quality, and interesting decor have their price; expect to pay Rs. 300 ($23.05) to Rs. 500 ($38.45) for two for a meal. If you split a beer, add Rs. 28 ($2.15), or stick to Chinese tea. Hours: 12:30 to 3 p.m. and 7:30 p.m. to midnight.

RICH MUGHLAI, KASHMIRI, AND TANDOORI MEALS—MEDIUM TO SPLURGE: Delhi Durbar, with branches near the Regal Cinema, Colaba (tel. 2025997), and at 197 P. Bapurao Marg, Grant Road (tel. 357977), is renowned in Bombay for its Mughlai foods and especially recommended for its mutton dishes for which this style of cooking is world famous. The distinctive flavors of Mughlai mutton dishes come from the elaborate masalas (spice mixtures) used in their preparation. At Delhi Durbar, you'll also enjoy the prices, which are generally under Rs. 40 ($3.05) for a number of the best mutton choices, including Durbar shahi mutton. On the menu are chicken dishes, also excellent in Mughlai cuisine, and Chinese foods (which are better eaten at one of the Chinese places in town). Open for lunch and dinner. The P. Bapurao branch is not air-conditioned.

At **Kwality** (in three locations: Colaba, Worli, and Kemp's Corner) there is a variety of Mughlai dishes for about Rs. 12 (90¢) to Rs. 48 ($3.70). Among these is sagwala mutton (made with a vegetable vaguely resembling spinach) and a prawn masala (curry). About the highest-priced item on the menu is a full chicken tandoori (made in the clay oven), which can serve two and makes a delicious meal served with nan (teardrop-shaped, tandoor-baked bread) and peas pulau, one portion large enough for two as a side dish. Open from 10:30 a.m. to midnight daily.

Berry's, on V. Nariman Road, near Churchgate Station (tel. 2046041), with wood-paneled walls and a Sun God mural, is open from 11:30 a.m. to 3:30 p.m. and 6:30 to 11:30 p.m. every day. Tandoori foods are the specialties, with a mixed grill this style at Rs. 50 ($3.85). Naan (rich Indian bread, teardrop in shape and baked right in the clay tandoori oven) is the preferred side dish. Biryani (chicken, rice, and spices, nuts, and fruits) cost Rs. 30 ($2.30). Murg musslam (a Mughlai chicken dish) is a Berry's Special, Rs. 70 ($5.40), and one of the highest-priced items on the menu. An excellent kulfi (Indian ice cream) is served at this restaurant. Ask for Berry's special menu to delve more deeply into the delicacies here. It lists elaborate, less well-known Mughlai dishes, Rs. 50 ($3.85) to Rs. 70 ($5.40). Each is explained: for instance, chicken maharaja is boneless chicken, made with dried fruit, eggs, and sauce. You eat in the main room or on the balcony.

Some very traditional Mughlai delicacies are served at **Sapna,** V. Nariman Road (tel. 2043687), where everyone is extremely attentive and eager to please. Inside there's a modern art mural using bold numerals; it has an outdoor café too. Try the chicken masala (a special curry) and you'll get one of the most famous dishes in Mughlai cookery, Rs. 22 ($1.70); roghan josh (a fragrantly spiced lamb curry cooked in ghee, which is clarified butter) costs around Rs. 24 ($1.85). Tandooris run from Rs. 22 ($1.70) for fish to Rs. 36 ($2.75) for a full chicken. Plain rice, at Rs. 12 (90¢) is good with any of the fancy dishes, and fresh fruit makes a good dessert, as do ice creams, Rs. 10 (75¢) to Rs. 18 ($1.40), the higher price for a special flavor such as tutti frutti. Sapna also serves continental cuisine and is proud of a dish called "chicken White House," stuffed with foie gras, for Rs. 32 ($2.45). The hours are noon to 11:30 p.m. every day. The bar is closed between 3 and 6 p.m.

Going up in price is **Kabab Corner,** in the Hotel Natraj (tel. 2044161), a rustic-looking place with thatched-roof alcoves to set off tweed banquettes. As the name implies, kebabs are a specialty here. The old nawabs were so fond of kebabs it is said they ate a different one every day of the year. A good way to act like a newab and to sample some of the tastiest tidbits on the menu is to order an assorted platter for about Rs. 50 ($3.85). There are also tandoor dishes, kebabs and others, for around Rs. 45 ($3.45). The Corner is open for breakfast from 7 to 10 a.m., for lunch from noon to 3 p.m., for snacks from 3 to 7:30 p.m., and for dinner from 8 p.m. to 12:30 a.m.

A bit of a splurge, and worth a Rs.-25 ($1.90) taxi ride on top of it, for those interested in eating well-prepared Mughlai dishes not found on every other menu in town is the **Copper Chimney,** Dr. Annie Besant Road (tel. 4924488), near the race course. A spacious room, with copper-shaded lanterns and wood and bamboo accents, it has a glassed-in kitchen complete with copper chimney as a focal point where you can watch chefs at work preparing your food. You probably can't go wrong with anything on the menu, which runs largely about Rs. 20 ($1.55) to Rs. 25 ($1.90) for vegetarian dishes and Rs. 35 ($2.70) to Rs. 45 ($3.45) for nonvegetarian. Each dish is described fully so you know the ingredients in your selections. For a three- to four-course dinner for two, consisting appetizers, entrees, side dishes, and dessert, figure on spending about Rs. 300 ($23.05) to Rs. 400 ($30.75). For this you might get some of my personal favorites, such as murg rashida (chicken baked with mint and herbs), roomali roti (handkerchief-thin bread), Banarasi (named for the holy Ganges city) pulao, which is assorted mixed vegetables with rice, and tandoori machi (whole fish tandoori style). Higher-priced items on the menu include jhinga sekela (shrimp with spices, cooked in the tandoori), at Rs. 85 ($6.55), and a house specialty, Peshawari raan (lamb in herbs and spices), for Rs. 75 ($5.75). For dessert, throw your calorie counter to the winds and try rasmalai (milk sweet) or malai firni (rice and rosewater sweet), each Rs. 14 ($1.05). Open from noon to 4 p.m. and 7 p.m. to 1 a.m. (last orders taken at midnight). A branch is soon to open in London.

Not under the same management, but sharing the same name, is the quietly tasteful, dimly lit **Copper Chimney,** at 18 K. Dubash Marg, Rampart Row (tel. 24468), also with well-prepared North Indian dishes cooked behind a glassed-in kitchen for your observation. Recommended highly here are charcoaled kebabs for about Rs. 40 ($3.05), and chelo kebab with rice, rich with cream and egg, at Rs. 45 ($3.45). A mutton chop costs Rs. 30 ($2.30), and a special vegetables in cream sauce is Rs. 25 ($1.90). Dinner for two will come to about Rs. 250 ($19.25). Hours are 12:30 to 3:30 p.m. and 7:30 p.m. to 12:30 a.m. every day. Behind the Prince of Wales Museum and handy for lunch after sightseeing there.

The foods at **Santoor,** Maker Arcade, Cuffe Parade (tel. 215449), near the Hotel President, are Mughlai and Kashmiri. A smallish restaurant, with a quiet brown color scheme and silk-shaded lamps, its mirrored walls give the room a spacious look. Specialties to try are chicken malai chop (with cream), at Rs. 30 ($2.30), and chana Peshawari, a puri with chickpeas, Rs. 16 ($1.25). Most entrees run Rs. 25 ($1.90) to Rs. 28 ($2.15). Regular patrons sip Kashmiri soda, made with salt and pepper, with their foods, but you may prefer yours plain. Open from 11:30 a.m. to 3:30 p.m. and 7:30 to 11:30 p.m.

Right on target for this book is the excellent value and good food at **Balwas' Restaurant**, Maker Bhawan, 3 Thackersey Marg (New Marine Lines; tel. 251108), where owner Yusuf Balwas is usually around to see that everything is running just right. Well-prepared tandooris are lower priced here than at some other restaurants, running an average of Rs. 14 ($1.05) to Rs. 20 ($1.55), in the non-air-conditioned section, where big overhead fans stir the breezes; and Rs. 4 (30¢) to Rs. 5 (40¢) more in the air-conditioned part. Open every day from 9:30 a.m. to 11 p.m.

Splurgey and pretty is the spacious **Moghul Room** at the Oberoi Towers, Nariman Point (tel. 2024343), open from 8 p.m. to midnight, where you can enjoy North Indian dancing and music with such delicious dishes as fish makhani and mutton begum bahar, accompanied by thin-as-paper roomali roti. There's a buffet here at lunch, but no entertainment then, though (see "Bombay's Buffets"). Next door, in the Oberoi (tel. 2024153) there's the elegant and hushed **Kandahar**, a soft setting of muted beiges, overlooking the pool, with delicious Northwest Frontier foods (kebabs and such) to tuck into Indian breads and enjoy along with highly attentive service and memorable surroundings. You'll pay Rs. 400 ($30.75) to Rs. 600 ($46.15) for three courses for two, not including beer.

Near the Welcomgroup SeaRock is the sophisticated **Daavat**, 21-25 Natasha Shopping Centre, 52 Hill Rd., Bandra (tel. 6402625). It's not easy to see from the road, so keep your eyes peeled for a discreet sign on a dark wooden door. This marble-floored restaurant has just a hint of Mughal architecture in the archways, and a pretty garden, pleasant for eating out when the weather's fine. Owner Amil N. Karamchandani takes food seriously, and has hired special traditional North Indian cooks to turn out some of the tastiest tandooris around, accompanied by biryani, naan, and roti. Figure on Rs. 200 ($15.40) for two, beer included. Open from 12:30 to 3:30 p.m. and 7:30 to 11:30 p.m.

CONTINENTAL AND ITALIAN CUISINE—HERE AND THERE: These restaurants feature continental-style and Western cooking, but of course offer Indian specialties too, and even Chinese dishes.

While an elaborate collection of woodcarvings from Nepal and South India adorn the walls at **Talk of the Town**, 143 Netaji Subhash Rd. (tel. 221074), the accent is on continental foods. Suggested are the filling soups at Rs. 17 ($1.30), grilled lobster at Rs. 120 ($9.25), and rich Indian sweets for dessert. A little outdoor café in front is a pleasant place for an espresso and sweet. Indian espresso is usually steamed with milk . . . so make it very clear to the waiter if you want it black or order *kona,* which is black. Open from 11 a.m. to midnight. Many Indian dishes on the menu are less expensive than the aforementioned. A band plays at Talk of the Town every night except Monday, from 8 p.m. to midnight.

An old favorite, **Gaylord's**, V. Nariman Road (tel. 294160), has been newly done up and sparkles with mirrors, gold accents, velvet chairs, and Renoir prints on the off-white wall walls. The big windows in front overlook a small outdoor café surrounded by well-manicured hedges—a nice place to sip a drink late in the afternoon. The Italian-continental specialties are about Rs. 35 ($2.70) and up; slightly over that range is cannelloni (with spinach and cheese) for Rs. 52 ($4), and then it's up a few notches to lobster, at Rs. 95

($7.30). The Indian vegetarian specialties rarely run higher than Rs. 29 ($2.25) and the non-vegetarian dishes hover around Rs. 55 ($4.25), with prawns tandoori at Rs. 85 ($6.55). Like some other restaurants, each dish is described so you know just what you'll be eating. Hours are 12:30 to 3 p.m. and 8 p.m. to midnight every day.

The oldest Italian Restaurant in Bombay is the **Lido Bar,** in the Ritz Hotel, J. Tata Road (tel. 220141), open from noon to 3 p.m. and 6:30 p.m. to midnight. The restaurant was started a number of years ago by a Ritz manager who missed his homeland. Today you find a rich minestrone, at Rs. 20 ($1.55), and spaghetti Napolitaine (with tomatoes) or con funghi (mushrooms), each Rs. 40 ($3.05). Chicken Florentine (with spinach), at Rs. 60 ($4.60), and vegetable lasagne, at Rs. 35 ($2.70), are featured on a menu including Italian, continental, and Indian dishes. Desserts and ice creams, are in the Rs.-20 ($1.55) range.

At the rustic-looking **Trattoria,** in the President Hotel, Cuffe Parade (tel. 4950808), a coffeeshop which resembles a country inn, with red-tile floors and ceramic plates hung on the walls, there's a buffet at noon and nicely prepared Italian dishes on the à la carte menu all through the day and night. Pizzas run Rs. 25 ($1.90) to Rs. 30 ($2.30); ravioli with riccotta, Rs. 42 ($3.25), which is also the price of some Italian seafood dishes; spaghetti with pesto sauce is Rs. 25 ($1.90). Also the hotel's coffeeshop, it's open 24 hours a day, in case you get a pizza attack at 3 a.m.

SPLURGING AROUND TOWN: In the super-splurge category, the **Café Royal** at the Oberoi Towers, Nariman Point (tel. 234343), flies the colors of the Bonaparte family—purple and green in case you're wondering—under an elaborate art nouveau ceiling, and offers only French foods in keeping with the theme. A three-course meal can easily run Rs. 500 ($38.45) to Rs. 700 ($53.85) for two, without wine or many cocktails, or a tip. Open from 12:30 to 3 p.m. for lunch and 8 p.m. to midnight for dinner.

At the stylish and sophisticated **La Rotisserie,** in the Oberoi, Nariman Point (tel. 2024343), a big crystal chandelier, and gorgeous jewels on some of the well-heeled guests are the only glittering objects in this understated room. The subtle cream-and-rust color scheme, complimented by blond woods and beautiful flower arrangements, complete the low-key theme—a lovely setting for a special meal. Prices are steep for high-quality, well-prepared food and attentive service. You can easily spend a minimum of Rs. 1,000 ($77) for a three- to four-course meal for two, not including wine, which can add Rs. 500 ($38.45) for a modest French import. Your memorable meal might include a choice of marinated prawns in two sauces; hot appetizers; Scottish smoked salmon; a charcoal grill, spit-roasted specialty, or exotic quail eggs with fresh mushrooms; and vegetable side dishes, followed by cheese and fruits, or mousse, parfait, or pastry—to cite only a few items on the menu. Hours: 12:30 to 3 p.m. and 8 p.m. to midnight.

Bombay's only restaurant specializing in seafood is the **Lobster Pot,** at the Welcomgroup SeaRock, Bandra (tel. 6425454), a striking restaurant done entirely in black and white accented with peacock-blue napkins. Lobsters, pomfrets (like Dover sole), prawns, and a host of other creatures of the deep are fresh and nicely prepared—and steep in price. Figure on spending Rs. 500 ($38.45) to Rs. 600 ($46.15) for a three-course dinner for two, without wine. Open from 12:30 to 3 p.m. and 8 p.m. to midnight.

ROOFTOP ROOMS WITH VIEWS, AND HIGH PRICES TOO: If you eat in the **Rendezvous** on top of the Taj Mahal Inter-Continental, Apollo Bunder

(tel. 24366), you get a wonderful view of Bombay, fine service, and elegant atmosphere. Plan on about Rs. 500 ($38.45) to Rs. 700 ($53.85) for a three-course meal for two, without wine. Add Rs. 500 ($38.45) to Rs. 600 ($46.15) for an imported vin ordinaire. Unfortunately wines produced in India are not table quality—they are too sweet or heavy, or taste like vermouth. The ambience is refined, and well-prepared French-accented foods are attentively served. Some choices you might enjoy are mushrooms vinaigrette, chilled tomato-and-orange soup, tiger prawns, lamb with sorrel and mint, plus vegetable timbale, sorbet, soufflés. Open from 12:30 to 3 p.m. for lunch and 7:30 p.m. to midnight for dinner. Dance band at night.

Adjoining the Rendezvous is the intimate and cozy **Apollo Bar,** where you can sip a drink and soak up the view between 11:30 a.m. and 3 a.m., and enjoy a light nouvelle cuisine lunch daily for about Rs. 100 ($7.70). At night there's a pianist. Drinks are expensive: for instance, a large sherry for Rs. 45 ($3.45), a small sherry for Rs. 30 ($2.30), VSOP for Rs. 60 ($4.60), and imported wines from Rs. 450 ($34.60); Indian spirits run about Rs. 30 ($2.30) a peg. A nice place for a special romantic interlude.

Two revolving restaurants offer distinctive views: **The Top,** atop the Ambassador, V. Nariman Road (tel. 291131), and the **Palace of the West Empress** at the Welcomgroup Searock, Bandra (tel. 6425454). Figure on Rs. 500 ($38.45) to Rs. 700 ($53.85) for two, without drinks.

SNACKING AND EATING ON AND AROUND VITHAL BHAI PATEL (LINKING) ROAD: Two snack shops—**Open House,** at 537 Vithal Bhai Patel Rd. (tel. 546118), and **Indian Fast Food,** opposite the National College—are both spic-and-span places for snacks and light meals. There are burgers and pizza as well as ice cream, sweets, and soft drinks, coffee, or tea. Open from 11 a.m. to midnight. Also on Vithal Bhai Patel Road is **Walk-In,** another clean snack place, open from 11 a.m. to 11 p.m. All three are nice to know about if you're staying out this way or want to stop for something on the way to Juhu or the airport. Prices are moderate: Rs. 15 ($1.15) to Rs. 20 ($1.55) for light entrees.

On Vithal Bhai Patel Road as well is a branch of Bombay's well-known **Chopsticks** Chinese restaurant. Menu, prices, and hours are about the same as at the Churchgate branch: Rs. 40 ($3.05) to Rs. 60 ($4.60) for entrees. Hours are 12:30 to 3 p.m. and 7:30 p.m. to midnight. There's a buffet on Sunday from 12:30 to 3 p.m. for Rs. 50 ($3.85).

The place to go for a splurge in this area is **Manjit da Dhaba,** at the corner of West and Main Avenue, opposite Grindlays Bank, Vithal Bhai Patel (Linking) Road, Santa Cruz (tel. 539362). Dhaba means roadside village restaurant, something akin to a U.S. truckstop café. And while the old legend is not necessarily true that American truckers know the best wayside eateries, they insist it's positively so in India—"for authentic North Indian food, go to a dhaba," I've long been told. Now someone's made it easier: they've brought the dhaba to me and you, in the guise of this restaurant (and a couple of others in Bombay I didn't have time to review) which strives to create authentic truckstop atmosphere and their typical foods. At Manjit's entrance is a curious menagerie—rabbits, monkeys, cockatoos—coexisting peacefully in a rockery. Inside the compound are actually three restaurants and a bar—Manjit's, Viashnu, (vegetarian) and Chinese, and Tabela, a permit (bar) room—but the others don't matter much. Manjit, named after the owner's son, is currently one of Bombay's "in" places. Here, you eat around a huge mango tree, in chairs with rush seats and backs, on crude wooden tables set under palm thatch hung with kitchen kettles and cages of exotic birds. Specialties are finger-foods—flatware is not used. Instead, generous hunks of tandooried kid, lamb, or murgh de tang chimney walla (stuffed chicken leg) are scooped up in Indian breads; or like dal Bukhara, a delicious black dal with tomato purée and pomegranate seeds, served in handis (casserole dishes). The fare, in the Mercedes, not truck driver's, realm is at top of the speedometer: about Rs. 400 ($30.75) for a three- to four-course meal for two, including a sweet and a beer.

Now for the other restaurants sharing the compound: vegetarian **Viashnu** has a costly silver thali, Rs. 100 ($7.70) for nine dishes and unlimited refills; cheaper thalis cost Rs. 75 ($5.75) for four dishes and Rs. 50 ($3.85). As for eating Chinese, you're better off at one of the restaurants specializing in this style of food.

Manjit de Dhaba is open from 8 p.m. to midnight, and somewhat later on weekends. Ask for Sheikh Noor Ahmed, the captain, and he'll see to your order personally. Better make a reservation so there'll be room for you among Bombay's movers and shakers who are here in abundance.

SWEETS AND LIGHT SNACKS: Here air conditioning ceases to exist for the most part—indeed some of the most enjoyable places are open air or open to the street.

Tea costs Rs. 2.50 (20¢) per cup at the plainer-than-plain **Tea Centre** on Resham Bhavan, right near all the restaurants on V. Nariman Road. Hours are 11 a.m. to 7 p.m.; closed Sunday.

On Homi Modi Street two or three doors away from the Piccolo Café is the **Coffee Centre,** where you can get good fresh-brewed Indian coffee and snacks for Rs. 3 (23¢) to Rs. 5 (40¢).

For Indian snacks—grains, nuts, spicy fritters, and the best panipuris (tiny puffs of dough filled with tamarind water) or bhelpuri (sweet-and-sour sauced mixture of grains, lentils, chopped vegetables, herbs, and chutney), or any number of other between-meal savouries—head to **Chowpatty Beach,** most famous snacking spot in town. Part of the fun of buying your treat is browsing for your snack among the gaily striped stalls, then downing it on the spot. A panipuri requires skill: it must be eaten in one bite to keep the luscious juices from squirting all over your shirt. The snack foods are safe to eat, with one reminder: it's more hygienic to have them served on banana leaves or in a paper cone than on crockery plates that have been washed in a bucket of dubious-looking lukewarm water. Rs. 3 (23¢) will get you a couple of panipuris, and for Rs. 1.50 (11¢) you can get a cone of some other savoury snack. Fresh coconuts opened on the spot can act as the fire extinguisher if your snack is too hot. Chowpatty stalls are open from about 3 p.m. to around midnight.

Other snack stalls around the city near the office buildings sell similar snacks for little pickups at any time of the day.

One of the nicest things about Bombay is the numerous clean fresh fruit-juice bars around the town. Best of all is the tidy **Sukh Sagar,** opposite Chowpatty on S. V. P. Road, partly hidden by a bus stand and decorated with seasonal fruits strung up around the entrance. A long, narrow place, the electric juicers are always in action from 8 a.m. to 1 a.m., churning out every kind of fresh juice. Prices start at Rs. 7 (55¢) and go to around Rs. 12 (90¢). Try the pomegranate (in season) for a tart taste treat. Down the lane, nearer the beach, is Sukh Sagar's snack shop offering some of the richest kulfi (ice cream) in town. Try saffron kulfi, Rs. 7 (55¢), or any other flavor. Served also are pizzas, idlis, vegetable curry, and bread—all under Rs. 13 ($1). Hours: 9 a.m. to 1 a.m. Very clean.

Almost next door at Chowpatty Seaface is M. K. Tripathi's tiny, tidy **New Kulfi Center,** tucked away under the fly-over, renowned throughout Bombay for excellence in Indian ice cream (kulfi). Familiar fruit flavors—mango, orange, and pineapple, to name a few—cost Rs. 5 (40¢) a serving; and exotic flavors such as cashew, pista (pistachio), almond, fig, and such cost about Rs. 9 (70¢) per serving. Serious browsers—those intent on buying—can have tastes before making their final decisions. Open every day from 10 a.m. to 2 a.m.

For pizza, try the **New Yorker,** across from Chowpatty Beach (tel. 35 6108), open from noon to midnight and all done up with a Statue of Liberty and Manhattan skyline mural. The "New Yorker Pizza" is made with onions, peppers, mushrooms, tomatoes, and cheese: Rs. 26 ($2) for a 7½-inch pie to serve two or possibly three. Other types of pizza as well. Recommended also is **Pizza King,** Nylor House, 254/DZ Dr. Annie Besant Rd., Worli (tel. 4939757), and 6 Tirupati Shopping Centre, Warden Road (tel. 4926058).

On Netaji Subhash Road, the **Hotel Natraj** (tel. 294161) has an ice-cream parlor that looks like a little amphitheater; and around the corner, **K. Rustom's & Co.,** Brabourne Stadium, Churchgate (opposite the Hotel Ambassador), a department store on N. V. Nariman Road, serves kulfi sandwiches, ice cream between two rich biscuits, for Rs. 6 (45¢); without the biscuits, various flavors are Rs. 3 (23¢) to Rs. 5 (40¢).

On B. Desai Road, **Snowman's** is the place to satisfy a craving for rich Western-style ice cream in familiar fruit, chocolate, and vanilla flavors, as well as more inspired concoctions, for Rs. 7 (55¢) per dip. There's also a machine for soft ice cream. Very popular, clean, and efficient.

Waikiki, clean and cheerful, with three locations—near Flora Fountain, opposite the New Empire Cinema, and opposite Amber Cinema in Andheri (not far from Juhu)—is open from 10 a.m. to midnight for ice cream, burgers, and soft drinks. Two can get a light meal here for Rs. 60 ($4.60) to Rs. 100 ($7.70).

Right in the center of everything at Flora Fountain is a Bombay institution, the **Fountain Dry Fruit Stall,** where the owner sits cross-legged overseeing a jumbo assortment of irresistible nuts and sweets. Badami (a rich almond confection) and pedah (a milk-and-sugar sweet) are sold by the gram at prices quoted by the owner, as are all the items here. Cashews, for instance, run Rs. 8 (60¢) per 100 grams (about a quarter of a pound), and sweets are higher.

For refreshment when shopping on S. Bhagat Singh Road, stop at **Edward VIII** (no. 113-A is the address) or **Canteena Juice Centre** (near Delhi Durbar), two more clean fresh-juice bars. Try fresh apple or carrot, each Rs. 6 (45¢) or splurge on pomegranate at Rs. 20 ($1.55), or have a falooda (ice cream, milk, and raspberry syrup), a Bombay favorite, for Rs. 8 (60¢).

With several immaculate sweetmeat shops, **Brijwasi** (all over Bombay, and in the suburb of Santa Cruz) is synonymous with high-quality sweets at prices running around Rs. 44 ($3.40) to Rs. 50 ($3.85) on the average per kilo. Halwa is only one of the items to buy in the shop. Any sweet is a perfect and appreciated gift if you're invited to tea or a meal at a local home. All Indian sweets are somewhat sweeter than sweet when it comes to describing their taste generally. Savouries are also sold.

While sightseeing around Malabar Hill, two treats await you on Babulnath Road. At tiny, unpretentious **Dave Farsan and Sweet Mart** (open from 6:30 a.m. to 9 p.m.) you can buy the jalebi (pretzel-shaped syrup-dipped sweet) many Bombayites insist are the best in town—Rs. 24 ($1.85) per kilo. And nearby you can see the Babulnath Temple with its 200-year-old statue of Krishna looking quite sweet in fine silks and jewels.

All the top hotels have coffeeshops, many open 24 hours a day. Most pleasant for coffee or tea, a snack, or light lunch is the stately low-key **Sea Lounge** in the old wing of the Taj Mahal Inter-Continental (not open around the clock). At the Sea Lounge, a great view of the sea with rowboats and yachts, comfort, good coffee, and old-world elegance give you the unbeatable combination for a refreshing pause in a hectic day. High-priced, however.

EATING, DISCOING, SNACKING, AND SPLURGING AT JUHU BEACH:

For a splurge meal, head for one of the big hotels. For well-prepared Mughlai foods at moderate prices, try **Moghal Mahal,** next to the Centaur, Juhu (tel. 6144924), open from 11:30 a.m. to 3:30 p.m. for lunch and 7:30 p.m. to midnight for dinner. For Rs. 65 ($5), you can get a complete meal consisting of a pre-dinner drink of fresh lime and soda, soup, a grilled item or tandoori chicken (or fish tikka or shish kebab), roti, nan or pulao, and ice cream. There are two levels for diners and grillwork dividers to add a decorative touch.

Also at Juhu, **Prithvi Café,** adjoining Prithvi Theatre (tel. 620969), serves snacks and light meals in a tiny, pleasant plant-filled patio café. Prices start around Rs. 12 (90¢); a thali meal is less, Rs. 10 (75¢). Soft drinks as well as Irish coffee without whisky (Irish coffee without Irish whisky?) cost Rs. 7 (55¢), Rs. 12 (90¢) with whisky or brandy. Plays are presented every night in the theater in both English and Hindi. You'll want to check to see what's playing to get tickets for an English-speaking night or you might end up seeing *Khoob Milai Jodi* (Neil Simon's *Odd Couple* in Hindi).

Hours: lunch from 1 to 2:30 p.m., snacks from 4 p.m. to midnight, and dinner from 8 p.m. to midnight.

Xanadu is the name of the discothèque at Horizon Hotel (tel. 571411), open from around 9 p.m. to the "wee" hours.

At any time for real snackers, there are stalls along **Juhu Beach** where you can buy "trash," those tasty snacks of grains, nuts, spiced fritters, or panipuris dripping with tamarind sauce. Be sure to eat them off clean palm leaves rather than barely washed dishes. On Sunday, in addition to a treat to eat, there's a feast for the eyes when the beach takes on a festive air and camels, horses, and merry-go-rounds take kids riding on family outing day.

3. Shopping

You can buy all over India, but you can shop in Bombay better than anywhere else in the country. Indeed, on first impressions the city seems one gargantuan bazaar, with an endless choice of stores bursting with merchandise for every budget. There are handcraft emporiums, antique and jewelry markets, and boutiques carrying the kinds of fashions Westerners really enjoy and want to take home with them.

The following are a few of my shopping suggestions. There are more in "Where to Buy," a pamphlet put out by the Government of India Tourist Office, 123 M. Karve Rd. Better yet are the shop discoveries you make on your own. Generally, shops in south Bombay are closed on Sunday; from Dadar onward, they're closed on Thursday and open on Sunday.

You bargain in all but the price-fixed stores and expect to find the most resistance in stores where many Westerners shop and merchants long ago discovered that they'll usually pay the asking price. As a general rule, merchandise is more expensive in the shops around the top hotels, but you're paying a little more for preselection of good-quality merchandise. Even so, prices are not totally out of line in the top shops and emporiums.

When buying antiques, be sure the merchant supplies the forms you need to export them from the country.

Should you decide to buy a lasting memory of your trip in the form of some gold jewelry set with diamonds or other precious stones, be aware that you need a certificate to get your glittering prize out of the country. Be sure to ask for it when making your purchase.

For a good survey of handcrafts from all over India, the place to head is the **Cottage Industries Emporium,** 34C S. Maharaj Marg (formerly Apollo Pier Road), where there is no bargaining for the interesting inventory. You'll find easy-to-pack beautifully embroidered placemats in cotton or silk, delicate-looking rings set with semiprecious stones. All kinds of scarves and ties in bold and subtle prints and solids in lustrous silks. Prices for silks vary greatly according to quality of the textile. You can also get ready-to-wear for everyone here. This is just a small sampling of the emporium's many wares. Open every day but Sunday from 10 a.m. to 6:30 p.m.

Many of the states have emporiums in Bombay, a number of them in the **World Trade Centre** on Cuffe Parade. They are supposed to be open from 10:30 a.m. to 1 p.m. and 3 to 5 p.m., but I found that this varied widely. All did open at 10:30 a.m., but some did not close for lunch; others did, but stayed open late until 8 p.m. Most were open until 2 p.m. on Saturday. All were closed on Sunday. Among the World Trade Centre shops are: **Chinar** (Kashmir and Jammu), 25 North World Trade Centre, and also **Kashmir** in the Co-operative Insurance Building on Sir P. Mehta Road, with rugs, papier-mâché, woodwork, and interesting shopping bags; **Trimurti** (Maharashtra), 30 World Trade Centre, with leather sandals, brasswares, mirror-studded silk salvar kamiz (tunic and trousers); **Mrignayani** (Madhya Pradesh), 14 World Trade Centre, offering hand-painted tussah silks, jute bags, spun copper figures; **Phulkari** (Punjab), 13 World Trade Centre, with charming costumed dolls, folk paintings, men's silk kurtas, and the intricate embroidered phulkari fabric for which the shop was named.

Also **Gangotri** (Uttar Pradesh), at 38 World Trade Centre, has lovely chiffon saris and kurtas (tunics) with delicate shadow embroidery, a specialty of the state. At **Himachal Pradesh Emporium,** also in the World Trade Centre, there are practical and attractive hand-loomed fringed woolen shawls. Also in the World Trade Centre, **Trimurti,** Maharashtra's boutique, has Kolhapuri sandals—you soak them in water and let them dry on your feet for a perfect fit—as well as charming red-painted clay Ganeshas ($2), made by villagers and wonderful gifts.

Still more state emporiums are **Bihar** (Dhun Nur), on Sir P. Mehta Road; **Black Partridge** (Haryana), Air-India Building, ground floor, Nariman Point; **Gurjari** (Gujarat), Khetan Bhavan, opposite the Ritz Hotel on J. Tata Road; **Kairali** (Kerala), in the Nirmal Building, ground floor, Nariman Point; **Poompuhar** (Tamil Nadu), U.N. Parsuram & Co., D. Naoriji Road; and **Rajasthan,** at 230 D. Naoroji Rd.

Back at the World Trade Centre, **Aabushan Curios and Jewelry,** open from 10:30 a.m. to 7 p.m., specializes in diamonds and colored stones. Diamonds range from Rs. 1,500 ($115.50) to Rs. 15,000 ($1,154), and one-of-a-kind silver jewelry, Rs. 200 ($15.40) to Rs. 2,000 ($153.85).

For everything from foods to fancy clothes, try **Akbarally's,** a department store with the atmosphere of a bazaar, at 45 V. Nariman Rd., and at Shri Sai Darshan Apartments, S. V. Road, Santa Cruz, the latter in the suburbs and open on Sunday.

At Chowpatty Seaface, the hushed marble interiors of **Amratlal Bhimj Zaveri** (open from 10:30 a.m. to 7:30 p.m.; closed Sunday) are dotted with plants and pools in an opulent setting for extravagant jewelry, much of it made especially for this shop. It's not unusual to spend Rs. 50,000 ($3,846) for a simple 22-karat necklace at this shop. There are also little 22-karat snowflakes for a cool Rs. 1,000 ($77) among the less expensive wares. The shop also has a branch in Jhaveri Bazaar.

Behind the Taj Hotel there's a quarter mile of bargains in shops running from the Regal Cinema to the Temple, on the road which in a former incarnation was Colaba Causeway and is now **S. Bhagat Singh Marg.** The stores are open every day but Sunday, from around 10 a.m. to 7 to 8:30 p.m. Addresses are listed where I found them, but the shops can be located by name as you stroll.

At **Sambena,** there are leather handbags in all sizes and shapes, from Rs. 100 ($7.70) to Rs. 700 ($53.85).

Across the road at **Olga's** (open from 10 a.m. to 8 p.m.), beguiling children's clothes include toddlers' dresses appliquéed with little ducks carrying umbrellas and other outfits for boys and girls ages 18 months to 6 years.

Metro Footwear, 19 Abubakar Mansion, S. Bhagat Singh Road, has fairly up-to-date Western footwear such as high-heeled sandals and men's shoes, and salesmen who skillfully intercept boxed merchandise tossed from the balcony to customers on the salesfloor. Hours: 10 a.m. to 8:30 p.m.

Right behind the Regal Cinema, **Dadlani Silk Store** has a huge selection of kurtas (tunics) and caftans in cotton, some low-priced, as well as higher priced silk. Silk scarves, if not of the finest quality, are pretty nonetheless and make nice gifts. The shop has a branch at Sun-N-Sand Hotel at Juhu Beach.

A must for serious collectors of antiques—and all inveterate browsers— is **Phillips,** in the Indian Merchants Mansion on Madame Cama Road, opposite the Regal Cinema (open from 9 a.m. to 1 p.m. and 2:30 to 6:30 p.m.; closed Sunday), which was established in 1860 and is a treasure trove of relics from the Raj period. There are, for example, 15,000 or more prints, sketches, and engravings documenting the 18th and 19th centuries, plus painted Staffordshire animals and Lowestoft porcelain—an 18th- and 19th-century import from China—bowls, platters, and tureens. Valuable and beautiful old glass, coins, buttons, rings, medals, jades and ivories, 19th-century vases, épergnes, and bowls abound here. Also for sale are Indian miniature paintings, which go up into the thousands for something old and detailed and valuable, and a rare collection of old bidriware (items elegantly inlaid with zinc, copper, lead, tin, and stones). Don't hurry when shopping at Phillips (or anywhere in India). A few minutes spent chatting with Mr. Issa, the owner, or one of his knowledgeable staff, can help you learn the history of your purchase, which will be reliably dated and documented for export formalities by the shop.

Near the Regal Cinema are a number of shops with good selections of Indian silver which, as in Mexico, is a mixture of alloys and silver, and in India, generally sold by weight. Behind the Regal Cinema, **AK Essajee,** Suleman Chambers, on Baltery Street, Apollo Bunder, opposite the Cottage Industries Emporium, has an excellent and huge selection of silver, bangles, necklaces, and belts. Nearby, **Framroz Sorabji Khan Co.,** in the Regal Cinema Building (open from 9:30 a.m. to 6 p.m.; closed Sunday), specializing in old pieces, guarantees its baubles to be 90% silver and claims to have pieces about 100 years old. Also nearby, **Jehangir Khan** has old textiles, sari borders, and silver, including silver fish which Parsis believe bring good luck, and luckily for you, can be bought in this shop.

From Apollo Bunder, buses 132 and 121 go to B. Desai Road, where there are abundant shopping opportunities in stores that are open generally from 10 a.m. to 8 p.m. every day but Sunday.

The **Cymroza Art Gallery,** 72 B. Desai Rd., features exhibitions that change frequently. When I looked in, table linens were on display and on sale, but when you get there some other type of item may be. It could be jewelry or handcrafts or any other number of wares. Open from 10 a.m. to 7:30 p.m.

At **Benzer,** 49 B. Desai Rd., a posh, pricey air-conditioned shop, churidars (tunic and trousers) are expensive and attractive.

At 63A/B B. Desai, **Amarson's Department Store** (open from 9 a.m. to 8 p.m.; closed Sunday) has an excellent selection of costume jewelry, especially bangles in silver, for Rs. 75 ($5.75) to Rs. 300 ($23.05) for a pair. It's popular with Bombay women who crowd around the counter looking for a favorite style among the many bangles.

While spending your rupees in and about the B. Desai Road shops, you might want to take a **sightseeing break** by taxiing a few blocks up the coastal road to Mahalaxmi Temple, Bombay's oldest temple and dedicated to Lakshmi, goddess of wealth. Nearby is Sadubella Temple (across from the Cadbury Chocolate sign), much newer than the other temple, and also an interesting and restful place to wander for a few moments.

An unusual shop in the B. Desai area is **Kimavanti,** 8 Peddah Rd. (formerly Carmichael Road), a shop located in jewelry designer Chandu Moraraji's garden and featuring some of her handsome one-of-a-kind modern pieces. There is also a tasteful selection of scarves, bags, and accessories, all at prices moderate to high. Hours are 10 a.m. to 6 p.m. Monday to Friday.

Back in the fort, **Ethnic Heart,** Chetana Art Gallery, near Jehangir Art Gallery, Kala Ghoda (open from 11 a.m. to 7 p.m.; closed Sunday), is a tiny little shop with a tasteful and interesting selection of items created by traditional weavers and crafts people of Andhra, Orissa, and Maharashtra such as hand-loomed saris, leather puppets, toys, scroll paintings, and embroideries. This is the shop for an unusual gift for yourself or a friend. Not cheap, however.

To concentrate on the jewelers (at least 200 of the more than 3,000 in Bombay), zero in on the intersection of Kalbadevi and Sheikh Memon Streets, commencing at the Cotton Exchange (near Mahatma Jyotiba Phule Market), which is officially known as **Jhaveri Bazaar.** This is one of Bombay's oldest most crowded and fascinating areas . . . which you should walk through browsing at the shops displaying gems, gold, and silver in such great abundance that even Shah Jahan would have been impressed. In some of the little shops that are open to the street, customers sit cross-legged on the floor bargaining over 24-karat gold bangles. Shops 39 and 47 have antique silver jewelry, and at Shop 62, Siroya Champalal Uttamchand sells new silver jewelry. In front of this shop sit craftsmen winding beads by hand on silky threads, working almost too fast for the eye to follow.

If all this is too rich for your blood, you can go over to **Mangaldass Market,** nearby, which has reasonably priced saris—even more reasonably priced after you bargain.

Reasonable is the last word you'd use to describe the extravagantly beautiful saris, silks, and brocades in the lineup of special shops over near the Back Bay on M. Karve Marg. The most popular of this group is **Kala Niketan,** 95 Pravin Court, M. Karve Marg, which is usually jammed with shoppers unless you get there at 9:30 a.m.—before opening time. In the store are fabulous assortments of saris, going as high as Rs. 25,000 ($1,923), for something filigreed in pure gold and silver and suitable for a wealthy bride. To make one square inch of some of these elaborate fabrics can take eight weavers one whole day. The prices go down to Rs. 65 ($5) to Rs. 130 ($10) for a little, packable portable cosmetic case in a lovely piece of patterned silk. Kala Niketan also has a store in Amarpali Shopping Centre. Other silk, sari, and brocade stores on M. Karve Marg worth looking into are **Roop Kala, Indian Art Palace, Indian States and Eastern Agency, John Roberts, Roop Milan, Anjali,** and **Kala Darshan.** Their hours are generally 10 a.m. to 7:30 p.m.

Back in the center of things is **Khadi-Village Industries Emporium,** 286 D. Naoriji Rd. (open from 10 a.m. to 6:30 p.m.; closed for lunch from 1:30 to 2:30 p.m. and all day Sunday), has two floors of price-fixed merchandise, with especially good selections of hand-spun and hand-woven textiles. Other items include mirror-studded shoulder bags, greeting cards painted on Bodhi leaves, Indian toys, and jewelry.

Another old standby, at 221 D. Naoroji Rd., is **Handloom House.** You might stop by for a good selection of textiles from every corner of India—saris, scarves, shawls, and more. The hours are 10 a.m. to 6 p.m. weekdays, to 7 p.m. on Saturday; closed Sunday.

For dedicated collectors and indefatigable bargain hunters, there's **Chor Bazaar** (Thieves Market), near Mohammed Ali Road, about a Rs. 15 ($1.15) taxi from the center, and open every day but Friday and Sunday. From the riot of merchandise, you can assemble an automobile, furnish a house, stock a china closet, find antique clocks, unstrung beads, half-strung guitars, ribbons, bangles, picture frames, china, and copper pots. The merchants heap their treasures in tiny shops, spread them on the streets, or wander among the crowds holding their wares aloft on wooden trees. Amid all this chaos, the most interesting shops are found on Mutton Street. They have woodcarvings, old coins, glass, silver, ivory, paintings, jewelry, and that's for starters only. Asking prices are very high. Haggle!

Finally, secondhand book vendors spread their wares on the walks near Flora Fountain. Look carefully, you may find a valuable treasure.

SUBURBAN SHOPPING: If you're staying near the airport or Juhu Beach, shopping at **Amarpali Shopping Center,** Juhu Vile Parle Scheme, V. M. Road, near Woodlands' Garden Café, is a convenient place to hunt bargains. A quick check of shops revealed a wide variety of wares from artworks to old watches. In the good assortment at **Desco,** there are little sandalwood souvenirs such as letter openers for about Rs. 13 ($1), as well as big rosewood elephants intricately inlaid with ivory chips for thousands of rupees. The shop is open from 10 a.m. to 8:30 p.m. and closed on Sunday. At another shop, **Indiana** (open from 9:30 a.m. to 8 p.m. every day), there are expensive antique church figures and contemporary bronzes, reasonably priced. Also in this center is a branch of the expensive silk shop Kala Niketan.

4. Seeing the City

An early stop on your exploration of Bombay should certainly be **Malabar Hill,** at the western side of town. Here there's a delightfully landscaped park clinging to the side of the hill.

Needless to say, there's a wonderful view of the city curving around the bay and the best place to see this is from a table in the little **Naaz** restaurant, open from 9 a.m. to 11 p.m.

Across the street on top of a covered reservoir are the renowned **Hanging Gardens** (now called Sir P. Mehta Gardens), where the old English art of topiary is practiced: here privet bushes are trained, cut, and trimmed in such shapes as cows, giraffes, monkeys, oxen, and elephants. Pleasant to stroll through in the evening but they're not much shelter in the broiling sun of early afternoon.

Just beyond the trees, at the far end of the garden, are the **Towers of Silence,** where devout Parsis take their dead to be eaten by vultures. Grisly as this sounds, it has been a Parsi custom—the sect originally came from Persia —for centuries and owes its origin to Parsi respect for sacred soil, which shouldn't be corrupted with rotting flesh.

The only part of this procedure that can be seen, of course, is the flock of vultures hovering ominously overhead, but a scale model of the towers can be seen in the **Prince of Wales Museum** downtown.

Just down Malabar Hill, in the opposite direction from the Towers of Silence, is an interesting **Jain temple** that is worth brief inspection. Back on the promenade—Netaji Subhash Road—the famous **Chowpatty Beach** is about one mile down, going toward town. Here it's always lively, with scores of stalls selling tasty tidbits, fortune tellers, jugglers, and even a masseur or two. The beach is renowned for its association with the fiery (verbal) struggles for Indian independence and still today is a popular spot for soapbox orators.

The **Taraporewala Aquarium** (open from 11 a.m. to 8 p.m., closed Monday; entry is Rs. 1, 7½¢) also on Netaji Subhash Road, is probably the best in the country, with the biggest crowds always around the fascinating tank of octopuses and striped sea snakes.

The **Prince of Wales Museum** (open from 10 a.m. to 6:30 p.m., October to February; 10 a.m. to 6 p.m., July to September; 10 a.m. to 6:30 p.m., March to June; always closed Monday) definitely needs a few hours for full appreciation. Unlike most museums, it can't be covered in a fast run around—at least, you won't want to rush when you see some of its treasures. The extensive collection of fascinating 18th- and 19th-century miniatures, one flight up, delays most art lovers for a while (inexpensive reproductions are for sale in the lobby), and on the same floor are elegantly carved ivory artworks as well as jade and Indian bronze images. A rich collection of Nepalese and Tibetan art occupies one whole gallery and probably has few equals anywhere. The museum was named after George V, who laid its foundation stone in 1905. Free Tuesday; Rs. 2 (15¢) otherwise.

Highest sightseeing viewpoint is the 260-foot clock tower, the **Rajabai Tower,** above the University Library on Mayo Road. Once the tower could be climbed via its spiral staircase, but that's no longer allowed.

The city's **zoo** (open from 7 a.m. to 7 p.m.) is only so-so, but far more than just so-so are the attractive **Veermata Jijabai Bhonsle Udyan** (formerly Victoria Gardens) in which it is situated. Take bus 1 or 4. The **Victoria and Albert Museum** on the grounds is open all days except Monday and eight public holidays, between 10:30 a.m. and 5 p.m. On Sunday it's 8:30 a.m. to 4:45 p.m.; on Thursday it's 10 a.m. to 4:45 p.m. and free. Admission stops at 4:45 on all days except Thursday when it's stopped earlier.

Exhibits are divided into sections, covering several vast subject areas— agriculture, village life, armory, cottage industries, costumes, fine arts, fossils, coins, minerals, old Bombay, geology, religion, and mythology—each of which can command your attention endlessly.

Up in the northwest section of the city, the **Breach Candy Swimming Pool,** Bhulabhai Desai Road (tel. 364381), is right on the beach (no. 121 bus to Cumballa Hill) and charges a small membership fee for tourists. A little farther up the coast you'll see a famous Muslim shrine, **Haji Ali,** on a causeway that connects it with the mainland 500 yards away. At this point, on the other side of the coast highway, is the **Mahalaxmi Race Course** (races on Sunday, November to April, 2 to 5 p.m.), which can be visited by tourists upon presentation of Rs. 6 (45¢) and an introduction card from the Tourist Office. This gets you in the first enclosure only. Special badges, costing Rs. 22 ($1.70) for the classics, are needed for members' enclosure.

A memorial to Mahatma Gandhi, containing pictures and books by and about the late guru, is **Mani Bhavan** (open from 9:30 a.m. to 6 p.m.), near the Gowalia Tank, a short walk up Laburnam Road from Chowpatty Beach. Admission is Rs. 2 (15¢).

Mahatma Jyotiba Phule Market (formerly Crawford) is located at the corner of Carnac and D. Naoroji Roads, about a mile north of Horniman Circle. Founded in 1871, it's a massive stone structure full of fruit, vegetable, and food stalls, but like most places of its kind is hard for a tourist to walk around without being pestered to death by overeager salesmen. Imported canned goods are available at many of the stalls, and the market is much cleaner than many markets of this type in other countries.

If you head south from Horniman Circle, down Old Customs House Road or Apollo Street—or, better still, from Flora Fountain down Mahatma Gandhi Road—you'll eventually reach the **Wellington Fountain,** from which you can see the celebrated **Gateway of India,** a massive stone arch built on the waterfront to commemorate the visit of Britain's King George V in 1911, when the Indian Empire was but one of the many jewels in the British crown. The Gateway, built of yellow basalt quarried locally, was created by an English architect in a style recalling 16th-century Gujarat architecture. The equestrian statue nearby is of the last great Maratha emperor, Shivaji, who conducted guerrilla warfare against the British in the 18th century, until his attention was diverted by Aurangzeb, a bitterer foe. Shivaji left his legacy in the manner the local sari is still worn—looped between the legs so as not to interfere with the riding capabilities of the warrior horsewomen.

On the way from the Flora Fountain to the Taj Mahal Hotel, you will encounter the **Jehangir Art Gallery,** probably the most modern art museum in India, around which many of the city's avant-garde currents ebb and flow. There are actually several galleries (including one on the roof) rolled into one, and all have different and interesting shows.

North of Flora Fountain is the great **Victoria Terminus,** a blend of Gothic and Indian architecture. About three million passengers and 1,000 trains a day go through "VT," as it's known. See the exterior carvings on the history of India's transportation.

CITY TOURS: A number of city tours are offered by various operators in Bombay. Usually covered on these tours are the Gateway to India, Aquarium (except Monday when it's closed), the Prince of Wales Museum (closed Monday), Jain Temple, Hanging Gardens, Kamla Nehru Park, and Mani Bhavan (Gandhi Museum).

To make your reservations, you call the tour operator at the number listed below. Be sure to call in advance during the peak season, October to February, and check on whether they're operating on schedule during the monsoon, roughly June to September.

Operating a city tour every day, from 2 to 6 p.m., costing Rs. 30 ($2.30) for adults, Rs. 25 ($1.90) for children, is **Travel Corporation of India** (tel. 245716).

Pickup points are: India Tourist Office, 123 M. Karve Rd., Churchgate; the Taj Mahal Hotel, Apollo Bunder; and Oberoi Towers, Nariman Point.

Operating a city tour every day but Monday, from 9 a.m. to 1 p.m. and 1:45 to 5:45 p.m., costing Rs. 35 ($2.70) for adults and Rs. 25 ($1.90) for children is **India Tourist Development Corporation,** the ITDC (tel. 2023343 or 2026679). Pickup points are the India Tourist Office and Taj Mahal Hotel.

Operating a city tour every day but Monday, from 9 a.m. to 2 p.m., except Sunday when it's 9 a.m. to 1 p.m., is **Maharashtra Tourism Development Corporation,** the MTDC (tel. 2026713 or 2027762). This tour costs Rs. 40

($3.05) and includes the World Trade Centre (except on Sunday when it's closed). The pickup point is the MTDC Office, CDO Hutments, Madame Cama Road, opposite the LIC office.

Another MTDC tour operates every day but Monday from 2 to 7 p.m., and 2 to 6 p.m. on Sunday, costs Rs. 40 ($3.05), and visits the Nehru Science Centre (planetarium) and Worli Dairy, but not the Jain Temple. Pickup at the MTDC Office, CDO Hutments, Madame Cama Road, opposite the LIC office.

For those staying at Juhu or near the airports, **Oshiwara Travel Tours** conducts five-hour city tours every day but Monday. The tour starts at 10 a.m. at the Oshiwara office, near Oshiwara Bridge, S.V. Road, and has pickups at the following hotels: Palm Grove, Centaur (Juhu and airport), Horizon, Sun N' Sand, and Leela Penta. Fare is Rs. 100 ($7.70) per person in an air-conditioned coach and Rs. 80 ($6.15) non-air-conditioned. For information and reservations, call 571989, or ask at the reception desk of the hotels mentioned above.

Should you wish to sightsee on your own but with a guide, the **Government of India Tourist Office,** 123 M. Karve Rd. (tel. 293144), can provide an approved guide at these rates: one to four persons, Rs. 48 ($3.70) for one to four hours, Rs. 72 ($5.55) for four to seven hours, and beyond eight hours, Rs. 10 (75¢) per hour. Lunch allowance is Rs. 20 ($1.55) for a full day; language allowance (does not involve English, but French, etc.), Rs. 25 ($1.90). It costs an extra Rs. 15 ($1.15) to take a guide to Elephanta Caves and Rs. 30 ($2.30) for Kanheri Caves.

5. Elephanta Caves

Six miles across the harbor from the Gateway to India lie the celebrated Elephanta Caves, meager fare compared to Ellora and Ajanta, but certainly worth a visit if only for the pleasant one-hour boat ride. And for those not going to Ellora and Ajanta, Elephanta gives a good sample of cave sculpture.

Tour launches leave the Gateway to India every hour from 9 a.m. to 2 p.m. and return after four hours. The fare is Rs. 30 ($2.30) for adults and Rs. 20 ($1.55) for children. Phone 2026384 for reservations. Currently this tour even goes during the monsoon, unless the sea is very rough. You can find out more by telephoning the above number.

Guides go with the groups, so there is no need to hire one for yourself. It is advised that you go on a weekday and not on a Sunday or public holiday, when the island gets very crowded. But if you can only go when the others go, do so . . . it's worth it.

Elephanta, green and lovely, is named after the huge elephant statue that once stood there—pieces of which can now be seen in the Veermata Jijabai Bhonsle Udyan (formerly Victoria Gardens) in Bombay. The six caves on the island date back to the 8th century but were vandalized by the Portuguese who used them as cattle sheds and artillery grounds.

Ordinary launches, without guides, cost Rs. 16 ($1.25) for adults, Rs. 10 (75¢) for children 2 to 7.

6. Nightlife and Entertainment

Rather conventional activities such as movies (several **cinemas** show English and American films, some pretty old and all with any sensuous parts censored). Movies are generally screened at 3, 6, and 9 p.m., and are listed in the daily newspapers.

In addition to the Indian dances with meals at the Taj Mahal and Oberoi

Towers, mentioned above, there's **dancing** to Western music in the restaurants at a number of the high-priced hotels. Some of these hotels also have **discothèques:** The Cellar in the Oberoi Towers, 1900s in the Taj Mahal Inter-Continental (elegant, gets an older, more sophisticated crowd), Xanadu in the Horizon Hotel, the Cavern in the SeaRock, and Take Off in the Airport Plaza. Typically, there's a charge unless you're a hotel guest: for instance, at SeaRock, Rs. 35 ($2.70) weeknights and Rs. 50 ($3.85) to Rs. 60 ($4.60) on weekends; ladies are free Tuesday through Thursday. At Xanadu, the fee is Rs. 50 ($3.85) during the week and Rs. 100 ($7.70) weekends. The hours are 9:30 p.m. to 4 a.m. at the Taj, 10:30 p.m. and onward at Xanadu, and 9:30 p.m. to around 2 a.m. at SeaRock.

For theater, it's **Prithvi Theatre,** at Juhu Beach, or the **National Center for the Performing Arts,** at Nariman Point, a handsome building designed by American architect Philip Johnson, also site of Western musical events.

A helpful brochure, "Welcome to Bombay," published fortnightly by the Government of India Tourist Office, lists such cultural events as classical dance performances in varying styles including bharata natyam, kathak, and kathakali; classical Indian music recitals featuring the karnatic style of the South and ghazals (songs) of North India; and art exhibits. Dates, timings, places, and prices are in the brochure.

7. Useful Information

AIRPORT TRANSFERS: Coach service is available to and from both airports: Sahar international terminal for Rs. 25 ($1.90), Santa Cruz domestic terminal for Rs. 20 ($1.55). The coach picks you up at the airport and drops you off at the Air-India or Indian Airlines office in the city, or the Taj Mahal Inter-Continental Hotel. Going to the airports, the hotel and airline offices are places you'll be picked up.

Taxis from Sahar airport can be prepaid in advance to save a hassle over the fare when you get in. A taxi should cost about Rs. 95 ($7.30) to Nariman Point, Rs. 115 ($8.85) to Colaba. Be sure to save your receipt—you'll be asked to give it to the driver when you get to your destination as proof you prepaid. From the domestic terminal there is no prepayment deal: a taxi costs about Rs. 75 ($5.75) to Nariman Point, Rs. 105 ($8.05) to Colaba. Tourist car operators generally charge a four-hour rate for airport transfers: Rs. 220 ($16.90) to the domestic airport, Rs. 240 ($18.45) to the international, are the lowest fares.

TRANSPORTATION: Black-and-yellow **taxis** are metered and fares begin at about Rs. 3.75 (30¢) for the first kilometer and Rs. 2.35 (18¢) for subsequent kilometers, but will probably be around three times what it says on the meter since they haven't been recalibrated for aeons. If you're picked up near any of the five-star hotels, taxi drivers will probably try to charge you five times the authorized amount. Don't give in! Ask the doorman to mediate and settle the dispute when getting out or when embarking, pick up the cab away from the hotel. Black-and-yellow taxis are permitted to ply the suburbs. **Auto-rickshaws** are metered and cheaper than taxis. However, they are confined to the suburbs only, and are not allowed beyond Mahim into South Bombay. Tourist taxis charges Rs. 3.50 (27¢) per kilometer, non-air-conditioned.

TOURIST INFORMATION: The **Government of India Tourist Office,** 123 M. Karve Rd., opposite Churchgate Station, Bombay 400020 (tel. 293144), is open from 8:30 a.m. to 6 p.m. Monday through Friday, and from 8:30 to 2 p.m. on Saturday and holidays; closed Sunday. At the airports, Tourist Office counters are located at both Sahar international terminal (tel. 6325331), open 24 hours a day, and Santa Cruz domestic terminal (tel. 6149200, ext. 278 or 279), open until the last flight at night. In addition to pamphlets, booklets, maps, and advice, the tourist office maintains a list of meet-the-people contacts should you wish to visit someone in your own line of work or sharing mutual interests during your stay. The office also has a list of paying guest accommodations should you be interested in staying with a family.

TRAIN AND PLANE SCHEDULES: Key times for trains and planes are published each Saturday in the *Indian Express.*

BEST TIME TO VISIT BOMBAY: Winter, November through February, is the best season as far as the weather goes, when temperatures are usually in the 80s; in summer, March to October, it can climb into the 90s and keep going up. Rainy season is June to September.

A special time to visit is not during the peak season but in August/September during Ganesh Chatur. This is the most spirited of Bombay's festivals, and it celebrates the birthday of the beloved elephant-headed Ganesh. Images of the chubby god of good luck are dressed in their finest, paraded through the streets, and immersed in the sea.

GETTING TO BOMBAY: A number of international airlines land at Bombay, so your visit to India can begin or end here. Indian Airlines has many **flights** connecting Bombay to such cities as Delhi, at Rs. 1,132 ($87); Madras, at Rs. 949 ($73); Aurangabad, at Rs. 296 ($22.75); Goa (Dabolim), at Rs. 398 ($30.60); Ahmedabad, at Rs. 409 ($31.45); and Udaipur, at Rs. 615 ($47.30), to name a few only.

Best **train** from Delhi is the twice-weekly completely air-conditioned *Rajdhani Express,* making the trip of 1,384 km (845 miles) in 17 hours, for Rs. 1,065 ($81.90) in air-conditioned class, Rs. 325 ($25) in a chair, and Rs. 605 ($46.55) in two-tier air-conditioned. You can also take the *Frontier Mail* from Delhi, a 24-hour ride, to Bombay Central or the *Punjab Mail* to Victoria Terminus, for Rs. 400 ($30.75) in first class, Rs. 97 ($7.45) in second. Both the *Madras Mail* and *Madras Express* leave Madras Central and pull into Victoria Terminus 28 hours later, after covering 1,279 km (780 miles), for Rs. 380 ($29.25) in first class, Rs. 91 ($7) in second.

If you are departing Bombay by train and going to the north or west, make your reservation at the Western Railway Office, Churchgate (tel. 291952), for first class; Bombay Central Station (tel. 391611) for second class. Hours are 9 a.m. to 4 p.m. If you are going east or south (and for a few trains heading north), make your reservations at Victoria Terminus Station, Bori Bunder (tel. 264321). There are railway tourist guides to assist tourists at both stations.

Buses connect Bombay to such cities as Aurangabad, Bangalore, Baroda, Gir Forest (home of the Asian lion), Goa, Hyderabad, Udaipur, and several other popular tourist centers.

TOURING BEYOND BOMBAY: The MTDC runs a daily bus tour to Aurangabad to see the Ellora and Ajanta Caves, departing at 8:30 a.m. and returning four days later at 8 a.m., costing Rs. 880 ($67.70), including room and meals at a top hotel, Rs. 765 ($58.85) for a lesser hotel. For Rs. 120

($9.25) one-way fare, you can take the tour and stay at the modest Holiday Camp, for Rs. 485 ($37.30), buying your own food. For reservations, call 2023343 or 2026679.

8. A Special Attraction

A rare, beautiful, and valuable private art collection can be visited by those who have their bankers write a letter of introduction to fans of this book, **Mr. and Mrs. H. K. Swali,** 102/A Bhublabhai Desai Rd., Mehra Sadan, First Floor, Bombay, 400026. Mr. Swali, a former banker himself, and his wife, Nalini, will take true pleasure in showing you their remarkable centuries-old bronzes, miniature paintings, and stone carvings, which ordinarily you'd see only in a museum. Here, you can hold the bronzes, which warm and seem to take on life in your hands, examine everything closely, and learn the history of each piece and how it was found in a country town or city bazaar. The Swalis have written articles on Indian art, lectured on the subject, and traveled abroad focusing on art. They're acquainted with some major collections outside India and full of worthwhile information for those interested in art.

9. Out of Town

Lovely palm-fringed **Juhu Beach,** about 33 miles (20.8 km) north of the city, beyond the airport, is a favorite excursion. Take the Western Railway suburban line to Santa Cruz and a bus or taxi from there. The Juhu Beach waters are probably polluted and so guests use the hotel pools. But there are lovely, lonely beaches away from Bombay for those who wish a swim in the clean, sparkling sea. The beautiful beaches of **Marve** and **Manori** are 25 miles (40 km) from the city and connected to each other by ferry. There's also **Madh Beach,** a little farther away. All three of these beaches can be reached by taking the train to Malad and taxiing from there for three or four miles.

Powai and Vihar Lakes, about one mile apart, are approximately 19 miles (30 km) from Bombay and popular sites for picnics. Powai, celebrated for fishing, is the quieter of the two. Vihar is one of Bombay's reservoirs. Take the Central Railway to Kurla or the Western Railway to Andheri and a taxi or bus from there. Buses run only on Sunday and holidays.

Aarey Milk Colony, a modern dairy farm, in beautiful surroundings with gardens, supplies milk to Bombay. The Central Dairy is open to visitors from 9 a.m. to noon. It is about 22 miles (35 km) from Bombay via Kurla and Andheri, served by the Central and Western suburban trains respectively, thence by taxi or bus.

Beyond Aarey Milk Colony are the **Kanheri Caves,** part of Krishnagiri Upavan National Park. The 109 caves, dating from the 2nd to the 9th century, are one of the largest groups of Buddhist caves in western India. Many of them, merely holes in the ravine, were monks' cells. Caves 1, 2, and 3 have massive pillars, sculptures, and stupas well worth seeing. Wear sneakers, take a flashlight to see the interiors, and take care walking over the moss-covered rocks to the caves. Sunday is an especially interesting time to visit as devotees go up the steep rocks to see the sadhus in two ashrams at the top.

Not far from the national park's entrance is the **Lion Safari Park,** where you can observe the Indian lions from closed vehicles. The lion park is open every day but Monday, including public holidays. It's closed on Tuesday if Monday happens to be a public holiday. The hours are 9 a.m. to 5 p.m.

You can see the safari park and other suburban sights on suburban tours, or you can take a train to Borivili and a taxi from the station to the park.

SUBURBAN TOURS: The suburban tour visits Sahar International Airport, Juhu Beach, Observation Point, Tulsi Lake National Park, Kanberi Caves, Lion Safari Park (except Monday), and the lakes, from 10 a.m. to 6 p.m. daily, for Rs. 65 ($5). The MTDC Office, CDO Hutments, M. Cama Road (tel. 2026713 or 2027762) is the operator and the pickup point, and the place to call for reservations.

Chapter XVI

CONTRASTS: CAVE TEMPLES AND SUNLIT BEACHES

1. Aurangabad
2. Ajanta and Ellora
3. Goa

DESPITE ITS SIZE and considerable population, Aurangabad (pop. 400,000) is still basically a market town, with few paved streets. Even with an industrial complex on the outskirts, the town has a pleasantly amiable, rural air about it. The narrow streets are still more familiar with herds of oxen than with cars, whose occasional noisy horns seem out of place among the gentler lullaby of tinkling cow bells.

But then hardly any of the thousands of visitors who come to the city come to see Aurangabad itself, or even to attend any of the apparently constant festivals thronged with the brightly colored green saris and magenta turbans, which seem so characteristic of the area.

The number-one tourist target, of course, is the famous cave temples of the region—those at the easily accessible Ellora (18 miles, 29.5 km) and relatively isolated Ajanta (66 miles, 108 km), which were already being abandoned by their builders more than 600 years before the discovery of America.

1. Aurangabad

THE SIGHTS: Aurangabad possesses a smaller edition of the Taj Mahal, built about 1660, the famous Agra tomb its model. It was built in memory of Aurangzeb's wife, sometimes known as Rabia-ud-Daurani, but there seems to be some dispute about who actually did the building. The official sign at the site attributes it to the emperor's son, but he is generally believed to have been too young for any such project at the time the building, known as the **Bibi-Ka-Maqbara,** was constructed. On the other hand, Aurangzeb was hardly the most lavish of monarchs and, in fact, imprisoned his father, Shah Jahan, original builder of the Taj. Admission is 50 paise (4¢), free on Friday. Open from sunrise to 10 p.m., and is floodlit at night.

The Bibi-Ka-Maqbara is by no means as impressive as the Taj, the building being more or less dominated by the four minarets around it, and although the tomb is constructed of marble from Jaipur at the base and dome, the remainder is stone covered with decorated stucco. At the left-hand side, the small mosque between two of the minarets totally destroys the balance of the vista. The grounds, although not particularly cultivated, are impressive, and the best view of all is to be obtained by climbing the 120 steps of the 72-foot minaret (only one is kept open because of numerous suicides) and gazing out over the nearby town and surrounding hills.

An absolute must in Aurangabad is the beautiful **Panchakki** or Water Mill (open from sunrise to 8 p.m.; entry is 75 paise, 6¢), which even today demonstrates the ingenuity of Mughal engineers. Underground pipes lead water from the hills five miles away to an elevated tower here, cascading it from a wide outlet as a gentle and caressing waterfall. The tower, freshly whitewashed, is still lower than the surrounding hills and so the principle of gravity is never in doubt. The water flows into an attractive pool with fountains, some of it being diverted to drive an old mill wheel, used for grinding millet until recent times. The remainder flows into an adjoining river, across which can be seen some remains of the ancient clay pipe system.

There is a small refreshment stand under the sheltering banyan tree and fat gray trout fight for tidbits from numerous tourists. At the rear is a lovely garden with more fountains, pine and cypress trees, and the red sandstone tomb of one of Aurangzeb's favorite saints, Baba Shah Musafir.

Aurangabad, too, has **caves,** only a few miles beyond Bibi-ka-Maqbara. And while they are nowhere near as awe-inspiring as those at Ellora and Ajanta, they are a must when sightseeing around town.

None of the city tours includes the caves. A taxi from your hotel to the site and back should cost around Rs. 70 ($5.40), including waiting charges. The caves are open for visitors from sunrise to sunset or 6 p.m.

You can drive only to the base of the cave site and then it's a healthy hike up steep stairs to inspect their interiors. There are two wings of caves, about a mile apart. With so much walking, it's best to plan this excursion early or late in the day while it's light but not too hot. A watchman will materialize to illuminate the dim interiors. Give him a rupee or two.

These caves are referred to by numbers, but they are not clearly designated. Just ask the attendant to point you in the right direction. Like their counterparts at Ellora and Ajanta, these rock-cut tabernacles were the handiworks of monks, but slightly later than those at the caves away from town. The caves here date from A.D. 700, except cave 4, which dates from the 2nd century A.D.

Of this group, cave 7 is most impressive, with Buddha preaching about the eight human fears (fire, sword, chains, shipwreck, lion, snake, elephant, and death).

Next to it, cave 6 shows Buddha with two Naga kings; cave 3 has a frieze telling a legend about a lioness licking the soles of a king's feet which made her pregnant. She ultimately gave birth to a lion-son who gorged himself on humans and had to be annihilated for this dietary indulgence.

WHERE TO STAY IN AURANGABAD: Keep in mind that taxes add 6% to hotel bills of Rs. 5 (40¢) to Rs. 30 ($2.30) and 15% to bills above Rs. 30 ($2.30). No sales tax is added if your room price is under Rs. 5. A good, clean budget-priced room is hard to find in Aurangabad.

The ITDC's **Aurangabad Ashok,** Dr. Rajendra Prasad Marg, Aurangabad 431001 (tel. 4520), is an airy, attractive, rather pricey place, with a coffeeshop and restaurant, a pool, and a garden where it's pleasant to sit out with tea and a beer and look over the tree-lined grounds. The hotel has 65 rooms renting for Rs. 320 ($24.60) single, a possibility for two at Rs. 385 ($29.60) double, both air-conditioned. Furnishings are motel-modern throughout.

Also on Dr. Rajendra Prasad Marg, and in a slightly lower price range, is the 40-room **Hotel Raviraj,** Aurangabad 431001 (tel. 3939), with modern furniture and attached bathrooms. Prices are Rs. 225 ($17.30) single and Rs. 275 ($21.15) double, air-conditioned; Rs. 145 ($11.15) single and Rs. 195 ($15) double, non-air-conditioned. The restaurant on the premises serves the usual Indian, continental, and Chinese cuisines at Rs. 25 ($1.90) to Rs. 60 ($4.60) for a three-course meal.

Hotel Amapreet, J. Nehru Marg, Aurangabad 431001 (tel. 4306), has a mural showing Kashmir in the lounge. All the rooms are only fairly clean and have with bathrooms attached. They run Rs. 250 ($19.25) for doubles and Rs. 200 ($15.40) for singles, Rs. 50 ($3.85) less without air conditioning. There is a restaurant, open from 6 a.m. to midnight, and a 24-hour coffeeshop.

At the meeting of two highways, the **Printravel Hotel,** Dr. Ambedkar Road, Aurangabad 431210 (tel. 4707), is a pleasant and tidy place to stay. The upper veranda gets the breezes from both sides and thus remains fairly cool. There are 38 basic, clean rooms, and showers in the adjoining private bathrooms. Rates are Rs. 49 ($3.75) single and Rs. 90 ($6.90) double. None is air-conditioned. Breakfast is Rs. 12 (90¢); lunch and dinner each cost about Rs. 30 ($2.30).

Here are three places for the unfussy. The hall walls at the **Hotel Nandanvan,** opposite the fire station on Railway Station Road, Aurangabad 431001 (tel. 3311), are in frightful condition and badly need a coat of paint. The rooms are fairly neat, but still not for the fastidious. The rates are too high for the quality of the accommodation, but if you are in need of a place to stay: Rs. 70 ($5.40) for singles and Rs. 130 ($10) for doubles, without air conditioning; Rs. 150 ($11.55) for air-conditioned doubles, Rs. 100 ($7.70) if an air-conditioned double is occupied by a single. Only the double rooms are air-conditioned, but all rooms have attached bathrooms with hot and cold running water. Vegetarian foods served.

The hall walls are also in need of a fresh paint job at the **Neelam Lodging and Boarding,** opposite Jubilee Park, Aurangabad 431001 (tel. 4561), where the rooms are fairly neat. There are 28 rooms, of which two are singles, 20 are doubles, and the remaining are family rooms. Rates are Rs. 40 ($3.05) single and Rs. 45 ($3.45) double. There are ceiling fans in the rooms. The windows don't have screens, so you should probably use some insect repellent at night in case mosquito nets aren't available. All rooms have attached bathrooms with Western-style toilets; the family room, renting for Rs. 100 ($7.70), with its six beds, has an Eastern toilet. A nice touch here is the outdoor lounge. The dining room has a very low ceiling and serves moderately priced meals. A vegetarian thali includes three vegetable dishes, chapatis, rice, and condiments, for Rs. 15 ($1.15). Your sweet is extra.

The **Hotel Deogiri,** Jalna Road (formerly Airport Road), Aurangabad 431210 (tel. 8622), has small, plain, but reasonably clean rooms for Rs. 75 ($5.75) single and Rs. 100 ($7.70) double, with attached Western-style bathrooms.

Splurging

There are two high-priced hotels within a stone's throw of the airport, catering mostly to package-tour groups. They are Welcomgroup **Rama International,** Chikalthana Road, Aurangabad 431210 (tel. 8241), with an elaborate mirrored lobby ceiling reflecting the peach marble floors and boldly colored furnishings. Central air conditioning and a swimming pool are features. Rooms rent for Rs. 500 ($38.45) single, Rs. 600 ($46.15) double. The restaurant has an interesting mural of the *Ramayana* and main dishes mainly in the Rs.-20 ($1.55) to Rs.-30 ($2.30) range.

Next door, on airport road, the **Ajanta Ambassador** (tel. 8211) has expensive works of art placed everywhere, as in its flagship Ambassador Hotel in Bombay. Even the bathroom plumbing is all dressed up—swan figures are the faucets on the sinks. Bedrooms have wallpaper, some of which needs repairing; the rates are Rs. 500 ($38.45) single and Rs. 625 ($48.05) double. There's a swimming pool and air conditioning. Tandoori foods are a specialty in the Diwan-e-Khas restaurant.

Low Budget

There are simple accommodations at the **Government Holiday Resort,** near the railway station (tel. 4259), which need a paint job and tender loving care. However, the price is right: Rs. 60 ($4.60) to Rs. 80 ($6.15) for a double, the higher price for a bathroom with a Western toilet. An air-conditioned double is Rs. 120 ($9.25), or Rs. 45 ($3.45) and Rs. 60 ($4.60) for a three- and four-bedded room, with common bathrooms with either Western or Indian toilets. There's a Re.-1 (7½¢) per person service charge. A very popular place with Indian families. For reservations you must write from seven days to three months in advance to Senior Executive, MTDC, Holiday Resort, Aurangabad (tel. 4713).

The best Indian-style hotel in town is probably the brand-new **Hotel Ira,** near the Central Bus Stand in the Samarth Nagar area (tel. 3114). Rooms are neat, clean, but unfancy, with rates to match: ten singles for Rs. 40 ($3.05), 14 doubles for Rs. 60 ($4.60). All have attached bathrooms with Indian toilets.

Better than many other Indian-style hotels is the simple **Natraj,** Station Road (tel. 4260), charging Rs. 25 ($1.90) single and Rs. 30 ($2.30) double. Inexpensive vegetarian meals are served.

A pleasant but in-need-of-cleaning-and-painting **Youth Hostel,** Padampura (tel. 3801), gives preference to members of the Youth Hostel Association and students. The 42 beds, mainly in dorms for men and women, go for Rs. 6 (45¢) per person per night for members and students, Rs. 10 (75¢) per person for others. Write to the Warden, Youth Hostel, Station Road, Aurangabad 431005, for reservations. A vegetarian thali here is Rs. 5 (40¢). And don't forget to bring bed linens or a sleeping bag, towel, and soap.

WHERE TO EAT: There's a Rs.-75 ($5.75) buffet for dinner in the Welcomgroup **Rama International.**

The **Shaolin,** on Pawandeep Jalna Road (tel. 7291), serves Punjabi, Mughali, Indian, and Chinese foods, at Rs. 25 ($1.90) to Rs. 30 ($2.30) for entrees. Beer is served also.

For vegetarian food, try the **Bhoj,** in the Printravel Hotel (tel. 6407), open from 11:30 a.m. to 3 p.m. and 7 to 11 p.m., where a thali is Rs. 10 (75¢) to Rs. 16 ($1.25). Seats about 70.

You might also want to try **Pinky,** on Station Road (tel. 5222), opposite the Holiday Resort, for both vegetarian and nonvegetarian foods: vegetarian thalis run Rs. 7 (55¢) to Rs. 11 (85¢); chicken and mutton entrees, Rs. 8 (60¢) to Rs. 14 ($1.05). Hours are 11 a.m. to midnight in off-peak season and 8 a.m. to midnight in peak tourist season.

SHOPPING: Aurangabad, as I've said, is still relatively undeveloped, considering its size, so tourists tend to spend more time in their hotels than wandering about the town itself—even in the evenings, since the movie theaters show mostly Indian films. There are, however, a couple of "commercial" expeditions to be made, the first might be to **Hind Bidri Works,** in Nawabpura, where they make delicate inlay work on metal called bidriware. It's also of interest to visit one of the places where shawls are made (and sold)—the **A. Himroo Factory,** in Nawabpura. Himroo shawls have been a cottage industry in Aurangabad since the 18th century. On site you can see weavers eight years old and up working on the intricate looms, drying skeins of silk on frames, or winding threads onto shuttles via an intricate bicycle-wheel contraption that looks like one of Marcel Duchamps' "ready-mades." The looms on which the shawls are woven here differ from most conventional looms in that the threads hang taut from above; the weaver sits on a plank, his feet, dangling into a hole in the floor, operating the mechanism. The weaver is directed by a series of handmade, IBM-type cards above, which apparently control the sequence. In this way only one worker can handle a loom, producing a couple of yards of shawl every few days. The shawls are remarkably beautiful and, under the circumstances, are a tremendous bargain at Rs. 65 ($5) to Rs. 275 ($21.15) in cotton and silk blended, and Rs. 550 ($42.30) in pure silk. Open from 8:30 a.m. to 9 p.m. every day.

Another excursion can be made to the **Ajanta Agate Handicrafts,** on Mondha Road, outside Safar Gate (tel. 3517), open from 7 a.m. to 8:30 p.m. every day, where there are all kinds of items made from semiprecious stones. The firm also has a store in Jhaveri Bazaar in Bombay. Semiprecious stones are mined around Aurangabad.

2. Ajanta and Ellora

THE FAMOUS AJANTA CAVES: A British army officer, on the trail of a panther in desolate country some miles from the village of Ajanta, stumbled on the overgrown entrance to a deep cave—now Cave 10, and one of the oldest—and his discovery quickly became worldwide news. The year was 1819 and the caves, a series of subterranean Buddhist temples, had lain forgotten by civilization for the better part of a thousand years. The discovery ranks among the major archeological finds of modern times and it's ironical that the caves' long-time neglect is responsible for their preservation. Within years of their discovery vandals had scratched their names across paintings that had survived intact for centuries. The Indian government eventually stepped in and took over their maintenance. Today they are one of the major tourist sights of the world.

There are 30 caves in all, carved out of a horseshoe-shaped cliff, itself surrounding a deep valley, which, with its little bridges, hillside-hugging pathways, scattered rocks, river, flowers, and elevated viewing pavilion, now looks like a giant-sized Japanese garden. From the far side of the valley it's possible to obtain an excellent perspective of the whole cave area, but the road from the viewing point to the valley—a distance of scarcely a mile, as the crow flies —meanders around the parched countryside for about ten miles. A cable railway or mule track would certainly help.

Most dramatic (but least popular) time to visit the caves is during the summer monsoons, when waterfalls pouring from the cliff above provide the caves with a natural curtain and the foliage all around is lush and green. As it is, the best times are October to March—and March is only okay for those who like it hot.

The caves, and their artworks, were not the product of one particular era but were created over a period of 800 or 900 years—from about 200 B.C. to about A.D. 650—and nothing is known about the monks and/or artisans who created them beyond the obvious fact that the Ajanta site was as remote in those days as it is today. The work, in other words, was that of an isolated religious order, executed through centuries of dedication.

The frescoes were prepared by first covering the rough surface of the rock with a layer of clay mixed with cow dung and rice husks. A coating of white lime plaster was added and then the outline of the drawings, filled in later with glowing colors made mostly from locally obtained vegetable and mineral ingredients. Few of the large murals have survived intact and some, indeed, look more like examples of abstract expressionism than meaningful pictures. What can be seen, though, is a mixed grab bag of myth and legend along with real life; of the latter there are elephant fights, singing and dancing, preparing food, buying and selling, and an occasional procession or court scene.

Openings in the cave walls allow enough sunlight for superficial inspection (reflected sun from outside was probably enough light for the original artists); to supplement this, uniformed attendants, who spend the entire day amid trailing cables, endlessly flash high-powered lamps onto the highspots. No wonder they look bored! Each cave is usually occupied by several groups of tourists listening attentively, awestruck, to commentaries by their various guides, and a cacophony of explanatory shreds floats back and forth in a variety of languages. Small children, bored by the lectures, run between the feet of bald-headed transients with determined faces and ever-exploring flash cameras. The government of India has been for years underwriting an ambitious project to copy the cave paintings exactly as they are, and a group of artists sometimes can be seen working from miniature scaffolds reproducing the fragments in surprisingly accurate hues. ("Windsor & Newton watercolors," one painter explained.)

Although there are 30 caves altogether, some are less interesting than others. For those with limited time, therefore, the best plan is to concentrate on Caves 1, 2, 9, 10, 16, 17, 19, and 26, which are sumptuous enough for three score.

WHERE TO STAY AND EAT IN AJANTA: For those who can't see enough of the caves in one day, there's the **State Guest House** in Fardapur, about three miles away, just past the road that turns off the main highway to the caves. Regular buses and tour buses stop outside the guesthouse, which happens to be on the main highway to Jalgaon. An 85-year-old structure, the guesthouse has a few suites, available for Rs. 50 ($3.85) daily. There's a cook on the premises and bed linen is provided at no extra charge. There's one hitch: the guesthouse is primarily for government officials, open to tourists only if no party is booked in. Reservations are a must: Executive Engineer, B & C. P.W.D. Padampura, Aurangabad (tel. 4874).

A simple but untidy **Travellers' Rest House**, charging Rs. 15 ($1.15) per night double, has a cook in attendance. Write to Executive Engineer, B & C. P.W.D. Padampura, Aurangabad (tel. 2874). Government officials get first consideration.

Not far from the caves, there's the very basic, clean **Holiday Resort** (tel. 30), in Fardapur, with rooms at Rs. 50 ($3.85) daily. The cook will make Eastern and Western food with two hours' notice. You should make a reservation, but you can just drop in. If there's room, you can have it. This would be the best place to stay. The bus to Ajanta, costs Rs. 1 (7½¢).

The manager at the Holiday Resort is very nice, giving information and advice to travelers who are backpacking through and seeing to the comforts of the guests. Reservations: Senior Executive, MTDC Regional Office, Station Road, Aurangabad 431001. You can also pitch a tent on the grounds for Rs. 5 (40¢).

The Forest Rest House (tel. 4701) is a gray building that has recently been renovated, with two clean suites and a dining hall. It's for officials in forestry, but if there's no one staying at the house, you can move in for Rs. 15 ($1.50) per night. The reservation authority is Divisional Forest Officer, Osmanpura, Aurangabad 431001. It's walking distance from the caves.

The MTDC **Travellers Lodge,** Ajanta Caves (tel. 26), has four rooms and seven beds, at Rs. 50 ($3.85) double, Rs. 35 ($2.70) single. Reservations can be made through the Maharashtra Tourist Development Corporation in Aurangabad. There's a restaurant on the premises serving Indian and continental cuisine, and open to one and all.

ON THE WAY TO ELLORA: Nine miles to the northwest of Aurangabad, on the road to Ellora, is one of the most impregnable castles in India, the **Daulatabad Fort.** Constructed in the 12th century by the Yadava dynasty's Bhilama Raja, and occupied by kings from the late 13th century, it's atop an isolated rocky hill with seven outer walls and an internal moat. The sheer rock cliff on which it is perched is so smooth and steep that, legend says, even a snake would slip off it.

The only access to the top of the fort, until recent times, was via a pitch-black, internal tunnel that spiraled around the inside of the hill until it culminated in a narrow opening at the top, 640 feet above. In the old days, potential intruders would see a patch of light ahead and rush forward, only to be doused with boiling hot pitch or oil poured in by the defenders above.

There is no record that any attacker reached the top, although the fort was captured—as forts inevitably are—by siege. In fact, the slender, pink **Chand Minar,** an elegant minaret 100 feet high that stands not far inside the spike-studded outer gates, was built by Allaudin Ahmed Shah Bahmani (1435–1457) to celebrate such a victory.

Although the impressive Mughal pavilion and upper sections remain in good condition, many of the buildings just inside the fort's outer walls are now in ruins. Among them is the palace in which the last ruler of another fort —Golconda, near Hyderabad—was kept captive until his death in the latter part of the 16th century.

Opposite the entrance to the fort, on the main road, are several refreshment stands, which serve beer and soft drinks. There are souvenir stalls nearby.

THE CAVES OF ELLORA: There are 34 cave temples at Ellora—12 Buddhist, 17 Hindu, and five Jain, built in that order, probably from the 7th to the 13th centuries A.D.—and despite what you may have heard and read you won't be prepared for what you will actually see. The caves are only 18 miles (29.5 km) from Aurangabad, just off the main road, and unlike those at Ajanta, they have never been "lost"—even though for many centuries they were so disregarded that local villagers actually lived in some of them, building fires for cooking and heating that have pretty well wrecked what remained of the paintings on the ceilings. It could be almost impossible, however, to remove the carvings and sculptures with anything less than a bulldozer, and it is these that will impress you most.

Cave 16

The first thing to remember—and to keep constantly in mind as you investigate these extraordinary works of art—is that each temple is carved out of what was once a solid mass of rock, without scaffolding, starting at the top and chiseling downward. The difficulties must have been monumental. Yet each figure is perfectly proportioned, and in some cases the carvings are as intricate as lace.

This is particularly awesome in the case of Cave 16, a Hindu temple known as Kailasa, which was supposedly built by King Krishna I in the 8th century after Lord Shiva, the destroyer of evil, flew over the rock and claimed it for his home. Three million cubic feet of rock were chiseled away before the complex of temple buildings, life-size elephants, and realistic sculptures were completed. The focal-point sculpture shows Ravana, the evil mythological king, being subdued by Shiva who's crushing him underfoot. The cause for this forceful confrontation involved Ravana's desire to lift this incredible temple on his head and shake it.

Ten lifetimes is what it may have taken to create this temple. Nobody can accurately tell how long this massive creation was in the making, but archeologists estimate at least seven to eight generations.

Incomparable Kailasa cannot be likened to ancient structures such as the Pyramids no matter how astonishing the others. It is aptly summed up in words of a well-known British historian as "the noblest Hindu memorial of ancient India."

There's a 50-paise (3½¢) charge to enter Cave 16; free on Friday (every day for children age 15 and under).

Cave 10

The most interesting introduction to the Buddhist series of temples, which were created between A.D. 350 and 700, is Cave 10, which is known locally as **Vishwakarma** (Carpenter's Cave). Some of the carving, indeed, is deliberately designed to simulate wood. Even the angels, with their graceful legs, on the exterior do not prepare you for the surprise when you first step inside the cave. A high-ceilinged nave-like chamber, similar in style to a Christian church, it is dominated at the far end by an enormous 15-foot-high Buddha in the preaching pose. Fluted stone beams curving across the ceiling give the impression of an upturned ship skeleton. Outside, beside the stone lions, which were damaged when part of the overhanging roof collapsed in a landslide, are steps leading to an upper gallery from which one can clearly see the rows of carved Naga queens (who were believed to have brought the monsoons) and the galaxy of dwarfs who represented court entertainers. This cave was completed in the 7th century A.D.

Caves 11 and 12

These two caves, especially the latter, are interesting examples of three-story temples, which not only contained cells for the monks in residence, but were also used as hostels for visiting pilgrims. Cave 12 is the more interesting. The façade is austere, but inside are many handsome carvings. Each of the floors contains Buddhas, the top story boasting of two fine sets of seven Buddhas all in a row. Adherents of Buddhism believe that Buddha visits the earth every 5,000 years; thus there have been seven visits so far in history (the next one is due about 2,500 years from now). This is the final Buddhist cave at Ellora.

Caves 14, 15, and 29

All are Hindu. Among the deities to see in Cave 14 are Vishnu, Lakshmi, and Shiva. In Cave 15, the second story shows reliefs of Shiva performing various deeds. Cave 29 echoes Elephanta on Bombay's bay, with massive proportions and three entrances. It shows Shiva as the Destroyer.

Caves 30 to 34

The Jain caves, nos. 30 to 34, are a little farther away and are devoted to Buddha's contemporary, **Mahavira,** who died about 700 B.C. Jain followers are more ascetic than their fellow Buddhists and don't believe in killing any living creatures, including mosquitoes. One statue displays Mahavira standing on an anthill (apparently not crushing the ants) and surrounded by a scorpion, a cobra, and two deer, all of which appear to be quite compatible. This is in Cave 32, the best of the Jain temples, built in the 12th century. From the outside it appears smaller and less elaborate than the earlier caves, but inside it is really quite impressive, with traces of color still to be seen on the walls and ceiling.

OVERNIGHTING IN ELLORA: People rarely overnight at Ellora, but there are some basic accommodations should you care to stop. **Khultabad Guest House,** for Rs. 50 ($3.85) per room, provides bed linen and has a cook in attendance. Preference is given to government officials, but if there is no party booked in you can stay. Write to: Executive Engineer, B & C, P.W.D., Padampura, Aurangabad (tel. 4874). It's within walking distance to the caves.

Travellers Bungalow (tel. 5511) at Khultabad, again humble, charges Rs. 50 ($3.85) per room. Cook in attendance. Write Executive Engineer, Zilla Parishad, Aurangabad. It's within walking distance of the Ellora Caves.

Hotel Kailas, also within walking distance of the caves, charges Rs. 150 ($11.55) single and Rs. 400 ($30.75) double. Meals are served in the adjoining restaurant. Reserve rooms by writing the manager or phoning Khultabad 43. All 16 rooms in bungalows have attached bathrooms. There's absolutely nothing to rave about except that the owner's nice and there's a little patch of grass to sit out on. Lunch prices for thalis are Rs. 15 ($1.15) to Rs. 20 ($1.55); buffet, Rs. 40 ($3.05) to Rs. 65 ($5).

Also, moseying around **Khultabad,** about two miles away, can be interesting. It's the burial place of Shah Jahan's son, Aurangzeb (1658–1707). The frugal Aurangzeb's grave, set in a Muslim saint's tomb, is marked with a plain stone slab that has no inscription. In his will, Aurangzeb stipulated that four rupees and two annas he earned during his lifetime from sewing caps be used to buy his shroud. Another Rs. 305 ($23.45—at today's rates) he earned copying the Koran was to be given to holy men.

BEST TIME TO VISIT: Aurangabad and the caves are at their best weatherwise from October through March. During the monsoon, roughly June through September, the rains rushing through the rocks at Ellora and Ajanta are a spectacularly beautiful sight. It's hot as blazes in April and May.

USEFUL INFORMATION: The **Government of India Tourist Office** is in Krishna Vilas, Station Road (tel. 4817), open from 10 a.m. to 5 p.m., and there's also an airport counter. . . . Take plenty of small change with you when sightseeing at the caves. Guards keep popping up out of the shadows with sheets of tin to catch the light and illuminate the carvings, and they expect a tip. At the fort, the guide/guard takes you through the dark passageways and he expects a tip. . . . Chanters and singers who demonstrate the caves' acoustics also want to be tipped.

TOURS: The **Maharashtra Tourist Development Corporation (MTDC)** (tel. 3219) operates three tours daily to Ellora, Aurangabad city sights, and Daulatabad Fort, from 7:30 a.m. to 5:30 p.m. by ordinary coach, costing Rs. 16.30 ($1.25). Another tour, operating in season, takes in the above sights in a luxury coach, for Rs. 24 ($1.85), from 9:30 a.m. to 6 p.m. The MTDC's daily luxury bus tour also combines Ellora, the city, and the fort at Rs. 50 ($3.85) for adults, Rs. 35 ($2.70) for children, from 9:30 a.m. to 6 p.m. These tours take off from the Railway Bus Stand, but it's best to double-check departure points when you make a reservation. Reservations are made at the Central Bus Stand (tel. 3241) for the less expensive tours, from 8 a.m. to noon and 2 to 9 p.m., and for other tours at the MTDC's Holiday Resort (tel. 4713), from 7 a.m. to 8:30 p.m.

A similar Ellora tour is conducted by the ITDC's **Ashok Travels and Tours,** on even-numbered days, in a luxury coach for Rs. 45 ($3.45); reservations are made at the Aurangabad Ashok Hotel travel counter (tel. 4143).

The MTDC conducts two daily tours to the Ajanta Caves: in an ordinary bus from 7:30 a.m. to 5:30 p.m. for Rs. 39 ($3), and in a luxury coach from 8 a.m. to 6 p.m. at Rs. 65 ($5) for adults, Rs. 40 ($3.05) for children. These tours leave from the Railway Bus Stand (but double-check when reserving). Make reservations at the Central Bus Stand for the less expensive tour, MTDC's Holiday Resort for the other.

The ITDC's Ashok Travels and Tours also runs an Ajanta tour for Rs. 60 ($4.60) in a luxury bus on odd-numbered days. Reservations at the Aurangabad Ashok Hotel travel counter.

GETTING AROUND AURANGABAD AND TO THE CAVES: Metered **cabs** are scarce, and charges are Rs. 2.6 (2¢) for the first 1.6 km and Rs. 1.6 (1¢) for each kilometer thereafter. Waiting charges are recorded on the meter. You can almost always find an unmetered **tourist taxi,** but they charge more: Rs. 2.4 (18½¢) per kilometer. A package deal would be to Ellora and back (half a day) for Rs. 150 ($11.55) and to Ajanta and return (one day) for Rs. 520 ($40).

From Aurangabad, **buses** to Ellora cost Rs. 5 (40¢), and to Ajanta, Rs. 10 (75¢).

Auto-rickshaws cost Rs. 2 (15¢) for the first 1.6 km and Re. 1 (7½¢) for each kilometer thereafter. Auto-rickshaws are permitted to go only within 20 miles (32 km) of Aurangabad and are not recommended for trips to the caves. Lack of safety on long trips is the reason for the restriction, although there were hints that it was to be lifted.

GETTING TO AURANGABAD AND THE CAVES: There are **flights** to Aurangabad from Bombay at Rs. 298 ($22.90); from Delhi, at Rs. 858 ($66); from Jaipur, at Rs. 690 ($53.05); from Udaipur, at Rs. 556 ($42.75); and from other cities.

Most **train** travelers depart from Bombay. Trains from Bombay take eight hours to Jalgaon, which is about 37 miles (59 km) from Ajanta. From Jalgaon station, there is frequent bus service to Ajanta and Aurangabad. The fare from Bombay is Rs. 165 ($12.70) in first class and Rs. 41 ($3.15) in second. The bus fare from Jalgaon to Ajanta is Rs. 9 (70¢), a bit higher to Aurangabad.

The *Punjab Mail* is one of the trains that goes through Jalgoan and continues to Delhi, stopping en route in Bhopal and Gwalior, offering the traveler other possible stopovers.

Alternatively, you can take the *Punjab Mail* or *Panchavati Express* from Bombay and change at Manmad to a narrow-gauge train for a snail's-pace 70-mile (115-km) journey to Aurangabad. Trains also connect Hyderabad (Secunderabad) with Manmad.

The roads are good between Bombay and Aurangabad and **bus** service is frequent. Deluxe air-conditioned buses take about 11 hours and operate mainly at night, for Rs. 96 ($7.40); ordinary buses cost Rs. 22 ($1.70). For information and reservations, check with the Maharashtra State Road Transport Corporation in Bombay or at the Aurangabad Central Bus Stand (tel. 4713), open from 8 a.m. to noon and 2 to 6 p.m.

3. Goa

Goa is something like a European picture framed against an Indian background. This is because the tiny state (pop. over 10 million)—only slightly bigger than Rhode Island—was ruled for 450 years by the Portuguese. They pulled out in 1961 and left behind their calling cards in the form of distinctive churches, convents, customs, and converts to the Catholic church.

Goa today is the place to cop out on sightseeing, apart from a token inspection of the things that made it the first important Christian colony in the East, and to head instead for its golden beaches, to bask in the sun among an abundance of coconuts, bananas, and pineapples. Even as Goa's development as a new resort goes on at a fairly rapid pace, there's still plenty of old-world charm.

Back in the 15th century, Goa was the starting point for Indian pilgrims en route to Mecca. It was a bone of contention among the English, Dutch, and Portuguese, who were vying for its possession. The Portuguese, in the person of Alfonso de Albuquerque, won out in 1510; the bearded viceroy entered Old Goa, then the capital city, after a triumphant procession up the Mandovi River with 1,200 men in 20 ships.

This was the beginning of Goa's glory as a rich trading center—spices from Malaya, coral and pearls from Persia, Chinese porcelain and silk. St. Francis of Xavier, on an evangelical mission, arrived, as did Garcia da Orta, the famed botanist who is reputed to have introduced Indian and Eastern herbs into Western pharmacology, and the epic poet Luís de Camões, who dedicated some of his noblest lyrics to an Indian slave girl.

Then Goa's decline began. The Inquisition was set up in the late 16th century—a grim reflection of the religious fanaticism that was sweeping Europe. Hundreds of innocent victims were tortured and killed on charges of paganism during a 250-year reign of terror. Then came an even worse terror—a disastrous plague in 1635 wiped out 200,000 people. Still the city went on and the religious inquisitions continued until 1812. In 1834 the seat of power moved six miles downriver to **Panaji,** and a year later Old Goa was abandoned altogether.

But Portugal's days of glory in India were coming to a close. Time and time again they found themselves in skirmishes not only with rival powers (the Dutch, Spanish, and English) but with the Goans themselves, who were becoming increasingly discontented with colonial rule. Despite the way the bazaars bulged with imported merchandise, the economy was hollow. There was no shortage of the most expensive foreign cars available—but hardly a decent road on which to drive them.

Just before the Portuguese were forced out, some drastic changes at last took place: rich deposits of manganese and iron ore were discovered and the mining and export of these became Goa's chief industry. Since then, industrial development has blossomed, with dozens of small plants set up: rice and flour mills, cashew nut and soap factories, tile and brick plants.

The main port for all this activity is **Marmagoa,** on a peninsula jutting into the Arabian Sea south of Dona Paula Bay. It is much more likely, however, that as a tourist you'll head for Panaji, the capital, almost at the mouth of the Mandovi River and at the northern side of Dona Paula Bay or a gorgeous beach away from the bustle.

HOTELS: Things have gotten pretty touristy over the past few years in some parts of Goa what with the publicity given the beaches and the promotion of package tours. Happily, however, this beach-studded seacoast state remains relatively unspoiled.

The good life also comes fairly cheap in Goa. Some of the more extravagant resorts aside, you can still get by well within this book's budget, especially if there are two of you. You also will find a number of Goa's hoteliers willing to bargain, particularly in the off-season.

Most hotels require one day's tariff as a deposit when you book your room, and a number levy cancellation charges up to 50%. You'll want to make sure of the policy when making reservations.

Some people head for a beach as soon as they get to Goa. Others prefer to stay in Panaji (Panjim) a few days at least, before getting away from the madding crowd. So, first, a few hotel choices in Panaji:

Hotels in Panaji

An old favorite in town is the **Hotel Mandovi** (P.O. Box 164), Panjim (tel. 4320), a white 1930s structure with balconies on the rooms overlooking the river. It's been renovated and a new wing was being added when I was last there. Totally air-conditioned, the rooms, all with telephones and attached bathrooms, are Rs. 150 ($11.55) to Rs. 165 ($12.70) for singles and Rs. 280 ($21.55) to Rs. 340 ($26.15) for doubles. There's a 10% service charge. A pleasant outdoor bar is a good place to stop for refreshment even if you don't stay here, but they do overdo the rock music in the restaurant.

Hotel Delmon, Caetano de Albuquerque Road, Panjim 403001 (tel. 5616), is one of those box-like modern buildings. The rooms are clean and all have cross ventilation, which is important when you don't have air conditioning. There are also attached bathrooms. Rates are Rs. 75 ($5.75) to Rs. 90 ($6.90) single, Rs. 99 ($7.60) to Rs. 120 ($9.25) double. There's a Rs.-5 (40¢) discount during the monsoon. There's a 10% service charge.

On the backwaters of the Mandovi River, the **Hotel Sona,** Rua de Ourem (tel. 4426), has a North Indian touch in the Mughali-inspired archways. Above average in cleanliness, the rooms are all doubles, at Rs. 105 ($8.05), each with a bathroom. Nine bathrooms have Indian toilets and 12 have Western. The adjoining restaurant has Goan, Indian, and continental foods.

Almost always booked to overflowing, the **Hotel Vistar,** Dr. Shirgaokar Road (tel. 5411), has a little lobby and clean rooms, all with bathrooms attached, renting for Rs. 80 ($6.15) to Rs. 100 ($7.70) single occupancy, Rs. 100 ($7.70) to Rs. 130 ($10) double, both without air conditioning; and Rs. 130 ($10) to Rs. 180 ($13.85) for double occupancy of an air-conditioned room. There's a 10% service charge.

Keni's Hotel, 18th June Road, Panjim 403001 (tel. 4581), has a lobby bar overlooking a garden. The rooms are neat, containing spartan but adequate furnishings, and each has a pretty patterned tile bathroom. Rates are Rs. 70

($5.40) single, Rs. 120 ($9.25) double. An air-conditioned double costs Rs. 180 ($13.85), and a suite, Rs. 225 ($17.30). There's a 10% service charge.

Hotel Aroma, Cunha Riviera Road (opposite the Municipal Gardens), Panaji 403001 (tel. 3519), has a garden view in front and cheerless little cells they insist on calling hotel rooms, renting for Rs. 75 ($5.75) single and Rs. 85 ($6.55) double if you share a bathroom, Rs. 120 ($9.25) with a private bathroom. It's better to eat than stay here since the rooms are not much, but the food is very good and is covered later under restaurants.

You'll like the prices at the **Neptune Hotel,** Malaca Road (tel. 4447), where the warmth and enthusiasm of the management makes up for the lack of decor. True, some rooms need a little tender loving care, and a paint job would do no harm, but for the money this is a good deal: Rs. 55 ($4.25) for single occupancy of a double, Rs. 80 ($6.15) for a double. There are a few air-conditioned rooms for Rs. 150 ($11.55). A small restaurant on site serves Goan, Muhgali, and Chinese foods, Rs. 5 (40¢) to Rs. 18 ($1.40).

On Dr. Dada Vaidya Road are two hotels for your consideration: the **Mayfair,** near the Mahalaxmi Temple (tel. 5952), has the old Portuguese look with its wrought-iron balconies and tile roof. This is simple place, with concrete floors and small rooms renting for Rs. 70 ($5.40) to Rs. 80 ($6.15) single, and Rs. 90 ($6.90) to Rs. 135 ($10.40) double, non-air-conditioned; Rs. 95 ($7.30) to Rs. 120 ($9.25) single and Rs. 115 ($8.85) to Rs. 170 ($13.05) double, with air conditioning. There's a 10% service charge.

The **Hotel Samrat,** Dr. Dada Vaidya Road, Panaji 403001 (tel. 3318), is another simple place, but it's clean and everyone seems friendly. Rates from March 1 to October 15 are Rs. 75 ($5.75) for singles and Rs. 120 ($9.25) for doubles; from October 16 to the end of February rates go up to Rs. 95 ($7.30) single and Rs. 150 ($11.55) double. There is also a special monsoon-season discount from July 1 to September 15. The Pink Darbar restaurant faces a courtyard and serves vindaloos and other Goan foods. Most dishes are in the Rs.-20 ($1.55) range unless they're vegetarian, and then they're around Rs. 15 ($1.15).

On the next street over, the **Hotel Golden Goa,** Dr. A. Borkar Road, Panaji 403001 (tel. 4575 to 4580), is a pricey place with clean, air-conditioned rooms, all with telephones, televisions, refrigerators, and attached bathrooms. Two restaurants on the premises service vegetarian and nonvegetarian foods. Single rooms are Rs. 270 ($20.75), and doubles, Rs. 320 ($24.60). There is a 20% discount from June 15th to September 15.

Also on Dr. A. Borkar Road the **Hotel Nova Goa** (tel. 4580), is centrally air-conditioned and has many amenities that go with its fairly high prices: Rs. 150 ($11.55) to Rs. 300 ($23.05) for singles, Rs. 200 ($15.40) to Rs. 350 ($26.90) for doubles. A 20% discount is given off-season. Seafood selections are specialties in the hotel's restaurant.

A block from the riverfront on Campal is the appropriately named **Hotel Campal,** Campal (tel. 4533), a big old mansion set in a spacious garden and topped by a roof garden which is promoted by the hotel as "the longest in Panjim." Non-air-conditioned doubles cost Rs. 110 ($8.45) and air-conditioned doubles, Rs. 175 ($13.45).

At Panaji's Beaches: About five minutes away from Panjim proper on Miramar Beach is the **Hotel Solmar,** Avenida Gaspar Dias, Bandodkar Marg, Panaji (tel. 4556), colorfully painted rust and cream and only a few steps from the sea. All the rooms, which could do with a sprucing-up, have attached bathrooms and some are air-conditioned. Rates are Rs. 50 ($3.85) to Rs. 75 ($5.75) single and Rs. 65 ($5) to Rs. 90 ($6.90) double, the higher rate for air conditioning. Service charge is 10%. The restaurant serves reasonably priced food.

Also on and opposite Miramar are these selections:

The **Mayur,** Miramar, Panaji 4003001 (tel. 3174), has the ambience of a private home, and charges Rs. 120 ($9.25) and Rs. 75 ($5.75), the higher rate for air conditioning.

London Hotel, Miramar Beach (tel. 6017), is the priciest of the three: Rs. 200 ($15.40) with air conditioning, Rs. 150 ($11.55) without. The rooms have cross ventilation, so you may not need it.

The **Royal Beach Hotel,** opposite Miramar (tel. 6316), charges a variety of rates: Rs. 45 ($3.45) to Rs. 50 ($3.85) off-season; Rs. 60 ($4.60) to Rs. 80 ($6.15) in-season. Some of the low-priced rooms don't have private bathrooms attached, and some of the higher-priced rooms not only have bathrooms, but balconies. The hotel is proud of its 28-inch color television set for the screening of English-language and Indian films.

About 2½ miles (four kilometers) from Panjim and six miles (ten kilometers) from Calangute beach, **Bamboo Motels and Hotels,** Verem Reis Magos, Goa (tel. 5770), consists of a main building and cottages called "Noah's Ark," nestled in the woods. All accommodations face the swimming pool, and there's a tennis court and billiard room. For cottages, the fee is Rs. 200 ($15.40) to Rs. 250 ($19.25), the higher rate for air conditioning; double rooms with attached bathrooms cost Rs. 100 ($7.70). Bus to the beach is about Re. 1 (7½¢). In the restaurant you can get Goan, Portuguese, and Indian foods in the Rs.-15 ($1.15) range for an entree.

Dona Paula is a beach a little over four miles (6.5 km) from Panjim and the site of the charming **Prainha Cottages** (tel. 4004), where doubles are about $20 for two. Simply furnished rooms contain all the essentials for a comfortable beach stay. Candlelight dinners of home-cooked Goan foods and fado serenades keep guests well fed and entertained. I've had this listing for some years, but I am happy to report that U. Hortstern, a reader from West Germany, found it delightful and especially enjoyed the family hospitality. He plans to return, so maybe some of you will meet him there. For reservations, contact Palmar Beach Resorts, "Glendela," first floor, Rua de Ormuz, Panaji 403001 (tel. 4004).

Finally, best for a splurge the center of Panaji, the pleasantly decorated **Hotel Fidalgo,** Swami Vivekanandji Road, Panjim, Goa 403001 (tel. 3321), has singles for Rs. 350 ($26.90) and doubles for Rs. 450 ($34.60). Special three-night plans for two people cost Rs. 888 ($68.30) per person. If you don't stay here, you might enjoy dropping in for the folksong concert held twice a week. Check with reception on time and dates.

Low-Budget Choices: The Directorate of Tourism runs three low-budget places. At Miramar Beach is the pleasant **Youth Hostel** (tel. 5433), where you can stay up to seven days (and perhaps longer depending on the management's decision), when rates are doubled for beach places during May and December. There are 60 beds in five dorms, at Rs. 10 (75¢) per person. For more information, or to make reservations (which are advised), write to either the Manager, Youth Hostel, Miramar, Panaji, Goa 403001; or Directorate of Tourism, Government of Goa, Daman and Diu, Tourist Home, Pato, Panaji, Goa 403001. Nearby is the Hotel Solmar for reasonably priced things to eat.

There's only one thing wrong with the Tourism Directorate's **Tourist Hostel** (tel. 3396)—it's almost always fully booked. But if you write two or three months in advance you might get in this pleasant, low-priced place. All the rooms are simply furnished with private bathrooms and balconies to catch the refreshing breezes. Some rooms have double refreshment with river views and breezes, as does the restaurant. There's an outdoor terrace as well. Singles are Rs. 32 ($2.45) to Rs. 50 ($3.85) and doubles cost Rs. 50 ($3.85) to Rs. 80 ($6.15), the higher rates during the season (September 15 to June 14).

Cots in the **Tourist Home,** Pato Bridge, Panaji (tel. 2535, 3183, or 4215), runs Rs. 8 (60¢) and Rs. 5 (40¢).

About 2½ miles (four kilometers) from Panaji is the **Motel La Joy,** Porvorim, Soccorro, Bardez, Goa (tel. 5583), a lovely big old house, about half of whose rooms are furnished with run-down antique beds and others with cots. This is strictly a place for the unfussy, and it's a bit out of the way for anyone at all. The price is low: rooms have cots for Rs. 50 ($3.85). The core of the building is a restaurant which extends to the patio and is discussed later in "Eating Out in Goa."

There are also a lot of flophouses at the lowest budget level, below my minimal fastidious standards. You'll have no trouble finding them on the streets around the General Post Office.

The Beach Life

In the '60s, and well into the '70s, Goa's beaches were the number-one circus in the East. Hippies freaking out all over the place were a sightseeing attraction on the package tours, and the press frequently wrote about their antics.

The maddest part of this carnival took place at Christmas, when hordes of hippies turned Calangute into a discothèque, head shop, and skin show with revelries to rival India's most revealing temple friezes. As conventional holiday-goers moved in, Calangute's hippies tripped on to popularize the more remote beaches. Although fewer than in the '60s, there are still many hardcore hippy dropouts in Goa. They're not as highly visible now as they've continued to shift their base away from civilization to the more inaccessible beaches.

Their current favorite is splendid beach at Terekhol, 32 miles (52 km) from Panaji at the northernmost point of Goa. If you wish to visit, you can stay in the **Terekhol Tourist Rest House,** the old Portuguese fort that has been converted by the government into a rest house. Rooms rates are Rs. 30 ($2.30) single, Rs. 40 ($3.05) double, Rs. 10 (75¢) per person in the dorm.

Now for some other places for your beach stay. My first suggestion for long-staying tourists is to rent a bungalow near almost any of the beaches. Each Goan beach has a distinct personality, so you should check them out to see which suits you before settling down: Baga and Anjuna are for those who like a cool slice of life; on the southeast coast, beautiful palm-shaded Colva is even more relaxed. On some of the semi-isolated beaches no one has bothered to name you can be just about alone, kissed by crystal-clear waters and visited occasionally by a fisherman wanting to sell some of his daily catch.

Rentals are generally advertised only by word of mouth. To find out what's available, just ask around at the local cafés and someone will steer you to a landlord. After bargaining, you can expect to pay about Rs. 360 ($27.70) to Rs. 600 ($46.15) per month, depending on the size and location of the house and the season.

The entire fee is payable in advance and usually nonrefundable, so select with care. Check a few houses before deciding on yours. But don't expect a palace, or even a real beach house. With a few exceptions, these modest cottages are located in little lanes and groves a stroll away from the beach.

The cottages are usually simple, single-story affairs with pillared verandas, and painted as brightly as pictures in a children's coloring book. One or two bedrooms and a rudimentary kitchen sum up their interior space and decor. The bathroom is usually an outhouse (if it exists at all). Once in a while you'll find an indoor toilet (some landlords have started to add them to please the tourists).

There's well water for cooking and cleaning up. If you'd rather not keep house, your landlord will probably know someone to do the chores for you. You have to supply bed linens and towels, which you can buy in Mapusa on market day rather than dragging from home. Being a householder in Goa for a month or more can be so enjoyable you may find it hard to tear yourself away.

If you don't want to rattle around in a house, you can be a paying guest in a tourist's or Goan's home. If you ask at the local cafés, someone will know of a vacancy somewhere around.

Now for a sampling of more conventional suggestions at various beaches.

Calangute, ten miles (17 km) from Panaji, the most built-up beach, offers a remarkable expanse of sand, but not much in the way of palms. Less than a mile away, Baga seems far more remote. Goans lovingly describe Baga as "nature's spoiled daughter" because its beach and palms both seem to do exactly as they please—a perfect description for the relaxed ambience at Baga as well.

The old standby in Calangute is the government-run **Tourist Resort** (tel. 24), right on the beach, a main building with a nice terrace overlooking the sea and cottage accommodations. Nothing fancy, you understand: Rs. 50 ($3.85) to Rs. 65 ($5) single, Rs. 60 ($4.60) to Rs. 85 ($6.55) double, the higher rates for sea views. Suites are Rs. 150 ($11.55); dorm rates, Rs. 10 (75¢) per person. These rates apply from September 15 to June 15. After that, if you don't mind braving the monsoon, the rates are reduced by Rs. 15 ($1.15) per person, and the dorm goes down to Rs. 8 (60¢). During the season your stay may be limited to seven days, at the discretion of the management. For advance reservations, which are necessary, write to: Manager, Travel Division, Goa, Daman and Diu, Tourism Development Corporation Ltd., Tourist Hostel, Panaji, Goa 403001 (tel. 3396 or 3902).

Higher in price and nicer at Calangute are the simple, clean **Palmar Cottages,** under the same management as the highly recommended Prainha Cottages at Dona Paula. They're closed at this writing, but due to reopen. Phone 4004 in Panaji for information, or write to Palmar Beach Resorts, "Glendela," first floor, Rua de Ormuz, Panaji 403001.

At the very unregal **Royal,** there are accommodations for the very unfussy: Rs. 30 ($2.30) single; during December, Rs. 50 ($3.85) double. You share toilets and showers.

There's also a **Tourist Dormitory** at Calangute, with basic accommodations: five rooms in all, three with eight beds and two with five beds, charging Rs. 10 (75¢) per person in season, Rs. 8 (60¢) out of season. Three have Indian-style toilets and two, Western. Canteen on the premises. For reservations, write to Manager, Travel Division, Tourism Development Corporation, Government of Goa, Daman and Diu, Tourist Hostel, Panaji 403001 (tel. 3396 or 3903).

Near the dormitory and the Royal is the **Canoa,** a square building with verandas all around and nine double rooms renting for Rs. 75 ($5.75), Rs. 100 ($7.70) in November and December.

Just next door is the **Concha Beach Resort** (tel. 56), with a palm-thatch roof and rooms decorated with Gujarati fabrics, for Rs. 100 ($7.70) to Rs. 150 ($11.55) without air conditioning.

As to one of the guesthouses renting rooms, there's **P. V. Fernandes' Guest House** (near the Tourist Resort), where the people are warm and friendly and the atmosphere decidedly relaxed and informal. Eight doubles and two singles rent for Rs. 45 ($3.45) and Rs. 25 ($1.90), respectively, in season; Rs. 20 ($1.55) double and Rs. 15 ($1.15) single, out of season. Fernandes prospered as a guesthouse keeper, so he's built a block of rooms known as **Calangute Beach Resort,** which has a homey atmosphere. There are nine rooms with attached bathrooms, for Rs. 65 ($5) to Rs. 85 ($6.55). It's closed off-season. An attraction at both the guesthouse and resort is the food, especially the delicious homemade cake. Breakfast is always available for Rs. 5 (40¢). The other meals have to be ordered in advance, as does the cake.

On Baga, there's the cozy **Baia do Sol** (tel. 3476). The main building houses the restaurant. Rooms in cottages are sleek and modern, and all doubles, at Rs. 250 ($19.25) with air conditioning, Rs. 150 ($11.55) to Rs. 200 ($15.40) without air conditioning.

At Calangute and Baga, for simple rooms for costing under Rs. 100 ($7.70), try: **Cavala Beach Resort,** Saunta Vaddo (tel. 90); **Holiday Beach Resort,** Candolim (tel. 88); **Hotel Riverside,** Baga (open only October through May); **Miranda Beach Resort,** Saunta Vaddo; and **O Camarão Beach Resort,** Umtavaddo.

For rooms under Rs. 50 ($3.85) at Calangute, try the ultra-simple **Barbosa Cottages,** Calangute Mahal, Cobra Vaddo; **O Seas Tourist Home,** near St. John's Chapel, Umtavaddo (tel. 65); **Sonny Lobo's Guest House,** Lobo Building, Sallgoa; **Hotel Souza Lobo,** Calangute Beach (tel. 79); or **Ancoro Beach Resort,** Saunta Vaddo (tel. 96).

Colva Beach, about four miles (6.5 km) from Margao, is being built up, but presently seems an endless, semi-isolated expanse: abundant with palms, kissed by clear water, and, provided you get away from the village, a good place to skinny-dip.

For accommodations on the low-budget side, there's the government-run **Tourist Cottages** (tel. 22287), all doubles with attached bathrooms. Off-season you can stay here for Rs. 50 ($3.85) double, Rs. 40 ($3.05) single, Rs. 110 ($8.45) air-conditioned; in season, September 15 to June 15, the rates go up to Rs. 65 ($5) single, Rs. 80 ($6.15) double, and Rs. 125 ($9.60) air-conditioned. Visitors can stay only seven days at these rates, and then they're doubled, during May and December. An 18-bed dormitory costs Rs. 8 (60¢) to Rs. 10 (75¢) per bed. The major recommendation for this place, outside of the price, is its proximity to the sea. You can eat in the beach cafés. To get in, reserve your room three months in advance by writing to: Manager, Travel Division, Goa, Daman and Dui, Tourism Development Corporation, Ltd., Tourist Hostel, Panaji, Goa 403001.

Hotel Silver Sands, Colva Beach (tel. 21645), is a bit pricey, but within this book's budget. This streamlined hotel is dramatically decorated in a black, white, and silver color scheme. Every room has a balcony from which to admire the silvery sands. The rates for the 55 air-conditioned rooms are Rs. 200 ($15.40) single and Rs. 250 ($19.25) double.

Singles for Rs. 65 ($5) to Rs. 85 ($6.55) and doubles for Rs. 80 ($6.15) to Rs. 110 ($8.45), non-air conditioned, make **Sukh Sagar** (tel. 21888) attractive. Air-conditioned rooms run Rs. 145 ($11.15) to Rs. 180 ($13.85) single and Rs. 160 ($12.30) to Rs. 180 ($13.85) double.

At Colva, for a room for Rs. 50 ($3.85) to Rs. 99 ($7.60), try **Longuinhos Beach Resort** (tel. 21038).

Anjuna Beach—red-cliffed and semi-secluded—is ideal for long stays in rental cottages. But there's a hitch: many of the regulars return year after year and have the best places all tied up. You can ask around on the beach to find out if anyone has a room to let. Or try these few under-Rs.-50 ($3.85) places: **Poonam Guest House; Nobel Nest and Restaurant** (opposite Chapel Chapora); or **Palmosol Beach Resort,** St. Anthony Vaddo.

Vagator, about 15 miles (24 km) going north from Panaji, along with neighboring Chapora Beach, attract hundreds of Westerners. Yet, remarkably, both retain much of their secluded flavor. Helping to keep it that way are the many coves and beaches spread out over a vast expanse, making it possible to play hide-and-seek with the other tourists. At Chapora, an old Portuguese fort provides a sightseeing break from the beach life.

Some of the regulars around here look like a bedraggled cast of *Hair* that's been on the road for the past 20 years. It is in fact a last stop for many free-wheeling hippies before they head farther north to Terekhol.

If you don't go the house route, there are a few other alternatives: **Vagator Beach Resort,** Fort Chapora, Vagator (tel. Siolim 41), Anjuna, is a series of red-tile-roofed cottages, each room with a fan, refrigerator, and attached bathroom. Prices vary according to season and cottage size, from Rs. 50 ($3.85) to Rs. 170 ($13.05) single and Rs. 100 ($7.70) to Rs. 290 ($22.30) for a double. There's a restaurant on the same site.

Another place is **Vales Happy Holiday Home,** House No. F/301, Vagator, which you can check out on your own.

Beach Splurges: North of Miramar Beach is Aguada, where poshness is administered by the Taj Group of hotels, in three distinctive places:

The **Fort Aguada Beach Resort,** Sinquerim, Bardez, Goa 403515 (tel. 4401), is built into the ruins of a 300-year-old fort, where galleons used to call for fresh water from natural springs. The structure is situated on a finger of topaz-colored sand and designed to harmonize with the landscape. There's a swimming pool, bar, and restaurant where the focal point is a chandelier made of local transparent seashells. The rates are Rs. 650 ($50) single and Rs. 725 ($55.70) double; Rs. 750 ($57.70) single and Rs. 850 ($65.40) double from December 20 through February 28.

Adjacent to the Fort Aguada is the **Aguada Hermitage** (tel. 4401 to 4412), where villas run Rs. 1,650 ($127) to Rs. 2,400 ($184.50), depending on size and layout. The rate is the same whether single or double. They go up to Rs. 2,500 ($192.25) to Rs. 3,000 ($230.75) from December 20 through February 28.

The **Taj Holiday Village,** Sinquerim, Bardez, Goa (tel. 4414), is a cluster of rustic cottages with air-conditioned rooms and a separate restaurant cottage. There's a swimming pool and other sports and fitness facilities. Singles run Rs. 450 ($34.60) to Rs. 575 ($44.25); doubles, Rs. 500 ($38.45) to Rs. 625 ($48.05). In Christmas season the rates go up to Rs. 650 ($50) single and Rs. 750 ($57.70) double.

The imaginative **Cidade de Goa,** Curta, Vainguinim Beach, Dona Paula, Goa 403111 (tel. 3301), takes its inspiration from a medieval Portuguese city and is built on levels to blend with the terrain. There are 96 rooms, simply and tastefully furnished to recall various local styles. The attractively mosaic-tiled bathrooms incorporate palm motifs. The hotel's shops jut in and out of streets as in an old Latin town. Rates are Rs. 375 ($28.85) to Rs. 650 ($50) for singles, Rs. 450 ($34.60) to Rs. 695 ($53.45) for doubles. The highest rates are in effect from December 16 through February 28. The hotel has two swimming pools, fresh and salt water, and many open patios and plazas.

On yet another superb beach, the **Oberoi Bogmalo Beach,** Bogmalo, Goa

403906 (tel. 2191), is built in modern style. All rooms have sea views and private balconies from which you can contemplate the waves. Five minutes from the airport, the hotel offers guests free transportation to and from their planes, and runs a free coach into Panaji daily. Though on a superb beach, the hotel has a swimming pool, plus a fully equipped health club and shopping arcade. Rates are Rs. 600 ($46.15) single and Rs. 700 ($53.85) double, but go up Rs. 100 ($7.70) to Rs. 125 ($9.60) in the peak period, from December 16 to January 31; they go down to Rs. 425 ($32.70) single and Rs. 475 ($36.55) double from May 1 to September 30.

EATING OUT IN GOA: Goa's distinctive dishes are quite tasty, often using superb seafood in complicated preparations. You'll want to try such local specialties as vindaloos (sharply spiced prawns, meat, or chicken and vegetables marinated in a vinaigrette before cooking), sanna (rice cakes steeped in toddy), foogaths (vegetables simmered with coconut and spices), buffads (stewed meat and vegetables), and becina (a sweet). Goans also make some delicious sausages similar to those in the West. If you crave something with a kick, sip feni, made from cashews and coconut—powerful stuff. The local wine is a bit on the sweet side with meals even when dry or "sec," but goes nicely with a sweet. Beer is good with spicy Goan dishes. Whisky prices are somewhat less than in other tourist centers in India—provided you stick to domestic brands.

Panjim Restaurants

Worth a 2½-mile (four-kilometer) trip from Panaji (or on the way to Mapusa) is **O Coqueiro** (tel. 5671), where you'll be able to taste delicious Goan dishes not often found in restaurants. Try the chicken carfrail (ginger, chilis, garlic), at Rs. 24 ($1.85), a local specialty. The restaurant also has Goan sausages and makes a delicious fish mayonnaise, at Rs. 16 ($1.25), as another specialty. A large seafood selection is offered as well for average prices of Rs. 16 ($1.25) to Rs. 20 ($1.55). Open every day from 11 a.m. to 3 p.m. and 6 to 11 p.m. The restaurant also has rooms to let in cottages nearby, but they're very shabby.

Also out this way, **Motel La Joy,** Porvorim (tel. 5583), has an indoor restaurant that extends outdoors. The chicken dishes run Rs. 10 (75¢) to Rs. 15 ($1.15). An excellent snack, pappadams stuffed with prawns is Rs. 3 (23¢) for three pieces, and delicious with a cool drink or beer. Open for lunch and dinner.

Back in town, for North Indian food the **Tandoor,** in the Hotel Aroma, opposite the Municipal Garden on Gunha Rivara Road (tel. 3519), serves some of the best tandoori food in town. Under the same management is **Shere-Punjab,** on 18th June Road.

The **New Punjab Bar and Restaurant** (tel. 3475) has no decor to speak of, but North Indian food that's worth talking about, moderately priced and well served. A meal of paratha, fish masala, and Indian beer runs around Rs. 26 ($2), a bargain when you realize the beer alone can cost that in many tourist places.

For Chinese food, it's **Goenchin,** in the Mandovi Apartments, near Mahalaxmi Temple (tel. 4218). For well-prepared vegetarian thalis at Rs. 8 (60¢) on the street level and Rs. 11 (85¢) upstairs, try the **Hotel Kamat,** Kamat Church Square.

For snacks such as samosas (turnovers), soft drinks, and ice creams, in the Rs. 5 (40¢) to Rs. 15 ($1.15) range, try **Cafe Jesmal,** Travessa de

Revolucaos (closed Sunday, but open from early morning to early evening other days).

Cakes, mutton, prawn, and chicken patties—for an elaborate tea or a light meal—are available at the almost-always-crowded **Café Perfect Confectionery,** where Disney characters decorate the walls. For Rs. 8 (60¢) to Rs. 16 ($1.25) you can get a sampling of the various items above and others on the menu.

If you're looking to splurge, try the **Taj Holiday Village Beach House,** a restaurant in a palm-thatched hut with a full table d'hotel; Cidade de Goa's Alfama, which is designed like a town square, has a cuisine that travels the old spice route—with dishes from Arabia to Portugal. Dancing to Western music and serenading with Portuguese fados in the evenings.

Eating at the Beaches

Calangute: As the most built-up of the beach areas, Calangute has a lot of places to eat, from the village to the waterfront, and at many places a wide range of beer and liquors are available.

A summary of a few beach cafés would include **Dinky's,** next to the Tourist Resort, which serves a good Western breakfast of eggs, toast, tea, coffee, and fruit for under Rs. 20 ($1.55). All kinds of liquor and beer are served, and beer is about Rs. 20 (75¢) per liter.

Seaview has a nice terrace, with appropriately enough, a sea view, a pleasant place to eat. Special dishes are pork sorpotel (local stew with cloves, red peppers, and other spices), and the well-known vindaloo. These cost about Rs. 15 ($1.15), as do fried prawns. Open from 8 a.m. (when breakfast foods are served) to 10 p.m.

A few steps from the Tourist Resort is the lantern-lit **Epicure,** popular at night. Many kinds of seafoods are available in the Rs.-12 (90¢) to Rs.-20 ($1.55) range; fish curry is Rs. 15 ($1.15).

Right in the **Tourist Resort,** you can eat on the terrace and admire the view from 7 a.m. to 11 p.m. every day. Try shakuti chicken (chicken, coconut, tomatoes, and spices), a specialty, for under Rs. 20 ($1.55). You might also try the **Palm Beach Café,** which has a lot of Western dishes, but isn't much to look at. Other choices are **Laxmi, Summervine,** and **Richdavi,** which is between Calangute and Baga, and lets travelers pin up notices for rides and rooms and fellow travelers.

Other restaurants on this beach are so similar in price, menu, and ambience that they don't merit special write-ups. Just try for yourself: you're bound to find a favorite among them. Also, they come and go like the tide, what's here today may not be there tomorrow, let alone when you use this book.

Baga Beach: St. Anthony's Café and Bar, near Baia do Sol, is one of the first of the beach restaurants hereabouts. It's right next to the area where fishing boats are readied to go into the sea. Appropriately enough, seafood is featured, for Rs. 10 (75¢) to Rs. 20 ($1.55); some excellent fish curries are less. The restaurant also makes a special fish smoked in banana leaves for a memorable beach meal. But if you order anything special at the restaurant, ask the price so you're not surprised by the bill.

A bit of a splurge for the beach is the upstairs restaurant at **Baga's,** in the Hotel Baia do Sol, where seafood is the specialty and you can expect to pay town prices of Rs. 20 ($1.55) or more for fish and prawn dishes. Lobster can run Rs. 80 ($6.15) or more.

A myriad of cafés along Baga allow you to pick and choose to fit your budget.

Colva: Oldest restaurant on this beach is **Vincy's,** which serves fish, chicken, and steak dishes and cool beer at the Rs.-15 ($1.15) to Rs.-30 ($2.30) level. It's some of the best food out this way. Cool beer also available.

For splurging, you can go to **Sand Pebbles** in the Silver Sands Hotel where they serve fish curry, prawns, and many seafood dishes, as well as pork vindaloo and other Goan specialties.

Anjuna: No special recommendation, but a wide variety of cafés to choose from.

Vagator: In addition to the **Vagator Beach Resort,** there are many restaurants around the beaches. Again, pick and choose for yourself.

WHAT TO DO IN PANAJI: The nearest beaches to Panaji are **Gaspar Dias** (also called Miramar) and **Dona Paula,** both southwest of the city. As near to the city as they are, they're rarely overcrowded. Farther afield are the beaches of **Calangute,** to the north, and **Colva,** to the south.

In Panaji itself, the most historic building is the **Secretariat,** once a Muslim Palace, then a Portuguese fort. Nearby, look for the strange **statue of Abbe Faria,** a priest, hypnotizing a woman. Climb the steps of the marble church, **Our Lady of Pilar,** for a panoramic view from the roof of the surrounding countryside. And be sure to see the sunset from **Dona Paula,** at the tip of the peninsula; you'll get a fine view of Vasco da Gama across the Marmagoa Harbor.

The **Handicrafts Emporium** in the Tourist Hotel will give you an overall knowledge of local prices that will serve you well when you pay a visit (Friday) to the renowned weekly market at **Mapusa** and the various shops in town and at the beaches.

Near Indian Airlines is the 160-year-old **Medical College Hospital,** said to be the oldest medical institute in Asia. And next to Police Headquarters is **Menzes Braganza Hall,** with an entryway done in tiles and paintings depicting scenes from a Portuguese poet's epic about Vasco da Gama's stormy voyage from Portugal to India.

Old Goa

If you make only one sightseeing trip during your stay, go to Old Goa. You can bus from Panaji for about 75 paise (6¢) or take a taxi—supposedly Rs. 3 (23¢) per kilometer, but you can probably negotiate with the driver for a flat round-trip rate. During some of the major Goan festivals, boats cruise from Panajai (where the Bombay steamer docks) to Old Goa. In Old Goa, you'll dock and enter, as did the viceroys of old, through the grand **Viceregal Arch.** The arch is only one of the highlights of Old Goa.

The **Bom Jesus Basilica,** dating back to the 16th century, is where the remains of St. Francis are interred—less the two toes that were reputedly stolen by fanatics and an arm that was sent to an early pope on special request. The upper portion of the shrine depicts scenes from the saint's life in varicolored marble, and more scenes are carved on the bronze covering of the elaborate three-tiered marble and silver monument and casket. Adjoining is a small museum containing sacred relics.

Across the square from the basilica is the huge **Cathedral of St. Catherine** (also called the Sé, "cathedral" in Portuguese) with its high-vaulted ceiling, spanning and covering numerous small chapels; in one of the chapels stands a cross that carries local fame because a vision of Christ is said to have been seen on it in 1919. There are 14 magnificent altars dedicated to the saint. The cathedral was built on a battlefield.

Also of interest are the **St. Francis of Assisi Church and Convent,** its porch retained from the original Muslim structure; an adjoining museum with archeological artifacts and portraits of former governors; **St. Cajetan Church,** where the Portuguese archbishops and viceroys were entombed. The area in front, calm and lovely now, was once the site of ugly inquisition trials. Also **St. Monica's Convent,** with enough of the original structure and murals intact to show how the nuns lived.

On a small hill above the basilica, **Monte Sante,** are the ruins of **St. Paul's College** and two other churches.

About 12 miles from Panaji are eight Hindu temples, constructed here after the Portuguese destroyed the ones in the coastal region. Finest is the **Manguesh Temple,** with a lovely tower, tank, and residential quarters for pilgrims, and lots of kids to pester tourists.

Where to Stay in Old Goa: A pricey hotel, practically a stone's throw from Old Goa, is the **Hotel Dolphin,** Panaji, Old Goa Road, San Pedro (tel. 4189), with a beautiful location on the Mandovi River and some rooms with balconies to admire the view. Rooms are simply furnished: singles or doubles, air-conditioned, cost Rs. 200 ($15.40); non-air-conditioned, Rs. 125 ($9.60) to Rs. 150 ($11.55). There's a 50% discount from June 15 to September 15. The Village restaurant, topped with a thatched roof, serves both Indian and Chinese foods. The main bus stand is seven kilometers (4¼ miles) away.

VASCO DA GAMA: About 18 miles (29 km) from Panaji, near the airport and Marmagoa Harbor, and as the railway terminus for Goa, Vasco da Gama is aptly described as "The Gateway to Goa." There is nothing here to detain you. But in case you have to spend the night or have a meal on your way to more interesting sites in or out of Goa, you'll want to know about accommodation.

Where to Stay

The **Hotel Zuari,** Vasco da Gama, Goa 403802 (tel. 2127) has some rooms with such amenities as radios, refrigerators, and air conditioning (13 of 18 rooms). The dining room is popular with visitors. Non-air-conditioned doubles cost Rs. 100 ($7.70); air-conditioned room, all with baths attached, run Rs. 105 ($8.05) to Rs. 160 ($12.30). Service charge is 10%.

La Paz, Swatantra Path, Panaji 403802 (tel. 2121), is cleaner than most of the hotels in this town and has 33 rooms: 12 doubles, and 19 singles, and two suites. Some of the bathrooms have bright-red tubs. All the rooms are air-conditioned and rent for Rs. 105 ($8.05) single, Rs. 168 ($12.90) double, and Rs. 250 ($19.25) to Rs. 300 ($23.05) for suites.

Hotel Rebelo, Main Road, Mundvei-Vadem, Vasco da Gama (tel. 2620), away from the center of town, is a restaurant and 25-room hotel. Upstairs, clean, simple rooms cost under Rs. 50 ($3.85).

The **Tourist Hostel,** near the State Transport Office (tel. 3119), is the most convenient place to collapse if you make the 16-hour bus trip from Bombay. From September 15 to June 15, the 50 rooms, with private balconies and attached bathrooms, cost Rs. 40 ($3.05) to Rs. 70 ($5.40), the highest rate for four-bedded rooms; from June 16 to September 14, rates go down Rs. 10 (75¢). Like the other government hostels, your stay is limited to seven days, at the discretion of management.

Where to Eat

The **Zuari Hotel** has a daily buffet lunch for Rs. 25 ($1.90); in the hotel's Anchorage Restaurant, the emphasis is on Indian seafood dishes, in a range from Rs. 20 ($1.55) to Rs. 60 ($4.60) for tandoori prawns. For Western visitors, the spices in Indian dishes are automatically toned down. If you want authentic seasoning, you can discuss it with the maître d'. Open for lunch and dinner daily.

In La Paz Hotel is the **Café Noir coffeeshop,** open from 6 a.m. to midnight and a good place for breakfast or snacks.

Little **Chef Bar and Restaurant,** Francesco L. Gomez Road (tel. 2127), is popular for North Indian dishes. Entrees rarely go higher than Rs. 15 ($1.15) to Rs. 20 ($1.55). Moderate, not cheap, but good as well. Espresso coffee and a number of less expensive snacks are available as well. Air-conditioned. Open from 11 a.m. to 2:30 p.m. and 5 to 10 p.m.

At the **Hotel Rebelo's** restaurant, modestly priced vegetarian entrees are Rs. 12 (90¢) to Rs. 15 ($1.15); nonvegetarian, Rs. 22 ($1.70) to Rs. 25 ($1.90).

MARGAO: This town, about 21 miles (34 km) from Panaji, is the industrial heart of Goa. It's most important to travelers as being en route to beautiful Colva Beach. Intrepid shoppers and browsers will appreciate Margao's wonderful covered market. Some people on business trips stay here and take time off at the beach.

Where to Stay in Margao

The nicest place is the well-kept **Mabai Hotels,** Praça Dr. George Baretto, opposite the Municipal Garden (P.O. Box 365), Margao 403601 (tel. 21653), with a large lobby and big breezy rooms overlooking the gardens. All kinds of amenities include attached bathrooms, private balconies, piped-in music, and telephones in the rooms. There are also a number of places to eat in the hotel. Singles cost Rs. 74 ($5.70) and doubles go for Rs. 175 ($13.45), air-conditioned; Rs. 45 ($3.45) single and Rs. 75 ($5.75) double, non-air-conditioned. The hotel transports guests to Colva Beach, which is only about four miles (six kilometers) away. The hotel is located near the bus station, post office, and shops, and is walking distance from the covered market.

Higher in price but not as pleasant is the **Hotel Metropole,** Avenida Concessão, Margao (tel. 21169), whose midtown setting is offset by gracious gardens. The rooms have all the amenities for a comfortable stay, attached modern bathrooms, central air conditioning, and on top of it all—literally—a roof garden. Rooms cost Rs. 100 ($7.70) for singles without air conditioning, Rs. 135 ($10.40) for doubles without air conditioning; with air conditioning, Rs. 150 ($11.55) single and Rs. 200 ($15.40) double.

At these two next hotels you can get a room for around Rs. 50 ($3.85) to Rs. 60 ($4.60).

At the **Hotel Neptune,** Rua Martires Dias, near Hari Mandir (tel. 21369), a branch of the Panaji hotel of the same name, you climb three flights of stairs to the rooms, most of which have balconies where you can stop for a while and admire your view. All the rooms have private bathrooms, and everything could use a good paint job.

The **Goa Woodlands Hotel,** Minguel Loyola Furtado Road (tel. 3121), is painted strawberry pink outside but is more subdued inside. All rooms are simply furnished, with private bathrooms. Some air-conditioned rooms go up to about Rs. 100 ($7.70).

Where to Eat in Margao

From the time it opens at 8 a.m. until closing at 11 p.m., **Longuinhos,** opposite the Municipality, is bursting with life, and the music blares as it would from a canteen in a small Portuguese town. The restaurant is famous for its prawns, prepared in a variety of ways—for example, grilled, fried, and in vindaloo—and there are other seafood dishes. Most main dishes are in the Rs. 20 ($1.55) range, but lobster can be much higher. At this restaurant you can get everything from breakfast to snacks, sweets, and whisky.

You'll find good vegetarian food in Margao at the clean and simple, air-conditioned **Kamat Millan Hotel,** Station Road (tel. 21295). Served here are well-prepared North and South Indian dishes—idli, dosas, puris, a host of curries—all no more than Rs. 5 (40¢) to Rs. 15 ($1.15), the latter enough to buy a hearty meal. Hours: 7 a.m. to 9:30 p.m.

Also near the Municipal Garden is **Marliz Bakery,** with cakes to satisfy your sweet tooth and delicious breads as well—a nice place to stop if you want to pack a picnic for a day at the beach.

MAPUSA: If you're staying for a while at Anjuna or Vagator Beach, then Mapusa (pronounced "Mapsa") will be your **shopping** center. Friday is market day at Mapusa. You can also use Mapusa for shopping if you're at Calangute or Baga, but from either of them it's a fairly easy trip to Panaji.

Should you get hungry wandering around the Mapusa market (and you may well after seeing all the fresh fruits and smelling the wonderful spices), you might want to stop for a bite to eat at **Casa Bella,** on Bank Street, from 9:30 a.m. to 10 p.m.

INFORMATION: Tourist information can be obtained in Goa at the Directorate of Tourism, Tourist Home (tel. 5583); Tourist Information Counter, 5 Interstate Bus Terminus (tel. 5620), open from 9:30 a.m. to 4 p.m.; Tourism Information Counter, Interstate Bus Stand Arrivals, open from 7 a.m. to 7 p.m.; Tourist Information Centre, Margao (tel. 22513); Tourist Information Centre, Tourist Hostel, Vasco da Gama (tel. 2673); and Tourist Information Centre, Dabolim Airport (tel. 2644).

GETTING AROUND GOA: The most enjoyable way to get from place to place is on **ferries** which cross the rivers of Goa. The ferry between Dona Paula and Mormugão operates only during fair weather, September to May, for passengers only. There are crossings all day long, but there can be waits of an hour or more between ferries at certain hours. Taking along a snack and something to read helps pass the waiting time if you hit a long delay. The crossing takes about 30 to 45 minutes and costs Rs. 1.50 (12¢) in first class and 90 paise (7¢) in second. Buses meet the ferries on either side.

The following ferries carry both passengers and vehicles and operate about every ten minutes from 7 a.m. to 11 p.m., but the timings and frequency should be double-checked for changes (buses also meet these ferries): The Agassaim-Cortalim ferry has replaced the Nehru Bridge that collapsed in 1986, which, ironically, earlier replaced it. It runs every few minutes; pedestrians are free and cars, Rs. 3 (23¢). Other ferries are the Colvale-Macasana, 40 paise (3¢) per person; Old Goa–Divar, also 40 paise (3¢); and Panaji-Betim, 30 paise (2¢). Cars cost Rs. 8 (60¢); vans, Rs. 10 (75¢); and bikes, Re. 1 (7½¢).

There is also **launch** service from Panaji's Central Jetty to Aldona (once a day), Britona and Naroa (twice a day), and Verem.

Bargain for yellow **cab** rates. They should run about Rs. 3.50 (27¢) for the first kilometer and Rs. 3 (23¢) per kilometer thereafter. There's a charge of Rs. 6 (45¢) per hour of waiting time and Re. 1 (7½¢) for large packages or luggage; beyond the city limits you pay 50% to 60% of the fare as a return fee.

Tourist taxis can usually be found near the Mandovi and Fidalgo Hotels and the Tourist Hostel. Agree to the price before getting in. You should be able to negotiate the use of a tourist taxi for eight hours for Rs. 200 ($15.40) with Rs. 2 (15¢) additional for every extra kilometer over 100; after eight hours, waiting time is Rs. 6 (45¢) per hour. To phone for a tourist taxi, call the Tourist Hostel (tel. 3396). There are 125 tourist taxis.

Auto-rickshaws (found near Azad Maidan and elsewhere) charge Rs. 2 (15¢) for the first kilometer and Rs. 1.75 (13½¢) per subsequent kilometer, with waiting charges of Rs. 3 (23¢) per hour, and same-as-taxi rules about return fees and luggage fees. But set the fare firmly before you get in.

There is frequent **bus** service from Panjim to everyplace in Goa. Some buses important to tourists are these: From Panaji to Old Goa, the service is every ten minutes. The trip takes about 30 minutes and costs 75 paise (5½¢). The Ponda bus can also be taken to Old Goa. To Miramar Beach (site of the Youth Hostel and some budget hotels), take the Dona Paula bus from Panaji. To get a bus going anywhere in North Goa, take the ferry from Panaji to Betim where you'll make connections. To Calangute/Baga takes about 45 minutes and costs around Rs. 1.35 (10¢); the first stop is Calangute. From Panjim to Mapusa is about a 30-minute trip and costs about Rs. 2 (15¢). Some buses to Chapora Village (near Vagator Beach) also go through Mapusa. Remember that locally it's "Mapsa," and that's what to ask for and what the driver will announce. Buses also to Margao, Vasco da Gama, and throughout Goa. Bus drivers announce their destinations. They pull out when full and, as elsewhere in India, are usually very crowded.

Share taxis (get them near ferry wharfs, the main hotels, and marketplaces) and pay by the seat, five passengers to a car. For example, from Panaji it's Rs. 4 (30¢) to Mapusa and vice versa; from Colva to Margao, Rs. 2 (15¢).

Motorcycle taxis (which means sharing a ride with a cycler, and very dangerous) within Panaji cost Rs. 2 (15¢) to Rs. 5 (40¢) per head—and it's yours to lose. Helmets are not generally worn.

Bicycles can be rented in town and at the popular beaches for Re. 1 (7½¢) per hour: **Motorcycles** can also be rented, for around Rs. 75 ($5.75) to Rs. 100 ($7.70) per day.

Going or coming, the Indian Airlines bus from Dabolim Airport, an 80-minute drive to or from Panaji, costs Rs. 15 ($1.15). A taxi should run about Rs. 120 ($9.25).

TOURS: Conducted tours, operated by the Tourism Development Corporation, offer a good way to see the main sights. They can be booked through the **Tourist Information and Tour Counter,** Tourist Home Pato, Panaji 403001 (tel. 5583), where you can also get all kinds of local information and a few pamphlets, and book guides. You can also book tours at the Tourist Hostel Tour Counter in Panaji (tel. 3396). Tours operate subject to a minimum booking of ten. Advance booking is necessary in season.

Tour 1, the **North Goa Tour,** takes in Altinho Hillock, Mayem Lake, Shri Datta Temple, Shri Vithal Temple, Mapusa, the Vagator, Anjuna, and Calangute beaches, and Aguada Fort. It operates daily, lasts nine hours (from 9 a.m. to 6 p.m.), and costs Rs. 35 ($2.70).

No. 2, the **South Goa Tour,** goes to Panaji, Old Goa, Shri Manguesh, **Shri** Shantadurga, Margao, Colva Beach, Mormugao Harbor, Vasco da Gama, Pilar Seminary, and Dona Paula and Miramar beaches. It lasts nine hours (9 a.m. to 6 p.m.), goes daily, and costs Rs. 35 ($2.70).

No. 3, the **Pilgrim Special,** takes in Old Goa and churches, and the Shri Manguesh, Manguesh, Ramnathi Shri Shantadurga Temples. It takes 3½ hours (9:30 a.m. to 1 p.m.), costs Rs. 15 ($1.15), and operates on demand.

No. 4, the **Beach Special,** visits Calangute, Anjuna, and Vagator beaches, lasts four hours (3 to 7 p.m.), costs Rs. 15 ($1.15), and operates on demand.

No. 5, the **Goa Darshan Tour,** goes to the beaches of Margao and Colva, Calangute, Miramar, Dona Paula, the main Hindu temples and Old Goa sights, and Panaji. This tour operates daily from the Tourist Hostels at Margao, Vasco, and Mapusa; cost is Rs. 35 ($2.70).

Three more tours, **Holiday Specials,** operate on demand and take in Bondla Sanctuary, for Rs. 20 ($1.55); Terekhol Fort and Arambol Beach, for Rs. 20 ($1.55); and Tambdi Surla, a famous temple not far from the Molem Wildlife Sanctuary, for Rs. 32 ($2.45). All three tours take 8½ hours (9 a.m. to 7 p.m.).

Another tour, sure to be a highlight of your stay, is a **River Cruise,** operating every evening for one hour along with a cultural performance, for Rs. 25 ($1.90); there is also four-day, full-moon River Cruise for Rs. 35 ($2.70). For details and bookings, check with the Tourist Home, Pato (tel. 5583); or the Tourist Hostel Tour Counter, Panaji (tel. 3396).

TREKKING: There are some beautiful trails through forest areas, and treks through them are organized frequently in December/January. For more information, contact the Hiking Association of Goa, Daman Dui, c/o Capt. A. Rebello (President), Captain of Ports Office, Government of Goa, Daman and Diu (tel. 5070).

SHOPPING: You'll find **Goa Handicrafts Rural and Small Scale Industries Development Corporation Ltd.** emporia in the Tourist Hostels at Panaji, Margao, Vasco, and Mapusa, and the Interstate Bus Terminus in Panaji.

WHEN TO VISIT: December to mid-January is very popular and most expensive. This period coincides with three major festivals: the Feast of St. Francis Xavier (December 3), Christmas, and Reis Magos (Feast of the Three Kings) on January 6. Unless you've booked in advance, it's almost impossible to find accommodation in Panaji. In February/March, the uninhibited antics at the four-day pre-Lenten carnival also draws crowds. Many budget travelers enjoy the monsoon season, when the rain falls and so do tariffs.

Every ten years Goa's most important festival is celebrated when the remains of St. Francis are displayed and huge numbers of pious the world over come to bear witness. A grand procession opens and closes the exposition. It will be held next in late November 1994 to mid-January 1995. Reservations must be booked far in advance. If you arrive without them . . . well, there's always a beach to stretch out on.

GETTING TO GOA: For the unhurried and unfussy, there's the Shipping Corporation of India's **steamer** from Bombay to Panaji, daily except Tuesday from Bombay (and Wednesday from Panaji), during fair weather. Service is suspended during the monsoon (June to September) or if the sea is very rough. Departure in either direction is at 10 a.m.; arrival is at 8 a.m. the following day.

This is such a delightful way to travel that one wishes the standard of cleanliness were higher. There are six classes of accommodation: Owner's Cabin (drawing room, bedroom, bathroom) at Rs. 300 ($23.05), Deluxe Cabins (with bathrooms) at Rs. 235 ($18.05) to Rs. 260 ($20), Upper Deck at Rs. 72 ($5.55), and Lower Deck at Rs. 48 ($3.70). Lower deck will make you know how it felt to be in steerage.

For inquiries and bookings in Bombay, contact Shipping Corporation of India Lines, New Ferry Wharf Office, Mallet Bunder, opposite Wadi Bunder Railway Goods Depot (opposite Gate 11), Bombay 400009 (tel. 864071). Deluxe and first class can be purchased any number of days in advance, daily (except Sunday and holidays), between 10 a.m. and 4 p.m. Deck classes can be purchased six days in advance, from 10 a.m. to 3 p.m. daily except Monday. At the last minute—one day in advance—you can book deck classes at the Girgaum Booking Office, Khadilkar Road, opposite Gaiwadi, Girgaum (tel. 356066), 8 a.m. to noon.

For inquiries and bookings in Panaji, go to the Passenger Jetty (near Panaji Port and Customs Office) in Campal; for tickets, V. S. Dempo, Campal (tel. 3842). You can buy tickets for deluxe and first class anytime in advance, daily except Wednesday; for deck classes, on Wednesday from 2 to 5:30 p.m.

From Bombay, Goa is 50 minutes **by plane,** via Indian Airlines, with flights Tuesday through Sunday, and an extra Mondays-only flight, for Rs. 398 ($30.60). Indian Airlines also flies in from Bangalore, Cochin, Delhi, and Trivandrum; Vayudoot flies from Hyderabad; and Air-India connects from Dubai, Kuwait, and Trivandrum.

The **train** from Bombay takes 22 hours to Vasco da Gama and somewhat longer to Marmugoa, for Rs. 267 ($20.55) in first class, Rs. 82 ($6.30) in second. By train from Bangalore takes 20 to 24 hours, covers only 352 km (214 miles), but involves a train change and wait along the way: Rs. 134 ($10.30) in first class; Rs. 31 ($2.40) in second.

Kadamba Transport Corporation (a Government of Goa undertaking) operates both deluxe and ordinary **buses** from Bombay to Goa. The trip takes about 16 to 17 hours, and prices range from Rs. 100 ($7.70) to Rs. 175 ($13.45), depending on the type of bus. Kadamba buses also connect to Bangalore, Belgaum, Mangalore, Mysore, Pune, and other places. The Maharashtra and Karnataka State Road Transport Corporations also operate buses on these routes in their respective states to Goa. Bookings can be made seven days in advance.

Chapter XVII

GUJARAT: GANDHI'S HOME STATE

1. Ahmedabad
2. Step Wells, Sarkhej, Lothal, and Modhera

UNTIL MAY 1, 1960, GUJARAT was a territory within the state of Maharashtra, from which it differed linguistically, and when the official partition took place, it was on these linguistic grounds.

1. Ahmedabad

Ahmedabad (pop. 1,750,000) is Gujarat's biggest city. Known to history as a city of mosques and minarets, it is equally well known today for a rather different sort of tower—the numerous factory chimneys of the 70 textile mills that make it, after Bombay, the major textile center in India.

The city is renowned also for other seemingly incompatible things—as the headquarters for 16 years of Mahatma Gandhi and his **Sabarmati Ashram,** and as a place blessed by Lakshmi, the goddess of wealth. Both seem to have their shrines: the original site of Gandhi's ashram is now a lovely complex of buildings popular with sightseers, and this area's wealth is symbolized by the architecturally unique headquarters of the **Mill Owners' Association,** designed by Le Corbusier. Both are on the western bank of the sometimes dry Sabarmati River.

The Gandhi Ashram dates back to 1917 (it was actually disbanded in 1933) and was the starting point for the celebrated 24-day, 241-mile march to Dandi in March 1930, when Bapu and 81 adherents—by the march's end, the active supporters numbered 90,000—protested the British administration's unjust Salt Tax laws. (The manufacture of salt was then a government monopoly.)

Although Gandhi himself maintained good relations with the British, having been educated in London, he was a firm advocate of Indian independence and never missed a chance to further that cause in some nonviolent way. By March 1930 he thought he had found the issue. "Salt," writes Vincent Sheenan, "was the commonest of necessities and it had been monopolized by the foreign government. Salt was something every peasant could understand. Salt was God's gift and the wicked foreign government had stolen it from the people."

On March 2, Gandhi wrote to the British viceroy and announced his plans for the march. It began ten days later, with 78 followers, ended at Dandi beach on April 6, when Gandhi went down to the sea and picked up a pinch of salt. He had broken the law, for which he was arrested one month later. But during that month his example was joyously followed by hundreds of thousands. The fledgling Congress Party, many of whose leaders were to become officials in India's first independent government 17 years later, organized the public—and illegal—sale of salt all over India. More than 60,000 people were arrested by the British, who, by doing so, underwrote their own demise.

A picture gallery containing large painted panels, a library, and photo gallery depict Gandhi's life in pictures; and a five-minute film devoted to his life is shown occasionally between 8 a.m. and 7 p.m.

Gandhi's original room—simple mats, small desk, and spinning wheel—remains undisturbed, overlooking the central prayer corner and the river beside which the local women still gather to wash their clothes.

An adjoining room displays some of Gandhi's own meager possessions: his dhoti, bedsheet, some beautifully inscribed bamboo tributes to him, and photostats of letters and cards from all over the world. The entire inspiring struggle for freedom is the subject of a Son et Lumière show at the ashram, in English every day at 8:30 p.m., for Rs. 5 (40¢). There are also daily showings in Gujarati at 7:30 p.m., for Rs. 3 (23¢).

From April 1 to September 30, the ashram is open from 8:30 a.m. to noon and 2:30 to 7 p.m. (last entry at 6 p.m.); from October 1 to March 31, 8:30 a.m. to noon and 2 to 6:30 p.m. (last entry at 6 p.m.). Admission is free.

WHERE TO STAY: Gujarat is very expensive—taxes can add as much as 30% to 40% to your room and food bills. So when a room rate looks low (and there are precious few of these), remember the added taxation when calculating your actual costs. In addition, most accommodations—even modest ones—are high-priced in comparison to many other cities of India.

Away from the bustle of town is the serene **Gandhi Ashram Guest House** (tel. 407742), opposite the Gandhi Ashram. A contemporary-style red-brick building with natural cement accents, the guesthouse (managed by the Tourism Corporation of Gujarat) was undergoing complete renovation when I stopped in. By now it should be as serene as ever, with simple furniture accented by modern paintings and photographs. The bulletin board is undoubtedly again hung with listings of everything travelers need to know for a pleasant visit to Ahmedabad—movie times, phone numbers, buses, Son et Lumière shows, tours, taxi hire services, etc. There are ten double bedrooms, all with attached bathrooms with hot and cold running water. Two rooms are air-conditioned, and rent for Rs. 201 ($15.45) double and Rs. 148 ($11.40) single occupancy. Non-air-conditioned, they're Rs. 110 ($8.45) for doubles, Rs. 85 ($6.55) for single occupancy. Vegetarian food runs Rs. 8 (60¢) at breakfast and Rs. 10 (75¢) at lunch or dinner. From here to town will cost Re. 1 (7½¢) by bus and Rs. 8 (60¢) by auto-rickshaw, both found in front of the guesthouse.

In a beautiful residential area, the **Circuit House,** Shahibagh, Ahmedabad (tel. 65033 or 65045), is a striking structure more than 100 years old, with a new block as well, overlooking sweeping lawns and gardens. Each clean room has an attached bathroom. Single occupancy costs Rs. 75 ($5.75) non-air-conditioned, Rs. 125 ($9.60) air-conditioned. Doubles run Rs. 90 ($6.90) to Rs. 135 ($10.40), the higher rate for air conditioning. These are usually booked by government officials, so write far in advance if you want to stay here. An auto-rickshaw to town will cost about Rs. 10 (75¢). A three- to four-course Western meal in the dining room runs Rs. 27 ($2.05); a vegetarian thali, Rs. 6 (45¢).

The **Hotel Roopalee**, Lal Darwaja, Ahmedabad 380001 (tel. 24607), is run-down and overpriced at Rs. 170 ($13.05) to Rs. 200 ($15.40). There are bathrooms attached to each bedroom and hot and cold water, plus telephones in the rooms.

In town, a basic good buy is the **Hotel Capital**, Chandanwadi, Khanpur, Ahmedabad 380001 (tel. 24633 to 24637). Set in a pretty garden, the hotel has 34 rooms, 15 with air conditioning and attached bathrooms with hot and cold water, and 19 with ceiling fans and common bathrooms. While the lobby lighting is sinister and some halls could easily star in horror movies with their scaling, peeling, and scratched walls, the rooms are pretty nice. Rates here for non-air-conditioned rooms with common bathrooms range from Rs. 45 ($3.45) to Rs. 65 ($5) for singles and Rs. 69 ($5.30) to Rs. 100 ($7.70) for doubles; with attached bathrooms, Rs. 130 ($10) single and Rs. 170 ($13.05) double. For air-conditioned rooms with attached bathrooms, Rs. 180 ($13.85) to Rs. 220 ($16.90) single and Rs. 220 ($16.90) to Rs. 260 ($20) double. Tax is added to these rates. There is a restaurant on the premises and many other places to eat nearby.

About a kilometer (half a mile) from town, the 27-room **Hotel Meghdoot,** Gupta Chambers, outside Sarangpur Gate, near New Cloth Market, Ahmedabad 380002 (tel. 364614 to 364617), has fairly moderately priced non-air-conditioned rooms to recommend it: Rs. 60 ($4.60) to Rs. 65 ($5) for singles and Rs. 140 ($10.75) for doubles. Nine rooms are air-conditioned: singles are Rs. 165 ($12.70), and doubles, Rs. 200 ($15.40). Most rooms have attached bathrooms.

Keep your eyes up in the **Ambassador Hotel,** Khanpur Road, Ahmedabad 380001 (tel. 392244), and you'll think you're in a rather grand home with elaborate encrusted ceilings. There are 30 rooms in all, ten of them air-conditioned. The rooms, however, are nothing fancy, and some need a good paint job. The big tile bathrooms are clean. Deluxe air-conditioned singles rent for Rs. 175 ($13.45), and doubles are Rs. 225 ($17.30); regular air-conditioned singles cost Rs. 150 ($11.55), and doubles, Rs. 200 ($15.40). Non-air-conditioned rooms go for Rs. 100 ($7.70) to Rs. 120 ($9.25) single and Rs. 150 ($11.55) double. There's a 24-hour room service, but no restaurant. Many places to eat nearby.

The 21-room **Ritz Hotel,** Lal Darwaja, Ahmedabad 380001 (tel. 393637), overlooking the river at Nehru Bridge, is a white stucco building with simply furnished rooms opening off a terrace and a pleasant garden, away from the road. Great green plants and the chirping of birds overhead fill the compound with sight and sound. There's a small patio overlooking the river and a comfortable dining room. The 14 air-conditioned rooms cost Rs. 190 ($14.60) to Rs. 215 ($16.55) single and Rs. 240 ($18.45) to Rs. 265 ($20.40) doubles; three singles are not air-conditioned and go for Rs. 95 ($7.30) to Rs. 125 ($9.60), and one double, for Rs. 160 ($12.30). The restaurant is being expanded for outside guests. A combination South and North Indian vegetarian breakfast is a specialty here, for Rs. 20 ($1.55). A full English breakfast runs Rs. 25 ($1.90) to Rs. 30 ($2.30).

The pricey **Panshikura,** beside Town Hall, near Underbridge, Ellis Bridge, Ahmedabad 380006 (tel. 77611), charges Rs. 250 ($19.25) single and Rs. 300 ($23.05) for reasonably clean, if not terribly imaginatively furnished, rooms. All have air conditioning, bathrooms attached, and such amenities as phones, TV, and piped-in music. Low ceilings make this hotel seem cramped. There is a coffeeshop and a restaurant on site.

In the upper range, the **Hotel Karnavati,** Ashram Road, Ahmedabad 380019 (tel. 402161), has fountains outdoors to screen the street noises and an attractive lobby with circular rugs, diwali lamps, and hanging banners in typical Gujarati textiles. The rooms, with printed drapes and bedspreads and built-in furniture, are fairly well maintained. Single rates are Rs. 390 ($30) plus Rs. 102 ($7.85) in tax, for a total of Rs. 492 ($37.85); doubles cost Rs. 440 ($33.85) plus Rs. 117 ($9) in tax, for a total of Rs. 557 ($42.85)—an example of how taxes increase rates in this city. The 24-hour Haveli Coffee Shop has a daily buffet (see "Where to Eat"); upstairs on the first floor, the dressy-looking Jade Room, with dark woods upholstered in green, is open from 7:30 to 10:45 p.m.

Also on Ashram Road, Ahmedabad 380019, is the overpriced **Natraj Hotel** (tel. 448747), centrally air-conditioned, with all rooms in proximity to the heavily traveled road. Music blares from the adjoining coffeeshop. Rates are Rs. 450 ($34.60) single, Rs. 500 ($38.45) double.

Spare lobby decor and compact modern rooms are found at the pricey **Rivera Hotel,** Khanpur Road, Ahmedabad 380001 (tel. 24201), on the riverbank. Centrally air-conditioned rooms cost Rs. 275 ($21.15) single and Rs. 350 ($26.95); a continental breakfast runs Rs. 16 ($1.25).

Next door is the top hotel in town, the 55-room **Cama Hotel,** Khanpur Road, Ahmedabad 380001 (tel. 25281), on the riverbank. The front of the hotel faces the road, and in back there's a terrace and garden with a swimming pool and view of the river. The lounge is handsomely done with big leather chairs, and each floor has a mini-lounge, some with antique furniture and accessories. The attractive comfortable rooms have bathrooms attached: Rs. 425 ($32.70) to Rs. 475 ($36.55) for singles, and Rs. 475 ($36.55) to Rs. 525 ($40.40) for doubles.

WHERE TO EAT: A great percentage of the population here is vegetarian, and Gujarati meatless dishes are some of the most distinctive in all of India. Local cooking is less spicy and a little sweeter than some other Indian styles, which makes it easier for many Westerners to enjoy. There's prohibition in the entire state so you'll need your liquor permit to purchase even a bottle of beer.

A good place to try typical Gujarati food is the simple, clean, air-conditioned **Gaurav Dining Hall,** Shiv Cinema Compound, Ashram Road (tel. 407197). There's no English sign, so you have to look for it near the movie. Inside near the entrance are basins for washing up before and after your finger-lickin' good Gujarati meal. The waiters don't speak English, but they will get you a Gujarati thali: Rs. 15 ($1.15) with unlimited refills. It features no fewer than seven vegetable dishes as well as one dal, one curry, roti (wheat bread), pappadam, farsan (a crisp biscuit-like dish), tiny puris, pickle, curds, and rice. This is a good deal in terms of price, and it permits you to taste a whole lot of good things you might not otherwise order. Foods are to be eaten in a certain order, but there's nothing too rigid about this pattern except for the rice. In Gujarat, ghee-topped rice is traditionally served after your wheat breads and farsan to mop up your wet foods, rather than with the meal as elsewhere. Nor is rice brought to table without notifying the waiters. They will continue to bring you puris and rotis like the "Sorcerer's Apprentice" until halted. Unless you know the local etiquette, it's very easy to overeat on puris and not have room for a grain of rice, let alone the mountain that's inevitably heaped on your tray. Hours: 10 a.m. to 3 p.m. and 6:30 to 10 p.m. every day.

For pure South Indian vegetarian food, the **Old Madras Brahmin's Hotel,** opposite the City Civil Court, Bhadra (tel. 391005), is the place to go. Prices are similar to Gaurav above. Hours are 8:30 a.m. to 10 p.m.

For a non-vegetarian splurge, the place to go is **Patang** ("kite"), Patang

Chinubhai Centre, Ashram Rd., Ahmedabad 38009 (tel. 77899), the city's revolving restaurant, 221 feet above the ground, offering a grand view, good surroundings, and a bountiful buffet. A colorful mural of children flying kites greets visitors, and a glassed-in elevator whisks them to the top where a curved copper ceiling forms an overhead canopy. The dining area's modern furnishings place the accent outdoors and on the food, which is Indian, continental, Punjabi, Mughlai, and ordered from a prize-winning kite-shaped menu or selected from the Rs.-55 ($4.25) buffet (served on weekends only). Otherwise you might try the ample three-course executive lunch, every day but Sunday, for Rs. 45 ($3.45). Taxes are added to all prices. Hours: 12:30 to 3 p.m. and 7 p.m. to 11 p.m. There's a minimum of Rs. 55 ($4.25) per adult and Rs. 35 ($2.70) per child. Live classical Indian music at night, and at Sunday lunch and dinner. Reservations essential (tel. 78866).

Lower-priced foods are available at the casual **Garden Café** on the pillar's first floor, where you can indeed eat outdoors surrounded by flowers and plants. Dishes include sandwiches for Rs. 10 (75¢) to Rs. 15 ($1.15); pizzas for Rs. 8 (60¢) to Rs. 15 ($1.15); noodles for Rs. 10 (75¢); sundaes for Rs. 14 ($1.05); and other treats—all pictured on the placemat menu which also has games for kids on the reverse side. Open from 6 p.m. to 1 a.m. At the base is a snack shop for sandwiches, and cutlets at Rs. 2.50 (20¢) and plate meals at Rs. 8 (60¢)—these and other foods are shown in realistic color photographs. Snack shop hours had not been determined when I stopped in.

Patang also operates the **Pastry Wagon Shops,** near Sadar Patel Stadium and elsewhere, featuring rich pastries such as Black Forest or chocolate cake, each Rs. 7 (55¢) per slice. Open from 8 a.m. to 9 p.m. Plans were to open snack shops with the same name.

Two buffets, 12:30 to 3 p.m. and 7:30 to 11 p.m., are offered at the **Cama Hotel,** Khanpur Road (tel. 25281).

If you'd like some Punjabi food, the air-conditioned Russian-named **Volga,** on Ashram Road (tel. 408533), is the place to go, 11:30 a.m. to 3:30 p.m. and 7 to 11 p.m. every day. Specialties are butter chicken, chicken tikka masala, and other familiar northern fare. The prices for entrees are Rs. 20 ($1.55) to Rs. 30 ($2.30).

On Relief Road, **Kwality** (tel. 20309) is another good bet if you're not interested in vegetarian foods. There are about 75 Chinese specialties and about 75 continental dishes on the menu, a dozen or so tandoori specialties, plus snacks and sweets galore. The highest prices are around Rs. 35 ($2.70). Air-conditioned, and open from noon to 4 p.m. and 7 to 11 p.m.

Try either of the two very popular **Havmors** around town for rich sundaes with all kinds of sweets, ice cream, sundaes, and snacks, for Rs. 6 (45¢) to Rs. 25 ($1.90). One is on Relief Road (tel. 26264), opposite the Krishna Cinema, and the other is near Town Hall, Ellis Bridge (tel. 76192), both open from 11 a.m. to 11 p.m.

For a sightseeing and eating experience, there's charming **Vishala,** about four miles from town, a re creation of a traditional village designed and owned by Surinder Patel, an architect/contractor. Displayed handcrafts are for sale and the well-designed Vechaar Utensil Museum is devoted to cooking and various household implements, hookahs, and other objects. You can sit outdoors on charpoys (cots) as you snack or sip fresh coconut juice; or have a thali meal under the trees—a bit of a splurge at Rs. 45 ($3.45). In the evening folk dancers entertain during dinner. Open every day. From town to Vishala, a scooter-rickshaw will cost about Rs. 45 ($3.45), but settle the price before you get in, and keep it for the trip home. Or you can take the bus headed for Sarkhej and ask the conductor to let you off at Hagi Bawakvai, then walk a short distance to the site. Busing it is risky because you may not get a bus going back when you want it.

GETTING AROUND AND GETTING HELP: Metered **tourist taxis** cost Rs. 2.35 (18¢) per kilometer, but who uses meters? So bargain and ask for the rate card to see how you're doing. **Diesel taxis** are unmetered and charge Rs. 1.60 (12¢) per kilometer, but often you can bargain this down to Re. 1 (7½¢). There's a taxi stand at Bhadra in the center of town.

Auto-rickshaws are plentiful and will bring out the religion in you— they careen around town and you say your prayers. Rickshaw meters need adjustment, so it's best to ask for the rate card. They should charge Rs. 2 (15¢) for the first and 75 paise (6¢) per kilometer thereafter. But meters will probably read about one-third less. Auto-rickshaw fares go up 150% at night.

Low-priced **tours** twice daily (including Sunday and holidays) taking in the major sights in and about Ahmedabad are conducted by the Ahmedabad Municipal Corporation (tel. 392709). They cost Rs. 15 ($1.15) each and run from 8 a.m. to 12:30 p.m. and 2:30 to 6 p.m. from the AMTS Terminus, Lal Darwaja. A number of hotels have information on these tours. The Tourism Corporation of Gujarat has tours to outlying areas and museums, which depart from the Gujarat Tourism Information Bureau, HK House, Ashram Road. Call 449683 for information. The Tourism Corporation also operates tours throughout the state commencing in Ahmedabad.

For **information** on tours, tourist attractions, and special events for tourists, the Tourist Office at the Ahmedabad Municipal Corporation (tel. 392709) and the Tourist OInformation Bureau at the Tourism Corporation of Gujarat (tel. 449683) are your best sources.

SHOPPING: The most attractive place in town, and very interesting too, is **Gujari,** National Chambers, near Dipalee Cinema on Ashram Road—three floors of beautifully displayed and carefully selected handcrafts from all over the area. Textiles, of course, and rugs are both outstanding, and very impressive as well is the local lacquered and inlaid furniture, as bright as a summer's day. Note the good creative reuse of old fabrics that have been worked into coats and vests, as well as the new fabrics that use traditional motifs. The rosewood beads here make lovely gifts, which are easy to pack and easy on the pocketbook too. Wool shawls are good buys for rough quality or merino. Open every day but Wednesday from 10:30 a.m. to 7 p.m. Closed for lunch between 2 and 3 p.m.

Nearby is **Handloom House,** on Ashram Road, with an impressive selection of textiles in a similar price range.

For bargaining, head to the shops on Relief Road, **Bhadra** and **Teen Darwaja;** to haggle, try the **Junk Bazaar** on Sunday on the banks of the Sabarmati, near B. K. Municipal Garden under Ellis Bridge.

AROUND TOWN: The various mosques around town are pretty much like mosques anywhere. Two, however, have special features: the delicately carved stone windows, in the pattern of a tree with spreading branches, of the **Sidi Saiyad** mosque, very near the Ritz Hotel; and the celebrated "Shaking Towers" of the **Jhulta Minara** (part of Siddi Bashir mosque), not far from the Ahmedabad Railway Station, outside the Sarangpur Gate. A sign at the latter describes the 75-foot twin minarets as "a challenge to modern architecture," and the structure certainly does seem unique. Visitors pay a modest fee to climb the 68 steps of the narrow staircase to the top of one tower, and while they are huffing and puffing, a youth starts up the other tower—and shakes it! The vibrations, transmitted by the stone bridge connecting the towers 40 feet below, can clearly and somewhat frighteningly be felt in the other tower. The skillful builder of this architectural phenomenon, in 1450, was Malik Shahnang Sahib, who lived at the time of Sultan Ahmed, founder of this city which now bears his name. The minarets, still in use to call the faithful at sunset (via microphone and loudspeaker) are closed between 12:30 and 2:30 p.m.

The 800-seat **Tagore Theatre** is an impressive piece of architecture too— soaring concrete beams, colored panels suspended from the ceiling, and a mural in the lobby ingeniously constructed from mirrors, beads, and beaten copper panels. Adjoining the theater—and both are situated just at the western end of the Sardar Bridge across the river—is a square, squat museum (open from 8 to 11 a.m. and 4 to 8 p.m.; closed Monday) containing some lovely miniatures, some suspended from the ceiling and others displayed in glass cases.

At the southeast side of town is **Kankaria Lake,** a circular tank built in 1451, at the center of which is a small island housing the **Nagira Wadi** temple. Connected to the mainland by a causeway, it's also accessible by little boats and at night is illuminated with orange lights. There's a small Kwality restaurant overlooking the lake, a pleasant spot in the evening.

Adjoining the lake, which is ringed with busy little stalls, are a children's garden, zoo, swimming pool, open-air theater, and children's swimming pool. A scooter rickshaw will cost about Rs. 5 (40¢) out from the town center.

Or perhaps you might be interested in one of the city's unusual museums. A most fascinating choice is the unique **Calico Textile Museum,** Shahibagh, in a lovely old haveli in the beautiful botanical flower- and peacock-filled botanical gardens that are part of the Sarabhai Foundation, an appropriate museum for this city in which prosperity is interwoven in three threads—cotton, silk, and gold. "Calico" is a real understatement when it comes to describing the displays in this museum. They are anything but humble cotton: lavish heavy brocades, delicate fine embroideries, carpets, turbans, saris, costumes of maharajas and other royalty. This is one of the finest museums of its type in the world, and deserves time for peaceful quiet investigation. Hours are 10 a.m. to 12:30 p.m. and 2:30 to 5 p.m.; closed Wednesday and bank holidays. Tours are given from 10:15 to 11:15 a.m. and 2:30 to 3:30 p.m. In this area also is a 15th-century Jain temple, included on the daily tour, and under renovation for the past 200 years.

Another interesting museum is the **Shreyas Folk Museum,** Shreyas Foundation, housing a comprehensive collection of folk arts and crafts of Gujarat. Open from 9 to 11 a.m. and 4 to 7 p.m.; closed Wednesday and bank holidays.

The **N.C. Gallery,** Sanskar, Paldi (tel. 78369), houses Gujarati and Rajput artworks in a building designed by Le Corbusier (open from 9 to 11 a.m. and 4 to 7 p.m.; closed Monday).

Also worth a visit are the **Tribal Research and Training Institute Museum,** Vidyapith, Ashram Road (tel. 79741), open from 11:30 a.m. to 7:30 p.m. (to 2:30 p.m. on Saturday; closed Sunday and holidays); and the **Institute of Indology,** University Campus, Vidyapith (tel. 446148), open from 11:30 a.m. to 7:30 p.m. (11:20 a.m. to 2:30 p.m. on Saturday; closed Sunday). Entry to both is free.

BEST TIME TO VISIT: October to March is best; April to June is hot. The monsoon is roughly mid-June to mid-September. For Gir, the lion sanctuary, the best time is March to May.

GETTING TO AHMEDABAD: There are frequent Indian Airlines flights from Bombay, at Rs. 409 ($31.45); from Jaipur, at Rs. 489 ($37.60); from Madras, at Rs. 1,242 ($95.55); and from a number of other cities.

From Bombay, the best **train** is the *Gujarat Express,* a nine-hour ride, or the *Saurashtra Express,* about an 11-hour ride, both departing in the morning and arriving in the afternoon, for Rs. 182 ($14) in first class, Rs. 45 ($3.45) in second. From Delhi, try to get the *Sarvodaya Express,* which takes 17 hours to cover the 585 miles (960 km), or you'll be stuck with a 24-hour train ride: Rs. 206 ($15.85) in first class and Rs. 50 ($3.85) in second.

2. Step Wells, Sarkhej, Lothal, and Modhera

Unique to Gujarat are **step wells.** Easiest to see, but by no means the most outstanding, is the five-story **Dada Hari** in the southern part of the city where it more or less blends in with the neighborhood. Built in 1501 it has retained traces of its former glory in the carved walls and pillars, best seen if you walk down the stairs. As with other step wells, it once offered a cool drink and respite from the heat to travelers.

A more handsome step well is **Adalaj Vav,** 19 km (11½ miles) north of Ahmedabad in the village of Adalaj. This is superior to the other step well in town: its carved pillars and walls are covered with birds and flowers, leaves and fishes, and designs that unify the whole.

About eight kilometers (five miles) southwest of the city is **Sarkhej Roza,** architecturally of interest because it lacks archways commonly associated with this kind of structure. Here is the renowned domed tomb of Ahmed Khattu Ganji Bakhsh (1445); spiritual adviser to Sultan Ahmed Shah. Inside the octagonal shrine, sunlight forms graceful patterns through some of the loveliest brass latticework to be seen today. Handsome marble inlay flooring embellishes the courtyard. The adjoining mosque from the 16th century is simple architecturally, and noted for its rows of supporting pillars and, like the other structures, its absence of arches. Also to be seen in the courtyard near the entrance is the tomb of Mehmud Shah Begada and his wife, Queen Rajabai, through a portico on the tank bank. In proximity are palace ruins and pavilions and the tombs of brothers 'Azam and Mu'azzam, believed to be the architects of Sarkhej.

You can get to Sarkhej by bus from Ahmedabad's Lal Darwaja Terminus; take bus 36/1 or 31/1, which run about every 45 minutes to an hour. At the site, a self-designated expert sells booklets for Rs.-7 (55¢) asking price, but will part with them for less, and the added information is good to have.

Southwest of Ahmedabad 87 km (53 miles) is **Lothal,** an important archeological find made only 20 years ago. This site dates from the Harappan era, going back to 1,000 years before Christ. This finding is of great significance, as it extends the borders of the Harappan civilization as far south as the Gulf of Cambay.

Remains of a dockyard and an inlet channel connecting to the River Bhogavo bear witness of Lothal's importance as an ancient port. An excavated Persian seal is evidence that there had been gulf trade. Also excavated have been a planned city with houses having such amenities as baths and fireplaces. On view at the small museum are jewelry, bowls, and other early artifacts.

Lothal is a day's excursion from Ahmedabad by rail to Bhurkhi on the Ahmedabad–Bhavnagar line of the Western Railway. Buses are available at Bhurkhi. It's a nice walk from there as well.

Should you want to spend the night, there's a tourist Bungalow at Lothal, charging Rs. 20 ($1.55) for a room, less for a dorm. The cook on the premises will prepare simple thali meals for Rs. 8 (60¢). But you'd better get the telephone number from the tourist office and ask your hotel reception to ring up and say in Gujarati that you're coming and how long you will stay. The Lothal bungalow is infrequently used and may need a sweeper's touch before your visit.

Modhera, 60 miles (104 km) northwest of Ahmedabad, boasts of a Sun Temple from A.D. 1026, two centuries older than the Sun Temple at Konarak and, like it, dedicated to Surya the Sun. Against a barren landscape, the temple is an outstanding sight, set off like a work of art in an outdoor museum. Built on a platform above a deep tank, the temple was attacked and nearly destroyed by Mehmud of Gazni, but remarkably still has beautiful carvings of goddesses, birds, blossoms, and beasts inside and outside. Surya's image is missing from the sanctum now, but originally it was strategically placed to be illuminated by the first rays of the rising sun. Some of the stone carvings standing around the structure now are to be placed in a museum. Archeologists have been restoring the temple and replacing some of the damaged stones with plain sandstone so you can tell which are new additions to the temple.

The Tourism Corporation of Gujarat runs **Toran,** a clean place for a snack or light meal, within walking distance of the temple. Try the local pakoras—they look like balls instead of fritters—for Rs. 4 (30¢) per plate; tea is Rs. 1.50 (11¢) a cup.

There are state transport buses from Ahmedabad to Modhera or you can get a direct (meaning few stops) bus to Mehsana for Rs. 11 (85¢) and then get a bus for the remaining 40 km (24 miles) to the temple for Rs. 2.50 (20¢). There are two direct buses a day from Ahmedabad to Mehsana, and a bus from there every hour to the Sun Temple. By train, you go via Mehsana and then transfer to a bus

HINDI VOCABULARY

Useful Terms and Expressions

		Pronounced
Greetings	**Namaste/Namaskar**	Nah-maas-tay
Thanks	**Shukriya**	Shook-ree-yah
Please	**Kripya**	Kreep-yah
Yes	**Ha (nasal *n*)**	Haa(nasal *n*)
No	**Nahin (silent *n*)**	Naa-hee
What is the price for this?	**Iska kya dam hai?**	Ees-ka ke-yah daam ha-ay
I want this	**Mujhe yeh chahiye**	Mooj-hey yea cha-ee-eh
I do not want this	**Mujhe yeh nahin chahiye**	Mooj-hey yea na-hee cha-ee-eh
How are you?	**Aap Kaise hai**	Aap kaa-eh-se ha-eh
Where	**Kahan (silent *n*)**	Kaa-ha
Why	**Kyon (nasal *n*)**	Key-ohn (nasal *n* but not emphatic)
What	**Kya**	Kay-ah
Water	**Pani**	Pa-nee
Where is the post office?	**Dak ghar kahan hai**	Daak ghar ka-ha ha-ay
Today	**Aaj**	Aaj
Tomorrow	**Kal**	Kaal
The day after tomorrow	**Purso**	Perso
Here	**Idhar**	Id-haar
There	**Udhar**	Ud-haar
I liked this	**Mujhe achchha laga**	Mooj-hey aachaa laaga
I did not like this	**Mujhe achchha nahin laga**	Mooj-hey aacha na-hee-laaga
Expensive	**Mehenga**	Mung-ah
I want more	**Mujhe aur chahiye**	Mooj-hey ah-ur cha-ee-eh
I do not want more	**Mujhe aur nahin chahiye**	Mooj-hey ah-uv na-hee cha-ee-eh

Help me	**Meri madad kijiye**	Mary maadaad key-jee-eh
Call doctor	**Doctor bulaiye**	Doctor boo-la-ee-eh
Take me to a hospital	**Mujhe haspatal le jaiye**	Mooj-hey haspaataal lee-ja-ee-eh
Call the police	**Police bulaiye**	Police boo-la-ee-eh

NOW, SAVE MONEY ON ALL YOUR TRAVELS!
Join Arthur Frommer's $35-A-Day Travel Club™

Saving money while traveling is never a simple matter, which is why, over 26 years ago, the **$35-A-Day Travel Club** was formed. Actually, the idea came from readers of the Arthur Frommer Publications who felt that such an organization could bring financial benefits, continuing travel information, and a sense of community to economy-minded travelers all over the world.

In keeping with the money-saving concept, the annual membership fee is low—$18 (U.S. residents) or $20 U.S. (Canadian, Mexican, and foreign residents)—and is immediately exceeded by the value of your benefits which include:

(1) The latest edition of any TWO of the books listed on the following pages.

(2) An annual subscription to an 8-page quarterly newspaper *The Wonderful World of Budget Travel* which keeps you up-to-date on fastbreaking developments in low-cost travel in all parts of the world—bringing you the kind of information you'd have to pay over $35 a year to obtain elsewhere. This consumer-conscious publication also includes the following columns:

Hospitality Exchange—members all over the world who are willing to provide hospitality to other members as they pass through their home cities.

Share-a-Trip—requests from members for travel companions who can share costs and help avoid the burdensome single supplement.

Readers Ask . . . Readers Reply—travel questions from members to which other members reply with authentic firsthand information.

(3) A copy of *Arthur Frommer's Guide to New York*.

(4) Your personal membership card which entitles you to purchase through the Club all Arthur Frommer Publications for a third to a half off their regular retail prices during the term of your membership.

So why not join this hardy band of international budgeteers NOW and participate in its exchange of information and hospitality? Simply send $18 (U.S. residents) or $20 U.S. (Canadian, Mexican, and other foreign residents) along with your name and address to: $35-A-Day Travel Club, Inc., Gulf + Western Building, One Gulf + Western Plaza, New York, NY 10023. Remember to specify which *two* of the books in section (1) above you wish to receive in your initial package of member's benefits. Or tear out the next page, check off any two of the books listed on either side, and send it to us with your membership fee.

Date_____

**FROMMER BOOKS
PRENTICE HALL PRESS
ONE GULF + WESTERN PLAZA
NEW YORK, NY 10023**

Friends:

Please send me the books checked below:

FROMMER'S $-A-DAY GUIDES™

(In-depth guides to sightseeing and low-cost tourist accommodations and facilities.)

☐ Europe on $30 a Day $13.95
☐ Australia on $30 a Day $11.95
☐ Eastern Europe on $25 a Day $10.95
☐ England on $40 a Day............... $11.95
☐ Greece on $30 a Day............... $11.95
☐ Hawaii on $50 a Day............... $11.95
☐ India on $25 a Day $10.95
☐ Ireland on $30 a Day............... $10.95
☐ Israel on $30 & $35 a Day $11.95
☐ Mexico (plus Belize & Guatemala)
   on $20 a Day..................... $10.95

☐ New Zealand on $40 a Day $11.95
☐ New York on $50 a Day............. $10.95
☐ Scandinavia on $50 a Day........... $10.95
☐ Scotland and Wales on $40 a Day..... $11.95
☐ South America on $30 a Day $10.95
☐ Spain and Morocco (plus the Canary
   Is.) on $40 a Day $10.95
☐ Turkey on $25 a Day............... $10.95
☐ Washington, D.C., & Historic Va. on
   $40 a Day $11.95

FROMMER'S DOLLARWISE GUIDES™

(Guides to sightseeing and tourist accommodations and facilities from budget to deluxe, with emphasis on the medium-priced.)

☐ Alaska...................... $12.95
☐ Austria & Hungary $11.95
☐ Belgium, Holland, Luxembourg $11.95
☐ Egypt....................... $11.95
☐ England & Scotland $11.95
☐ France...................... $11.95
☐ Germany..................... $12.95
☐ Italy....................... $11.95
☐ Japan & Hong Kong $13.95
☐ Portugal, Madeira, & the Azores $12.95
☐ South Pacific.................. $12.95
☐ Switzerland & Liechtenstein $12.95
☐ Bermuda & The Bahamas........... $11.95
☐ Canada $12.95
☐ Caribbean $13.95

☐ Cruises (incl. Alaska, Carib, Mex,
   Hawaii, Panama, Canada, & US) $12.95
☐ California & Las Vegas $11.95
☐ Florida..................... $11.95
☐ Mid-Atlantic States $12.95
☐ New England.................. $12.95
☐ New York State $12.95
☐ Northwest.................... $11.95
☐ Skiing in Europe $12.95
☐ Skiing USA—East $11.95
☐ Skiing USA—West $11.95
☐ Southeast & New Orleans............ $11.95
☐ Southwest.................... $11.95
☐ Texas...................... $11.95

FROMMER'S TOURING GUIDES™

(Color illustrated guides that include walking tours, cultural & historic sites, and other vital travel information.)

☐ Egypt....................... $8.95
☐ Florence $8.95
☐ London $8.95

☐ Paris....................... $8.95
☐ Venice $8.95

TURN PAGE FOR ADDITIONAL BOOKS AND ORDER FORM.

THE ARTHUR FROMMER GUIDES™

(Pocket-size guides to sightseeing and tourist accommodations and facilities in all price ranges.)

☐ Amsterdam/Holland	$5.95	☐ Mexico City/Acapulco	$5.95
☐ Athens	$5.95	☐ Minneapolis/St. Paul	$5.95
☐ Atlantic City/Cape May	$5.95	☐ Montreal/Quebec City	$5.95
☐ Boston	$5.95	☐ New Orleans	$5.95
☐ Cancún/Cozumel/Yucatán	$5.95	☐ New York	$5.95
☐ Dublin/Ireland	$5.95	☐ Orlando/Disney World/EPCOT	$5.95
☐ Hawaii	$5.95	☐ Paris	$5.95
☐ Las Vegas	$5.95	☐ Philadelphia	$5.95
☐ Lisbon/Madrid/Costa del Sol	$5.95	☐ Rome	$5.95
☐ London	$5.95	☐ San Francisco	$5.95
☐ Los Angeles	$5.95	☐ Washington, D.C.	$5.95

SPECIAL EDITIONS

☐ A Shopper's Guide to the Caribbean	$12.95	☐ Motorist's Phrase Book (Fr/Ger/Sp)	$4.95
☐ Bed & Breakfast—N. America	$8.95	☐ Swap and Go (Home Exchanging)	$10.95
☐ Guide to Honeymoon Destinations (US, Canada, Mexico, & Carib)	$12.95	☐ The Candy Apple (NY for Kids)	$11.95
☐ Beat the High Cost of Travel	$6.95	☐ Travel Diary and Record Book	$5.95
☐ Marilyn Wood's Wonderful Weekends (NY, Conn, Mass, RI, Vt, NH, NJ, Del, Pa)	$11.95	☐ Where to Stay USA (Lodging from $3 to $30 a night)	$10.95

☐ Arthur Frommer's New World of Travel (Annual sourcebook previewing: new travel trends, new modes of travel, and the latest cost-cutting strategies for savvy travelers) $12.95

SERIOUS SHOPPER'S GUIDES

(Illustrated guides listing hundreds of stores, conveniently organized alphabetically by category.)

☐ Italy	$15.95	☐ Los Angeles	$14.95
☐ London	$15.95	☐ Paris	$15.95

ORDER NOW!

In U.S. include $1.50 shipping UPS for 1st book; 50¢ ea. add'l book. Outside U.S. $2 and 50¢, respectively.

Enclosed is my check or money order for $_____

NAME _____

ADDRESS _____

CITY _____ STATE _____ ZIP _____

It's 2 am.
It's far from home.
It's more than
a tummyache.

American Express Cardmembers can get emergency medical and legal referrals, worldwide. Simply by calling Global Assist.℠

What if it really is more than a tummyache? What if your back goes out? What if you get into a legal fix?

Call Global Assist – a new emergency referral service for the exclusive use of American Express Cardmembers. Just call. Toll-free. 24 hours a day. Every day. Virtually anywhere in the world.

Your call helps find a doctor, lawyer, dentist, optician, chiropractor, nurse, pharmacist, or an interpreter.

All this costs nothing, except for the medical and legal bills you would normally expect to pay.

Global Assist. One more reason to have the American Express® Card. Or, to get one.

 TRAVEL RELATED SERVICES   For an application, call 1-800-THE-CARD.

Don't leave home without it.®

If you lose cash on vacation, don't count on a Boy Scout finding it.

Honestly.

How many people can you trust to give back hundreds of dollars in cash? Not too many.

That's why it's so important to help protect your vacation with American Express® Travelers Cheques.

If they're lost, you can get them back

from over 100,000 refund locations thro⟶ out the world. Or you can hope a Boy S⟨ finds it.

Protect your vacation.

 Travelers Cheques